lonely planet

Iceland

Alexis Averbuck, Carolyn Bain, Jade Bremner, Belinda Dixon

PLAN YOUR TRIP

CHALIE CHULAPORNSIRI/SHUTTERSTOCK ©

ICELANDIC PHALLOLOGICAL MUSEUM, REYKJAVÍK P61

SHOTAROBKK/SHUTTERSTOCK ©

HALLGRIMSKIRKJA, REYKJAVÍK P59

ON THE ROAD

Contents

UNDERSTAND

SURVIVAL GUIDE

SPECIAL FEATURES

Welcome to Iceland

Hitting headlines, topping bucket lists, wooing nature lovers and dazzling an increasing number of visitors – there seems no end to the talents of this breathtaking northern destination.

A Symphony of Elements

An underpopulated island marooned near the top of the globe, Iceland is, literally, a country in the making. It's a vast volcanic laboratory where mighty forces shape the earth: geysers gush, mudpots gloop, ice-covered volcanoes rumble and glaciers cut great pathways through the mountains. Its supercharged splendour seems designed to remind visitors of their utter insignificance in the greater scheme of things. And it works a treat: some crisp clean air, an eyeful of the cinematic landscapes, and everyone is transfixed.

The Power of Nature

It's the power of Icelandic nature to turn the prosaic into the extraordinary. A dip in a pool becomes a soak in a geothermal lagoon; a casual stroll can transform into a trek across a glittering glacier; and a quiet night of camping may mean front-row seats to the aurora borealis' curtains of light, or the soft, pinkish hue of the midnight sun. Iceland has a transformative effect on people too – its sagas turned brutes into poets, and its stories of *huldufólk* (hidden people) may make believers out of sceptics. Here you'll find some of the world's highest concentrations of dreamers, authors, artists and musicians, all fuelled by their surrounds.

A Personal Experience

The warmth of Icelanders is disarming, as is their industriousness – they've worked hard to recover from financial upheaval, and to transform Iceland into a destination that, thanks to its popularity with visitors, can host more than six times its population each year. Pause and consider a medium-sized city in your country – then give it far-flung universities, airports and hospitals to administer, 30-odd active volcanoes to monitor, and hundreds of hotels to run. How might they cope? Could they manage as well as the Icelanders – and still have time left over to create spine-tingling music and natty knitwear?

Nordic Nirvana

Don't for a minute think it's all about the great outdoors. The counterpoint to so much natural beauty is found in Iceland's cultural life, which celebrates a literary legacy that stretches from medieval sagas to contemporary thrillers by way of Nobel Prize winners. Live music is everywhere, as is visual art, handicrafts and locavore cuisine. The world's most northerly capital is home to the kind of egalitarianism, green thinking and effortless style that its Nordic brethren are famous for – all of which is wrapped in Iceland's assured individuality.

KAVRAM/SHUTTERSTOCK ©

Why I Love Iceland

By Carolyn Bain, Writer

It's not a unique claim these days: I've been smitten with Iceland since I first visited. My visits were increasing, for both work and fun, but my cravings weren't subsiding, and I started to entertain the notion of moving there permanently. Icelandic friends gave me wise advice to experience more wintry conditions before committing, so in February 2017 I took the ferry north from Denmark. I sailed into Seyðisfjörður at sunrise on Valentine's Day under incredible candy-pink skies, and my decision was made. I moved to Reykjavík from Australia later that year, and am now overjoyed to call Iceland home.

For more about our writers, see p448

Above: Svartifoss (p188)

Iceland

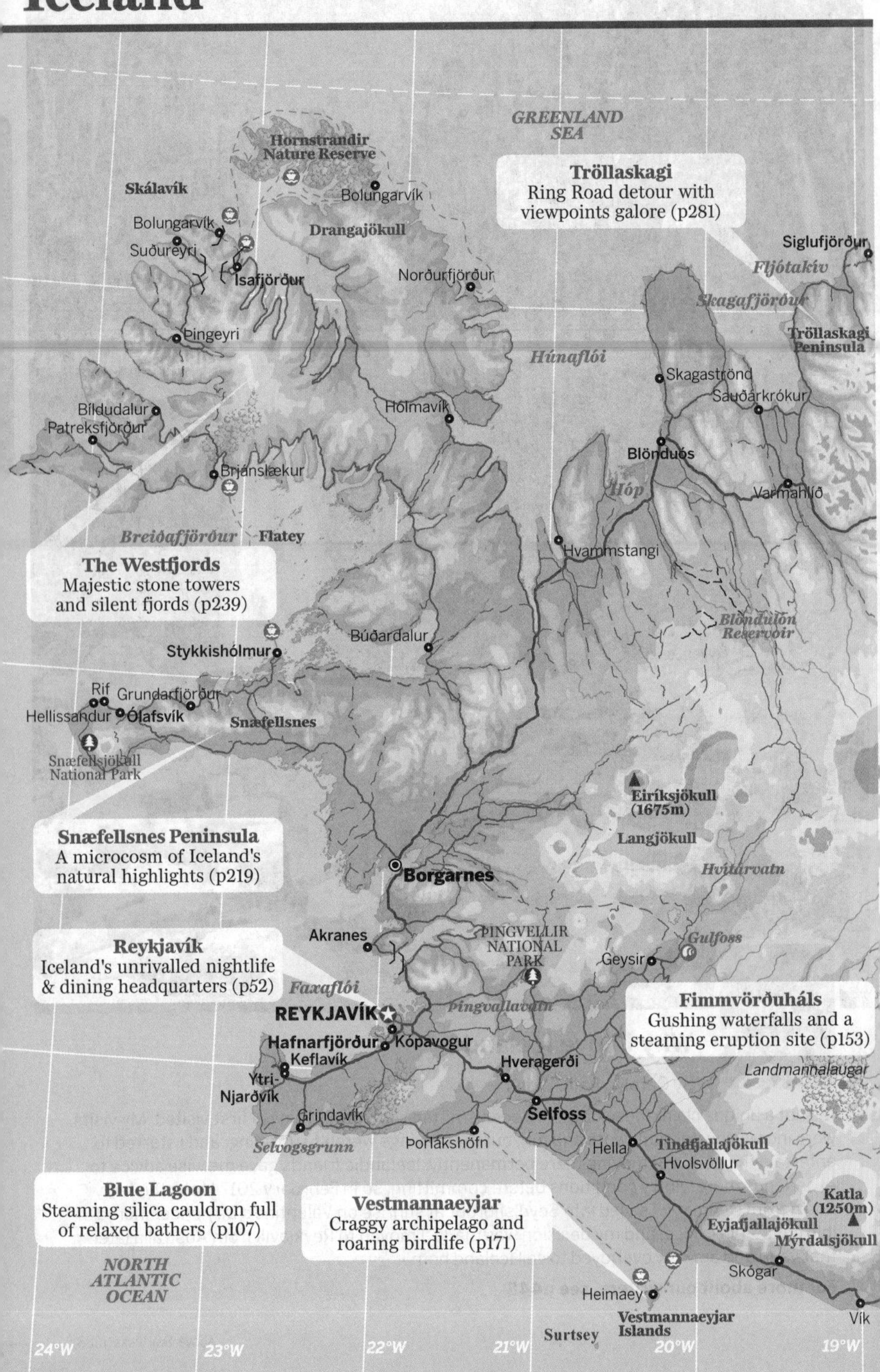

GREENLAND SEA
Hornstrandir Nature Reserve
Skálavík
Bolungarvík
Bolungarvík
Suðureyri
Ísafjörður
Drangajökull
Norðurfjörður
Þingeyri
Tröllaskagi
Ring Road detour with viewpoints galore (p281)
Siglufjörður
Fljótakív
Skagafjörður
Tröllaskagi Peninsula
Húnaflói
Skagaströnd
Sauðárkrókur
Bíldudalur
Patreksfjörður
Hólmavík
Blönduós
Brjánslækur
Hóp
Varmahlíð
Breiðafjörður
Flatey
Hvammstangi
The Westfjords
Majestic stone towers and silent fjords (p239)
Blöndulón Reservoir
Búðardalur
Stykkishólmur
Rif
Grundarfjörður
Hellissandur
Ólafsvík
Snæfellsnes
Snæfellsjökull National Park
Eiríksjökull (1675m)
Langjökull
Snæfellsnes Peninsula
A microcosm of Iceland's natural highlights (p219)
Borgarnes
Hvítárvatn
Akranes
Pingvellir National Park
Gulfoss
Reykjavík
Iceland's unrivalled nightlife & dining headquarters (p52)
Geysir
Faxaflói
Fimmvörðuháls
Gushing waterfalls and a steaming eruption site (p153)
Þingvallavatn
REYKJAVÍK
Hafnarfjörður
Kópavogur
Keflavík
Hveragerði
Landmannalaugar
Ytri-Njarðvík
Selfoss
Grindavík
Selvogsgrunn
Þorlákshöfn
Hella
Tindfjallajökull
Hvolsvöllur
Blue Lagoon
Steaming silica cauldron full of relaxed bathers (p107)
Vestmannaeyjar
Craggy archipelago and roaring birdlife (p171)
Katla (1250m)
Eyjafjallajökull
Mýrdalsjökull
Skógar
NORTH ATLANTIC OCEAN
Heimaey
Vestmannaeyjar Islands
Vík
Surtsey
24°W
23°W
22°W
21°W
20°W
19°W

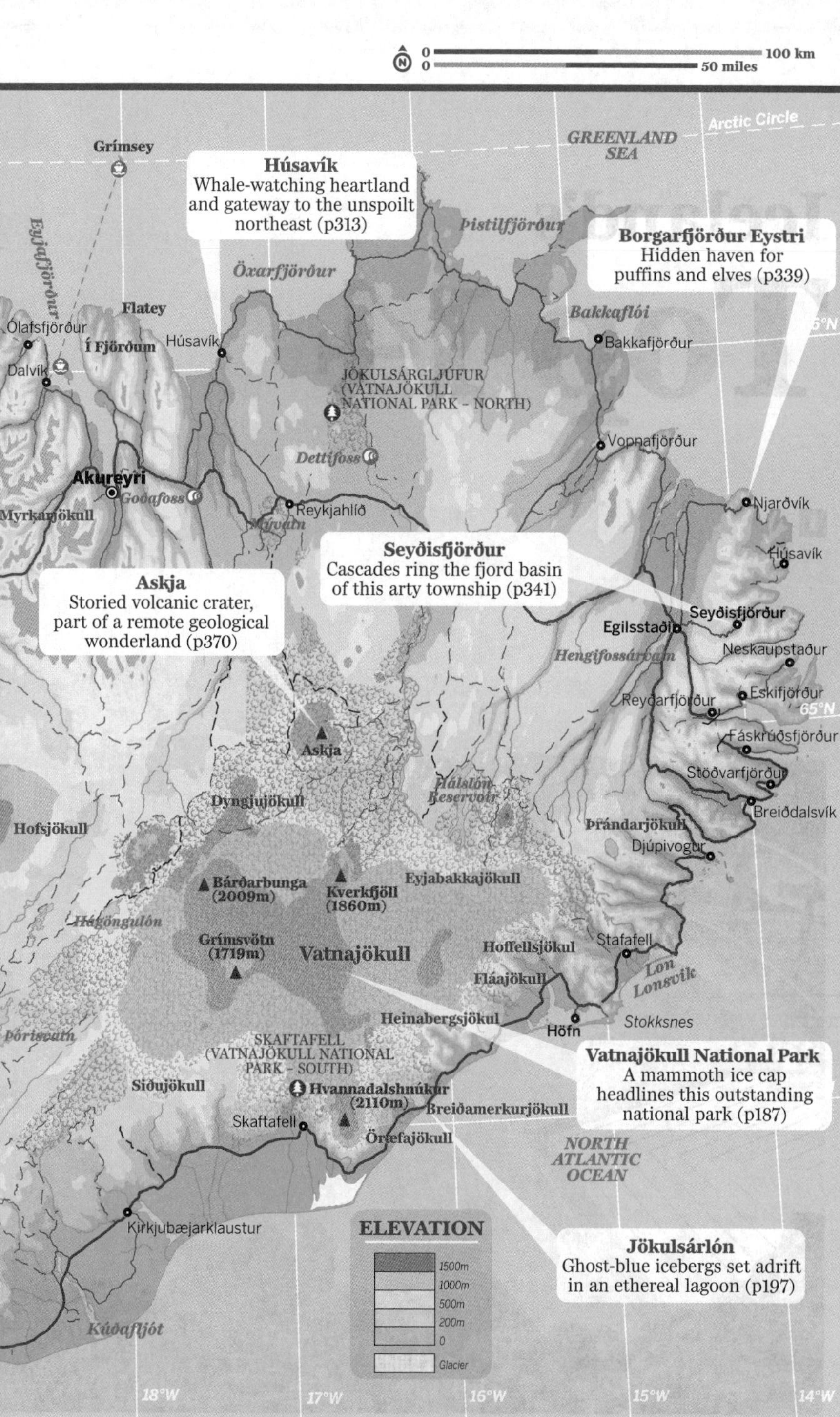

0
100 km
0
50 miles
Arctic Circle
GREENLAND SEA
Grímsey
Húsavík
Whale-watching heartland and gateway to the unspoilt northeast (p313)
Þistilfjörður
Borgarfjörður Eystri
Hidden haven for puffins and elves (p339)
Eyjafjörður
Öxarfjörður
Flatey
Bakkaflói
Ólafsfjörður
Í Fjörðum
Húsavík
Bakkafjörður
Dalvík
JÖKULSÁRGLJÚFUR (VATNAJÖKULL NATIONAL PARK - NORTH)
Vopnafjörður
Dettifoss
Akureyri
Goðafoss
Reykjahlíð
Njarðvík
Myrkárjökull
Mývatn
Seyðisfjörður
Cascades ring the fjord basin of this arty township (p341)
Húsavík
Askja
Storied volcanic crater, part of a remote geological wonderland (p370)
Seyðisfjörður
Egilsstaðir
Neskaupstaður
Hengifossárfoss
Eskifjörður
Reyðarfjörður
65°N
Fáskrúðsfjörður
Askja
Stöðvarfjörður
Hálslón Reservoir
Dyngjujökull
Breiðdalsvík
Hofsjökull
Þrándarjökull
Djúpivogur
Bárðarbunga (2009m)
Kverkfjöll (1860m)
Eyjabakkajökull
Hágöngulón
Grímsvötn (1719m)
Vatnajökull
Hoffellsjökull
Stafafell
Lón
Lonsvík
Fláajökull
Heinabergsjökull
Höfn
Stokksnes
Þórisvatn
SKAFTAFELL (VATNAJÖKULL NATIONAL PARK - SOUTH)
Vatnajökull National Park
A mammoth ice cap headlines this outstanding national park (p187)
Síðujökull
Hvannadalshnúkur (2110m)
Breiðamerkurjökull
Skaftafell
Öræfajökull
NORTH ATLANTIC OCEAN
Kirkjubæjarklaustur
ELEVATION
1500m
1000m
500m
200m
0
Glacier
Jökulsárlón
Ghost-blue icebergs set adrift in an ethereal lagoon (p197)
Kúðafljót
18°W
17°W
16°W
15°W
14°W

Iceland's Top 14

1

Getting into Hot Water

1 Iceland's unofficial pastime is splashing around in its surplus of geothermal water. You'll find 'hot-pots' everywhere, from downtown Reykjavík to the isolated peninsular tips of the Westfjords. Not only are they incredibly relaxing, they're the perfect antidote to a hangover and a great way to meet the locals (this is their social hub, the equivalent of the local pub or town square). The Blue Lagoon (p107) is the big cheese: its steaming lagoon full of silica deposits sits conveniently close to Keflavík airport, making it the perfect send-off before flying home.

Northern Lights

2 Everyone longs to glimpse the Northern Lights (p282), the celestial kaleidoscope known for transforming long winter nights into natural lava lamps. The lights, also known as aurora borealis, form when solar flares are drawn by the earth's magnetic field towards the North Pole. What results are ethereal veils of green, white, violet or red light, shimmering and dancing in a display not unlike silent fireworks. A good deal of luck is involved in seeing them, but look for the lights in clear, dark skies anytime between mid-September and mid-April.

PURIPAT LERTPUNYAROJ/SHUTTERSTOCK ©

2

EVRENKALINBACAK/SHUTTERSTOCK ©

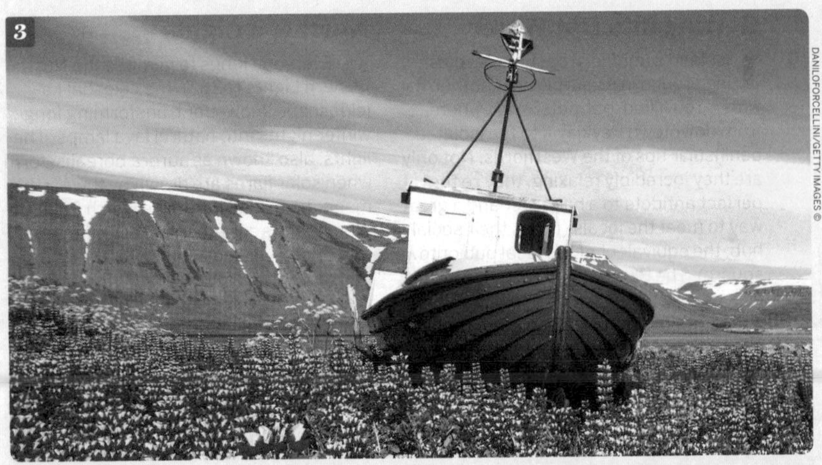

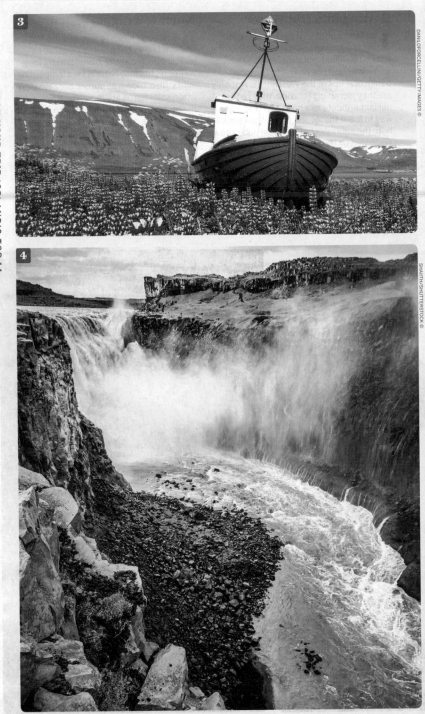

DANILOFORCELLINI/GETTY IMAGES ©

SHAIITH/SHUTTERSTOCK ©

Westfjords

3 Iceland's sweeping spectrum of superlative nature comes to a dramatic climax in the Westfjords (p239) – the island's off-the-beaten-path adventure par excellence. Broad, multi-hued beaches flank the southern coast, roaring bird colonies abound, fjordheads tower above and then plunge into the deep, and a network of ruddy roads twists throughout, adding an extra edge of adventure. The region's uppermost peninsula, Hornstrandir, is the final frontier; its sea cliffs are perilous, the Arctic foxes are foxier, and hiking trails forge through pristine patches of wilderness that practically kiss the Arctic Circle.

Driving the Ring Road

4 There's no better way to explore Iceland than to hire a set of wheels and road-trip Rte 1, affectionately known as the Ring Road (p36). This 1340km tarmac trail loops around the island, passing through verdant dales decked with waterfalls, glacier tongues dripping from ice caps like frosting from a cake, desert-like plains of grey outwash sands, and velvety, moss-covered lava fields. It's supremely spectacular – but don't forget to detour (to places such as Dettifoss, pictured p322). Use the Ring Road as your main artery and follow the veins as they splinter off into the wilderness.

Jökulsárlón

5 A ghostly procession of luminous-blue icebergs drifts serenely through the 25-sq-km Jökulsárlón (p197) lagoon before floating out to sea. This surreal scene (handily, right next to the Ring Road) is a natural film set; in fact, you might have seen it in *Batman Begins* and the James Bond film *Die Another Day*. The ice calves come from Breiðamerkurjökull glacier, an offshoot of the mighty Vatnajökull ice cap. Boat trips and kayaking among the bergs are popular, or you can simply wander the lakeshore, scout for seals and exhaust your camera's memory card.

6

RNDMS/SHUTTERSTOCK ©

Tröllaskagi Peninsula

6 Touring Tröllaskagi (p281) is a joy, especially now that road tunnels link the spectacularly sited townships of Siglufjörður and Ólafsfjörður. The peninsula's dramatic scenery contrasts with the gentle hills that roll through most of northern Iceland. Pit stops include Hofsós' perfect fjord-side swimming pool, Lónkot's plates of fine local produce and Siglufjörður's outstanding herring museum. Plus you'll find glorious panoramas, quality hiking, ski fields, microbreweries and beer baths, whale-watching tours, and ferries to offshore islands Grímsey and Hrísey.

Snæfellsnes Peninsula

7 With its cache of wild beaches, bird sanctuaries, horse farms and lava fields, the Snæfellsnes Peninsula (p219) is one of Iceland's best escapes – either as a day trip from the capital or as a relaxing long weekend. It's little wonder it's called 'Iceland in miniature' – it even hosts a national park and glacier-topped stratovolcano. Jules Verne was definitely onto something when he used Snæfellsjökull's icy crown as his magical doorway to the centre of the earth. Top right: Seacoast near Arnarstapi, Snaefellsnes Peninsula

Reykjavík's Cafe Culture & Beer Bars

8 Petite Reykjavík boasts all the treats you'd expect of a European capital – such as excellent museums and great shopping – but the city's ratio of coffee houses to citizens is nothing short of staggering. In fact, the local social culture is built around such low-key hang-outs (p91) that crank up the intensity after hours, when tea is swapped for tipples and the dance moves are broken out. Caffeine hits and designer microbrews are prepared with the utmost seriousness for accidental hipsters sporting well-worn *lopapeysur* (Icelandic woollen sweaters).

7

UHRYN LARYSA/SHUTTERSTOCK ©

8

HENN PHOTOGRAPHY/GETTY IMAGES ©

Borgarfjörður Eystri & Seyðisfjörður

9 A tale of two east-side fjords. Stunning, art-fuelled Seyðisfjörður grabs most of the attention – only 27 (sealed) kilometres from the Ring Road, it welcomes the weekly ferry from Europe into its mountain-lined, waterfall-studded embrace. Beautiful Borgarfjörður Eystri (p339), on the other hand, is 70km from the Ring Road, and much of that is unsealed. Its selling points are understated: puffins, mythical elves, rugged rhyolite peaks. Both fjords have natural splendour and bumper hiking trails. Below: Mt Dyrfjöll, Borgarfjörður Eystri

Vatnajökull National Park

10 Europe's largest national park covers around 14% of Iceland and safeguards mighty Vatnajökull (p189), the largest ice cap outside the poles (it's three times the size of Luxembourg). Scores of outlet glaciers flow down from its frosty bulk, while underneath it are active volcanoes and mountain peaks. Yes, this is ground zero for those 'fire and ice' clichés. You'll be spellbound by the diversity of landscapes, walking trails and activities inside this supersized park. Given its dimensions, access points are numerous – start at Skaftafell in the south or Ásbyrgi in the north.

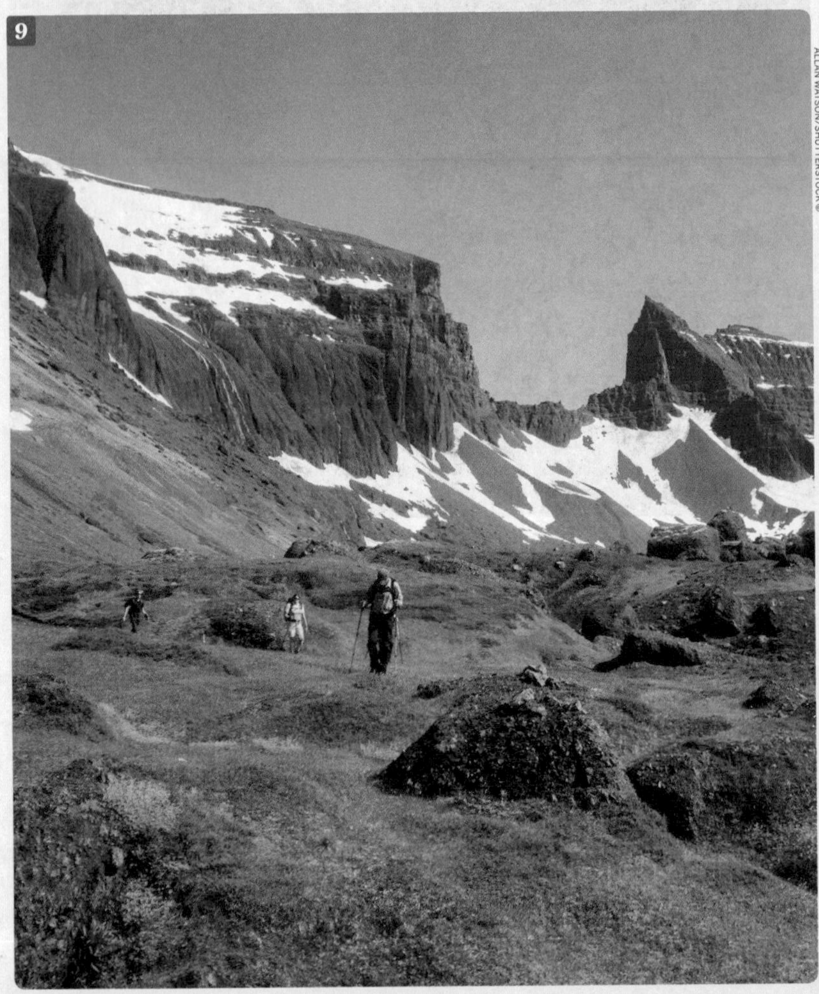

9

GUITAR PHOTOGRAPHER/SHUTTERSTOCK ©

WITOLD ZIOMEK/SHUTTERSTOCK ©

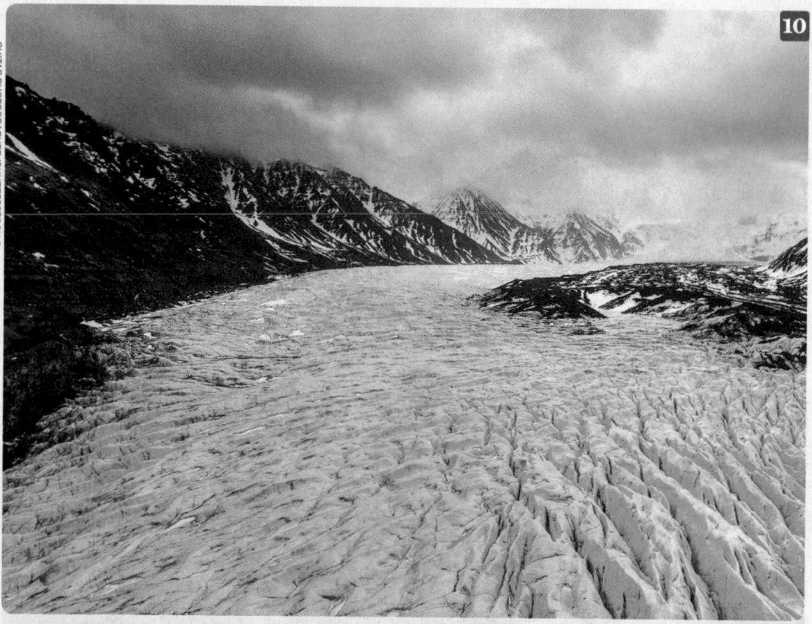

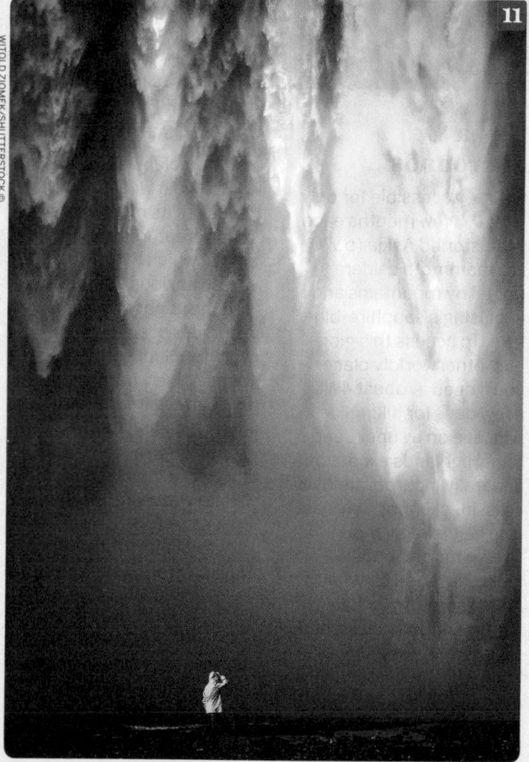

Fimmvörðuháls

11 If you haven't time to complete one of Iceland's multiday treks, the 23km, day-long Fimmvörðuháls trek (p153) will quench your wanderer's thirst. Start at the shimmering cascades of Skógafoss (pictured; p151); hike up into the hinterland to discover a veritable parade of waterfalls; gingerly tiptoe over the steaming remnants of the Eyjafjallajökull eruption; and hike along the stone terraces of a flower-filled kingdom that ends in silent Þórsmörk, a haven for campers, hemmed by a crown of glacial ridges.

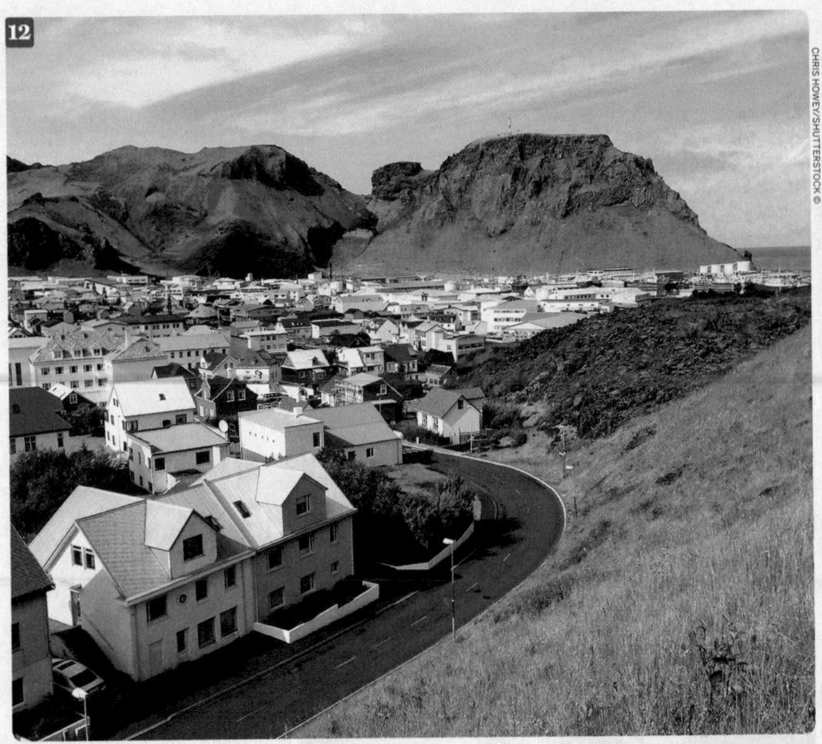

CHRIS HOWEY/SHUTTERSTOCK ©

Vestmannaeyjar

12 An offshore archipelago of craggy peaks, Vestmannaeyjar (p171) is a mere 30-minute ferry ride from the mainland, but feels miles away in sentiment. A boat tour of the scattered islets unveils squawking seabirds, towering cliffs and postcard-worthy vistas of lonely hunting cabins perched atop rocky outcrops. The islands' 4000-plus population is focused on Heimaey, a small town of windswept bungalows with a scarring curl of lava that flows straight through its centre – a poignant reminder of Iceland's volatile landscape.

Askja & Surrounds

13 Accessible for only a few months each year, storied Askja (p370) is a mammoth caldera ringed by mountains and enclosing a sapphire-blue lake. To access this glorious, otherworldly place, you'll need a robust 4WD, a few days for hiking, or passage on a super-Jeep tour. Highlands excursions generally incorporate river crossings, impossibly vast lava fields, regal mountain vistas and outlaw hideouts – and possibly a naked soak in geothermal waters. Added bonus: head south from Askja to visit Iceland's freshest lava field at Holuhraun.

Puffins & Whales

14 Iceland's two biggest wildlife drawcards are its most charismatic creatures: the twee puffin, which flits around like an anxious bumblebee, and the mighty whale, a number of species of which, including the immense blue whale, glide through the frigid blue ringing Iceland's coast. Opportunities to see both abound on land and sea. Whale-watching heartland is Húsavík (p313), and other northern towns and Reykjavík also offer cruises. Colonies of puffins are at numerous coastal cliffs and offshore isles, including Heimaey, Grímsey, Drangey, Látrabjarg and Borgarfjörður Eystri.

13

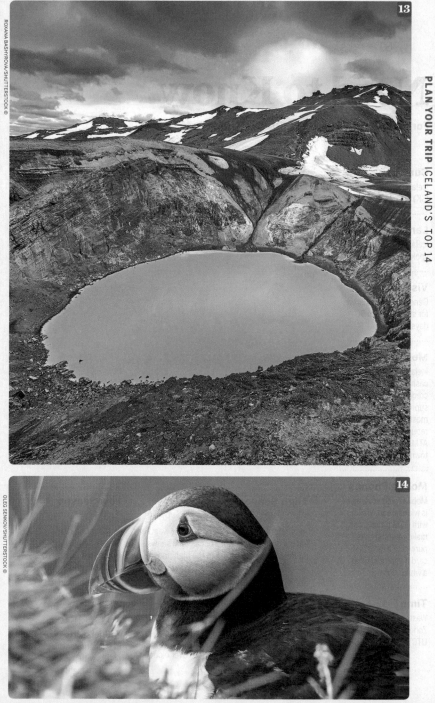

ROXANA BASHYROVA/SHUTTERSTOCK ©

14

OLEG SENKOV/SHUTTERSTOCK ©

Need to Know

For more information, see Survival Guide (p415)

Currency

Icelandic króna (kr or ISK)

Language

Icelandic; English widely spoken

Visas

Generally not required for stays of up to 90 days.

Money

Iceland is an almost cashless society where credit cards reign supreme, even in the most rural reaches. PIN required for purchases. ATMs available in all towns.

Mobile Phones

Mobile (cell) coverage is widespread. Visitors with GSM phones can make roaming calls; purchase a local SIM card if you're staying a while.

Time

Western European Time Zone (equal to GMT/UTC)

When to Go

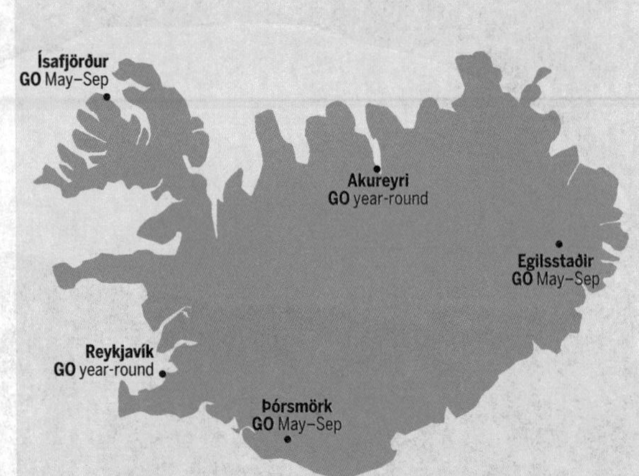

High Season
(Jun–Aug)

➡ Visitors descend en masse, especially to Reykjavík and the south. Prices peak; prebookings are essential.

➡ Endless daylight, plentiful festivals, busy activities.

➡ Highland mountain roads open to 4WDs from mid-June or later; hikers welcome.

Shoulder
(May & Sep)

➡ Breezier weather; occasional snows in the highlands (access via mountain roads is weather-dependent).

➡ Optimal visiting conditions if you prefer smaller crowds and lower prices over cloudless days.

Low Season
(Oct–Apr)

➡ Mountain roads closed; some minor roads shut due to weather conditions.

➡ Winter activities on offer, including skiing, snowshoeing and visiting ice caves.

➡ Brief spurts of daylight; long nights with possible Northern Lights viewings.

Useful Websites

Visit Iceland (www.visiticeland.com) Official tourism portal.

Visit Reykjavík (www.visitreykjavik.is) Official site for the capital.

Icelandic Met Office (http://en.vedur.is) Best resource for weather forecasts.

Icelandic Road Administration (www.road.is) Details road openings and current conditions.

Reykjavík Grapevine (www.grapevine.is) Great English-language newspaper and website.

Lonely Planet (www.lonelyplanet.com/iceland) Destination information, hotel bookings, traveller forum and more.

Important Numbers

To call from outside Iceland, dial your international access code, Iceland's country code (354) then the seven-digit number. There are no area codes in Iceland.

Emergency services (police, ambulance, fire, search & rescue)	☎112
Directory enquiries	☎118
Iceland country code	☎354
International access code	☎00
Weather (press 1 after the intro)	☎902 0600
Road condition information	☎1777

Exchange Rates

Australia	A$1	79kr
Canada	C$1	81kr
Eurozone	€1	124kr
Japan	¥100	97kr
NZ	NZ$1	73kr
UK	UK£1	141kr
USA	US$1	107kr

For current exchange rates, see www.xe.com.

Daily Costs

Budget: Less than 18,000kr

- Camping: 1500–1800kr
- Dorm bed: 4000–7000kr
- Hostel breakfast: 1800–2000kr
- Grill-bar meal or soup lunch: 1500–2200kr
- One-way Reykjavík–Akureyri bus ticket: 10,120kr

Midrange: 18,000–35,000kr

- Guesthouse double room: 18,000–28,000kr
- Cafe meal: 2000–3500kr
- Museum entry: 1000kr
- Small vehicle rental (per day): from 8000kr

Top End: More than 35,000kr

- Boutique double room: 30,000–45,000kr
- Main dish in top-end restaurant: 3500–7000kr
- 4WD rental (per day): from 15,000kr

Opening Hours

Opening hours vary throughout the year (some places are closed outside the high season). In general hours tend to be longer from June to August, and shorter from September to May.

Banks 9am–4pm Monday to Friday

Cafe-bars 10am–1am Sunday to Thursday, 10am to between 3am and 6am Friday and Saturday

Cafes 10am–6pm

Offices 9am–5pm Monday to Friday

Petrol stations 8am–10pm or 11pm (automated pumps open 24 hours)

Post offices 9am–4pm or 4.30pm Monday to Friday (to 6pm in larger towns)

Restaurants 11.30am–2.30pm and 6pm–9pm or 10pm

Shops 10am–6pm Monday to Friday, 10am–4pm Saturday; some Sunday opening in Reykjavík

Supermarkets 9am–9pm

Arriving in Iceland

Keflavík International Airport Iceland's primary international airport is 48km southwest of Reykjavík. The most common transport to the capital is bus (45 to 60 minutes). Flybus and Airport Express deliver you to their terminals (2700kr to 2950kr) or to your city accommodation (3300kr to 3950kr). Flybus can also deliver you to the domestic airport in Reykavík (3950kr), and a separate service runs to/from the Blue Lagoon (4990kr). Taxis from Keflavík are possible, but pricey. Car rental from the airport is also popular.

Seyðisfjörður ferry port The weekly Smyril Line car ferry that connects Denmark with Iceland via the Faroe Islands arrives in Seyðisfjörður in East Iceland.

Getting Around

Car The most common way for visitors to get around. Vehicles can be expensive to rent but provide great freedom. A 2WD vehicle will get you almost everywhere in summer. Driving into the highlands and on F roads requires 4WDs.

Bus A decent bus network operates in July and August, shuttling you between major destinations and into the highlands. Outside these months, services are less frequent.

Air If you're short on time, domestic flights can help you get around efficiently.

For much more on **getting around**, see p428

What's New

Tourism Slowdown?

After a few years of astronomical growth in visitor numbers (20% to 30% annually), figures indicate the tourism boom may have slowed down a little. Iceland is still a hugely popular destination, and growth does continue, but the figures were less head-spinning in 2018 than in previous years.

Ring Road Re-Route

Road-trippers: the Ring Road has been re-routed in East Iceland (p329), and now travels between Breiðdalsvík and Egilsstaðir via the fjords Reyðarfjörður, Fáskrúðsfjörður and Stöðvarfjörður. It's an increase of only around 10km, but it's a safer and more convenient route, especially outside the summer months.

Booming Bathing

Canny developers are meeting the demand for more opportunities to soak in geothermal waters. In the capital, Sundhöllin has had a makeover, while Krauma has opened in West Iceland. GeoSea (p314) is new to Húsavík, and Vök Baths (p332) is under construction outside Egilsstaðir. Bjórböðin (p289), the beer baths north of Akureyri, have also made a splash.

Shrinking Bus Services

There was a noticeable drop in bus services in North and East Iceland in summer 2018. Visitors who are planning to tour the country by bus are advised to do their homework, and to allocate more time to getting around.

Microbrew Magic

There's been a countrywide microbrew boom, with great beers being made in unlikely places, including tiny Breiðdalsvík (p354) in the east, Jón Ríki (p202) in the southeast, and Siglufjörður (p285) in the north. Southern road-trippers can check out Ölverk (p134) in Hveragerði and Smiðjan (p169) in Vík, or prearrange a tour at Ölvisholt Brugghús (p139). In Akureyri, a new brewer's lounge (p298) stocks Einstök beers.

Parking Fees

Parking fees are now being charged at a handful of sites, including Þingvellir National Park (p119), the Skaftafell area of Vatnajökull National Park (p187), and at Seljalandsfoss (p149). Stand by for more of these arrangements at tourist hot spots.

Icy Activities

A few years ago the first iceberg-lagoon kayaking began at Heinabergsjökull (p199), but similar paddling tours are now possible at Jökulsárlón (p197) and Sólheimajökull (p165). The popularity of wintertime ice cave visits (p189) continues unabated.

Arctic Coast Way

A new North Iceland tourism initiative (www.northiceland.is/en/about/arctic-coast-way-nordurstrandarleid) launches in mid-2019, celebrating 21 villages near the Arctic Circle; travelling via 800km of road.

More Beds

A hotel-construction boom mirrors the tourist boom: existing lodgings continue to expand, and new developments spring up. A 250-room Marriott hotel is taking shape in Reykjavík, while the Retreat Hotel (p110) at Blue Lagoon and Deplar Farm (p285) have taken luxury to new heights. Elsewhere, Hótel Geysir (p126) impresses, as does Fosshotel Mývatn (p310).

For more recommendations and reviews, see lonelyplanet.com/iceland

If You Like...

Stunning Scenery

You realise that choosing between incomparable vistas is like trying to pick a favourite child? This list could be endless...

Þingeyri to Bíldudalur Zipper-like fjordheads resemble fleets of earthen ships engaged in a celestial battle. (p248)

Breiðafjörður Thousands of islets dot the sweeping bay as rainbows soar overhead in summertime sun showers. (p219)

Skaftafell to Höfn Glittering glaciers, brooding mountains and an iceberg-filled lagoon line this stretch along the Ring Road's southeast coast. (p187)

Eastfjords Supermodel Seyðisfjörður steals the limelight, but its fine fjord neighbours are just as photogenic. (p338)

Þórsmörk In the 'valley of Thor', lush green plants nestle under volcanic peaks, and among wild stretches of desert and looming glaciers. (p163)

Askja A remote, sapphire-blue lake at the heart of an immense caldera, accessed across vast, barren lava fields. (p370)

Tröllaskagi Peninsula The road hugs steep mountainsides, then emerges from tunnels to capture magical vistas of glistening waters. (p281)

Wildlife

Vestmannaeyjar's puffins The largest puffin colony in the world lives in this eye-catching archipelago. (p171)

Húsavík's whales View underwater marvels and birdlife on a boat expedition from Iceland's whale-watching heartland. (p314)

Hornstrandir's Arctic foxes Iceland's only native mammal thrives in a faraway kingdom of towering cliffs and mossy stones. (p262)

Lake Mývatn's birds Twitchers adore the marshy surrounds of the lake, a magnet for migrating geese and all kinds of waterfowl. (p303)

Vatnsnes Peninsula's seals Take a seal-spotting cruise from Hvammstangi or drive the peninsula to scout for sunbaking pinnipeds. (p274)

Lagoons & Swimming Pools

Blue Lagoon It's hard not to adore a soak in this steaming silica soup surrounded by dramatic flourishes of frozen lava. (p107)

Mývatn Nature Baths Ease your aching hiking muscles at the north's scenic answer to the Blue Lagoon. (p311)

Krossneslaug A Valhalla at the edge of the world where lapping Arctic waters greet a toasty geothermal source. (p269)

Lýsuhólslaug Swimming in this pool's mineral-rich waters is like soaking in a warm gin fizz with a twist of algae. (p236)

Hofsós Swimming Pool This perfectly sited fjord-side swimming pool puts the sleepy northern town of Hofsós on the map. (p281)

Gamla Laugin Mist rises from the 'Secret Lagoon' in Flúðir, surrounded by wildflower-filled meadows. (p129)

Víti The milky-blue waters are tepid, but the location – a crater beside the Askja caldera in the remote interior highland – is sizzling. (p370)

Sundhöllin Central Reykjavík's deco delight has had a makeover, and now features indoor and outdoor pools. (p66)

History

Settlement Exhibition A cleverly curated exhibit constructed around the excavation site of an ancient Viking hall. (p55)

Settlement Centre Gain insight into Iceland's settlement and famous *Egil's Saga* through beautiful wooden sculptures. (p211)

Herring Era Museum Recreates the heyday of herring fishing, which once brought frenzied activity and riches to Siglufjörður. (p285)

Víkingaheimar A museum whose centrepiece is a perfect reconstruction of the oldest known Viking-age ship. (p112)

Lakagígar Attempt to comprehend one of the most catastrophic volcanic events in human history. (p184)

Eldheimar The 'Pompeii of the North' museum gives insight into the devastating 1973 eruption on Heimaey. (p171)

Fáskrúðsfjörður The French flavour of this fjord is celebrated with a chic hotel and museum development. (p353)

National Museum Great historical context and content, spanning Settlement to the modern age. (p54)

Icelandic Emigration Center How and why so many headed to the New World for a new life in the late 19th century. (p284)

Wilderness Center Step back in time at this unique farm, home to creative, history-tinged accommodation and exhibits. (p336)

Waterfalls

Dettifoss With the greatest volume of any waterfall in Europe, thundering Dettifoss is nature at its most awesome. (p322)

Goðafoss The 'Waterfall of the Gods', loaded with spiritual symbolism, looks like it's been ripped straight from a shampoo commercial. (p303)

Skógafoss Camp near this gorgeous gusher then hike up into the highlands for 20 more waterfalls just beyond. (p151)

Dynjandi Veins of Arctic water cascade 100m over terraces of stone and offer some of the most gorgeous fjord views. (p249)

GARY LATHAM/LONELY PLANET ©

ROBERTO LA ROSA/SHUTTERSTOCK ©

Top: Carving depicting *Egil's Saga* at the Settlement Centre (p211), Borgarnes

Bottom: Harpa (p60), Reykjavík

Seljalandsfoss A (slippery) path in the rockface gives behind-the-scenes access to this postcard-perfect chute. (p149)

Hengifoss Iceland's second-highest falls plummet into a photogenic, brown-and-red-striped gorge. (p336)

Hiking

Landmannalaugar A striking realm offering endless foot fodder; the hike to Þórsmörk is the original flavour of wilderness walking. (p156)

Hornstrandir Pristine nature as far as the eye can see in this hiking paradise orbiting the Arctic Circle. (p262)

Skaftafell Follow trails through twisting birch woods or don crampons to tackle offshoots of mammoth Vatnajökull ice cap. (p187)

Jökulsárgljúfur Offers a veritable smorgasbord of geological wonders, including thundering waterfalls and Iceland's 'Grand Canyon'. (p318)

Kerlingarfjöll A remote highland massif with geothermal activity, and a growing reputation among the hiking community. (p363)

Borgarfjörður Eystri The base for a superb series of trails – don't miss the giant boulders and green ponds of Stórurð. (p339)

Local Food

Fish soup Any restaurant worth its salt has fish soup on the menu – try it at Narfeyrarstofa (p223) or Tjöruhúsið (p256).

Lamb Iceland's headliner meat is a locavore's dream; it falls off the bone at myriad restaurants, including Fjallakaffi. (p313)

Langoustine The Höfn fishing fleet pulls countless crustaceans from the icy local waters; Höfn's restaurants simply grill and add butter. (p202)

Skyr A delicious yoghurty snack available at any supermarket in Iceland. Taste it in creative, upmarket form at Slippurinn. (p177)

Hverabrauð Sample this cake-like rye bread, baked underground using geothermal heat, around Mývatn. (p303)

Tomatoes Friðheimar serves up tomato soup and top-notch Bloody Marys in a geothermally heated greenhouse. (p128)

Dairy delights Stop in at farm cafes doling out creamy treats – Efstidalur II (p123) and Kaffi Kú (p302) are exemplary.

Barley and herbs Vallanes is an organic farm deliciously setting the record straight on what can be grown in Iceland. (p334)

Unique Sleeps

Hótel Egilsen A run-down merchant's house transformed into a gorgeous harbour inn with boutique-chic fixtures. (p223)

Hótel Djúpavík This legendary bolthole fulfils fjord fantasies; Sigur Rós shot part of their documentary here. (p268)

Dalvík HI Hostel A charming, vintage-inspired hostel like no other. Budget prices belie boutique decor. (p288)

Silfurberg Soak in a glass-dome-enclosed hot-pot at this luxurious boutique guesthouse in view-blessed Breiðdalur valley. (p355)

Ion Luxury Adventure Hotel Swim in geothermal waters and dine on organic, local fare at this award-winning design hotel. (p122)

Wilderness Center Bunk down in a recreated *baðstofa* (historic living/sleeping room) on a farm in a glorious, remote eastern valley. (p336)

Buubble Hotel Scouting for Northern Lights might prevent you catching any shut-eye in these unique clear domes. (p128)

Tungulending A secluded waterfront outpost designed to make you slow down and enjoy the knockout views. (p318)

Þakgil Camp in an emerald-green valley among stark mountains and dramatic rock formations. (p170)

Retreat Hotel The exclusive way to access the Blue Lagoon, complete with private lagoon and decadent subterranean spa. (p110)

Architecture & Design

Churches Some of Iceland's most intriguing architecture can be seen in Stykkishólmur (p219), Akureyri (p290) and Reykjavík churches (p54).

Iceland Design Centre Promotes Iceland's designers and architects, and the brains behind the annual DesignMarch event. (p402)

Harpa Reykjavík's dazzling concert hall and cultural centre glows like the switchboard of an alien ship after dark. (p60)

Turf houses A paradigm of pre-modern Iceland, these hobbit houses, such as Glaumbær, offer a wonderfully whimsical insight into Iceland's past. (p277)

Reykjavík design boutiques Icelandic designs from sleek, fish-skin purses to knitted *lopapeysur* (woollen sweaters) and nature-inspired jewellery. (p96)

Þórbergssetur Honouring a local writer, this museum has an inspired exterior (resembling a giant bookshelf) that's a traffic-stopper. (p198)

Month by Month

TOP EVENTS

Bræðslan, July

Þjóðhátíð, August

Reykjavík Culture Night, August

Northern Lights, mid-September to mid-April

Iceland Airwaves, November

January

After December's cheer, the festive hangover hits. The first few weeks of the year can feel like an anticlimax – not helped by long dark nights and inclement weather.

Þorrablót

This Viking midwinter feast from late January to mid- or late February is marked nationwide with stomach-churning treats such as *hákarl* (fermented Greenland shark), *svið* (singed sheep's head) and *hrútspungar* (rams' testicles). All accompanied by shots of *brennivín* (a potent schnapps nicknamed 'black death'). Hungry?

February

The coldest month in many parts of Iceland, though everyday life in the capital can seem untouched. The countryside may be scenic under snow, but it's mostly dark – there are only seven to eight hours of daylight per day.

Winter Lights Festival

Reykjavík sparkles with this four-day winter-warmer encompassing Museum Night and Pool Night (late-opening museums and swimming pools), plus light installations and concerts. See www.winterlightsfestival.is.

Food & Fun

International chefs team up with local restaurants and vie for awards at this capital feast held in February or March. Teams are given the finest Icelandic ingredients (lamb and seafood, natch) to create their masterpieces. See www.foodandfun.is.

March

Winter is officially over in other parts of the world, but it's not time to start celebrating here. The country wakes from its slumber; winter activities such as skiing are popular as daylight hours increase.

Beer Day

It's hard to imagine, but beer was illegal in Iceland for 75 years. On 1 March, Icelanders celebrate the day in 1989 when the prohibition was overturned. With little prompting required, pubs, restaurants and clubs around Reykjavík are especially beer-lovin' on this night.

Iceland Winter Games

Snowy activities take centre stage in Akureyri, Iceland's winter-sports capital, including international freeski and snowboard competitions. Tour operators offer ways to get out into snowy scenes (dog-sledding, snowmobiling, super-Jeep and helicopter tours). See www.iceland-wintergames.com.

DesignMarch

The local design scene is celebrated in Reykjavík at this four-day fest of all things aesthetically pleasing: from fashion to furniture, architecture to food design. It's organised by the Iceland Design Centre, see www.designmarch.is.

Sónar Reykjavík

Music, creativity and technology are all brought together for three days in

March or April at Harpa concert hall, with more than 70 electronica and hip-hop bands and DJs from Iceland and abroad. See www.sonarreykjavik.com.

April

Easter is celebrated in a traditional fashion (Easter-egg hunts and roast lamb), and spring is in the air. Days lengthen and the mercury climbs, meaning greenery after the snow melts, plus the arrival of thousands of migrating birds.

Reykjavík International Literary Festival

Feeling bookish? This venerable festival gathers international writers for four days of readings and panels in the capital. Check www.bokmenntahatid.is for schedules.

Sumardagurinn Fyrsti

Rather ambitiously, Icelanders celebrate the first day of summer (the first Thursday after 18 April) with celebrations and street parades. A case of winter-induced madness? No, it's a nod to the Old Norse calendar, which divided the year into just two seasons: winter and summer.

Puffins on Parade

To the delight of twitchers and photographers, the divinely comedic puffin arrives in huge numbers (an estimated 10 million birds) for the breeding season, departing for warmer climes by mid-August. There are puffin colonies all around the country.

May

May is shoulder season, and isn't a bad month to visit, just before the tourist season cranks up in earnest. Enjoy prices before they escalate, plus lengthening days, spring wildflowers and first-rate birdwatching.

Reykjavík Arts Festival

Culture vultures flock to Iceland's premier cultural festival, a biennial event (even-numbered years) that showcases local and international theatre performances, film, dance, music and visual art. See www.listahatid.is for the program.

June

Hello summer! The short, sharp, three-month-long tourist season begins. Pros: the best weather, near-endless daylight, the pick of tours and excursions, the best choice of accommodation. Cons: big crowds, peak prices, the need to book all lodging.

Seafarers' Day

Fishing is integral to Icelandic life, and Seafarers' Day (Sjómannadagurinn) is party time in fishing villages. On the first weekend in June, every ship in Iceland is in harbour and all sailors have a day off. Salty-dog celebrations on the Sunday include drinking, rowing and swimming contests, tugs-of-war and mock sea rescues.

Hafnarfjörður Viking Festival

The peace is shattered as Viking hordes invade this seaside town near Reykjavík for a four-day market festival in mid-June. Expect family-friendly storytelling, staged battles, archery and music. See www.visithafnarfjordur.is.

Whale Watching

Some 11 species of whale are regularly spotted in waters around Iceland. Sightings happen year-round but the best time is from June to August. Whale-watching boat tours leave from the Reykjavík area, from Akureyri and surrounds, and from Húsavík, the country's whale-watching HQ.

National Day

The country's biggest holiday commemorates the founding of the Republic of Iceland, on 17 June 1944, with parades and general patriotic merriment. Tradition has it that the sun isn't supposed to shine. And it usually doesn't.

Opening of Mountain Roads

The highland regions of Iceland are generally blanketed in snow well into the warmer months. The opening of 4WD-only mountain roads is weather dependent, but generally occurs around mid-June; roads are closed again by late September/October. The website www.road.is keeps you updated.

Secret Solstice

This excellent music festival (www.secretsolstice.is) with local and international acts coincides with the summer solstice, so there's 24-hour daylight for partying. It's held at Laugardalur in Reykjavík.

Midsummer

Although midsummer isn't as major an event as in the rest of the Nordic countries, the longest day of the year is celebrated in Iceland with solstice parties and bonfires (staged anytime between 21 and 24 June).

Humar Festival

The tasty *humar* (often translated as lobster, but technically it's langoustine) is pulled fresh from Icelandic waters and served a delectable number of ways in the fishing town of Höfn during the Humarhátíð festival in late June/early July.

July

Iceland's festival pace quickens alongside a (hopefully) rising temperature gauge and a distinct swelling of tourist numbers. Expect busy roads, crowded trails, packed camp grounds, no-vacancy guesthouses etc, and book ahead.

Landsmót Hestamanna

Horse lovers: the week-long national Icelandic horse competition is held in even-numbered years at rotating host towns. It's a beloved spectator event and excuse for a country festival. See www.landsmot.is.

Folk Music Festival

The small but well-regarded five-day folk music festival in Siglufjörður welcomes Icelandic and foreign musicians. Enjoy traditional tunes, courses on Icelandic music, dance and handicrafts. See www.folkmusik.is.

Skálholt Summer Concerts

The cathedral at the historic religious centre of Skálholt hosts public concerts, lectures and workshops over a five-week period from July to August. The focus is on contemporary religious music and early music. See www.sumartonleikar.is.

Eistnaflug

The town of Neskaupstaður goes *off* in the second week of July, when the population doubles to celebrate the heavy-metal festival Eistnaflug. See www.eistnaflug.is.

Bræðslan

The beloved Bræðslan pop/rock festival has earned a reputation for great music and an intimate atmosphere. Some big local names (and a few international ones) come to play in tiny, out-of-the-way Borgarfjörður Eystri in late July. Check out www.braedslan.com.

August

The busy tourist season continues apace, with Southern Europeans flying north for holidays. By mid-month the puffins have departed (and some whales too); by late August the local kids are back at school, and the nights are lengthening.

Verslunarmannahelgi

This public-holiday long weekend (the first weekend in August) sees Icelanders flock to rural festivals, family barbecues, rock concerts and wild campground parties.

Þjóðhátíð

This earth-shaking event occurs in Heimaey, Vestmannaeyjar, on the August long weekend, commemorating the day in 1874 when foul weather prevented the islanders from partying when Iceland's constitution was established. Up to 16,000 people descend to watch bands and fireworks, and drink gallons of alcohol. See www.dalurinn.is.

Herring Festival

On the August long weekend, Siglufjörður celebrates its heady herring-induced heyday with dancing, feasting, drinking and fishy-flavoured activities.

Reykjavík Pride

Out and proud since 1999, this festival brings Carnaval-like colour to the capital on the second weekend of August. Up to 100,000 people (more than a quarter of the country's population) attend the Pride march and celebrations. See www.hinsegindagar.is/en.

Reykjavík Culture Night

On Culture Night (Menningarnótt), held mid-month, Reykjavikers turn out in force for a day and night of art, music, dance and fireworks. Many galleries, ateliers, shops, cafes and churches stay open until late. See www.menningarnott.is for a full program.

Reykjavík Marathon

Your chance to get sporty, mid-month in Reykjavík sees more than 15,000 people sweat it out in full- and half-marathons, as well as fun runs. See www.rmi.is.

Jökulsárlón Fireworks

Could there be a more beautiful location for a fireworks display than Jökulsárlón glacier lagoon? For one night in mid- to late August, an annual fundraising event is staged, with buses shuttling spectators from Höfn, Kirkjubæjarklaustur and Skaftafell. See www.visitvatnajokull.is.

September

Tourist arrivals decrease significantly and prices drop, making this a good time to visit. The weather can still be agreeable, but summer-only hotels, attractions and services are closed. Highland roads are closed by month's end.

Reykjavík Jazz Festival

Early in the month, Reykjavík toe-taps its way through five days dedicated to jazz, man. Local and international musicians blow their own trumpets at events across town. Check out www.reykjavikjazz.is.

Réttir

An autumn highlight, the *réttir* is the farmers' round-up of sheep that have grazed wild over summer. The round-up is often done on horseback and the animals are herded into a coral where the sorting takes place (participants and spectators welcome). Naturally, it's all accompanied by much rural merrymaking.

Reykjavík International Film Festival

This intimate 11-day event from late September features quirky programming that highlights independent filmmaking, both homegrown and international. There are also panels and masterclasses. Check the program at www.riff.is.

October

October marks the official onset of winter, with cooler temperatures, longer nights and the appearance of the Northern Lights.

Northern Lights

Also called aurora borealis, these colourful, dancing lights are caused by charged particles from solar flares colliding with the earth's atmosphere. They can only be viewed in the darkness of night with no cloud cover. The best months for viewing are from October to April (from mid-September, if you're lucky).

November

Summer is a distant memory. November sees nights lengthening (the sun sets around 4pm) and weather cooling, but Reykjavík parties hard, with big crowds gathering for its flagship music festival.

Iceland Airwaves

You'd be forgiven for thinking Iceland is just one giant music-producing machine. Since the first edition of Iceland Airwaves was held in 1998, this fab festival has become one of the world's premier annual showcases for new music (Icelandic and otherwise). Check out www.icelandairwaves.is.

Days of Darkness

East Iceland (Egilsstaðir and the fjords) perversely celebrates the onset of winter over 10 days in early to mid-November, with dark dances, ghost stories, magic shows and torch-lit processions during its unusual Days of Darkness (Dagar Myrkurs) festival.

Ice Caves

The frozen blue wonder of natural ice caves becomes accessible close to glacier edges from around November through to March. For safety reasons you *must* visit with a guide – tours can be arranged with local operators in the southeast, between Skaftafell and Höfn. (p189)

December

A festive atmosphere brings cheer to the darkest time of the year. Christmas markets, concerts and parties keep things bright and cosy, followed by New Year's Eve celebrations. Note that some hotels are closed between Christmas and New Year.

DENNIS VAN DE WATER/SHUTTERSTOCK ©

Plan Your Trip
Itineraries

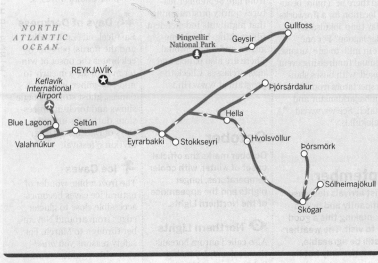

NORTH ATLANTIC OCEAN
Gullfoss
Þingvellir National Park
Geysir
REYKJAVÍK
Keflavík International Airport
Þjórsárdalur
Hella
Blue Lagoon
Seltún
Valahnúkur
Eyrarbakki
Stokkseyri
Hvolsvöllur
Þórsmörk
Sólheimajökull
Skógar

Reykjavík Minibreak

Whether you're on a lengthy layover or enjoying a long weekend away, don't miss the chance to get out into the countryside and take in some of the natural wonders located within a stone's throw of the capital. It's simple to string together the top sights, including the Golden Circle, with more off-the-beaten-path diversions, and still have a bit of time left to lap up Reykjavík's unique charm.

After landing at **Keflavík International Airport** make a beeline for the **Blue Lagoon** to soak away the jet lag in surreal waters and silica mud. Wander the Reykjanes Peninsula's steaming earth near **Valahnúkur** or **Seltún** before barrelling down the coastal highway for fresh seafood in **Eyrarbakki** or **Stokkseyri**. Choose a base near **Hella** or **Hvolsvöllur** to get out in the open air on horseback: the lush waterfall-rimmed Fljótshlíð valley is a key candidate. Or try to spot the Northern Lights (in the colder months). Active bodies will enjoy the stunning Fimmvörðuháls hike from **Skógar** up through the ridge

Strokkur geyser (p126)

between two brooding ice caps (and the site of the Eyjafjallajökull eruption in 2010) then down into **Þórsmörk**, a soaring valley dotted with wild Arctic flowers. Or you can take a super-Jeep tour or amphibious bus to Þórsmörk, and head out on day hikes around the valley. Those who are tighter on time can trek along the glacial tongue of **Sólheimajökull** instead.

On your way back west, roam the **Þjórsárdalur**, a broad volcanic river valley with a handful of disparate sights, including a Settlement Era farmstead, hidden waterfalls, and the foothills of Hekla volcano. Or, swing up to the gushing cascades at **Gullfoss**, the spurting **Geysir** from which all others got their name and **Strokkur** geysir nearby, and the rift valley and ancient parliament site **Þingvellir National Park** – the classic Golden Circle route.

Wrap up your minibreak with a night in **Reykjavík**. Iceland's capital bustles with an all-star assortment of boutiques, museums and galleries, lively bars and restaurants serving scrumptious food, plus there's easy access to whale-watching trips from the Old Harbour.

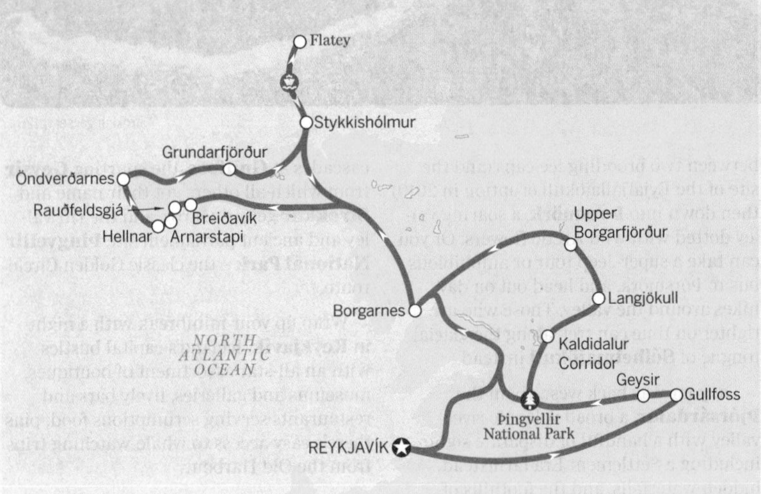
Flatey
Stykkishólmur
Grundarfjörður
Öndverðarnes
Rauðfeldsgjá
Breiðavík
Hellnar
Arnarstapi
Upper
Borgarfjörður
Langjökull
Borgarnes
NORTH
ATLANTIC
OCEAN
Kaldidalur
Corridor
Geysir
Gullfoss
Þingvellir
National Park
REYKJAVÍK

MANDRITOIU/SHUTTERSTOCK ©

NIDO HUEBL/SHUTTERSTOCK ©

Top: Stykkishólmur (p219)
Bottom: Þingvellir National Park (p119)

1 WEEK Best of the West

With one week to spend, you'll be able to roam further than the popular Golden Circle and the busy southwest. Try heading northwest from Reykjavík to lesser-travelled west Iceland, which is chock-a-block with history and boasts landscapes ranging from lava fields to broad fjords and ice caps, and gives a sense of the wonderful solitude that Iceland offers.

Start in **Reykjavík**, enjoying the city's museums, cafes and bars while getting acclimatised. Then complete the day-long Golden Circle with stops at glittering **Gullfoss**, surging **Geysir**, and historic **Þingvellir National Park**, where you'll witness the tearing apart of the continental plates. If you're feeling adventurous, go inland and bump along the rutted **Kaldidalur Corridor** for stunning vistas through the pinnacles of several ice caps. Stop in at **Langjökull** for exploration of its glistening tunnel and caves, or a taste of icy activities such as snowmobiling. You'll emerge at **Upper Borgarbyggð**, where you can sleep in the quiet countryside, explore enormous lava tubes or soak in a sleek spa complex. If you're not up for the back-country aspects of the Kaldidalur Corridor, instead head to **Borgarnes** along the coastal route, and learn about the sagas at its excellent Settlement Centre.

Next up, explore the wonderful Snæfellsnes Peninsula. Start by horse riding around the bay of **Breiðavík** or creeping into the bizarre gorge, **Rauðfeldsgjá**. Then head west to **Arnarstapi**, where you can hike the coastal trail to **Hellnar** or pick up a Snæfellsjökull glacier tour, exploring Jules Verne's fabled centre of the earth. The area is part of Snæfellsjökull National Park and offers a multitude of hikes, taking in bird cliffs, volcanic craters, lava tubes and protected native flower terrain.

On the tip of the peninsula near **Öndverðarnes** look for pods of orcas, or catch a whale-watching or puffin-viewing tour near **Grundarfjörður**. Then alight in charming **Stykkishólmur**, where you can take in interesting museums and sup on tasty mussels. If time permits, hop aboard the *Baldur* ferry for a day trip to quaint **Flatey** island; it's a great way to really disconnect from the world before returning to the capital.

Classic Ring Road

For such a wild, wonderful land, much of Iceland is surprisingly compact; the classic Ring Road trip loops you near the most popular sights. With extra time, you can add on myriad adventures along the way.

Start in **Reykjavík**, enjoying the city's creature comforts, before heading out in a clockwise fashion. Stop in **Borgarnes** for its fascinating Settlement Centre, historical sights and tasty restaurants. Then zip up to **Stykkishólmur**, an adorable village overlooking a bay studded by islets. With extra time, from here you could detour to the Snæfellsnes Peninsula. Either way, rejoin the Ring Road, breaking free of it once more to explore the quaint townships and coastal vistas of the **Tröllaskagi Peninsula** before gliding through **Akureyri**, Iceland's unofficial northern capital. Head to the geological treasure chest of the **Mývatn** region next, with a stop at **Dettifoss** to experience nature's awesome power firsthand. Push eastwards, detouring to **Borgarfjörður Eystri** for summer puffins galore. Take a break in **Seyðisfjörður**, then tackle the long journey through the rest of the east as the road curls along magical fjords.

Pause in **Höfn** for langoustine, and make plans to discover the icy realms of the vast **Vatnajökull** ice cap, be it via snowmobile or superjeep. Don't miss the glacial lagoon at **Jökulsárlón**, or neighbouring Fjallsárlón, where giant bergs break off glaciers and float out to sea. You can warm up your hiking legs in **Skaftafell** with glacier hikes aplenty then head south across mossy lava fields and enormous river deltas to **Vík**, which has a fantastical basalt-columned beach and puffin cliffs. Still feeling spry? Tackle the awesome trek from **Skógar** to **Þórsmörk**, a verdant interior valley. Or continue west along the Ring Road, passing enormous waterfalls at **Skógafoss** and **Seljalandsfoss**, then veer away one last time to check out the Golden Circle: **Gullfoss**, **Geysir** and the yawning continental divide and ancient governmental seat at **Þingvellir National Park**. Roll back into Reykjavík to spend the remainder of your holiday chatting with the locals, whether in the city's geothermal pools or during late-night pub crawls.

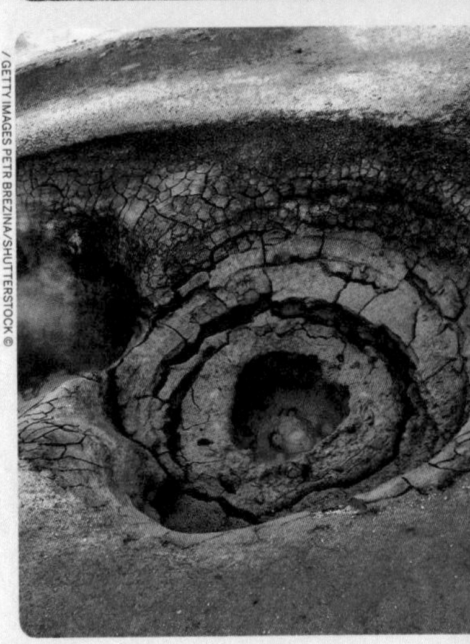

Top: Dettifoss (p322)
Bottom: Lava at Hverir (p311)

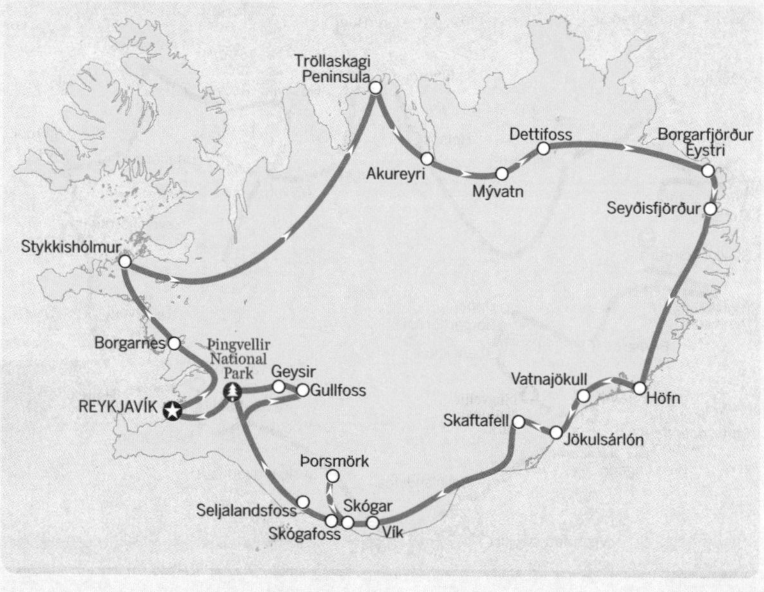

Tröllaskagi Peninsula
Akureyri
Dettifoss
Mývatn
Borgarfjörður Eystri
Seyðisfjörður
Stykkishólmur
Borgarnes
Þingvellir National Park
Geysir
Gullfoss
REYKJAVÍK
Vatnajökull
Höfn
Skaftafell
Jökulsárlón
Þorsmörk
Seljalandsfoss
Skógar
Skógafoss
Vík

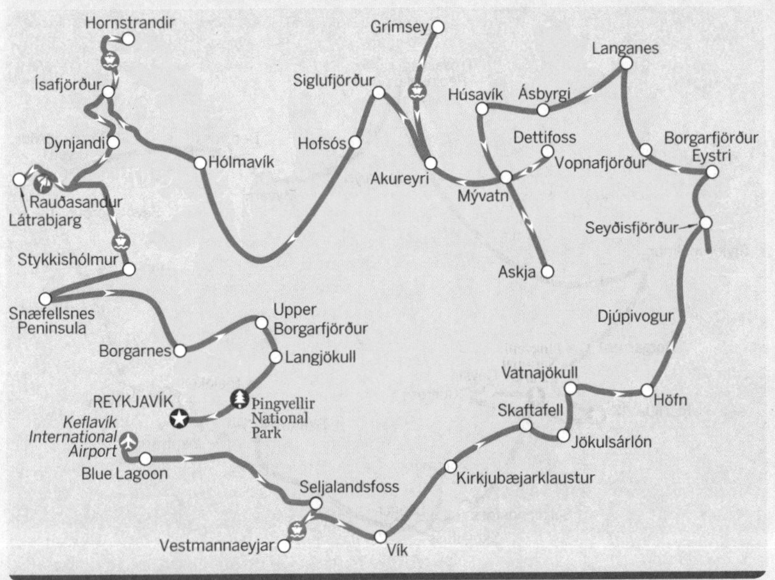
Hornstrandir
Ísafjörður
Dynjandi
Rauðasandur
Látrabjarg
Hólmavík
Stykkishólmur
Snæfellsnes Peninsula
Borgarnes
Upper Borgarfjörður
Langjökull
REYKJAVÍK
Þingvellir National Park
Keflavík International Airport
Blue Lagoon
Seljalandsfoss
Vestmannaeyjar
Vík
Kirkjubæjarklaustur
Skaftafell
Jökulsárlón
Vatnajökull
Höfn
Djúpivogur
Seyðisfjörður
Borgarfjörður Eystri
Langanes
Ásbyrgi
Húsavík
Dettifoss
Vopnafjörður
Mývatn
Askja
Akureyri
Grímsey
Siglufjörður
Hofsós

1TOMM/SHUTTERSTOCK ©

ANDREW MAYOVSKYY/SHUTTERSTOCK ©

Top: Hiking Hornstrandir (p262)
Bottom: Víkurkirkja, Vík (p168)

The Grand Tour

Remote and fantastical swaths of Iceland open to you with an extended stay. In addition to seeing major sights, venture further from the Ring Road, into the gorgeous, isolated Westfjords, or four-wheel-drive in the Highlands.

From **Keflavík airport**, rent wheels and head to the **Blue Lagoon** to unwind. Follow the coastal road, then head inland to chase waterfalls like **Seljalandsfoss**. Catch the boat to **Vestmannaeyjar**, where puffins flip-flap over fresh lava. Then sojourn near **Vík**, with its iconic black beach and stone sea stacks.

At **Kirkjubæjarklaustur** explore emerald trails and a fiery history. **Skaftafell** offers hiking, glacier walking and winter ice caves. Don't miss the icebergs at **Jökulsárlón** and consider a snowmobile or super-Jeep safari on frosty **Vatnajökull**, Europe's largest ice cap. Pause in **Höfn** for legendary langoustine, then negotiate hairpin fjord roads with epic views. Enjoy panoramas aplenty in inspiring **Seyðisfjörður**, and puffins and glorious hiking in **Borgarfjörður Eystri**.

Climb through **Vopnafjörður** to the grassy plains of **Langanes**, then follow the quiet northeastern circuit to the natural wonders of **Ásbyrgi**. Charming **Húsavík** is perfect for whale watching. Scenic **Mývatn** is a great base for exploring geothermal wonders and pounding waterfall **Dettifoss**. It's also a jump-off point for Highland treasures like mammoth caldera **Askja**. Get a slice of civilisation in **Akureyri** before touching the Arctic Circle on the island of **Grímsey**. Tour Tröllaskagi to check out **Siglufjörður**, then treat yourself to a relaxing swim in **Hofsós**.

Head to the Westfjords to learn about ancient witchcraft in **Hólmavík**, and use buzzing **Ísafjörður** as a launch pad to **Hornstrandir**, Iceland's majestic reserve. Explore the gushing waters of **Dynjandi**, then weave through fjords to bird cliffs at **Látrabjarg** and the mind-blowing pink-red beach **Rauðasandur**.

Ferry to charming **Stykkishólmur** and discover the treasures of the **Snæfellsnes Peninsula**, including golden beaches and craggy lava fields. **Borgarnes** and **Upper Borgarbyggð** blend saga sites and hidden caves, then **Langjökull** presents its ice tunnel. Get a history lesson at **Þingvellir National Park**, then finish up in **Reykjavík**, the ebullient capital.

Plan Your Trip

Ring Road Planner

Unless you've visited Iceland before, you'll likely struggle to name an Icelandic town besides Reykjavík. You may worry about planning your visit when so much of the country is vast and unknown. Fear not, the path is clear: take the Ring Road.

Best Ring Road Detours

Snæfellsnes Peninsula

A veritable ring road unto itself that takes in lava fields, wild coastline and an infamous ice cap; 200km detour.

Tröllaskagi Peninsula

Follow Rte 76/Rte 82 as it climbs up towards the Arctic – hair-raising road tunnels and scenic panoramas await; 90km detour.

Borgarfjörður Eystri

Take Rte 94 through rhyolite cliffs and down into this quiet hamlet where there are visiting puffins and superb hiking trails; 150km detour.

Vestmannaeyjar

Hop on the ferry at Landeyjahöfn to discover a rugged archipelago of islets; 30km detour plus a 30-minute boat ride each way.

Þórsmörk

Park at Seljalandsfoss and take the bus into a forested kingdom rife with scenic walks; 50km detour along a rutty road accessible only by certified vehicles; hiking also an option.

The 'Diamond Circle'

Dreamed up by marketers, the Diamond Circle barrels north from Mývatn to take in the whale-filled bay of Húsavík, the grand canyon and trails of Ásbyrgi, and the roaring falls at Dettifoss; 180km detour.

Route 1

Route 1 (Þjóðvegur 1), known as the Ring Road, is the country's main thoroughfare, comprising a super-scenic 1340km (832 miles) of paved highway. It's rarely more than one lane in either direction. Countless gems line its path, while secondary roads lead off it to further-flung adventures.

When to Go

The Ring Road is generally accessible year-round (there may be exceptions during winter storms); many of the secondary roads are closed during the colder months. Check out www.road.is for details of road closures, and www.vedur.is for weather forecasts.

Clockwise or Anticlockwise?

It doesn't matter which way you tackle the Ring Road – the landscape reveals itself in an equally cinematic fashion from both directions.

If you're travelling during the latter part of summer (August into September), we recommend driving the loop in a clockwise manner – check off your northern must-sees first as warmer weather sticks around a tad longer in the south.

How Long Do I Need?

Driving the Ring Road without stopping (or breaking the speed limit) would take approximately 16 hours. Thus, a week-long trip around the countryside means an average of about 2½ hours of driving per day. While this might seem a bit full-on for some, remember that the drive is extraordinarily scenic and rarely feels like a haul. In summer there's plenty of daylight.

A minimum of 10 days is recommended to do justice to the Ring Road (two weeks is better). For travellers planning an itinerary that's less than a week, it's better to commit to one or two regions in detail (eg Reykjavík and the south or west; or a week in the north), rather than trying to hoof it around the island.

By Car

Discovering Iceland by private vehicle is by far the most convenient way to go. It is, as you may have expected, also the most expensive option.

Renting a Car

It's best to start planning early if searching for low rates. The internet is your best resource, but take care to double-check that all fees are included in the quoted price.

Book early for summer hires – companies sometimes run out of vehicles.

2WD or 4WD?

A 2WD vehicle is fine in summer if you're planning to drive just the Ring Road and major secondary roads. If you want to explore the interior (driving on 'F' mountain roads), you'll need a robust 4WD; alternatively, hire a 2WD and book bus trips or super-Jeep tours to less accessible areas.

In winter, 2WDs aren't recommended; consider a 4WD for safety (note, rental prices are considerably lower than in summer). Winter tyres are fitted to winter rentals.

Breaking Up the Journey

The most important thing to remember when travelling the Ring Road is to use it as a conduit to explore memorable detours. Choosing five mini-bases along the journey to break up the drive is recommended. Try selecting one stop in each region through which the Ring Road passes: the west, north, east, southeast and southwest. Depending on the length of your trip, you can spend several nights at each base, engaging in the area's best activities and detours.

RING ROAD TIPS

➡ Don't confuse the Ring Road, which loops the country, with the Golden Circle (a tourist route in the country's southwest).

➡ The Ring Road doesn't traverse Iceland's interior – if you're keen to see more, two highland routes cut through the centre. These roads are only open in summer, and only to 4WDs and all-terrain buses.

By Bus

Far less convenient than car rental, Iceland's limited bus service is the most cost-effective option for solo travellers – however, in summer 2018 a reduction in services in the east meant it became very hard (but not altogether impossible) to travel the entire Ring Road by bus.

You should budget double the time of a private vehicle to loop around. For comparison, two travellers bussing around the island roughly equals the price (excluding petrol) of a small rental car for a week.

By Bicycle

Unfortunately cyclists will have a tougher time than expected travelling the Ring Road. The changeable weather makes for tough going, and although the path is paved, there is hardly any room on the shoulder of the road to provide a comfortable distance from vehicular traffic.

By Hitching & Ride-Sharing

The most cost-effective way to venture around the Ring Road is to stick out your thumb. In summer it's quite easy to hitch all the way around the Ring Road but be aware of the potential risks (p435) involved.

Many hostels have ride-share poster boards in their lobbies. A great resource is www.samferda.is, an online ride-share messageboard.

Jökulsárlón (p197)

Plan Your Trip

Outdoor Adventures

Iceland's spectacular natural beauty encompasses Western Europe's largest national park and the mightiest ice cap outside the poles, plus a whale-filled ocean and the world's biggest puffin colonies. Prepare to greet soaring mountains, hidden valleys, dark canyons, roaring waterfalls, twisting rivers and fjord-riven coastlines. Getting out into it is easy, and utterly exhilarating.

Best Time to Go

For multiday hiking Wait for spring thaw; hiking is best July to mid-September.

For highlands exploration Mountain roads open sometime from mid-June to early July, and close by late September or early October.

For midnight sun Around the summer solstice (21 June) the daylight is endless (especially in the north).

For Northern Lights You'll need dark, clear nights; viewings occur between about mid-September and April.

For skiing December to April, with best conditions (and increasing daylight) in February and March.

For whale watching Year-round, with peak viewing from June to August.

For puffin viewing Mid-May to early or mid-August.

For icy endeavours Glacier hikes and snowmobile trips can generally be done year-round (conditions permitting). Boat trips are scheduled on Jökulsárlón May to October. Mid-November to March is best for ice caving.

For horse riding Multiday treks are great in the shoulder season (May and September to early October) when the weather is cool but mild, and visitor numbers are fewer.

Activities

Hiking

Opportunities for hiking are endless, from leisurely hour-long strolls to multiday wilderness treks. Setting off on foot will open up vast reaches of unspoilt nature; however, the unpredictable weather is always a consideration, and rain, fog and mist can turn an uplifting hike into a miserable trudge. Always be prepared.

Ferðafélag Íslands (www.fi.is) runs huts, campgrounds and hiking trips throughout the country. Offers solid advice on hikes – especially Laugavegurinn.

Top Short Walks

Skaftafell Everyone's favourite part of Vatnajökull National Park; offers a slew of short walks around glinting glaciers and brooding waterfalls.

Þórsmörk An emerald kingdom tucked between the unforgiving hills of the interior; moderate-to-difficult walks abound.

Skógar Hike up into the interior for a parade of waterfalls; continue on to Fimmvörðuháls and down into Þórsmörk for one of Iceland's most rewarding day-long hikes.

Snæfellsnes Peninsula Half-day hikes galore through crunchy lava fields; don't miss the coastal walk from Hellnar to Arnarstapi.

Mývatn Flat and easy, the marshy Mývatn lakeshore hosts a variety of geological wonders as well as prolific bird life.

Borgarfjörður Eystri Superb trails among the rhyolite cliffs, and hikes up to the fjordhead for views.

Best Multiday Treks

Laugavegurinn Iceland's classic walk takes you through caramel-coloured dunes, smoking earth and devastating desert. Duration: two to five days.

Ásbyrgi to Dettifoss A sampler of Iceland's geological phenomena starts at the northern end of Jökulsárgljúfur (in Vatnajökull National Park) and works its way down the gorge, ending with Europe's most powerful waterfall. Duration: two days.

Royal Horn Words can't do justice to Hornstrandir's fan-favourite route and the views of lonely fjords, emerald-green bluffs and swooping gulls. Duration: two to four days.

Fimmvörðuháls A parade of waterfalls turns into a blustery desert as you pass between hulking glaciers. Then, the steaming stones from the 2010 eruption appear before the path leads down into flower-filled Þórsmörk. Duration: one to two days.

Kerlingarfjöll Loop Largely untouched, this remote interior circuit unveils postcard-worthy vistas that rival those of well-trodden Laugavegurinn. Duration: three days.

Wildlife Watching

Iceland's range of wildlife is narrow but bewitchingly beautiful.

Arctic Foxes

Lovable like a dog but skittish like a rodent, the Arctic fox is Iceland's only native mammal. Sightings are rare, but these are the best spots to try your luck:

HIKING CHECKLIST

The specifics of gear required in Iceland will vary, depending on your activity, the time of year, the remoteness of the trail, and how long you'll be exploring (day hike versus multiday trek; staying in a hut versus camping). One constant: the changeability of the weather, and the risk it poses.

Essentials

- Take proper navigation tools; topo map and GPS are vital.
- Dress in layers. This is essential. First base layer: thermal underwear (wool or synthetic). Second layer: light wool or fleece top; quick-drying trousers. Third layer: waterproof and windproof jacket (eg Gore-Tex). You'll need a breathable rain shell, including waterproof overtrousers. Your day pack should also be waterproof.
- Avoid cotton clothes such as jeans, T-shirts and socks – these lose insulation properties when wet and take hours to dry. Polypropylene, which is quick-drying (but can be flammable) or merino wool, which warms even when wet (but dries slowly), are recommended.
- Take gloves, hat, sunglasses and sunscreen. Woollen or synthetic socks, and waterproof, broken-in hiking boots or shoes.

For Longer Trips

- Packs need a waterproof cover or a plastic liner to keep things dry. A dry set of clothes is essential.
- Always carry a first-aid kit, a headlamp/torch and a survival kit (survival blanket, whistle etc).
- Sleeping bags should be capable of handling negative Celsius temperatures. Campers will need a tent (wind- and weatherproof), stove and cooking utensils (hut users may or may not need the latter).
- Pack a swimsuit (for hot springs), lightweight sandals (for river crossings, to keep your boots dry), and hiking poles for steep descents and river crossings.
- Take plastic bags, which are handy for separating wet and dry gear, and for carrying out rubbish.

Buying or Hiring Gear

You can buy hiking and camping gear in larger towns – Reykjavík is best for this; Akureyri also has options. Note that prices in Iceland aren't cheap – strongly consider bringing what you need from home, and/or hiring gear.

A few car-rental places offer camping equipment for rent (this is particularly true of campervan-hire companies). Otherwise, two good rental places in Reykjavík are Fjallakofinn (p98) and Iceland Camping Equipment Rental (p98).

Hornstrandir The fox's main domain – join the team of researchers who set up camp here each summer.

Suðavík Home of the Arctic Fox Center – there are often orphaned foxes living in a small habitat on-site.

Breiðamerkursandur One of the main breeding grounds for skuas, the area has drawn a rising number of Arctic foxes hungry for a snack.

Birds

On coastal cliffs right around the country you can see huge numbers of seabirds, often in massive colonies. The best time for birdwatching is between June and mid-August, when puffins, gannets, guillemots, razorbills, kittiwakes and fulmars get twitchers excited.

The best bird cliffs and colonies include:

Vestmannaeyjar Puffins arc across cliff faces as you sail into the harbour at Heimaey. Birds nest on virtually every turret of stone emerging from the southern sea.

Hornstrandir This preserve offers an endless wall of stone that shoots down from the verdant bluffs straight into the waves – countless birds have built temporary homes within.

Borgarfjörður Eystri This hamlet offers one of the best places in Iceland to spot puffins, who build their intricate homes just metres from the viewing platform.

Látrabjarg Famous in the Westfjords for the eponymous bird cliffs.

Mývatn A different ecosystem than towering coastal bird cliffs, Mývatn's swampy landscape is a haven for migratory birds.

Langanes Remote windswept cliffs are home to prolific bird life; there's a viewing platform above a colony of northern gannets.

Ingólfshöfði Take a tractor ride to this dramatic promontory, where skuas swoop and puffins pose.

Grímsey Visit for the treat of crossing the Arctic Circle, and to admire hardy locals outnumbered by countless puffins and Arctic terns.

Drangey Climbing to the top of this storied Skagafjörður islet involves ropes, ladders and close-ups with puffins, guillemots, gannets and more.

Seals

Seals aren't as ubiquitous as Iceland's birds, but they're fun to spot.

Hvammstangi and Vatnsnes Peninsula A seal museum, boat tours and a peninsula studded with basking pinnipeds.

Ísafjarðardjúp Curling coastline and rock-strewn beaches offer good seal spotting.

Jökulsárlón As if the ice lagoon wasn't photogenic enough – look out for seals swimming among the bergs.

Húsey This remote, panoramic farm encourages you to do your seal spotting on horseback.

Whales

Iceland is one of the best places in the world to see whales and dolphins. The most common sightings are of minke and humpback whales, but you can also spot fin, sei and, very rarely, blue whales, among others.

Iceland's best spots for whale watching include:

Húsavík Iceland's classic whale-watching destination, complete with an excellent whale museum; 99% success rate during summer.

Eyjafjörður Whale-watching cruises ply the scenic waters of Iceland's longest fjord from Akureyri, Dalvík and Hauganes.

Icelandic horse

Reykjavík Easy viewing for visitors to the capital; boats depart from the old harbour downtown.

Snæfellsnes Peninsula Boat rides in Breiðafjörður seek whales, especially orcas, and puffins too.

Horse Riding

Horses are an integral part of Icelandic life; you'll see them all over the country. Many farms around the country offer short rides, including a handful of stables within a stone's throw of Reykjavík. Reckon on around 8000kr to 13,000kr for a one- or two-hour ride.

Best Horse-Riding Regions

Southern Snæfellsnes The wild beaches under the shadow of a glinting glacier are perfect places for a ride. Several award-winning stables are located here.

Hella The flatlands around Hella that roll under brooding Hekla host a constellation of horse ranches offering multiday rides and short sessions.

Skagafjörður The only county in Iceland where horses outnumber people has a proud tradition of breeding and training.

Best Swimming & Spas

Thanks to Iceland's abundance of geothermal heat, swimming is a national institution, and nearly every town has at least one *sundlaug* (heated swimming pool – often outdoors). Most pools also offer *heitir pottar* (hot-pots; small heated pools for soaking, with the water around 40°C), saunas and Jacuzzis. Admission is usually from 800kr to 1300kr (half-price for children).

The clean, chemical-free swimming pools and natural hot springs require a strict hygiene regimen, which involves a thorough shower with soap and without swimsuit before you enter the swimming area. Instructions are posted in a number of languages. Not following these rules is a sure-fire way to offend the locals.

Best Resources

Swimming in Iceland (www.swimminginiceland.com) Info on Iceland's thermal pools.

Thermal Pools in Iceland (by Jón G Snæland and Þóra Sigurbjörnsdóttir) Comprehensive guide to Iceland's naturally occurring springs; sold in most bookshops.

Blue Lagoon (www.bluelagoon.com) Iceland's favourite soaking venue and undisputed top attraction.

Visit Reykjavík (www.visitreykjavik.is) Click through to 'What to Do' for pools in the capital region.

Glacier Walks & Snowmobiling

Trekking across an icy white expanse can be one of the most ethereal experiences of your Iceland visit. The island has several options that offer a taste of winter even on the warmest of days – strap on the crampons!

Common-sense safety rules apply: don't get too close to glaciers or walk on them without the proper equipment and guiding.

Best Glaciers & Ice Caps to Explore

Vatnajökull Europe's biggest ice cap is perfect for snowmobile rides; it also has dozens of offshoot glaciers primed for guided hikes and ice climbs – arrange these from Skaftafell and points east towards Höfn.

Eyjafjallajökull The site of a volcanic eruption in 2010; take a super-Jeep to discover the icy surface then wander over to Magni, nearby, to see the still-steaming earth.

Snæfellsjökull Jules Verne's *Journey to the Centre of the Earth* starts here; try the snowcat tour from Arnarstapi.

Langjökull Close to Reykjavík; draws icy crowds thanks to its 'Into the Glacier' ice-cave experience.

Sólheimajökull An icy tongue unfurling from Mýrdalsjökull ice cap, ideal for an afternoon trek.

Boating, Kayaking & Rafting

A new perspective on Iceland's natural treasures is offered from the water.

Best Boating

Heimaey Zip across the Vestmannaeyjar archipelago, taking in the craggy cliffs and swooping birds.

Stykkishólmur Wind through the islands of silent Breiðafjörður.

Húsavík and Eyjafjörður Traditional wooden ships or high-speed Zodiacs sail through whale-filled waters.

Jökulsárlón and Fjallsárlón Cruise between freshly calved icebergs on these glacial lagoons.

Best Kayaking

Hornstrandir, Ísafjörður and Ísafjarðardjúp Sea kayaking at its finest; try multiday tours or a one-day adventure to Vigur, an offshore islet.

Seyðisfjörður The charismatic tour guide will leave you wondering what's more charming – the fjord or him.

Glacier lagoons The Southeast offers a number of superscenic opportunities to paddle among icebergs, including at Jökulsárlón.

Best River Trips

Varmahlíð Northern Iceland's white-water rafting base, with two glacial rivers to choose from (family-friendly rapids or full throttle).

Reykholt White-water rafting thrills on the Hvítá; you can also get your adrenalin pumping on Iceland's only jet-boat rides.

Cycling

Short cycling excursions can be a fun, healthy way to explore. In Reykjavík you'll find a couple of biking outlets, some offering day trips to nearby attractions such as the Golden Circle. Bike hire is possible in many other towns around the country.

ALFONS HAUKE/GETTY IMAGES ©

TATONKA/SHUTTERSTOCK ©

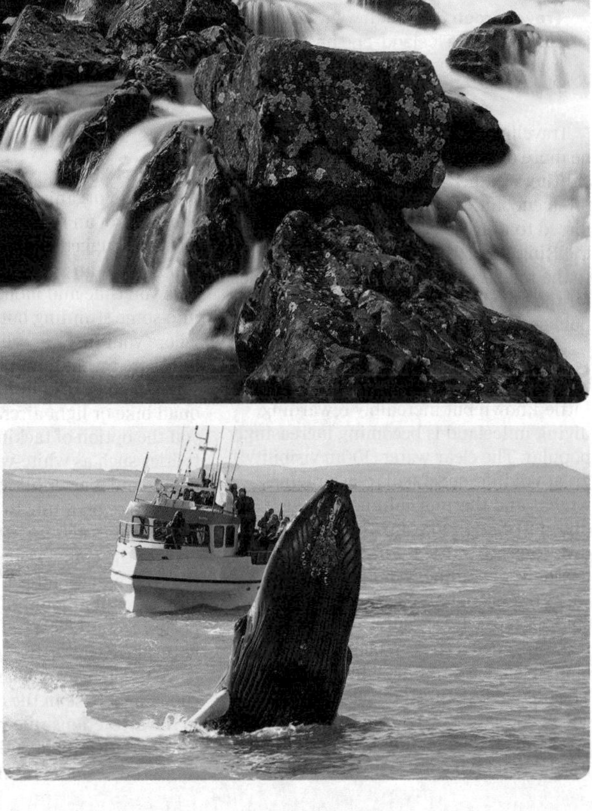

Top: Waterfall in Vestdalur (p343)

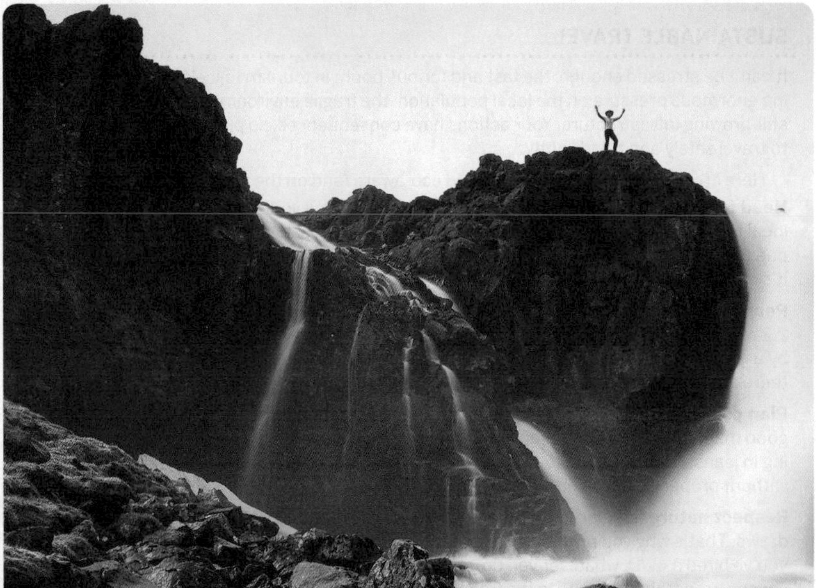

Bottom: Whale-watching near Husavik

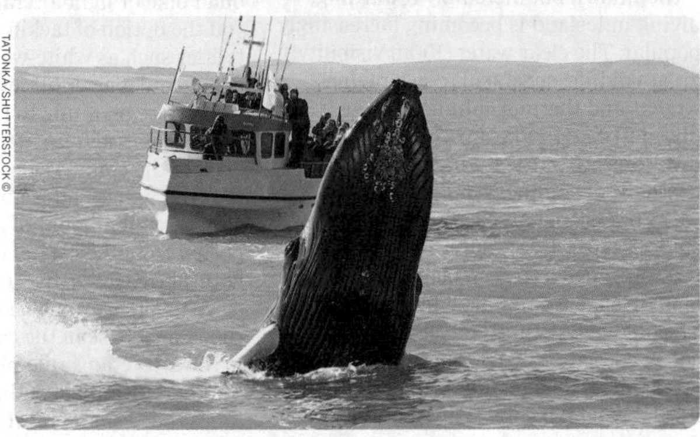

SUSTAINABLE TRAVEL

It can't be stressed enough: the fast and furious boom in tourism to Iceland is placing enormous pressure on the local population, the fragile environment, and the still-growing infrastructure. Your actions have consequences, so please endeavour to travel safely and tread lightly.

Here are a few tips on staying safe and eco-aware (and on the good side of locals):

Heed local warnings and advice No one is trying to spoil your holiday – when a local tells you that your car isn't suitable for a particular road, or an area is off limits due to fear of a glacial outburst flood, it's because they know this country and what it's capable of. Be flexible, and change your plans when necessary.

Recognise your impact The numbers speak for themselves: 350,000 locals versus 2.2 million tourists in 2017. You may think that staying overnight in your campervan by a roadside isn't a problem. But it is when thousands of people do it – that's why there are laws (p417) banning it.

Plan properly Check weather-forecast and road-condition websites (p19). Pack a good map, the appropriate gear, common sense and a degree of flexibility. No hiking in jeans, no attempting to cross rivers in small cars, no striding out onto glaciers without proper guidance and equipment (p40).

Respect nature Subglacial volcanoes, geothermal areas and vast lava fields are big draws. That's why you're visiting Iceland, no? So take care not to damage them. If you've hired a 4WD, whatever you do, stick to marked roads; off-roading is illegal and causes irreparable damage to the fragile landscape.

Travel green Check out www.nature.is – it's chock-full of amazing tips on travelling sustainably in Iceland, and has an online map and apps with a goal of making eco-friendly choices easier for everyone.

Travelling around Iceland by bicycle can be more of a challenge than it might seem – shifting weather patterns mean that you'll often encounter heavy winds, and you'll be forced to ride closely alongside traffic on the Ring Road (there are no hard shoulders to the roads). Check www.cyclingiceland.is for the excellent *Cycling Iceland* map, also published and distributed locally.

Scuba Diving & Snorkelling

Little-known but incredibly rewarding, diving in Iceland is becoming increasingly popular. The clear water (100m visibility!), great wildlife, spectacular lava ravines, wrecks and thermal chimneys make it a dive destination like no other. The best dive sites are Silfra at Þingvellir and the geothermal chimneys in Eyjafjörður.

A Professional Association of Diving Instructors (PADI) Dry Suit Diver certificate is recommended – you can obtain this in Iceland through a handful of diving companies. The unique PADI Tectonic Plate Awareness course (designed by Dive.is – www.dive.is) gives you an understanding of plate tectonics and what it means to dive between them.

Tours

Joining an organised tour may not be your idea of an independent holiday, but Iceland's rugged terrain and high costs can make it an appealing option. Tours can save you time and money, and can get you into some stunning but isolated locations where your hire car will never go. Many tours are by bus, others are by 4WD or super-Jeep, and some are by snowmobile, quad bike or light aircraft. Most tours give you the option of tacking on adventure activities such as white-water rafting, horse riding and glacier hiking.

If you're planning to base yourself in Reykjavík and use day-long tours to explore the countryside, it's vital to note that you will spend (some may say waste) a significant amount of time being transported from the capital out to the island's natural treasures. If a series of short tours is what you're after, you are better off choosing a base in the countryside closer to the attractions that pique your interest. Another advantage of this approach: sometimes the best and most personalised tours

Silfra fissure (p121), Þingvellir National Park,

are offered by small-scale local operators who have grown up exploring the ice caves, glaciers, mountains and/or trails in their backyards, and can give you a real local insight (as opposed to large city-based companies that shuttle busloads to popular destinations).

There are hundreds of tour operators in Iceland, ranging from small-scale to large. The following list represents some of the largest, most reputable tour operators; check their websites to get a sense of what is on offer. And don't forget to look out for the little guys too.

Reykjavík Excursions (www.re.is) Reykjavík's most popular day-tour agency, with a comprehensive range of year-round tours.

Arctic Adventures (www.adventures.is) Specialises in action-filled tours – from straight-up sightseeing to mountain biking, sea kayaking and even surfing.

Grayline Iceland (www.grayline.is) Bus-tour operator offering comprehensive day trips and plenty of activities.

Icelandic Mountain Guides (www.mountainguides.is) Offers an incredibly diverse range of activities, plus multiday hiking, mountain climbing, biking and skiing tours. Hard-core expeditions too.

Midgard Adventure (www.midgardadventure.is) Local operator in South Iceland with immense expertise and a great vibe to boot.

Saga Travel (www.sagatravel.is) A company with strong ties to North Iceland, and a diverse year-round program of tours from Reykjavík, Akureyri and Mývatn.

Air Iceland Connect (www.airicelandconnect.is) Iceland's largest domestic airline runs air, bus, hiking and 4WD day tours from Reykjavík and Akureyri. Also tours to Greenland.

Outdoor Activities

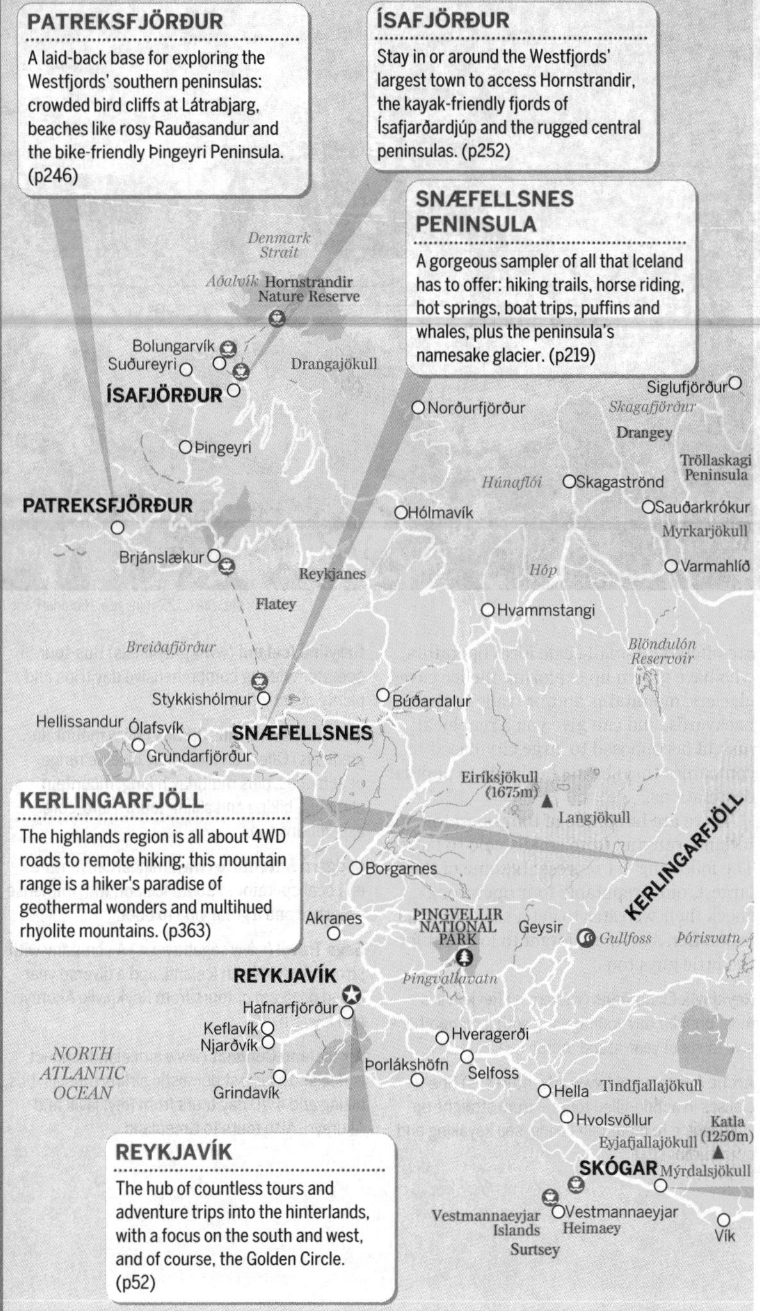
PATREKSFJÖRÐUR
A laid-back base for exploring the Westfjords' southern peninsulas: crowded bird cliffs at Látrabjarg, beaches like rosy Rauðasandur and the bike-friendly Þingeyri Peninsula. (p246)
ÍSAFJÖRÐUR
Stay in or around the Westfjords' largest town to access Hornstrandir, the kayak-friendly fjords of Ísafjarðardjúp and the rugged central peninsulas. (p252)
SNÆFELLSNES PENINSULA
A gorgeous sampler of all that Iceland has to offer: hiking trails, horse riding, hot springs, boat trips, puffins and whales, plus the peninsula's namesake glacier. (p219)
KERLINGARFJÖLL
The highlands region is all about 4WD roads to remote hiking; this mountain range is a hiker's paradise of geothermal wonders and multihued rhyolite mountains. (p363)
REYKJAVÍK
The hub of countless tours and adventure trips into the hinterlands, with a focus on the south and west, and of course, the Golden Circle. (p52)
Denmark Strait
Aðalvík
Hornstrandir Nature Reserve
Bolungarvík
Suðureyri
Drangajökull
ÍSAFJÖRÐUR
Norðurfjörður
Siglufjörður
Skagafjörður
Drangey
Þingeyri
Tröllaskagi Peninsula
Húnaflói
Skagaströnd
PATREKSFJÖRÐUR
Hólmavík
Sauðarkrókur
Myrkarjökull
Brjánslækur
Reykjanes
Hóp
Varmahlíð
Flatey
Hvammstangi
Breiðafjörður
Blöndulón Reservoir
Stykkishólmur
Búðardalur
Hellissandur
Ólafsvík
Grundarfjörður
SNÆFELLSNES
Eiríksjökull (1675m)
Langjökull
KERLINGARFJÖLL
Borgarnes
Akranes
ÞINGVELLIR NATIONAL PARK
Geysir
Gullfoss
Þórisvatn
Þingvallavatn
REYKJAVÍK
Hafnarfjörður
Keflavík
Njarðvík
Hveragerði
NORTH ATLANTIC OCEAN
Þorlákshöfn
Selfoss
Grindavík
Hella
Tindfjallajökull
Hvolsvöllur
Katla (1250m)
Eyjafjallajökull
SKÓGAR
Mýrdalsjökull
Vestmannaeyjar Islands
Vestmannaeyjar
Heimaey
Surtsey
Vík

0 100 km
0 50 miles
AKUREYRI
Iceland's second city is a gateway for tours all over the north, plus whale watching, horse riding and unique scuba diving. The ski fields are a wintertime magnet. (p290)
SEYÐISFJÖRÐUR
A cool, arty base for short and long hikes in waterfall-lined mountains, kayaking and sea-angling on calm fjord waters, or mountain biking into scenic valleys. (p341)
Arctic Circle
Grímsey
Raufarhöfn
Skoruvík
Þistilfjörður
Öxarfjörður
Þórshöfn
Flatey
Bakkaflói
Skjálfandi
Húsavík
Bakkafjörður
Ólafsfjörður
JÖKULSÁRGLJÚFUR (VATNAJÖKULL NATIONAL PARK – NORTH)
Dalvík
Eyjafjörður
Dettifoss
Vopnafjörður
Vopnafjörður
Reykjahlíð
AKUREYRI
MÝVATN
MÝVATN
Check out prolific birdlife and a cycle-friendly lakeshore, plus trails through lava fields to geological wonders. Bonus: easy highlands access via super-Jeep tours. (p303)
Egilsstaðir
SEYÐISFJÖRÐUR
Lagarfljót
Neskaupstaður
Eskifjörður
Reyðarfjörður
Fáskrúðsfjörður
Stöðvarfjörður
Hálslón Reservoir
Breiðdalsvík
Þrándarjökull
Hofsjökull
Dyngjujökull
Bárðarbunga (2009m)
Kverkfjöll (1860m)
Djúpivogur
Tungnafellsjökull
Hágöngulón
SKAFTAFELL (VATNAJÖKULL NATIONAL PARK – SOUTH)
Hoffellsjökull
Stafafell
Grímsvötn (1719m)
Vatnajökull
Fláajökull
Heinabergsjökull
Höfn
Hvannadalshnúkur (2110m)
SKAFTAFELL
SKAFTAFELL
This national-park headliner has trails aplenty, plus it's a stone's throw to Vatnajökull's icy treasures: glacier hikes, boat trips in ice-filled lagoons, snowmobiling and ice caves. (p187)
Kirkjubæjarklaustur
SKÓGAR
The area from Hella to Skógar is tops for horse riding, waterfalls and forays to Hekla or the famous Laugavegurinn trail, connecting Landmannalaugar and Þórsmörk. (p151)

Regions at a Glance

Reykjavík

Culture
Nightlife
Easy Escapes

Culture Capital

With miles of nothing but nature all around, Reykjavík is Iceland's confirmed repository of all things cultural, from winning museums and sleek gallery spaces to a sparkling music scene, a fat year-round festival calendar and a colourful guild of craftsfolk and designers.

White Nights

Reykjavík is notorious for its small but fierce nightlife scene. The best nights start with coffee at one of the dozens of cafes, 'pre-gaming' drinks at a friend's apartment, an unholy pilgrimage between several beer bars, and a late sticky-floored jam to DJs or live music.

Long Weekends

The perfect layover between Europe and North America: urban walking and biking tours take in the capital's top sights, but the magic of Iceland unfolds just beyond, and the city's well-oiled travel machine can instantly launch you into the wilderness.

p52

Southwest Iceland & the Golden Circle

Landscape
Activities
Wildlife

Volcanoes & Vistas

If the southwest were to print bumper stickers, they would say 'the further you go, the better it gets'. Wander into the interior and you'll find vistas of mythic proportions sitting under the watchful glare of several grumbling volcanoes.

Hiking, Riding & Vikings

High in the hills a hiker's paradise awaits, while around Hella are plenty of bucolic horse ranches. Toss in a smattering of Saga-era relics and you have endless itinerary fodder for every type of visitor.

Puffin Magic

The stunning Vestmannaeyjar archipelago has the largest colony of puffins in the world, and the birds offer a spirited welcome as they shoot over the arriving ferries like wobbly firecrackers.

p106

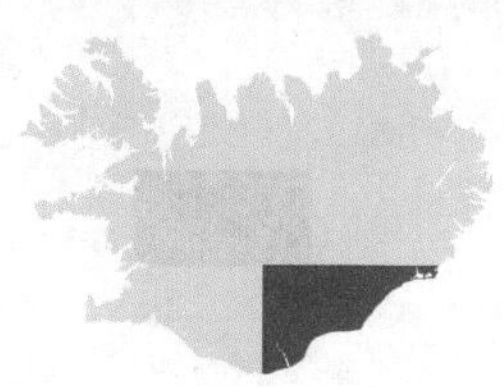

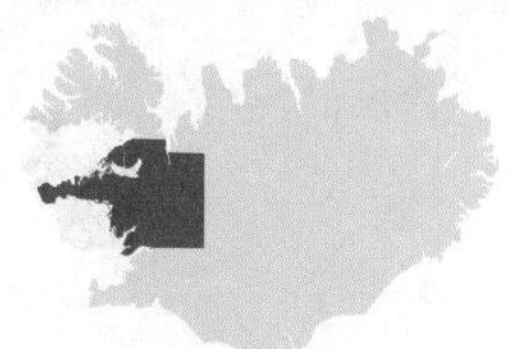

Southeast Iceland

Landscape
Wildlife
Activities

Glacial Glory

Home to glittering glaciers, toppling waterfalls, the iceberg-filled Jökulsárlón lagoon and Iceland's favourite walking area of Skaftafell, it's little wonder the southeast is among Iceland's most visited regions. Contrasting this beauty is the stark grey sands of the sandar (sand deltas).

Scene-Stealing Wildlife

Seals are a photogenic addition to the camera-friendly waters of Jökulsárlón, while great skuas make their homes in the sandar and harass visiting humans and birds. Ingólfshöfði is overrun with nesting puffins and other seabirds – getting there in a tractor-drawn cart is a blast.

Ice-Cap Endeavours

Icy activities include glacier walks, snowmobiling and winter ice-cave visits. Boat and kayaking trips among glacial lagoon bergs are in demand. There's ace mountain biking from Kirkjubæjarklaustur, and the underrated activity of cracking langoustine claws in Höfn.

p178

West Iceland

Landscape
History
Activities

Infinite Islets

The Snæfellsnes Peninsula is a technicolour realm composed of exotic splashes of sere lava, green waterfall-cut meadows, Arctic-blue water, and a dazzling ice cap. One of its most impressive vistas is Breiðafjörður – a bay reflecting cloud-filled skies and speckled with thousands of isles.

Viking Sagas

History buffs can take a trip back in time: the west is often dubbed Sagaland for its rich Viking history. Make a beeline for the Settlement Museum in buzzy Borgarnes to let the stories unfold.

Horseback Exploring

The southern shores of the Snæfellsnes Peninsula are among the best places to ride the small, tough Icelandic horse – follow the crests of sand or trot into the hills to find hidden geothermal sources.

p207

The Westfjords

Landscape
Activities
Wildlife

The End of the Line

On maps, the undulating coastline of the Westfjords makes the region resemble giant lobster claws snipping away at the Arctic Circle. The landscapes of this dramatic enclave of sea and stone inspire fables of magical, faraway lands.

Explore the Subarctic

Sitting at the edge of the Arctic, its jagged peninsulas stretching north, Iceland's final frontier is the perfect setting for rugged mountain biking, sea kayaking, sailing and springtime skiing. Hornstrandir hiking reserve is the jewel in the crown.

Foxy Friends

Wild-maned horses rove throughout, but the main draws are the impressive bird cliffs dotting the region and the fleet Arctic foxes scurrying between grassy hillocks. With preplanning, you can volunteer to monitor Iceland's only native mammal.

p239

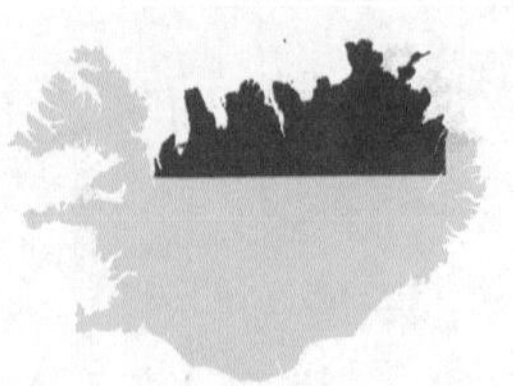

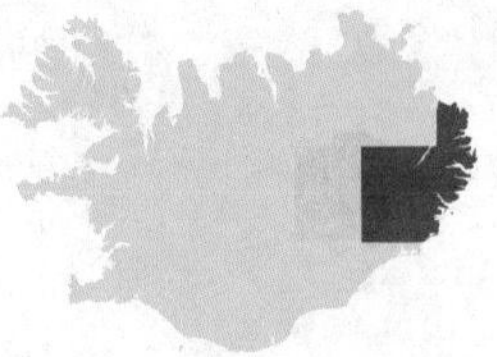

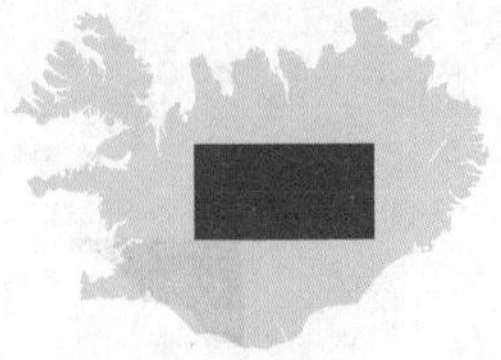

North Iceland

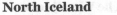

Landscape
Wildlife
Activities

A Land with the Lot

What landscape *doesn't* North Iceland offer? There are offshore islands, lonely peninsulas, icy peaks, pastoral horse farms, belching mudpots, sleepy fishing villages, epic waterfalls, shattered lava fields, breaching whales…

Whale Wonderland

Seals inhabit Vatnsnes Peninsula; puffins and seabirds nest all over. Waterbirds take to Mývatn like, well, ducks to water. The biggest draw lurks beneath: Húsavík is the whale-watching hub and towns along western Eyjafjörður, including Akureyri, are its apprentice.

The Active North

Horse riding is best in the northwest. Birdwatching around Lake Mývatn is world-class, but remote Langanes and Arctic Grímsey hold their own. Hike the northern reaches of Vatnajökull National Park, or ski the Tröllaskagi Peninsula.

p270

East Iceland

Landscape
Activities
Wildlife

Fan-fjord-tastic

The Eastfjords' scenery is particularly dramatic around the northern fjord villages, backed by sheer-sided mountains etched with waterfalls. Inland, scenic lake Lagarfljót (and the forest on its eastern shore) is ripe for exploration, as is the 1833m mountain Snæfell, part of Vatnajökull National Park.

On Land & Water

Kayaking the waters of Seyðisfjörður is a breathtaking highlight; mountain biking here is good for landlubbers; and seal spotting on horseback at Húsey is a unique treat. Trails in and around the fjords offer peak panoramas and hiking delights – Borgarfjörður Eystri is a local favourite.

Creatures of the East

Wild reindeer roam the mountains, and Iceland's version of the Loch Ness monster calls Lagarfljót home. Bird life is enjoyed at remote farms like Húsey or from the perfectly placed puffin-viewing platform at Borgarfjörður Eystri.

p328

The Highlands

Landscape
Solitude
Activities

Lunar Landscapes

This region is practically uninhabited – there are no towns or villages, only summertime huts and accommodation. NASA astronauts once trained here, and the recent Holuhraun eruption has added a whole new dimension to ancient lava fields.

Barren Beauty

Touring the highlands will give you a new understanding of the word 'desolation'. The solitude is exhilarating, the views are vast. Some travellers are disappointed by the interior's ultra-bleakness and endless grey-sand desert, others are humbled by the sight of nature in its rawest form.

Remote Hiking

It's immensely tough but equally rewarding to hike, bike or ride horses along interior routes. Kerlingarfjöll and the Askja region have first-class hiking; Hveravellir lures with hot springs. Many visitors may be happiest visiting the sights from the comfort of a super-Jeep tour!

p358

On the Road

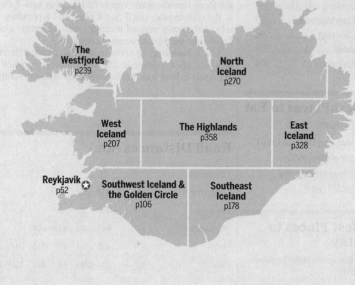

Reykjavík

POP CITY CENTRE: 124,847; GREATER REYKJAVÍK: 217,711

Includes ➡

Best Places to Eat

- ➡ Dill (p90)
- ➡ Matur og Drykkur (p86)
- ➡ Sægreifinn (p85)
- ➡ Flatey Pizza (p85)
- ➡ SKÁL! (p89)

Best Places to Stay

- ➡ Consulate Hotel Reykjavík (p76)
- ➡ Icelandair Hotel Reykjavík Marina (p77)
- ➡ Eyja Guldsmeden (p81)
- ➡ Alda Hotel (p80)
- ➡ Forsæla Apartmenthouse (p79)

Why Go?

The world's most northerly capital combines colourful buildings, quirky, creative people, eye-popping design, wild nightlife and a capricious soul.

Reykjavík is strikingly cosmopolitan for its size. It's merely a town by international standards, compared with London or Paris, yet it's loaded with captivating art, rich culinary choices, and cool cafes and bars. When you slip behind the shiny tourist-centric veneer (it is a great base for tours to the countryside) you'll find a place and a populace that mix aesthetically minded ingenuity with an almost quaint, know-your-neighbours sense of community.

Add a backdrop of snow-topped mountains, churning seas and crystal-clear air, and the chances are you'll fall helplessly in love, heading home already saving to return.

Road Distances (km)

	Reykjavík	Borgarnes	Ísafjörður	Akureyri	Egilsstaðir	Höfn
Borgarnes	74					
Ísafjörður	457	384				
Akureyri	389	315	567			
Egilsstaðir	698	580	832	265		
Höfn	459	519	902	512	247	
Vík	187	246	630	561	511	273

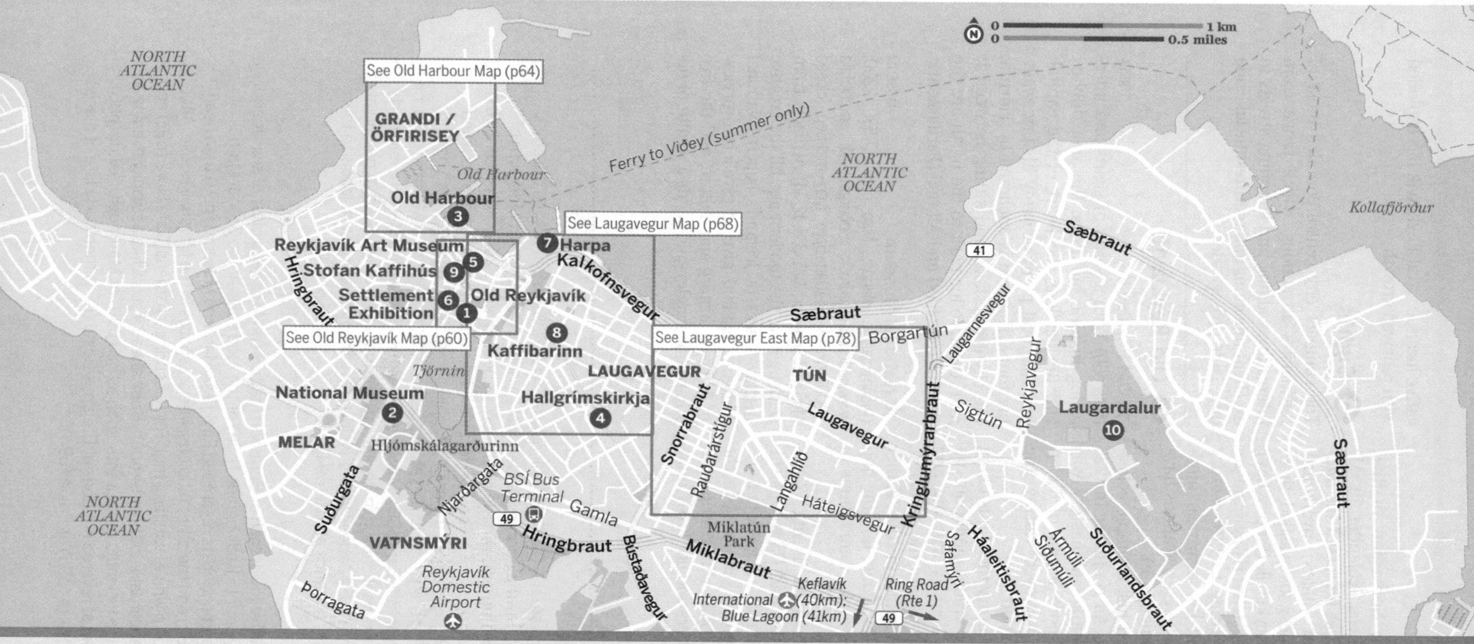

Reykjavík Highlights

1. **Old Reykjavík** (p54) Exploring this historic quarter and shopping in Laugavegur.
2. **National Museum** (p54) Learning about Iceland's fascinating history.
3. **Old Harbour** (p58) Hitting the museums, microbrewery and restaurants.
4. **Hallgrímskirkja** (p59) Scaling the heights of this landmark's modernist steeple.
5. **Reykjavík Art Museum** (p55) Immersing yourself at these standout museums.
6. **Settlement Exhibition** (p55) Perusing artefacts from Reykjavík's first days.
7. **Harpa** (p60) Enjoying a performance at the capital's twinkling concert hall.
8. **Partying** (p95) Joining a wild pub crawl at nightspots such as Kaffibarinn or Kiki.
9. **Cafes** (p87) Sipping coffee at quirky cafes like Stofan Kaffihús.
10. **Laugardalur** (p63) Soaking at the geothermal pool or visiting botanical gardens.

History

Ingólfur Arnarson, a Norwegian fugitive, became the first official Icelander in AD 871. The story goes that he tossed his *öndvegissúlur* (high-seat pillars) overboard, and settled where the gods washed them ashore. This was at Reykjavík (Smoky Bay), which he named after steam rising from geothermal vents. According to 12th-century sources, Ingólfur built his farm near modern-day Aðalstræti (where excavations have unearthed a Viking longhouse).

Reykjavík remained just a simple collection of farm buildings for centuries. In 1225 an important Augustinian monastery was founded on the offshore island of Viðey, although this was destroyed during the 16th-century Reformation.

In the early 17th century the Danish king imposed a crippling trade monopoly on Iceland, leaving the country starving and destitute. In a bid to bypass the embargo, local sheriff Skúli Magnússon, the 'Father of Reykjavík', created weaving, tanning and wool-dyeing factories – the foundations of the city – in the 1750s.

Reykjavík really boomed during WWII, when it serviced British and US troops stationed at Keflavík. The capital grew at a frenetic pace until it took a slamming in the credit crisis of 2008. Today, with continuously rising visitor numbers and endlessly innovative locals, central Reykjavík has exploded with renewed growth.

Sights

The compact city centre contains most of Reykjavík's attractions, which range from interesting walking and shopping streets to excellent museums and picturesque lakeside or seaside promenades.

Old Reykjavík

★Old Reykjavík AREA

(Map p60) With a series of sights and interesting historic buildings, the area dubbed Old Reykjavík is the heart of the capital, and the focal point of many historic walking tours. The area is anchored by Tjörnin, the city-centre lake, and sitting between it and Austurvöllur park to the north are the Raðhús (city hall) and Alþingi (Parliament).

★National Museum MUSEUM

(Þjóðminjasafn Íslands; Map p56; ☎530 2200; www.nationalmuseum.is; Suðurgata 41; adult/child 2000kr/free; ⏰10am-5pm May–mid-Sep, closed Mon mid-Sep–Apr; 🚌1, 3, 6, 12, 14) Artifacts from settlement to the modern age fill the creative display spaces of Iceland's superb National Museum. Exhibits give an excellent overview of Iceland's history and culture, and the free smartphone audio guide adds a wealth of de-

REYKJAVÍK IN...

One Day

Start with a walk around the Old Reykjavík quarter near Tjörnin then peruse the city's best museums, such as the impressive National Museum, Reykjavík Art Museum (p55) or Settlement Exhibition (p55). In the afternoon, wander up arty Skólavörðustígur to the immense Hallgrímskirkja (p59). For a perfect view, take an elevator up the tower, then circle down to stroll Laugavegur, the main shopping drag. Sit for people-watching and drinks at Bravó (p94) then head to dinner. For casual eats, hit Hlemmur Mathöll (p88), or try Icelandic fusion at Mat Bar (p89). Many cafes – like Kaffi Vínyl (p93) – turn into party hangouts at night. On weekends, join Reykjavík's notorious pub crawl. Start at perennial favourite Kaffibarinn (p93) or beer-lovers' Kaldi (p93), then tag along with locals to the latest drinking holes, or dance at Kiki (p94).

Two Days

After a late night out, enjoy brunch at Bergsson Mathús (p84) or get a blast of sea air and stroll to the Old Harbour to Kaffivagninn (p86) or the food stalls at the Grandi Mathöll (p85). Take in the harbor and its revamped Reykjavík Maritime Museum (p59) then head to Kling & Bang (p62) and the other fabulous, free art spaces in the Marshall House. Alternatively, head out on a whale-watching tour. For hot springs, gardens, Café Flóra (p91) and cool art, head to Laugardalur in the afternoon. Book ahead if you'd like a swanky evening at one of Reykjavík's top Icelandic restaurants, such as Dill (p90) or Matur og Drykkur (p86). Or try Reykjavík's most revered hot dogs at Bæjarins Beztu (p84) then party late at places like Paloma (p91), Húrra (p95) or Prikið (p94).

tail. The strongest section describes the Settlement Era – including the rule of the chieftans and the introduction of Christianity. Upstairs, collections span from 1600 to today and give a clear sense of how Iceland struggled under foreign rule and finally gained independence. Simple objects utilise every scrap of materials; check out the gaming pieces made from cod ear bones, and the wooden doll that doubled as a kitchen utensil. There are free guided tours in English at 11am on Wednesday, Saturday and Sunday. Entry also covers admission to the Culture House (p61).

★Settlement Exhibition MUSEUM
(Landnámssýningin; Map p60; ☎411 6370; www.reykjavikmuseum.is; Aðalstræti 16; adult/child 1650kr/free; ⏰9am-6pm) This fascinating archaeological ruin-museum is based around a 10th-century Viking longhouse unearthed here from 2001 to 2002 and other settlement-era finds from central Reykjavík. It imaginatively combines technological wizardry and archaeology to give a glimpse into early Icelandic life. Don't miss the fragment of **boundary wall** at the back of the museum that is older still (and the oldest human-made structure in Reykjavík). Among the captivating high-tech displays, a wraparound panorama shows how things would have looked at the time of the longhouse.

Interactive multimedia tables explain the area's excavations, and a space-age panel allows you to steer through different layers of the longhouse construction. There are guided tours on weekdays at 11am June to August.

★Reykjavík Art Museum – Hafnarhús GALLERY
(Map p60; ☎411 6400; www.artmuseum.is; Tryggvagata 17; adult/child 1650kr/free; ⏰10am-5pm, to 10pm Thu; 🚌1, 3, 6, 11, 12, 13, 14) Reykjavík Art Museum's Hafnarhús is a marvellously restored warehouse converted into a soaring steel-and-concrete exhibition space. Though the well-curated exhibitions of cutting-edge contemporary Icelandic art change frequently (expect installations, videos, paintings and sculpture), you can always count on the comic-book-style paintings of Erró (Guðmundur Guðmundsson), a political artist who has donated several thousand works to the museum.

★Tjörnin LAKE
(Map p56) The placid lake at the centre of the city is sometimes locally called the Pond. It echoes with the honks and squawks of more than 40 species of visiting birds, including swans, geese and Arctic terns; feeding the ducks is a popular pastime for the under-fives. Pretty sculpture-dotted parks like Hljómskálagarður (p58) line the southern shores, and their paths are much used by cyclists and joggers. In winter hardy souls strap on ice skates and the lake transforms into an outdoor rink.

REYKJAVÍK ART MUSEUM

The excellent Reykjavík Art Museum (Listasafn Reykjavíkur; www.artmuseum.is; adult/child 1650kr/free; 📶) is split over three superbly curated sites: the large, modern downtown Hafnarhús, focusing on contemporary art; Kjarvalsstaðir (p62), in a park just east of Snorrabraut which displays rotating exhibits of modern art; and Ásmundarsafn (p63), a peaceful haven near Laugardalur for viewing sculptures by Ásmundur Sveinsson. One ticket (valid for 24 hours) gains entry to all three sites.

Austurvöllur PARK
(Map p60) Grassy Austurvöllur was once part of first-settler Ingólfur Arnarson's hay fields. Today it's a favourite spot for cafe lounging or lunchtime picnics and summer sunbathing next to the Alþingi, and is sometimes used for open-air concerts and political demonstrations. The statue in the centre is of Jón Sigurðsson, who led the campaign for Icelandic independence.

Alþingi HISTORIC BUILDING
(Parliament; Map p60; ☎563 0500; www.althingi.is; Kirkjustraeti) FREE Iceland's first parliament, the Alþingi, was created at Þingvellir in AD 930. After losing independence in the 13th century, the country gradually won back its autonomy, and the modern Alþingi moved into this current basalt building in 1881. A stylish glass-and-stone annexe was completed in 2002. Visitors can attend sessions (four times weekly mid-September to early June) when parliament is sitting; see website for details.

Ráðhús NOTABLE BUILDING
(City Hall; Map p60; Vonarstræti; ⏰8am-4pm Mon-Fri) FREE Reykjavík's waterside Ráðhús is a beautifully positioned postmodern construction of concrete stilts, tinted windows and mossy walls rising from Tjörnin. Inside you'll find an interesting 3D topographical map of Iceland and the main tourist office (p101).

Reykjavík

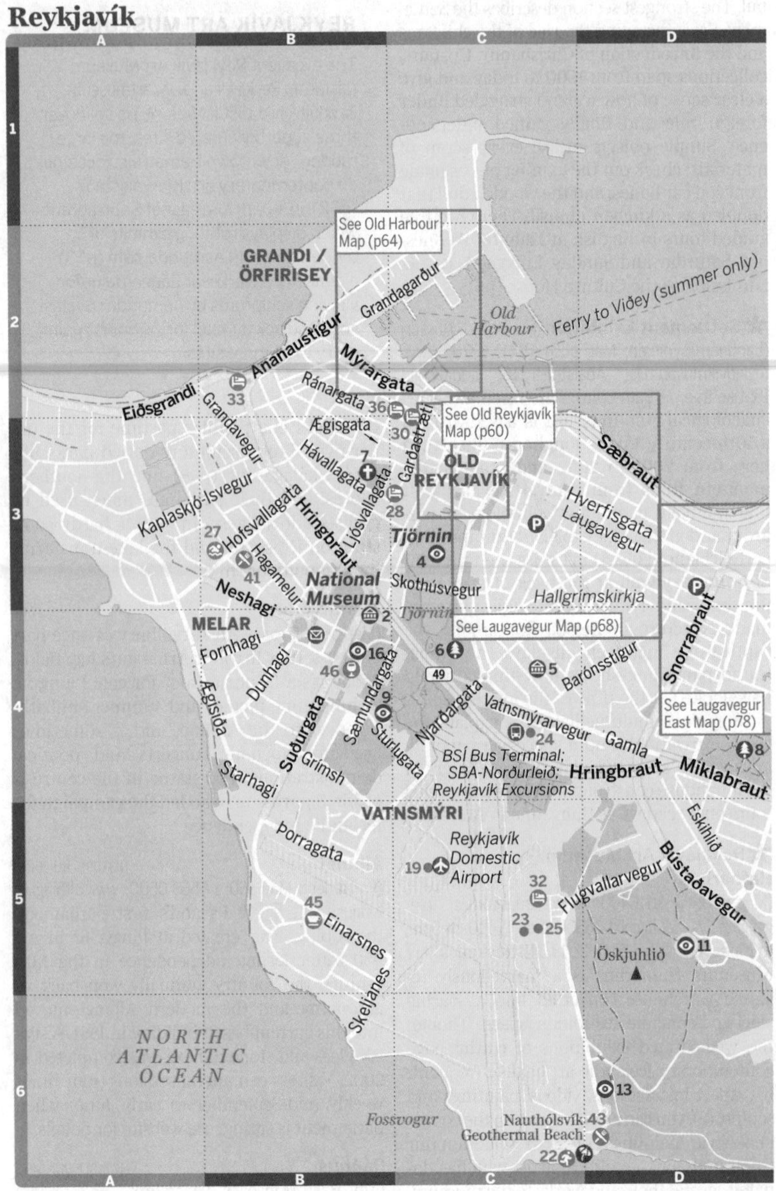

Reykjavík Museum of Photography MUSEUM

(Ljósmyndasafn Reykjavíkur; Map p60; ☎411 6390; www.photomuseum.is; 6th fl, Tryggvagata 15, Grófarhús; adult/child 1000kr/free; ⏰10am-6pm Mon-Thu, 11am-6pm Fri, 1-5pm Sat & Sun; 📶) This gallery room, high above Reykjavík City Library, is well worth a visit for its top-notch exhibitions of regional photographers. If you take the lift up, descend by the stairs, which are lined with vintage B&W photos.

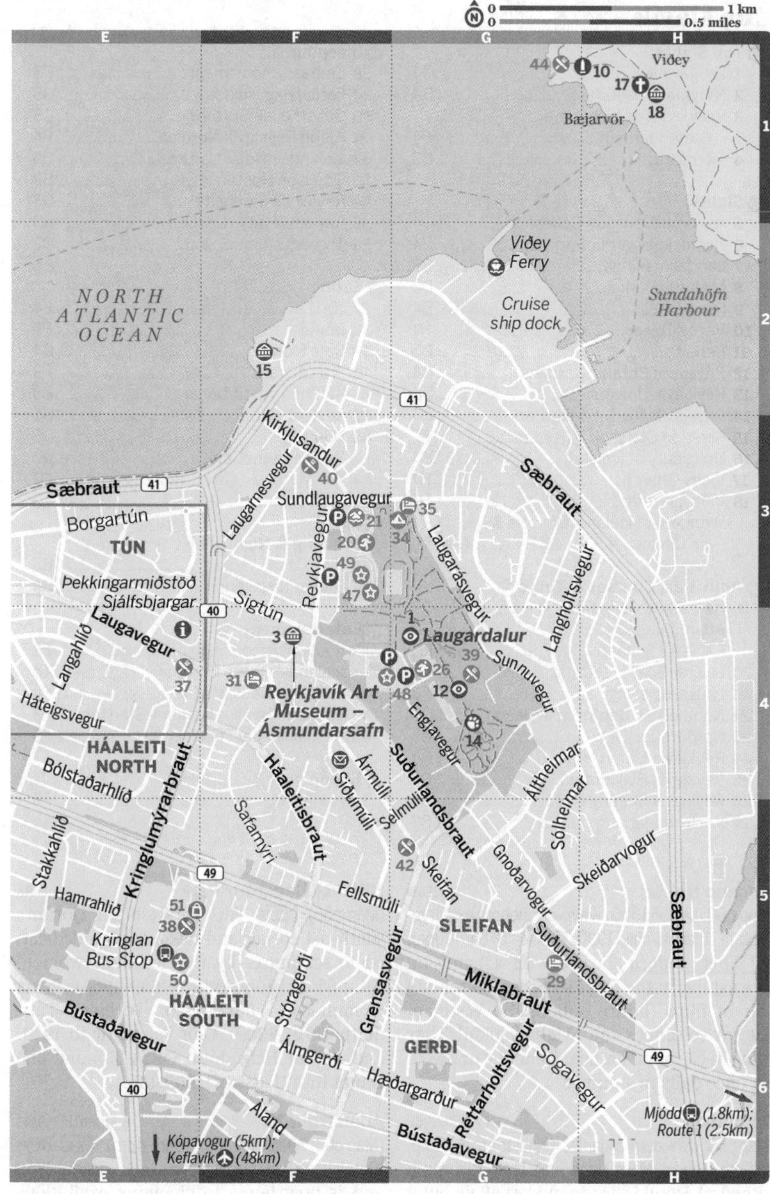

Gröndalshús MUSEUM

(Writer's Home; Map p60; ☎411 6020; www.bokmenntaborgin.is; Fischersund; ⏲1-5pm Thu-Sun mid-Jun–Aug) FREE The small, red former home of writer, illustrator and naturalist Benedikt Gröndal beautifully evokes turn-of-the-century Reykjavic life. Gröndal lived here from 1880 to 1907 and exhibits include his famous *Fauna of Iceland* collection of colour drawings. Look out for the majestic great auk, a flightless bird hunted to extinction by the mid-19th century.

Reykjavík

Top Sights
1 Laugardalur G4
2 National Museum B4
3 Reykjavík Art Museum – Ásmundarsafn F4
4 Tjörnin C3

Sights
5 Ásgrímur Jónsson Collection C4
6 Hljómskálagarður Park C4
7 Landakotskirkja B3
8 Miklatún Park D4
9 Nordic House B4
10 Peace Tower H1
11 Perlan D5
12 Reykjavík Botanic Gardens G4
13 Reykjavík University D6
14 Reykjavík Zoo & Family Park G4
15 Sigurjón Ólafsson Museum F2
16 University of Iceland B4
17 Viðey Church H1
18 Viðeyarstofa H1
Wonders of Iceland: Glaciers & Ice Cave .... (see 11)

Activities, Courses & Tours
19 Air Iceland Connect C5
Atlantsflug .... (see 19)
Eagle Air Iceland .... (see 19)
20 Laugar Spa F3
21 Laugardalslaug F3
22 Nauthólsvík Geothermal Beach C6
23 Norðurflug C5
24 Reykjavík Excursions C4
25 Reykjavík Helicopters C5
26 Reykjavík Skating Hall G4
27 Vesturbæjarlaug B3

Sleeping
28 Embassy Apartments C3
29 Ferðafélag Íslands G5
30 Guesthouse Butterfly C3
31 Hilton Reykjavík Nordica F4
32 Icelandair Hotel Natura C5
33 Oddsson Hostel B2
34 Reykjavík Campsite G3
35 Reykjavík City Hostel G3
36 Three Sisters C2

Eating
37 10-11 .... E4
38 Bónus E5
39 Café Flóra G4
40 Frú Lauga F3
41 Kaffihús Vesturbæjar B3
42 Le Kock G5
43 Nauthóll D6
Viðeyarstofa Café .... (see 18)
44 Viðeyjarnaust Day Hut G1
Vox .... (see 31)

Drinking & Nightlife
45 Bike Cave B5
46 Stúdentakjallarinn B4

Entertainment
47 Football Association of Iceland F3
Icelandic Dance Company .... (see 50)
48 Laugardalshöllin F4
49 Laugardalsvöllur National Stadium F3
50 Reykjavík City Theatre E5

Shopping
51 Kringlan E5

Volcano House MUSEUM
(Map p60; ☎555 1900; www.volcanohouse.is; Tryggvagata 11; adult/child 1990/1000kr; ⏱9am-10pm; 📶) This modern theatre with a hands-on lava exhibit in the foyer screens a 55-minute pair of films (hourly) about the Vestmannaeyjar volcanoes and Eyjafjallajökull. They show in German, French, Icelandic or Swedish once daily in summer.

Dómkirkja CHURCH
(Map p60; www.domkirkjan.is; Kirkjustræti; ⏱10am-4.30pm Mon-Fri, Mass 11am Sun) Iceland's main cathedral, Dómkirkja is a modest affair, but it played a vital role in the country's conversion to Lutheranism. The current building (built in the late 18th century and enlarged in the 1840s) is small and perfectly proportioned, with a plain wooden interior animated by glints of gold.

Hljómskálagarður Park PARK
(Map p56) FREE This Park sits on Tjörnin's southeast corner and has a section dedicated to sculptures by five Icelandic women: Gunnfríður Jónsdóttir (1889–1968), Nína Sæmundson (1892–1962), Þorbjörg Pálsdóttir (1919–2009), Ólöf Pálsdóttir (b 1920) and Gerður Helgadóttir (1928–75); and one Dane, Tove Ólafsson (1909–92).

Aðalstræti 10 HISTORIC BUILDING
(Map p60; Aðalstræti 10; ⏱9am-4pm) FREE Reykjavík's oldest timber house dates to 1762 and is now home to changing exhibitions charting the course of the city's history.

Old Harbour

★Old Harbour AREA
(Map p64; Geirsgata; 🚌1, 3, 6, 11, 12, 13, 14) Largely a service harbour until recently, the Old

Harbour and the neighbouring Grandi area have blossomed into tourist hot spots, with key art galleries, several museums, volcano and Northern Lights films, and excellent restaurants. Whale-watching and puffin-viewing trips depart from the pier. Photo ops abound with views of fishing boats, the Harpa concert hall and snowcapped mountains beyond.

On the western edge of the harbour, the Grandi area, named after the fish factory there, is burgeoning with eateries and shops.

★Omnom Chocolate FACTORY

(Map p64; ☎519 5959; www.omnomchocolate.com; Hólmaslóð 4, Grandi; adult/child 3000/1500kr; ⏲11am-6pm Mon-Fri, noon-4pm Sat) Reserve ahead for a tour (2pm Monday to Friday) at this full-service chocolate factory where you'll see how cocoa beans are transformed into high-end scrumptious delights. The shop sells its stylish bars (packaged with specially designed labels) which come in myriad sophisticated flavours.

Reykjavík Maritime Museum MUSEUM

(Sjóminjasafnið í Reykjavík; Map p64; ☎411 6300; www.maritimemuseum.is; Grandagarður 8; adult/child 1650kr/free; Óðínn & museum 2600kr; ⏲10am-5pm, Óðínn tours at 11am, 1pm, 2pm & 3pm; 👪; 🚌14) The crucial role fishing plays in Iceland's economy is celebrated through the imaginative displays in this former fish-freezing plant. The new exhibition **Fish & folk** evokes 150 years of the industry, using artefacts, sepia photos and interactive games to chart a course from the row boats of the late 1800s to the trawlers of the 21st century. Make time for one of the daily guided tours of the former coastguard ship Óðínn (1300kr).

Whales of Iceland MUSEUM

(Map p64; ☎571 0077; www.whalesoficeland.is; Fiskislóð 23; adult/child 2900/1500kr; ⏲10am-5pm; 📶; 🚌14) Ever strolled beneath a blue whale? This museum houses full-sized models of the 23 species of whale found off Iceland's coast. The largest museum of this type in Europe, it also displays models of whale skeletons, and has good audio guides and multimedia screens to explain what you're seeing. There's a cafe and gift shop too.

Look out for online ticket discounts and family tickets (5800kr).

Saga Museum MUSEUM

(Map p64; ☎511 1517; www.sagamuseum.is; Grandagarður 2; adult/child 2200/800kr; ⏲10am-6pm; 📶; 🚌14) The endearingly bloodthirsty Saga Museum is where Icelandic history is brought to life by eerie silicon models and a multi-language soundtrack featuring the thud of axes and hair-raising screams. Don't be surprised if you see some of the characters wandering around town, as moulds were taken from Reykjavík residents (the owner's daughters are the Irish princess and the little slave gnawing a fish).

Aurora Reykjavík MUSEUM

(Northern Lights Centre; Map p64; ☎780 4500; www.aurorareykjavik.is; Grandagarður 2; adult/child 1600/1000kr; ⏲9am-9pm; 🚌14) Learn about the classical tales explaining the Northern Lights, and the scientific explanation, then watch a 35-minute surround-sound panoramic high-definition re-creation of Icelandic auroras.

> **ℹ LOCAL RESOURCES**
>
> **Visit Reykjavík** (www.visitreykjavik.is) Official tourism site.
>
> **Grapevine** (www.grapevine.is) Excellent English-language content.
>
> **Iceland Review** (www.icelandreview.com) Daily Icelandic news with current affairs, entertainment and more.
>
> **I Heart Reykjavík** (www.iheartreykjavik.net) Fun local blog.

Laugavegur & Skólavörðustígur

★Hallgrímskirkja CHURCH

(Map p68; ☎510 1000; www.hallgrimskirkja.is; Skólavörðustígur; tower adult/child 1000/100kr; ⏲9am-9pm May-Sep, to 5pm Oct-Apr) Reykjavík's immense white-concrete church (1945–86), star of a thousand postcards, dominates the skyline and is visible from up to 20km away. An elevator trip up the 74.5m-high tower reveals an unmissable view of the city. In contrast to the high drama outside, the Lutheran church's interior is quite plain. The most eye-catching feature is the vast 5275-pipe organ installed in 1992. The church's size and radical design caused controversy, and its architect, Guðjón Samúelsson (1887–1950), never saw its completion.

The columns on either side of the tower represent volcanic basalt, part of Samúelsson's desire to create a national architectural style. At the front, gazing proudly into the distance, is a statue of the Viking Leifur Eiríksson, the first European to discover America.

Old Reykjavik

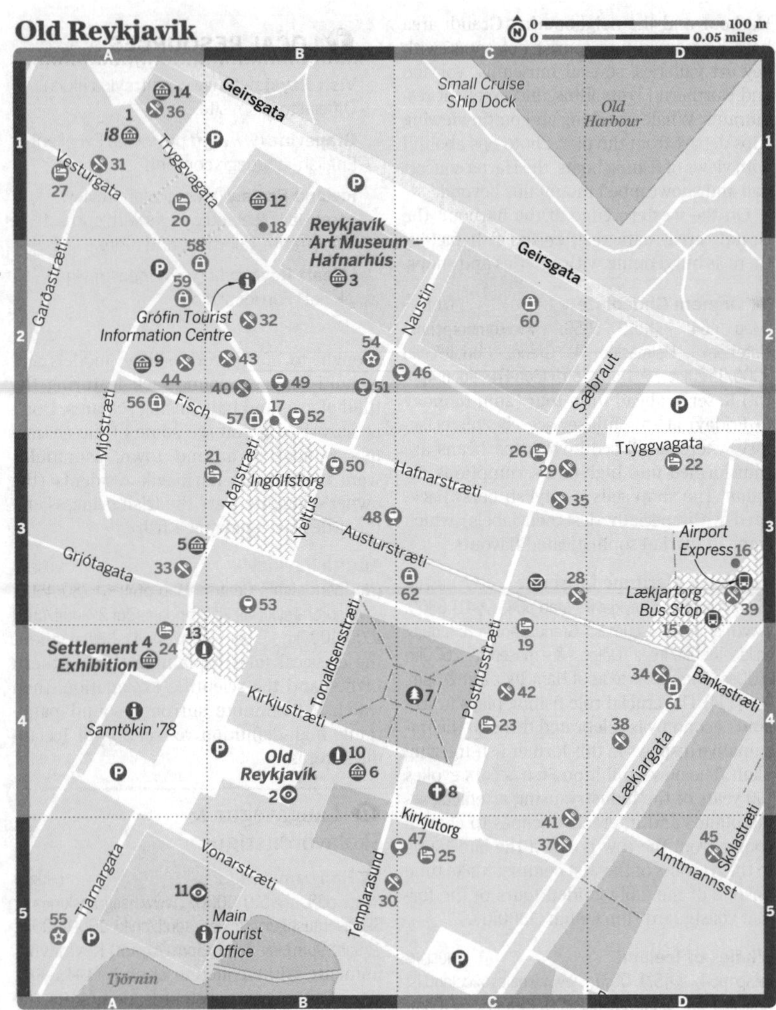

Hallgrímskirkja (pronounced *hatl-krims-kirkya*) was named after poet Reverend Hallgrímur Pétursson (1614–1674), who wrote Iceland's most popular hymn book: *Passíusálmar* (Passion Hymns).

From mid-June to late August, hear half-hour **choir concerts** (www.scholacantorum.is; 2500kr) at noon on Wednesday and **organ recitals** (www.listvinafelag.is) at noon on Thursday and Saturday (2000kr), and for one hour at 5pm on Sunday (2500kr). Services are held on Sunday at 11am, with a small service Wednesday at 8am. There is an English service the last Sunday of the month at 2pm.

★Harpa — ARTS CENTRE

(Map p68; box office 528 5050; www.harpa.is; Austurbakki 2; 8am-midnight, box office noon-6pm;) With its ever-changing facets glistening on the water's edge, Reykjavík's sparkling Harpa concert hall and cultural centre is a beauty to behold. In addition to a season of top-notch shows (some free), the shimmering interior with harbour vistas is worth stopping in for, or take a highly recommended, 30-minute guided tour (1500kr); these run two to three times daily year-round, with up to eight daily tours between mid-June and mid-August.

Old Reykjavik

Top Sights
1 i8 ... A1
2 Old Reykjavík ... B4
3 Reykjavík Art Museum – Hafnarhús ... B2
4 Settlement Exhibition ... A4

Sights
5 Aðalstræti 10 ... A3
6 Alþingi ... B4
7 Austurvöllur ... C4
8 Dómkirkja ... C4
9 Gröndalshús ... A2
10 Ingibjörg H Bjarnason Statue ... B4
Jón Sigurðsson Statue ... (see 7)
11 Ráðhús ... A5
12 Reykjavík Museum of Photography ... B1
13 Skúli Magnússon Statue ... A4
14 Volcano House ... A1

Activities, Courses & Tours
15 Free Walking Tour Reykjavik ... D4
16 Grayline Iceland ... D3
17 Haunted Walk ... B2
18 Literary Reykjavík ... B1

Sleeping
19 Apotek ... C4
20 Black Pearl ... A1
21 CenterHótel Plaza ... B3
22 Consulate Hotel Reykjavík ... D3
23 Hótel Borg ... C4
24 Hótel Reykjavík Centrum ... A4
25 Kvosin Downtown ... C5
26 Radisson Blu 1919 ... C3
27 Reykjavík Downtown Hostel ... A1

Eating
28 10-11 ... C3
Apotek ... (see 19)
29 Bæjarins Beztu ... C3
30 Bergsson Mathús ... B5
31 Bio Borgari ... A1
32 Fiskfélagið ... B2
33 Fiskmarkaðurinn ... A3
34 Grillmarkaðurinn ... D4
35 Hornið ... C3
36 Icelandic Fish & Chips ... A1
37 Icelandic Street Food ... C5
38 Jómfrúin ... D4
39 Lobster Hut ... D3
40 Matarkjallarinn ... B2
41 Messinn ... C5
42 Nora Magasin ... C4
43 Stofan Kaffihús ... B2
44 Tapas Barinn ... A2
45 Torfan Lobsterhouse ... D5

Drinking & Nightlife
46 Frederiksen Ale House ... C2
47 Klaustur ... C5
48 Loftið ... B3
49 Micro Bar ... B2
50 Pablo Diskobar ... B3
51 Paloma ... B2
52 Sæta Svínið Gastropub ... B2
53 Skúli Craft Bar ... B3

Entertainment
54 Gaukurinn ... B2
Húrra ... (see 54)
55 Tjarnarbíó ... A5

Shopping
Akkúrat ... (see 57)
Eymundsson ... (see 19)
56 Fischer ... A2
57 Iceland Design Centre ... B2
58 Kirsuberjatréð ... A2
59 Kogga ... A2
60 Kolaportið Flea Market ... C2
61 Nordic Store ... D4
62 Vínbúðin – Austurstræti ... C3

★ **Culture House** GALLERY
(Þjóðmenningarhúsið; Map p68; ☎530 2210; www.culturehouse.is; Hverfisgata 15; adult/child incl National Museum 2000kr/free; ⏲10am-5pm May–mid-Sep, closed Mon mid-Sep–Apr;) This fantastic collaboration between the National Museum, National Gallery and four other organisations creates a superbly curated exhibition covering the artistic and cultural heritage of Iceland from settlement to today. Priceless artefacts are arranged by theme, and highlights include 14th-century manuscripts, contemporary art, and the skeleton of a great auk (now extinct). Check the website for free guided tours. The renovated 1908 building is beautiful with great views of the harbour and has a classy cafe (p88) on the ground floor. Entry also covers admission to the National Museum (p54).

★ **Icelandic Phallological Museum** MUSEUM
(Hið Íslenzka Reðasafn; Map p78; ☎561 6663; www.phallus.is; Laugavegur 116; adult/child 1500kr/free; ⏲10am-6pm, from 9am Jun-Aug) Oh, the jokes are endless here, but although this unique museum houses a huge collection of penises, it's actually very well done. From pickled pickles to petrified wood, there are 286 different members on display, representing all

Icelandic mammals and beyond. Featured items include contributions from sperm whales and a polar bear, minuscule mouse bits, silver castings of each member of the Icelandic handball team and a single human sample – from deceased mountaineer Páll Arason.

★Reykjavík Art Museum – Kjarvalsstaðir GALLERY

(Map p78; ☎411 6420; www.artmuseum.is; Flókagata 24, Miklatún Park; adult/child 1650kr/free; ⏲10am-5pm; 📶) The angular glass-and-wood Kjarvalsstaðir, which looks out onto Miklatún Park, is named for Jóhannes Kjarval (1885–1972), one of Iceland's most popular classical artists. He was a fisherman until his crew paid for him to study at the Academy of Fine Arts in Copenhagen, and his wonderfully evocative landscapes share space alongside changing installations of mostly Icelandic 20th-century paintings.

★National Gallery of Iceland MUSEUM

(Listasafn Íslands; Map p68; ☎515 9600; www.listasafn.is; Fríkirkjuvegur 7; adult/child 1800kr/free; ⏲10am-5pm daily mid-May–mid-Sep, 11am-5pm Tue-Sun mid-Sep–mid-May; 📶) This pretty stack of marble atriums and spacious galleries overlooking Tjörnin offers ever-changing exhibits drawn from a 10,000-piece collection. The museum can only exhibit a small sample at any one time; shows range from 19th- and 20th-century paintings by Iceland's favourite artists (including Jóhannes Kjarval and Nína Sæmundsson) to sculptures by Sigurjón Ólafsson and others.

The museum ticket also covers entry to the Ásgrímur Jónsson Collection (p62) and Sigurjón Ólafsson Museum (p63).

Ásgrímur Jónsson Collection GALLERY

(Map p56; ☎515 9625; www.listasafn.is; Bergstaðastræti 74; adult/child 1000kr/free; ⏲1-5pm mid-May–early Sep, 2-5pm Sat & Sun early Sep–Nov & Feb–mid-May) Iceland's first professional painter, Ásgrímur Jónsson (1876–1958) was the son of a farmer. He lived and worked here, and you can visit his former atelier to see his work incorporating folk tales and Icelandic nature.

Einar Jónsson Museum GALLERY

(Map p68; ☎551 3797; www.lej.is; Eriksgata 3; adult/child 1000kr/free; ⏲10am-5pm Tue-Sun) Einar Jónsson (1874–1954) is one of Iceland's foremost sculptors, famous for intense symbolist works. Chiselled representations of Hope, Earth and Death burst from basalt cliffs, weep over naked women and slay dragons. Jónsson designed the building, which was built between 1916 and 1923, when this hill was on the outskirts of town. It also contains his austere penthouse flat and studio, with views over the city.

The **sculpture garden** (Map p68; www.lej.is; Freyjugata; ⏲24hr) FREE behind the museum contains 26 bronzes, in the shadow of Hallgrímskirkja.

REYKJAVÍK'S ART GALLERIES

Reykjavík has many small contemporary-art galleries, and local designer shops.

Kling & Bang (Map p64; ☎554 20 03; http://this.is/klingandbang; Grandagarður 20, Marshall Húsið, Grandi; ⏲noon-6pm Wed & Fri-Sun, to 9pm Thu) FREE Perennially cutting-edge young artists' exhibitions in a new gallery space; a favourite with locals.

Stúdió Ólafur Elíasson (Map p64; ☎551 3666; www.olafureliasson.net; Grandagarður 20, Marshall Húsið, Grandi; ⏲noon-6pm Tue, Wed & Fri-Sun, noon-9pm Thu; 🚌14) FREE Provides an insight into the works of the much-lauded Icelandic-Danish artist.

i8 (Map p60; ☎551 3666; www.i8.is; Tryggvagata 16; ⏲11am-6pm Tue-Fri, 1-5pm Sat) FREE This gallery represents some of the country's top modern artists, many of whom show overseas as well.

Hverfisgallerí (Map p68; ☎537 4007; www.hverfisgalleri.is; Hverfisgata 4; ⏲1-5pm Tue-Fri, 2-5pm Sat) Browse contemporary Icelandic art in a large, central space.

Gallerí Fold (Map p78; ☎551 0400; www.myndlist.is; Rauðarárstígur 12; ⏲10am-6pm Mon-Sat) FREE Large Icelandic art dealer and auction house.

Nýló (Nýlistasafnið – The Living Art Museum; Map p64; ☎551 4350; www.nylo.is; Grandagarður 20, Marshall Húsið, Grandi; ⏲noon-6pm Tue, Wed & Fri-Sun, to 9pm Thu) FREE Emerging and established contemporary artists. Also holds occasional live music or theatre.

Árnarhóll LANDMARK

(Map p68) A statue of Iceland's first settler, Ingólfur Arnarson, takes pride of place at Árnarhóll, a greensward that is also a central gathering place for parades and demonstrations.

Tün

Reykjavík is adorned with fascinating sculptures, but it's Jón Gunnar Árnason's shiplike *Sun Voyager (Sólfar;* (Sólfar; Map p68; Sæbraut)*)* sculpture that seems to catch visitors' imaginations. Scooping in a skeletal arc along the seaside, it offers a photo shoot with snowcapped mountains in the distance.

Laugardalur

★Laugardalur AREA, PARK

(Map p56; 2, 5, 14, 15, 17) Laugardalur encompasses a verdant stretch of land 4km east of the city centre. It was once the main source of Reykjavík's hot-water supply: it translates as 'Hot-Springs Valley', and in the park's centre you'll find relics from the old wash house. The park is a favourite with locals for its huge swimming complex (p65), fed by the geothermal spring, alongside a spa, cafe (p91), skating rink, botanical gardens, sporting and concert arenas, and a zoo/entertainment park for kids.

★Reykjavík Art Museum – Ásmundarsafn GALLERY

(Ásmundur Sveinsson Museum; Map p56; 411 6430; www.artmuseum.is; Sigtún; adult/child 1650kr/free; 10am-5pm May-Sep, 1-5pm Oct-Apr; ; 2, 4, 14, 15, 17, 19) There's something immensely playful about the vast collection of sculptures by Ásmundur Sveinsson (1893–1982) housed in the studio and museum he designed – the rounded, white Ásmundarsafn. Monumental concrete creations fill the garden, while the peaceful haven of the interlocking cupolas showcases works in wood, clay and metals, some of them mobile, exploring themes as diverse as folklore and physics.

Reykjavík Botanic Gardens GARDENS

(Grasagarður; Map p56; 411 8650; www.grasagardur.is; Laugardalur; 10am-10pm May-Sep, to 3pm Oct-Apr; 2, 5, 14, 15, 17) FREE More than 5000 varieties of subarctic plants fill the city's botanic gardens, delivering a wealth of colourful seasonal flowers and plenty of birdlife, particularly grey geese and their fluffy little goslings. In the summer the acclaimed Café Flóra (p91) sets up shop in the greenhouse.

DISCOUNT CARDS

- **Reykjavík City Card** (www.citycard.is; 24/48/72hr 3800/5400/6500kr) offers admission to 10 of Reykjavík's municipal swimming/thermal pools and to most of the main galleries and museums, plus discounts on some tours, shops and entertainment. It also gives free travel on the city's Strætó buses and on the ferry to Viðey. The 24-hour **Children's City Card** (1600kr) is less useful, since kids enter free at many museums anyway. Cards are available at the Main Tourist Office (p100), some travel agencies, 10-11 supermarkets, HI hostels and some hotels.
- The Reykjavík Art Museum ticket covers all three of its sites.
- A joint ticket for the National Gallery, nearby Ásgrímur Jónsson Collection and further-afield Sigurjón Ólafsson Museum costs 1800kr.

Reykjavík Zoo & Family Park ZOO

(Fjölskyldu og Húsdýragarðurinn; Map p56; 411 5900; www.mu.is; Laugardalur; adult/child 880/660kr, 1/10 ride ticket 330/2520kr; 10am-6pm Jun–mid-Aug, to 5pm mid-Aug–May; ; 2, 5, 15, 17) Sunny days see happy local families flocking to this children's park in Laugardalur. Don't expect lions and tigers; think seals, foxes and farm animals in simple enclosures, and tanks of cold-water fish. The family park section is jolly, with a mini-racetrack, child-size bulldozers, a giant trampoline, boats and fairground rides for kids.

Sigurjón Ólafsson Museum GALLERY

(Listasafn Sigurjóns Ólafssonar; Map p56; 553 2906; www.lso.is; Laugarnestanga 70; adult/child 1000kr/free; 1-5pm daily mid-May–mid-Sep, 2-5pm Sat & Sun mid-Sep–Nov & Feb–mid-May; 12, 16) Sculptor Sigurjón Ólafsson (1908–82) used this peaceful seafront building as a studio. Now it showcases his varied, powerful work: portrait busts, driftwood totem poles and abstract pillars. A salty ocean breeze blows through the modern rooms, and the area is interlaced with waterfront paths giving clear views back to Reykjavík.

South of the Centre

Nordic House CULTURAL BUILDING

(Norræna Húsið; Map p56; 551 7030; www.nordichouse.is; Sæmundargata 11; 10am-5pm, to 9pm

Old Harbour

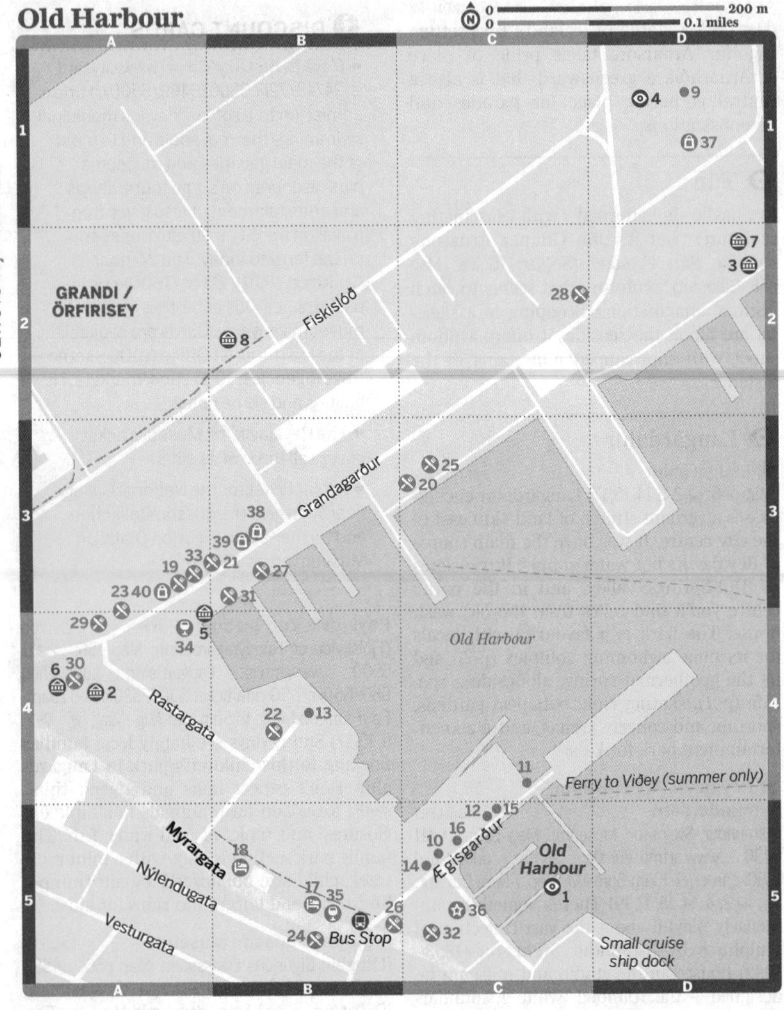

Wed; ; 1, 3, 6, 12, 14) This cultural centre fosters connections between Iceland and its Nordic neighbours with a rich program of events, a library, exhibition space and bistro.

Perlan NOTABLE BUILDING

(Map p56; 566 9000; www.perlanmuseum.is; Öskjuhlíð; adult/child 3900/1950kr; 8am-8pm; 18) Perlan's mirrored dome, designed by Ingimundur Sveinsson, covers huge geothermal-water tanks some 2km from the city centre. Inside, the Wonders of Iceland exhibit features high-tech, audiovisual recreations of chilly artificial glaciers and an ice cave, augmented reality depictions of the massive Látrabjarg bird cliffs, and immersive exhibits on volcanoes, earthquakes and geothermal zones. The wraparound **viewing deck** (adult/child 490kr/free) offers a tremendous 360-degree panorama of Reykjavík and the mountains.

Numerous **walking and cycling trails** criss-cross the hillside; one path leads down to Nauthólsvík geothermal beach (p66).

There are wraparound views from Perlan's 5th-floor bistro-style restaurant and cafe. A free shuttle bus (9am to 5pm) leaves for Perlan from the Harpa concert hall.

Old Harbour

Top Sights
1 Old Harbour C5

Sights
2 Aurora Reykjavík A4
Kling & Bang .... (see 7)
3 Nýló D2
4 Omnom Chocolate D1
5 Reykjavík Maritime Museum A4
6 Saga Museum A4
7 Stúdíó Ólafur Elíasson D2
8 Whales of Iceland B2

Activities, Courses & Tours
Bryggjan Brugghús .... (see 34)
9 Dive.is D1
10 Elding Adventures at Sea C5
11 Reykjavík Bike Tours C4
12 Reykjavík By Boat C5
13 Reykjavík Sailors B4
14 Reykjavík Sea Adventures C5
15 Special Tours C5
16 Whale Safari C5

Sleeping
17 Icelandair Hotel Reykjavík Marina B5
18 Reykjavík Marina Residence B5

Eating
19 17 Sortir A3
20 Bergsson RE C3
Burið .... (see 39)
21 Coocoo's Nest B3
22 Fish & Chips B4
23 Flatey Pizza A3
24 Forréttabarinn B5
25 Grandi Mathöll C3
26 Hamborgara Búllan B5
27 Kaffivagninn B3
28 Kumiko C2
29 Lamb A4
30 Matur og Drykkur A4
31 Messinn Granda B3
32 Sægreifinn C5
Salt .... (see 32)
33 Valdís A3

Drinking & Nightlife
34 Bryggjan Brugghús A4
Café Haiti .... (see 36)
Marshall .... (see 3)
35 Slippbarinn B5

Entertainment
36 Cinema at Old Harbour Village No 2 .... C5

Shopping
37 Farmers & Friends D1
38 Jen's B3
39 Kjötkompaní B3
40 Steinunn A3

Outskirts

Seltjarnarnes AREA
(www.seltjarnarnes.is; 11) Seltjarnarnes, 5km west of central Reykjavík, is a coastal area that feels a world away. The offshore island of **Grótta** boasts a red-and-white lighthouse and is a haven for birdwatching, with 106 visiting species. It is accessible at low tide, but is closed May to mid-July to protect nests. Get here along the pretty coastal path, popular with walkers, joggers and cyclists.

Árbær Open Air Museum MUSEUM
(Árbæjarsafn; 411 6300; www.reykjavikmuseum.is; Kistuhylur 4, Ártúnsholt; adult/child 1650kr/free; 10am-5pm Jun-Aug, from noon Sep-May; ; 12, 24) Around 20 quaint old buildings have been transported from their original sites to open-air Árbæjarsafn. Alongside 19th-century homes are a turf-roofed church and various stables, domestic animals, smithies, barns and boathouses – all very picturesque. In the summer there are arts and crafts demonstrations and year-round tours run at 1pm. It's 4km southeast of the city centre.

Activities

Locally you can tour the city, rent bikes to zoom along lake or seaside trails, or pop into hot-pots all over town. Reykjavík is also the main hub for every kind of activity tour to all manner of destinations beyond the city limits. Most operators provide pick-up either from your accommodation or, if in the central zone, from a designated bus stop very nearby.

★ **Laugardalslaug** GEOTHERMAL POOL, HOT-POT
(Map p56; 411 5100; www.reykjavik.is/stadir/laugardalslaug; Sundlaugavegur 30a, Laugardalur; adult/child 950/150kr, suit/towel rental 850/570kr; 6.30am-10pm Mon-Fri, 8am-10pm Sat & Sun; ; 12, 14) One of the largest pools in Iceland, with the best facilities: an Olympic-sized indoor pool and several outdoor pools, a string of hot-pots, a saltwater tub, a steam bath and a curling 86m water slide.

★ **Laugar Spa** SPA, GYM
(Map p56; 553 0000; www.laugarspa.com; Sundlaugavegur 30a, Laugardalur; day pass 5800kr; 6am-11pm Mon-Fri, 8am-9.30pm Sat & Sun)

THE LOW-DOWN ON REYKJAVÍK'S POOLS

Reykjavík's naturally hot water is the heart of the city's social life (as in many Icelandic towns); children play, teenagers flirt, business deals are made and everyone catches up on the latest gossip at the baths. Volcanic heat keeps the temperature at a mellow 29°C, and most baths have *heitir pottar* (hot-pots): Jacuzzi-like pools kept a toasty 37°C to 42°C. Bring towels and bathing suits or rent them on-site. For further information and more locations, see www.spacity.is.

Reykjavikers get very upset by dirty tourists in their clean, chemical-free pools. To avoid causing huge offence, you must wash thoroughly with soap and without a swimsuit (yes, that means getting naked) before hopping in.

Super-duper Laugar Spa, next door to the Laugardalslaug geothermal pool, offers myriad ways to pamper yourself. There are six themed saunas and steam rooms, a seawater tub, a vast and well-equipped gym, fitness classes, and beauty and massage clinics with detox wraps, facials and hot-stone therapies. The spa is only open to visitors over 18; entry includes access to Laugardalslaug.

There's a cafe (dishes 2500 to 3000kr) and Icelandic-language child care.

★Sundhöllin GEOTHERMAL POOL
(Sundhöll Reykjavíkur; Map p78; ☎411 5350; www.reykjavik.is/stadir/sundholl-reykjavikur; Barónsstígur 16; adult/child 950/150kr; ⏲6.30am-10pm Mon-Fri, from 8am Sat & Sun; 👪) Our top pick for a Reykjavík city-centre swim. Sundhöll reopened in 2017 after a year-long revamp which added an entire outdoor area with hot tubs, sauna and a swimming pool. The original indoor pool remains open, as well as the secret upstairs hot tub with excellent city views.

Nauthólsvík Geothermal Beach BEACH
(Map p56; ☎551 3177; www.nautholsvik.is; summer/winter free/600kr; ⏲10am-7pm mid-May–mid-Aug, 11am-1pm Mon-Fri, plus 5-7.30pm Mon & Wed, 11am-3pm Sat mid-Aug–mid-May; 👪; 🚌5) The small sandy arc of Nauthólsvík Geothermal Beach, on the edge of the Atlantic, gets packed on sunny summer days. During opening hours in summer only, geothermal water is routed in to keep the lagoon between 15°C and 19°C. There is also a busy hot-pot (38°C year-round), a snack bar and changing rooms.

Vesturbæjarlaug GEOTHERMAL POOL, HOT-POT
(Map p56; ☎411 5150; Hofsvallagata; adult/child 900/140kr; ⏲6.30am-10pm Mon-Fri, 9am-10pm Sat & Sun; 👪; 🚌11, 13) Within walking distance of the city centre, Vesturbæjarlaug has a 25m pool, steam, sauna, three hot-pots and one cold plunge.

Árbæjarlaug GEOTHERMAL POOL, HOT-POT
(☎411 5200; www.reykjavik.is/stadir/arbaejarlaug; Fylkisvegur 9, Elliðaárdalur; adult/child 950/150kr; ⏲6.30am-10pm Mon-Thu, to 8pm Fri, 9am-6pm Sat & Sun; 👪; 🚌5) Ten kilometres southeast of the city centre, slickly designed Árbæjarlaug is known as one of the area's best family pools: it's half inside and half outside, and lots of watery amusements (slides, waterfalls and massage jets) keep kids entertained.

Reykjavík Skating Hall SKATING
(Skautahöllin; Map p56; ☎588 9705; www.skautaholl.is; Múlavegur 1, Laugardalur; adult/child 1000/700kr, skate hire 500kr; ⏲1-2.30pm Mon-Wed & Fri, 1-2.30pm & 5-7.30pm Thu, 1-5pm Sat & Sun Sep–mid-May) The Reykjavík Skating Hall throws open its doors from September to mid-May.

Mink Viking PHOTO STUDIO
(Map p68; ☎786 2525; www.mink.is; Laugavegur 11; per person 10,900kr; ⏲10am-6pm Mon-Fri) It's niche, but if you yearn to unleash your inner Viking drop by this quirky studio dedicated to the notorious Norse sea explorers to dress in authentic costumes, wield weapons and pose for some stern pics – the photographers are good at snapping their subjects without a smile. The price includes a digital copy of six selected images. Book ahead.

Borgarhjól CYCLING
(Map p68; ☎551 5653; www.borgarhjol.is; Hverfisgata 50; per 4hr/day 2600/3600kr; ⏲8am-6pm Mon-Fri, 10am-2pm Sat) Rents and repairs bikes.

Courses

★Creative Iceland ARTS & CRAFTS
(☎615 3500; www.creativeiceland.is) Get involved with knitting (19,500kr), cooking (24,900kr), graphic design, arts, crafts, music...you name it. This service hooks you up with local creative people offering workshops in their specialities.

Icelandic Culture & Craft Workshops ARTS & CRAFTS
(☎869 9913; www.cultureandcraft.com; Hotel Laxnes, Háholt 7) Knitting workshops using Icelandic wool. Durations range from three hours (19,500kr) to four days (145,000kr).

Tours

City Tours

The tourist office (p101) has info on guided walking tours, plus loads of free maps and self-guided walking-tour brochures, from *Literary Reykjavík* to *The Neighbourhood of the Gods*. Hard-core walkers can buy the more in-depth *Reykjavík Walks* (2014; 3100kr) by Guðjón Friðriksson at local bookshops.

There are downloadable smartphone apps, including Guides by Lonely Planet and Locatify (Smartguide).

★Literary Reykjavík WALKING
(Map p60; www.bokmenntaborgin.is; Tryggvagata 15; ⏲3pm Thu Jun-Aug) FREE The Dark Deeds city-centre walking tour focuses on crime fiction and starts at the main library. There's also a downloadable Culture Walks app and themes include Settlement, Crime Fiction and Queer Literature.

Free Walking Tour Reykjavik WALKING
(Map p60; www.freewalkingtour.is; ⏲noon & 2pm Jun-Aug, 1pm Sep-May) FREE A 90-minute, 1.5km walking tour of the city centre, starting at the little clock tower on Lækjartorg Sq.

Haunted Walk WALKING
(Map p60; www.hauntedwalk.is; adult/child 2500kr/free; ⏲8pm Sat-Thu early Jun-Aug) Ninety-minute tour, including folklore and ghost spotting,

CHOOSING YOUR DAY TOUR

If you have more than a day in Reykjavík, get out into Iceland's incredible natural beauty. Popular day-tour destinations get swamped in high season, but if you have the luxury of a rental car you can visit outside peak hours or head to lesser-stomped grounds. You can also use the **Strætó** (☎540 2700; www.straeto.is), Reykjavík Excursions (p72), Iceland By Bus (p101) and Trex (p430) buses for transport, instead of tours.

The Golden Circle (p118) With three beloved attractions – Þingvellir (beautiful site of the original outdoor parliament and the continental rift), Geysir (huge eponymous geyser area) and Gullfoss (enormous waterfalls) – the Golden Circle is the ultimate and much-marketed taste of Icelandic countryside. You can combine a Golden Circle tour with virtually any activity from quad-biking to caving and rafting. Full-day trips generally depart around 8.30am and return around 6pm; shorter trips leave around noon, returning at 7pm. In summer there are evening trips (7pm to midnight). In your own car it takes about four hours.

Blue Lagoon (p107) Hugely popular, with crowds to match. Many day trips from Reykjavík tie in a visit to the lagoon. It's also seamless to visit on your journey to/from Keflavík International Airport. In high season it's best at night; you should always book ahead or risk being turned away.

Snæfellsnes Peninsula (p219) A less -travelled, gorgeous portion of the country that you can add to the popular Golden Circle loop or visit on its own. Expect short hikes along crunchy lava fields, snowmobiling on the glacier, seaside villages, and whale-watching or boat tours to offshore puffin-inhabited islets.

South Coast (p242) A wild assortment of geological wonders, including active volcanoes, glorious hikes and shivery ice caps. Tours run year-round from Reykjavík and regional hubs.

Þórsmörk (p163) Though beautiful back-country volcanic valley Þórsmörk has loads of hiking routes that take more time, you should be able to squeeze in one short walk on a day trip by super-Jeep or bus.

Landmannalaugar (p156) For day trippers, a (very short) visit to the geothermal Landmannalaugar region can only be done on a super-Jeep tour or bus, and you'll spend most of the day on the road. Jeep stops along the way, though, often include Hekla. Beware: Landmannalaugar is packed in summer.

Jökulsárlón (p197) This incredible glacial lagoon is quite far from the capital, making it one of the longest day trips. You'll arrive when the lagoon is at its most crowded. If at all possible, it's much better to overnight on the south coast and go to the lagoon in the off-peak hours.

Laugavegur

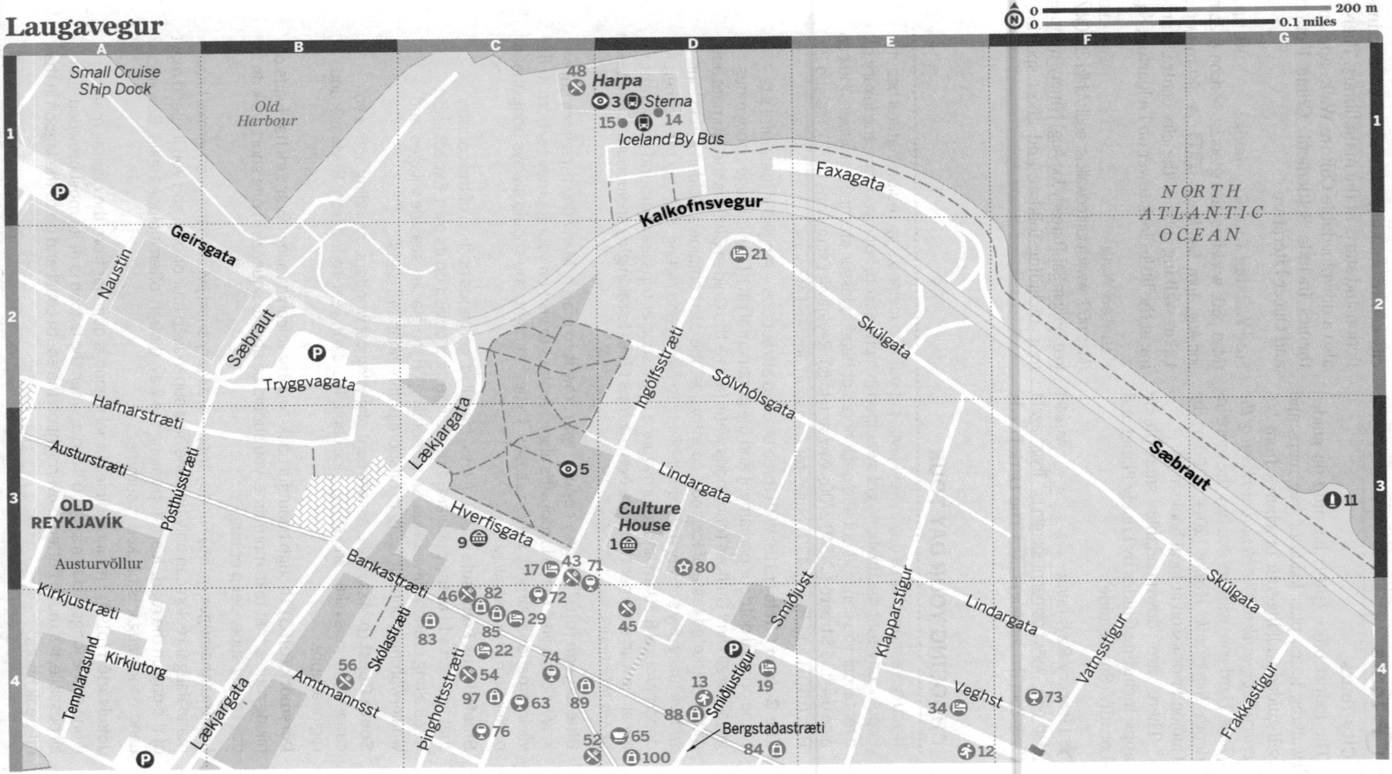

0 200 m
0 0.1 miles

Small Cruise Ship Dock
Old Harbour
48 Harpa
3 Sterna
15 14
Iceland By Bus
Faxagata
Kalkofnsvegur
NORTH ATLANTIC OCEAN
Geirsgata
Naustin
Sæbraut
Tryggvagata
21
Skúlgata
Ingólfsstræti
Sölvhólsgata
Hafnarstræti
Austurstræti
Pósthússtræti
Lækjargata
5
Lindargata
Sæbraut
11
OLD REYKJAVÍK
Culture House
1
9
Hverfisgata
Austurvöllur
Bankastræti
17 43 71
80
Kirkjustræti
46 82
72
29
45
Smiðjust
Klapparstígur
Lindargata
Skúlgata
Skólastræti
83
85
22
Templarasund
Kirkjutorg
56
Þingholtsstræti
54
74
Smiðjustígur
13
19
Vatnsstígur
Frakkastígur
Amtmannsst
97
63
89
88
Veghst
34
73
Lækjargata
76
52
65
100
Bergstaðastræti
84
12

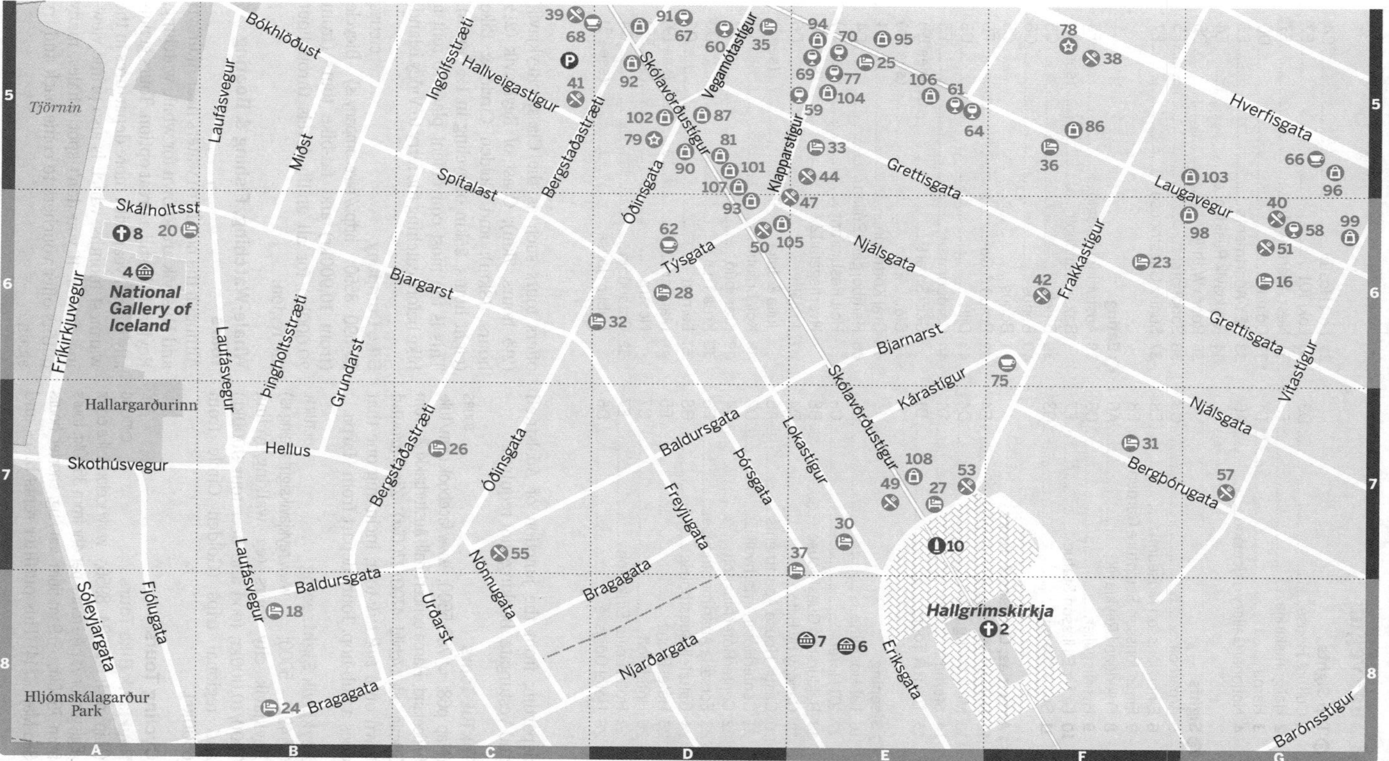
Tjörnin
Bókhlöðust
Laufásvegur
Miðst
Ingólfsstræti
Hallveigastígur
Bergstaðastræti
Skólavörðustígur
Vegamótastígur
Klapparstígur
Hverfisgata
Laugavegur
Grettisgata
Spítalast
Óðinsgata
Skálholtsst
National Gallery of Iceland
Frikirkjuvegur
Bjargarst
Týsgata
Njálsgata
Frakkastígur
Vitastígur
Þingholtsstræti
Grundarst
Bjarnarst
Kárastígur
Hallargarðurinn
Hellus
Skothúsvegur
Baldursgata
Þórsgata
Lokastígur
Bergþórugata
Freyjugata
Nönnugata
Bragagata
Urðarst
Njarðargata
Eriksgata
Hallgrímskirkja
Sóleyjargata
Fjólugata
Hljómskálagarður Park
Barónsstígur

Laugavegur

Top Sights
1 Culture House....D3
2 Hallgrímskirkja....F8
3 Harpa....D1
4 National Gallery of Iceland....A6

Sights
5 Árnarhóll....C3
6 Einar Jónsson Museum....E8
7 Einar Jónsson Sculpture Garden....E8
8 Fríkirkjan í Reykjavík....A6
9 Hverfisgallerí....C3
10 Leifur Eiríksson Statue....E7
11 Sun Voyager....G3

Activities, Courses & Tours
12 Borgarhjól....E4
13 Mink Viking....D4
14 Sterna....D1
15 TukTuk Tours....D1

Sleeping
16 101 Hostel....G6
17 101 Hotel....C3
18 Baldursbrá Guesthouse....B8
19 Canopy by Hilton....D4
20 Castle House Apartments....A6
21 CenterHótel Arnarhvoll....D2
22 CenterHótel Þingholt....C4
23 Forsæla Apartmenthouse....F6
24 Galtafell Guesthouse....B8
25 Hótel Frón....E5
26 Hótel Holt....C7
27 Hótel Leifur Eiríksson....E7
28 Hótel Óðinsvé....D6
29 Loft Hostel....C4
30 Loki 101....E7
31 Nest Apartments....F7
32 Óðinn....D6
33 REY Apartments....E5
34 Reykjavík Residence....E4
35 Room With A View....D5
36 Sandhotel....F5
37 Sunna Guesthouse....E7

Eating
38 Austur Indíafélagið....F5
Bakarí Sandholt....(see 36)
39 Block....C5
40 Bónus....G6
41 Bónus....C5
42 Brauð & Co....F6
43 Dill....C3
44 Garðurinn....E5
Geiri Smart....(see 19)
Gló....(see 94)
45 Grái Kötturinn....D4
46 Hamborgara Búllan....C4
Holt Restaurant....(see 26)
Hverfisgata 12....(see 71)
47 Joylato....D6
Julia & Julia....(see 1)
48 Kolabrautin....C1
49 Krambúð....E7
50 Krua Thai....D6
51 Lemon....G6
Mat Bar....(see 19)
Nostra....(see 58)
52 Ostabúðin....C4
Public House....(see 25)

departing from the junction of Aðalstræti and Vesturgata. Bookings not required.

TukTuk Tours TOURS
(Map p68; ☎788 5500; www.facebook.com/tuktukiceland; Harpa concert hall, Austurbakki 2; from 30min adult/child 4700/2700kr) Zip around town on a *tuk tuk* tour, including one that does a pub-hop. Tours depart from Harpa.

Reykjavík Sightseeing CULTURAL
(☎497 5000; www.reykjaviksightseeing.is) Reykjavík city tours (eg walking/cycling 7000/10,000kr, food and beer tour 9000kr) and regional trips (Golden Circle from 6500kr).

Cycling Tours

Reykjavík Bike Tours CYCLING
(Map p64; ☎694 8956; www.icelandbike.com; Ægisgarður 7; bike rental per 4hr from 3500kr, tours from 7500kr; ⏰9am-5pm Jun-Aug, shorter hours Sep-May; 🚌14) This outfitter rents bikes and offers tours such as the Classic Reykjavík (2½ hours, 7km); Coast of Reykjavík (2½ hours, 18km); and Golden Circle & Bike (eight hours, 25km of cycling in 1½ hours). This is the most convenient place to rent a bike before catching the ferry to Viðey island.

Bike Company CYCLING
(☎590 8550; http://bikecompany.is) Bicycle (from 10,900kr) and fat-bike tours (from 20,000kr) for all ability levels throughout the region.

Whale-Watching, Fishing & Boating Tours

Although the northern waters near Akureyri and Húsavík are known for whale watching, Reykjavík is still a great option. Tours generally run all year with more departures in the warmest months, which is also prime viewing season. If you don't spot whales, many outfits offer vouchers to come back and try again.

53 ROK ... E7
Snaps ... (see 28)
Súpa ... (see 91)
54 Sushi Social ... C4
55 Þrír Frakkar ... C7
56 Torfan Lobsterhouse ... B4
57 Vitabar ... G7

Drinking & Nightlife

58 Artson ... G6
59 Bar Ananas ... E5
60 Bastard ... D5
61 Boston ... E5
Bravó ... (see 70)
62 C is for Cookie ... D6
63 Den Danske Kro ... C4
64 Dillon ... E5
65 Kaffi Mokka ... D4
66 Kaffi Vínyl ... G5
67 Kaffibarinn ... D5
68 Kaffifélagið ... C5
69 Kaldi ... E5
70 Kiki ... E5
71 Mikkeller & Friends ... C3
72 Petersen Svítan ... C4
73 Port 9 ... F4
74 Prikið ... C4
75 Reykjavík Roasters ... F6
76 Spánski ... C4
77 Veður ... E5

Entertainment

78 Bíó Paradís ... F5
79 Mengi ... D5
80 National Theatre ... D3

Shopping

81 12 Tónar ... D5
82 66° North ... C4
83 Aurum ... C4
84 Blue Lagoon Shop ... D4
85 Cintamani ... C4
86 Dogma ... F5
87 Eymundsson ... D5
88 Fjallakofinn ... D4
89 Fóa ... C4
90 Geysir ... D5
91 Geysir ... D5
92 Geysir Heima ... D5
93 Handknitting Association of Iceland ... D6
94 Heilsuhúsið ... E5
95 Hrím ... E5
96 Húrra Reykjavík ... G5
97 Kiosk ... C4
98 Kron ... G6
99 KronKron ... G6
Mál og Menning ... (see 35)
100 Ófeigur Björnsson ... D4
101 Orrifinn ... D5
102 Rammagerðin ... D5
103 Reykjavík Foto ... G5
104 Reykjavík Record Shop ... E5
105 Skúmaskot ... D6
106 Spúútnik ... E5
107 Stígur ... D5
108 Tulipop ... E7

Several companies also offer sea-angling and puffin-viewing trips, though you'll often see puffins on small islets while whale watching.

★Elding Adventures at Sea WILDLIFE
(Map p64; ☎519 5000; www.whalewatching.is; Ægisgarður 5; adult/child 11,000/5500kr; ⊙harbour kiosk 8am-9pm; 🚌14) The city's most established and ecofriendly whale-watching tours feature a whale exhibition set in a converted fishing vessel; refreshments are sold on board. Elding also offers angling (adult/child 14,900/7450kr) and puffin-watching trips (adult/child from 6500/3250kr) and combo tours. It also runs the ferry to Viðey (p104). Pick-up available.

Special Tours WILDLIFE
(Map p64; ☎560 8800; www.specialtours.is; Ægisgarður 13; ⊙harbour kiosk 8am-8pm; 🚌14) One of the smaller, faster boats in the fleet of operators, used for sea angling (adult/child 13,000/6175kr) and whale watching (adult/child 11,000/5200kr). It also runs puffin tours (adult/child 5700/2700kr) and offers multiple combo deals.

Reykjavík Sailors WILDLIFE
(Map p64; ☎571 2222; www.reykjaviksailors.is; Hlésgata, Old Harbour; adult/child 9900/4950kr; ⊙9am-7pm, winter hours vary; 🚌14) Whale-watching tours plus those aimed at spotting puffins and the Northern Lights.

Whale Safari WILDLIFE
(Mr Puffin; Map p64; ☎497 0000; www.whalesafari.is; Ægisgarður 7; per passenger 22,000kr; ⊙harbour kiosk 8am-8pm mid-Apr–Oct; 🚌14) Small, fast Zodiac boats go in search of whales and puffins.

Reykjavík By Boat BOATING
(Map p64; ☎841 2030; www.reykjavikbyboat.is; Ægisgarður 9; adult/child 5600/2800kr; 🚌14) Offers a 1½-hour trip on a small wooden boat from the Old Harbour, around Engey islet (with a puffin colony), to Viðey and back.

Reykjavík Sea Adventures BIRDWATCHING, FISHING
(Map p64; ☎775 5777; www.seaadventures.is; Ægisgarður 3; ⏲9.30am-5pm, hours vary in winter; 🚌14) Sea-angling (adult/child 12,990/6500kr, mid-May to mid-September) and puffin tours (adult/child 5700/3000kr, May to August).

Fish Partner FISHING
(☎571 4545; www.fishpartner.com; fishing day tour from 32,000kr) Offers fishing day tours and a huge array of custom and multiday possibilities: sea angling, trout fishing, volcano fishing, heli-fishing.

Iceland Angling Travel FISHING
(☎568 6050; www.icelandangling.com) Custom holidays for fishing of all sorts around Iceland. A three-day package, including transport, accommodation, permits and guides costs from 369,000kr.

Bus & Activity Tours

A daylong bus tour from Reykjavík is one of the most cost-effective, efficient ways to see spectacular natural wonders if you're on a short holiday. They're also good if you want to combine sightseeing with activities like snowmobiling, horse riding, rafting or scuba diving.

Reykjavík Excursions BUS
(Kynnisferðir; Map p56; ☎580 5400; www.re.is; BSÍ Bus Terminal, Vatnsmýrarvegur 10; tours 8000-47,300kr) The largest and most popular bus-tour operator (with large groups) has an enormous booklet full of summer and winter programs. Extras include horse riding, snowmobiling and themed tours tying in with festivals. It also offers 'Iceland on Your Own' bus tickets and passports for transport, and operates the Flybus (p103) to Keflavík International Airport.

Icelandic Mountain Guides ADVENTURE
(Iceland Rovers; ☎587 9999; www.mountainguides.is; Stórhöfði 33) Highly respected, full-action outfit specialising in mountaineering, trekking, ice climbing (from 24,900kr) and the like. It also markets itself as 'Iceland Rovers' for its super-Jeep tours (Essential Iceland tour 35,000kr).

Grayline Iceland BUS
(Iceland Excursions; Map p60; ☎540 1313; www.grayline.is; Hafnarstræti 20) Bus-tour operator with comprehensive day trips (Golden Circle 8700kr) that often combine destinations and activities such as white-water rafting and horse riding. Book online for the best prices; expect large groups.

Sterna BUS
(Map p68; ☎551 1166; www.sternatravel.com; Harpa Concert Hall, Austurbakki 2; ⏲7am-midnight Jun-Aug, 8am-10pm Sep-May) Straight-up bus tours all around Iceland (eg Golden Circle and Green Energy 11,900kr). Also runs Iceland By Bus (p102), providing bus tickets and passports for independent travellers.

Saga Travel ADVENTURE
(☎558 8888; www.sagatravel.is) Small groups and a wide range of tours including a Game of Thrones trip (11,000kr). Runs some larger tours, in partnership with other local operators.

Arctic Adventures ADVENTURE
(☎562 7000; www.adventures.is) With young and enthusiastic staff, this company specialises in action-filled tours including kayaking (from 13,000kr), rafting (from 14,000kr), horse riding, quad-biking and glacier walking (16,000kr).

Gateway to Iceland BUS
(☎534 4446; www.gtice.is) Gets great reviews from independent travellers for its interesting guides and because its minibus tours (eg Golden Circle 12,800kr, South Iceland 13,700kr) are smaller than mass-market ones.

Hidden Iceland TOURS
(☎770 5733; www.hiddeniceland.is) Highly recommended operator using enthusiastic guides to take small groups on off-the-beaten path tours, as well as the more conventional routes. Experiences range from the Golden Circle (20,000kr) to a two-day trip to the Jökulsárlón Glacier Lagoon (from 52,000kr), and four days in the Westfjords (250,000kr). Provides pick-up.

Icelandic Knitter CULTURAL
(www.icelandicknitter.com; 6 days from 255,800kr) Designer Hélène Magnússon offers multiday knitting tours that take in spinning, woolwork, design, folklore and hiking/sightseeing, in partnership with Icelandic Mountain Guides (p72).

Bustravel BUS
(☎511 2600; www.bustravel.is; Golden Circle from per half-/full day 6750/10,000kr) Very popular among the hostelling crowd for the informative driver-guides. Large groups, low prices.

Go Green BUS
(☎694 9890; www.gogreen.is; tours from 44,000kr) Small, high-end operator that uses methane-powered vehicles and follows environ-

mentally conscious practices. Options range from the Golden Circle to fishing and kayaking. Provides pick-up.

Reykjavík Hiking HIKING
(☎893 2200; www.reykjavikhiking.is) Climb Mt Esja (15,000kr) or take an easier trek through lava-rich Búrfellsgjá canyon (12,000kr), both near Reykjavík.

Dog Sledding ADVENTURE
(☎863 6733; www.dogsledding.is; tours from 19,900kr) Runs dog-sledding tours; visitors sit on the rig but do not drive the team. When there's snow tours operate from Skálafell ski area near Reykjavík, when there's no snow they operate on dry land at Hólmasel in the Southwest; check the website. From mid-May to mid-July they're often on Langjökull glacier in West Iceland.

Ferðafélag Íslands ACCOMMODATION SERVICES
(Iceland Touring Association; Map p56; ☎568 2533; www.fi.is; Mörkin 6) Iceland Touring Association runs huts and campsites throughout the South, particularly along the Laugavegurinn hiking trail. The service can help with bookings, opening months and other information.

Extreme Iceland ADVENTURE
(☎588 1300; www.extremeiceland.is; Golden Circle/Snæfellsnes Peninsula bus tour 12,250/15,250kr) Host of bus, super-Jeep, caving, quad-bike and Northern Lights tours. Provides pick up.

Green Energy Travel BUS
(☎453 6000; www.get.is; tours from 14,900kr) Ecofriendly operator with a focus on small groups, quieter roads and less-visited sights as well as the blockbuster attractions.

Iceland Horizons BUS
(☎825 8886; www.icelandhorizon.is) Small minibus operator with only 20 seats, and four, highly rated tours (Golden Circle 10,900kr, South Shore 13,900kr, Snæfellsnes Peninsula 16,000kr, Northern Lights 10,900kr).

Super-Jeep & Supertruck Tours

Super-Jeep tours offer small groups (four to six people) a more customised experience. You'll reach your destinations a lot faster, and you can get out further into wild terrain. Prices are correspondingly higher than bus trips.

Icelandic Mountain Guides and Superjeep.is are among those offering super-Jeep trips. The tourist office has brochures for loads more.

Mountaineers of Iceland ADVENTURE
(☎580 9900; www.mountaineers.is) Excellent, knowledgable guides, many with experience on the national rescue team. Lots of super-Jeep (from 30,000kr) and snowmobiling (from 25,000kr) tours, with an emphasis on Langjökull, where it has several base camps.

Superjeep.is DRIVING
(☎660 1499; www.superjeep.is; tours per half-/full day from 28,000/29,000kr) Full range of super-Jeep trips with all the add-ons (snowmobiling, quad-biking etc).

Into the Wild DRIVING
(☎866 3301; www.intothewild.is) Full roster of super-Jeep excursions, from the Golden Circle (35,000kr) to Eyjafjallajökull and Landmannalaugar (32,500kr).

Caving & Lava-Tunnel Tours

Exploring the wild underground world of Iceland's volcanic terrain is a wonderful way to experience the geology of the island. Many lava tubes and caverns are seen by tour only. Main sites from Reykjavík include Reykjanes Peninsula and upper Borgarfjörður. Arctic Adventures, Icelandic Mountain Guides and many bus and super-Jeep tour operators lead caving expeditions.

Inside the Volcano ADVENTURE
(☎519 5609; www.insidethevolcano.com; tours 42,000kr; ⊗mid-May–mid-Oct) This one-of-a-kind experience takes adventure-seekers into a perfectly intact 4000-year-old magma chamber. Hike 3km (about 50 minutes) or go via helicopter (86,900kr) to the Thrihnukagigur crater where an elevator lowers groups of six down 120m into the bottom of a vase-shaped chasm that once gurgled with hot lava. Lights are dim and time inside is limited. Must be aged 12 and up.

Iceland Expeditions ADVENTURE
(☎777 0708; www.icelandexpeditions.is) Adventure tours include lava-tube caving (18,900kr).

Horse-Riding Tours

Trotting through lava fields on an Icelandic horse under the midnight sun is an unforgettable experience. Stables offer everything from 90-minute outings to multiday tours, and you can combine riding with other activities, such as visiting the Golden Circle and Blue Lagoon.

Eldhestar HORSE RIDING
(☎480 4800; www.eldhestar.is; Vellir, Hveragerði) Located near Hveragerði, Eldhestar is one of the most established riding outfits in Iceland. Trots take place on the surrounding grasslands (one hour 8000kr, half-day from 13,500kr) and throughout the region. A highlight is the Horses and Hot Springs day tour (22,750kr), which includes a dip in steaming natural pools.

Íshestar HORSE RIDING
(☎555 7000; www.ishestar.is; Sörlaskeið 26, Hafnarfjörður; half-/full day 12,200/22,000kr) One of the largest, oldest stables in the country with well-organised trots and multiday tours through crumbling lava fields.

Íslenski Hesturinn HORSE RIDING
(Icelandic Horse; ☎434 7979; www.theicelandichorse.is; Surtlugata 3; from 14,500kr) With experienced local guides, this outfit near the capital takes special care to match you with a horse that suits your capabilities; small groups.

Viking Horses HORSE RIDING
(☎537 9590; www.vikinghorses.is; Almannadalsgata 19; half-day 18,900kr) This family-run stable is popular for its higher-end, small-group rides around Hólmsheiði hill and surrounding lakes.

Reykjavík Riding Center HORSE RIDING
(☎477 2222; www.reykjavikridingcenter.is; Brekknaás 9; half-/full day 13,900/23,900kr) Located near Reykjavík's main equestrian centre, this outfit takes small groups (no more than 10) of all levels around the Rauðholar (Red Hills). A midnight sun tour is also offered.

Glacier Walks & Ice-Climbing Tours

Crunching across a rugged glacier is a thrill. Tours often take visitors to Sólheimajökull (p165), the most accessible glacial tongue of massive Mýrdalsjökull. Glacier walks run year-round; ice climbing runs September to April. For ice climbing you have to be able to pull and push your own weight up. Prices are significantly lower if you base yourself near the glacier and go with local guides.

Reykjavík-based operators include Arctic Adventures (p72) and Icelandic Mountain Guides (p72).

Asgard Beyond ADVENTURE
(☎779 6000; www.asgardbeyond.com) Glacier hikes (from 30,000kr), rock climbing (from 35,000kr) and other outdoor activities.

Quad-Biking Tours

Quad-biking tours explore the lava fields of Reykjanes Peninsula. Many of the main bus/activity tour operators (eg Arctic Adventures, Reykjavík Excursions) offer quad-bike options.

Safari Quads QUAD-BIKE TOUR
(Safari Buggy; ☎414 1533; www.quad.is; Lambhagavegur) ATV and buggy outings in the hills near Mosfellsbær. Rides last from between one hour (from 16,900kr) and a day (from 51,500kr); there are also evening rides with sunset and city-light views. Single-rider supplements start at 4000kr.

ATV Reykjavík QUAD-BIKE TOUR
(☎861 0006; www.atvreykjavik.is) All terrain vehicle (ATV) tours around Hafrafell mountain (20,000kr, solo supplement 5900kr) and beyond.

Rafting & Speedboating Tours

Fun for the family, these trips run from Reykholt with Arctic Rafting (p128) or Iceland Riverjet (p128), and offer Reykjavík pick-ups.

Scuba-Diving & Snorkelling Tours

Iceland has some of the most unique snorkelling and scuba diving in the world. Operators offer dives at Silfra, a fissure filled with crystalline water near Þingvellir on the Golden Circle, and a more technical one in the nearby lake. Advance booking is essential; outfitters can pick you up in town or meet you on-site. In summer it's possible to do a midnight dive.

PADI certification is required for scuba diving. Some of the bigger activity-tour companies – such as Arctic Adventures (p72) through its subsidiary, **Dive Silfra** (www.divesilfra.is) – also offer dive options.

Dive.is DIVING
(Map p64; ☎578 6200; www.dive.is; Hólmaslóð 2; 2 dives at Þingvellir 34,000kr) The oldest and most established operator in Iceland offers snorkelling in the glacial waters filling the fissure between the tectonic plates at Þingvellir (from 15,000kr), as well as diving and combo tours.

Scuba Iceland DIVING
(☎562 7000; www.scuba.is; 2 dives from 35,000kr, snorkelling from 13,900kr) Scuba Iceland offers dives at Silfra, Kleifarvatn geothermal lake and in the ocean. Has a good reputation for small groups and runs snorkelling trips too.

Snowmobiling Tours

Though most opportunities to jump on a snowmobile lie far beyond the capital, there are several operators that go to nearby Langjökull. One hour with two riders costs from about 25,000kr per rider; for solo riders it's around 35,000kr. The best operators in Reykjavík are Mountaineers of Iceland (p73) and **Snowmobile.is** (☎562 7000; www.snowmobile.is).

Northern Lights Tours

During winter, most bus and activity companies offer Northern Lights trips taking onlookers into the countryside to escape urban light interference when viewing the aurora borealis. Trips last around four hours, usually starting at 9pm or 10pm. Since there's no guarantee when you'll see these magnificent curtains of light, or where they'll be, we recommend spending a night or two in the countryside to maximise viewing possibilities.

If you're not in Iceland during aurora season, you can have a multimedia immersion at Aurora Reykjavík (p59).

Air Tours

Larger budgets offer the possibility of day trips and tours by air to far-flung or remote destinations like Lake Mývatn, the Westfjords, the steam-shrouded south coast and highlands, Vestmannaeyjar and even Greenland.

Atlantsflug FLIGHT TOUR
(Map p56; ☎854 4105; www.flightseeing.is; Reykjavík Domestic Airport; adult/child from 26,900/13,450kr) Offers flightseeing tours from Reykjavík, Bakki Airport and Skaftafell. From Reykjavík Domestic Airport you can fly over the Golden Circle, the Hengill, Bláfjöll and Esja mountains, or take a day trip with tours around Skaftafell and Jökulsárlón glacial lagoon. Also runs scheduled flights to Vestmannaeyjar.

Air Iceland Connect FLIGHT TOUR
(Map p56; ☎570 3030; www.airicelandconnect.is; Reykjavík Domestic Airport) Iceland's largest domestic airline runs a wide range of combination air, bus, hiking, rafting, horse-riding, whale-watching and glacier day tours around Iceland from Reykjavík and Akureyri. It also runs day tours to Greenland and the Faroe Islands.

Eagle Air Iceland FLIGHT TOUR
(Map p56; ☎562 2640; www.eagleair.is; Reykjavík Domestic Airport) Eagle Air Iceland offers sightseeing flights over volcanoes (61,800kr) and glaciers, and many combo tours. Also runs set routes from Reykjavík: Vestmannaeyjar (return 37,700kr); Höfn (return 54,400kr); Húsavík (return 52,600kr); and in the Westfjords, Bíldudalur (return 50,600kr) and Gjögur (return 50,600kr).

Reykjavík Helicopters FLIGHT TOUR
(Map p56; ☎589 1000; www.reykjavikhelicopters.com; Reykjavík Domestic Airport) Helicopter trips all over, including Reykjavík (27,000kr), a glacier landing (99,000kr) and volcanoes such as Eyjafjallajökull (139,000kr) and Hekla.

Norðurflug FLIGHT TOUR
(Map p56; ☎562 2500; www.helicopter.is; Nauthólsvegur 58d, Reykjavík Domestic Airport; Reykjavík flight 27,900kr) Helicopters fly over Reykjavík, or zip to craters (69,900kr), waterfalls, glaciers and beyond. Its multitude of trips go as far as the Westfjords, Mývatn (439,900kr) and Askja.

FAROE FORAY

Flights and ferries give Arctic adventurers three or four days to explore the truly magical Faroe Islands. A half-week is just enough time to see the following highlights:

Tórshavn The first thing you'll notice are striking turf roofs adorning almost every bright-coloured building in the marina. Although light on sights, Tórshavn makes a great base if you're planning a series of day trips.

Gjógv It may be hard to pronounce (say 'jaykf'), but Gjógv is oh so easy to love. Tiny turf-roofed cottages cluster around a harbour that looks as though a lightning bolt ripped straight through the terrain. There's good hiking and an inn.

Mykines Marking the western limits of the island chain, Mykines (*mee*-chi-ness) offers innumerable bird colonies (puffins!), haunting basalt sea stacks and solitary cliffs. Considered remote by Faroes standards (11 inhabitants), it is connected to Vágar by helicopter and ferry.

Hestir Just south of Streymoy, Hestir is best known for hollow grottoes carved into the cliffs by pounding waves.

DAY-TRIP TO GREENLAND

You can grab a day tour to Greenland from Reykjavík since it takes just under two hours to fly there. In summer **Air Iceland Connect** (www.airiceland connect.is) offers regular tours to Kulusuk in east Greenland (from about 70,750kr). Hidden in a tapestry of icy whites and cool blues, on a mountainous island, Kulusuk has only 250 inhabitants. The village of brightly coloured wood-box houses and its icy bay reveal themselves to day trippers during the stunning walk over from the airport. Although the traditional Greenlandic drum-dance demo is a tad kitsch, the rest of the experience is like one giant dream sequence. Greenland Travel offers multiday tours.

Greenland Travel TOURS
(☎ in Denmark 45 3313 1011; www.greenland-travel.com; tours from 109,400kr) Part of Air Greenland, this tour operator offers multiday tours from Reykjavík to Greenland.

Sleeping

June through August accommodation books out entirely; reservations are essential. Prices are high. Plan for hostels, camping or short-term apartment rentals to save money. Most places open year-round and many offer discounts or variable pricing online.

Old Reykjavík

Hótel Reykjavík Centrum HOTEL €€
(Map p60; ☎ 514 6000; www.hotelcentrum.is; Aðalstræti 16; d/apt/ste from 27,400/39,300/51,800kr; P Wi-Fi) Mezzanines and a glass roof unite two historic central buildings, giving this hotel a spry, light feel. Its 89 neatly proportioned rooms, suites and apartments all have mini-fridges, satellite TV and coffee-making gear. Prices vary wildly online depending on date.

CenterHótel Plaza HOTEL €€
(Map p60; ☎ 595 8500; www.centerhotels.com; Aðalstræti 4; s/d incl breakfast from 25,400/26,300kr; @ Wi-Fi) One of the blander members of the CenterHótel chain, with business-oriented rooms but great views from the higher levels. It's in an enviably central spot.

★Consulate Hotel Reykjavík LUXURY HOTEL €€€
(Map p60; ☎ 514 6800; www.curiocollection3.hilton.com; Hafnarstraeti 17; d incl breakfast from 44,700kr, ste from 112,700kr; A/C @ Wi-Fi) Hilton's new Curio hotel is a plush place where the service is impeccable and conversations are held in quiet tones. A supremely sympathetic conversion of a 1900s department store has created welcoming bedrooms rich in antique flourishes and modern comforts – espresso machines, blackout curtains and big TVs. There's also a gym and spa.

★Apotek BOUTIQUE HOTEL €€€
(Map p60; ☎ 512 9000; www.keahotels.is; Austurstræti 16; d incl breakfast from 42,200kr; Wi-Fi) Apotek is set in one of the city's most iconic buildings – a well-renovated, former pharmacy smack in the centre of Old Reykjavík, which dates from 1917 and was designed by Guðjón Samúelsson. It offers slick contemporary rooms in muted tones and a popular ground-floor tapas-style restaurant-bar (p85).

★Kvosin Downtown HOTEL €€€
(Map p60; ☎ 571 4460; www.kvosinhotel.is; Kirkjutorg 4; 2-/4-/6-person ste incl breakfast 43,600/49,800/67,300kr; Wi-Fi) Firmly a part of Reykjavík's luxury-accommodation wave, the suites at this superbly located historic hotel range from 'Junior' and 'Executive' to 'Valkyrie'. Espresso machines adorn the kitchenettes and all the mod cons are standard, including Sóley Organics toiletries.

Black Pearl APARTMENT €€€
(Map p60; ☎ 527 9600; www.blackpearlreykjavik.com; Tryggvagata 18a; apt 50,000-150,000kr; P @ Wi-Fi family) These 17 fully kitted-out apartments fill several black towers just back from the waterfront. The reception can organise cleaning service, laundry and child care, while the spacious, cleanly decorated suites come with king-sized beds, designer furniture and balconies, some with water views. Apartments sleep four to six people.

Hótel Borg LUXURY HOTEL €€€
(Map p60; ☎ 551 1440; www.hotelborg.is; Pósthússtræti 11; d from 49,800kr; @ Wi-Fi) This historic hotel dates from 1930 and is now tricked out with super-smart beige, black and cream decor, parquet floors, leather headboards and flat-screen Bang & Olufsen TVs. The tower suite is two storeys of opulence with panoramic views.

Radisson Blu 1919 HOTEL €€€
(Map p60; ☎ 599 1000; www.radissonblu.com; Pósthússtræti 2; d from 32,200kr; @ Wi-Fi) Although

part of a large chain, a strong sense of style lingers here, thanks in part to the hotel's 1919 facade. Inside heritage meets modern styling – contemporary rooms sport large beds and flat-screen TVs, while an ornate stairwell leads to large, comfy suites.

Old Harbour

★Reykjavík Downtown Hostel HOSTEL €
(Map p60; 553 8120; www.hostel.is; Vesturgata 17; 4-/10-bed dm 9200/5700kr, d with/without bathroom 20,800/18,400kr; @ ; 14) The reviews are so good for this squeaky clean, charming and well-run hostel that it regularly lures large groups and the nonbackpacker set. Enjoy friendly service, a guest kitchen and excellent rooms. Discount 800kr for HI members.

Oddsson Hostel HOSTEL €
(Map p56; 511 3579; www.oddsson.is; Hringbraut 121; dm from 6000kr, d with/without bathroom 32,340/24,500kr; ; 14) You can't miss this large, quirky hostel near the Old Harbour with its brightly coloured facade. There are dorm rooms, tiny private pod-like doubles and regular hotel rooms, some with excellent sea views. Everyone shares a kitchen, hot tub, rooftop, and yoga and karaoke rooms.

Guesthouse Butterfly GUESTHOUSE €€
(Map p56; 894 1864; www.butterfly.is; Ránargata 8a; d with/without bathroom incl breakfast 21,900/15,250kr;) On a quiet, central residential street, you can't miss Butterfly's flamboyant mural. Neat, brightly furnished rooms, a guest kitchen and friendly Icelandic-Norwegian owners make you feel right at home. Self-contained apartments (from 25,000kr) with kitchen and some with balconies are ideal for the family.

Three Sisters APARTMENT €€
(Þrjár Systur; Map p56; 565 2181; www.threesisters.is; Ránargata 16; 2-/4-person apt 24,400/49,800kr; mid-May–Aug; @) A warmly welcoming owner who goes the extra mile to meet guests' needs helps lift Three Sisters above the crowd. The seven studio apartments in the corner townhouse have comfy beds, homey decor and flat-screen TVs. Each studio has a kitchen.

★Icelandair Hotel Reykjavík Marina BOUTIQUE HOTEL €€€
(Map p64; booking 444 000, hotel 560 8000; www.icelandairhotels.is; Mýrargata 2; d 34,850-42,500kr, ste from 47,600kr; @ ; 14) Captivating art, cool nautical-chic decor and up-to-the-second mod cons ensure this harbourside design hotel is a gorgeous retreat. Clever ways to conserve space make the small rooms winners. The attic bedrooms facing the harbour have excellent sea views. The lobby is home to the happening Slippbarinn (p93) cocktail bar.

Reykjavík Marina Residence APARTMENT €€€
(Map p64; 560 8500; www.reykjavikmarinaresidence.is; Mýrargata 14; ste 77,400-103,000kr; @ ; 14) Seven refined suites in two restored historical houses expand the nearby Icelandair Hotel Reykjavík Marina offerings into the luxury accommodation market. Concierge service, access to the facilities at the other hotel, Sóley Organics toiletries and designer furnishings make them deeply comfortable. The Aðalbjörg Suite is the largest, spanning two floors.

Laugavegur & Skólavörðustígur

★KEX Hostel HOSTEL €
(Map p78; 561 6060; www.kexhostel.is; Skúlagata 28; 4-/16-bed dm 7900/4800kr, d with/without bathroom 34,500/20,000kr; @) An unofficial headquarters of backpackerdom and popular local gathering place, KEX is a megahostel with heaps of sociability and style (think retro vaudeville meets rodeo). The bathrooms may be shared by many, but KEX remains a favourite for its lively restaurant-bar with interior courtyard and water views.

Loki 101 GUESTHOUSE €
(Map p68; 864 0944, 553 9344; www.loki101.is; Lokastígur 24a; s/d from 11,600/14,800kr;) The location couldn't be better, in a quiet street to one side of Skolavörðustígur and with Hallgrímskirkja just steps away. Inside find simple rooms with hardwood floors, shared bathrooms and a well-equipped guest kitchen. On the downside, the soundproofing isn't that good.

SHORT-TERM RENTALS

Reykjavík's sky-high summertime accommodation prices have led enterprising locals in the capital's prized neighbourhoods to rent their apartments (or rooms) to short-stay visitors. Prices often beat commercial rates, though of course there's no maid, concierge etc. Aim for a Reykjavík 101 postal code to be centrally located.

Laugavegur East

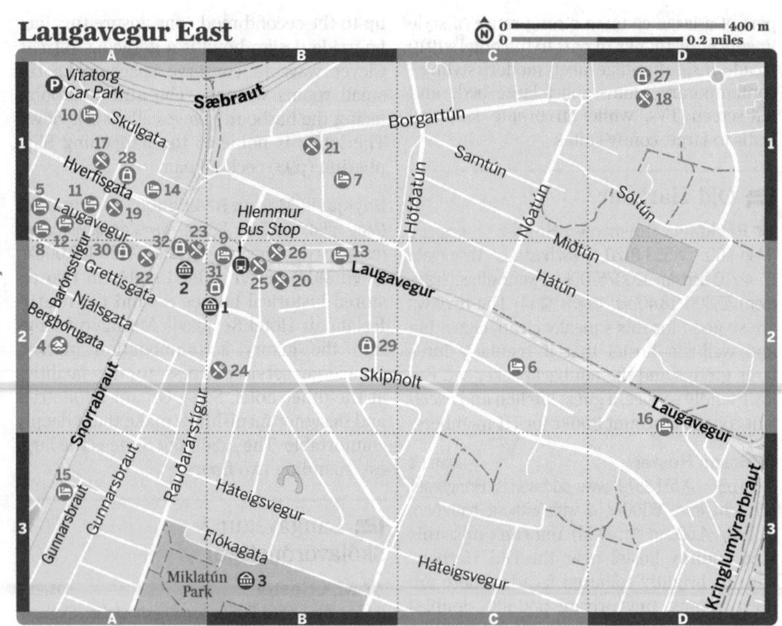

Laugavegur East

Sights
1 Gallerí Fold B2
2 Icelandic Phallological Museum A2
3 Reykjavík Art Museum – Kjarvalsstaðir B3

Activities, Courses & Tours
4 Sundhöllin A2

Sleeping
5 Alda Hotel A1
6 Eyja Guldsmeden C2
7 Fosshotel Reykjavík B1
8 Grettir Apartments A1
9 Hlemmur Square B2
10 KEX Hostel A1
11 Luna Hotel Apartments A1
12 OK Studios A1
13 Opal Apartments B2
14 Skuggi Hotel A1
15 Snorri's Guesthouse A3
16 Útivist D2

Eating
17 10-11 .... A1
18 10-11 .... D1
19 Argentína A1
20 Ban Thai B2
Hlemmur Mathöll .... (see 25)
21 Johansen Deli B1
22 Matwerk A2
23 Noodle Station A2
24 Restó B2
25 SKÁL! B2
26 Yummi Yummi B2

Drinking & Nightlife
KEX Bar .... (see 10)

Shopping
27 Handknitting Association of Iceland D1
28 Iceland Camping Equipment Rental A1
29 Iðnú Bookshop B2
30 Jokla Icelandic Design A2
31 Lucky Records B2
32 Orr A2

101 Hostel HOSTEL €
(Map p68; ☎661 4767; 101hostel@mail.com; Laugarvegur 58b; dm 5800-6700kr; 📶) The fabulously friendly family that runs this compact hostel is supremely proud of the heritage features dating back to the 1840s. Homey dorms have either six or 10 beds, while three wet-room showers have heated floors. Chill in the 1950s kitchen or on the deck – there's a positive vibe either way.

★ **Nest Apartments** APARTMENT €€
(Map p68; ☎893 0280; www.nestapartments.is; Bergthorugata 15; apt from 20,000kr; 📶) Four

modern apartments with neat antique touches make a superb home away from home on this central, peaceful street. Ranged over a tall townhouse, the apartments sleep two to four people – the one in the loft steals the show with water and mountain views. There's a two-night minimum.

★**Loft Hostel** HOSTEL €€
(Map p68; ☎553 8140; www.lofthostel.is; Bankastræti 7; dm 8500-9900kr, d/q 26,200/36,700kr; @📶) Perched high above the action on bustling Bankastræti, this modern hostel attracts a decidedly young crowd, including locals who come for its trendy bar and cafe terrace. This sociable spot comes with neat dorms with linen included and en suite bathrooms.

★**Forsæla Apartmenthouse** GUESTHOUSE, APARTMENT €€
(Map p68; ☎551 6046; www.apartmenthouse.is; Grettisgata 33b; d/tr without bathroom incl breakfast 25,700/34,500kr, apt/house from 45,150/90,300kr; 📶👪) A 100-year-old wood-and-tin house is the star of the show here. It sleeps four to eight people and comes with old beams and tasteful mod cons. Smaller apartments have cosy bedrooms and sitting rooms, kitchens and washing machines. Or opt for the B&B lodging alongside. There's a minimum three-night stay.

★**Grettir Apartments** APARTMENT €€
(Map p78; ☎694 7020; contact@grettisborg.is; Grettisgata 53b; apt 23,500-57,700kr; 📶👪) Sleeping here is like sleeping in a magazine for Scandinavian home design. The thoroughly modern studios and apartments boast fine furnishings and sleek built-ins. The largest sleeps six or seven.

★**REY Apartments** APARTMENT €€
(Map p68; ☎771 4600; www.rey.is; Grettisgata 2a; apt 30,000-55,800kr; 📶👪) For those preferring private digs over hotel stays, REY is a smart choice thanks to its cache of modern, two- to eight-person apartments scattered across several Escher-like stairwells. They're well maintained and stylishly decorated.

Luna Hotel Apartments APARTMENT €€
(Map p78; ☎852 7572; www.luna.is; reception 3rd fl, Laugavegur 77; apt from 24,200kr) A strong entry on Reykjavík's luxury-apartment scene, Luna maintains 15 excellent apartments in the streets near Skólavörðustígur. Locations are relatively quiet, and the apartments are bright and cheerful, ranging from small studios to four-bedroom pads that sleep eight.

Baldursbrá Guesthouse GUESTHOUSE €€
(Map p68; ☎552 6646; baldursbra@centrum.is; Laufásvegur 41; s/d/tr without bathroom incl breakfast from 9,700/17,800/19,000kr; 📶) Decent-sized comfy rooms with washbasins characterise this little guesthouse on a quiet street near Tjörnin. You'll also find a sitting room and garden with hot-pot and barbecue. The owners provide friendly, attentive service.

Castle House Apartments APARTMENT €€
(Map p68; ☎511 2166; www.hotelsiceland.net; Skálholtsstígur 2a; apt from 20,500kr; 📶👪) Modern, self-contained apartments are satisfyingly central and commendably quiet. More personal than a hotel, they still come with room service: fresh towels appear daily and washing up seems to magically look after itself. The same people run **Embassy Apartments** (Map p56; ☎511 2166; www.hotelsiceland.net; Garðastræti 40; apt from 24,400kr; 📶) on the northwest side of Tjörnin.

Galtafell Guesthouse GUESTHOUSE €€
(Map p68; ☎699 2525; www.galtafell.com; Laufásvegur 46; d with/without bathroom from 25,300/24,600kr, apt from 29,000kr; 📶) The four one-bedroom apartments in this converted historic mansion have fully equipped kitchens, cosy seating areas and the use of a lovely garden. The three double rooms share a guest kitchen. It's all tucked away in a quiet lakeside neighbourhood within easy walking distance of the city centre.

Óðinn APARTMENT €€
(Map p68; ☎561 3400; www.odinnreykjavik.com; Óðinsgata 9; 6-/8-/10-person apt 25,200/41,200/80,000kr; 📶👪) Simple white rooms, stripped floors, large TVs and bright, fun artwork define these four swish apartments in a quiet but still central street. All come with well-equipped kitchens and washing machines; the four-bedroom penthouse has a terrace with Hallgrímskirkja views.

Hlemmur Square HOSTEL €€
(Map p78; ☎415 1600; www.hlemmursquare.com; Laugavegur 105; dm 5200-5600kr, d 22,000-33,000kr, apt from 38,000kr; @📶) Rooms can be noisy and the quality is a little patchy, but friendly staff, a great location and an upbeat vibe more than compensate. Also a plus are the big dorm rooms with crisp linens and spacious doubles featuring king-sized beds; some even have balconies and sea views.

Sunna Guesthouse GUESTHOUSE €€

(Map p68; ☎511 5570; www.sunna.is; Þórsgata 26; d with/without bathroom 33,400/27,000kr, apt 51,000kr; P@📶👪) All the various room and apartment configurations here are simple and sunny with honey-coloured parquet floors. Several have good Hallgrímskirkja views. There's limited free parking and breakfast is included in the price. Families can choose between studios or spacious apartments with room for eight.

Hótel Leifur Eiríksson HOTEL €€

(Map p68; ☎562 0800; www.hotelleifur.is; Skólavörðustígur 45; s/d incl breakfast from 24,700/26,800kr) In one of the best locations in Reykjavík, Hótel Leifur Eiríksson is set at the end of arty Skólavörðustígur just in front of Hallgrímskirkja – more than half the rooms have excellent church views. Rooms are fairly small and basic, but you're paying for the coordinates not the interior design.

Hótel Frón HOTEL €€

(Map p68; ☎511 4666; www.hotelfron.is; Laugavegur 22a; d/apt from 27,100/28,600kr; @📶👪) This hotel is excellently located overlooking Laugavegur (although this also means rooms at the front can be noisy at weekends). The newer wing has good doubles and large, stylish apartments with kitchenettes; older rooms are less inspiring.

Snorri's Guesthouse GUESTHOUSE €€

(Map p78; ☎552 0598; www.guesthousereykjavik.com; Snorrabraut 61; s with/without bathroom 22,600/16,600kr, d with/without bathroom 28,200/21,000kr; P📶👪) The impeccably maintained rooms in this pebble-dashed building are decked out in muted shades. The 'family' rooms (from 30,100kr) and friendly owner make it a good base.

★**Alda Hotel** BOUTIQUE HOTEL €€€

(Map p78; ☎553 9366; www.aldahotel.is; Laugavegur 66; d/tr 40,500/47,400kr, ste from 87,300kr; 📶) A wealth of boutique touches lift sleek Alda well above the crowd: knitted lamp covers, a sauna and hot tub, and the free cell phones given to guests (all local calls and data are free). The vast King suite is made sumptuous by a huge TV, coffee machine and free-standing slipper bath.

★**Reykjavík Residence** APARTMENT €€€

(Map p68; ☎561 1200; www.rrhotel.is; Hverfisgata 45; 2-/3-/8-person apt 33,500/37,300/87,000kr; @📶👪) Plush city-centre living feels just right in this array of apartments set in six historic mansions. Linens are crisp, service attentive and the light a glowing gold. The pick of the lot are the Royal Suites in the former home of an Icelandic Prime Minister – named after one-time visitors, the king and queen of Denmark

★**Hótel Holt** LUXURY HOTEL €€€

(Map p68; ☎552 5700; www.holt.is; Bergstaðastræti 37; s 31,000-34,000kr, d 35,000-45,000kr; @📶) Expect a totally cool blast to the luxurious past. Built in the 1960s as one of Reykjavík's first hotels, Holt is decked out with original paintings, drawings and sculptures (it boasts the largest private art collection in Iceland), set off by warm-toned decor.

Sandhotel BOUTIQUE HOTEL €€€

(Map p68; ☎519 8090; www.sandhotel.is; Laugavegur 34; r from 40,000kr; 📶) When the folks behind one of Iceland's best bakeries (p87) open a hotel, you know it's going to be great. At Sandhotel art deco echoes meet Nordic design and 21st-century luxury: in-room espresso machines, bluetooth speakers, fine linens and soft towels. The breakfast breads and pastries are, of course, superb.

Canopy by Hilton BOUTIQUE HOTEL €€€

(Map p68; ☎528 7000; www.canopybyhilton.com; Smiðjustígur 4; d from 42,500kr; @📶) The elaborately comfortable rooms here are styled in tones echoing ocean, volcanic rock and ice and some have sea or mountain views. You also get loaner bikes, wholesome breakfasts, afternoon beer tastings and a gym.

Opal Apartments APARTMENT €€€

(Map p78; ☎860 1300; www.opalapartments.is; Laugavegur 151; apt from 41,300kr; P📶) Despite a work-a-day location beside a busy road, the eight cheerful apartments on the Hlemmur Sq end of Laugavegur are immaculate and fully equipped with all the cooking equipment and comforts you could need.

CenterHótel Arnarhvoll HOTEL €€€

(Map p68; ☎595 8540; www.centerhotels.com; Ingólfsstræti 1; d incl breakfast from 37,500kr; @📶) A glossy hotel on the waterfront, 100-room Arnarhvoll offers unimpeded views of the bay and Mt Esja. Cool, Scandinavian-designed rooms with clean lines and large windows let in lovely Nordic light. Rooms are a bit small, but extremely comfortable beds compensate. Adding flair are the mini-sauna, steam room and top-floor Ský bar.

OK Studios APARTMENT €€€

(Map p78; ☎578 9850; Laugavegur 74; 2-/4-person studios from 24,800/28,800kr; 📶) A creative vibe pervades rooms kitted out in individual style and featuring cool mismatched furniture with La Giaconda art. Despite the up-cycled air it's all very agreeable, with comfy beds, balconies and a daily cleaning service.

Skuggi Hotel BOUTIQUE HOTEL €€€
(Map p78; ☎590 7000; www.keahotels.is; Hverfisgata 103; d incl breakfast from 30,700kr; P 📶) King-sized beds, sleek furnishings, satellite TV and an excellent location just off Laugavegur make this a good bet. Plus there's free parking.

CenterHótel Þingholt BOUTIQUE HOTEL €€€
(Map p68; ☎595 8530; www.centerhotels.com; Þingholtsstræti 3; d/ste from 34,400/50,400kr; @ 📶) Full of character, Þingholt was designed by architect Gulla Jónsdóttir, who used natural materials to create one of Reykjavík's more distinctive hotels. Compact rooms feel cosy with atmospheric lighting, stylish dark-grey flooring, and black-leather headboards. Some have sleek tubs in the bedrooms.

Hótel Óðinsvé HOTEL €€€
(Map p68; ☎511 6200; www.hotelodinsve.is; Þórsgata 1; d/ste from 36,000/47,000kr; @ 📶) There's a welcome sense of individuality and personality at Oðinsvé – in its 50 sunny rooms classic furnishings meet wooden floors and original art. Some are split-level, some have bathtubs or balconies, while the top-floor suites have sea views. Breakfast is 2800kr.

101 Hotel BOUTIQUE HOTEL €€€
(Map p68; ☎580 0101; www.101hotel.is; Hverfisgata 10; d from 47,500kr; @ 📶) The 101 aims to tickle the senses – with yielding downy beds, a stark black-and-white colour scheme, Bang & Olufsen sound systems and glass-walled showers. A spa, small gym and glitterati restaurant-bar add to the opulence.

Room With A View APARTMENT €€€
(Map p68; ☎552 7262; www.roomwithaview.is; Laugavegur 18; apt 34,000-75,000kr; 📶 👪) The location is superbly central, the design is pure luxe-Scandinavian and the trappings are tempting: kitchenettes, CD players, high-end toiletries and a sundeck and Jacuzzi. The only fly in the ointment is nightlife noise.

Eyja Guldsmeden BOUTIQUE HOTEL €€€
(Map p78; ☎519 7300; www.hoteleyja.is; Brautarholt 10; s/d incl breakfast from 40,700/45,500kr; P 📶) 🍃 If Reykjavík's check-yourself-in apartments aren't your thing, try Eyja Guldsmeden, where attentive service, excellent breakfasts and four-poster beds sit beside chic bedrooms finished with wood and stone. An edge-of-downtown location and free parking might seal the deal.

🛏 Tün

Fosshotel Reykjavík HOTEL €€€
(Map p78; ☎531 9000; www.islandshotel.is; Þórunnartún 1; ⏰d/f incl breakfast from 31,200/42,800kr; 🚌4, 12, 16) This 320-room behemoth is one of the new breed of high-rise hotels, especially centred around the Tún neighbourhood east of the city centre. Modern rooms with all the normal mod cons (flat-screen TV, hairdryer) get better, bigger and more expensive as you get higher in the tower. Smaller, older Fosshotels dot the capital.

🛏 Laugardalur

Reykjavík Campsite CAMPGROUND €
(Map p56; ☎568 6944; www.reykjavikcampsite.is; Sundlaugavegur 32; sites per adult/child 2400kr/free; ⏰May-Sep; P @ 📶; 🚌14) 🍃 Reykjavík's only campground is vast, with space for 650 people in three fields. Extensive, modern facilities include free showers, bike hire (five hours 4000kr), kitchens and barbecue areas. It's 2km east of the city centre in Laugardalur, next to the swimming pool (p65).

Reykjavík City Hostel HOSTEL €€
(Map p56; ☎553 8110; www.hostel.is; Sundlaugavegur 34; dm from 4500kr, d with/without bathroom 23,100/19,100kr; P @ 📶 👪; 🚌14) 🍃 Reykjavík's original hostel is a large, ecofriendly complex with a fun backpacker vibe. Two kilometres east of the city centre in Laugardalur, it abuts the swimming pool, and is served by the Flybus and many tour operators. It boasts bike rental, guest kitchen, barbecue and spacious deck.

Hilton Reykjavík Nordica HOTEL €€€
(Map p56; ☎444 5000; www.hilton.com; Suðurlandsbraut 2; d from 31,500kr; @ 📶; 🚌2, 5, 14, 15, 17) Spacious, easygoing Scandinavian chic makes this Hilton an effortless stay: amenities include 24-hour room service, gym, spa, bar and gourmet restaurant Vox (p91). Light-filled rooms in subtle shades of cream and mocha have enormous beds; those on the upper floors have super sea views. It's about 2km from the city centre, near Laugardalur.

🛏 South of the Centre

Icelandair Hotel Natura HOTEL €€
(Map p56; ☎444 4500; www.icelandairhotels.com; Nauthólsvegur 52; d from 22,100kr; P @ 📶 🏊; 🚌15) A bit out of the way, Natura is best for

1

LOTTIE DAVIES/LONELY PLANET ©

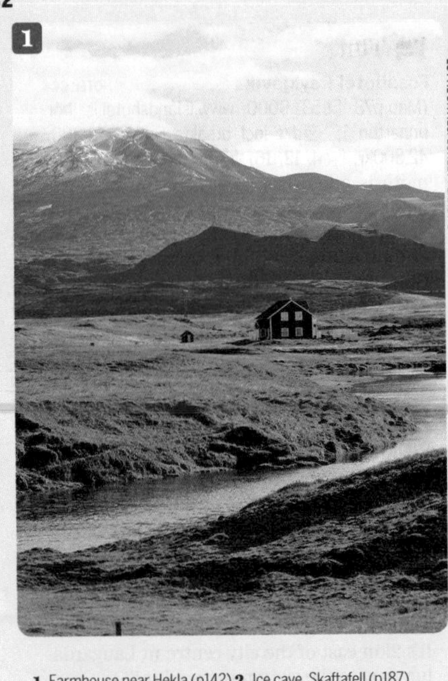

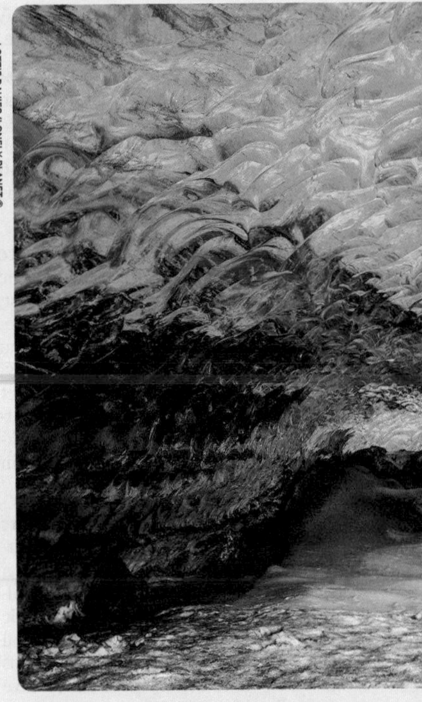

1. Farmhouse near Hekla (p142) 2. Ice cave, Skaftafell (p187) 3. Eyjafjallajökull (p167) 4. Magni (p153)

3

J. HELGASON/SHUTTERSTOCK ©

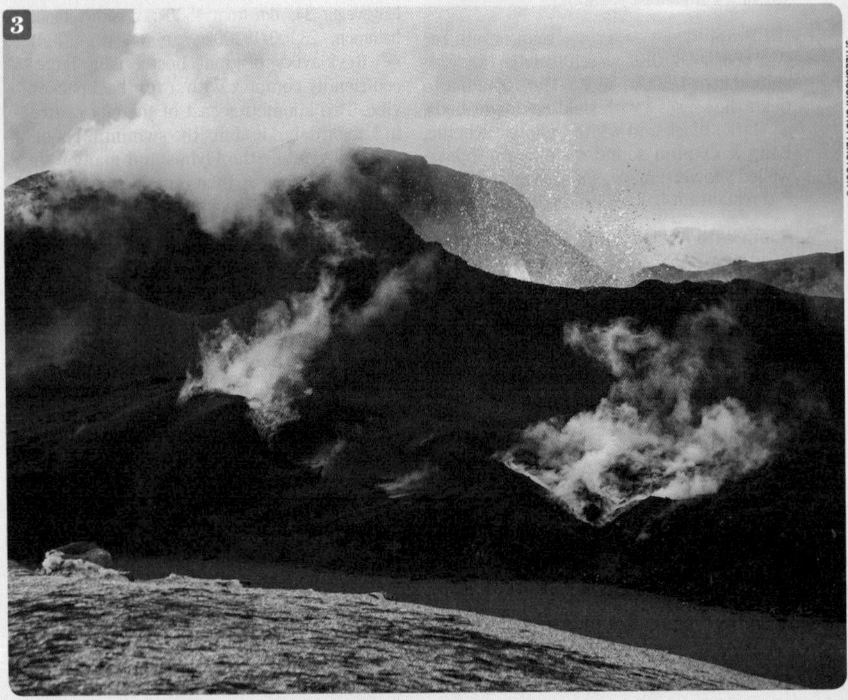

ANNA OM/SHUTTERSTOCK ©

Fire & Ice

'Land of fire and ice' might be an overused marketing slogan, but it's not hyperbole. Serene, majestic scenery belies Iceland's fiery heart – there are some 30 active volcanoes, and many of them lie under thick ice. When their fire-breathing fury is unleashed, the world often has no choice but to take notice (remember Eyjafjallajökull?).

Vatnajökull

The island's ice queen is Europe's largest ice cap and the namesake for its largest national park (p187). Don't miss the chance to explore this endless kingdom of white aboard a snowmobile.

Eyjafjallajökull

We've all heard the name (or at least heard people try to pronounce the name) of the treacherous eruption that spewed impenetrable tufts of ash over Europe in 2010, causing the cancellation of thousands of flights (p167).

Hekla & Katla

Like wicked stepsisters from some Icelandic fairy tale, Hekla (p142) and Katla (p167) are volatile beasts that dominate many of the southern vistas, threatening to belch forth steam, smoke and oozing lava that melts the nearby glaciers and floods the southern plains.

Snæfellsjökull

Jules Verne's famous journey to the centre of the earth starts here – the Snæfellsnes Peninsula's prominent glacial fist (p227) that can be easily glimpsed from Reykjavík on clear days.

Magni & Móði

Iceland's newest mountains (p153) were formed during the eruptions of 2010. Bring a pack of *pýlsur* (hot dogs) with you as you mount Magni – the still-steaming earth will cook them in no time flat.

Continued from p81

those using the domestic airport. It's a large hotel with modern rooms, local art, a spa and Sóley organic bath products.

Eating

From take-it-to-go hot dogs to gourmet platters on white-clothed tables, little Reykjavík has an astonishing assortment of eateries. Loads of seafood and Icelandic or 'New Nordic' restaurants serve tried-and-true variations on local fish and lamb, but the capital is also the main spot for finding international eats. Kolaportið Flea Market (p97) also has a section with traditional Icelandic foods.

Old Reykjavík

Bæjarins Beztu HOT DOGS €

(Map p60; www.bbp.is; Tryggvagata; hot dogs 450kr; ⌚10am-1am Sun-Thu, to 4.30am Fri & Sat) Icelanders swear the city's best hot dogs are found at this truck near the harbour (patronised by Bill Clinton and late-night bar-hoppers). Use the vital phrase *'eina með öllu'* (one with everything) to get the quintessential favourite with sweet mustard, ketchup and crunchy onions.

Icelandic Street Food STREET FOOD €

(Map p60; ☎691 3350; www.icelandicstreetfood.com; Laekjargata 8; mains from 1300kr; ⌚8am-11pm) For a budget taste of old Iceland, squeeze into this tiny canteen that just loves showcasing home-cooked food. Owner Unnar has drafted in his grandmother to cook some of the dishes that range from fish stew and lamb soup to rolled up pancakes dusted with sugar. Her principle that no one leaves her house hungry means free food refills.

Bio Borgari BURGERS €

(Map p60; ☎519 5195; www.facebook.com/bioborgari; Vesturgata 12; burgers from 1500kr; ⌚11am-2pm & 5-9pm Wed-Fri, noon-9pm Sat & Sun; 🅥) Conventional burgers get a fresh new feel at this enterprising eatery. Organic meat or lentil patties are sandwiched between soft, seeded buns and slithers of crispy root veg come as a side.

Jómfrúin SANDWICHES €

(Map p60; ☎551 0100; www.jomfruin.is; Lækjargata 4; sandwiches from 2230kr; ⌚11am-10pm) Wayward Danes seek out this no-frills joint specialising in *smørrebrød:* traditonal Danish open-face sandwiches with any number of Nordic toppings.

10-11 SUPERMARKET €

(Map p60; www.10-11.is; Austurstræti 17; ⌚24hr) Ever-present 10-11 are similar to 7-Elevens in other countries. They are often open all night and have inflated prices. Other locations include **Barónsstígur** (Map p78), **Borgartún** (Map p78) and **Laugalækur** (Map p56).

★**Messinn** SEAFOOD €€

(Map p60; ☎546 0095; www.messinn.com; Lækjargata 6b; lunch mains 1850-2200kr, dinner mains 2700-4200kr; ⌚11.30am-3pm & 5-10pm; 📶) Make a beeline to Messinn for the best seafood that Reykjavík has to offer. The speciality here is the amazing pan-fried dishes: your pick of fish is served up in a sizzling cast-iron skillet, accompanied by buttery potatoes and salad. The mood is upbeat and comfortable and the staff friendly.

Nora Magasin BISTRO €€

(Map p60; www.facebook.com/NoraRvk; Pósthússtræti 9; mains 1900-2750kr; ⌚11.30am-11pm Sun-Thu, to 3am Fri & Sat) Hip and open plan, this buzzy bistro-bar serves up a tasty selection of pub food, from creative small plates to burgers and fresh fish. Coffee and cocktails run all night, but the kitchen closes at 10pm or 11pm.

Bergsson Mathús CAFE €€

(Map p60; ☎571 1822; www.bergsson.is; Templarasund 3; mains 2200-2800kr; ⌚7am-7pm Mon-Fri, to 5pm Sat & Sun; 🅥) There's nothing fancy here, but the homemade breads and fresh produce mean you'll be eating among locals as they flip through magazines, gossip and devour tasty brunch plates.

Icelandic Fish & Chips SEAFOOD €€

(Map p60; ☎511 1118; www.fishandchips.is; Tryggvagata 11; mains 1600-6300kr; ⌚11.30am-9pm) 🍃 Pick your fish and, voila, spelt-batter fried it becomes. Pair it with local beer, organic salads (990kr) and 'Skyronnaises' – *skyr*-based sauces (eg basil and garlic) that add a zing to this most traditional of dishes.

Lobster Hut SEAFOOD €€

(Map p60; humarkofi@gmail.com; Lækergata; mains 1800-2800kr; ⌚11am-1am Mon-Thu, to 6am Fri & Sat) What's it gonna be? Lobster soup? Lobster salad? Lobster sandwich? This little food truck dishes it all out, for fine diners on the run. By day it's opposite Harpa, after 9pm it's on Lækergata in the city centre.

Hornið ITALIAN €€

(Map p60; ☎551 3340; www.hornid.is; Hafnarstræti 15; mains 1900-5200kr; ⌚11am-11.30pm; 📶)

There's an easygoing air at this bright art deco cafe-restaurant. Pizzas are freshly made before your eyes, the prettily presented pasta meals will set you up for the day, and there are also seafood and meat mains.

★**Apotek** FUSION €€€

(Map p60; ☎551 0011; www.apotekrestaurant.is; Austurstræti 16; mains 2800-6000kr; ⏰noon-11pm Sun-Thu, to midnight Fri & Sat) This beautiful restaurant and bar with shining glass fixtures and a cool ambience is equally known for its delicious menu of small plates that are perfect for sharing and its top-flight cocktails. It's on the ground floor of the hotel of the same name.

★**Grillmarkaðurinn** FUSION €€€

(Grill Market; Map p60; ☎571 7777; www.grillmarkadurinn.is; Lækargata 2a; mains 3500-9500kr; ⏰11.30am-2pm & 6-10.30pm, closed Sat & Sun lunch) Top-notch dining is the order of the day here, from the moment you enter the glass atrium with its golden-globe lights to your first snazzy cocktail, and on throughout the meal. Service is impeccable, and locals and visitors alike rave about the food, which uses Icelandic ingredients prepared with culinary imagination by master chefs.

★**Fiskfélagið** SEAFOOD €€€

(Map p60; ☎552 5300; www.fishcompany.is; Vesturgata 2a; mains lunch 2700-4600kr, dinner 4800-6600kr; ⏰11.30am-2.30pm & 5.30-10.30pm, closed Sat & Sun lunch) The 'Fish Company' takes Icelandic seafood recipes and spins them through a variety of far-flung inspirations from Fiji coconut to Spanish chorizo. Dine out on the terrace or in an intimate-feeling stone-and-timber room with copper light fittings and quirky furnishings.

★**Fiskmarkaðurinn** SEAFOOD €€€

(Fishmarket; Map p60; ☎578 8877; www.fiskmarkadurinn.is; Aðalstræti 12; mains 4800-9900kr, tasting menu 11,900kr; ⏰5-10.30pm) Dramatic presentations of elaborate dishes fill the tables of this intimate, artistically lit restaurant, where chefs excel at infusing Icelandic seafood with Asian flavours such as lotus root. The tasting menu is acclaimed, and the place is renowned for its excellent sushi bar (3600kr to 4100kr).

Tapas Barinn TAPAS €€€

(Map p60; ☎551 2344; www.tapas.is; Vesturgata 3b; tapas 2000-3400kr; ⏰5-11.30pm Sun-Thu, to 1am Fri & Sat) Look for the life-sized fibreglass bull, painted in Spanish yellow and red, then settle down to sample some of the 50 tapas-style nibbles. To olives and *patatas bravas* (friend potatoes with spicy sauce), add Icelandic lamb, pickled tomatoes, saltfish and pan-fried lobster tails. Book ahead for a spot.

Matarkjallarinn ICELANDIC €€€

(Map p60; ☎558 0000; www.matarkjallarinn.is; Aðalstræti 2; mains lunch 2300-4000kr, dinner 4200-6500kr; ⏰11am-3pm Mon-Fri, 5-11pm daily) Elegance is everywhere at Matarkjallarinn (the 'Food Cellar'). Brasserie-style dishes, Icelandic ingredients, magical decor and oh-so-skillful cocktails could draw you here. As could the slow-cooked cod, moss-cured salmon or smoked Arctic char.

Old Harbour

★**Grandi Mathöll** STREET FOOD €

(Map p64; ☎577 6200; www.grandimatholl.is; Grandagarður 16; mains from 1200kr; ⏰11am-9pm Mon-Thu, to 10pm Fri-Sun) There's no neater encapsulation of Grandi's rejuvenation than the transformation of this old fish factory into a pioneering street-food hall. Long trestle tables sit beside stalls selling a diverse range of lamb, fish and veggie delights; look out for the Gastro Truck, its succulent signature chicken burger has quite a jalapeño kick.

★**Sægreifinn** SEAFOOD €

(Seabaron; Map p64; ☎553 1500; www.saegreifinn.is; Geirsgata 8; mains from 1500kr; ⏰11.30am-10pm) Sidle into this green harbourside shack for the most famous lobster soup in the capital, or choose from a fridge full of fresh fish skewers to be grilled on the spot. Though the original sea baron sold the restaurant some years ago, the place retains its unfussy, down-to-earth charm.

★**Flatey Pizza** PIZZA €

(Map p64; ☎588 2666; www.flatey.pizza; Grandagarður 11; pizzas 1750-2650kr; ⏰11am-10pm) Flatey raises pizza making to something akin to an art form. Its sourdough circles are made from organic wheat and are baked for just one minute at 500°C to keep the toppings tasty. It's very hip and very classy. As you can't book, be prepared to queue.

Hamborgara Búllan BURGERS €

(Hamborgarabúlla Tómasar; Map p64; ☎511 0800; www.bullan.is; Geirsgata 1; burgers/meals from 1300/2000kr; ⏰11.30am-9pm; 📶👪) The Old Harbour's outpost of burgerdom and Americana proffers savoury patties that are perennial local favourites. Hollywood film stars have been known to come here to feed too.

Lamb STREET FOOD €

(Map p64; ☎557 9777; www.facebook.com/lamb streetfood; Grandagarður 7; mains from 1900kr; ⌚11am-10pm) A cheerful street-food-style restaurant dishing up lamb and falafel flatbread combos with fresh, crunchy veg and zingy *skyr*-based sauces.

Fish & Chips SEAFOOD €

(Map p64; www.fishandchipsvagninn.is; Hlésgata, Old Harbour; mains 1200-2200kr; ⌚11am-9pm; 🚌14) Delicious, piping-hot fish and chips are on offer at this simple food truck near the Víkín Maritime Museum.

Valdís ICE CREAM €

(Map p64; ☎586 8088; www.valdis.is; Grandagarður 21; scoops 490kr; ⌚11.30am-11pm; 👪) Throughout summer happy families flock here, take a number and join the crush waiting for a scoop chosen from the huge array of homemade ice creams. Totally casual, totally fun.

Burið CHEESE €

(Map p64; ☎551 8400; http://blog.burid.is; Grandagarður 35; ⌚11am-6pm Mon-Fri, noon-5pm Sat; 🚌14) Select from a broad range of Icelandic cheeses and *skyr* (Icelandic yoghurt), and other deli and sweet treats.

17 Sortir BAKERY €

(Map p64; ☎571 1701; www.sautjansortir.is; Grandagarður 19; ⌚10am-6pm Mon-Fri, 11am-5pm Sat & Sun) From Toblerone cupcakes and vegan pastries to four-layer chocolate cake – the daily selection here includes something for every sweet tooth. The name '17 Sortir' refers to a diligent housewife in a novel by Nobel Prize–winner Halldór Laxness who believed offering 17 types of cake was the bare minimum when guests arrived.

★**Matur og Drykkur** ICELANDIC €€

(Map p64; ☎571 8877; www.maturogdrykkur.is; Grandagarður 2; lunch/dinner mains from 1900/3400kr, tasting menu 10,000kr; ⌚11.30am-3pm & 6-10pm, closed Sun lunch; 📝; 🚌14) One of Reykjavík's top high-concept restaurants, Matur Og Drykkur means 'Food and Drink', and you'll surely be plied with the best of both. The brainchild of brilliant chef Gísli Matthías Auðunsson, who also owns the excellent Slippurinn (p177), it creates inventive versions of traditional Icelandic fare. Book ahead in high season and for dinner.

Messinn Granda SEAFOOD €€

(Map p64; ☎546 0095; www.messinn.com; Grandagarður 8; lunch/dinner buffet 2300/5000kr; ⌚lunch 11.30am-2pm, dinner 6-10pm) Sample the catch of the day at this buffet-style harbour restaurant, serving its freshly caught selection on steaming skillets with root vegetables and spinach. The fabulously simple preparation was developed at Messinn's popular saloon-sized downtown restaurant (p84).

Bergsson RE SEAFOOD €€

(Map p64; ☎571 0822; www.bergsson.net; Grandagarður 16; mains 1500-2600kr; ⌚9am-4pm Mon-Fri; 🚌14) An acclaimed seafood spot with great harbour views and a daily-changing lunch menu featuring the freshest catch. The same family runs Bergsson Mathús (p84) in Old Reykjavík.

Coocoo's Nest CAFE €€

(Map p64; ☎552 5454; www.coocoosnest.is; Grandagarður 23; mains 1500-4500kr; ⌚11am-10pm Tue-Sat, to 4pm Sun; 📶) Pop into this cool eatery for delicious brunches (11am to 4pm Friday to Sunday) and decadent cocktails. It's casual, small and groovy, with mosaic plywood tables. Nightly themes range from pizza to tacos, but it's always first rate.

Kaffivagninn DINER €€

(Map p64; ☎551 5932; www.kaffivagninn.is; Grandagarður 10; mains 1600-3000kr; ⌚7.30am-9pm Mon-Fri, from 9am Sat & Sun; 📶) A harbourside eatery with broad windows looking onto the bobbing boats, good breakfasts and hearty seafood-based lunches.

Salt SEAFOOD €€

(Map p64; ☎552 0011; www.saltkitchenandbar.is; Geirsgata 3; mains 2000-3500kr; ⌚11.30am-10.30pm Thu-Mon, from 5pm Tue & Wed) Cod, ling, lobster soup? Salt is an excellent Old Harbour option for fruits of the sea and is among the many 'whale-friendly' restaurants in Reykjavík.

Forréttabarinn TAPAS €€

(Starter Bar; Map p64; ☎517 1800; www.forrettabarinn.is; Nýlendugata 14, entrance from Mýrargata; plates 1750-2650kr; ⌚4-10pm; 📶) Tapas restaurants are popular in the capital, and this hip joint near the harbour is a favourite for its menu of creative plates like cod and pork belly with white beans. There is also an airy and relaxed bar (4pm to 11pm), with weathered wood tables and broad couches.

Kumiko CAFE €€

(Map p64; ☎517 2424; www.kumiko.is; Grandagarður 101; mains from 1200kr; ⏰10am-6pm Wed-Mon; ✎) Theme cafe Kumiko is a Japanese tea house and cake shop that revels in a bright, cartoon-like decor. The vibe extends to their creations: Princess Cakes, speciality teas, power brunches and cocktails made from Omnom Chocolate (p59) and schnapps liqueur.

Laugavegur & Skólavörðustígur

★Gló ORGANIC, VEGETARIAN €

(Map p68; ☎553 1111; www.glo.is; Laugavegur 20b; mains 1000-2400kr; ⏰11.30am-10pm; 📶✎) Join the cool cats in this airy upstairs restaurant serving fresh daily specials loaded with Asian-influenced herbs and spices. Though not exclusively vegetarian, it's a wonderland of raw and organic foods, with a broad bar of elaborate salads, from root veggies to Greek.

★Bakarí Sandholt BAKERY €

(Map p68; ☎551 3524; www.sandholt.is; Laugavegur 36; snacks 700-2700kr; ⏰7am-7pm Sun-Thu, 6.30am-9pm Fri & Sat; 📶) Reykjavík's favourite bakery is usually crammed with folks hoovering up the generous assortment of fresh baguettes, croissants, pastries and sandwiches. The soup of the day (1850kr) comes with delicious sourdough bread.

★Brauð & Co BAKERY €

(Map p68; www.braudogco.is; Frakkastígur 16; ⏰6am-6pm Mon-Fri, to 5pm Sat & Sun) Head for the building smothered in rainbow spray paint then queue for the locals' tip for the best *snúður* (cinnamon buns) in town – watch Viking hipsters make them while you wait.

Súpa SOUP €

(Súpubarinn; Map p68; www.facebook.com/supubarinn; Bergstaðastræti 4; mains 1500kr; ⏰noon-8pm Mon-Sat; ✎) Six pots of steaming soups make this snazzy downtown corner a top

REYKJAVÍK'S COFFEE CULTURE

Reykjavikers take their coffee seriously, and there are many sweet corners in which to dwell and sip your joe, or grab it on the go.

Reykjavík Roasters (Map p68; ☎517 5535; www.reykjavikroasters.is; Kárastígur 1; ⏰7am-6pm Mon-Fri, 8am-5pm Sat & Sun) These folks take their coffee seriously. This tiny hipster joint is easily spotted on warm days with its smattering of wooden tables and potato sacks dropped throughout the paved square. Swig a perfect latte with a flaky croissant.

Kaffi Mokka (Map p68; ☎552 1174; www.mokka.is; Skólavörðustígur 3a; ⏰9am-6.30pm, to 9pm Jun-Aug) The decor at Reykjavík's oldest coffee shop has changed little since the 1950s, and its original mosaic pillars and copper lights have a distinctive retro charm. The clientele ranges from local families and artists to tourists, while the sandwiches, cakes and waffles are top notch.

Kaffi Vínyl (p93) This hip fixture of the Reykjavík coffee, restaurant and music scene is popular for its chill vibe, great music and delicious vegan and vegetarian food.

Stofan Kaffihús (Map p60; ☎546 1842; www.facebook.com/stofan.cafe; Vesturgata 3; dishes 1650-1900kr; ⏰10am-10pm Sun-Wed, to midnight Thu-Sat; 📶) Spacious and relaxed, this welcoming coffee house fills a character-laden historic building in the city centre.

Café Haiti (Map p64; ☎588 8484; www.cafehaiti.is; Geirsgata 7c, Marshall Húsið, Grandi; ⏰8am-10pm Sun-Thu, to midnight Fri & Sat) If you're a coffee afficionado, this tiny cafe in the Old Harbour is the place for you. Owner Elda buys her beans from her home country Haiti, and roasts and grinds them on-site, producing what regulars swear are the best cups of coffee in the country.

C is for Cookie (Map p68; www.facebook.com/cookie.reykjavik; Týsgata 8; ⏰7.30am-5pm Mon-Sat, 10am-6pm Sun) A cheerful spot named in honour of Sesame Street's Cookie Monster. It does super coffee, plus great homemade cakes, salad, soup and grilled sandwiches.

Kaffifélagið (Map p68; www.kaffifelagid.is; Skólavörðustígur 10; ⏰7.30am-6pm Mon-Fri, 10am-4pm Sat) A popular hole-in-the-wall place for a quick cuppa on the run, with a couple of outdoor tables too.

lunch spot for non-meat eaters. The place is entirely vegetarian (some options are vegan) and sourdough sandwiches and salads are served along with the signature soups. It's also popular for take away.

Garðurinn VEGETARIAN €
(Map p68; ☎561 2345; www.kaffigardurinn.is; Klapparstígur 37; mains 1400-2200kr; ⏲11am-8.30pm Mon, Tue, Thu & Fri, to 5pm Wed, noon-5pm Sat; ☑) Asian, Middle Eastern and Mediterranean flavours infuse ever-changing vegetarian and vegan soups (950kr) and dishes of the day at this friendly eatery.

Grái Kötturinn CAFE €
(Map p68; ☎551 1544; www.facebook.com/graikotturinn; Hverfisgata 16a; mains 1100-2500kr; ⏲7.15am-2pm Mon-Fri, 8am-2pm Sat & Sun) Blink and you'll miss this tiny six-table cafe (a favourite of Björk's). It looks like a cross between an eccentric bookshop and an underground art gallery, and dishes up delicious breakfasts of toast, bagels, pancakes, or bacon and eggs served on thick, buttery slabs of freshly baked bread.

Julia & Julia CAFE €
(Map p68; ☎866 5703; www.juliaogjulia.com; Hverfisgata 15; soup 1200kr; ⏲8am-5pm) Icelandic Júlía and Swedish Julia run this stylish cafe, whose name also references a book and a film starring Meryl Streep. Soups and cakes draw from Nordic family recipes, appropriate to the cafe's location inside the Culture House, the oldest building on Hverfisgata.

Vitabar BURGERS €
(Map p68; Bergþórugata 21; mains 900-3400kr; ⏲11.30am-11pm, bar to 1am or 2am Fri & Sat) Sidle up to the bar to order your short-order burger with some of the best hand-cut fries you'll find. This is a tile-and-formica kind of joint, with American rock on the stereo and locals quaffing pints of cold Einstök and Viking.

Block BURGERS €
(Map p68; ☎511 0011; www.blockburger.is; Skolavörðustígur 8; burgers/meals from 1200/1900kr; ⏲11am-9pm) Succulent burgers, tangy sauce, crisp fries and, for Reykjavík, good prices make this bare bones burger joint a hit. It's a bit hard to find, tucked in behind the deli Ostabúðin, set slightly back from Skolavörðustígur.

Hamborgara Búllan BURGERS €
(Tommi's Burger Joint; Map p68; www.tommis.is; Bankastræti 5b; burgers from 1300kr, meals from 2000kr; ⏲11.30am-9pm) This tiny burger booth, part of the famous local chain, is tucked back inside and behind the B5 nightclub. It serves up tasty patties.

Yummi Yummi THAI €
(Map p78; ☎588 2121; www.yummy.is; Hverfisgata 123; mains 1000-1800kr; ⏲11.30am-9pm Mon-Fri, from 5pm Sat & Sun) Quick and easy Thai noodles and mains to eat in or take away.

Noodle Station THAI €
(Map p78; ☎551 3198; www.noodlestation.is; Laugavegur 103; mains 960-1640kr; ⏲11am-10pm Mon-Fri, noon-10pm Sat & Sun) No-frills but delicious Thai noodle soups are dished out by the bowlful at this trusty popular establishment.

Bónus SUPERMARKET €
(Map p68; www.bonus.is; Hallveigarstígur 1; ⏲11am-6.30pm Mon-Thu, 10am-7.30pm Fri, 10am-6pm Sat, noon-6pm Sun) Good central bargain supermarket.

Joylato ICE CREAM €
(Map p68; www.joylato.is; Njálsgata 1; scoops from 650kr; ⏲noon-10pm) Scoops of high-end homemade ice cream and sorbets in delectable flavours, including Icelandic strawberries.

Lemon HEALTH FOOD €
(Map p68; www.lemon.is; Laugavegur 56; juices 900-1000kr, sandwiches 800-1500kr; ⏲8am-9pm Mon-Fri, from 10am Sat, from noon Sun; ☎) Lemon is tops for smoothies and healthy sandwiches on the go.

Bónus SUPERMARKET €
(Map p68; www.bonus.is; Laugavegur 59; ⏲11am-6.30pm Mon-Thu, 10am-7.30pm Fri, 10am-6pm Sat, noon-6pm Sun) The best-value supermarket in the city centre. Also at Hallveigarstígur (p88), Grandi near the Old Harbour and **Kringlan shopping centre** (Map p56; ☎527 9000; www.bonus.is; Kringlunni 4; ⏲11am-6.30pm Mon-Thu, 10am-7.30pm Fri, 10am-6pm Sat, noon-6pm Sun; 🚌1, 3, 6).

Krambúð SUPERMARKET €
(Map p68; www.samkaup.is; Skólavörðustígur 42; ⏲24hr) Pricey but central.

★**Hlemmur Mathöll** FOOD HALL €€
(Map p78; www.hlemmurmatholl.is; Laugavegur 107; mains from 800kr; ⏲8am-11pm) If only all bus terminals had a food court like this. Some 10 vendors rustle up multicultural foods including Danish *smørrebrød* (rye bread), Mexican tacos and Vietnamese street food. The pick is innovative SKÁL! (p89). Most stalls kick into action by lunchtime.

★SKÁL! STREET FOOD €€

(Map p78; ☎775 2299; www.skalrvk.com; Laugavegur 107; mains 1000-2500kr; ⏲noon-10pm Sun-Wed, to 11pm Thu-Sat; ☑) SKÁL! demands your attention – with its capital lettering and punctuation but most emphatically with its food. Experimental offerings combine unusual flavours (fermented garlic, birch sugar, arctic thyme salt) with Icelandic ingredients to impressive effect, best sampled at a stool beside its neon-topped bar. There's an impressive list of vegan creations and the cocktails feature foraged herbs.

★Hverfisgata 12 PIZZA €€

(Map p68; ☎437 0203; www.hverfisgata12.is; Hverfisgata 12; pizzas 2450-3450kr; ⏲5-10.30pm Mon-Fri, 11.30am-10.30pm Sat & Sun; ☑) There's no sign, but those in the know come to this cream-coloured converted corner house for some of the city's best gourmet pizza and fabulous cocktails. Cheerful staff pull pints of craft beer from behind the copper bar, and the weekend brunches (11.30am to 3pm) are a big draw.

Mat Bar FUSION €€

(Map p68; ☎788 3900; www.matbar.is; Hverfisgata 26; tapas from 1600kr; ⏲3-10pm Tue-Thu, to 11pm Fri & Sat) At this intimate, atmospheric place, traditionally Italian dishes are prepared with elements from Nordic cuisine – the tomatoes are pickled and the capers dried. Plates are tapas-sized and designed for sharing. It's a good spot for drinks too.

Matwerk SCANDINAVIAN €€

(Map p78; ☎555 1550; www.matwerk.is; Laugavegur 96; mains 3700-5800kr; ⏲5.30-10pm Sun-Thu, to 11pm Fri & Sat) For well-priced New Nordic cuisine, head to the classy Matwerk for a duck salad or Arctic char and everything in between. The two-store venue is ambitiously large but with its open-plan kitchen and clever lighting the ambience is welcoming and laid-back. The lunch menu is particularly good value.

Snaps FRENCH €€

(Map p68; ☎511 6677; www.snaps.is; Þórsgata 1; mains lunch from 2000kr, dinner 3900-6200kr; ⏲7-10am daily, 11.30am-10pm Sun-Thu, to 11pm Fri & Sat) Reserve ahead for this French bistro that's a megahit with locals. The secret of Snaps is simple: serve perfectly cooked seafood and classic bistro mains – think steak or *moules frites* (mussels and fries) – at surprisingly decent prices. Lunch specials (2000kr) and tempting brunches (11.30am to 4pm Saturday and Sunday) are a big draw too.

Geiri Smart EUROPEAN €€

(Map p68; ☎528 7050; www.geirismart.is; Hverfisgata 30; mains 3100-5900kr; ⏲6.30-10am, 11.30am-2pm & 6-10pm) Part of the Canopy by Hilton (p80), but far more than just a hotel restaurant, Geiri Smart gets creative with local ingredients and is renowned for its service and sommeliers. The setting is cool too – a subtle mix of contemporary and '70s design. The upstairs bar is perfect for a quiet drink by the fireplace, and the two-course theatre menu (5500kr) is a great deal. Booking recommended.

Public House FUSION, TAPAS €€

(Map p68; ☎555 7333; www.publichouse.is; Laugavegur 24; small plates 1100-2500kr; ⏲11.30am-11pm) Excellent Asian-style tapas and great local draught beers are just part of the draw at this central gastropub. It's also a fun place to hang out, with its pounding pop soundtrack and no less than *two* happy hours (3pm to 6pm and 11pm to 1am)

Ostabúðin DELI €€

(Cheese Shop; Map p68; ☎562 2772; www.ostabudin.is; Skólavörðustígur 8; mains 1550-4700kr; ⏲restaurant noon-10pm, deli 10am-6pm Mon-Thu, to 7pm Fri, 11am-4pm Sat) Half restaurant, half gourmet deli, Ostabudin has a friendly owner and serves up cheese and meat platters, soups and fish of the day with homemade bread. Pick up other local goods, perhaps terrines and duck confit, on the way out.

Ban Thai THAI €€

(Map p78; ☎552 2444; www.banthai.is; Laugavegur 130; mains 2000-3100kr; ⏲6-10pm Sun-Thu, to 11.30pm Fri & Sat) Ban Thai is by far the local favourite for Thai food and a fair few Hollywood stars have dropped in too. Find it just east of Hlemmur Sq. It also has a cheaper canteen and takeaway outlet, Yummi Yummi (p88), across the street.

Krua Thai THAI €€

(Map p68; ☎552 2525; www.kruathai.is; Skólavörðustígur 21a; mains 1600-2600kr; ⏲noon-9.30pm Mon-Sat, from 5pm Sun) Serves up tasty Thai curries and noodles with crunchy veg and plump prawns in a small shopfront or the sunny restaurant upstairs.

Restó SEAFOOD €€

(Map p78; ☎546 9550; www.resto.is; Rauðarárstígur 27; mains 3500-5400kr; ⏲5.30-10pm Sun-Thu, to 10.30pm Fri & Sat) This comfortable little restaurant over by Hlemmur Sq is worth the trek for delicious changing menus of seafood and the friendly family that runs the place. The owner-chef Jóhann Helgi Jóhannesson was the chef at celebrated seafood joint Ostabúðin, and he and his wife Ragnheiður Helena Eðvarðsdóttir have created a new anchor in this up-and-coming district.

ROK ICELANDIC €€
(Map p68; ☎544 4443; www.rokrestaurant.is; Frakkastígur 26a; dishes 1300-2400kr; ⏰11.30am-11pm) Duck into the small timber house with a turf roof and sunny terrace across from Hallgrímskirkja for high-concept small plates and good beer and wine. Book ahead in summer and on weekends.

Austur Indíafélagið INDIAN €€
(East India Company; Map p68; ☎552 1630; www.austurindia.is; Hverfisgata 56; mains 4000-5500kr; ⏰6-10pm Sun-Thu, to 11pm Fri & Sat) The aromas wafting from the northernmost Indian restaurant in the world draw you inside to find a refined, upmarket experience, with a choice of sublime dishes (a favourite: tandoori salmon). It's all achieved without any pretension – the atmosphere is relaxed and the service warm.

★Dill ICELANDIC €€€
(Map p68; ☎552 1522; www.dillrestaurant.is; Hverfisgata 12; 5/7 courses 11,900/13,900kr; ⏰6-10pm Wed-Sat) Exquisite 'New Nordic' cuisine is the major drawcard at Reykjavík's elegant Michelin-starred bistro. Skilled chefs use a small number of ingredients to create highly complex dishes in a parade of courses. The owners are friends with Copenhagen's famous Noma clan and take Icelandic cuisine to similarly heady heights. It's hugely popular; book well in advance.

★Nostra NEW NORDIC €€€
(Map p68; ☎519 3535; www.nostrarestaurant.is; Laugavegur 59; 4/6/8 courses 8900/11,900/13,900kr; ⏰5.30-10pm Tue-Sat; 🌶) Fine-dining Nostra is where fresh, local ingredients – à la New Nordic Cuisine – are turned into French-inspired multicourse tasting menus, including those for vegans, vegetarians and pescatarians. Nostra refers to its menus as 'experiences' and with their intense flavours and picture-perfect presentation, it's not wrong.

★Þrír Frakkar ICELANDIC, SEAFOOD €€€
(Map p68; ☎552 3939; www.facebook.com/3frakkar.is; Baldursgata 14; mains 4200-6250kr; ⏰11.30am-2.30pm & 6-10pm Mon-Fri, 6-11pm Sat & Sun) Owner-chef Úlfar Eysteinsson has built up a consistently excellent reputation at this snug little restaurant. Specialities range throughout the aquatic world from salt cod and halibut to *plokkfiskur* (fish stew) with black bread. Non-fish items run towards guillemot, horse, lamb and whale.

Holt Restaurant INTERNATIONAL €€€
(Map p68; ☎571 3800; www.holtrestaurant.is; Hótel Holt, Bergstaðastræti 37; dinner mains 4300-6200kr; ⏰11.30am-2pm & 6-9.30pm Wed-Sat) Expect to eat lavishly at high-end Holt, where a combination of Icelandic ingredients and largely European flourishes transforms stalwarts such as rhubarb, cod and Arctic char. The tasting menu is suitably elaborate (5/7 courses 10,900/12,900kr); the lunch mains are a tad simpler but still first class.

Kolabrautin ITALIAN €€€
(Map p68; ☎519 9700; www.kolabrautin.is; Harpa concert hall, Austurbakki 2; mains 3900-5700kr; ⏰5.30-10pm Tue-Sat) Kolabrautin, high up on the top of the Harpa concert hall, creatively teams Icelandic ingredients with Mediterranean techniques. Start with a flashy cocktail before digging into dishes like blackened salmon with lemon cream.

Sushi Social FUSION €€€
(Map p68; ☎568 6600; www.sushisocial.is; Þingholtsstræti 5; sushi 1600-3300kr, multicourse menus 9000-10,000kr; ⏰5-11pm Sun-Thu, to midnight Fri & Sat) Sushi Social is a perennial capital favourite for nuggets of rice-wrapped raw fish. It puts an Icelandic and South American spin on the delicacy, alongside meat and seafood mains.

Argentína STEAK €€€
(Map p78; ☎551 9555; www.argentina.is; Barónsstígur 11a; mains 4500-7700kr; ⏰6-10.30pm Sun-Thu, 5.30-11.30pm Fri & Sat) This dimly lit steakhouse rightly prides itself on its succulent locally raised beef and fresh grilled fish, with a wine list to match. The bar stays open to midnight or 1am.

Torfan Lobsterhouse SEAFOOD €€€
(Map p60; ☎561 3303; www.torfan.is; Amtmannsstígur 1; mains 4200-11,000kr; ⏰11.30am-3pm & 5-10pm, closed Sun lunch) Understatedly elegant, Torfan is justly celebrated for its choice of shellfish, langoustine and lobster. Although crustaceans feature strongly, you can also order game, beef, fish or a vegetarian option.

Tün

The aromas wafting from the bright tiled **Johansen Deli** (Map p78; ☎517 0102; www.facebook.com/johansendeli; Þórunnartún 2; mains 1600kr; ⏰8am-6pm Mon-Fri) draw you inside for gourmet breakfasts and picnic supplies. It's a handy pit stop in the high-rise hotel district.

Laugardalur

★**Frú Lauga** MARKET €

(Map p56; ☎534 7165; www.frulauga.is; Laugalækur 6; ⏰10am-6pm Mon-Fri, to 4pm Sat; 📶) 🌿 Reykjavík's trailblazing farmers market sources its ingredients from all over the countryside, featuring treats such as *skyr* (Icelandic yoghurt) from Erpsstaðir, organic vegetables, rhubarb conserves, honey and meat. It also stocks a range of carefully curated international pastas, chocolates and wine.

★**Café Flóra** CAFE €€

(Flóran; Map p56; ☎553 8872; www.floran.is; Botanic Gardens; cakes from 950kr, mains 1550-3150kr; ⏰8am-10pm May-Sep; 📶) 🌿 Sun-dappled tables fill a greenhouse in the Botanic Gardens and spill onto a flower-lined terrace at this lovely cafe specialising in wholesome local ingredients – some grown in the gardens themselves. Soups come with sourdough bread, while snacks range from cheese platters with nuts and honey to pulled-pork sandwiches. Weekend brunch, good coffee and homemade cakes round it all out.

Vox ICELANDIC €€€

(Map p56; ☎444 5050; www.vox.is; Suðurlandsbraut 2; mains 4700-13,800kr, lunch buffet 3950kr; ⏰11.30am-10.30pm) The Hilton's five-star restaurant has a contemporary but welcoming vibe and continues to pack 'em in for New Nordic cuisine and a famous weekend brunch (4400kr).

South of the Centre

★**Le Kock** BURGERS €€

(Map p56; ☎555 4774; www.lekock.is; Ármúli 42; mains from 2400kr; ⏰11.30am-9pm; 🚌2, 12, 15) The three founding chefs at this charismatic joint have impressive restaurant pedigrees, Icelandic and otherwise. Their skills shine through in reinvented fast food: burgers with Korean slaw, fries with avocado and wasabi nuts, and donuts with salted liquorice and chocolate. Go – it's fun.

Nauthóll ICELANDIC €€

(Map p56; ☎599 6660; www.nautholl.is; Nauthólsvegur 106; mains 2950-6800kr; ⏰11am-10pm) Out of the city centre beside Nauthólsvík Geothermal Beach, this reliable option for Icelandic faves sits in a delicate glass box with views out to the waterway. It's casual by day.

Outskirts

Kaffihús Vesturbæjar BISTRO €€

(Map p56; ☎551 0623; www.kaffihusvesturbaejar.is; Melhagi 20; mains 2500-4000kr; ⏰8am-11pm Mon-Fri, 9am-11pm Sat & Sun; 🚌11,15) This popular hang-out in the Vesturbær neighbourhood is a real hipster stronghold, with thrifty, mismatched decor. Delightful dishes range from soups and top-notch sandwiches to vegan burgers which are arguably the best in town.

Drinking & Nightlife

Sometimes it's hard to distinguish between cafes, restaurants and bars in Reykjavík, because when night rolls around (whether light or dark out) many coffee shops and bistros turn lights down and volume up, swapping cappuccinos for cocktails. Craft-beer bars, high-end cocktail bars and music and dance venues flesh out the scene. Some hotels and hostels also have trendy bars.

Old Reykjavík

★**Paloma** CLUB

(Map p60; http://palomaclub.is; Naustin 1; ⏰8pm-1am Thu & Sun, to 4.30am Fri & Sat) At one of Reykjavík's best late-night dance clubs DJs lay down reggae, electronica and pop upstairs, and a dark deep house dance scene in the basement. Find it in the same building as the Dubliner.

BUYING ALCOHOL

- Alcohol is pricey in bars and restaurants, with happy hours bringing the best deals.
- The only shops licensed to sell alcohol are government-owned liquor stores called Vínbúðin (www.vinbudin.is), with five branches around central Reykjavík.
- Buy when you arrive at Keflavík International Airport Duty Free for the steepest discounts.

Pablo Diskobar COCKTAIL BAR

(Map p60; ☎552 7333; www.facebook.com/discobarrvk; Veltusundi 1; ⏲4pm-1am Sun-Thu, to 3am Fri & Sat) In the world's northernmost capital, Pablo Discobar offers an escape from darkness and disappointing weather for the price of a cocktail. Neon-bright and nostalgic, tropical-themed Pablo is Reykjavík's top stop for exotic drinks. Weekends bring DJ sets, Wednesday night brings deals on drinks. The bar also serves the downstairs tapas restaurant, Burro, until midnight.

Loftið COCKTAIL BAR

(Jacobsen Loftið; Map p60; ☎551 9400; www.facebook.com/loftidbar; 2nd fl, Austurstræti 9; ⏲4pm-1am Wed-Sat) Loftið is all about high-end cocktails and good living. Dress up to join the fray at this airy upstairs lounge, which features a zinc bar, retro tailor-shop-inspired decor, vintage tiles and a swank, older crowd. The basic booze here is top-shelf liquor elsewhere, and jazzy bands play from time to time.

Skúli Craft Bar CRAFT BEER

(Map p60; ☎519 6455; www.facebook.com/skulicraft; Aðalstræti 9; ⏲3-11pm Sun-Thu, to 1am Fri & Sat) The big draw here is the 14 craft beers on tap, the majority of which are normally Icelandic. Or you might want to opt for one of the bottled beers – there are around 130 brands to choose from (who's counting?). A six-beer flight costs 4500kr; happy hour is 4pm to 7pm.

Micro Bar BAR

(Map p60; ☎865 8389; www.facebook.com/MicroBarIceland; Vesturgata 2; ⏲3pm-midnight Sun-Thu, to 1am Fri & Sat) Boutique brews are the name of the game at this low-key spot in the heart

ICELANDIC BOOZE: WHAT TO CHOOSE

Icelanders have a lot of time in winter to perfect their crafts. It's no wonder then that a slew of good local distilleries and breweries have sprung up. Here's a quick cheat sheet for your next bar-room order:

Spirits

64° Reykjavík (www.reykjavikdistillery.is) Microdistillery producing Katla vodka, aquavit, herbal liqueurs and schnapps from foraged fruits and botanicals.

Brennivín Caraway-flavoured 'black death' schnapps, nicely neon green and a whopping 80 proof.

Flóki Icelandic single malt whisky, produced by **Eimverk Distillery** (☎698 9691; www.flokiwhisky.is; Lyngas 13).

Opal Flavoured vodka in several menthol and licorice varieties (52 proof).

Reyka Iceland's first distillery, in Borgarnes, with crystalline vodka.

Beer

Egils, Gull, Thule and Viking are the most common beers (typically lagers) in Iceland. But craft breweries are taking the scene by storm and you can ask for them in most Reykjavík and larger city bars.

Borg Brugghús (www.borgbrugghus.is) Award-winning craft brewery with scrumptious beers from Bríó pilsner to Úlfur India Pale Ale and Garún stout, all whimsically named. Its sheep-dung-smoked IPA Fenrir is an acquired taste.

Bryggjan Brugghús (p93) Microbrewery at Reykjavík's Old Harbour that offers tours.

Einstök Brewing Company (www.einstokbeer.com) Akureyri-based craft brewery with a fab Viking label and equally distinctive Icelandic pale ale, among other ales and porters.

Kaldi (www.bruggsmidjan.is) Produced using Czech techniques, Kaldi's popular microbrews are widely available. Its cool Kaldi (p93) bar offers seasonal draught beers on offer nowhere else.

Ölvisholt Brugghús (www.brugghus.is) Solid range of microbrews from South Iceland, including eye-catching Lava beer.

Steðji Brugghús (www.stedji.com) This small, family-run Borgarnes brewhouse crafts good seasonal beers, from strawberry beer to lager.

of the action. On tap you'll find 14 creations from the island's top microbreweries, and a happy hour (4pm to 7pm) of 900kr beers. Try the sampler trays of five mini-draught beers for 3000kr (or 10 beers for 5000kr).

Klaustur WINE BAR
(Map p60; ☎571 4421; www.klaustur.bar; Kirkjutorg 4; ⏲4pm-midnight Sun-Thu, to 2am Fri & Sat) One of Old Reykjavík's most beguiling night-time hideaways, low-key, welcoming Klaustur is primarily a wine bar, but drinks also include a bold selection of spirits, including the local Flóki malt whisky and smooth Katla vodka.

Stúdentakjallarinn BAR
(Map p56; ☎570 0890; www.studentakjallarinn.is; University Sq; ⏲11am-11pm Sun-Wed, to 1am Thu-Sat) You don't have to be a student to drop by the University of Iceland's on-campus bar. In the dimly-lit, stylish basement you'll find academics of all ages and nationalities brewing bright ideas. Drinks are a bargain during happy hour. Events, from DJ sets to stand-up comedy, are free. Stúdentakjallarinn stays open during the summer holidays.

Frederiksen Ale House PUB
(Map p60; ☎571 0055; www.frederiksen.is; Hafnarstræti 5; ⏲11am-1am Mon-Sat, to 11pm Sun) A modest selection of draught beers (happy hour is two-for-one; 4pm to 7pm) meets lots of bottled offerings and a decent pub-food menu, including brunch. Despite the address, you'll actually find the ale house on the junction of Tryggvagatta and Naustín.

Sæta Svínið Gastropub PUB
(Map p60; www.saetasvinid.is; Hafnarstræti 1; ⏲11.30am-11.30pm) Tuck into meaty and creative pub food while quaffing a litre of the local ale at this three-storey feature of Reykjavík's gastropub scene. Happy hour is 3pm to 6pm.

Old Harbour

★**Bryggjan Brugghús** CRAFT BEER
(Map p64; ☎456 4040; www.bryggjanbrugghus.is; Grandagarður 8; ⏲11am-midnight Sun-Thu, to 1am Fri & Sat; 📶) Cavernous, dimly lit and dotted with vintage pub paraphernalia, harbourside Bryggjan Brugghús is a roomy microbrewery where 12 taps dispense its own fresh-tasting beers. Join one of the regular **brewery tours** (tours 3500-5000kr; ⏲noon-10pm) then settle back to sip a house beer – 600kr during happy hour (3pm to 7pm).

★**Slippbarinn** COCKTAIL BAR
(Map p64; ☎560 8080; www.slippbarinn.is; Mýrargata 2; ⏲noon-midnight Sun-Thu, to 1am Fri & Sat; 📶) Jet-setters unite at this buzzy bar at the Old Harbour's Icelandair Hotel Reykjavík Marina (p77). It's bedecked with vintage record players and cool locals sipping some of the best cocktails in town. For cut-price creations drop by during happy hour (3pm to 6pm).

Marshall BAR
(Map p64; ☎519 7766; www.marshallrestaurant.is; Grandagarður 20; ⏲11.30am-11pm Tue-Sun; 📶; 🚌14) The perfect pit stop for art aficionados, Marshall sits in the same building as three cutting-edge galleries. It's appropriately aesthetically appealing: an industrial-chic spot with coppery colours, a beautiful back-lit bar and great city views.

Laugavegur & Skólavörðustígur

★**Mikkeller & Friends** CRAFT BEER
(Map p68; ☎437 0203; www.mikkeller.dk; Hverfisgata 12; ⏲5pm-1am Sun-Thu, 2pm-1am Fri & Sat; 📶) Climb to the top floor of the building shared with excellent pizzeria Hverfisgata 12 (p89) to find a Danish craft-beer pub with 20 taps serving Mikkeller's own offerings and local Icelandic brews. Then enjoy the cool, colourful, laid-back vibe.

★**Kaffi Vínyl** CAFE
(Map p68; ☎537 1332; www.facebook.com/kaffivinyl; Hverfisgata 76; ⏲8am-11pm Sun-Thu, to 1am Fri & Sat; 📶) 'Vegan is the new black' reads the neon sign, vinyl disks spin on the decks and a cool crowd tucks into meat-free noodles, burgers and pasta (mains from 1400kr). Happy hour lasts from 4pm to 7pm here – an ideal time to try an Icelandic beer or a vegan whiskey sour.

★**Kaffibarinn** BAR
(Map p68; ☎551 1588; www.kaffibarinn.is; Bergstaðastræti 1; ⏲3pm-1am Sun-Thu, to 4.30am Fri & Sat; 📶) This old house with the London Underground symbol over the door contains one of Reykjavík's coolest bars; it even had a starring role in the cult movie *101 Reykjavík* (2000). At weekends you'll feel like you need either a famous face or a battering ram to get in. At other times it's a place for artistic types to chill with their Macs.

★**Kaldi** BAR
(Map p68; ☎581 2200; www.kaldibar.is; Laugavegur 20b; ⏲noon-1am Sun-Thu, to 3am Fri & Sat)

Effortlessly cool with mismatched seats and teal banquettes, plus a popular courtyard, Kaldi is awesome for its range of five Kaldi microbrews, not available elsewhere. Happy hour (4pm to 7pm) gets you a beer for 750kr. Anyone can play the in-house piano.

★Port 9 WINE BAR

(Map p68; ☎832 2929; www.facebook.com/portniu; Veghúsastígur 7; ⏲4-11pm Tue-Sat, to 9pm Sun & Mon) Port 9 sauntered onto Reykjavík's drinking scene supremely confident in the quality of its wines and the knowledge of its staff – offerings here range from affordable tipples by the glass to vintages to break the bank. Low lighting, an arty clientele and a secret hang-out vibe (it's tucked down a tiny street) make it worth tracking down.

★KEX Bar BAR

(Sæmundur í Sparifötunum; Map p78; www.kexhostel.is; Skúlagata 28; ⏲11.30am-11pm; 📶) Locals love this hostel bar-restaurant (mains 2000kr to 2500kr) in an old cookie factory (*kex* means 'biscuit') for its broad sea-view windows, inner courtyard and own-brew beer. Happy hipsters soak up the 1920s Vegas vibe: saloon doors, old-school barber station, happy chatter and scuffed floors. Look out for regular, free, live jazz sessions.

Bravó BAR

(Map p68; Laugavegur 22; ⏲11am-1am Mon-Thu, to 3am Fri & Sat; 📶) What's claimed to be the city's longest happy hour (11am to 8pm, local draught beer 800kr) isn't Bravó's only asset. You'll also find friendly bartenders, great people watching, cool tunes on the sound system and a laid-back vibe.

Kiki GAY

(Map p68; www.kiki.is; Laugavegur 22; ⏲8pm-1am Wed, Thu & Sun, to 4.30am Fri & Sat) Ostensibly a queer bar, Kiki is also *the* place to get your dance on (with pop and electronica the mainstays), since much of Reyjavík's nightlife centres around the booze, not the groove.

Prikið PUB

(Map p68; ☎551 2866; www.prikid.is; Bankastræti 12; ⏲8am-1am Mon-Thu, to 4.30am Fri, 11am-4.30am Sat, 11am-1am Sun) Being one of Reykjavík's oldest joints, Prikið feels somewhere between diner and saloon, which is great if you're up for greasy eats (mains 2000kr to 4000kr) and socialising. Things get hip-hop dance-y in the wee hours, and if you survive the night, it's popular for its next-day 'hangover killer' breakfast (3000kr).

Dillon BAR

(Map p68; ☎697 6333; www.dillon.is; Laugavegur 30; ⏲noon-1am Sun-Thu, to 3am Fri & Sat) Beer, beards and the odd flying bottle. Atmospheric Dillon is a RRRRROCK pub with a great beer garden out the back. Loud live bands hit its tiny corner stage. More than 170 whiskeys are stocked.

Artson COCKTAIL BAR

(Map p68; ☎519 3535; www.nostrarestaurant.is/artson; Laugavegur 59; ⏲5pm-1am Tue-Sat) Stylish, roomy Artson features a list of crafted cocktails that's as long as your arm. Six are seasonal, 10 are alcohol free and they're all served up with flair. Happy hour (5pm to 7pm) brings the price down to 1500kr.

Veður BAR

(Map p68; www.vedurbarinn.is; Klapparstígur 33; ⏲noon-1am Sun-Thu, to 3am Fri & Sat) Cosily cool Veður has a beautifully lit bar, welcoming vibe, acclaimed cocktails and a long happy hour (noon to 7.30pm).

LGBTI REYKJAVÍK

Reykjavík is very gay friendly. The annual **Reykjavík Pride** (www.hinsegindagar.is; ⏲Aug) festival and parade is one of Iceland's most attended events, with some 100,000 people (the equivalent of more than 25% of the country's population) joining the celebrations. Visit Gayice (www.gayice.is) and Gay Iceland (www.gayiceland.is) for LGBT tips and news.

Literary Reykjavík (p67) has a Culture Walks app with a Queer Literature feature. For a queer night out, head to Kiki dance club.

The LGBT organisation **Samtökin '78** (Map p60; ☎552 7878; www.samtokin78.is; Suðurgata 3; ⏲office 1-4pm Mon-Fri, Queer Centre 8-11pm Thu, closed Jul) provides information during office hours and operates a community centre on Thursday nights.

Pink Iceland (☎562 1919; www.pinkiceland.is; Hverfisgata 39; ⏲9am-5pm Mon-Fri) is Iceland's first gay-and-lesbian-owned-and-focused travel agency and welcomes all. It arranges all manner of travel, events and weddings and offers tours, including a two-hour happy-hour walking tour of Reykjavík (6000kr).

DJAMMIÐ: HOW TO PARTY IN REYKJAVÍK

Reykjavík is renowned for its weekend party scene that goes strong into the wee hours, and even spills over onto some of the weekdays (especially in summer). *Djammið* in the capital means 'going out on the town', or you could say *pöbbarölt* for a 'pub stroll'.

Thanks to the high price of alcohol, things generally don't get going until late. Icelanders brave the melee at the government alcohol store Vínbúðin (www.vinbudin.is), then toddle home for a prepub party. People hit town around midnight, party until 5am, queue for a hot dog, then topple into bed.

Rather than settling into one venue for the evening, Icelanders like to cruise from bar to bar, getting progressively louder and less inhibited as the evening goes on. 'In' clubs may have long queues, but they tend to move quickly with the constant circulation of revellers.

Most of the action is concentrated near Laugavegur and Austurstræti. Places usually stay open until 1am Sunday to Thursday and 4am or 5am on Friday and Saturday. You'll pay around 1200kr to 1600kr per pint of beer, and cocktails hit the 2000kr to 2800kr mark. Some venues have cover charges (around 1000kr) after midnight, and many have early-in-the-evening happy hours that cut costs by 500kr or 700kr per beer. Download the smartphone app Reykjavík Appy Hour.

The legal drinking age is 20 years.

Bastard CRAFT BEER

(Map p68; ☎558 0800; www.bastard.is; Vegamótastígur 4; ⊙11.30am-1am Sun-Thu, to 4am Fri & Sat) Bastard's in-house microbrewery produces two zippy beers for the taps here and around a dozen others sit alongside. It's a swish spot, with an upbeat soundtrack and buzzy vibe. Happy hour is 4pm to 7pm.

Boston BAR

(Map p68; www.facebook.com/boston.reykjavik; Laugavegur 28b; ⊙2pm-1am Sun-Thu, to 3am Fri & Sat) In dimly lit Boston fairy lights glint off mirrored pillars, and a pool table, sunny patio and occasional live music keep things cool.

Petersen Svítan LOUNGE

(Gamla Bíó; Map p68; ☎563 4000; www.gamlabio.is; Ingólfsstræti 2a; ⊙noon-1am Sun-Thu, to 3am Fri & Sat) The sweeping roof terrace at this lounge-bar at the top of a restored old theatre is supremely stylish with decking, rattan sofas and expansive views, making it one of the hottest spots in town when the sun shines.

Den Danske Kro BAR

(Danski Barinn; Map p68; www.danski.is; Ingólfsstræti 3; ⊙noon-1am Sun-Thu, to 4.30am Fri & Sat) 'The Danish bar' has good cocktails, a boozy atmosphere and a buzzy front deck but the beer is firmly centre stage.

Spánski WINE BAR

(Map p68; ☎8328881; www.spanski.is; Ingólfsstræti 8; ⊙11am-11pm Mon-Wed, to 1am Fri & Sat, 2-11pm Sun) Sip Tempranillo and Rioja by the glass (from 1200kr) and tuck into tapas (from 800kr) at this Spanish-themed wine bar.

Bar Ananas BAR

(Map p68; www.facebook.com/barananas.tikibar; Klapparstígur 38; ⊙4pm-1am Sun-Thu, to 3am Fri & Sat) A tropical-themed bar that's a good bet for warming up for a night out.

Outskirts

Bike Cave CAFE

(Map p56; ☎770 3113; www.facebook.com/bikecavereykjavik; Einarsnes 36; ⊙9am-10pm, shorter hours in winter; 🚌12) This unusual cafe (dishes 990kr to 3700kr) caters to cyclists, with coffee, beer, wine, a shower, laundry and a workshop for DIY repairs.

☆ Entertainment

The ever-changing vibrant Reykjavík performing-arts scene features shows at bars and cafes, local theatres and the Harpa concert hall.

For the latest in Icelandic music and performing arts, and to see who's playing, consult free English-language newspaper *Grapevine* (www.grapevine.is) and its events listing app Appening; websites Visit Reykjavík (www.visitreykjavik.is), What's On in Reykjavík (www.whatson.is/magazine) and Musik.is (www.musik.is); or city music shops.

★Húrra LIVE MUSIC

(Map p60; www.facebook.com/hurra.is; Tryggvagata 22; ⊙6pm-1am Mon-Thu, to 4.30am Fri & Sat, to

11.30pm Sun;) Dark and raw, this large bar opens up its back room to create a much-loved concert venue, with a wide range of live music or DJs most nights. It's one of the best places in town to close out the evening. There's a range of beers on tap and happy hour runs till 9pm.

★Bíó Paradís CINEMA

(Map p68; ☎412 7711; www.bioparadis.is; Hverfisgata 54; adult 1600-1800kr;) This totally cool cinema, decked out in movie posters and vintage officeware, screens specially curated Icelandic films with English subtitles and international flicks. It's a chance to see movies that you may not find elsewhere.

Cinema at Old Harbour Village No 2 CINEMA

(Map p64; ☎898 6628; www.thecinema.is; Geirsgata 7b; adult/child 1800/900kr; 14) A tiny theatre perches in the top of one of the rehabbed Old Harbour warehouses. Nature films cover volcanoes (Eyjafjallajökull, Westmann Islands), the creation of Iceland, and the Northern Lights, and are mostly shown in English with occasional German screenings. See schedule online.

Tjarnarbíó THEATRE

(Map p60; ☎527 2100; www.tjarnarbio.is; Tjarnargata 12; tickets from 2000kr) Drama, stand-up comedy, improv and dance all get a showing at this long-standing, independent performing-arts theatre. Look out for the many shows performed in English. The vibrant theatre cafe-bar is open during the day, too.

Gaukurinn LIVE MUSIC

(Map p60; www.gaukurinn.is; Tryggvagata 22; ⊙2pm-1am Sun-Thu, to 3am Fri & Sat) Grungy and glorious, Gaukurinn is a solid stop for live music, comedy, karaoke and open mikes. Happy hour is 7pm to 9pm.

Mengi LIVE PERFORMANCE

(Map p68; ☎588 3644; www.mengi.net; Óðinsgata 2; ⊙noon-5pm Tue-Sat & for performances) It may be small, but Mengi offers an innovative program of music and visual and performing arts.

National Theatre THEATRE

(Þjóðleikhúsið; Map p68; ☎551 1200; www.leikhusid.is; Hverfisgata 19; ⊙closed Jul) The National Theatre puts on everything from modern Icelandic works to musicals, opera and Shakespeare. The five separate performance areas include the main stage and studio, children's and puppet spaces.

Reykjavík City Theatre THEATRE, DANCE

(Borgarleikhúsið; Map p56; ☎568 8000; www.borgarleikhus.is; Listabraut 3, Kringlan; ⊙closed Jul & Aug) Stages plays and musicals, and is home to the **Icelandic Dance Company** (Map p56; ☎588 0900; www.id.is; Listabraut 3, Kringlan).

Laugardalsvöllur National Stadium STADIUM

(Map p56; ☎510 2914; Laugardalur) Iceland's football (soccer) passion is huge. Cup and international matches are played at this national stadium in Laugardalur. See the sports sections of Reykjavík's newspapers or **Football Association of Iceland** (Knattspyrnusamband Íslands, KSÍ; Map p56; ☎510 2900; www.ksi.is), and buy tickets directly from the stadium.

Laugardalshöllin CONCERT VENUE

(Map p56; ☎585 3300; www.ish.is; Engjavegur 8, Laugardalur) Huge venue for major international acts.

Shopping

Reykjavík's vibrant design culture makes for great shopping: from sleek fish-skin purses and knitted *lopapeysur* (Icelandic woollen sweaters) to unique music or Icelandic schnapps *brennivín*. Laugavegur is the most dense shopping street. You'll find interesting shops all over town, but fashion concentrates near the Frakkastígur and Vitastígur end of Laugavegur. Skólavörðustígur is strong for arts and jewellery, while Bankastræti and Austurstræti have touristy shops.

All visitors are eligible for a 15% tax refund on their shopping, these are under certain conditions (see www.iceland.is/iceland-abroad/be/tourist-information/vat-refund---tax-free).

Old Reykjavík

★Fischer CONCEPT STORE

(Map p60; www.fischersund.com; Fischersund 3; ⊙noon-6pm Mon-Sat) Formally the recording studio of Icelandic musician Jónsi, best known as the Sigur Rós frontman, this concept store feels like walking through an immersive exhibition. Perfumes, Icelandic herbs, hand-crafted soap bars and candles, ethereal music and visual artwork all play with all the senses.

★Kirsuberjatréð ARTS & CRAFTS

(Cherry Tree; Map p60; ☎562 8990; www.kirs.is; Vesturgata 4; ⊙10am-7pm Mon-Fri, to 5pm Sat & Sun) Talented designers show their works at this long-running women's art-and-design collective. Highlights include the bracelets and purses made from soft, supple, brightly coloured fish skin leather, music boxes made from string, and, our favourite, beautiful coloured bowls made from radish slices.

★Kolaportið Flea Market MARKET
(Map p60; www.kolaportid.is; Tryggvagata 19; ⌚11am-5pm Sat & Sun) Kolaportið is a Reykjavík institution. Weekends see a huge industrial building by the harbour filled with a vast tumble of secondhand clothes, old toys and cheap imports. A food section sells traditional eats like *rúgbrauð* (geothermally baked rye bread) and *brauðterta* ('sandwich cake'; a layering of bread with mayonnaise-based fillings).

Akkúrat DESIGN
(Map p60; ☎868 7613; www.facebook.com/akkuratreykjavik; Aðalstræti 2; ⌚10am-7pm Mon-Fri, to 6pm Sat, 11am-5pm Sun) Browse the best of Nordic design, from hand-painted mugs to fisherman sweaters, at this concept store supported by the Iceland Design Centre (p402). Be sure to check out the hats and sweaters from local clothing brand Döðlur.

Eymundsson BOOKS
(Map p60; www.eymundsson.is; Austurstræti 18; ⌚9am-10pm Mon-Sat, 10am-10pm Sun; 📶) Head to this big central bookshop for a superb choice of English-language books, newspapers, magazines and maps, along with a great cafe.

A second branch can be found on **Skólavörðustígur** (Map p68; www.eymundsson.is; Skólavörðustígur 11; ⌚9am-10pm Mon-Fri, 10am-10pm Sat & Sun; 📶).

Kogga CERAMICS
(Map p60; ☎552 6036; www.kogga.is; Vesturgata 5; ⌚9am-6pm Mon-Fri, 11am-3pm Sat) This tiny ceramics studio in the lower level of an old Reykjavík house offers imaginative pottery.

Vínbúðin – Austurstræti ALCOHOL
(Map p60; www.vinbudin.is; Austurstræti 10a; ⌚11am-6pm Mon-Thu & Sat, to 7pm Fri) The most central branch of the national liquor store chain. There's another store on the way towards Laugardalur at Borgartún 26.

Old Harbour

Farmers & Friends CLOTHING
(Farmers Market; Map p64; ☎552 1960; www.farmersmarket.is; Hólmaslóð 2; ⌚10am-6pm Mon-Fri, 11am-5pm Sat & Sun) Gorgeous boots, clothes and accessories in earthy tones fill the shelves of this design company's store. The emphasis is firmly on natural fabrics and materials.

Steinunn CLOTHING
(Map p64; ☎588 6649; www.steinunn.com; Grandagarður 17; ⌚11am-6pm Mon-Fri, 1-4pm Sat) Browse the couture collection of celebrated Icelandic designer Steinunn Sigurðardóttir, featuring innovative knitwear.

WOOLLY JUMPERS

Lopapeysur are the ubiquitous Icelandic woolly sweaters you will see worn by locals and visitors alike. Made from naturally water-repellant Icelandic wool, they are thick and cosy, with simple geometric patterns or regional motifs. They are no longer the bargain they were in the 1960s, so when shopping, be sure to make the distinction: do you want hand-knit or machine made? You'll notice the price difference (some cost well over 27,500kr), but either way these beautiful but practical items (and their associated hats, gloves and scarves) are exceptionally wearable souvenirs.

Handknitting Association of Iceland (Handprjónasamband Íslands; Map p68; ☎552 1890; www.handknit.is; Skólavörðustígur 19; ⌚9am-10pm Mon-Fri, to 6pm Sat, 10am-6pm Sun) Traditional handmade hats, socks and sweaters are sold at this knitting collective, or you can buy yarn, needles and knitting patterns and DIY. The association's smaller **branch** (Handprjónasamband Íslands; Map p78; ☎552 1890; www.handknit.is; Borgartún 31; ⌚9am-6pm Mon-Fri, 10am-5pm Sat) sells made-up items only.

Nordic Store (Map p60; ☎445 8080; www.nordicstore.net; Lækjargata 2; ⌚9am-10pm) Sells loads of hand- or machine-made *lopapeysur* and other wool products from it's base in Old Reykjavík.

Álafoss (☎566 6303; www.alafoss.is; Álafossvegur 23, Mosfellsbær; ⌚8am-8pm Mon-Fri, 9am-8pm Sat & Sun; 🚌15) in the suburb of Mosfellsbær also has a great range.

OUTDOOR OUTFITTERS

Iceland's premier outdoor-clothing company **66° North** (Map p68; ☎535 6680; www.66north.is; Bankastræti 5; ⏲9am-8pm Mon-Sat, 10am-8pm Sun) began by making all-weather wear for Arctic fishermen. This metamorphosed into costly, fashionable streetwear: jackets, fleeces, hats and gloves. Similar brands flourish, like **Cintamani** (Map p68; ☎533 3800; www.cintamani.is; Bankastræti 7; ⏲9am-9pm).

If you're looking to rent equipment for hiking or camping (tents, sleeping bags, stoves, backpacks, boots, climbing gear, GPS, wi-fi hot spots etc), your best bets are **Iceland Camping Equipment Rental** (Map p78; ☎647 0569; www.iceland-camping-equipment.com; Barónsstígur 5; ⏲9am-5pm May-Oct, by appointment Nov-Apr) in Laugavegur and **Rent-A-Tent** (☎848 5805; www.rentatent.is; Smiðjuvegur 6; ⏲9am-4pm Mon-Fri Jun-Aug, shorter hours in winter) in Kópavogur. **Fjallakofinn** (Map p68; ☎510 9505; www.fjallakofinn.is; Laugavegur 11; ⏲9am-6pm Mon-Fri, 10am-5pm Sat, noon-6pm Sun) offers (pricey) brand-name camping and climbing gear, GoPros and more, plus equipment rental.

Jen's JEWELLERY

(Map p64; ☎546 6446; www.jens.is; Grandagarður 31; ⏲11am-5pm Mon-Fri) Fine jewellery featuring Icelandic runes and stones from a well-established family of designers.

Kjötkompaní FOOD & DRINKS

(Map p64; www.kjotkompani.is; Grandagarður 29; ⏲11.30am-6.30pm Mon-Fri, 10am-5pm Sat) Deli with a tempting array of meat dishes, pickles, sauces and oils.

Laugavegur & Skólavörðustígur

★Skúmaskot ARTS & CRAFTS

(Map p68; ☎663 1013; www.facebook.com/skumaskot.art.design; Skólavörðustígur 21a; ⏲10am-6pm Mon-Fri, to 5pm Sat, noon-4pm Sun) Local designers create unique handmade porcelain items, women's and kids' clothing, paintings and cards. It's in a large renovated gallery that beautifully showcases the creative Icelandic crafts.

★Kiosk CLOTHING

(Map p68; ☎571 3636.; www.kioskreykjavik.com; Ingólfsstræti 6; ⏲11am-6pm Mon-Fri, to 5pm Sat) This wonderful designers' cooperative is lined with creative women's fashion in a glass-fronted boutique. Designers take turns staffing the store.

★Geysir CLOTHING

(Map p68; ☎519 6000; www.geysir.com; Skólavörðustígur 16; ⏲10am-7pm Mon-Sat, 11am-6pm Sun) One of the city's best bets for traditional Icelandic clothing and unique modern designs. Geysir's menswear store boasts an elegant selection of sweaters, blankets, clothes, shoes and bags. The **womenswear** (Skólavörðustígur 7) and **homeware** (☎519 6033; Skólavörðustígur 12) stores are one block down.

★12 Tónar MUSIC

(Map p68; ☎511 5656; www.12tonar.is; Skólavörðustígur 15; ⏲10am-6pm Mon-Sat, from noon Sun) A very cool place to hang out, in two-storey 12 Tónar you can listen to CDs, drink coffee and on summer Fridays sometimes catch a live performance. It is responsible for launching some of Iceland's favourite bands.

★KronKron CLOTHING

(Map p68; ☎561 9388; www.kronkron.com; Laugavegur 63b; ⏲10am-6pm Mon-Fri, to 5pm Sat) This is where Reykjavík goes high fashion, with labels such as Marc Jacobs and Vivienne Westwood. But we really enjoy its Scandinavian designers (including Kron by KronKron) and the offering of silk dresses, knit capes, scarves and even woollen underwear. The handmade shoes are off the charts; they are also sold down the street at **Kron** (Map p68; ☎551 8388; www.kron.is; Laugavegur 48; ⏲10am-6pm Mon-Fri, to 5pm Sat).

★Orrifinn JEWELLERY

(Map p68; ☎789 7616; www.orrifinn.com; Skólavörðustígur 17a; ⏲10am-6pm Mon-Fri, 11am-4pm Sat) Orrifinn's subtle, beautiful jewellery captures the natural wonder of Iceland and its Viking history. Delicate anchors, axes and pen nibs dangle from understated matte chains. There are some workbenches here so you're likely to see the jewellers creating pieces.

★Fóa ARTS & CRAFTS

(Map p68; ☎571 1433; www.facebook.com/foaiceland; Laugavegur 2; ⏲10am-6pm Mon-Fri, 11am-7pm Sat, noon-6pm Sun) A great place to stock up on witty souvenirs and cool handmade stationary, jewellery and ceramics.

★ **Mál og Menning** BOOKS
(Map p68; ☎580 5000; www.bmm.is; Laugavegur 18; ⏲9am-10pm Mon-Fri, 10am-10pm Sat; 📶) A friendly, well-stocked independent bookshop with a strong selection of English-language books offering insights to Iceland. It also sells maps, CDs, games and newspapers and has a good cafe (soup and bread 1000kr).

★ **Rammagerðin** GIFTS & SOUVENIRS
(Iceland Gift Store; Map p68; ☎535 6690; www.icelandgiftstore.com; Skólavörðustígur 12; ⏲10am-9pm) One of the city's better souvenir shops, Rammagerðin offers loads of woollens, crafts and collectibles. It also has branches at Skólavörðustígur 20, Bankastræti 9 and Keflavík International Airport.

Tulipop GIFTS & SOUVENIRS
(Map p68; www.tulipop.com; Skólavörðustígur 43; ⏲10am-6pm) The stationary, tableware and toys here feature cute Icelandic cartoon creations from the magical island of Tulipop: Gloomy, Bubble, Mama Skully and Mr Tree.

Húrra Reykjavík CLOTHING
(Map p68; ☎571 7101; www.hurrareykjavik.is; Hverfisgata 50; ⏲11am-6pm Mon-Thu & Sat, to 7pm Fri) Cool streetwear and top international brands in a beautifully arranged space.

Jokla Icelandic Design CLOTHING
(Map p78; www.facebook.com/jokla.iceland; Laugavegur 86-94; ⏲11am-6pm Mon-Fri, to 5pm Sat) Chunky jewellery, fine boots and elegant women's clothes in both subtle natural tones and bold, bright colours.

Blue Lagoon Shop COSMETICS
(Map p68; ☎420 8849; www.bluelagoon.com; Laugavegur 15; ⏲10am-6pm Mon-Fri, to 4pm Sat, 1-5pm Sun) Forgot to stock up on facial masks and unguents at the Blue Lagoon? Here's your chance! You'll also find its line of beauty products at Lyfa pharmacies, Hagkaup and Keflavík International Airport duty-free.

Spúútnik VINTAGE
(Map p68; ☎533 2023; Laugavegur 28; ⏲10am-6pm) This jam-packed secondhand store offers a less expensive way to pick up that Icelandic sweater you've been hankering for.

Hrím DESIGN
(Map p68; www.hrim.is; Laugavegur 25; ⏲10am-6pm Mon-Sat, 1-6pm Sun) With one large high-concept design store, and one smaller kitchenware store (Laugavegur 32), Hrim stands out for its creative Scandinavian and high-end *tchotchkes*, linens and other eminently take-home-able gear.

Lucky Records MUSIC
(Map p78; ☎551 1195; www.luckyrecords.is; Rauðarárstígur 10; ⏲10am-6pm Mon-Fri, 11am-5pm Sat & Sun) This deep den of musical goodness holds loads of modern Icelandic music, but plenty of vintage vinyl too. The huge collection spans hip hop to jazz and electronica. Occasional live music.

Reykjavík Record Shop MUSIC
(Map p68; ☎561 2299; www.facebook.com/reykjavikrecordshop; Klapparstígur 35; ⏲11am-6pm Mon-Fri, 1-6pm Sat) Scratch your vinyl itch at this hole-in-the-wall record store in the city centre.

Ófeigur Björnsson FASHION & ACCESSORIES
(Map p68; ☎551 1161; www.ofeigur.is; Skólavörðustígur 5; ⏲10am-6pm Mon-Fri, 11am-4pm Sat) Ófeigur Björnsson and other local goldsmiths make jewellery with lava and other natural materials. Hildur Bolladóttir is a master dressmaker and also shows modern bags and felted hats. There's an art gallery upstairs.

Aurum JEWELLERY
(Map p68; ☎551 2770; www.aurum.is; Bankastræti 4; ⏲10am-8pm Mon-Fri, to 6pm Sat & Sun Jun-Aug, shorter hours Sep-May) Guðbjörg at Aurum is one of Reykjavík's more interesting designers; her whisper-thin silver jewellery is sophisticated stuff, its shapes often inspired by leaves and flowers. Collectibles fill the other side of the shop.

Orr JEWELLERY
(Map p78; ☎511 6262; www.orr.is; Skólavörðustígur 17b; ⏲10am-6pm Mon-Sat) A creative couple craft delicate, nature-inspired jewellery using pearls, semiprecious stones and lustrous metals.

Stígur ARTS & CRAFTS
(Map p68; ☎551 5675; Skólavörðustígur 17b; ⏲10am-6pm Mon-Sat, to 4pm Sun) Seven local artists work in textiles, graphics, ceramics, glass and paint. We're particularly fond of the vases.

Heilsuhúsið FOOD
(Map p68; ☎552 2966; www.heilsuhusid.is; Laugavegur 20; ⏲10am-6pm Mon-Fri, 11am-4pm Sat, noon-4pm Sun) Stop by to shop with the locals for health food, smoothies and supplements beneath the equally organic and health-

conscious Gló restaurant. It carries the excellent local organic line of Sóley bath products.

Dogma CLOTHING
(Reykjavík T-Shirts; Map p68; ☎562 6600; www.dogma.is; Laugavegur 32; ⏲10am-8pm Jun-Sep, to 6pm Oct-May) This quirky T-shirt specialist is the go-to spot for scouting out funky local designs with a cartoonish appeal. It also does a nice line in comedy fridge magnets and drinks coasters that gently mock the tourist trade. It also has a branch in the Kringlan centre.

Iðnú Bookshop MAPS
(Map p78; ☎517 7210; www.ferdakort.is; Brautarholt 8; ⏲10am-4pm Mon-Fri) You'll find a large selection of road and hiking maps at the specialist Ferðakort map department at Iðnú Bookshop.

Reykjavík Foto ELECTRONICS
(Map p68; ☎577 5900; www.reykjavikfoto.is; Laugavegur 51; ⏲10am-6pm Mon-Fri, 11am-4pm Sat) Loads of cameras, tripods and water-resistant bags, with helpful service.

South of the Centre

Kringlan SHOPPING CENTRE
(Map p56; ☎517 9000; www.kringlan.is; Kringlunni 4-12; ⏲10am-6pm Mon-Wed & Sat, to 9pm Thu, to 7pm Fri, 1-6pm Sun; 🚌1, 3, 4, 6) Reykjavík's main shopping centre, 1km from town, has some 170 shops. A free shuttle runs on the hour from the tourist office at the Ráðhús.

Information

EMERGENCY

Police Station (☎emergency 112, nonemergency 444 1000; Hverfisgata 113) Central police station.

INTERNET ACCESS

There's free wi-fi at the main tourist office, almost all accommodation and many cafes. You can also use terminals at libraries (per hour 350kr); the main library **Aðalbókasafn** (Reykjavík City Library; ☎411 6100; www.borgarbokasafn.is; Tryggvagata 15; per hour 350kr; ⏲10am-7pm Mon-Thu, 11am-6pm Fri, 1-5pm Sat & Sun; 📶) is excellent.

LAUNDRY

Laundry is a perennial (pricey) problem in Iceland. At the time of writing, there were no laundromats in the entire country. Luckily most apartments and hostels and many guesthouses have washing machines.

Úðafoss (☎551 2301; www.udafoss.is; Vitastígur 13; ⏲8am-6pm Mon-Fri) provides dry cleaning services.

LUGGAGE STORAGE

BSÍ bus terminal, Reykjavík Domestic Airport and several other locations in Reykjavík have luggage lockers (www.luggagelockers.is). Many Reykjavík hotels will keep bags for you if you take off for the countryside for a few days.

MEDICAL SERVICES

Dentist (☎575 0505)
Health Centre (Heilsugæslan Miðbæ; ☎513-5950; Vesturgata 7; ⏲by appointment) Book in advance.
Læknavaktin (☎doctor on duty 1770; ⏲5-11.30pm Mon-Fri, 8am-11.30pm Sat & Sun) Nonemergency after-hours medical advice.
Landspítali University Hospital (☎543 1000, doctor on duty 1770; www.landspitali.is; Fossvogur) Hospital and emergency centre.

MONEY

Credit cards are accepted everywhere (except municipal buses); ATMs are ubiquitous. Currency-exchange fees at hotels or private bureaux can be obscenely high.

POST

By the time you read this, the city's **main post office** (Map p60; www.postur.is; ⏲9am-6pm Mon-Fri) should have moved from Pósthússtræti in Old Reykjavík to the ground floor of the **Radisson Blu Saga Hotel** (Map p56; www.postur.is; Hagatorg 107). There's another **branch** (Map p56; ☎580 1000; Síðumúla 3; ⏲9am-6pm Mon-Fri) on the fringes of Laugardalur.

TELEPHONE

Public phones are rare. Try the Main Tourist Office, post office, by the southwestern corner of Austurvöllur, on Lækjargata, or at Kringlan shopping centre.

TOURIST INFORMATION

The official tourism site for the country is Inspired By Iceland (www.inspiredbyiceland.com), which has comprehensive information.

Main Tourist Office (Upplýsingamiðstöð Ferðamanna; Map p60; ☎411 6040; www.visitreykjavik.is; Ráðhús, Tjarnargata 11; ⏲8am-8pm; 📶) The city's official tourist office is located in the Ráðhús (City Hall). Friendly staff and mountains of free brochures, plus maps, the Reykjavík City Card and Strætó city bus tickets for sale. Books accommodation, tours and activities too. The SafeTravel desk, an initiative led by the Icelandic Search & Rescue, is gold for those planning outdoor adventures such as overnight hikes or driving in the highlands.

Grófin Tourist Information Centre (Iceland Travel Assistance Head Office; Map p60; ☎570 7700; www.ita.is; Grófin 1; ⏲8am-8pm) Large tourist information centre with friendly staff, currency exchange, printing and luggage storage. Under the wing of Iceland Travel Assistance, running several outlets in Reykjavík, it acts primarily as a booking service. For specific travel advice, head for the publicly funded Main Tourist Office (p101) inside the nearby Ráðhús.

TRAVEL AGENCIES

Icelandic Travel Market (ITM; ☎522 4979; www.icelandictravelmarket.is; Bankastræti 2; ⏲8am-9pm Jun-Aug, 9am-7pm Sep-May) Information, tour bookings and luggage storage (per day/additional day 1000/500kr).

Trip (☎433 8747; www.trip.is; Laugavegur 54; ⏲9am-7pm) Books tours and transport.

Getting There & Away

AIR

Keflavík International Airport

Iceland's primary international airport, Keflavík International Airport (p428), is 48km west of Reykjavík, on the Reykjanes Peninsula.

The airport has ATMs, money exchange, car hire, an **information desk** (☎425 0330, booking service 570 7799; www.visitreykjanes.is; Reykjanesbraut; ⏲6am-8pm Mon-Fri, noon-5pm Sat & Sun) and cafes. The duty-free shops in the arrival area sell liquor at far better prices than you'll find in town. There's also a desk for collecting duty-free cash back from eligible purchases in Iceland. The 10-11 convenience store sells SIM cards, and major tour companies like Reykjavík Excursions and Grayline have desks.

Reykjavík Domestic Airport

Reykjavík Domestic Airport (Reykjavíkurflugvöllur; Map p56; www.isavia.is; Innanlandsflug) Is in central Reykjavík, just 2km south of Tjörnin. Sightseeing services, domestic flights and those to/from Greenland and the Faroe Islands fly here.

Air Iceland Connect (p75) Serves Akureyri, Egilsstaðir, Ísafjörður and Greenland. There's a desk at the airport, but you can usually save money by booking online.

Atlantic Airways (☎in Faroe Islands 298 34 10 00; www.atlantic.fo) Flies to the Faroe Islands.

Eagle Air Iceland (p75) Operates sightseeing services and five set routes from Reykjavík: Vestmannaeyjar Islands; Höfn; Húsavík; and in the Westfjords, Bíldudalur and Gjögur.

BUS

Bus services are ever-changing in Iceland, so it pays to get up-to-date information on schedules and fares, from bus-company websites or tourist offices. The free Public Transport in Iceland (www.publictransport.is) map has a good overview of routes.

You can travel from Reykjavík by day tour (most offer hotel pick-up), or use Strætó (p67) or one of the other companies, getting on and off its scheduled buses. It also offers a multitude of bus transport passes.

The bus network operates frequently from around mid-May to mid-September. Outside these months services to remoter regions can be less frequent (or nonexistent).

For destinations on the northern and eastern sides of Iceland (eg Egilsstaðir, Mývatn and Húsavík), you usually change in Höfn or Akureyri; for the West and Westfjords change in Borgarnes.

Strætó (p429) Operates Reykjavík long-distance buses from **Mjódd bus terminal** (☎540 2700; www.bus.is; ⏲ticket office 7am-6pm Mon-Fri, 10am-6pm Sat, 12.30-6pm Sun), 8km southeast of the city centre, which is served by local buses 3, 4, 11, 12, 17, 21 and 24. Strætó also operates city buses and has a smartphone app, which you can use for timetables and to buy tickets. For long-distance buses only you can use cash, credit/debit card with PIN or (wads of) bus tickets.

BSÍ Bus Terminal (Map p56; ☎580 5400; www.bsi.is; Vatnsmýrarvegur 10; 📶) Reykjavík Excursions (and its Flybus) uses the BSÍ bus terminal (pronounced 'bee-ess-ee'), around 2km south of the city centre. There's a ticketing desk, tourist brochures, lockers, luggage storage (www.luggagelockers.is), Budget car hire and a cafeteria with wi-fi. The terminal is served by Reykjavík buses 1, 3, 5, 6, 14 and 15. Reykjavík Excursions offers pre-booked hotel pick-up to bring you to the terminal. Some Grayline (p72) buses also stop there.

Sterna (Sterna; Map p68; ☎551 1166; www.icelandbybus.is; 📶) Sales and departures from the Harpa concert hall. Bu-ses around the southern Ring Road and to tourist highlights.

Trex (p430) Departs from the Main Tourist Office, Kringlan's Shell petrol station or Reykjavík Campsite. Buses to Þórsmörk and Landmannalaugar in the South.

Getting Around

TO/FROM THE AIRPORT

Keflavík International Airport

The journey from Keflavík International Airport to Reykjavík takes about 50 minutes. Three easy bus services connect Reykjavík and the airport and are the best transport option; kids get discounted fares.

Flybus (☎580 5400; www.re.is; one-way ticket 2950kr; 📶) Meets all international flights. Hotel pick-up/drop off costs 3950kr and shuttles you from/to the Flybus at the

BSÍ bus terminal; book hotel pick-up at least a day ahead. A separate service runs to the Blue Lagoon (4990kr), from where you can continue to the city centre or the airport. Buy tickets online, at many hotels, or at the airport booth. Flybus will also drop off/pick up in Garðabær and Hafnarfjörður, just south of Reykjavík. Operated by Reykjavík Excursions (p72).

Airport Express (Map p60; ☎540 1313; www.airportexpress.is; 📶) Links the airport with Lækjartorg Sq (2700kr) in central Reykjavík or Mjódd bus terminal, or via hotel pick-up/drop off (3300kr; book ahead). Also has connections to Borgarnes and points north, including Akureyri. Operated by Grayline Iceland (p72).

Airport Direct (☎497 5000; www.reykjavik-sightseeing.is/airport-direct; one way/return from 5500/10,000kr; 📶) Minibuses operated by Reykjavík Sightseeing link accommodation and the airport.

BUS SERVICES FROM REYKJAVÍK

Below are sample routes and fares; check with bus companies for current rates. Strætó (p67) usually offers the lowest fares. Private companies like Reykjavík Excursions (p72), RE and Sterna (p101) also ply some of these routes, and may offer pick-up, but usually cost more unless you buy a bus passport.

DESTINATION	COMPANY & LINE	COST ONE WAY (KR)	DURATION	FREQUENCY	YEAR-ROUND
Akureyri	Strætó 57	10,120	6½hr	daily	yes
Blue Lagoon	RE	3000	45min	daily	yes
Borgarnes	Strætó 57	1840	1½hr	daily	yes
Geysir/Gullfoss	RE 610	5000	2½hr	daily	mid-Jun–early Sep
Höfn	Strætó 51	13,340	7hr	daily	yes
Hólmavík	Strætó 57/59 via Borgarnes	6900	3½hr	2-5 weekly	yes
Keflavík	Strætó 55/1	1840	1hr	daily	yes
Kirkjubæjarklaustur	Strætó 51/ Sterna 12	7820/7800	4¼/6½hr	daily	yes/Jun-Aug
Landmannalaugar	Trex/RE/ Sterna	8400/8500/ 7950	4½hr	daily	late Jun-early Sep
Selfoss	Strætó 51/52, also Sterna& RE	1840	1hr	many daily	yes
Skaftafell	Strætó 51/ Sterna 12/ RE 20	10,120/10,000/ 11,200	5¼/7¾/ 7¾hr	daily	yes/Jul-Aug/ Jul-Aug
Skógar	Strætó 51/ Sterna/RE	5520/5300/ 6700	2½/3/ 3½hr	daily	yes/Jun–mid-Sep/Jun-early Sep
Stykkishólmur	Strætó 57 to 58	4140	2½hr	daily	yes
Landeyjarhöfn port for Vestmannaeyjar	Strætó 52	4600	2¼hr	daily	yes
Vík í Mýrdal	Strætó 51/ Sterna/RE	6440/6000/ 7800	3/4¼/4hr	2 daily	yes/late Jun–early Sep
Þingvellir	Tours only (eg RE)	6700	half-day	daily	May-Sep
Þórsmörk	Trex/RE/ Sterna	7400/8000/ 6950	4/7/12hr	daily	Jun–mid-Sep

Strætó (p67) Bus 55 also connects the BSÍ bus terminal and the airport (1840kr, 1¼ hours, nine daily Monday to Friday). It's less frequent.

Taxis from Keflavík airport to Reykjavík cost around 16,100kr.

Reykjavík Domestic Airport

From the Reykjavík Domestic Airport it's a 2km walk into town. Otherwise bus 15 stops near the Air Iceland Connect terminal and goes to the Hlemmur bus stop. A cab into the city centre costs around 1300kr.

BICYCLE

Reykjavík has a steadily improving network of cycle lanes; ask the Main Tourist Office (p101) for a map. You are allowed to cycle on pavements as long as you don't cause pedestrians problems.

The bike share scheme **WOW City Bike** (☎590 3085; www.wowcitybike.com; per hr 850kr) has docks in eight places around town. Or you can rent from Reykjavík Bike Tours (p70) in the Old Harbour, or **Örninn** (☎588 9890; www.orninn.is; Faxafen 8; ⊙10am-6pm Mon-Fri, 11am-3pm Sat) in southeast Reykjavík. The Bike Cave (p95), near Reykjavík Domestic Airport, can help with repairs.

BUS

Strætó (p67) operates regular buses around Reykjavík and its suburbs (Seltjarnarnes, Kópavogur, Garðabær, Hafnarfjörður and Mosfellsbær); it also operates long-distance buses. It has online schedules, a smartphone app and a printed map. Many free maps like *Welcome to Reykjavík City Map* also include bus-route maps.

Buses run from 7am until 11pm or midnight daily (from 11am on Sunday). Services depart at 15-minute or 30-minute intervals. A limited night-bus service runs until 4.30am on Friday and Saturday. Buses only stop at designated bus stops, marked with a yellow letter 'S'.

Bus Tickets & Fares

The fare is 460kr; you can buy tickets at the bus terminal, pay on board (though no change is given) or by using the Strætó app. Buy one-/three-day passes (1700/4000kr) at Mjódd bus terminal, the Main Tourist Office, 10-11 convenience stores, many hotels, Kringlan (p103) and Smáralind shopping malls, and bigger swimming pools. If you need to take two buses to reach your destination, get a *skiptimiði* (transfer ticket) from the driver; it's good for 75 minutes in the city, 120 minutes in the countryside.

The Reykjavík City Card (p63) also acts as a Strætó bus pass.

Bus Stations & Lines

Two central Strætó stops are at **Hlemmur** (Map p78), at the eastern end of Laugavegur, and **Lækjartorg Sq** (Map p60), in the centre of town. Mjódd (p101), 8km southeast of the city centre, is the main bus terminal, and where you'll catch long-distance Strætó buses. Many buses make a loop around Tjörnin lake and serve the city centre, the National Museum and BSÍ bus terminal before heading onwards.

A free shuttle bus also runs from the tourist office to the Kringlan Shopping Centre (Map p56).

CAR & MOTORCYCLE

A car is unnecessary in Reykjavík as it's so easy to explore on foot and by bus. Car and camper hire for the countryside are available at both airports, the BSÍ bus terminal and some city locations.

Parking

Street parking in the city centre is limited and costs 320kr per hour in the Red Zone and 170kr per hour in the Blue, Green and Yellow Zones. You must pay between 9am and 6pm from Monday to Friday and from 10am to 4pm Saturday; outside those hours it's free. Pay with coins or card (with PIN only). Parking outside the city centre is free.

Vitatorg Car Park (Skúlgata; 1st hour 80kr, subsequent hours 50kr; ⊙7am-midnight) is a relatively central, covered parking lot.

TAXI

Taxi prices are high. Flagfall starts at around 700kr. Tipping is not required. From BSÍ bus terminal to Harpa concert hall costs about 2200kr. From Mjódd bus termimal it's about 4300kr.

There are usually taxis outside bus stations, airports and bars on weekend nights (huge queues for the latter), plus on Bankastræti near Lækjargata.

BSR (☎561 0000; www.taxireykjavik.is)
Hreyfill (☎588 5522; www.hreyfill.is)

GREATER REYKJAVÍK

The area around the capital encompasses fascinating Reykjavík and its bustling suburbs, Mosfellsbær to the north, Kópavogur, Garðabær and Hafnarfjörður to the south. Plan to base yourself in Reykjavík proper, as that's where the main points of interest are for tourists.

Viðey

On fine-weather days, the tiny uninhabited island of Viðey makes a wonderful day trip. Just 1km north of Reykjavík's Sundahöfn Harbour, it feels a world away. Well-preserved historic buildings, surprising modern art, an abandoned village and great birdwatching add to its remote spell. The only sounds are the wind, the waves and the golden bumblebees buzzing among the tufted vetch and hawkweed.

Little Viðey was settled around 900 and was farmed until the 1950s. It was home to a powerful monastery from 1225, but in 1539 it was wiped out by Danish soldiers during the Reformation. In the 18th and 19th century several significant Icelandic leaders lived here.

See www.videy.com for more information about opening hours, prices and ferry schedules.

Sights & Activities

Viðey is great for birdwatching (30 species breed here) and botany (over one-third of all Icelandic plants grow on the island). In late August, some Reykjavikers come to pick wild caraway, which was originally planted here by Skúli Magnússon.

Viðeyarstofa HISTORIC BUILDING
(Map p56; ☎411 6360; www.videy.com; Viðey; ferry & admission adult/child 1550/775kr; ⏲10.30am-5pm mid-May–Sep, 1.30-4pm Sat & Sun Oct–mid-May) Just up from Viðey's harbour sits Viðeyarstofa, Iceland's oldest stone house. Icelandic Treasurer Skúli Magnússon was given the island in 1751 and he built Viðeyarstofa as his residence. It now houses a cafe (p104).

Viðey Church CHURCH
(Map p56; ☎411 6360; www.videy.com; Viðey; ferry & admission adult/child 1550/775kr; ⏲10.30am-5pm mid-May–Sep, 1.30-4pm Sat & Sun Oct–mid-May) The second-oldest wooden church in Iceland, Viðey Church dates from the 18th century. Look out for the original decor and the tomb of the former owner of Viðey, Skúli Magnússon – he died here in 1794. Excavations of the old monastery foundations unearthed 15th-century wax tablets and a runic love letter, now kept in the National Museum (p54).

Peace Tower MONUMENT
(Map p56; ☎411 6360; www.videy.com; Viðey; ferry & admission adult/child 1550/775kr; ⏲10.30am-5pm mid-May–Sep, 1.30-4pm Sat & Sun Oct–mid-May) Yoko Ono's Imagine Peace Tower (2007) is a 'wishing well' that blasts a dazzling column of light into the sky every night between 9 October (John Lennon's birthday) and 8 December (the anniversary of his death). See Viðey's website for Peace Tower tours from Reykjavík.

Island Paths
The whole island is criss-crossed with walking paths. Some you can bicycle, others are more precarious. When boats are running from the Old Harbour, you can hire a bike there at Reykjavík Bike Tours (p70) and bring it to the island.

From the harbour, trails to the southeast lead past the natural sheep fold **Réttin**, the tiny grotto **Paradíshellir** (Paradise Cave) and then to the abandoned fishing village at **Sundbakki**.

Trails leading to the northwest take you to **Vesturey**, the northern tip of the island. You'll pass low ponds, monuments to several shipwrecks, and the low cliffs of **Eiðisbjarg**. Richard Serra's **Áfangar** (Standing Stones; 1990) sculptures, made from huge pairs of basalt pillars, dot this northern part of the island.

Sleeping & Eating

There is no lodging or camping on Viðey.

There is one mediocre **cafe** (Map p56; mains 2450-3900kr; ⏲11.30am-5pm mid-May–Sep, 1.30-4pm Sat & Sun Oct–mid-May; 📶) on the island, but it's in a beautiful historic building. You can bring supplies to picnic or barbecue at the shoreside **Viðeyjarnaust Day Hut** (Map p56) FREE, some 400m northwest of the ferry landing stage.

Getting There & Away

Viðey is accessed from Reykjavík by ferry. The **Viðey Ferry** (Map p56; ☎533 5055; www.videy.com; Skarfabakki; return adult/child 1500/750kr; ⏲from Skarfabakki hourly 10.15am-5.15pm mid-May–Sep, 1.15-4.30pm Sat & Sun Oct–mid-May) takes five minutes from Skarfabakki, 4.5km east of the city centre. During summer, two boats a day also start from Elding at the Old Harbour and the Harpa concert hall. Bus 16 runs to Skarfabakki, and it's a point on the **City Sightseeing Reykjavík** (☎580 5400; www.city-sightseeing.com; adult/child per 24hr 4080/2040kr; ⏲half-hourly 10am-4.30pm) bus route.

Kópavogur

POP 35,966

Kópavogur, the first suburb south of Reykjavík, is just a short bus ride away but feels far from the tourist trail. You might be drawn here by the museum and concert house in the Menningarmiðstoð Kópavogs cultural complex or the huge **Smáralind** (☎528 8000; www.smaralind.is; Hagasmára 1, Kópavogur;

HAFNARFJÖRÐUR'S HIDDEN WORLDS

Many Icelanders believe that their country is populated by hidden races: *jarðvergar* (gnomes), *álfar* (elves), *ljósálfar* (fairies), *dvergar* (dwarves), *ljúflingar* (lovelings), *tívar* (mountain spirits), *englar* (angels) and *huldufólk* (hidden people). Although some are embarrassed to say they believe, most refuse to say hand on heart that they *don't* believe. You'll see many Icelandic gardens feature small wooden *álfhól* (elf houses).

Hafnarfjörður, 12km south of Reykjavík, is believed to lie at the confluence of several strong ley lines (mystical lines of energy) and, according to tradition, rests on one that is 7300 years old and hides an entire elfin universe. As you walk through **Hellisgerði**, a peaceful park filled with lava grottoes, be aware it is also apparently one of the favourite places of the hidden people. A 1½-hour **Hidden Worlds tour** (694 2785; www.alfar.is; per person 4500kr; 2.30pm Tue & Fri Jun-Aug) leaves from the **tourist office** (585 5500; www.visithafnarfjordur.is; Strandgata 6; 8am-4pm Mon-Fri), which also sells elf maps. At weekends when the office is closed, get info at Pakkhúsið (p105).

Hafnarfjörður Museum, the town's other main attraction, is divided over several old tin-clad houses near the harbour, exploring local history. Start at **Pakkhúsið** (585 5780; http://museum.hafnarfjordur.is; Vesturgata 6; 11am-5pm Jun-Aug, Sat & Sun Sep-May) FREE, the primary site. **Hafnarborg Centre of Culture & Fine Art** (585 5790; www.hafnarborg.is; Strandgata 34; noon-5pm Wed-Mon; 1) FREE features rotating exhibitions of well-chosen art, and there are hot springs and mud pools south of town in **Krýsuvík**.

In a pinch, overnight at **Lava Hostel & Campsite** (565 0900; www.lavahostel.is; Hjallabraut 51; campsites per adult/child 1700/1000kr, dm from 5800kr, d without bathroom 15,500kr;). Find good eats at popular cafe **Súfistinn** (565 3740; www.sufistinn.is; Strandgata 9; dishes 1400-1750kr; 8.15am-11.30pm Mon-Fri, from 10am Sat, from 11am Sun;). Get here on Strætó (www.bus.is) bus 1 (30 minutes from Reykjavík). Other Strætó lines circulate within town. **Flybus** (580 5400; www.re.is) to Keflavík International Airport will stop in Hafnarfjörður if prearranged.

11am-7pm Mon-Wed, to 9pm Thu & Fri, to 6pm Sat, 1-6pm Sun; 2) shopping mall. See www.kopavogur.is for general information.

Gerðarsafn Art Museum GALLERY

(441 7600; www.gerdarsafn.is; Hamraborg 4; adult/child kr1000/free; 11am-5pm Tue-Sun) In this beautifully designed museum you'll find excellent rotating modern-art exhibitions and a notable permanent collection of 20th-century Icelandic works. It's dedicated to stained-glass artist and sculptor Gerður Helgadóttir and has a small cafe with mountain views.

Menningarmiðstoð Kópavogs CULTURAL CENTRE

(Hamraborg 6) Menningarmiðstoð Kópavogs contains Kópavogur's **Natural History Museum** (Náttúrufræðistofa Kópavogs; 441 7200; www.natkop.is; Hamraborg 6a; 9am-6pm Mon-Thu, 11am-5pm Fri & Sat) FREE, where displays include an orca skeleton, stuffed animals and some of Mývatn lake's odd *marimo* balls (round, cannon-ball sized clusters of algae). You'll also find Iceland's first specially designed concert hall, **Salurinn** (441 7500; www.salurinn.is; Hamraborg 6), which has been built entirely from Icelandic materials such as driftwood and spruce.

Gló HEALTH FOOD €

(553 1111; www.glo.is; Hæðasmári 6; mains 1400-2400kr; 11am-9pm;) Thai, Indian and Mexican flavours jazz up the raw and organic ingredients dished up here to create a wonderland of largely vegetarian wraps, soups and elaborate salads. The decor is as casually cool as the food.

Getting There & Away

Strætó (p67) buses to Kópavogur call at the Hamraborg stop (look for the church). Fares cost 460kr from the Greater Reykjavíka area. Buses run every 15 minutes and the journey takes around 20 minutes.

- Bus 1 from both the Lækjartorg stop in central Reykjavík, and the Hlemmur bus stop.
- Bus 2 from Hlemmur.
- Bus 4 from Hlemmur, via the Kringlan shopping centre.

Southwest Iceland & the Golden Circle

Includes ➡

Best Places to Eat

- ➡ Slippurinn (p176)
- ➡ Við Fjöruborðið (p136)
- ➡ Bryggjan (p117)
- ➡ Efstidalur II (p123)

Best Places to Stay

- ➡ Héraðsskólinn (p123)
- ➡ Mengi (p126)
- ➡ Hótel Geysir (p126)
- ➡ Buubble Hotel (p128)

Why Go?

Black beaches stretch along the Atlantic, geysers spout from geothermal fields and waterfalls glide across escarpments while brooding volcanoes and glittering ice caps score the inland horizon. The beautiful Southwest has many of Iceland's legendary natural wonders, so it's a relatively crowded and increasingly developed area. The Golden Circle – a tourist route comprising three famous sights: Þingvellir, Geysir and Gullfoss – draws the largest crowds outside of Reykjavík, but visit during off-hours or venture into the wilderness and you'll find quiet hiking routes and otherworldly scenes.

The further you go, the better it gets. Tourist faves such as the silica-filled Blue Lagoon and the rift valley and ancient parliament at Þingvellir are just beyond the capital. Churning seas lead to the Vestmannaeyjar archipelago offshore. At the region's far reaches lie the powerful Hekla and Eyjafjallajökull volcanoes, busy Skógar and Vík, and the hidden valleys of Þórsmörk and Landmannalaugar.

Road Distances (km)

	Keflavík	Selfoss	Gullfoss	Landmannalaugar	Vík
Selfoss	100				
Gullfoss	156	71			
Landmannalaugar	230	130	147		
Vík	226	130	177	218	
Reykjavík	51	57	113	185	186

REYKJANES PENINSULA

The Reykjanes Peninsula expands in drama as you move away from the highway between Reykjavík and Keflavík International Airport. You'll find not only the Blue Lagoon, Iceland's most famous attraction, but numerous other gorgeous and interesting sights, many of them based around active volcanoes. The busiest towns are amenity-rich Keflavík and nearby Njarðvík, but the sweet, windswept fishing hamlets of Garður and Sandgerði – great for whale watching – are just minutes to the west of the airport on a small northwestern spur. The rest of the Reykjanes, from dramatic Reykjanestá in the southwest to the Reykjanesfólkvangur wilderness reserve in the east, is an untamed landscape of multihued volcanic craters, mineral lakes, bubbling hot springs, rugged mountains and coastal lava fields.

The Reykjanes Peninsula is a Unesco Global Geopark (www.reykjanesgeopark.is), formed to research and protect the region's local culture and unusual geology (pillow lava, oceanic ridge, meeting of tectonic plates, and a whopping four volcanic systems).

Getting There & Away

Public transport to Keflavík and the Blue Lagoon is fast and frequent from Reykjavík. There is a limited public bus service to other villages, but you'll do best with private transport to reach the more remote parts of the peninsula.

Blue Lagoon

Paris has the Eiffel Tower, Iceland has the Blue Lagoon...with all the positive and negative connotations implied. Surrounded by jagged, moss-dusted black-lava scenes, the milky-teal spa is delivered water via the Svartsengi geothermal plant. Look out for the billowing wafts of steam emerging from the plant's silver towers, while spa-goers prance around covered in white silica mud.

Activities

★**Blue Lagoon** GEOTHERMAL POOL
(Bláa Lónið; ☎420 8800; www.bluelagoon.com; Nordurljosavegur 9; adult/child from 7000kr/free, premium entry from 9600kr/free; ⊙7am-midnight Jul–mid-Aug, to 11pm late May-Jun, 8am-10pm Jan-late May & mid-Aug–Sep, to 9pm Oct-Dec) In a magnificent black-lava field, the cyan Blue Lagoon spa is fed water from the futuristic Svartsengi geothermal plant; with its silver towers, roiling clouds of steam, and people daubed in white silica mud, it's an otherworldly place. Those who say it's too commercial and too crowded aren't wrong, but you'll be missing something special if you don't go. Pre-booking is essential.

Reykjanes Peninsula

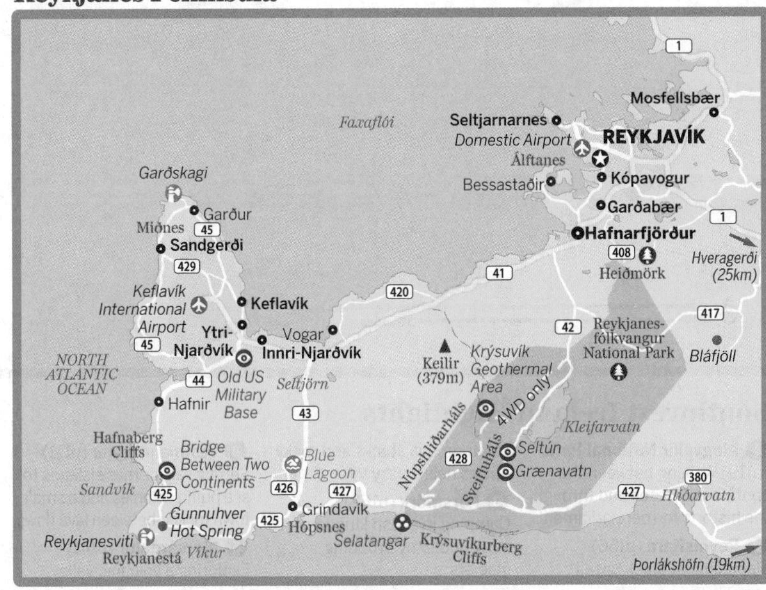

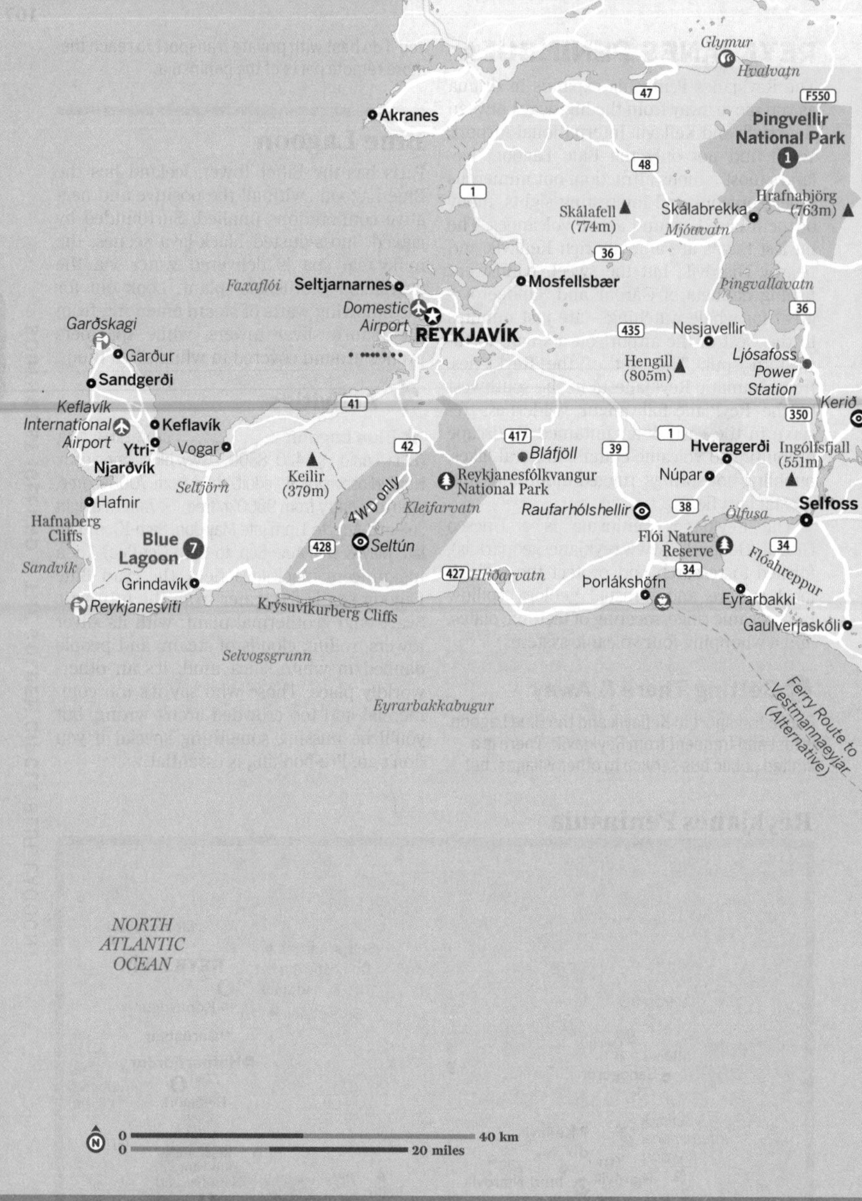

Southwest Iceland Highlights

1 Þingvellir National Park (p119) Walking between the continental plates and through the historic former parliament.

2 Reynisfjara (p166) Marvelling at black basalt columns, sea stacks and rocky buttes near buzzy Vík.

3 Þórsmörk (p162) Camping in a lush kingdom surrounded by brooding glaciers.

4 Vestmannaeyjar (p171) Setting sail for these islands to see puffin colonies and a small town tucked between lava flows.

5 Þjórsárdalur (p141) Exploring a volcanic valley

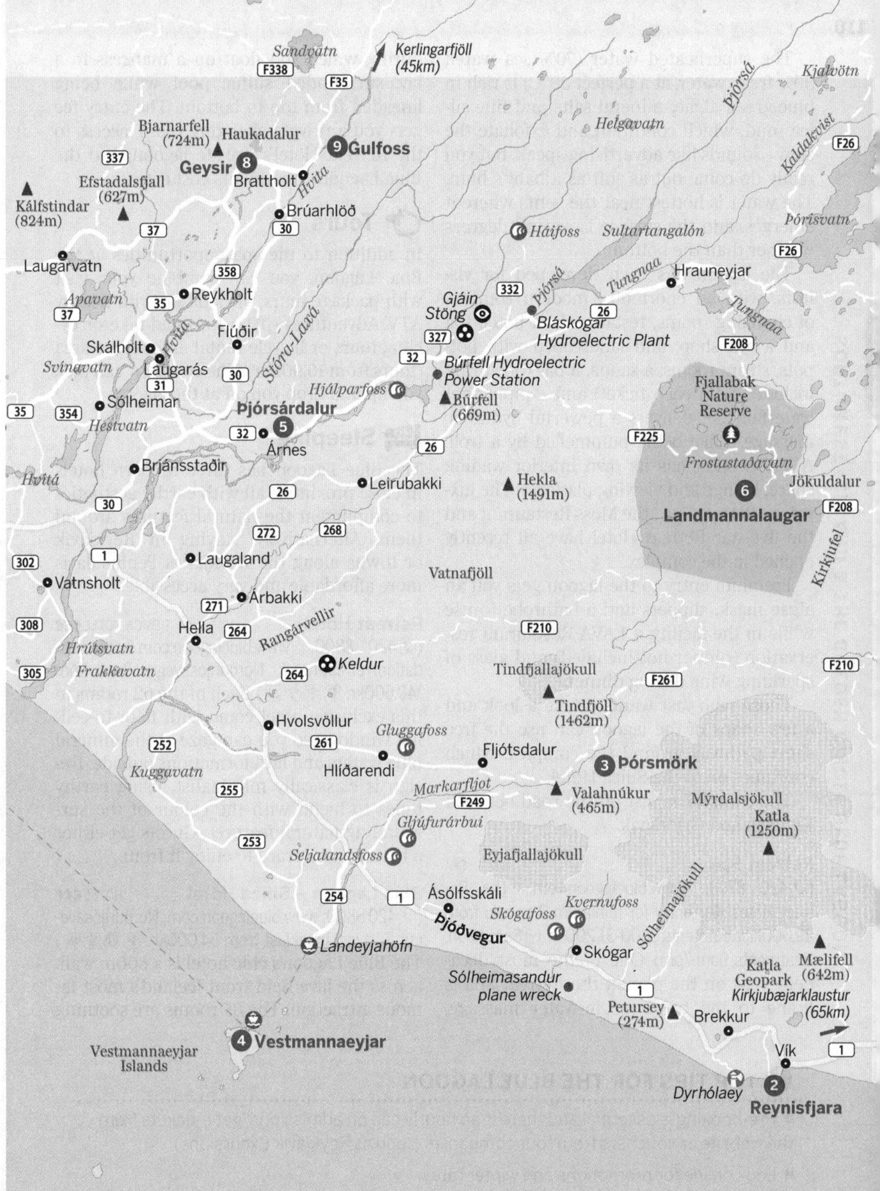

of raw terrain carved by the powerful Þjórsá river.

6 Landmannalaugar (p156) Traversing multicoloured peaks past pristine lakes, then setting off on Iceland's most famous hike, the Laugavegurinn.

7 Blue Lagoon (p107) Washing away your cares at the Vegas version of Icelandic hot-pots.

8 Geysir (p126) Waiting for water to shoot skywards.

9 Waterfalls (p127) Seeing brilliant cascades from Háifoss, Seljalandsfoss and Skógafoss to Gullfoss.

The superheated water (70% sea water, 30% fresh water, at a perfect 38°C) is rich in blue-green algae, mineral salts and fine silica mud, which condition and exfoliate the skin – sounds like advertising speak, but you really do come out as soft as a baby's bum. The water is hottest near the vents where it emerges, and the surface is several degrees warmer than the bottom.

The lagoon has been developed for visitors, with an enormous, modern complex of changing rooms, restaurants, a hotel, spa and a gift shop, and landscaped with hotpots, steam rooms, a sauna, a bar (one drink included with each ticket) and a piping-hot waterfall that delivers a powerful hydraulic massage – like being pummelled by a troll. A VIP section has its own interior wading space, lounge and viewing platform. The luxurious Retreat Spa , the Moss Restaurant and the five-star Retreat Hotel have all recently opened in the complex.

Premium entry to the lagoon gets you an algae mask, slippers and a bathrobe to use while in the facility, a LAVA Restaurant reservation (dinner not included) and glass of sparkling wine during dinner.

Those who just want to take a look and a few snaps of the lagoon can use the free short pathway around the complex, which continues on to the Silica Hotel.

The complex is just off the road between Keflavík and Grindavík.

Retreat Spa SPA

(☎420 8703; www.bluelagoon.com; The Retreat Hotel; 4hr entry for minimum 2 people from 29,000kr, treatments 5300-31,200kr; ⏰8am-noon, treatments 9am-7pm) One of the most decadent spas on the planet, the Retreat Spa is home to the two-hour in-water massage, during which you float on a mattress in a lava-surrounded sulfur pool while being kneaded from top to bottom. The entry fee gets you a private changing room, access to the Retreat Hotel's private lagoon, and the Blue Lagoon. Treatments cost extra.

Tours

In addition to the spa opportunities at the Blue Lagoon, you can combine your visit with package tours, or hook up with nearby ATV Adventures (p117) for quad-bike or cycling tours or bicycle rental around the area (tours from 10,900kr). The company can pick you up and drop you off at the lagoon.

Sleeping

The Blue Lagoon has three modern hotels in close proximity, all with earthy aesthetics to compliment the natural features around them. Alternatively, staying in Reykjavík or towns along the Reykjanes Peninsula is more affordable and very accessible.

Retreat Hotel DESIGN HOTEL €€€

(☎420 8800; www.bluelagoon.com/accommodation/retreat-hotel; Norðurljósavegur 9; r from 140,600kr; P ❄ ☎ ≋) Each of the 62 rooms in this exclusive hotel come with floor-to-ceiling windows so you can gaze at the mineral blue waters and lava formations outside. Design is classically minimalist, using earthy tones to blend with the colour of the surrounding natural features. Guests get either a balcony or terrace to enjoy it from.

Blue Lagoon – Silica Hotel HOTEL €€€

(☎420 8800; www.bluelagoon.com; Norðurljósavegur 7; d incl breakfast from 54,000kr; P @ ☎ ≋) The Blue Lagoon's chic hotel is a 600m walk across the lava field from Iceland's most famous attraction. The 35 rooms are soothing

TOP TIPS FOR THE BLUE LAGOON

- Pre-booking is essential and there is an hourly cap on admissions; get e-tickets from the website or vouchers from tour companies (such as Reykjavík Excursions).
- Look online for promotions and winter rates.
- Avoid summertime mayhem (worst from 10am to 2pm); try to go first thing or after 7pm.
- Lagoon water can corrode silver and gold; leave watches and jewellery in your locker.
- You must practise standard Iceland pool etiquette: thorough naked pre-pool showering.
- Going to the lagoon on a tour or in transit to the airport can sometimes save time and money. By bus, Reykjavík Excursions (p429) connects Keflavík International Airport, the Blue Lagoon and Reykjavík.
- At the car park you'll find a luggage check (550kr per bag per day); perfect if you're going to the lagoon on your way to/from the airport.

and sleek, with heated-floor bathrooms, and each has a small porch for viewing the surrounding moonscape. The hotel has its own pool of blue lagoon water. Rates include one entry to the Blue Lagoon.

Northern Light Inn HOTEL €€€
(☎426 8650; www.northernlightinn.is; d incl breakfast from 28,000kr; P @) Forty-two spacious, stylish rooms line the lava field at this bungalow hotel. There's a sunny sitting room, honesty bar, free afternoon waffles and the hotel contributes towards taxi transfers to Keflavík airport. The lagoon is only 1km away. The onsite **Max's Restaurant** (☎426 8650; www.nli.is/restaurant; mains 2200-5300kr; noon-9.30pm) boasts a smattering of Nordic fare, and floor-to-ceiling windows look out over lava and the steam-spewing geothermal plant.

Eating & Drinking

Blue Café CAFE €
(☎420 8800; Nordurljosavegur 9; snacks 850kr, sandwiches 1200kr, cold meal trays 2200kr; 7am-midnight Jun–mid-Aug, reduced hours mid-Aug–May;) Simple, cafeteria-style eating at the Blue Lagoon, with smoothies, sandwiches, baked salmon and rice, vegetable trays and pre-made sushi.

LAVA Restaurant ICELANDIC €€€
(☎420 8800; www.bluelagoon.com; Norðurljósavegur 9; mains lunch/dinner 4500/5900kr, tasting menu 10,300kr; 11.30am-9.30pm Jun-Aug, to 8.30pm Sep-May;) The Blue Lagoon's cavernous dining room can feel like a function hall, but views to the lagoon are serene, the waitstaff are excellent and the menu features Iceland's favourite dishes prepared with well-conceived recipes; think baked celeriac, grilled beef and fish of the day.

Moss Restaurant ICELANDIC €€€
(☎420 8700; www.bluelagoon.com/restaurant/moss; Norðurljósavegur 11; 7-course tasting menu 15,900kr; 6.30-9.30pm) Gourmet tasting menus are served in the top part of the Retreat Hotel where guests can gaze at volcanic views out of the floor-to-ceiling windows. Frequently changing dishes are made using fresh, local and seasonal produce, like beetroots and blue cheese or langoustine with wild garlic and butter, and lamb with white onion, swede, mustard and broth.

Getting There & Away

The lagoon is 47km southwest of Reykjavík and 23km southeast of Keflavík International Airport.

> **SOUTHWEST RESOURCES**
>
> **South Iceland Tourist Information** (www.south.is) Has excellent free detailed maps for each subregion. Get them at local tourist offices.
>
> **Visit Reykjanes** (www.visitreykjanes.is) Information on the Reykjanes Peninsula.

The complex is just off the road between Keflavík and Grindavík. Bus services run year-round, as do tours (which sometimes offer better deals than a bus ticket plus lagoon admission). You must book in advance. If your bus or tour does not include lagoon entry, you must pre-book.

Blue Lagoon partners with Reykjavík Excursions (p429), which runs buses to the lagoon from/to Reyjavík and from/to the airport (one-way/return 3000/4990kr). With frequent buses (around 10 a day between 7am and 8pm), it's possible to do a round trip from either Reykjavík or the airport, or stop off at the lagoon on your way between the two. Return to Reyjavík bus tickets can be booked online and you can choose to book lagoon entry when booking your bus ticket (10,980kr with Blue Lagoon entry).

Bustravel (p72) also runs transfers from the airport or Reykjavík with its partner Destination Blue Lagoon (one-way/return 2750/5500kr). Buses leave every hour from Reykjavík between 6am and 11pm.

Keflavík & Njarðvík (Reykjanesbær)

POP 19,500

The twin towns of Keflavík and Njarðvík, on the coast about 47km southwest of Reykjavík, are both rather ungainly expanses of suburban boxes and eateries. Together they're known as 'Reykjanesbær'. While they're good places for amenities, unless you've got an early flight it's worth the 40-minute ride into Reykjavík.

Sights

Keflavík

The waterfront strip in Keflavík has most of the town's hotels and restaurants, and also the museum Duushús (p112). To the east on the seashore is an impressive **Ásmundur Sveinsson sculpture** (btwn Hafnargata & Ægisgata), sometimes used as a climbing frame by the local kids. Just beyond, on the edge of the little harbour, find a black cave where a larger-than-life **Giantess** (Skessa; Gróf small

Keflavík

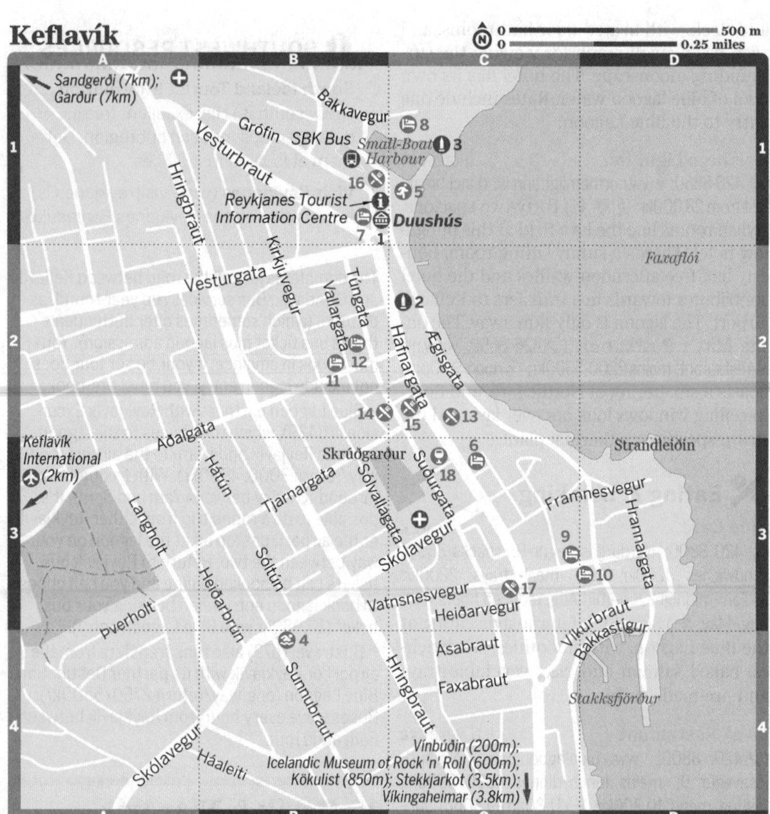

boat harbour; ⏰10am-5pm) FREE, a character from Herdís Egilsdóttir's children's books, sits in a rocking chair.

Duushús MUSEUM

(☎420 3245; Duusgata 2-8; adult/child 1500kr/free; ⏰noon-5pm) In a long red warehouse by the harbour, Duushús is Keflavík's historic cultural centre. There's a permanent exhibition of around 60 of Grímur Karlsson's many hundreds of miniature ships, made over a lifetime, as well as Reykjanes Art Museum galleries with international art exhibitions, and a changing local-history display.

Icelandic Museum of Rock 'n' Roll MUSEUM

(Rokksafn Íslands; ☎420 1030; www.rokksafn.is; Hjallavegur 2; adult/child 2000kr/free; ⏰11am-6pm) This museum delves into the history of the awesome Icelandic music scene, from Björk to Sigur Rós and Of Monsters and Men. Admission includes a walking-guide app with music. There's also the Music Hall of Fame, instruments for you to jam on, a cafe, and a shop where you can stock up on local tunes.

Njarðvík

★Víkingaheimar MUSEUM

(Viking World; ☎422 2000; www.vikingworld.is; Víkingabraut 1; adult 1500kr, family ticket 3000kr; ⏰7am-6pm) At the eastern end of Njarðvík's waterfront, the spectacular Víkingaheimar is a Norse exhibition centre built in one beautiful, sweeping architectural gesture. The centrepiece is the 23m-long *Íslendingur,* an exact reconstruction of the Viking Age *Gokstad* longship. It was built almost single-handedly by Gunnar Marel Eggertsson, who then sailed it from Iceland to New York in 2000 to commemorate the 1000th anniversary of Leif the Lucky's journey to America.

Keflavík

Top Sights
1 Duushús ... B1

Sights
2 Ásmundur Sveinsson Sculpture ... C2
3 Giantess ... C1

Activities, Courses & Tours
4 Swimming Pool ... B4
5 Whale Watching Reykjanes ... C1

Sleeping
6 Bjorkinn Apartments & Rooms ... C3
7 Guesthouse 1x6 ... B1
8 Hótel Berg ... C1
9 Hótel Keflavík ... C3
10 Hótel Keflavík Guesthouse ... D3
11 Nupan Deluxe ... B2
12 Svítan Guesthouse & Apartments ... B2

Eating
13 Biryani ... C2
14 Bonus ... B2
15 Fernando's Restaurant ... C2
16 Kaffi Duus ... B1
17 Olsen Olsen ... C3
Thai Keflavík ... (see 6)
Vikings Pizza ... (see 18)

Drinking & Nightlife
18 Paddy's ... C3

Activities

Whale Watching Reykjanes WHALE WATCHING
(779 8272; www.whalewatchingreykjanes.is; Ægisgata; adult/child 10,900/5450kr; whale-watching tours 9am & 1pm) From Keflavík Harbour you can go on three- to four-hour whale-watching tours around the Reykjanes Peninsula. Puffin and sea-angling tours are also possible. Maximum 23 passengers so book ahead.

Swimming Pool SWIMMING
(420 1500; Sunnubraut 31; 800kr; 6.30am-8.30pm Mon-Thu, to 7.30pm Fri, 9am-5.30pm Sat & Sun) Keflavík has a good 25m outdoor swimming pool with hot tubs, a sauna and a 50m indoor pool.

Sleeping

There are tonnes of guesthouses and hotels in Keflavík; check www.visitreykjanes.is. Many hotels in the area provide free airport transfers.

Stapakot B&B B&B €
(421 4647; www.facebook.com/stapakot; Stapagötu 20; d from 11,500kr) In a residential area, only a 10-minute drive to Keflavík International Airport, this well-decorated red guesthouse has a handful of rooms with shared bathrooms. Coffee, tea and biscuits are free and there's a friendly resident cat.

Bjorkinn Apartments & Rooms GUESTHOUSE €
(864 6663; www.bjorkinn.com; Hafnargata 41; studios from 13,000kr;) With two studios sleeping two to four people, one on each floor with private entrances and kitchenettes, Bjorkinn is a good and inexpensive option for families and small groups. It's a clean, well-finished space right on Keflavík's main street, where there are plenty of restaurants and shops.

Svítan Guesthouse & Apartments APARTMENT €
(663 1269; www.svitan.is; Túngata 10; s/d without bathroom incl breakfast from 6100/13,100kr, apt with bathroom from 26,800kr;) Choose from simple rooms or fully furnished apartments at this centrally located building. Rooms have kitchen and terrace access, and some have private bathrooms. Apartments sleep four.

Guesthouse 1x6 GUESTHOUSE €€
(857 1589; www.1x6.is; Vesturbraut 3; d without bathroom from 16,500kr;) This guesthouse has been created using recycled timber, driftwood and volcanic stones, creating a special environment where every room is unique. The friendly owners have also built a stone hot-pot, and will do airport pick-ups with advance notice.

Hótel Berg B&B €€
(422 7922; www.hotelberg.is; Bakkavegur 17; d incl breakfast from 27,000kr;) This homey guesthouse overlooking a little inlet harbour has common spaces with charming touches, and modern rooms with flat-screen TVs and original photography on the walls. It's located at the northern (and most charming) end of Keflavík, and is a wonderfully welcoming place to stay. Free airport shuttles.

Nupan Deluxe B&B €€
(565 3333; www.hotelnupan.com; Aðalgata 10; s without bathroom incl breakfast 10,500kr, d/tr incl breakfast 24,700/26,700kr;) Sleek, clean and simple is the order of the day at this residential-area B&B on the main drag out of town. It has a hot tub. Free airport transfers available. Plus complimentary coffee and tea.

B&B Keflavík Airport HOTEL €€

(☎426 5000; www.bbhotel.is; Valhallarbraut & Keilisbraut; d/q incl breakfast from 18,400/26,500kr; P@📶) In one of Keflavík's former military base buildings, this large, spruced-up hotel with modern interiors and exposed concrete walls offers an assortment of simple accommodation and is close to the airport. It also has a bar and lounge area.

Hótel Keflavík HOTEL €€

(☎420 7000; www.hotelkeflavik.is; Vatnsnesvegur 12-14; s/d incl breakfast from 18,600/46,200kr; @📶) The most bling sleeping option in town has gold-coloured fittings, a particularly gaudy reception area, and serviceable, central rooms, some with ocean views. There's also a gym and sauna on-site. Rates vary wildly online. The hotel also runs a small **guesthouse** (www.hotelkeflavik.is; Vatnsnesvegur 9; d without bathroom from 15,200kr; P📶) across the street, with simple rooms and shared bathrooms.

Alex HOTEL €€

(☎421 2800; www.alex.is; Aðalgata 60; d without bathroom incl breakfast from 13,900kr, d sleeping-bag cottage incl breakfast from 14,900kr; @📶) On the main road between Keflavík (1.5km) and the airport, this complex has rooms with shared bathrooms in a no-frills main building and cool tiny cottages out back.

Airport Hotel Aurora Star HOTEL €€€

(☎595 1900; www.hotelairport.is; Blikavöllur 2, Keflavík International Airport; s/d/tr incl breakfast 30,500/33,000/39,000kr; P@📶) The only hotel actually at the airport, Hotel Aurora Star is about 100m from the terminal and offers a tower of solid business-style rooms with flat-screen TVs. Superior rooms are bigger, with two double beds. There's a small bar, lounge area and a restaurant serving typical main dishes (lamb, fish and chips, burgers) from 2300kr.

Eating & Drinking

Kökulist BAKERY €

(☎555 6655; www.kokulist.is; Hólagata 17; baked goods from 350kr; ⏰7am-6pm Mon-Fri, 8.30am-4pm Sat & Sun) On the way out of town, a few minutes' walk from the Icelandic Museum of Rock 'n' Roll (p112), is this excellent bakery and cafe. It serves dozens of sweet pastries and cakes plus sandwiches and coffee in an earthy-toned modern space.

Vikings Pizza PIZZA €

(☎561 3636; Hafnargata 36; pizzas from 1650kr; ⏰11.30am-10pm Mon-Thu, to 11pm Fri & Sat, 2am-10pm Sun) Good oven-cooked pizzas with fun names to honour Norse gods and warriors like the Ingólfr Arnarson (with ground beef, chicken, red onion, Béarnaise sauce and extra cheese), the Odin (with chicken, jalapeños and cream cheese), the Thor (ham, pepperoni, ground beef, bacon) and Berserker (with three cheeses and mushroom sauce). There's also a small hamburger menu.

Biryani INDIAN €

(☎774 2242; www.facebook.com/biryanikeflavik; Hafnargata 31; mains 1100-1600kr; ⏰11am-11pm Sun-Thu, to 5am Fri & Sat; 🌱) Cheap-eats counter-service joint selling tasty Middle Eastern and Indian dishes, from falafel wraps to curries. Open until the wee hours, it's one of the only late-night spots to get a bite in the area. Vegetarian and vegan options available.

Olsen Olsen FAST FOOD €

(☎421 4457; www.olsenolsendiner.com; Hafnargata 62; mains 900-2700kr; ⏰11am-10pm) In the 1950s, thanks to American-introduced rock and roll, Keflavík was the coolest place in Iceland. This US-style diner transports locals back to the glory days, with shiny silver tables, red plastic seats and pictures of Elvis. Eats are of the fast-food variety, with 12 different kinds of burgers, plus hoagies galore.

Bonus SUPERMARKET €

(☎527 9000; Túngata 1; ⏰11am-6.30pm Mon-Thu, 10am-7.30pm Fri, 10am-6pm Sat, noon-6pm Sun) Groceries.

Fernando's Restaurant ITALIAN €€

(☎555 1044; www.facebook.com/hafnargata28; Hafnargata 28; mains 2200-5900kr; ⏰11.30am-10pm Sun-Wed, to 11pm Thu-Sat) Small and popular place serving pasta, pizzas, burgers and lunch options like grilled chicken skewers in pita and grilled salmon teriyaki. Spice fanatics should try the hot 'lava' pizza, with homemade sauce, pepperoni, jalapeños, green peppercorns, habanero chilli and chilli seasoning.

Thai Keflavík THAI €€

(☎421 8666; www.thaikeflavik.is; Hafnargata 39; mains 1900-2800kr; ⏰11.30am-10pm Mon-Fri, 4-10pm Sat & Sun; 📶) If you're up to your eyeballs in fish and lamb, this restaurant is a great choice with authentic Thai dishes. There's outdoor seating during warm weather.

Kaffi Duus SEAFOOD, INDIAN €€

(☎421 7080; www.duus.is; Duusgata 10, Duushús; mains 2850-7500kr; ⏰11am-11pm) This friendly, nautical-themed cafe-restaurant-bar, decorated with walrus tusks, overlooks the small-boat harbour. It serves generous platefuls of fresh fish, plus pasta, salads, burgers and, incongruously, Indian dishes. It's a popular evening hang-out.

Paddy's BAR
(☎421 8900; Hafnargata 38; ⏱6pm-1am Mon-Thu, to 4am Fri, noon-4am Sat, noon-1am Sun) A hole-in-the-wall that can get raucous at weekends and has occasional live music. Some sports are shown during big tournaments.

Shopping

Vínbúðin ALCOHOL
(☎421 5699; www.vinbudin.is; Krossmói 4; ⏱11am-6pm Mon-Thu, to 7pm Fri, to 4pm Sat) National liquor chain.

Information

Reykjanes Tourist Information Centre
(☎420 3246; www.visitreykjanes.is; Duusgata 2-8, Keflavík; ⏱9am-5pm Mon-Fri, noon-5pm Sat & Sun summer, noon-5pm winter) Located inside the Duushús (p112). Reykjanes Peninsula information, maps and brochures.

Getting There & Away

AIR

Iceland's primary international airport, Keflavík International Airport (p428), is 48km west of Reykjavík, on the Reykjanes Peninsula. All of Iceland's international flights use this airport, apart from those to Greenland and the Faroes.

The airport is being expanded every year, and has all the modern facilities: ATMs, currency exchange, duty free, car rental, cafes and mini-marts.

BUS

Strætó (p429) bus 55 runs between Keflavík airport and Reykjavík's BSÍ bus terminal (adult/child 1840/880kr, 1¼ hours, 12 daily Monday to Friday), running from 6.30am to 10pm. On Saturday (10 daily, 6.30am to 10pm) and Sunday (seven daily, 10.30am to 10pm) buses only go as far east as Hafnarfjörður.

Bus 88 goes from Keflavík to Grindavík (460kr, two daily, one in the morning and one in the afternoon, 20 minutes). On weekends it only goes from Grindavík to the crossroads where you can connect to bus 55 (around four transfers a day).

Bus 89 goes from Keflavík to Garður and Sandgerði (both services 460kr, 11 daily Monday to Friday 6am to 10pm, four Saturday 8.30am to 11pm, three Sunday 10.30am to 11pm)

SBK (☎420 6000; www.sbk.is; Grófin 2-4, Keflavík) also runs tour buses buses out of Keflavík.

Airport buses can drop you near the town limits.

Northwestern Reykjanes

The western edge of the Reykjanes Peninsula is rugged and exposed – perfect if you love wild rain-lashed cliffs and beaches. There are several fishing villages and some intriguing sights among the lava fields.

To best see the countryside around Northwestern Reykjanes bring your own wheels – either pedal-pushed or motor-operated. Strætó (p429) bus 89 goes from Keflavík to Garður and Sandgerði.

Garður

POP 1600

From Keflavík, if you follow Rte 41 for 9km, through the village of Garður, you'll reach beautiful wind-battered **Garðskagi headland**, one of the best places in Iceland for birdwatchers. It's a big breeding ground for seabirds, and it's often the place where migratory species first touch down. It's also possible to see seals (and maybe whales) from here, as well as superb views over the ocean to Snæfellsjökull. Two splendid **lighthouses**, one tall and one tiny, add drama, and you can get near-360-degree sea views from the tallest.

Garðskagi Museum MUSEUM
(Heritage and Maritime Museum; ☎422 7220; www.svgardur.is; Skagabraut 100; adult/child 12-16/child under 12 1000/500kr/free; ⏱1-5pm Apr-Oct; P ♿) This small museum is filled with a pleasing mishmash of boating memorabilia, farming equipment and vintage Icelandic goods. The entry fee includes access to the **Gardur Lighthouse** (The Old Lighthouse Cafe; www.facebook.com/TheOldLighthouseCafe; ⏱noon-8.30pm Jun-Sep) outside.

Campground CAMPGROUND €
(sites per person 1000kr) Right in front of Gardur Lighthouse is a primitive campground with limited facilities – washing up sinks and a shared bathroom with the Garðskagi Museum – but you can't argue with the price.

Rostin Restaurant ICELANDIC €€
(☎893 8909; Skagabraut 100; mains 2300-3450kr; ⏱11.30am-8.30pm) Located above the Garðskagi Museum, this simple space has large glass windows and awesome views out to sea, plus a nice deck for the summer months. Menu items include standard offerings like fish and chips, grilled lamb chops and burgers.

Sandgerði & Around

POP 1750

Sandgerði is an industrious fishing village, 5km south of Garður. There are pleasant beaches on the coast south of Sandgerði, and the surrounding marshes are frequented by more than 190 species of bird. About 5km south you'll find a lonely church at **Hvalsnes** that featured in a famous Icelandic hymn by Hallgrímur Pétursson (1614–74), written at the death of his young daughter, who was buried here. Two kilometres south, you can walk to the ruins of Saga Age fishing village **Básendar**, which was destroyed by a tidal wave in 1799.

There's a simple **campground** (☎854 8424; www.istay.is; Byggdavegur; sites per person 1500kr, cabins from 17,500kr; ⊙Apr-Sep; P ⓦ) that also has small cabins for rent.

Sudurnes Science & Learning Center MUSEUM
(☎423 7551/5; www.thekkingarsetur.is; Garðskagavegur; adult/child 6-15 years/ child under 6 years 600/300kr/free; ⊙10am-4pm Mon-Fri, 1-5pm Sat & Sun May-Sep, 10am-2pm Mon-Fri Oct-Apr) This scientific learning centre has a fascinating exhibit about Polar explorer Jean-Baptiste Charcot, whose ship *Pourquois Pas?* wrecked near here in 1936 (all but one sailor perished). There are original artefacts from the wreck, and memorabilia. Other displays include stuffed and jarred Icelandic creatures (look out for the walrus) and a small aquarium.

★**Vitinn** SEAFOOD €€
(☎423 7755; www.vitinn.is; Vitatorg 7; mains 2700-6900kr; ⊙11.30am-2pm & 6-9pm Mon-Sat) The nautical-themed Vitinn is not to be missed. A friendly team serves heaps of seafood (stored in tanks out back in the courtyard) in marine-fancy surrounds. The crab and shellfish bisque with a dollop of cream is delicious. Alternatively, splash out on the Icelandic lobster (langoustine) with spiced rice, fresh salad and homemade bread and garlic butter.

Southwestern Reykjanes

The southwestern tip of the Reykjanes Peninsula is a wild and interesting landscape of volcanic terrain surrounding the rift between the North American and European tectonic plates. Bubbling mud pools, an attractive lighthouse and birdwatching opportunities can also be discovered.

Visit the Southwestern Reykjanes area with your own wheels or on a private tour. There is no public transport.

⊙ Sights

If you turn off Rte 41 onto Rte 44 just outside Keflavík, you'll first pass the deserted **US military base** before reaching the fading fishing village of **Hafnir**. There's nothing much to see here – just humps and bumps in a field, thought to be a 9th-century longhouse belonging to Ingólfur Arnarson's foster brother, and the anchor of the 'ghost ship' *Jamestown,* which drifted ashore mysteriously in 1870 with a full cargo of timber but no crew.

There are bird cliffs at **Hafnaberg**, south of which you'll reach the **Bridge Between Two Continents** (Negur), where a teeny footbridge spans a sand-filled gulf between the North American and Eurasian tectonic plates.

In the far southwest of the peninsula, the landscape alternates between lava fields and wild volcanic crags and craters, thus it's been named **100 Crater Park**. Several power plants here exploit geothermal heat to produce salt from seawater and to provide electricity for the national grid.

One of the most wild and wonderful spots on the peninsula is **Valahnúkur** (Reykjanesvitavegur), where a windy road leads off Rte 425 through 13th-century lava fields. Turn right at the T-intersection and go 900m on an unpaved road to dramatic, climbable cliffs and the 1878 **Reykjanesviti Lighthouse** (near Reykjanesvitavegur).

From Valahnúkur and the nearby coast you can see the flat-topped rocky islet **Eldey**, 14km offshore, home to the world's largest gannet colony. Some claim the last great auk was killed there, though Faroese dispute this, insisting that the event occurred at Stóra Dímun. Today Eldey is a protected bird reserve.

If you take the left branch of the above T-intersection, in 500m you reach a steaming multicoloured geothermal area. This includes the **Gunnuhver** (Reykjanesvitavegur) hot spring, named after the witch-ghost Gunna, who was lured into the boiling water and trapped by a priest.

Grindavík

POP 3300

The only settlement on the south coast of Reykjanes, Grindavík is one of Iceland's most important fishing centres. Here all flimflam is rejected in favour of working jetties, cranes and warehouses, though its proximity to the Blue Lagoon and relatively inexpensive accommodation options have drawn more tourism in recent years.

Sights

Kvíkan MUSEUM
(Magma; ☎420 1190; www.visitgrindavik.is; Hafnargata 12a; adult/child 1500kr/free; ⊙10am-5pm) Grindavík's only tourist attraction is Kvíkan, a museum with two exhibits: a well-curated one on the fish-salting industry, and another about the earth's energy. It's in the same building as the information centre.

Tours

ATV Adventures QUAD-BIKE TOUR
(4x4 Adventures Iceland; ☎857 3001; www.4x4adventuresiceland.is; Tangasund; 1hr ATV tour 13,000kr, 2-3hr bike tour 10,900kr, bike rental 4/24hr 4900/6900kr) The major provider for quad-bike rides around the peninsula: explore lava fields and see shipwrecks. A driver's licence is required. Also runs cycling tours around the Blue Lagoon area and has bicycle rental.

Arctic Horses HORSE RIDING
(☎848 0143; www.arctichorses.is; Hópsheiði 16; adult/child under 14 9000/6000kr) Small, family-run outfit with horseback rides along the peninsula. The popular lighthouse tour crosses moss-covered lava fields and lasts one to 1½ hours.

Víkur Hestar HORSE RIDING
(☎691 2196; http://vikurhestar.is; Hópsheiði 16; adult/child horse-riding tours from 9000/5000kr) Tours range from one hour to five hours around the starkly beautiful local landscape.

Salty Tours TOURS
(☎820 5750; www.saltytours.is; full-day tour for up 7 people 95,000kr) Private day group tours of Reykjanes and beyond. Picks up at the airport or from Reykjavík.

Sleeping

Grindavík has solid lodging options and is just a quick drive to the Blue Lagoon, so it's an increasingly popular place to sleep over.

Mar Guesthouse GUESTHOUSE €
(☎856 5792; www.marguesthouse.is; Hafnargata 28; d without bathroom from 13,000kr, studios from 23,500kr; 📶) Some of the modern rooms and studios with kitchenettes have harbour views. Everything is tidy, staff are helpful, and there's kitchen and laundry access for all.

Guesthouse Borg GUESTHOUSE €
(☎895 8686; www.guesthouseborg.com; Borgarhraun 2; s/d without bathroom incl breakfast 9500/14,500kr; @📶) Borg is an older home in the centre of town with the cosiness of 'grandma's place'. There's a good brekkie, with cereal, bread, meat and cheese. There's also a lounge area with a TV and books, plus a kitchen and laundry access.

Tjaldsvæði Campsite CAMPGROUND €
(☎660 7323; www.visitgrindavik.is/site/grindavik-campground; Austurvegur 26; sites per adult/child 1800kr/free; ⊙mid-May–Oct) Grindavík's fresh-faced campsite near the harbour is a patch of green with good amenities, including an indoor kitchen and warm common area, plus barbecues and a playground. Electricity is 1100kr, washing machines 550kr per load. Every guest after the first pays 1500kr.

Harbour View Cabins CABIN €€
(☎773 3993; www.harbourview.is; Hópsvegur; d from 28,500kr; P📶) Next to Grindavík's campground, on a small hill overlooking the harbour, sit 10 perfectly kitted out cabins. Each sleek minimalist-designed unit has a bathroom with walk-in shower, a well-stocked kitchen and a small lounge area.

Eating

★**Bryggjan** CAFE €
(☎426 7100; www.facebook.com/bryggjancafegrindavik; Miðgarður 2; cakes/sandwiches 850/1000kr, soup 1700-2000kr; ⊙8am-10pm Mon-Fri; 📶) Facing the harbourfront, in a block of warehouses, this adorable small cafe is decorated in fishing buoys, sailing memorabilia and framed photos. It serves up homemade lobster soup and cakes (carrot, apple, chocolate and meringue), plus open-faced fish sandwiches. It's often busy, especially in summer, so expect a queue.

Papa's SEAFOOD €€
(☎426 9955; Hafnargata 28; pizzas from 1290kr, burgers from 1600kr, mains 2290kr; ⊙11.30am-9pm Mon-Fri, noon-9pm Sat & Sun) Fish and chips at Papa's are a treat, although you'll also find locals crowding in for pizza, salad, burgers and pulled-pork sandwiches. The space is pretty casual, with TV screens, wooden tables and a bar made of stacked pallets. Papa's also does deliveries.

Salthúsið SEAFOOD €€
(☎426 9700; www.salthusid.is; Stamphólsvegur 2; mains 2400-7600kr; ⊙noon-9pm mid-May–mid-Sep) The classy wooden Salthúsið specialises

in local *saltfiskur* (saltfish), which is prepared in different ways, plus there's salmon, lobster, chicken and lamb. Tuck in surrounded by red soft furnishings and cabin-style decor.

Information

Tourist Information Centre (420 1190; www.visitgrindavik.is; Hafnargata 12; 10am-5pm mid-May–mid-Sep) The helpful staff here will give you tips on the local area. It houses the Kvíkan museum upstairs.

Getting There & Away

Strætó (p429) bus 88 goes directly to Keflavík (20 minutes, two daily on weekdays). Alternatively there are daily services via Reykjanesbær, where you can connect to bus 55 and go through Keflavík and onto Keflavík International Airport (one-way adult/child 460/220kr); the journey including transfer is approximately 40 minutes.

Reykjanesfólkvangur Reserve

For a taste of Iceland's raw countryside, visit this 300-sq-km wilderness reserve, a mere 40km from Reykjavík. Established in 1975, the reserve protects the elaborate lava formations created by the dramatic Reykjanes ridge volcanoes. Its three showpieces are Kleifarvatn, a deep mineral lake with submerged hot springs and black-sand beaches; the spitting, bubbling Krýsuvík geothermal zone at Seltún; and the Southwest's largest bird cliffs, the epic Krýsuvíkurberg. The whole area is criss-crossed by walking trails. Get good maps at Keflavík, Grindavík or Hafnarfjörður tourist offices. You'll see parking turnouts at the head of the most popular walks, including the loop around Kleifarvatn, and the tracks along the craggy Sveifluháls and Núpshliðarháls ridges.

Sights & Activities

Kleifarvatn LAKE

(Krýsuvíkurvegur) This deep, brooding lake sits in a volcanic fissure, surrounded by wind-warped lava cliffs and black-sand shores. A walking trail runs around the edge, offering dramatic views and the crunch of volcanic cinders underfoot. Legend has it that a wormlike monster the size of a whale lurks below the surface – but the poor creature is running out of room, as the lake has been shrinking ever since two major earthquakes shook the area in 2000.

Seltún HOT SPRINGS

(Krýsuvíkurvegur) The volatile geothermal field Austurengjar, about 2km south of Kleifarvatn, is often called Krýsuvík after the nearby abandoned farm. At Seltún, the main sight, boardwalks meander round a cluster of seething hot springs. The mud pots and steaming sulphuric solfataras (volcanic vents) shimmer with rainbow colours from the minerals in the earth.

Grænavatn LAKE

(off Vigdisarvallavegur) Just to the north of the Seltún hot springs, this lake is an old explosion crater filled with gorgeous teal water, caused by a combination of minerals and warmth-loving algae. The gravel road to the lake may only be drivable with 4WD and could be impassible at various times of year.

Krýsuvíkurberg Cliffs BIRDWATCHING

(off Suðurstrandarvegur) About 3km south of Seltún across the Krýsuvíkurhraun lava fields, a dirt track leads down to the coast at Krýsuvíkurberg (marked on the main road as Krýsuvíkurbjarg). These sweeping black cliffs stretch for 4km and are packed with some 57,000 seabird breeding pairs in summer, from guillemots to occasional puffins. A walking path runs the length of the cliffs.

THE GOLDEN CIRCLE

Diving in glacial waters, walking the Mid-Atlantic Ridge canyon, absorbing the grandeur of the first-ever parliamentary site and watching the earth belch boiling water 40m high – the Golden Circle has it all.

The route spans roughly 300km and takes in three main sights, which are all true knockouts: Þingvellir where tectonic plates meet, Geysir where water erupts more than 100 times a day, and the roaring and staggeringly voluminous waterfall Gullfoss.

With the mega-attractions all within a couple of hours' drive from the capital, places get crowded and it can feel more commercial than other areas. Still, despite the hordes, the Golden Circle remains one of the most memorable routes on the planet. Dozens of tour buses stop here, but visiting during off-hours allows a more subdued experience. Save time for nearby activities: rock climbing, rafting and soaking in geopools, plus visiting a hydropower museum, fishing and exploring a 6500-year-old explosion crater.

Þingvellir National Park

Þingvellir National Park, 40km northeast of central Reykjavík, is Iceland's most important historical site and a place of vivid beauty. The Vikings established the world's first democratic parliament, the Alþingi (pronounced *ál-thingk-ee,* also called Alþing), here in AD 930. The meetings were conducted outdoors and, as with many Saga sites, there are only the stone foundations of ancient encampments left. The site has a superb natural setting, in an immense, fissured rift valley, caused by the meeting of the North American and Eurasian tectonic plates, with rivers and waterfalls. The country's first national park, Þingvellir was made a Unesco World Heritage Site in 2004.

History

Many of Iceland's first settlers had run-ins with royalty back in mainland Scandinavia. These chancers and outlaws decided that they could live happily without kings in the new country, and instead created district *þings* (assemblies) where justice could be served by and among local *goðar* (chieftains).

Eventually, a nationwide *þing* became necessary. Bláskógur – now Þingvellir (Parliament Fields) – lay at a crossroads by a huge fish-filled lake. It had plenty of firewood and a setting that would make even the most tedious orator dramatic, so it fitted the bill perfectly. Every important decision affecting Iceland was argued out on this plain – new laws were passed, marriage contracts were made, and even the country's religion was decided here. The annual parliament was also a great social occasion, thronging with traders and entertainers.

Over the following centuries, escalating violence between Iceland's most powerful groups led to the breakdown of law and order. Governance was surrendered to the Norwegian crown and the Alþingi was stripped of its legislative powers in 1271. It functioned solely as a courtroom until 1798, before being dissolved entirely. When it regained its powers in 1843, members voted to move the meeting place to Reykjavík.

Sights

From the park Visitor Centre (p122) on Rte 36 (parking 500kr), follow the path from the outlook down to the Lögberg (Law Rock), and the only standing structures in the great rift. You can also approach the waterfall Öxarárfoss from a parking area on Rte 36, and hike down into the rift valley from there. Or, come in on Rte 361 on the eastern edge of the site, and park on Rte 362 there (parking 300kr). Get mapped reference points at www.thingvellir.is.

Free one-hour guided tours run most days from June to August; these were at 10am and 3pm at the time of research, but check ahead at the visitor centre (p122) for the schedule.

★ Tectonic Plates CANYON, WATERFALL
(accessible via Rte 35 & Rte 361; parking 300kr)
The Þingvellir plain is situated on a tectonic-plate boundary where North America and Europe are tearing away from each other at a rate of 1mm to 18mm per year. As a result, the plain is scarred by dramatic fissures, ponds and rivers, including the great rift **Almannagjá**. An atmospheric path runs through the dramatic crevice and along the fault between the clifftop visitor centre (p122) and the Alþingi site (p120).

The river **Öxará** cuts the western plate, tumbling off its edge in a series of pretty cascades. The most impressive is **Öxarárfoss**, on the northern edge of the Alþingi site. The pool **Drekkingarhylur** was used to drown women found guilty of infanticide, adultery or other serious crimes.

There are other smaller fissures on the eastern edge of the site. During the 17th century, nine men accused of witchcraft were burned at the stake in **Brennugjá** (Burning Chasm). Nearby are the fissures of **Flosagjá** (named after a slave who jumped his way to freedom) and **Nikulásargjá** (after a drunken sheriff discovered dead in the water). The

WORTH A TRIP

HALLDÓR LAXNESS' HOUSE

Nobel Prize–winning author Halldór Laxness (1902–98) lived in Mosfellsbær all his life. His riverside home is now the **Gljúfrasteinn Laxness Museum** (☎586 8066; www.gljufrasteinn.is; Þingvallavegur, Mosfellsbær; adult/child 900kr/free; ⏰9am-5pm Jun-Aug, 10am-4pm Tue-Sun Sep-May), on the road from Reykjavík to Þingvellir (Rte 36). The author built this upper-class 1950s house and it remains intact with original furniture, writing room and Laxness' fine-art collection (needlework, sweetly, by his wife Auður). An audio tour leads you round. Look for his beloved Jaguar parked out the front.

DIY GOLDEN CIRCLE

It's very easy to tour the Golden Circle on your own (by bike or car) – plus, it's fun to tack on additional elements that suit your interests. In the Golden Circle area, signs are well marked, roads well paved and the distances relatively short (it takes about four hours to drive the loop without any add-on stops). You can also cobble some of it together by bus (and buses do go into the highlands, which are not accessible by 2WD). The excellent, free *Uppsveitir Árnessýslu* map details the region; find it at tourist offices.

The primary points of the Golden Circle are Þingvellir, Geysir and Gullfoss. DIYers can add the following elements to their tour:

Laugarvatn (p122) Located between Þingvellir and Geysir, this small lakeside town has two must-tries: Lindin (p123), an excellent Icelandic restaurant, and Fontana (p122), an upmarket geothermal spa.

Þjórsárdalur (p140) Largely untouristed, the quiet valley along the Þjórsá river is dotted with ancient Viking ruins and mysterious natural wonders such as Gjáin (p141). Ultimately, it leads up into the highlands (a main route to Landmannalaugar, the starting point of the famous Laugavegurinn (near Laugavegur hut) hike).

Reykholt (p128) & Flúðir (p129) On your way south from Gullfoss, you can go river-rafting (p128) on the Hvítá river from Reykholt or swing through the geothermal area of Flúðir, for its beautiful natural spa and to pick up fresh veggies for your evening meal.

Eyrarbakki (p134) & Stokkseyri (p135) South of Selfoss, these two seaside townships are strikingly different from others nearby. Feast on seafood, peruse seasonal local galleries and birdwatch in nearby marshes.

Kaldidalur Corridor (p218) Not all rentals are allowed to drive this bumpy dirt track (Rte 550), but if you have a sanctioned vehicle, you can explore this isolated road that curves around hulking glaciers. It starts near Þingvellir and ends near Húsafell, so if you have time, do the traditional Golden Circle in reverse, then head westward, where many more adventures await.

Kerlingarfjöll (p363) You'll need a 4WD (or to go by bus) to travel beyond Gullfoss, but if you have one, it's worth continuing on to this highland reserve, a hiker haven, about two hours beyond the falls.

southern end of Nikulásargjá is known as **Peningagjá** (Chasm of Coins) for the thousands of coins tossed into it by visitors (an act forbidden these days). There are a few different car parks around the sights; a parking fee may be payable at some of them.

★Alþingi Site LANDMARK

(accessible via Rte 36 and Rte 362) Near the dramatic Almannagjá fault and fronted by a boardwalk is the **Lögberg** (Law Rock), where the Alþingi (Parliament) convened annually. This was where the *lögsögumaður* (law speaker) recited the existing laws to the assembled parliament (one-third each year). After Iceland's conversion to Christianity, the site shifted to the very foot of the Almannagjá cliffs, which acted as a natural amplifier, broadcasting the voices of the speakers across the assembled crowds. That site is marked by the Icelandic flag.

Þingvallakirkja CHURCH

(☎482 2660; www.thingvellir.is; parking 300kr; ⏲9am-5pm Jun-Aug) Behind the Þingvallabær farmhouse, Þingvallakirkja is one of Iceland's first churches. The original was consecrated in the 11th century, but the current wooden building dates from 1859. Inside are several bells from earlier churches, a 17th-century wooden pulpit and a painted altarpiece from 1834. Independence-era poets Jónas Hallgrímsson and Einar Benediktsson are buried in the cemetery behind the church. Use the car park at the end of Rte 363, cross the Óxará river bridge and follow the footpath on the left.

Þingvallabær HISTORIC BUILDING

(accessible via Rte 363; parking 300kr) The little farmhouse in the bottom of the rift, Þingvallabær was built for the 1000th anniversary of the Alþing in 1930 by state architect Guðjón Samúelsson. It's now used as the park warden's office and prime minister's summer house. Use the car park at the end of Rte 363, cross the Óxará river bridge and follow the footpath on the left.

Búðir RUINS

Straddling both sides of the Öxará river are the ruins of various temporary camps called *búðir* (literally 'booths'). These stone foundations were covered during Alþingi sessions and were where parliament-goers camped. They also acted like stalls at today's music festivals, selling beer, food and vellum to the assembled crowds. Most of the remains date from the 17th and 18th centuries; the largest, and one of the oldest, is **Biskupabúð**, which belonged to the bishops of Iceland and is located north of the church.

Þingvallavatn LAKE

(accessible via Rte 361; parking 300kr) Filling much of the rift plain, Þingvallavatn is Iceland's largest lake, at 84 sq km. Pure glacial water from Langjökull filters through bedrock for 40km before emerging here. It's joined by the hot spring **Vellankatla**, which spouts from beneath the lava field on the northeastern shore. Þingvallavatn is an important refuelling stop for migrating birds (including the great northern diver, barrow's golden-eye and harlequin duck).

Weirdly, the waters here are full of *bleikja* (Arctic char) that have been isolated for so long that they've evolved into four subspecies. It's possible to submerge into the depths of the the lake with Dive Silfra and potentially see them up close.

Ljósafoss Power Station MUSEUM

(Ljósafossstöð; ☎896 7407; www.landsvirkjun.com; Ljósafoss; ⊙10am-5pm Jun-Aug, shorter hours Sep-May) FREE The 1937 Ljósafoss Power Station catches the outflow of lake Úlfljótsvatn and turns it into electricity. In 2016, an elaborate state-of-the-art multimedia exhibition called Powering the Future opened, bringing the principles of electricity, hydropower, and geothermal and renewable energy to life.

Activities

Fishing

Check in with park centres for lake fishing rules (some areas are off limits, and any imported equipment must be disinfected), and get a permit (2000kr per pole per day; May to mid-September) from the Information Centre. The fishing card offering fishing access to multiple locations (www.veidikortid.is) also covers part of Þingvallavatn.

Diving & Snorkelling

One of the most otherworldly activities in Iceland is donning a scuba mask (or snorkel) and dry suit and exploring the crystalline **Silfra fissure**, one of the cracks in the rift valley. There's also a rift, **Davíðsgjá**, out in Þingvallavatn lake, which is harder to reach. You must book ahead with a Reykjavík dive operator like **Dive Silfra** (accessible via Rte 363; snorkeling/diving from 13,900/34,900kr; ⊙9am-6pm). People with their own equipment must have licences, dive in groups of at least two, and buy the permit (1000kr) from the visitor centre (p122) or www.thingvellir.is

Horse Riding

In the valley on the Rte 36 approach from Reykjavík, you can go horse riding and mountain biking with **Laxnes** (☎566 6179; www.laxnes.is; Mosfellsbær; 2hr ride 11,900kr).

Sleeping

There is camping in Þingvellir National Park, and hotels, guesthouses and cabin accommodation around the southern part of Þingvallavatn lake.

Þingvellir Campsite CAMPGROUND €

(www.thingvellir.is; Rte 361; sites per adult/tent/child 1300/300kr/free; ⊙Jun-Sep) A primitive campground opposite the information centre (p122), where there are bathrooms and camping supplies.

Ljósafossskóli Hostel GUESTHOUSE €

(☎699 2720; www.ljosafossskoli.is; Brúarási 1, Ljósafossskóli; d without bathroom from 10,500kr; P 📶) Many of the good, simple rooms in this modern, converted schoolhouse have excellent lake and mountain views. A particularly unusual feature is the full-sized sport hall (with basketball hoops) on the ground floor, which guests are free to use. Breakfast is 1500kr. Find it 28km south of Þingvellir and 21km north of Selfoss, on the edge of Úlfljótsvatn lake.

Útilífsmiðstöð Skáta Úlfljótsvatni CAMPGROUND €

(☎482 2674; www.ulfljotsvatn.is; off Rte 360, Úlfljótsvatn; sites per adult/child 1600kr/free, dm incl breakfast 4400kr; P 📶 ☒) This scouts centre has camping in summer and basic dorm huts in winter. It offers a full program of lakefront activities and extensive playgrounds. Find it on the southern side of Þingvellir's lake, Þingvallavatn. There's a small camp shop on-site.

Lake Thingvellir Cottages COTTAGE €€

(☎892 7110; www.lakethingvellir.is; Heiðarás; cottages 19,500kr, plus per person per night 2500kr;

(P) Four modern pine cottages with kitchenettes and views of the lake sit near the national-park entrance along Rte 36. Two-night minimum stay June to September.

Ion Adventure Hotel BOUTIQUE HOTEL €€€
(482 3415; www.ioniceland.is; Nesjavellir 801; d from 44,000kr; P@) Ion is hip, ultra modern and remote. Using sustainable practices throughout, it has a geothermal pool, organic spa, and a **restaurant** (482 3415; www.ioniceland.is; Ion Luxury Adventure Hotel, Nesjavellir við Þingvallavatn; mains lunch 2600-4500kr, dinner 4000-12,000kr, 3-course dinner from 9900kr; 11.30am-10pm) with slow-food local ingredients. The uber-cool bar has designer cardboard lampshades and floor-to-ceiling windows for Northern Lights watching. Rooms are a tad small, but kitted out impeccably.

Hótel Grimsborgir HOTEL €€€
(555 7878; www.grimsborgir.com; Ásborgir 30; d incl breakfast from 58,500kr, 2-bedroom apt 66,000kr;) Hótel Grimsborgir offers fully kitted-out luxury rooms, suites and apartments with terraces or balconies, flat-screen TVs, hardwood floors and high-end soft furnishings. There's an on-site restaurant serving Icelandic and international dishes. Find it on Rte 36, 5.5km south of Ljósafossstöð, and 5km north of the junction with Rte 35.

Eating

There is a small **cafe** (Rte 36, Þingvellir Information Centre; grilled sandwiches from 400kr; 9am-10pm Apr-Oct, shorter hours Nov-Mar) with a mini-mart at the Þingvellir Information Centre, serving sandwiches, hot dogs and soup, but the closest proper restaurant is at Ion Adventure Hotel. Otherwise bring your own food.

Information

Þingvellir Visitor Centre (Gestastofa; 482 3613; off Rte 36; 9am-7pm Jun-Aug, to 6.30pm Sep-May) Sitting above the Almannagjá rift is a basic visitor centre with restrooms (200kr per visit).

Þingvellir Information Centre (Leirar Þjónustumiðstöð; www.thingvellir.is; Rte 36; 9am-10pm May-Aug, to 6pm Sep-Apr) On the northern side of the lake, this is a larger information centre with plenty of helpful info, plus a cafe and small store.

Getting There & Away

The easiest way to get here is with a rental car. Parking per vehicle costs between 300kr and 750kr.

No buses currently stop here, but Þingvellir is a sight on almost every tour of the Golden Circle.

Laugarvatn

POP 190

Laugarvatn (Hot Springs Lake) is fed not only by streams running from the misty fells behind it, but by the hot spring Vígðalaug, famous since medieval times. A village, also called Laugarvatn, sits on the lake's western shore in the lap of the foothills. It is one of the more popular bases in the Golden Circle area.

Activities & Tours

★ **Fontana** GEOTHERMAL POOL
(486 1400; www.fontana.is; Hverabraut 1; adult/child 3800/2000kr; 10am-11pm early Jun-late Aug, 11am-10pm late Aug-early Jun) This swanky lakeside soaking spot boasts three modern wading pools, and a cedar-lined steam room that's fed by a naturally occurring vent below. The cool cafe (buffet lunch/dinner 2900/3900kr) has lake views. You can rent towels or swimsuits (800kr each) and dressing gowns (1500kr) if you left yours at home.

Laugarvatn Swimming Pool GEOTHERMAL POOL
(480 3041; Hverabraut 2; adult/child 1000/550kr; 10am-9pm Mon-Fri, to 6pm Sat & Sun Jun–mid-Aug, shorter hours mid-Aug–May) If you want skip the Fontana hot-pot hoopla, there's a regular geothermal swimming pool, hot-pots and sauna next door that costs a third of the price, with none of the glitz.

Laugarvatn Adventures ROCK CLIMBING, CAVING
(862 5614; www.caving.is; Laugarvatnshellir; caving trips from 9900kr; 10am-6pm) Runs two- to three-hour caving and rock-climbing trips in the hills around town. Tours often start from Laugarvatnshellir – a house built into the rock and cave within, where two families have lived the past 100 years.

Sleeping

Laugarvatn HI Hostel HOSTEL €
(486 1215; www.laugarvatnhostel.is; Laugarvatnsvegur; dm/d without bathroom 5100/9900kr, d/t/q 14,200/16,100/20,300kr; Feb-Nov; P@) This large, clean and friendly hostel is housed in a renovated two-storey building with plenty of kitchen space (great lake views while washing up or from the dining room). There's also a pool table, bar and breakfast buffet (for an additional 1500kr), plus a room discount for HI members.

Laugarvatn Campsite CAMPGROUND €
(Dalbraut; sites per adult/child 1300/700kr; ⊙late May–mid-Sep; P) By the highway just outside the village, this campground is a plain grassy expanse with some tree protection and portable toilets.

★**Héraðsskólinn** HOSTEL, GUESTHOUSE €€
(☎537 8060; www.heradsskolinn.is; 840 Laugarvatn; dm/d/q without bathroom from 4700/11,100/23,000kr, d with bathroom 18,500kr; P wifi) A beautifully unique lakeside boutique (originally built in 1928 by Guðjón Samúelsson) identifiable by its distinctive peaked green roofs. The interiors are sleek retro, with subtle nods to its old schoolhouse days. Design features include wooden desks, vintage maps and '50s-style chairs. It offers both private rooms with shared bathrooms (some sleep up to six) and dorms.

★**Efstidalur II** GUESTHOUSE €€
(☎486 1186; www.efstidalur.is; Efstidalur 2, Bláskógabyggð; s/d/tr incl breakfast from 19,800/24,200/34,200kr; P wifi) Located 12km northeast of Laugarvatn on a working dairy farm, Efstidalur offers wonderfully welcoming digs, tasty meals and amazing ice cream. Adorable semi-detached cottages have brilliant views of hulking Hekla, and the **restaurant** (☎486 1186; www.efstidalur.is; Efstidalur 2; ice cream per scoop 500kr, mains 2250-5800kr; ⊙ice cream bar 10am-10pm, restaurant 11.30am-10pm; P wifi) serves beef from the farm and trout from the lake. The ice-cream bar scoops farm ice cream and has windows looking into the dairy barn.

Galleri Laugarvatn Guesthouse GUESTHOUSE €€
(☎486 1016; www.gallerilaugarvatn.is; Háholt 1; d with/without bathroom from 18,800/15,600kr, tw without bathroom 22,800kr; wifi) At the eastern end of town, Galleri Laugarvatn has simply decorated rooms, with white walls and natural-toned bed linens. Each is well kitted out with a hairdryer, kettle and refrigerator. Some rooms have terraces with awesome mountain views. Breakfast costs 1600kr.

Golden Circle Apartments APARTMENT €€
(☎537 8060; www.goldencircleapartments.is; Laugarbraut 1; 1-/2-/3-bedroom apt from 22,400/28,400/47,200kr; P wifi) Several bland, white block buildings stepping up the slope next to Laugarvatn lake contain spacious, modern apartments with full kitchens. It's convenient for staying over in the Golden Circle area, as the name suggests.

Eating & Drinking

Good Burger BURGERS €
(☎666 1234; Dalbraut 6; burgers from 1100kr; ⊙11am-9pm) Serving the best burgers for miles, this simple joint has only four types of flavoursome beef patties. Choose them small, medium or large (like really large!). The Aruba burger (with an onion ring on top of the patty) is our choice. Veggies, bacon, cheese, Béarnaise sauce and fries can be ordered as extras. Get Boli beer and soda on tap.

★**Lindin** ICELANDIC €€
(☎486 1262; www.laugarvatn.is; Lindarbraut 2; mains 2200-5600kr; ⊙noon-10pm May-Sep, shorter hours Oct-Apr; P wifi) Owned by Baldur, an affable, celebrated chef, Lindin could be the best local restaurant. In a sweet little silver house, with simple decor and wooden tables, the restaurant faces the lake and is purely gourmet, with high-concept Icelandic fare featuring local or wild-caught ingredients. Order everything from soup to an amazing reindeer burger. Book ahead for dinner in high season.

Galleri Laugarvatn Cafe CAFE
(www.gallerilaugarvatn.is; Háholt 1; menu items from 950kr; ⊙8am-6pm Thu-Tue) Simple cafe with a nice outdoor terrace, serving good coffee plus hot-spring-baked rye bread with smoked trout or brie. Soup, waffles, cookies and muffins also available.

Shopping

Gallerí Laugarvatn ARTS & CRAFTS
(☎486 1016; www.gallerilaugarvatn.is; Háholt 1; ⊙8am-6pm Thu-Tue) Local handicrafts, from Icelandic sweets and ironwork to ceramics and woollens.

Samkaup Strax FOOD & DRINKS
(www.samkaup.is; Dalbraut 8; ⊙9am-9pm Mon-Fri, 10am-9pm Sat & Sun) Groceries, camping supplies and a fast-food counter serving hot dogs and burgers. ATM outside.

Getting There & Away

Strætó (p429) Bus 73 from Selfoss (adult/child 1840/880kr, 1¼ hours, two to three daily Monday to Friday, one Saturday and Sunday) stops in Laugarvatn.

Reykjavík Excursions (p429) Runs the 'Iceland On Your Own' service between Reykjavík and Akureyri, stopping at Laugarvatn en route. There's one daily mid-June to early September, leaving at 8am from Reykjavík's BSÍ bus terminal. Fares cost 17,900kr all the way to Akureyri, or a one-way fare to Laugarvatn costs 3500kr.

GIEDRIIUS/SHUTTERSTOCK ©

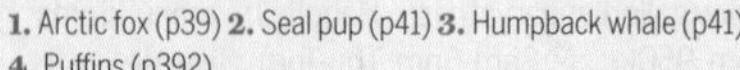

1. Arctic fox (p39) **2.** Seal pup (p41) **3.** Humpback whale (p41) **4.** Puffins (p392)

MAKSIMILIAN/SHUTTERSTOCK ©

2

EMKA74/SHUTTERSTOCK ©

4

Wildlife Watching

Iceland's magical natural realm is the playground for some headlining acts, including breaching whales, basking seals, elusive Arctic foxes and bumper bird life (the scene stealer: cute, clownish puffins, of course). The supporting cast of wandering sheep and wild-maned horses are still impossibly photogenic against a cinematic, mountainous backdrop.

The bird life in Iceland is abundant, especially during the warmest months when migrating species arrive to nest. On coastal cliffs and islands around the country, you can see a mind-boggling array of seabirds. Posted coastal hikes offer access to some of the most populous bird cliffs in the world – don't miss a chance to cavort with puffins (p392).

Whale watching has become one of Iceland's most cherished pastimes – boats depart throughout the year (limited service in the colder months) to catch a glimpse of these lurking beasts as they wave their fins and spray the air. The northern waters around Húsavík and Akureyri are a haven for feeding creatures (usually minke and fin species); travellers who are short on time can hop on a boat that departs directly from downtown Reykjavík (p70). In winter, it's possible to see orcas crash through the frigid waters – the best point of departure is the Snæfellsnes Peninsula (p219).

BEST WILDLIFE-WATCHING SPOTS

Vestmannaeyjar (p171) Zoom between islets as you snap photos of a Peterson Field Guide's worth of bird life.

Borgarfjörður Eystri (p339) It's like you've died and gone to puffin heaven, where encounters with these clumsy birds are up close and personal.

Húsavík (p313) Sample Iceland's original flavour of whale watching at this charming fishing village. There are tours aplenty, especially in summer.

Geysir

One of Iceland's most famous tourist attractions, Geysir (*gay*-zeer; literally 'gusher') is the original hot-water spout after which all other geysers are named. It sits in the Haukadalur geothermal area – a valley of hot springs with translucent blue pools, mud pots and colourful mineral details. Watch your step, some natural water features hover around the 100°C mark.

The **Great Geysir** has dramatically ejected water for around 800 years. In the year 2000 (after an earthquake), the Geysir erupted more than 120m into the sky. But the geyser goes through dormant periods and at the time of writing it was considered inactive. No matter, the very active **Strokkur** (Biskupstungnabraut) FREE geyser nearby still performs every five to 10 minutes, typically shooting a sizeable 15m to 30m in height before crashing back into the cavern below. Strokkur, like all hot geysers, is caused by water meeting magma-heated rock, then boiling and erupting under pressure. Stand downwind only if you want a shower.

Tours

Geysir Hestar HORSE RIDING
(☎847 1046; www.geysirhestar.com; Kjóastaðir 2; ⏲1/2/3hr rides 10,000/15,000/18,000kr) Four kilometres east of Geysir at Kjóastaðir horse farm, this outfit offers horse riding in the area as well as along Hvítá river canyon to Gullfoss, with trips for all skill levels. It also has great lodging, guesthouse rooms (from 8600kr without bathroom) or a cottage (sleeping up to six guests from 38,000kr).

Iceland Safari DRIVING
(☎896 4019; www.icelandsafari.com; Golden Circle bus tours per person from 9900kr, super-Jeep tours per person from 38,000kr) Super-Jeep tours and minibus tours around the southwest.

Sleeping

Gljasteinn Skálinn CABIN, GUESTHOUSE €
(☎486 8757; www.gljasteinn.is; Myrkholt; dm adult/child 6500/4000kr, d without bathroom 11,000kr; 📶) This beautiful farm in the widening sweep of the valley between Geysir and Gullfoss has a clutch of tidy houses, one of which has sleeping-bag accommodation dorms (four beds each) and doubles with shared bathrooms, plus a kitchen and living room. It also has cabins with dorm beds in the highlands on the Kjölur route (F35).

Skjól Camping CAMPGROUND €
(☎899 4541; www.skjolcamping.com; Kjóastaðir, near Biskupstungnabraut; sites per adult/child 1500kr/free; ⏲mid-May–mid-Sep; 📶) Field camping 3.5km northeast of Geysir, next to Kjóastaðir horse farm. Electricity for campers is 900kr, showers are 400kr. There's also a summertime bar on-site serving Scandinavian larger, plus pizzas and main dishes.

Geysir Campground CAMPGROUND €
(Biskupstungnabraut; adult/child 1800/500kr; 📶) Almost opposite the Geysir Centre is a campground with laundry and shower facilities (400kr per shower) and a kids' play area.

★ **Hótel Geysir** HOTEL €€
(☎480 6800; www.hotelgeysir.is; Biskupstungnabraut; s/d incl breakfast from 18,000/22,900kr; P @ 📶) This four-star, 77-room hotel is minimalist cool. The facade has an entirely wooden front with only a small single doorway, which opens into a grand lobby, and the relics of the walls from the original building – once a Glima (Scandinavian martial art used by the Vikings) training facility. B&W photography of historic athletes decorates the walls.

There's a restaurant serving a daily buffet (4200kr) from noon until late. At the time of writing, a new spa was being planned. It's located next to the Geysir Center.

Mengi GUESTHOUSE €€
(☎780 1414; www.mengi-kjarnholt.com; Kjarnholt; d without bathroom from 17,500kr; P 📶) This freshly renovated farmhouse in the countryside 10km south of Geysir has 10 rooms with sweeping pastoral views. Each is stylish with colourful artwork, wooden floors and crisp white sheets and walls. The on-site bar and hang-out space can be used by guests and there's a shared geothermal hot tub.

Litli Geysir HOTEL €€
(☎480 6800; www.geysircenter.is; Biskupstungnabraut; s/d incl breakfast from 19,600/21,500kr; P 📶) This simple, modern hotel is part of the vast Geysir Center and offers tidy rooms, some with good countryside and Geysir views. There's also a hot tub, sauna and lounge. It's next to the Geysir Hotel.

Eating & Drinking

Geysir Center FOOD & SHOPPING
(☎519 6020; www.geysircenter.com; Biskupstungnabraut; ⏲9am-10pm Jun-Aug, to 6pm Sep-May; 📶 👪) This large centre has been erected to corral the masses across the street from

the geysers. Here you'll find a restaurant named Kantína, a cafe and ice-cream shop, and Supa (a fast-food soup outlet), plus a souvenir shop of mall-like proportions with Icelandic name brands. There are also bathroom facilities here.

Getting There & Away

Reykjavík Excursions (p429) runs the 'Iceland On Your Own' service between Reykjavík and Geysir, which continues on to Gullfoss and then Akureyri. There's one daily mid-June to early September, leaving at 8am from Reykjavík's BSÍ bus terminal. Fares cost 17,900kr all the way to Akureyri, with around a 30-minute stop at big sights, so you can get off the bus and explore. A one-way fare to Geysir costs 4800kr per person; the journey takes roughly two hours.

All Golden Circle tours stop here.

Gullfoss

Situated on the Hvítá River, the mesmerising and voluminous **Gullfoss** (Golden Falls; www.gullfoss.is; Rte 35/Kjalvegur) FREE tumbles down a two-tiered drop into a rugged canyon. Each day, thousands of gallons (around 80 cubic meters per second) of water plummet 32m, before continuing their charging journey along a narrow chasm. On sunny days, when the waterfall's mist hits the rays, it's possible to spy rainbows. In winter the water often twinkles as the light hits ice particles.

It's one of the most easily accessible falls, with a large parking area and two access points by car, one from the Gullfoss tourist information centre and the other road to a lower viewing point overlooking Gullfoss, reserved for disabled access.

History

Visited since 1875, the falls came within a hair's breadth of destruction during the 1920s, when a team of foreign investors wanted to dam the Hvítá river for a hydroelectric project. The landowner, Tómas Tómasson, refused to sell to them, but the developers went behind his back and obtained permission directly from the government. Tómasson's daughter, Sigríður, walked (barefoot!) to Reykjavík to protest, even threatening to throw herself into the waterfall if the development went ahead. Thankfully, the investors failed to pay the lease, the agreement was nullified, and the falls escaped destruction. Gullfoss was donated to the nation in 1975 and has been a nature reserve ever since.

Sleeping & Eating

Hótel Gullfoss HOTEL €€

(486 8979; www.hotelgullfoss.is; Brattholt; d incl breakfast 20,000kr;) A few kilometres south of the falls, Hótel Gullfoss is a stylish bungalow hotel. Its clean en suite rooms overlook the moors (get one facing the valley) and all have tea-and-coffee-making facilities and private bathrooms. There are two hot-pots and an on-site restaurant (mains 2500kr to 4900kr) with sweeping views.

Tourist Information Centre CAFE €

(www.gullfoss.is; Kjalvegur/Rte 35; menu items from 990kr; 9am-9pm Jun-Aug, to 6.30pm Sep-May;) Above Gullfoss, the small tourist information centre boasts a large souvenir shop and a cafe serving coffee and a good selection of soups, salads, sandwiches and cakes.

Getting There & Away

Gullfoss is usually the final stop on a typical Golden Circle tour. Those wanting more adventure (and who are travelling with their own 4WD wheels) can continue along Rte F35 beyond the falls (the Kjölur route p359) for more of Iceland's raw beauty and the highlands. The first 14.8km is paved and doable in a sedan, after which a higher suspension is necessary; remember that on all F roads a 4WD is required.

Reykjavík Excursions (p429) runs the 'Iceland On Your Own' service between Reykjavík and Geysir, which continues on to Gullfoss and then Akureyri. There's one daily from mid-June to early September, departing at 8am from Reykjavík's BSÍ bus terminal. Fares cost 17,900kr all the way to Akureyri, with around a 30-minute stop at big sights, so you can get off the bus and explore. A one-way fare to Gullfoss from Reykjavik costs 5000kr; the journey takes roughly 2½ hours.

Hvítá River Valley (Gullfoss to Selfoss)

If you're completing the Golden Circle in the traditional direction, then the route from Gullfoss back to the Ring Road at Selfoss will be the final stage of your trip. Along the way you'll find plenty to lure you to stop. Most people follow surfaced Rte 35, which passes through Reykholt, with its river rafting. You can also detour slightly to Flúðir with its geothermal greenhouses and hot spring, and Skálholt, once Iceland's religious powerhouse.

If you'd like to continue east rather than return to Reykjavík, the western Þjórsárdalur area is the next valley of interesting sights.

Reykholt

POP 100

The rural township of Reykholt – one of several Reykholts around the country – is centred on the hot spring Reykjahver and has a geothermal pool. For visitors the main attraction, however, is the spectacular and atmospherically deep Hvítá river – South Iceland's centre for white-water rafting.

Tours

Arctic Rafting RAFTING TOUR
(☎562 7000; www.arcticrafting.com; Drumboddsstaðir; rafting/rafting & horse riding/rafting & ATV tours per person from 19,000/30,000/34,000kr; ⊙mid-May–mid-Sep) At the end of a dirt road is this activity centre, with changing facilities and a bar. It offers a full range of Hvítá river rafting and combination (horse-riding, quad-bike, beer-tasting) tours lasting three to four hours. Reykjavík pick-up available. Its Reykjavík office is at Arctic Adventures (p72). Children must be 11 years or older, but go half-price.

Iceland Riverjet BOAT TOUR
(☎562 7000; www.icelandriverjet.com; Drumboddsstaðir; speed boat/Golden Circle & speed boat per person 14,900/20,000kr; ⊙mid-Apr–Sep) Sharing an activity centre with Arctic Rafting, Iceland Riverjet offers 40-minute jet-boat rides that zip along the Hvítá. The company also offers pick-up and combo tours with the Golden Circle. Minimum age eight years old; kids go half-price.

Sleeping

Fellskot Guesthouse GUESTHOUSE €
(☎899 8616; www.fellskot.com; off Biskuptungnbraut/Rte 35, Fellskot 2 Farm; d/f without bathroom 13,700/19,000kr; P 🛜) This sweet farmhouse 2.5km north of Reykholt, just off Rte 35, makes a cosy base, featuring comfortable rooms with country views and a shared kitchen space. Guests are welcome to pat the horses.

Við Faxa CAMPGROUND €
(☎774 7440; Faxavegur; sites per person 1200kr) Overlooking the scenic Faxi waterfall, this campsite and small restaurant-cafe is set in a beautiful location. There's no kitchen, but the cafe serves fish and chips, soup, burgers, pizzas and lamb chops (10am to 10pm, dishes 1600kr to 3800kr). Electricity is 1000kr.

★**Fagrilundur Guesthouse** B&B €€
(☎486 8701; www.fagrilundur.is; Skólabraut 1; s/d without bathroom 13,700/17,500kr, 4-person f with bathroom 23,000kr, all incl breakfast; 🛜) A flower-pot-lined walk through the forest leads to a fairy-tale wooden cottage. Cosy rooms have patterned quilts and there's a shared porch. The attentive owners offer a warm welcome, celebrated breakfasts and loads of local advice.

★**Buubble Hotel** TENTED CAMP €€€
(www.buubble.com; Blaskogabyggd, near Reykholt; bubbles from 32,900kr) This once-in-a-lifetime sleeping experience offers you a clear bubble tent in the countryside near the Golden Circle. Recline and watch the midnight sun or, in winter, look for the aurora borealis. A small, modern hut has bathrooms and a kitchen. Each bubble can accommodate two adults and one child under 12. Prices are high, but the experience is unique.

★**The White House** B&B €€
(☎660 7866; Dalbraut; d with bathroom incl breakfast from 18,500kr; P ⊖ 🛜 🐾) In a quiet residential area, this big white wooden house is immaculate – and looks like a building straight out of the US. Classic design is used throughout, with wooden floors, neutral tones and crisp white bedspreads. There are six rooms of varying sizes; the whole house sleeps 12 to 14 and can be booked out for groups. There's also a hot tub.

Eating

Friðheimar CAFE €€
(☎486 8894; www.fridheimar.is; Friðheimar, off Rte 35; dishes from 2200kr; ⊙noon-6pm) This farm is a surreal sight: huge, bright greenhouses grow tomatoes and a range of other crops throughout the year using geothermal energy. Staff sell the produce and offer a good buffet lunch of tomato soup, cucumber salsa and fresh bread. It also has reservation-only greenhouse tours for groups of 10 or more, and reservation-only horse shows for groups of 15 or more.

Café Mika INTERNATIONAL €€
(☎486 1110; https://mika.is; Skólabraut 4; mains 1950-7000kr; ⊙11.30am-9pm; 🛜) Café Mika is popular with locals for its sizeable menu, outdoor pizza oven, sandwiches and Icelandic mains. The roasted langoustines (lobster) with garlic butter is recommended. For an extra treat, try the homemade chocolates.

Getting There & Away

From Selfoss, take Strætó (p429) bus 72 or 73 (adult/child 2300/1100k, 45 minutes, two daily Monday to Friday, one daily Sunday) to Reykholt; bus 73 also has a Saturday service.

Check the Strætó website or download the app to purchase tickets in advance. Bus drivers do not cary change.

Skálholt

An important religious centre, **Skálholt** (☎486 8870; www.skalholt.is; Skálholtskirkjuvegur; museum entry 500kr; 9am-6pm mid-May–mid-Sep, to 5pm mid-Sep–mid-May) FREE was one of two bishoprics (the other was Hólar in the north) that ruled Iceland's souls from the 11th to the 18th centuries. It rose to prominence under Gissur the White, the driving force behind the Christianisation of Iceland. The Catholic bishopric lasted until the Reformation in 1550, when Bishop Jón Arason and his two sons were executed by order of the Danish king. Skalhólt continued as a Lutheran centre until 1797, when the bishopric shifted to Reykjavík.

Unfortunately, the great cathedral that once stood at Skálholt was destroyed by a major earthquake in the 18th century. Today there's a modern Protestant theological centre with a **visitor centre**, a **turf-house re-creation** of Þorlagsbúð, and a prim **church** with a **museum** in the basement containing the stone sarcophagus of Bishop Páll Jónsson (bishop from 1195 to 1211). According to *Páls Saga*, an Old Norse account of the bishop's life, the earth was wracked by storms and earthquakes when he died. Spookily, a huge storm broke at the exact moment that his coffin was reopened in 1956.

The centre also hosts summertime concerts and has a small restaurant serving basic meals.

There is no public transport to Skálholt. Laugarás (3km from Skálholt) is served by Strætó (p429) buses 72 (two daily Monday to Friday, one Sunday) and 73 (two to four daily Monday to Friday, one daily Saturday and Sunday) from Selfoss (adult/child 2300/1100k, 40 minutes), Flúðir and Reykholt.

Slakki Petting Zoo ZOO
(☎486 8783; www.facebook.com/slakki; Laugarás; adult/child 1200/600kr; 11am-6pm) For more than 20 years, this petting zoo in small-town Iceland has been a popular hang-out for families passing through the village of Laugarás. Orphaned foxes live in the outside garden, locked away from goats, bunnies, parrots, rodents and kittens.

Sólheimar Eco-Village GUESTHOUSE €€
(☎422 6000; www.solheimar.is; Rte 354, off Rte 35, Sólheimar; dm 11,500kr, d with/without bathroom from 18,700/22,500kr, apt from 28,600kr; P) Sólheimar Eco-Village is a collection of homes and greenhouses utilising ecologically sound practices. The two guesthouses in the village offer clean rooms, dorms or doubles with private or shared bathrooms and one apartment suitable for four people. There are shared kitchens and living areas, as well as a nice pool and hot tub.

Engi MARKET
(☎486 8913; www.beintfrabyli.is/engi; Ferjuvegur, Laugarás; noon-6pm Fri, Sat & Sun Jun-Aug) Laugarás is essentially a community of farms, many of which sell their fresh organic produce on-site. Engi regularly offers a selection of top-grade fruits and vegetables grown in greenhouses. Adorable souvenirs – including rocks painted like ladybirds – are also for sale. It's 3km southeast of Skálholt.

Kerið

Around 15.5km north of Selfoss on Rte 35, Kerið (Biskupstungnabraut; adult/child 400kr/free; 8.30am-9pm Jun-Aug, daylight hours Sep-May) is a 6500-year-old explosion crater with vivid red and sienna earth and containing an ethereal green lake. Björk once performed a concert from a floating raft in the middle. Visitors can easily walk around the entire rim (it takes between 10 and 20 minutes), and go down to the lake in the crater.

Flúðir

POP 790

The approaches to little agrarian Flúðir become increasingly dramatic, with interesting rock buttes rising from the rolling green plains. Flúðir is known throughout Iceland for its geothermal greenhouses that grow the majority of the country's mushrooms, and it's also a popular weekend getaway for Reykjavikers with private cottages. More recently it's become a super stop for good food and for its beautifully refurbished hot springs.

Activities

★**Gamla Laugin** GEOTHERMAL POOL
(Secret Lagoon; ☎555 3351; www.secretlagoon.is; Hvammsvegur; adult/child 2800kr/free; 10am-10pm May-Sep, noon-8pm Oct-Apr) Soak in this

broad, calm geothermal pool, mist rising and ringed by natural rocks. The walking trail along the edge of this lovely hot spring passes the local river and a series of sizzling vents and geysers. Surrounding meadows fill with wildflowers in summer. Increasingly popular, the lagoon gets packed with tour-bus crowds in mid-afternoon, so come earlier or later.

Sleeping

Grund – Guesthouse Flúðir GUESTHOUSE €€
(Gistiheimilið Flúðum; ☎565 9196; www.gistingfludir.is; Skeiða-og Hrunamannavegur/Rte 30; d with/without bathroom incl breakfast 16,000/22,000kr; P 📶) This adorable guesthouse has five cosyrooms filled with antiques, and a wing of modern rooms with private bathrooms and decks with mountain views. The popular restaurant here prides itself on offering fresh local food.

Flúðir Camping CAMPGROUND €
(www.tjaldmidstod.is; off Skeiða-og Hrunamannavegur/Rte 30; sites per adult/child 1750/1000kr; ⏱Jun-Sep, weather dependent May-Oct; P 📶) Well-located campground with electricity hook-ups (100kr), laundry facilities (300kr per load) and wi-fi (500kr per 75 hours).

Eating & Drinking

Sindri Bakari Cafe CAFE €
(☎859 5417; www.facebook.com/sindribakari; Sneiðin; pastries from 380kr; ⏱9am-9pm) Good little cafe with a pleasant outdoor patio and marquee for eating in fine weather. It serves pastries, cakes, hot soups, coffee and sandwiches.

★**Minilik Ethiopian Restaurant** ETHIOPIAN €€
(☎846 9798; www.minilik.is; Skeiða-og Hrunamannavegur, Rte 30; mains 2000-2500kr; ⏱6-9pm Tue-Fri, 2-9pm Sat & Sun; 🌿) In the most unlikely location, Azeb cooks up traditional Ethiopian specialities in a welcoming, unpretentious setting decorated with African farming tools and colourful linens. There are vegetarian options, plus dishes such as *awaze tibs* (spicy lamb with onion, garlic and ginger) or *doro kitfo* (chicken). This is the only Ethiopian restaurant in Iceland, and it beckons all lovers of spice.

Flúðasveppir Farmers Bistro ICELANDIC €€
(☎519 0808; www.farmersbistro.is; Garðastígur; mains from 1900kr; ⏱noon-6pm Jun-Aug, to 4pm Sep-May) This restaurant is attached to Iceland's only mushroom farm. The mushroom soup is made with a secret recipe and served from a buffet with homemade bread and a selection of *álegg*, the Icelandic word for 'things that go on bread', all sourced from local greenhouses and dairy farms. Chicken salads, lamb wraps and vegetable patties are also on offer.

Grund Restaurant ICELANDIC €€
(☎565 9196; www.gistingfludir.is; Skeiða-og Hrunamannavegur/Rte 30; mains 2000-4900kr; ⏱12.30pm-9pm Jun–mid-Aug, hours may vary) This popular restaurant serves fresh local food from farm to table in a simple, cheerful dining room. The herby lamb chops with vegetables, salad, potatoes and rhubarb jam hit the spot.

Vínbúðin ALCOHOL
(☎487 8701; www.vinbudin.is; Akurgerði; ⏱11am-6pm Mon-Thu, to 7pm Fri, to 4pm Sat) Liquor store.

Samkaup-Strax FOOD
(Skeiða-og Hrunamannavegur/Rte 30; ⏱9am-9pm Mon-Fri, 10am-9pm Sat & Sun) Groceries. Located next to Grund Restaurant.

Getting There & Away

Strætó (p429) buses 72 and 73 froom Selfoss (2300/1100kr, 40 to 60 minutes, two daily, plus one Sunday) serve Flúðir; the 73 also has one Saturday service. Bus 76 links up to those routes to reach Árnes.

THE SOUTH

As you work your way east from Reykjavík, Rte 1 (the Ring Road) emerges into austere volcanic foothills punctuated by surreal steam vents, around Hveragerði, then swoops through a flat, wide coastal plain, full of verdant horse farms and greenhouses, before the landscape suddenly begins to grow wonderfully jagged, after Hella and Hvolsvöllur. Mountains thrust upwards on the inland side, some of them volcanoes (like Eyjafjallajökull, the site of the 2010 eruption that disrupted much of Europe), and the first of the awesome glaciers appears, as enormous rivers such as the Þjórsá cut their way to the black-sand beaches rimming the Atlantic.

Throughout the region, roads pierce deep inland, to realms of lush waterfall-doused valleys such as Þjórsárdalur and Fljótshlíð, and awe-inspiring volcanoes such as Hekla. Two of the most renowned inland spots are Landmannalaugar, where vibrantly coloured rhyolite peaks meet bubbling hot springs; and Þórsmörk, a dramatic valley tucked safely away from the brutal northern elements under a series of wind-foiling ice caps. They are linked by the famous Laugavegurinn hike, Iceland's most popular trek. These areas lie inland on roads that are sometimes impassable by standard vehicles and most visitors access them on tours or amphibious buses from the southern towns. Þórsmörk, a seriously good hiking destination, can be visited as a day trip.

Public transport (and traffic) can be solid along the Ring Road (Rte 1), which is studded with interesting settlements: Hveragerði, famous for its geothermal fields and hot springs; Skógar, with stunning waterfalls and the leaping-off point for Þórsmörk; and Vík, surrounded by glaciers, vertiginous cliffs and black-sand beaches. South of the Ring Road, the tiny fishing villages of Stokkseyri and Eyrarbakki feel refreshingly local. The South Coast is also filled with family farms, some rich with Saga heritage, offering lovely rural guesthouses and true Icelandic hospitality.

Hveragerði & Around

POP 2500

The grid of boxy buildings that is Hveragerði emerge from otherworldly lava fields and hills pierced, surreally, by natural steaming vents. You're not here for the architecture, you're here because Hveragerði is the hot-springs capital of the world, with a highly active geothermal field, which heats hundreds of greenhouses. Nationally, the town is famous for its horticultural college and naturopathic clinic. There are also some fantastic hikes in the area, though routes are sometimes packed in summer.

Sights

★Geothermal Park HOT SPRINGS

(Hveragarðurinn; ☎483 4601, 483 5062; Hverarmörk 13; adult/child 300kr/free; ⏲9am-6pm Mon-Sat, 10am-6pm Sun Jun-Aug, shorter hours Apr, May & Sep, closed Oct-Mar) The geothermal park Hverasvæðið, in the centre of town, has mud pots and steaming pools where visitors can dip their feet (but no more). Groups of 15 or more can book ahead for a guided walk to learn about the area's unique geology and greenhouse power (850kr per person). There's also a small cafe serving tea, coffee and geothermally baked bread.

SLEEPING IN THE SOUTH

The south is the most developed region outside of Reykjavík, with lodging in all of the towns along the Ring Road, plus many farms with guesthouses. Increasingly, hotels are staying open year-round.

Book well ahead during summer and holidays, especially in the far south, as visitor numbers often exceed beds.

Camping is easy in fine weather, with municipal campgrounds in each town. Wild camping is discouraged (and illegal for campervans).

★Listasafn Árnesinga GALLERY

(☎483 1727; www.listasafnarnesinga.is; Austurmörk 21; ⏲noon-6pm May-Sep, Thu-Sun Sep-Apr) FREE This airy modern-art gallery puts on superb exhibitions. When it's quiet the staff are more than happy to walk guests around the gallery, offering an insight into the art. It also has a fine cafe serving hot drinks and cakes.

The Lava Tunnel CAVE

(Raufarhólshellir; ☎519 1616; www.thelavatunnel.is; Raufarhólshellir, off Rte 39; tours from adult/child 6400/3200kr; ⏲9am-5pm) Known as Raufarhólshellir, this 11th-century lava tube is 1360m long (Iceland's third largest) and contains wonderful lava columns. Regular one-hour tours run on the hour every hour. The thrilling 'extreme' tour (adult/child 19,500/9950kr) guides visitors deep into the cave, where they have to climb over boulders and squeeze though tight spaces. Helmets and flashlights are provided but bring sturdy boots.

Hveragerði Stone & Geology Exhibition MUSEUM

(Ljósbrá Stone Exhibition; ☎847 3460; www.ljosbra.is; Breiðamörk 1b; tours available by request; ⏲1-5pm) FREE One of Iceland's largest private collections of stones is owned by the Thor family and you can view their crystals and other geological artefacts in an unlikely location next to the N1 petrol station. Unusual handmade gifts, made by the son Hafsteinn, are available for purchase.

Hellisheiði Geothermal Power Plant MUSEUM

(ON Power Geothermal Exhibition; ☎412 5800; www.onpower.is; Rte 378; admission incl tour 1950kr; ⏲9am-5pm) The sleek shell of Hellisheiði Geothermal Power Plant is one of the few plants that provides 30% of Iceland's electricity. A multimedia exhibition and tour

Hverageröi

Top Sights
- 1 Geothermal Park A2
- 2 Listasafn Árnesinga A3

Sights
- 3 Hveragerði Stone & Geology Exhibition A3

Activities, Courses & Tours
- 4 Geothermal Swimming Pool B2
- 5 HNLFÍ Health Clinic & Spa B3
- 6 Iceland Activities A3

Sleeping
- 7 Campsite B2
- 8 Frost & Fire Hotel A1
- 9 Gistiheimilið Frumskógar A2

Eating
- 10 Almar A3
- Bonus .... (see 14)
- 11 Fiskverslun Hveragerðis A3
- Ölverk .... (see 11)
- 12 Rósagarðurinn A3
- 13 Skyrgerðin A2
- Varmá .... (see 8)

Shopping
- 14 Vínbúðin A3

lay out the details of harnessing the earth's hot-water power and the origins of geothermal energy. Plus you can see the turbine room, and view Iceland's rocks and minerals. There's a cafe on-site. It's 17km west of Hveragerði off Rte 1.

Activities

★Reykjadalur GEOTHERMAL POOL

(Hot River Valley; Breiðamörk) Reykjadalur is a delightful geothermal valley where there's a hot river you can bathe in; bring your swimsuit. There are maps at the tourist information office to find the trail; from the trailhead car park, it's a 3km hike through fields of sulphur-belching plains (it takes roughly one hour one-way). Stick to marked paths, lest you melt your shoes, and leave no rubbish.

In recent years the area has taken a beating, and at times the route is overrun with visitors. Warm up at the nearby **Dalakaffi** (☎862 8522; www.dalakaffi.is; Reykjakoti 2; flatbread from 500kr, hot chocolate 700kr, soup & bread from 1200kr; ⏰1-6pm Sun-Fri, 11am-6pm Sat), which serves a great hot chocolate.

HNLFÍ Health Clinic & Spa SPA

(Heilsustofnun Náttúrulækningafélags Íslands; ☎483 0300; www.heilsustofnun.is; Grænumörk 10; herbal/mud bath from 4000/6500kr, massages from 7500kr; ⏰by appointment) Iceland's most famous clinic treats both prescription-bearing patients and visitors seeking relaxing massages, deep-heat mud baths and more. It offers many packages and has excellent facilities, including indoor and outdoor pools, hot-pots, a sauna, a steam bath and modest accommodation for those having treatments (rooms from 5500kr).

Geothermal Swimming Pool SWIMMING

(Sundlaugin Laugaskarði; ☎483 4113; https://sundlaugar.is; Reykjamörk; adult/child 900/350kr; ⏰6.45am-9.30pm Mon-Fri, 9am-7pm Sat & Sun Jun-Aug, shorter hours Sep-May) Hveragerði's open-air geothermal swimming pool, beside the Varmá river just north of town, is among Iceland's favourites. Goodies include a massaging hot-pot and a steam room built directly over a natural hot spring.

Tours

Iceland Activities ADVENTURE TOUR

(☎777 6263; www.icelandactivities.is; Mánamörk 3-5; tours from 15,600kr; ⏰9am-5pm Mon-Fri, to 4pm Sat) This family-run adventure company specialises in biking, surfing and hiking tours in the Southwest. Hot-springs tours, overnight volcano tours, super-Jeep tours and customised tours are also available.

Eldhestar HORSE RIDING
(☎480 4800; http://eldhestar.is/tours; Vallavegur, off Hringvegur; 1hr tour adult/child from 8000/6400kr; ⊙8.45am-4.30pm) Multiday, day and half-day horse-riding tours for a range of abilities, including countryside, heritage, hot springs, river and volcano tours. Combo tours like biking and riding, riding and rafting, and other adventure sport, can also be arranged with Eldhestar.

Sólhestar HORSE RIDING
(☎892 3066; www.solhestar.is; Borgargerði, Ölfus, off Hvammsvegur/Rte 374; 1-/2hr tours from 9000/12,000kr) Various half- and full-day riding tours through the volcanic wilds or down on the beach. It's 8km south of Hveragerði, on the Ring Road; head half a kilometre north on Rte 374.

Sleeping

Gistiheimilið Frumskógar GUESTHOUSE €
(☎896 2780; www.frumskogar.is; Frumskógar 3; d/apt without bathroom incl breakfast from 13,600/22,200kr;) This cosy apartment-style guesthouse has simple decor and earthy tones. It also has a hot-pot and steam bath.

Hjarðarból Guesthouse GUESTHOUSE €
(☎567 0045; www.hjardarbol.is; Rte 374; d from 14,900kr, d/q without bathroom 12,100/23,700kr; P) This buttercup-yellow set of cottages and guesthouse buildings, with small kitchen, hot tub and friendly hosts, is pastoral and welcoming. It is located in the rolling fields 8km southeast of Hveragerði, just north off the Ring Road.

Campsite CAMPGROUND €
(hveracamping@gmail.com; Reykjamörk 1, off Rte 377; sites per adult/child 1500/700kr) Just east of the centre, this campsite has toilets, showers, a cooking area and a laundry.

Hótel Hlíð HOTEL €€
(☎860 4644; Krókur, off Rte 38; s/d/t from 17,800/24,600/30,600kr;) This slim band of modern rooms sits against a brilliant backdrop, with rocky foothills behind and the sweep of a lush valley reaching towards the coast. There's a hot tub, lounge areas and restaurant (7pm to 9pm).

★**Frost & Fire Hotel** BOUTIQUE HOTEL €€€
(Frost og Funi; ☎483 4959; www.frostogfuni.is; Hverhamar, Hveragerði; d/tr incl breakfast 24,800/46,100kr; P@) This lovely little hotel sits on a bubbling stream and beneath fizzing geothermal spouts. The comfortable rooms with subtle Scandi-sleek details and original artworks stretch along the river ravine. The heat-pressured sauna and simmering hot-pots are fed by the hotel's private borehole.

SOUTH ICELAND VISITOR CENTER

Hveragerði has the regional **tourist office** (Upplýsingamiðstöð Suðurlands; ☎483 4601; www.southiceland.is; Sunnumörk 2-4; ⊙8.30am-5pm Mon-Fri, 9am-1pm Sat & Sun Jun-Aug, shorter hours Sep-May) for the entire south. Pop in for handy info on wild flowers in the area and to see a small exhibition about the earthquake that took place in 2008.

Eating & Drinking

The town has several busy bakeries, fast-food joints and supermarkets. Many restaurants offer bread cooked using geothermal heat.

★**Almar** BAKERY €
(☎483 1919; Sunnumörk 2; cakes from 250kr, salad bar 1900kr; ⊙7.30am-6pm;) A large, bustling bakery that also serves sandwiches, salads and soup of the day with fresh bread. The cakes here range from enormous Icelandic pastries to doughnuts, cookies and rice crispy cakes – they are all delicious (and reasonably priced). Sit in the cafe area or take out. It's in the complex with the tourist office.

Rósagarðurinn CAFE €
(☎483 3300; www.rosagardurinn.com; Breiðamörk/Rte 376; coffee from 300kr, ice creams from 480kr, hamburgers from 1600kr; ⊙9am-6pm Mon-Fri, 11am-5pm Sat) Rose garden, coffee shop and gift shop all rolled into one. Selling plants, cushions, candles and trinkets, cakes and food in an enormous conservatory area. Next door are impressive geothermal greenhouses, which grow roses year-round. It's possible to take a tour (1000kr per person) to learn about the botanical processes, then taste some homemade rose products like jam.

Fiskverslun Hveragerðis FISH & CHIPS €
(☎851 1415; www.fiskverslunhveragerdis.com; Breiðamörk 2; fish & chips 1600kr; ⊙11.30am-6pm Mon-Fri) This fishmongers sells the freshest morsels from the sea, plus one cooked dish only – tasty fish and chips. Pick your battered fish from the catch of the day.

Bonus SUPERMARKET €
(https://bonus.is; Sunnumörk; ⏲11am-6.30pm Mon-Thu, 10am-7pm Fri, 10am-6pm Sat, noon-6pm Sun) Groceries.

Skyrgerðin CAFE €€
(☎481 1010; www.skyrgerdin.is; Breiðamörk 25; mains 2000-2500kr; ⏲11am-10pm Mon-Thu, to 11pm Fri-Sun; 📶) This chilled-out cafe-cum-restaurant incorporates rough wood furniture, antiques and vintage photos. Creative meals are crafted from fresh Icelandic ingredients and include fresh *skyr* (Icelandic yoghurt) smoothies and drinks, sliders, lasagne and fish, plus grand cakes that are just too tempting to resit. The building also contains the oldest *skyr* factory, hence its name.

Ölverk PIZZA €€
(☎483 3030; www.olverk.is; Breiðamörk 2; pizzas from 1900kr; ⏲11.30am-10pm Sun-Thu, to 11pm Fri-Sat) This minimalist pizzeria and micro-brewery is a fine combination of bar and restaurant. Pizza toppings are creative (ever had banana on a pie?) and the house beer sets a high standard. Groups of 10 or more can book a brewery tour, which explains the brewing process and history of beer in Iceland; it takes 30 to 40 minutes and costs 2700kr per person.

★**Varmá** ICELANDIC €€€
(☎483 4959; www.frostogfuni.is; Hverhamar, off Rte 376; mains 3800-7650kr, wild game menu 10,500kr; ⏲6-9pm; P📶) At the Frost & Fire Hotel, this wonderfully scenic restaurant boasts floor-to-ceiling windows looking over the stream and gorge. Icelandic dishes are made using fresh, local ingredients and herbs and often with geothermal cooking techniques. The four-course wild game menu has hot smoked goose breast with brie and reindeer steak. Book ahead in summer.

Shopping

Vínbúðin ALCOHOL
(☎481 3932; www.vinbudin.is; Sunnumörk 2; ⏲11am-6pm Mon-Thu, to 7pm Fri, to 4pm Sat) National liquor chain.

Getting There & Away

The **bus stop** (off Rte 1, Hveragerði) is at the petrol stations on the main road into town (check whether your stop is the Shell or N1).

Strætó (p429) Buses 51 (Reykjavík–Vík/Höfn) and 52 (Reykjavík–Landeyjahöfn) stop in Hveragerði (1380kr, 35 minutes, 13 daily Monday to Friday, around nine daily Saturday and Sunday).

Sterna (p430) Bus 12/12A (Reykjavík–Höfn) stops in Hveragerði (1700kr, 55 minutes, daily June to September).

Reykjavík Excursions (p429) Buses 9/9A (Reykjavík–Þórsmörk), 11/11a (Reykjavík–Landmannalaugar), 17/17a (Reykjavík–Mývatn), 18 (Reykjavík–Álftavatn–Emstrur), 20/20a (Reykjavík–Skaftafell), 21/21a (Reykjavík–Vík) and 610/610a (Reykjavík–Kjölur–Akureyri) all stop in Hveragerði (2500kr). Journeys take 45 minutes to 1½ hours, with more than a dozen services per day between June and September. Trex (p430) buses T21 (Reykjavík–Landmannalaugar) and T11 (Reykjavík–Þórsmörk) can stop at Hveragerði with a prebooking (5100kr, two daily June to August).

Thule Travel (☎519 3399; www.thuletravel.is) Services run to Hveragerði from Landannalaugar (7650kr, three hours, two daily mid-June to mid-September) and Þórsmörk (6400kr, four hours, two daily June to mid-September.)

Þorlákshöfn

In the past, most people came to the fishing town of Þorlákshöfn, 20km south of Hveragerði, to catch the ferry to the Vestmannaeyjar. Now the ferry departs from Landeyjahöfn on the southwest coast near Hvolsvöllur. When it's stormy, the ferry does leave from here, though. There's little other reason to come.

Þorlákshöfn is served by Strætó (p429) bus 71 from Hveragerði (920kr, around 25 minutes, four daily Monday to Friday). Selfoss (920kr, 20 minutes) is connected to Hveragerði via bus 52 (three daily Monday to Saturday) and 51 (around 10 daily Monday to Friday, six daily Saturday and Sunday).

Eyrarbakki

POP 570

It's hard to believe, but tiny Eyrarbakki was Iceland's main port and a thriving trading town well into the 20th century. Farmers from all over the south once rode here to barter for supplies at the general store – crowds were so huge it could take three days to get served! Today the seaside town is known for its prison – the largest in Iceland – and its good museums and nearby nature reserve.

Sights

★**Flói Nature Reserve** NATURE RESERVE
(☎562 0477; www.fuglavernd.is; off Rte 34) Birdwatchers should head 3km northwest of Eyrarbakki to Flói Nature Reserve, an important estuary and marshland on the eastern bank of

the Ölfusá. It's visited by many wetland birds (common species include red-throated divers and various kinds of ducks and geese) most of which are present during nesting season (May to July). There's a 2km circular hiking trail through the marshes. To get there, take the small signposted turning off Rte 34, which meanders 5km through sheep farms before reaching an observation hut.

For information on Flói Nature Reserve and birding in Iceland check out **Icelandic Society for the Protection of Birds** (☎562 0477; https://fuglavernd.is).

★Húsið á Eyrarbakka MUSEUM

(House at Eyrarbakki; ☎483 1504; www.husid.com; Eyrargata; adult/child incl Sjöminjasafnið á Eyrarbakka 1000kr/free; ⏲11am-6pm mid-May–mid-Sep) One of Iceland's oldest houses, built by Danish traders in 1765, Húsið á Eyrarbakka has glass display cabinets explaining the town's history, interesting rooms restored with original furniture, and a stuffed bird collection. Keep an eye out for Ólöf Sveinsdóttir's shawl, hat and cuffs, knitted from her own hair. The entry fee includes access to other town attractions, including the Sjöminjasafnið á Eyrarbakka maritime museum.

Sjöminjasafnið á Eyrarbakka MUSEUM

(☎483 1082; Túngata 59; adult/child incl Húsið á Eyrarbakka 1000kr/free; ⏲11am-6pm May-Sep) Just behind Húsið á Eyrarbakka, this small maritime museum has displays on the local fishing community. Its main exhibit is the beautiful 12-oared fishing boat, *Farsæll*. The entry fee includes access to the Húsið á Eyrarbakka museum.

Sleeping & Eating

Eyrarbakki is a fishing port, and the limited restaurants do a great job with seafood.

Bakki Hostel & Apartments HOSTEL, APARTMENTS €

(☎788 8200; www.bakkihostel.is; Eyrargata 51-53; dm/studio/d 4500/18,000/19,000kr; P 📶) This broad building offers six-bed dorms that share a living area and kitchen, and studios (sleeping up to four) or one-bedroom self-catering apartments (sleeping up to four), some with sea views.

★Sea Side Cottages COTTAGE €€

(☎898 1197; www.seasidecottages.is; Eyrargata 37a; cottages from 26,000kr; 📶) Living up to their name, these two quaint cottages are just metres away from the pounding Atlantic, behind a protective berm. Each is tricked out in fine fashion, with thoughtful antiques, flat-screen TVs, fully equipped kitchens and outdoor seating.

★Hafið Bláa SEAFOOD €€

(☎483 1000; www.hafidblaa.is; Rte 34; mains 2300-3900kr; ⏲noon-9pm Jun-Aug, shorter hours Sep-May) Three kilometres west of Eyrarbakki on Rte 34 at the Ölfusá Bridge, this seafood restaurant sits on the water's edge in an ovoid building, with a beautiful arcing-wood interior. Even if you don't get a table overlooking the ocean, the sweeping estuary views on the opposite side are equally impressive. The menu offers a small range of seafood and lamb.

★Rauða Húsið SEAFOOD €€

(☎483 3330; www.raudahusid.is; Búðarstígur 4; mains 2700-5800kr; ⏲noon-9pm; 📶) This elegant and romantic white-linen restaurant fills a red house (hence the name) and has cheery staff and great fresh seafood prepared to perfection. The menu is broad with plenty to choose, from beef tenderloin and langoustine to pasta and nut steak.

Getting There & Away

Strætó (p429) bus 75 travels from Selfoss to Eyrarbakki (460kr, 30 minutes, eight daily Monday to Friday, four Saturday).

Stokkseyri

POP 450

Stokkseyri can seem like Eyrarbakki's twin to the east, but look a little closer and you'll find unusual attractions. While it, too, is a small fishing village, it has a quirky side, including an elves museum and a hostel filled with unusual art.

Sights & Activities

Draugasetrið MUSEUM

(Ghost Museum; ☎854 4510; http://icelandicwonders.is; Hafnargata 9, off Rte 33; adult/child 2000/1200kr; ⏲1-6pm Jun-Aug) Inside a huge maroon-and-black warehouse in the centre of town, Draugasetrið is a veritable haunted house run by a gaggle of bloodthirsty youngsters. A 50-minute audio guide (in many languages) recites 24 spooky stories in a series of dry-ice-filled stations. Not recommended for small fry. In the same building, the **Elves Museum** (☎483 1202; www.icelandicwonders.com; Hafnargata; adult/child 1500/1200kr; ⏲1-6pm Jun-Aug) explains more about Iceland's fascination with these mysterious creatures and folklore.

There's a gift shop out front too. Combined entry costs adult/child 2800/1800kr.

Kajakferðir Stokkseyri KAYAKING TOUR
(☎868 9046, 695 2058; www.kajak.is; Heiðarbrún 24, off Rte 33; tours from 4950-12,900kr; ⊗Apr-Oct) Explore the nearby lagoon by kayak or get out on the ocean. The Löngudæl Lake trip takes you through nearby narrow canals flanked by grass. The base is opposite the town pool, **Sundlaug Stokkseyrar** (☎480 3260; Ranakot, Rte 33; adult/child 980/150kr; ⊗1-9pm Mon-Fri, 10am-5pm Sat & Sun Jun–mid-Aug, 1-8.30pm Mon-Fri, 10am-3pm Sat & Sun mid-Aug–May).

Sleeping & Eating

Art Hostel HOSTEL, APARTMENTS €
(☎854 4510; www.arthostel.is; Hafnargata 9; sleeping-bag accommodation 3000kr, dm 4500kr, s/tw without bathroom 10,000/14000kr, s/d with bathroom 14,000/20,000kr; 📶) On the 2nd floor of the central culture complex and warehouse, above mosaic, painting and photography galleries, you'll find a 15-person dorm, small twins, and larger studios with microwaves and bathrooms. Decor is dated, but brightened up with little touches of art on some of the corridor and room walls.

Stokkseyri Camping CAMPGROUND €
(☎896 2144; www.facebook.com/tjaldastokkseyri; off Sólvellir; adult/child 1400/900kr; ⊗May-Oct) Simple campground with heated toilet cubicles, washing facilities (showers 200kr) and laundry facilities (200kr per wash).

Freyja B&B B&B €€
(☎567 1060; www.bbfreyja.com; Blomsturvellir 2; d without bathroom incl breakfast from 12,700kr; ⊗May-Sep; 📶) Tina and Tofi welcome guests to an immaculate ranch house, with simple clean rooms, in the village of Stokkseyri. Activities include board games and reflexology massages. The only downside is there's no shared kitchen.

Kvöldstjarnan GUESTHOUSE €€
(Evening Star; ☎483 1800; www.kvoldstjarnan.is; Holtsvegur, Rte 314; s/d without bathroom incl breakfast 11,000/17,000kr, 3-bedroom apt 31,400kr; 📶) The three bright, white rooms here come with washbasins and fluffy feathery duvets. There's a shared living room and terrace, hot-pot, barbecue and sparkling kitchen. There's also a modern apartment with contemporary Icelandic art for rent, sleeping up to five.

★ **Við Fjöruborðið** SEAFOOD €€€
(☎483 1550; www.fjorubordid.is; Eyrabraut 3a; mains 2900-7900kr; ⊗noon-9pm; P📶) This large seafood restaurant sits on the shore, just behind the ocean berm, and is known for making some of the best lobster bisque (langoustine tails sautéd in garlic and butter) in Iceland. Slurp your bisque alongside chatting locals, glass fishing buoys and marine memorabilia. Good homemade cakes too. Reserve for dinner.

Shopping

Icelandic Handcraft & Wool Shop ARTS & CRAFTS
(☎843 0398; Hafnargata 1; ⊗1-6pm Sat & Sun or by appointment) Features a vast array of handmade Icelandic wool items, from baby socks and mittens to cardigans, hats and scarves.

Information

Information Centre & Kaffigott (☎468 1486; www.facebook.com/kaffigott; Hafnargata; ⊗noon-6pm) Basic coffee shop and info centre offering advice about the local area, plus cakes, coffee (from 440kr) and soft drinks. The cakes are delicious and all homemade.

Getting There & Away

Strætó (p429) bus 75 from Selfoss (460kr, 20 minutes, eight daily Monday to Friday, four Saturday) stops in Stokkseyri on its way to Eyrarbakki.

Stokkseyri is easily accessible by car via Rte 33 on the South Coast.

Flóahreppur

For being so close to the most travelled portion of the Ring Road (Rte 1), it's a wonder you can feel like you've fallen into a rural region of rolling pastures leading to the ocean. Bordered by the Ring Road in the north, Rte 34 in the west, the Þjórsá river in the east, and the Atlantic Ocean in the south, this small agricultural area has a few laid-back farms with easily accessible accommodation.

Turf House HISTORIC BUILDING
(☎892 2702; www.islenskibaerinn.is; Meðalholt; adult/child 1600/600kr; ⊗1pm-6pm Sun) This farmstead is a constant work in progress: every summer, an international group of students practices the building of Icelandic turf houses from local material. A large, modern eco-house hosts an exhibition on the history of these traditional homes.

Admission can be requested in advance outside regular hours, and includes a peek inside the renovated turf house up the road.

Sleeping & Eating

Head to Selfoss or Stokkseyri for food – Flóahreppur is quite rural.

★Julia's Guesthouse B&B €
(☎856 4788; www.julias-guesthouse.com; Hnaus; d without bathroom 13,000kr, tr with bathroom from 16,400kr, all incl breakfast; P wifi) Friendly Julia from Switzerland runs this charming guesthouse in the countryside to perfection. A menagerie including birds, cats and a bunny fill this immaculate house with life, and Julia and her husband Mike have decorated with great love, plus they create a sumptuous homemade breakfast. Some rooms have wonderful views, and the triple room has its own toilet. Cash only.

Vatnsholt GUESTHOUSE €€
(☎482 4829; www.hotelvatnsholt.is; Rte 305; d with/without bathroom 16,700/13,500kr, cottages from 17,000kr; ⏲mid-Feb–mid-Dec; @ wifi) A wonderful place if you have the kids in tow, Vatnsholt is located about 16km southeast of Selfoss, just 8km off the Ring Road. Here you'll find over 30 sun-filled bedrooms and cottages scattered throughout a sweeping farmstead with views to Eyjafjallajökull, Hekla and Vestmannaeyjar. It does buffet meals, too.

Bitra B&B B&B €€
(☎4800 700; https://guesthousebitra.is; Rte 1; d with/without bathroom from 20,000/16,500kr; P wifi) This building was originally meant to be a women's prison, but it never became one and now it's a welcoming guesthouse with 17 clean, simple rooms – some with views over Hekla. Great buffet breakfast too. There's a large lounge room and a book swap, but no kitchen for guest use. Find it on Rte 1, around 15km east of Selfoss.

Shopping

Þingborg CLOTHING
(☎482 1027; http://thingborg.net; off Rte 1, Þingborg; ⏲10am-5pm Mon-Fri, to 4pm Sat & Sun) This non-profit wool workshop by the Ring Road sells hand-knitted clothes made by over 25 local men and women. There's a wide selection of traditional *lopapeysa* (Icelandic woollen sweaters), plus a ready-made *lopapeysa* kit, with yarn and all the essentials to make one yourself. Appointments can be arranged outside opening hours.

Selfoss

POP 6940

Selfoss is the largest town in southern Iceland, an important centre for getting business done, and relatively unattractive, unless you get into the neighbourhoods. Iceland's Ring Road (Rte 1) is its main street, so the primary reason to stop is to transfer buses, load up on groceries or get a decent meal.

Sights & Activities

Bobby Fischer Center MUSEUM
(☎894 1275; www.fischersetur.is; Austurvegur 21; adult/child 1000kr/free; ⏲1-4pm mid-May–mid-Sep) This little museum houses the memorabilia of chess champion Bobby Fischer, who is buried 2km northeast in Laugardælirkirkja's cemetery. It is also a hang-out for chess players. There are occasional chess classes and tournaments; enquire within for details.

Sundhöll Selfoss GEOTHERMAL POOL, HOT-POT
(☎480 1960; https://sundlaugar.is/sundlaugar/sundholl-selfoss; Tryggvagata 15; adult/child 900/150kr; ⏲6.30am-9.30pm Mon-Fri, 9am-7pm Sat & Sun) Selfoss has a fine geothermal swimming pool, with hot-pots, water slides and a kids' play pool.

Sleeping

There are loads of accommodation options in and around Selfoss, from hostels and camping to big hotels, making it a convenient base for taking day trips around the south.

★Geirakot GUESTHOUSE €
(☎482 1020; geirakot@simnet.is; Geirakot farm; sleeping-bag space 4000kr, s/d without bathroom incl breakfast 8000/15,000kr; ⏲Feb-Oct; P wifi) Sweet Geirakot is a nice alternative to Selfoss town. A friendly family on a dairy farm has renovated the grandparents' small farmhouse into a cosy guesthouse. Breakfast is lovely, local and served on china. Cooking facilities available. Book through Icelandic Farm Holidays (www.farmholidays.is).

Gesthús CAMPGROUND, GUESTHOUSE €€
(☎482 3585; www.gesthus.is; Engjavegur 56; sites per person 2000kr, d from 16,200kr; P wifi) At this friendly place by the park, choose between camping, doubles in two-room cabins with shared kitchen and bathroom, or a full summer house with kitchenette and TV. A warm lounge and cooking room acts as a cosy hang-out for campers. Hot-pots cost 300kr for

Selfoss

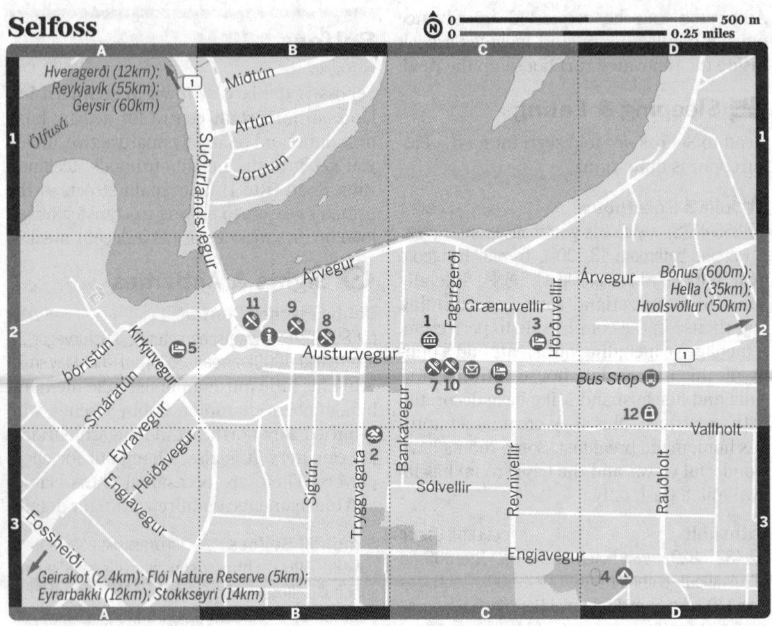

SOUTHWEST ICELAND & THE GOLDEN CIRCLE SELFOSS

Selfoss

Sights
1 Bobby Fischer Center C2

Activities, Courses & Tours
2 Sundhöll Selfoss B3

Sleeping
3 Bella Apartments & Rooms C2
4 Gesthús D3
5 Hótel Selfoss A2
6 Selfoss HI Hostel C2

Eating
7 Bókakaffið C2
8 Kaffi Krús B2
9 Krónan B2
10 Surf & Turf C2
11 Tryggvaskáli B2

Shopping
12 Vínbúðin D2

campers and are open 5pm to 11pm; they are free for other guests. Breakfast costs 1700kr.

Selfoss HI Hostel HOSTEL €
(482 1600; www.hostel.is; Austurvegur 28; dm/s/d without bathroom from 4100/5500/12,600kr;) Selfoss's HI hostel has plenty of common space, with games and comfortable lounge chairs, plus a hot tub. There's also a kitchen, barbecue and laundry facilities. Private rooms include a washbasin. HI members get a discount. The breakfast, including homemade waffles, is 1350kr.

★ **Icelandic Cottages** COTTAGE €€€
(898 0728; www.icelandiccottages.is; Hraunmörk, off Rte 30; cottages from 30,000kr;) These ubercool modern cottages dot the lava fields 18km east of Selfoss, just north of the Ring Road on Rte 30. They're beautifully kitted out (with everything from ironing boards and hairdryers to dishwashers), have terraces and barbecues, and sleep up to six people. Three-night minimum.

★ **Bella Apartments & Rooms** APARTMENT €€€
(859 6162; http://bellahotel.is; Austurvegur 33-35; d/apt incl breakfast 23,500/37,300kr;) This sparkling-clean property on the main street has comfortable double rooms and luxury two-bedroom apartments, complete with balconies and furnished kitchens. The apartments can sleep up to seven people, and there are washer-dryer facilities for all.

Hótel Selfoss HOTEL €€€
(☎480 2500; www.hotelselfoss.is; Eyravegur 2; s/d from 29,400/35,600kr; @📶) This 99-room behemoth near the bridge has a calm interior with snappy business-style rooms and great facilities, including a good in-house restaurant. There's lava art and Icelandic photography throughout. The hotel spa has a steam bath, sauna, relaxation showers and a bar serving snacks and drinks. Riverview rooms beat those overlooking the car park.

Eating & Drinking

Selfoss is the best place in the south to stock up on groceries before setting off for remote areas. It has most major supermarkets, including **Bónus** (Larsenstræti 5; ⌚11am-6.30pm Mon-Thu, 10am-7.30pm Fri, to 6pm Sat, 11am-6pm Sun) and **Krónan** (☎585 7000; Austurvegur 3-5; ⌚9am-8pm Mon-Fri, to 7pm Sat & Sun), plus farm-to-table restaurants and plenty of fast-food options.

Bókakaffið CAFE €
(☎482 3079; Austurvegur 22; cakes from 900kr; ⌚11am-6pm Mon-Fri, noon-6pm Sat & Sun; 📶) This independent bookshop (with both new and secondhand books) serves coffee and cake.

★Tryggvaskáli ICELANDIC €€
(☎482 1390; www.tryggvaskali.is; Austurvegur 1; mains 3450-6250kr; ⌚11.30am-10pm Sun-Thu, to 11pm Fri & Sat) Housed in Selfoss' first house (built for bridge workers in 1890), Tryggvaskáli has been lovingly renovated with antiques. Some tables in the intimate dining rooms have riverfront views and a romantic feel. The fine-dining Icelandic menu made with local produce includes dishes like slow-cooked pork belly and plums or mushroom-crusted cod and chorizo. The owners also operate Kaffi Krús.

★Kaffi Krús INTERNATIONAL €€
(☎482 1266; www.kaffikrus.is; Austurvegur 7; mains 1200-4900kr; ⌚10am-10pm Jun-Aug, shorter hours Sep-May) The 'Coffee Jar' is a popular cafe and restaurant in a charming, cosy old orange house along the main road. There's great outdoor space and a large selection of Icelandic and international dishes, from salads and pastas, to fish and farmers-market dishes. The pizza (try the duck or langoustine) and burgers are excellent too.

Surf & Turf AMERICAN €€
(☎482 2899; Austurvegur 22; mains 1900-5200kr; ⌚11am-10pm) Sleek American-style joint with hardwood floors, stripped-back minimalist decor and designer-cool chipboard walls. It serves up various burgers (like blue cheese, Béarnaise, and 'Mexico' burgers), pulled-pork sandwiches, fish dishes, barbecue ribs, lamb and horse steak.

Ölvisholt Brugghús MICROBREWERY
(☎767 5000; www.olvisholt.is; Ölvisholti, off Rte 1; ⌚groups only by appointment) Solid range of microbrews from South Iceland, including the eye-catching Lava beer. Tours last 30 to 40 minutes (per person 3000kr) and include details about the history of the brewery, the brewing process, and a chance to sample some beers. Visitors must be 20 years or older.

Shopping

Vínbúðin ALCOHOL
(☎482 2011; www.vinbudin.is; Vallholt 19; ⌚11am-6pm Mon-Thu, to 7pm Fri, to 4pm Sat) National liquor chain.

Information

Árborg Tourist Information Centre (☎480 1990; www.arborg.is; Austurvegur 2; ⌚8am-6pm Mon-Fri May-Aug, shorter hours Sep-Apr) In the same building as the library. It has maps and local area info, but the tourist office in Hveragerði is better.

Getting There & Away

Most buses between Reykjavík and Höfn, Skaftafell, Fjallabak, Þórsmörk, Flúðir, Gullfoss, Laugarvatn and Vík stop at the **N1 station** (cnr Austurvegur & Rauðholt) in Selfoss.

Strætó (p429) Buses include 51 Reykjavík–Vík/Höfn and 52 Reykjavík–Landeyjahöfn (1840kr, 50 minutes, 13 daily Monday to Friday, nine daily Saturday and Sunday). Also buses 72 and 73 Selfoss–Flúðir (2300kr, 40 to 60 minutes, two to four daily Monday to Friday, one Saturday, two Sunday) and bus 75 Selfoss–Eyrarbakki (460kr, 20 minutes, eight daily Monday to Friday, four daily Saturday).

Sterna (p430) Runs bus 12/12a Reykjavík–Vík–Höfn (2200kr, 55 minutes, one daily June to mid-September).

Reykjavík Excursions (p429) Services include buses 9/9a Reykjavík–Þórsmörk, 11/11A Reykjavík–Landmannalaugar, 17/17a Reykjavík–Mývatn, 18 Reykjavík–Álftavatn–Emstrur, 20/20a Reykjavík–Skaftafell, 21/21a Reykjavík–Skógar and 610/610a Reykjavík–Kjölur–Akureyri; all stop in Selfoss (2800kr, one to 1½ hours, around 13 daily).

Trex (p430) Buses include the T21 Reykjavík–Landmannalaugar (Selfoss–Landmannalaugar 8700kr, three hours, two daily mid-June to mid-September). Bus T11 Reykjavík–Þórsmörk (Selfoss–Þórsmörk 7400kr, 3¼ hours, two daily mid-June to mid-September).

Thule Travel (p134) Runs route Reykjavík–Landannalaugar (Selfoss–Landannalaugar, 7650kr, three hours, two daily June to mid-September).

Western Þjórsárdalur

The powerful Þjórsá is Iceland's longest river, a fast-flowing, churning mass of milky glacial water that courses 230km from Vatnajökull down to the Atlantic. Including its tributaries, it accounts for almost one-third of Iceland's hydroelectric power. Rte 32 follows the western side of the river, and as it moves upstream and into the highlands you'll traverse broad plains, split by the enormous river, that lead to volcanic fields and finally the foothills of the mountains beyond. It is a relatively untouristed area, with Viking ruins, hidden waterfalls and prehistoric-like river landscapes.

Rte 32 is one of the preferred ways to reach Landmannalaugar (the starting point for the famous Laugavegurinn hike) by vehicle (via the 4WD-only Rte F26). It's also possible (if you don't have a 4WD) to make a day's loop up this side of the valley, cross over the river after the Búrfell Hydroelectric Plant and return down the other side of the valley to Hella on Rte 26.

There are also hiking trails in the area, and horse-riding companies peppering the journey along Rte 32.

There is no public transport to or beyond Árnes. Bring your own wheels or book a custom trip with a local tour operator.

Árnes

Stop in the tiny settlement of Árnes, near the junction of Rtes 30 and 32, the last place to stock up on basic groceries before exploring Western Þjórsárdalur. Visitors can also get advice at **Þjórsárstofa** (Þjórsá Visitor Centre; ☎486 6115; www.thjorsarstofa.is; ⏲10am-6pm Jun-Aug) FREE, a large white building that houses an information centre, restaurant and an excellent display about nearby attractions. There's also camping in the village, a good local pool, and horse riding nearby.

Tours

Núphestar HORSE RIDING
(☎852 5930; www.nupshestar.is; Breiðanes; 1-/2-/3hr rides from 7000/9500/13000kr) This friendly, family-run horse farm offers short rides around the nearby countryside and Þjórsá river area, as well as multiday tours. It's near the junction of Rtes 30 and 32.

Steinsholt HORSE RIDING
(☎486 6069; www.steinsholt.is; Steinsholt II, off Rte 326; 1-/2hr rides 6500/11,000kr) This tidy horse farm offers multiday riding trips, hourly tours and cosy accommodation (double with/without bathroom including breakfast 13,900/16,200kr). Find it at the end of Rte 326, just north of Árnes.

Sleeping & Eating

Árnes Camping CAMPGROUND €
(☎845 9116, 697 7004; Rettarholt, off Rte 32; adult/child 12-16 years old/child under 12 years 1500/900kr/free; ⏲May-Aug) Simple campground with three grassy fields, toilets, washing facilities and free showers. Electricity hook-up 900kr. Pay at the Þjórsárstofa museum and visitor centre.

Guesthouse Denami FARMSTAY €€
(☎698 7090; www.denami.is; Háholtsvegur, Rte 326; s with shared bathroom incl breakfast 9000kr, d with/without bathroom incl breakfast 19,500/14,000kr; 📶) Stay on a lovely family-run farm in the lush rolling countryside on the northern edge of Árnes. The nine rooms are simple but tidy, and views of the nearby volcanoes can be magnificent. Some 80 horses, two dozen sheep, and a friendly cat called Sigg live on the 350-hectare farm. The buffet breakfast includes local produce.

Fosshotel Hekla HOTEL €€
(☎486 5540; www.hotelhekla.is; Brjánsstaðir; d/q incl breakfast from 22,000/41,500kr; P@📶) As you head up the Þjórsá valley, this hotel complex sits just off Rte 30, 17km before Árnes. Forty-two rooms include large, modern doubles with crisp white linen, plus flat-screen TVs. Family rooms are bigger still.

Búrfell & Around

As the Þjórsá's valley gets more remote, the drama and unusual sights increase. The austere black-stone river delta around Búrfell Hydroelectric Power Station leads to jagged mountains, ancient ruins, crashing waterfalls and hidden valleys. Due to the lack of transport to this area it's far less touristy.

Sights

The following sights are arranged in the order you'll encounter them driving northeast on Rte 32.

Hjálparfoss WATERFALL
(off Rte 32) Twenty-six kilometres northeast of Árnes along Rte 32, take a short (1km) detour along a signposted track to this delightful waterfall. The azure falls tumble in two chutes over twisted basalt columns (formed from the cooling of lava) and into a deep pool.

Þjóðveldisbærinn NOTABLE BUILDING
(488 7713; www.thjodveldisbaer.is; adult/child 1000kr/free; 10am-5pm Jun-Aug) Þjóðveldisbærinn is a reconstruction of Stöng (see below), exactly reproducing its turf-covered layout and its neighbouring church. Staff here wear period dress and often keep a fire going in the reconstructed farmhouse for added effect. It's located near Rte 32.

★**Stöng** RUINS
(Rte 327, off Rte 32) FREE Buried by white volcanic ash in 1104 during one of Hekla's eruptions, this ancient farm once belonged to Gaukur Trandilsson, a 10th-century Viking who lived a tempestuous life. Excavated in 1939 (Iceland's first proper archaeological dig), it's an important site, used to help date Viking houses elsewhere. The ruins include the foundations of a farm, house, barn, smithy and church. Find it at the end of a rough 5km dirt road (Rte 327), off Rte 32 about 26km northeast of Árnes

★**Gjáin** CANYON
(Rte 327) A walking path from Stöng farm takes you a couple of kilometres to a lovely little lush valley, Gjáin, full of twisting lava, otherworldly caves and spectacular waterfalls. The dirt road (4WD recommended) from Stöng also continues on to the upper ridge of the valley and to a small waterfall. *Gjáin* simply means 'rift'.

★**Háifoss** WATERFALL
(Rte 332, off Rte 32) Iceland's second-highest waterfall, Háifoss is a magnificent 128m-high cascade that plunges off the edge of a majestic plateau into an undulating lava canyon. Some of the thick lava formations here in the Þjórsárdal valley are two million years old. By 4WD or on foot, follow the pothole-laden Rte 332 (off Rte 32 or leading on from Gjáin) for around 10km. You'll reach a parking area and a footpath leading to a jaw-dropping view of the falls and canyon.

Sleeping & Eating

There are no grocery stores or restaurants anywhere nearby, so stock up or eat before arriving.

OFF THE BEATEN TRACK

TRAUSTHOLTSHÓLMI PRIVATE ISLAND

Go with Hákon to check his salmon fishing nets and explore his grass-covered **Traustholtshólmi Private Island** (699 4256; www.thh.is; tour per person 19,800kr; by reservation) in the Þjórsá river, before settling down to a dinner of fresh-caught fish and island-grown herbs, and perhaps a campfire. You can book longer stays on the island, which include sleepovers in his yurt (double 66,000kr).

Sandartunga Camping CAMPGROUND €
(asolfsstadir@simnet.is; off Rte 32; sites per adult/child 1250kr/free; mid-May–Aug) This simple sheltered campground has water and toilets and a children's play area. The blessing is its grand setting in the broad lava fields and river valley of the Þjórsá, but the flies can be irritating. Find it off Rte 32, around 8km west of Þjóðveldisbærinn.

Eastern Þjórsárdalur

Between the township of Hella to the southwest and Landmannalaugar to the northeast, you'll find the sweeping seaside floodplains of the river Þjórsá merging into increasingly mind-blowing volcanic formations and lava fields until you reach Hekla – one of Iceland's most ominous volcanoes.

The road to Hekla – Rte 26 – winds its way beyond a cluster of horse farms, offering a variety of riding trips, and connects with Rte 32, which can take you down the equally dramatic western side of the river valley. The easiest way to Landmannalaugar is via Rte 26. The last outpost (and last petrol) before heading into the highlands is at Highland Center Hrauneyjar (p366).

Sights

Hellnahellir CAVE
(847 5015, 487 6583; www.hellar.is; Hellavegur; adult/child 1100kr/free; by appointment) On the farm of Hellar in Landsveit, this 50m long human-made cave was built up to 11m below the soil at its deepest point. Inside a barn, visitors walk through a secret doorway leading to a dark passage illuminated by lights. Dating back 700 to 1100 years, five ancient chimneys and various carvings remain intact, supposedly made by monks.

HEKLA

The name of Iceland's most famous and active volcano means 'Hooded One', as its 1491m-high summit is almost always shrouded in ominous-looking clouds. **Hekla** (F255, off Rte 26) has vented its fury numerous times throughout history, and during the Middle Ages it was commonly believed to be the gateway to hell.

Viking-era settlers built farms on the rich volcanic soils around Hekla, only to be wiped out by the eruption of 1104, which buried everything within a radius of 50km. Since then there have been 15 major eruptions; the 1300 eruption covered more than 83,000 sq km in ash.

In recent years hellish Hekla has been belching out ash in steady 10-year intervals. This ash has a high fluorine content and has poisoned thousands of sheep. The most recent eruption (in 2000) produced a small pyroclastic flow (a high-speed and highly destructive torrent of rock particles and gas, which typically travels at over 130km per hour and can reach temperatures of 800°C). As you travel the region, look for grey pumice…it's probably from Hekla.

Locals live with the knowledge that the mighty mound could erupt at any time; it is long overdue.

For more on Hekla, check out the exhibition at the Hekla Center.

Climbing Hekla

You can climb Hekla, but there's never much warning before eruptions, usually indicated by multiple small earthquakes 30 to 80 minutes before it blows. Stick to days when the summit is free of heavy clouds, and carry plenty of water – the area's ash makes you thirsty. Most climbs are done June to September.

There's a small car park where mountain road F225 branches off Rte 26 (about 45km northeast of Hella). Most hire cars aren't allowed on F roads and need to be parked here, but it's a long and dusty walk (16km) to the foot of the volcano (or try your luck at hitching).

With a large 4WD you can continue along F225 to the trailhead at the bottom of Hekla (about 14.7km); the largest vehicles can continue a few kilometres further, but most have to park here. From this lower trailhead, a well-marked path climbs steadily up to the ridge on the northeastern flank of the mountain, then onto the summit crater; expect snow walking at altitude. Although the peak is often covered in snow, the floor of the crater is still hot. The trip to the summit takes about 3½ hours.

Alternatively, you may be able to organise bespoke super-Jeep tours here, although some tour companies avoid the area due to the chance of eruption.

Hekla Center MUSEUM
(Heklusetrið; ☎487 8700; www.leirubakki.is; Leirubakki; adult/child 900/450kr; ⊙noon-9pm Mon-Fri; P) The Hekla Center is part of the Leirubakki compound (camping, hotel and restaurant). It details the explosive history of Hekla in a deliberately dark building with flashing lights and multimedia exhibits. You'll learn that the volcano is long overdue to erupt. The centre also has regional information, and offers horse riding and local walks. It opens for groups out of hours with advance notice.

Tours

The many horse farms around the Þjórsárdalur offer rides, and most have high-quality guesthouse accommodation.

Skeiðvellir HORSE RIDING
(Icelandic HorseWorld; ☎487 6572, horse riding 899 5619; www.skeidvellir.is; Rte 26, Skeiðvellir farm; stable visit adult/child 2000kr/free, 1-/2hr horse rides 9500/15,000kr) This well-regarded horse-breeding farm has a visitor centre, teaches about horse maintenance and their purpose in Iceland, allows visitors to meet its newborns, touch and groom horses, and offers rides. It also has excellent accommodation; a cottage sleeping up to six people with a kitchen and free breakfast costs 11,000kr per person. Find it on Rte 26 about 9km north of Rte 1.

Hekluhestar HORSE RIDING
(☎487 6598; www.hekluhestar.is; Austvaðsholt; multiday rides from 275,000kr) Hidden along Rtes 271 and 272, 9km northeast of Hella,

this place run by a friendly French-Icelandic family specialises in six- to eight-day highland rides. Sleeping-bag accommodation is available (4500kr, linen 2000kr) in a cosy dorm. Book ahead for tours as they fill up months in advance.

Kálfholt HORSE RIDING

(☎487 5176; www.kalfholt.is; Rte 288, Kálfholt 2, Ásahreppi; beginner/2hr rides from 7100/9300kr;) This family-run farm offers one of the best ranges of hourly rides, day trips and two- to eight-day treks for every skill level. Comfy lodging is in two little cabins (per person 4000kr). Find it on Rte 288, 17km west of Hella and south of the Ring Road.

Herríðarhóll HORSE RIDING

(☎487 5252; www.herridarholl.is; Herríðarhóli) Multiday horse tours (from 217,500kr) and short rides, plus a warm welcome from this German-Icelandic family to those who simply want a farmstay (doubles with shared bathroom, including breakfast 8100kr for one person, or 11,250kr for two guests). Find it west of Hella, then 6km north of the Ring Road on Rte 284.

Hestheimar HORSE RIDING

(☎487 6666, 854 5491; www.hestheimar.is; Rte 281) Take family-run riding trips (two-hour/one-day ride 12,000/20,000kr), rent horses, or bunk in a variety of comfortable accommodation (double from 23,000kr) at this horse farm above a bubbling stream. On Rte 281, 7km northwest of Hella.

Sleeping & Eating

Most of the horse farms on the plains around Hella have good accommodation options for riders and other travellers as well. There's also a couple of camping options.

Eating options are scarce, but meals can be found at some hotels and guesthouses.

Laugaland CAMPGROUND €

(☎895 6543; www.tjalda.is/en/laugaland; Rte 26; sites per adult/child 1500kr/free; early May–mid-Sep) Family camping complex northwest of Hella, with cooking facilities, swimming pool and hot-pots (adult/child 900/400kr). Electricity 1000kr. Find it on Rte 26 around 6km north of Rte 1.

Rjúpnavellir COTTAGE, CAMPGROUND €

(☎892 0409; www.rjupnavellir.is; Rte 26, Landsveit; sites per person/sleeping-bag accommodation 1300/4900kr, cottage per person 10,000-12,000kr;) Just where the paved road ends, and the closest accommodation to the Rte 26–F225 junction, you'll find these two large cabins with sleeping-bag space for 44 people (showers 400kr). There's also cooking facilities, camping, and a six-person cottage with a kitchen.

Hótel Leirubakki HOTEL €€

(☎487 8700; www.leirubakki.is; Leirubakki; s/d without bathroom 17,800/23,400kr, s/d with bathroom 25,600/31,000kr, all incl breakfast;) Opposite the Hekla Centre, this modern hotel block and large farmstead next door are some of the last outposts before you hit volcanoes and highland, making it a good base for Hekla climbers. Guests can also use a sauna and swimming pool, named the Viking Pool. Rooms have a stripped-back design with wooden floors and white walls.

Getting There & Away

Landmannalaugar buses stop in Leirubakki and/or Hrauneyjar.

Reykjavík Excursions (p429) Bus 11 from Reykjavík to Landmannalaugar (8500kr) stops in Leirubakki (6000kr, 2½ hours) and Hrauneyjar (7000kr, three hours). There are three to five daily mid-June to mid-September.

Bus 14 and 11a Landmannalaugar–Mývatn (16,400kr, 10 hours) Stop in Hrauneyjar (3500kr, one hour, one daily late June to August). Or catch it from Hrauneyjar to Mývatn (12,900kr, 8½ hours).

Sterna (p430) Bus 13/13a from Reykjavík stops in Landmannalaugar (15,500kr, roughly five hours) and Leirubakki (6500kr, 2½ hours, one daily late June to early September).

Trex (p430) Bus T21 from Reykjavík stops in Landmannalaugar (9100kr one-way, 4½ hours) and Leirubakki (5100kr, two hours, two daily mid-June to mid-September).

Hella & Around

POP 860

The Ring Road (Rte 1) runs right beside this small agricultural community on the banks of the pretty Ytri-Rangá river, in an important horse-breeding area in the plains around the Þjórsá river. It's the nearest town to shadow-wreathed volcano Hekla, 35km north, and remains relatively sleepy despite the arrival of new hotels in the area. Staying here is a quiet option, with easy access to the South's attractions.

Activities & Tours

FFF Skydive Iceland SKYDIVING

(☎699-5867; http://skydive.is; dropzone near Dynskálar, off Rte 1 Hella; tandem jumps from 55,000kr; ⏲Apr-Sep) See the South from the sky by hurtling from 10,000ft to 12,000ft towards the drop zone in Hella. The whole descent, including about 30 seconds of free fall, takes roughly 25 minutes – but will no doubt be an experience you'll remember forever. FFF Skydive Iceland also does midnight jumps in June and July. Advance booking essential.

Sundlaugin Hellu GEOTHERMAL POOL, HOT-POT

(☎487 5334; Útskálum 4; adult/child 900/300kr; ⏲6.30am-9pm Mon-Fri, 10am-7pm Sat & Sun Jun–mid-Aug, shorter hours mid-Aug–May) Hella's top attraction might be its geothermal swimming pool, with hot-pots, sauna and a cool water slide (April to October) to keep the kids happy. Towel rental 600kr.

Hella Horse Rental HORSE RIDING

(☎864 5950; www.hellahorserental.is; Gaddstaðaflatir, off Rte 1; 1.5-/3hr tours from 8500/15,000kr; 👪) Offering daily horse rides for beginners and experienced riders and everything in between. Tours run during the summer season around the area and to the Ægisíðufoss waterfall.

Mud Shark FISHING, JEEP TOUR

(☎691 1849; www.mudshark.is; fishing/Jeep tours per person 47,000/15,000kr) Offerings include highland fishing trips and black-beach Jeep tours (minimum two people).

Sleeping & Eating

Árhús CAMPGROUND, CABINS €

(South Door; ☎487 5577; www.arhus.is; Rangárbakkar 6; sites per tent 2500kr, cottages with/without bathroom from 18,000/13,400kr; 📶) Set along the river, just south of the Ring Road, Árhús has a cluster of cottages (from a simple room to a complete cabin with kitchenette and bathroom), ample camping space, a guest kitchen, and a good nearby restaurant serving steak, pasta, salmon and pizzas (mains 1800kr to 4900kr). The office doubles as an Arctic Adventures booking office.

★ **River Hotel** HOTEL €€

(☎487 5004; www.riverhotel.is; Þykkvabæjarvegur, Rte 25; d/f from 20,000/26,000kr; P📶) Relax and watch the river glide by through giant plate-glass windows in the lounge areas of this immaculate hotel on the banks of the Ytri-Rangá river. Contemporary rooms and a separate cottage are super-comfortable and there's an on-site restaurant for dinner. It's ideal for Northern Lights watching as well, and the owners are avid anglers. It gets booked up quickly.

Guesthouse Nonni GUESTHOUSE €€

(☎894 9953; Arnarsandur 3; s/d without bathroom incl breakfast 14,700/18,000kr; 📶) Run by friendly Nonni, who loves cooking a large

THE EDDAS

The medieval monastery at **Oddi**, in Rangárvellir about 8km south of Hella on Rte 266, was the source of the Norse Eddas, the most important surviving books of Viking poetry. The *Prose Edda* was written by the poet and historian Snorri Sturluson around 1222. It was intended to be a textbook for poets, with detailed descriptions of the language and meters used by the Norse *skalds* (court poets). It also includes the epic poem 'Gylfaginning', which describes the visit of Gylfi, the king of Sweden, to Ásgard, the citadel of the gods. In the process, the poem reveals Norse creation myths, stories about the gods, and the fate in store for men at Ragnarök, when this world ends.

The *Poetic Edda* was written later in the 13th century by Sæmundur Sigfússon. It's a compilation of works by unknown Viking poets, some predating the settlement of Iceland. The first poem, 'Voluspá' (Sibyl's Prophecy), is like a Norse version of Genesis and Revelations: it covers the beginning and end of the world. Later poems deal with the story of how Óðinn discovered the power of runes, and the legend of Siegfried and the Nibelungs, recounted in Wagner's *Ring Cycle*. The most popular poem is probably 'Þrymskviða', about the giant Thrym, who stole Þór's hammer and demanded the goddess Freyja in marriage in exchange for its return. To get his hammer back, Þór disguised himself as the bride-to-be and went to the wedding in her place. Much of the poem is devoted to his appalling table manners at the wedding feast, during which he consumes an entire ox, eight salmon and three skins of mead.

Today Oddi is simply a church and farmsteads.

OFF THE BEATEN TRACK

FJALLABAK ROUTE

In summer the Fjallabak Rte F208 (pronounced *fiat*-la-back; Fjallabaksleið Nyrðri) makes a spectacular alternative to the coast road between Hella, in southwest Iceland, and Kirkjubæjarklaustur, if you have a large 4WD. Its name translates as 'Behind the Mountains', and that's exactly where it goes.

Leave the Ring Road (Rte 1) west of Hella on Rte 26 (the eastern side of the Þjorsá), then take Rte F208 from near the Sigölduvirkjun power plant until you reach Landmannalaugar. From there, F208 continues east past the **Kirkjufell** marshes and beyond **Jökuldalur**, before coursing through the icy veins of a riverbed for 10km, climbing up to the **Hörðubreið lookout**, then descending down into **Eldgjá**. Rte F235 to **Langisjór** lake turns off from Rte F208 about 3km west of Eldgjá. You can camp (1600kr) or sleep in a hut (6800kr) in **Hólaskjól** (www.holaskjol.com).

The 40km stretch of Rte F208 from Eldgjá to **Búland** is in reasonable shape, but there are some rivers to ford before the road turns into Rte 208 and emerges back along the Ring Road (Rte 1) southwest of Kirkjubæjarklaustur.

Note that a 2WD vehicle wouldn't have a hope of completing even a small portion of the route, and car-hire companies prohibit taking 2WD vehicles on F roads. Since much of the Fjallabak Rte is along rivers (or rather, in rivers!), it's not ideally suited to mountain bikes either. People attempt it, but it's not casual cycling by any stretch.

You can follow the entire route by bus by leaving Reykjavík on an early Rte 11 bus with Reykjavík Excursions (p429) to Landmannalaugar (8500kr, around five hours). You can break it up by spending nights at the Landmannalaugar base and exploring the area before taking the return journey or continuing on to Skaftafell (9500kr, around 5½ hours).

Well-established trekking company **Fjallabak** (☎511 3070; www.fjallabak.is; 4-day trek from 140,000kr) leads multiday guided treks and assisted backpacking tours throughout the southern back country, with a speciality in the Fjallabak Nature Reserve area, which the Fjallabak Rte passes through. Midgard Adventure (p146) is another great option.

breakfast (fresh bread and flower-shaped waffles) for his guests, this small guesthouse on a residential street has four wooden-walled rooms tucked up a cork stairwell.

★Hótel Rangá HOTEL €€€
(☎487 5700; www.hotelranga.is; Hjarðarbrekka; d/ste incl breakfast from 54,000/119,000kr; @☎) Just south of the Ring Road, 8km east of Hella, Hótel Rangá, with its stuffed polar bear in the lobby, looks like a log cabin but caters to Iceland's high-end travellers. Service is top-notch, and the wood-panelled rooms and luxurious common areas are cosy. The restaurant (mains 2600kr to 10,500kr) has broad windows looking across open pastures.

Stracta Hótel HOTEL €€€
(☎531 8010; www.stractahotels.is; Rangárflatir 4; d with/without bathroom from 23,700/20,200kr, studio/apt from 31,300/61,000kr, all incl breakfast; ☎) Stracta is one of the new breed of Iceland's higher-end tourist hotels. Rooms range from modern, comfortable doubles to studios with microwaves and refrigerators, on up to family-friendly apartments (sleeping six). The upstairs restaurant has sweeping views of Vestmannaeyjar and volcanoes, while downstairs there's a bistro serving lunch and dinner. Relaxation areas include a lounge and hot tub.

Restaurant Árhús INTERNATIONAL €€
(☎487 5577; http://arhusrestaurant.is; Rangárbakkar, off Rte 1; mains 1800-4900kr; ⏲11am-10pm; P) Set on the river bank of the Rangá, Árhús serves tasty pasta, meat and fish dishes, plus burgers and pizzas. In nice weather the terrace overlooking the river has the best view in the house (though the tables next to the big windows inside are a good second choice).

Kjarval SUPERMARKET €
(☎585 7585; Suðurlandsvegur 1; ⏲9am-8pm Mon-Fri, to 6pm Sat, to 5pm Sun) Local supermarket with bakery and liquor store attached.

ℹ Getting There & Away

BUS

Buses stop at the Olís petrol station.

Strætó (p429) Runs buses 51 Reykjavík–Vík–Höfn and 52 Reykjavík–Landeyjahöfn (Reykjavík–Hella 3220kr, 1½ hours, five daily Monday to Friday, two Saturday and Sunday).

Sterna (p430) Runs bus 12/12a Reykjavík–Vík–Höfn (Reykjavík–Hella 3300kr, 1½ hours, one daily June to mid-September).

Reykjavík Excursions (p429) Services include buses 9 Reykjavík–Þórsmörk, 11 Reykjavík–Landmannalaugar, 17/17a Reykjavík–Mývatn, 18 Reykjavík–Álftavatn–Emstrur, 20 Reykjavík–Skaftafell and 21 Reykjavík–Hvolsvöllur all stop in Hella (5000kr, routes take between 1½ hours to 2½ hours). At least five daily.

Trex (p430) Bus T21 runs Reykjavík–Landmannalaugar (Hella–Landmannalaugar 6900kr, 2¼ hours, two daily mid-June to mid-September). Bus T11 runs Reykjavík–Þórsmörk (Hella–Þórsmörk 5400kr, two hours, two daily mid-June to mid-September).

Thule Travel (p134) Runs route Reykjavík–Landannalaugar (Hella–Landannalaugar 6300kr, three hours, two daily June to mid-September). Also from Reykjavík–Þórsmörk (Hella–Þórsmörk 4650kr, 2¾ hours, two daily mid-June to mid-September).

TAXI

Mountain Taxi (☎862 1864) Jón Pálsson offers a taxi service into the mountains and Highlands. He is based in Hella but can pick up anywhere.

Hvolsvöllur & Around

POP 950

The farms around Hvolsvöllur were the setting for the bloody events of *Njál's Saga*, one of Iceland's favourites; today, though, the Saga sites exist mainly as place names, peaceful grassed-over ruins or modern agricultural buildings. Hvolsvöllur itself had not been much more than a pit stop, with a couple of petrol stations and a cluster of houses, but is now home to an enormous volcano education centre and numerous guesthouses, which make it an increasingly popular base for South Iceland adventures.

Sights

The area offers ruin exploring and hunting for secret waterfalls, plus has great access to adventures around the south.

LAVA Centre MUSEUM

(Iceland Volcano & Earthquake Centre; ☎415 5200; www.lavacentre.is; Austurvegur 14, Hvolsvöllur; adult/child 2400kr/free, cinema only 1200kr/free, exhibition & cinema 3200kr; ⏲exhibition 9am-7pm, lava house to 9pm) Essentially displaying Iceland's birth story, the LAVA Centre is a full-blown multimedia experience on volcanic and seismic life. Divided into multiple chambers, the museum includes an earthquake simulator (equivalent to four on the Richter scale) and a fog of smoke resembling volcanic ash. Visitors will likely leave with a sharper understanding of how earthquakes and volcanoes interconnect.

Keldur RUINS

(☎530 2200; www.thjodminjasafn.is; Rangárvallavegur/Rte 264; admission 1200kr; ⏲10am-6pm mid-Jun–mid-Aug) About 5km west of Hvolsvöllur, unsurfaced Rte 264 winds about 8km north along the Rangárvellir valley to the medieval turf-roofed farm at Keldur. This historic settlement once belonged to Ingjaldur Höskuldsson, a character in *Njál's Saga*. The structure is managed by the National Museum Historic Buildings Collection and has interesting historical exhibits and a pastoral setting.

Tours

★Midgard Adventure HIKING TOUR, ADVENTURE TOUR

(☎578 3370; www.midgardadventure.is; Dufþaksbraut 14; tours 14,000-34,000kr) One of the South's best bespoke adventure operators. Founder Siggi Bjarni and the other guide-owners know the area incredibly well and are top for guided hikes along Fimmvörðuháls or Laugavegurinn and beyond. Loads of day tours with pick-up are on offer, including super-Jeep trips, canyoning and ice climbing. Midgard also operates a hostel and cafe.

Sleeping

There are excellent sleeping options in the village of Hvolsvöllur and the verdant countryside nearby, such as Fljótshlíð. The municipal campsite is just off the Ring Road (Rte 1) in the heart of town while there's a hip adventure hostel at the east of town.

Campground CAMPGROUND €

(☎866 8945, 898 2454; https://tjalda.is/en/hvolsvollur; Vestri-Garðsauki, off Rte 1; adult/child 1500/500kr; ⏲Jun-Nov) A sheltered green space just a minute's walk from Hvolsvöllur's shops and restaurants. Laundry facilities (300kr per wash) and showers (400kr) on-site. Electricity 1000kr per day.

Midgard Base Camp HOSTEL €€

(☎578 3180; www.midgard.is; Dufþaksbraut 14; dm/d from 5300/23,300kr; P 🛜) Smart bunk beds, crafted by local iron smiths, in dorms of four to six. Private rooms have fabulous views, also enjoyed from the communal rooftop with hot tub and sauna. Downstairs there's foosball and a comfy lounge area, plus a restaurant offering hearty meals that hit the spot after a day of outdoor adventures. The highland tours run from here get glowing reviews.

Spói Guesthouse B&B €€
(☎861 8687; www.spoiguesthouse.is; Hlíðarvegur 15/Rte 261; s/d without bathroom 13,200/18,900kr; P 📶) This impeccable family-run guesthouse has a collection of pristine rooms grouped around a large dining room with a broad wooden table where a lavish breakfast is served. The owners offer a wealth of local knowledge.

Asgarður COTTAGES €€
(☎487 1440; www.asgardurinn.is; Hvolstróð, off Rte 261; d without bathroom incl breakfast 17,900kr; 📶) Next to the town church, the cute picket-lined individual cottages here cluster under a stand of trees. They have two bedrooms and private bathrooms and kitchenettes. A quaint restored 1927 schoolhouse sits in the centre. Made-up beds cost 11,000kr and sleeping-bag accommodation is 5500kr.

Eating

Katla Restaurant BUFFET €
(☎415 5252; http://katlarestaurant.is; LAVA Centre, off Rte 1; mains from 2000kr, buffet per person 3600kr; ⏲9am-9pm) Those looking for a hearty feed should head inside the LAVA Centre, where a large modern dining area serves a decent buffet. Fill up on soup, bread, salad, a number of mains like fish, pork, meatballs and chicken, plus get a dessert and drink. À la carte options available. There's also a cafe attached serving drinks, cakes and coffee to go.

Kronan Supermarket SUPERMARKET €
(https://kronan.is; Austurvegur 4; ⏲9am-8pm) Groceries.

NJÁL'S SAGA

One of Iceland's best-loved (and longest) sagas is also one of the most complicated. The story involves two friends and neighbours, Gunnar Hámundarson and Njál Þorgeirsson. A petty squabble between their wives is a prelude to the feuds and battles that ultimately leave almost every character dead. Written in the 13th century, it recounts 10th-century events that took place in the hills around Hvolsvöllur.

Doomed hero Gunnar of Hlíðarendi (near Fljótsdalur) falls for and marries the beautiful, hot-tempered Hallgerður, who has long legs but – ominously – a 'thief's eyes'. Hallgerður has a falling-out with Bergþóra, wife of Njál. Things become increasingly strained between Gunnar and Njál as Hallgerður and Bergþóra begin murdering each other's servants.

In one important episode, Hallgerður sends a servant to burgle food from a man named Otkell. When Gunnar comes home and sees Hallgerður's stolen feast, his temper snaps. 'It's bad news indeed if I've become a thief's accomplice', he says, and slaps his wife – an act that later comes back to haunt him. (Spoiler alert: Hallgerður's two previous husbands were killed as a result of slapping her.)

Through more unfortunate circumstances, Gunnar ends up killing Otkell and is sentenced to exile. As he rides away from home, his horse stumbles. Fatally, he takes one last glance back at his beloved farm Hlíðarendi and is unable to leave the valley after all. His enemies gather their forces and lay siege to the farm, but Gunnar manages to hold off the attackers until his bowstring breaks. When he asks Hallgerður for a lock of her hair to repair it, she refuses, reminding him of the slap she received (years earlier) – and Gunnar is killed.

The feud continues as Gunnar and Njál's clan members try to avenge their slaughtered kin. Njál himself acts as a peace broker, forming treaties between the two families, but in the end, the complicated peacemaking is all for naught. Njál and his wife are besieged in their farm. Tucking themselves in bed with their little grandson between them, the couple allow themselves to be burnt alive.

The only survivor of the fire is Njál's son-in-law Kári, who launches a legal case against the arsonists, commits a bit of extrajudicial killing himself and is finally reconciled with his arch-enemy, Flosi, who ordered the burning of the Njál family.

★**Eldstó Art Café** CAFE €€
(☎482 1011; www.eldsto.is; Austurvegur 2, Hvolsvöllur; mains 2150-4250kr; ⊙10am-10pm Jun-Aug; P 📶) Eldstó serves fresh-brewed coffee, homemade daily specials (such traditional Icelandic flatbread with smoked lamb and hot chocolate for 1350kr) and main courses like slowly roasted lamb shank or oven-baked salmon. Burgers and salads are on the menu too, plus triple-stacked homemade cakes. There are several tables in the cosy, welcoming space.

Gallerí Pizza FAST FOOD €€
(☎487 8440; www.gallerypizza.weebly.com; Hvolsvegur 29; mains 1300-4460kr; ⊙11.30am-10pm, to 9pm Mon-Fri Nov-Mar) The town pizzeria, one street back from the main road, is a busy, no-frills place with vinyl booths and 20 different pies to try, from mixed seafood or the lava (with pepperoni, mushrooms, garlic, olives, jalapeños and cream cheese) to Hawaiian and classic margherita. There are nine burgers on offer too – including a Béarnaise burger.

Shopping

Una Local Products ARTS & CRAFTS
(Sveitabúðin Una; ☎544 5455; www.unalocalstore.is; Austurvegur 4, Hvolsvöllur; ⊙10am-6pm; 📶) This large hangar on the Ring Road is loaded with all manner of handmade Icelandic crafts, from fish-skin purses to woolly sweaters, jewellery and leather goods.

Vínbúðin ALCOHOL
(☎486 1886; www.vinbudin.is; Austurvegur 1; ⊙11am-6pm Mon-Thu, to 7pm Fri, to 4pm Sat) National liquor chain.

Getting There & Away

Buses from Reykjavík to Þórsmörk stop in Hvolsvöllur.

Strætó (p429) Services buses 51 Reykjavík–Vík–Höfn and 52 Reykjavík–Landeyjahöfn (Reykjavík–Hvolsvöllur 3680kr, 1¾ hours, seven daily Monday to Friday, five Saturday and Sunday).

Sterna (p430) buses 12/12a Reykjavík–Vík–Höfn (Reykjavík–Hvolsvöllur 3700kr, 2¾ hours, one daily June to mid-September).

Reykjavík Excursions (p429) Buses 9/9a Reykjavík–Þórsmörk, 18 Álftavatn–Reykjavík, 20/20a Reykjavík–Skaftafell and 21/21a Reykjavík–Skógar all stop in Hvolsvöllur (Reykjavík–Hvolsvöllur 5000kr, approximately two hours, around nine daily).

Trex (p430) Bus T11 Reykjavík–Þórsmörk (5400kr, two hours, two daily mid-June to mid-September) stops in Hvolsvöllur.

Thule Travel (p134) Buses travel Reykjavík–Þórsmörk (Hvolsvöllur–Þórsmörk, 4650kr, 2¾ hours, two daily mid-June to mid-September).

Hvolsvöllur to Skógar

After Hvolsvöllur, the Ring Road (Rte 1) loops east toward Vik with three important side roads. The first is Fljótshlíð (Rte 261), just at the eastern end of Hvolsvöllur; the second is Rte 254, which shoots south 12km to Landeyjahöfn where the ferry leaves for Vestmannaeyjar; and the third is Rte 249 north to Þórsmörk passing Seljalandsfoss. Staying on the Ring Road will bring you along the base of hulking Eyjafjallajökull, made famous with its ashy 2010 explosion, and will continue on to Skógar.

Fljótshlíð

Rte 261 follows the mossy green edge of the lush Fljótshlíð hills, offering great views of their waterfalls, such as **Gluggafoss**, on one side, and the Markarfljót river delta and Eyjafjallajökull on the other.

The surfaced section of the road ends soon after the farm and church at **Hlíðarendi**, once the home of Gunnar Hámundarson from *Njál's Saga*. With an amphibious vehicle or large 4WD you can continue along road F261 towards Landmannalaugar and **Tindfjöll** – a hiker's paradise. Though it seems tantalisingly close, Þórsmörk can only be reached via Rte F249.

Tours

Midgard Adventure (p146) and Southcoast Adventure run hiking and canyoning tours in Tindfjöll and around the region.

Óbyggðaferðir QUAD-BIKE TOURS
(ATV Travel; ☎661 2503; www.atvtravel.is; tours per person from 32,500kr, 2 people per bike 25,500kr) Quad-bike tours around Eyjafjallajökull, Þórsmörk and beyond. Trips run for two to three hours or nine to 14 hours.

Sleeping & Eating

Along the length of the valley there is a series of good guesthouses and hotels, some with camping.

Some of the region's hotels have eating options, or head into Hvolsvöllur for restaurants.

★Fljótsdalur HI Hostel HOSTEL €
(☎487 8498; www.hostel.is; Rte 261; dm from 4200kr; ⊙Apr-Oct) It's very basic, but if you're looking for a peaceful, remote base for highland walks, with a beautiful garden, homey kitchen, cosy sitting room and mountain views that make your knees tremble, then you'll find it here. There are only seven bare mattresses in the attic (bring a sleeping bag) and two four-bed rooms on the main floor. Book ahead. HI members get a discount.

Find it 27km east of Hvolsvöllur. The road gets rough toward the end and only 4x4s can make it up the steep hill to the hotel's parking area; those with regular cars should park at the bottom and walk the 50m up. Bring all supplies.

Kennarabústaður GUESTHOUSE €
(off Fljótshiðarvegur; d without bathroom from 9000kr; P 📶) Good-value sparkling clean former teachers' house with simple rooms. There's a shared kitchen and bathrooms, plus a large dining area and superfriendly staff.

★Hótel Fljótshlíð HOTEL €€
(Guesthouse Smáratún; ☎487 1416; www.smaratun.is; Rte 261, Smáratún; sites per adult/child 1350/670kr, s/d/t with bathroom 22,400/27,400/34,500kr; P 📶) This attractive white farmhouse with a blue-tin roof has smart hotel-style rooms, guesthouse rooms (with shared facilities), four- to six-person summerhouses, sleeping-bag places (4600kr) and spots for tents. Unwind in the hot tub, or let the kids loose on the playground or pool table. There's an on-site restaurant serving Icelandic fare, plus a breakfast buffet (1850kr). It's 12.5km east of Hvolsvöllur.

Fagrahlíd Guesthouse B&B €€
(☎863 6669; www.fagrahlid.is; Rte 261, Fagrahlíd Farm; d without bathroom from 13,500kr, 2-bedroom apt from 22,300kr, all incl breakfast; P 📶) This pretty clutch of white buildings clusters on a slope with sweeping views of the valley and the volcanoes in the distance. The friendly owner keeps everything tip-top, and comfortable rooms and the two-bedroom apartment share a communal hot tub. It's 6.5km east of Hvolsvöllur on Rte 261.

Hótel Eyjafjallajökull B&B, CAMPGROUND €€
(☎487 8360; www.hoteleyjafjallajokull.is; Rte 261, Hellishólar; sites per adult/child 1300/800kr, s/d incl breakfast from 16,200/18,800kr; P 📶) This long, narrow, wooden hotel is accompanied by a high-quality campground with hot tubs and laundry. Hotel rooms have en suite bathrooms and flat-screen TVs. Kids can burn some energy in the playground. Guests can also book bike rental, horse-riding and ATV tours here and enjoy a nine-hole golf course. Find it 11km east of Hvolsvöllur on Rte 261.

Seljalandsfoss

You'll see the glistening 60m-high Seljalandsfoss waterfall thundering off the lower escarpments of Eyjafjallajökull volcano from miles away. A (slippery) path runs around the back of the waterfall. A few hundred metres further down the Þórsmörk road, **Gljúfurárbui** gushes into a hidden canyon.

Seljalandsfoss is a popular stop on the Ring Road and a pick-up point for Þórsmörk-bound buses (Þórsmörk is impossible to reach by regular vehicles due to the big rivers that are necessary to cross). The road to Þórsmörk (Rte 249/F249) begins just east of the Markarfljót river and alongside Seljalandsfoss, and leads north, quickly turning into a spectacular 4WD-only road.

Tours

★Southcoast Adventure ADVENTURE TOUR
(☎867 3535; www.southadventure.is; Hamragarðar Campground, Rte 249; 3-/5hr tours from 22,900/32,900kr, price based on 2 people) South Coast Adventure is a small tour operator run by enthusiastic locals with loads of regional knowledge and excellent reputations. Book tailor-made super-Jeep tours. Popular routes include Þórsmörk to Landmannalaugar and the famous Eyjafjallajökull glacier. Also offers snowmobiling, volcano tours and hikes. The info desk is at Hamragarðar on 2WD-friendly Rte 249, next to Seljalandsfoss.

Sleeping & Eating

There's a small outdoor cafe selling cakes, sandwiches and soups in the car park at the waterfall. For more substantial meals head to Hvolsvöllur or Skógar.

★Hamragarðar CAMPGROUND €
(☎866 7532; Rte 249; sites per adult/child 1500kr/free; ⊙May-Sep) Camp right next to the hidden waterfall at Gljúfurárbui at the start of Rte 249. There's a small cafe (9am to 11pm

WORTH A TRIP

FLIGHTSEEING THE VOLCANOES

From Bakki Airport, on the coast 5km northwest of Landeyjahöfn, **Atlantsflug** (☎555 1615; www.flightseeing.is; Rte 253; scenic flights from 19,900kr) offers the chance to see Iceland as a bird would. Scenic flights cruise over waterfalls, canyons and mountains, plus the crater of Eyjafjallajökull ice cap and the nation's highlands. Flights also run to Heimaey in Vestmannaeyjar.

June to August) that sells cake and coffee, plus laundry services (500kr), showers (300kr), electricity hook-up (1000kr), shared kitchen and an info area for Southcoast Adventure (p149).

Nicehostel Seljaland HOSTEL €
(☎419 0100; https://nicetravel.is; off Rte 1; dm/d incl breakfast 5900/16,500kr) Around 2km south of Seljalandsfoss, this smart hostel has four immaculate private rooms and 12-people dorms with private reading lights. Kitchen facilities and free coffee and tea are available. Find it off Rte 1 on the way to Skógar.

★ **Stóra-Mörk III** GUESTHOUSE, COTTAGE €€
(☎487 8903; www.storamork.com; off Rd 248; d with/without bathroom incl breakfast 19,500/14,500kr; 📶) About 5km along Rte 249 beyond the cluster of traffic at Seljalandsfoss falls, a dirt track leads to the historic Stóra-Mörk III farmhouse (mentioned, of course, in *Njál's Saga*), which offers large, cosy rooms with pictures of nature scenes on the walls. The main house has some rooms with private bathrooms, a large kitchen and a dining room with excellent mountain-to-sea views.

Getting There & Away

There's now a 700kr per day parking fee for cars stopping at Seljalandsfoss. Bus companies are also charged higher rates to stop; the Strætó bus no longer stops here and there is discussion among certain bus companies about ceasing their routes to this location as well.

At the time of writing Sterna and Trex still ran services to Seljalandsfoss from Reykjavík, plus a new company Thule Travel, with routes from Seljalandsfoss to Reykjavík and Húsadalur/Þórsmörk.

South of Eyjafjallajökull

The Ring Road (Rte 1) goes directly through the flood zone south of Eyjafjallajökull (*ay-ya-fiat*-la-yo-gootl) volcano that was inundated with muddy ash during the infamous eruption in 2010. The gorgeous area skirts its lower cliffs and foothills, and is scored by waterfalls and dotted with farms.

Sights & Activities

Seljavallalaug GEOTHERMAL POOL
(Seljavallavegur, off Rte 242) FREE Seljavallalaug, a peaceful 1923 pool, is filled by a natural hot spring and has become very popular with tourists. From Edinborg (7km west of Skógar) follow Rte 242 and signs 2km to Seljavellir; park by the farm, and walk up the beautiful river valley for about 15 minutes. There are very basic changing facilities at the spring.

Skálakot HORSE RIDING
(☎487 8953; www.skalakot.com; Skálakotsvegur; 1hr tours from 7000kr, half-day rides from 19,000kr, 4-day rides to Þórsmörk 183,500kr) Horse farm Skálakot (15km west of Skógar on Rte 246) offers an array of one-hour rides, half-day treks to the glacier, and four-day riding trips to Þórsmörk, the wild land named after Norse god Thor. It also offers a range of **accommodation** (☎487 8953; www.skalakot.com; Moldnúpsvegur, off Rte 246; standard d/ste incl breakfast from 52,500/68,250kr; 🅿📶).

Sleeping & Eating

There's a loose string of guesthouses and farmsteads along the Ring Road (Rte 1).

Hótel Lambafell HOTEL €€
(☎487 1212; www.lambafell.is; Lambafell, off Rte 242; d/q from 23,600/48,600kr; 📶) This big, airy and super clean log-cabin-style hotel offers spacious rooms with private bathrooms. There's a hot tub on the patio.

Guesthouse Edinborg GUESTHOUSE €€
(☎487 1212; www.greatsouth.is; Rte 242, Lambafell; d incl breakfast 16,100kr; @📶) Formerly named Hótel Edinborg (and still signposted that way on the main road), this tall, tin-clad farmhouse has inviting wood-floored rooms with comfy beds and private bathrooms, and an attic seating area with glacier views. It feels out in the remote countryside despite being just off the Ring Road. It also operates the nearby Hótel Lambafell.

Country Hotel Anna HOTEL €€

(☎487 8950; www.hotelanna.is; Moldnúpur, off Rte 246; s/d incl breakfast 23,200/30,000kr; 📶) This inn's namesake, Anna, wrote books about her worldwide voyages – and her descendants' country hotel upholds her passion for travel, with seven sweetly old-fashioned rooms furnished with antiques and embroidered bedspreads. The hotel and its little restaurant (11am to 8.30pm, until 9pm between June and August; mains 3900kr to 5100kr) sit at the foot of Eyjafjallajökull volcano just off Rte 246.

★**Gamla Fjósið** ICELANDIC €€€

(Old Cowhouse; ☎487 7788; www.gamlafjosid.is; Hvassafell, off Rte 1; mains 3900-6900kr, burgers from 2070kr, volcano soup 2400kr; ⊙11am-9pm Jun-Aug, shorter hours Sep-May; 📶) Built in a former cowshed that was in use until 1999, this charming eatery's focus is on farm-fresh and grass-fed meaty mains, from burgers to Volcano Soup, a spicy meat stew. The hardwood floor and low beams are balanced by polished dining tables, large wooden hutches and friendly staff.

Getting There & Away

While buses from Reykjavík pass through here, there are currently no planned stops in the area. A rental car or 4WD is the best way to explore.

Skógar

POP 25

Skógar nestles under the Eyjafjallajökull ice cap just off the Ring Road. This little tourist settlement is the start (or occasionally the end) of the breathtaking hike over the Fimmvörðuháls Pass to Þórsmörk, and is one of the activity hubs of the Southwest. At its western edge, you'll see the dizzyingly high waterfall, Skógafoss, and on the eastern side you'll find a fantastic folk museum and a hidden waterfall named Kvernufoss.

Sights

★**Skógafoss** WATERFALL

(Skogafossvegur, off Rte 1) This 62m-high waterfall topples over a rocky cliff at the western edge of Skógar in dramatic style. Climb the steep staircase alongside for giddy views, or walk to the foot of the falls, shrouded in sheets of mist and rainbows. Legend has it that a settler named Þrasi hid a chest of gold behind Skógafoss. The top of the waterfall is the start of the dramatic Fimmvörðuháls trek (p153), which continues 23km on to Þórsmörk, the land of the gods.

★**Skógar Folk Museum** MUSEUM

(Skógasafn; ☎487 8845; www.skogasafn.is; Skógavegur, near Rte 1; adult/child 2000kr/free; ⊙9am-6pm Jun-Aug, 10am-5pm Sep-May) The highlight of little Skógar is the wonderful Skógar Folk Museum, which covers all aspects of Icelandic life. The vast collection was put together by Þórður Tómasson over roughly 75 years – he retired as the museum's curator at the age of 92. There are also restored buildings – a church, a turf-roofed farmhouse, cowsheds – and a huge, modern building that houses an interesting transport and communication museum, a basic cafe and a shop.

★**Kvernufoss** WATERFALL

(Skógavegur, off Rte 1) Pretty much off the tourist radar (you'll likely have the place to yourself) is this hidden 20m waterfall that you can walk behind. The short trail to it starts behind the grey building at the far east of the Skógar Folk Museum car park. Climb the stile over the fence and follow the walking path (roughly 15 minutes) towards the cliff, and through a glorious moss-covered canyon to a magnificent rushing stream of water pounding into the pool below.

Tours

Several major operators have their bases near Skógar and offer tours to natural wonders in the area, from glaciers to volcanoes and beyond. Excellent companies operating in the general Skógar area include Southcoast Adventure (p149), Midgard Adventure (p146) and Arctic Adventures (p72), doing everything from guided treks and super-Jeep tours to ice climbing. Pick-up from Skógar can be arranged.

Icelandic Mountain Guides ADVENTURE TOUR

(☎587 9999, Skógar desk 894 2956; www.mountainguides.is; Rte 221; glacier kayaking from 12,900kr, guided Fimmvörðuháls hikes from 89,900kr; ⊙9.30am-5pm) One of the largest and best operators in Iceland, Icelandic Mountain Guides has partnered up with Arcanum (p166), located at Sólheimajökull, and also has booking facilities at Hótel Skógafoss (p152). Locally it runs kayaking around the glacier, guided Fimmvörðuháls hikes and many tours further afield. Offers Reykjavík pick-up.

Sleeping

Although Skógar is set up for tourists, with various places to stay, it's essential to book well ahead in high season.

★Skógar Campsite CAMPGROUND €
(Skógafossvegur, near Rte 1; sites per person 1500kr; ⏲May-Sep) Basic grassy lot in a superb location, right next to Skógafoss. The sound of falling water makes a soothing lullaby to drift off to. There's a no-frills toilet and shower (300kr per person) block, plus a couple of washbasins for pots and pans. Pay at the small office window next to the showers.

Skógar HI Hostel HOSTEL €
(☎487 8780; www.hostel.is; Skógafossvegur, off Rte 1; dm/d from 5900/17,800kr; 📶) A solid link in the HI chain, this spot is located a stone's throw from Skógafoss in an old school with utilitarian rooms. There's a guest kitchen and a laundry.

★Skógar Guesthouse GUESTHOUSE €€
(☎894 5464; www.skogarguesthouse.is; Ytri Skógar, off Skógaveur; d/tr without bathroom incl breakfast 23,800/35,700kr; 📶) This charming white farmhouse is tucked in a strand of trees, beyond the Hótel Edda, almost to the cliff face. A friendly family offers quaint, impeccably maintained rooms with crisp linens and cosy quilts, and a large immaculate kitchen. A hot tub on a wood deck sits beneath the maples. It feels out of the tourist fray, despite being just a 10-minute walk from Skógafoss.

Hótel Skógafoss HOTEL €€
(☎487 8780; www.hotelskogafoss.is; Skógafossvegur, off Rte 1; d incl breakfast 27,200-29,500kr; 📶) Nineteen well-put-together, modern rooms (half of which have views of Skógafoss) and good bathrooms. There's a well-located bistro-bar, with plate-glass windows looking onto the falls, and local beer on tap.

Hótel Edda Skógar HOTEL €€
(☎444 4000; www.hoteledda.is; Skógavegur, off Rte 1; d without bathroom from 21,800kr; ⏲early Jun-late Aug; 🅿📶) Perfectly serviceable but rather bland and worn, the local school is turned into a hotel for summer each year. It's close to the museum and split over two buildings. All rooms have washbasins but shared bathrooms.

Hótel Skógar HOTEL €€€
(☎487 4880; www.hotelskogar.is; Skógarfossvegur, near Rte 1; s/d/tr incl breakfast 24,300/27,600/34,100kr; 📶) This architecturally interesting hotel has 12 small, eclectic rooms with quirky antiques, some with hill views. From the garden you can see Eyjafjöll glacier and the Skógafoss waterfall. A hot tub and sauna plus an elegant restaurant (noon to 3pm and 6pm to 10pm; mains 1600kr to 4900kr) round it out. Good breakfast too.

Eating

Mia's Country Kitchen FISH & CHIPS €
(☎696 6542; Skógafossvegur, near Rte 1; fish & chips 2000kr; ⏲noon-4pm) Mia's red-and-while polka-dotted food truck sells one thing only – fresh fish and chips, with crunchy wedges and sauce (choose Icelandic tartar, sweet chilli or ketchup). It's permanently located on the road to Skógafoss.

Fossbúð ICELANDIC, ENGLISH €€
(☎487 4880; Skógafossvegur, off Rte 1; mains 1500-3000kr; ⏲9am-9pm Jun-Aug; 📶) Fossbúð doesn't have the most glamorous decor, but it does have friendly staff and serves reasonably priced hearty plates. Order soup, hamburgers, sandwiches and cakes, or more solid meals like fish and chips or full English breakfasts (with beans, tomatoes, toast, sausages, bacon and eggs). There's also free wi-fi, a **tourist information** (Skógafossvegur, off Rte 1; ⏲9am-9pm Jun-Aug) desk and a shop with groceries and camping supplies.

Hótel Skógafoss Bistro-Bar ICELANDIC €€
(☎487 8780; www.hotelskogafoss.is; Skógar, off Rte 1; mains 1900-3300kr; ⏲11am-9pm) The bistro-bar at Hótel Skógafoss is in a very convenient location, and rather tempting with its large windows looking onto the nearby falls. However, food is mediocre (burgers, pastas, fish), service can be slow and the staff often unfriendly. That said, it does serve local beer on tap (from 1100kr).

Getting There & Away

Strætó (p429) Bus 51 from Reykjavík (5520kr, 2½ hours, two daily) stops in Skógar, as does Sterna (p430) bus 12/12a from Reykjavík (5300kr, three hours, one daily June to mid-September).

Reykjavík Excursions (p429) Also has services from Reykjavík, including bus 20/20a (6700kr, 3¼ to four hours, one daily June to early September) and direct bus 21/21a (6700kr, 3¼ to four hours, two daily June to August).

FIMMVÖRÐUHÁLS TREK

Fimmvörðuháls (www.fimmvorduhals.is) – named for a pass between two brooding glaciers – dazzles the eye with a parade of wild inland vistas. Linking Skógar and Þórsmörk, the truly awesome hike is 23.4km long and showcases all of Iceland's varied terrain in one fell swoop. It can be divided into three distinct sections of somewhat equal length. Plan for around 10 hours to complete the trek (although it can be done quicker); this includes stops to rest and to check out the steaming remnants of the Eyjafjallajökull eruption. It's best to tackle the hike from late June to early September, but get local advice on conditions, and check www.safetravel.is. Download the 112 Iceland app and check in your location at the beginning and at various points on the trail (the app has a one touch emergency button too, in case you need it). There should be mobile-phone signal intermittently on the trail. Pack wisely; you can experience all four seasons over the course of this hike. While it's a completely manageable walk in good weather (if you're reasonably fit), if in doubt, go with a guide, who will help negotiate two treacherous passes.

Part 1: Waterfall Way Starting on the right side of splashy Skógafoss, the path zooms up and over the falls quickly, revealing a series of waterfalls just behind. Stay close to the tumbling water as you climb over small stones and twisting trees – there are 22 chutes in all, each one magnificent. The path flattens out as the trees turn to windswept shrubs, then set your sights on the 'bridge', which is a crude walkway over the gushing river below. It's imperative that you make the crossing on the walkway, otherwise you won't make it over and down into Þórsmörk later on.

Part 2: The Ashtray After crossing the crude bridge onto the left side of the moving water you start to enter the gloomy heart of the pass between two glaciers: Eyjafjallajökull and Mýrdalsjökull. The weather can be quite variable here – it could be raining in the pass when there is sunshine in Skógar. Expect to bundle up at this point as you move through icy rifts, probably snow in the earlier parts of summer. If you want to break up the hike over two days, book ahead for either the 20-person **Baldvinsskáli** (☎568 2533; www.fi.is; N 63°36.622', W 19°26.477'; sleeping-bag dm 7000kr; ⏲mid-Jun–mid-Sep) or **Fimmvörðuháls** (☎893 4910, booking 562 1000; www.utivist.is; N 63°37.320', W 19°27.093'; sleeping-bag accommodation per person 6500kr; ⏲mid-Jun–Aug) huts; booking in advance is advisable. The latter is positioned 600m away from the main trail about halfway through the walk (it can be difficult to find in bad weather; note the GPS coordinates before you set off). There's no campsite. Continuing on, the initial site from the Eyjafjallajökull eruption reveals itself; here you'll find steaming earth and the world's newest mountains – Magni and Móði. Climb up to the top of Magni, where people have been know to roast sausages over one of the sizzling vents.

Part 3: Goðaland After climbing down from Magni, the last part of the hike begins. The barren ashiness continues for a while, then an otherworldly kingdom reveals itself – a place ripped straight from the pages of a fairy tale. Here in Goðaland – the aptly named 'Land of the Gods' – wild Arctic flowers bloom as stone cathedrals emerge in the distance. Vistas of green continue as you descend into Þórsmörk to complete the journey.

GPS markers Although the hike is relatively short compared to some of Iceland's famous multiday treks, it's important to bring a GPS along – especially for the second portion of the hike when the way isn't always obvious. The following nine GPS markers can keep DIYers on track:

1 N 63°31.765, W 19°30.756 (start)

2 N 63°32.693, W 19°30.015

3 N 63°33.741, W 19°29.223

4 N 63°34.623, W 19°26.794 (the 'bridge')

5 N 63°36.105, W 19°26.095

6 N 63°38.208, W 19°26.616 (beginning of eruption site)

7 N 63°39.118, W 19°25.747

8 N 63°40.561, W 19°27.631

9 N 63°40.721, W 19°28.323 (terminus at Básar)

1

KOTENKO OLEKSANDR/SHUTTERSTOCK ©

2

4

KAVRAM/SHUTTERSTOCK ©

ANDREY BAYDA/SHUTTERSTOCK ©

BEKETOFF /SHUTTERSTOCK ©

1. Hverir (p311)
The magical world of Hverir has safe trails through its lunar-like landscape of belching mudpots and sulphur.

2. Fjaðrárgljúfur (p183)
The river Fjaðrá flows through the picturesque Fjaðrárgljúfur canyon.

3. Gatklettur (p228)
The rock arch Gatklettur is on Djúpalón Beach, on the southwest coast.

4. Reynisfjara beach (p166)
Black-sand beach Reynisfjara is backed by a stack of basalt columns that look like a magical church organ.

Landmannalaugar

Mind-blowing multicoloured mountains, soothing hot springs, rambling lava flows and clear-blue lakes make Landmannalaugar one of Iceland's most unique destinations, and a must for explorers of the interior. It's a favourite with both Icelanders and visitors – as long as the weather cooperates.

Part of the Fjallabak Nature Reserve, Landmannalaugar (600m above sea level) includes the largest geothermal field in Iceland outside the Grímsvötn caldera in Vatnajökull. Its multihued peaks are made of rhyolite – a mineral-filled lava that cooled unusually slowly, causing those intense pigments. It is as though you've stepped into a watercolour painting.

The area is the official starting point for the famous Laugavegurinn hike, and there are also some excellent day hiking opportunities, plus a natural pool.

Sights

Hnausapollur VOLCANO

(off F208) Sitting behind a volcanic ledge, right off the road to Landmannalaugar, hides an enormous crater. Hnausapollur erupted around 11,000 years ago, now it's filled with piercing blue turquoise water. Those in a 4WD can drive right up to the edge of the crater and peer into it from the car. It's also possible to carefully walk around the rim or obtain a permit (3500kr) from the Mountain Mall and go fishing in the lake below.

There's no road sign on the F208 pointing out this magnificent sight, which is around 200m from the road. Look for a dirt path leading up to a hill on the left before you reach Frostastaðavatn lake.

Natural Pool HOT SPRINGS

(off F224) FREE Boardwalks from Landmannalaugar's info hut lead to a geothermal hot pool flanked by volcanic hills. It's not officially a 'bathing area', but visitors are fine to take a dip in the water at their own risk. Signs around the area warn that the water is not disinfected, and entirely natural. Swimmer's Itch has been previously identified in these waters – but that doesn't stop the hordes of hikers bathing here every day.

Stútur VOLCANO

(off F224) Roughly translated as 'bottleneck', the Stútur crater sits on the Norðurnámshraun lava field and is signposted off the F224 road. Two fairly steep trails lead up both the west and east of the volcano to the crater's edge. On clear days it's possible to see Frostastaðavatn lake from the top. There are a couple of car parking spots on the side of the road. Alternatively, hike from Landmannalaugar.

Activities

There's plenty to do in and around Landmannalaugar, though many hikers skip the area's wonders and set off right away for their Laugavegurinn hike. If you plan to stick around, you'll be happy to know that the crowds dwindle in the evenings and, despite the base's chaotic appearance, you'll find peace in the hills above.

Hiking

If you're day hiking in the Landmannalaugar area, stop by the info hut to purchase the useful day-trip map (300kr), which details all of the best hikes in the region. Guided hikes (through operators from Hvolsvöllur to Skógar areas) can also be a great way to explore the area.

The start of the Laugavegurinn hike (p158) is behind the Landmannalaugar hut, marked in red.

★ Ljótipollur HIKING

(off F208) Day-hike to the ill-named Ljótipollur (Ugly Puddle), an incredible magenta crater filled with bright-blue water. The intense, fiery-red colour comes from iron-ore deposits. Oddly enough, although it was formed by a volcanic explosion, the lake is rich in brown trout. The walk to the Puddle offers plenty of eye candy, from tephra desert and lava flow to marsh and braided glacial valleys.

To get there from Landmannalaugar, you can climb over the 786m-high peak **Norðurnámur** or just traverse its western base to emerge on the road (a 10km to 13.3km return trip, depending on the route). For a shorter hike, it's possible to park near the trail on the F208 and hike to the crater – look for the signposts to the trail on the way into Landmannalaugar.

Brennisteinsalda HIKING

When the weather is clear, opt for a walk that takes in the region's spectacular views. From Landmannalaugar, climb to the summit of rainbow-streaked Brennisteinsalda – covered in steaming vents and sulphur deposits – for a good view across the rugged and variegated landscape. It's a 6.5km return trip from Landmannalaugar.

From Brennisteinsalda it's another 1½ hours along the Þórsmörk route to the impressive Stórihver geothermal field. Ask at the Landmannalaugar Hut to point you in the direction of the trailhead.

Frostastaðavatn HIKING

(off F208) This blue lake lies behind the rhyolite ridge north of the Landmannalaugar Hut. Walk over the ridge and you'll be rewarded with far-ranging views as well as close-ups of the interesting rock formations and moss-covered lava flows flanking the lake.

Fishing

Buy fishing licences (3500kr per person) for local lakes from the Mountain Mall at Landmannalaugar or at Landmannahellir.

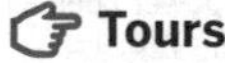

Tours

Landmannalaugar has **horse-riding tours** (☎868 5577; www.hnakkur.is; 1-/2hr tour 9000/13,000kr) from July to mid-August. The horse farms on the plains around Hella also offer riding (usually longer trips) in and around the Landmannalaugar area.

Sleeping

Landmannalaugar has a large base with camping and hut facilities. The camp opens for the season depending on when the roads are clear, usually sometime in June. It closes for sure by mid-October, but it may be earlier if there's a lot of snow or the water has to be turned off.

Landmannalaugar Hut & Camping Complex HUTS, CAMPGROUND €

(☎booking 568 2533, huts Jul-Sep 860 3335; www.fi.is; F244; sites/huts per person 2000/9000kr, facilities day use 500kr) In the middle of summer this campground can look surprisingly raggle-taggle, with hundreds of tents, several structures inundated with hikers, and laundry dangling throughout. The hut accommodates 78 people in close quarters and it is essential to book ahead. There's a kitchen area for hut guests and showers (500kr for five minutes of hot water) available to all.

Campers pitch tents in designated areas and have access to a sheltered tented dining-room area – ideal for when the weather is ghastly. Wild camping is strictly prohibited, as the entire area is in the protected Fjallabak Nature Reserve. There are several wardens on-site. At the time of writing there was no limit on the number of campers at Landmannalaugar, and you cannot reserve. By road, Landmannalaugar Hut is accessible with 4WD via the F244.

Landmannahellir CAMPGROUND €

(☎893 8407; www.landmannahellir.is; sites per adult 1500kr, sleeping-bag accommodation per person 6100kr, plus tax per person per booking 333kr; ⏰mid-Jun–early Sep) This remote campsite has basic facilities, including a shower (500kr) and toilets, as well as hut lodging (sleeping bag required). It also sells fishing licences (3500kr one-day). Trex (www.trex.is) bus T21 Reykjavík–Landmannalaugar can stop at Landmannahellir (7450kr, 3¾ hours, one or two daily mid-June to early September) if arranged in advance.

Eating

There are no formal restaurants at Landmannalaugar; bring all of your own food. The Mountain Mall sells soup and some basic food supplies at a premium, and the Landmannalaugar Hut & Camping Complex has cooking facilities for guests.

Shopping

Mountain Mall FOOD & DRINKS

(www.landmannalaugar.info; off F224; ⏰8am-8pm Jun–mid-Sep, 10am-5pm mid-Sep–May) The Mountain Mall on the Landmannalaugar grounds is set up inside three buses. Here you can buy basic supplies from hats, long johns, maps and camping gear to hot chocolate (500kr), fresh soup (from 1300kr), groceries and snacks. It also sell fishing licences (2000kr per person per day).

Information

The Landmannalaugar **wardens** (off F224; ⏰8am-7pm & 8-9.30pm Jun-Sep) can answer questions and provide directions and advice on hiking routes. They also sell a map of day hikes (300kr) and the Laugavegurinn hike (1800kr), as well as a booklet in English and Icelandic on the hike (3000kr). Note that wardens do not know if it will rain (yes, this is the most frequently asked question here). At the time of writing there was no wi-fi, but there was some mobile-phone reception.

The **Information Hut** (www.fi.is; off F224; ⏰8am-7pm & 8pm-10pm Jun-Sep) – simply known as Landmannalaugar – is operated by Ferðafélag Íslands (p162) and provides hiking, accommodation and general info, plus maps of the local area. The same company runs the campsite and sleeping hut next door, plus huts on the Laugavegurinn hike. The company website is also loaded with information.

Getting There & Away

BUS

Landmannalaugar can be reached by rugged, semi-amphibious buses from three different directions. They run when the roads are open to Landmannalaugar (check www.road.is) in the summer, when snow has cleared.

From Reykjavík Buses travel along the western part of the Fjallabak Rte, which first follows Rte 26 east of the Þjorsá to F225.

From Skaftafell Buses follow the Fjallabak Rte (F208).

From Mývatn Buses cut across the highlands via Nýidalur on the Sprengisandur Rte (F26).

It's possible to travel from Reykjavík and be in Landmannalaugar for two to 10 hours before returning to Reykjavík, or three to five hours before going on to Skaftafell. That's about enough time to take a dip in the springs and/or a short walk. Schedules change, but morning buses usually reach Landmannalaugar by midday. Alternatively, stay overnight and catch a bus out when you're done exploring.

Reykjavík Excursions (p429) Services include bus 10/10a Skaftafell–Landmannalaugar (9500kr, 5¾ hours, one daily late June to early September), and bus 11/11a Reykjavík–Landmannalaugar (8500kr, 4½ to five hours, five daily mid-June to mid-September). Meanwhile, bus 14/14a runs between Mývatn and Landmannalaugar (16,100kr, 10 hours, one daily late June to early September).

Sterna (p430) Runs bus 13/13a Reykjavík–Landmannalaugar (7950kr, 4¾ hours, one daily late June to early September).

Trex (p430) Runs bus T21 Reykjavík–Landmannalaugar (9100kr, 4¼ hours, two daily mid-June to early September).

Thule Travel (p134) Runs route Reykjavík–Landannalaugar (8200kr, four hours, two daily mid-June to mid-September), from Hella (6300kr, three hours), from Selfoss (7650kr, three hours), from Hvergerði (7650kr, three hours).

CAR

Roads to Landmannalaugar are open in summer only (approximately late June to September) depending on weather and road conditions (check www.safetravel.is and www.road.is). There are three routes to Landmannalaugar from the Ring Road (Rte 1), all requiring a minimum of a 4WD. Driving from Mývatn to Landmannalaugar takes all day along the Sprengisandur Rte route (4WD only). If you have a small 4WD, you will have to leave your vehicle in a parking area about 1km before Landmannalaugar, as the river crossing here is too perilous for small cars, and cross by footbridge. Two-wheel-drive rentals are not allowed to drive on F roads to Landmannalaugar.

There's no petrol at Landmannalaugar. The nearest petrol pumps are 40km north at **Hrauneyjar** (Hotel Highland; 487 7782; www.hrauneyjar.is; Rte 26, Hrauneyjar; P), close to the beginning of the F208 and also in the Fjallabak Reserve; and 90km southeast at Kirkjubæjarklaustur. To be on the safe side you should fill up along the Ring Road (Rte 1) if approaching from the west or the north.

F208 Northwest In summer, it's a fairly well-travelled route and you'll likely see numerous vehicles entering and leaving Landmannalaugar on this road. You can follow the western side of the Þjorsá (Rte 32), passing Árnes, then take Rte F208 down into Landmannalaugar from the north. This is the easiest path to follow for small 4WDs. After passing the power plant, the road from Hrauneyjar becomes horribly bumpy and swerves between power lines all the way to Ljótipollur ('Ugly Puddle').

F225 On the eastern side of the Þjorsá, follow Rte 26 inland through the low plains behind Hella, loop around Hekla, then take Rte F225 west until you reach the base. This route is harder to tackle (rougher roads).

F208 Southeast The hardest route comes from the Ring Road between Vík and Kirkjubæjarklaustur. This is the Skaftafell–Landmannalaugar bus route.

You can also take a super-Jeep tour with local tour operators, which will take you out to Landmannalaugar from Reykjavík, or from anywhere in the south.

Laugavegurinn Hike: Landmannalaugar to Þórsmörk

The two- to five-day hike from Landmannalaugar to Þórsmörk – commonly known as Laugavegurinn – is where backpackers earn their stripes in Iceland. It means 'Hot Spring Road', and it's easy to understand why. The harsh, otherworldly beauty of the landscape morphs in myriad ways as you traipse straight through the island's interior, with much of the earth steaming and bubbling from the intense activity below its surface. Expect wildly coloured mountainsides, glacial rivers and the glaciers themselves, and to finally emerge at a verdant nature reserve in Þórsmörk. It is the most popular hike in Iceland and the infrastructure is sound, with carefully positioned huts along the zigzagging 55km route. But it is

Laugavegurinn Hike

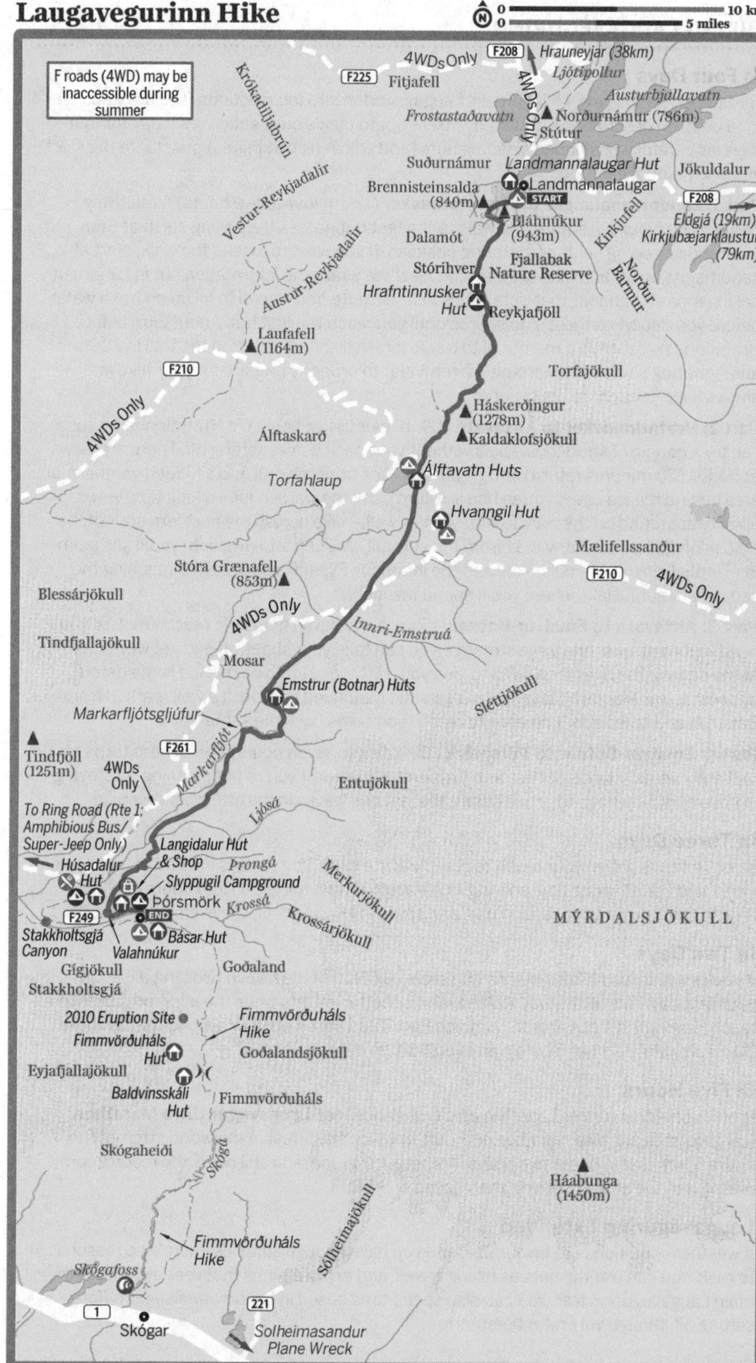

HIKING LAUGAVEGURINN

In Four Days

Ferðafélag Íslands (www.fi.is) breaks Laugavegurinn into four sections (see the website for a detailed description), and many hikers opt to tackle one section each day for four days, as carefully positioned sleeping huts (and adjoining campsites) punctuate the start and end point of each leg.

Part 1: Landmannalaugar to Hrafntinnusker (12km; four to five hours) A relatively easy start to your adventure, the walk to the first hut passes the boiling earth at Stórihver and sweeping fields of glittering obsidian. If you want to extend the walk, start at Landmannalaugar and hike to Hrafntinnusker via Skalli; the information hut in Landmannalaugar has a handout that details this quieter route. You'll need to fill up on fresh water before you depart as there's no source until you reach the first hut. About 2km before Hrafntinnusker there's a memorial to a solo Israeli hiker who died on the trail in 2005 after ignoring a warden's warning – a reminder to properly prepare for your hike and always keep your ear to the ground.

Part 2: Hrafntinnusker to Álftavatn (12km; four to five hours) At Hrafntinnusker you can try a couple of short local hikes without your pack before setting off. There are views at Södull (20 minutes return) and Reykjafjöll (one hour return), and a hidden geothermal area behind the ice caves (three hours return); ask the warden for walking tips. Views aplenty are found on the walk to Álftavatn as well – hike across the northern spur of the Kaldaklofsfjöll ice cap for vistas from the summit. Walking into Álftavatn you'll see looming Tindfjallajökull, Mýrdalsjökull and the infamous Eyjafjallajökull before reaching the serenely beautiful lake where you'll spend the night.

Part 3: Álftavatn to Emstrur-Botnar (15km; six to seven hours) To reach Emstrur you'll need to ford at least one large stream – you can take your shoes off and get wet or wait at the edge of the river for a 4WD to give you a lift over. Not to be missed is the detour to spectacular Markarfljótsgljúfur – a gigantic multihued canyon. It's well marked from Emstrur, and takes about an hour to reach (you come back the same way).

Part 4: Emstrur-Botnar to Þórsmörk (15km; six to seven hours) Barrenness turns to brilliantly verdant lands dotted with lush Arctic flowers. If you're not planning on staying in Þórsmörk, you need to arrive before the last bus leaves in the afternoon/evening.

In Three Days

If you're fit, it's within your reach to complete the hike in three days instead of four. Cover Part 1 and Part 2 in one day, arriving at Álftavatn after a full eight to 10 hours of hiking. Hike to Emstrur on your second day, and arrive in Þórsmörk on the evening of your third.

In Two Days

If you're a fast, avid hiker, you can complete all 55km of the hike in two long days. On your first day, hike all the way to Álftavatn, or better yet, continue the additional 5km to reach Hvanngil. It's possible to combine Part 3 and Part 4 on your second day, as these 30km are relatively flat. There's an overall 100m decline.

In Five Hours

Professional trail runner? Join the epic endurance race **Laugavegur Ultra Marathon** (Laugavegshlaupið; www.marathon.is; ⏲ Jul), in which the fittest in the world attempt the entire 55km trail in under five hours. Þorbergur Ingi Jónsson still holds the record, completing it in the almost superhuman speed of 3:59:13.

Laugavegurinn Extended

If weather conditions are favourable, and you have enough supplies, there's no reason to rush. You can use the huts as hiking bases, and explore paths that veer away from the main Laugavegurinn trail. You can also spend time based in Landmannalaugar before setting off, though we prefer Þórsmörk.

essential that you book months in advance if you intend to use them. Campers do not need to reserve.

Check www.safetravel.is before setting out (and log your plan with them). Also download the 112 app and check in en route; it has a one-touch emergency button, in case you need it. In addition, be sure to register at the information hut in Landmannalaugar. It is imperative not to attempt the hike out of season (opening dates vary according to weather, but tend to be early July to early September), as the conditions can be lethal and there will be no services on the route. Even in summer there will be snow and fog along the way, and rivers to cross – prepare accordingly.

Sleeping & Eating

As the Laugavegurinn trail is very well travelled, you'll find a constellation of carefully positioned huts along the way, all owned and maintained by Ferðafélag Íslands (www.fi.is). These huts sleep dozens of people, but (while you might get lucky) most people book (and prepay) months in advance. You can get on a waiting list the year before, and bookings officially open in October or November prior to the summer. We cannot stress enough that these beds go quickly. Also note that you need to bring a sleeping bag for the bunk beds in the huts, and most bunks sleep four people each – two (side by side) on each level. If you are alone, expect to be paired with a stranger.

Huts usually have a solar panel for wardens to charge their communications equipment and perhaps lights for the hut, but there is no electricity for hikers. There is a strict quiet rule from midnight to 7am in all huts.

There is camping in designated areas around the huts, though with the increasing popularity of the hike, these can become full as well (no limit was in place at the time of writing). Note that campers *do not* have access to hut kitchens or facilities and must bring all their own camping and cooking equipment. Campers can use bathrooms and running water. Camping areas are often exposed to the elements – streamline your tent with the wind, then pin it down with extra boulders. All camping costs 2000kr per person, and does not need to be reserved. Wardens usually accept cash and credit cards.

Huts are usually open late June to early September, but this is weather dependent; check ahead. Huts are locked in winter. Wild camping is strictly forbidden along the whole trail, as these are protected nature reserves.

There is no food for sale along the trail so you have to bring everything.

Hrafntinnusker HUT, CAMPGROUND €
(Höskuldsskáli; ☎499 0679; www.fi.is; N 63°56.014', W 19°10.109'; sites/sleeping-bag huts per person 2000/9000kr) This hut holds 52 people (around 22 of whom sleep on mattresses on the floor in a converted attic space). There's cold running water during the summer months, an outhouse and geothermal heating, but no refuse facilities and no showers – you must carry your rubbish to Hvangil.

It is at an elevation of 1027m – be prepared for particularly inhospitable conditions if you are camping – and it's the barest-bones of the huts. Some campers cook their food on the natural steam vents nearby; ask the warden (July and August only) to point you in the right direction. When there is no warden, water must be sourced from a stream or snow.

Álftavatn HUT, CAMPGROUND €
(☎823 4008; www.fi.is; N 63°51.470', W 19°13.640'; sites/sleeping-bag huts 2000/9000kr) Two huts here hold 72 people in total; both have drinking water and mattresses. Kitchen facilities have gas stoves. Showers cost 500kr. Opening coincides with the opening of local F roads (anywhere from early to late June, depending on weather), making it accessible with 4WD. It closes in mid-September.

Hvanngil HUT, CAMPGROUND €
(☎860 3336; www.fi.is; N 63°50.026' W 19°12.507'; sites/huts per person 2000/8500kr) This hut is on an alternative path on the Laugavegurinn hike, 5km south of the Álftavatn hut. It sleeps 60 people and has a kitchen and shower (500kr). It's a good choice for people tackling Laugavegurinn in two days. It tends to be much less busy than Álftavatn.

Emstrur HUT, CAMPGROUND €
(Botnar; ☎490 0137; www.fi.is; N 63°45.980', W 19°22.450'; sites/huts per person 2000/8500kr) Emstrur has 60 beds divided across three huts. There are two showers (500kr for five minutes of hot water), toilets and a gas stove. There are no garbage facilities or power outlets. Although it's located under the glacier, the other huts have a more striking position along the trail. Note that mobile-phone reception is particularly spotty here.

Jeeps may be able to negotiate the dirt road to this hut (which leads off Emstruleið/ F261) during summer.

Information

Ferðafélag Íslands (Iceland Touring Association; ☎568 2533; www.fi.is) runs the facilities in the area and its website is loaded with information, including details on the hike. It publishes (and sells at Landmannalaugar) a small booklet (3000kr) about the hike in English and Icelandic, offering detailed information and descriptions of the landscape, sights and path, and also sells a map (1800kr). Ferdakort trail maps are available for purchase at major online book retailers, if you want to start reading before you arrive (approximately 2300kr).

Most adventure operators throughout South Iceland offer experienced Laugavegurinn guiding, at a hefty premium. In addition to the traditional hike, some can do longer variations off the beaten track (literally), to hiker-free mountain passes that run parallel to the main trail.

Most hikers walk from north to south to take advantage of the net altitude loss and the facilities at Þórsmörk. From Þórsmörk you can catch an amphibious bus to towns in the south such as Hvolsvöllur, Hveragerði, Hella and Reykjavík (one-way fares starting from 4500kr out of Þórsmörk with Reykjavik Excursions). Hardened hikers continue walking to Skógar on the glorious Fimmvörðuháls trek (p153), which takes an extra day or two (about an additional 23km).

WEATHER & GEAR

Although the trail is well marked, we highly recommend bringing along a map and GPS if you plan on tackling the walk without a guide. Weather conditions (like snow, fog and whiteouts) may make the path hard to find, despite it being well trodden.

The track is almost always passable for hiking from early July through to mid-September. Early in the season (late June to early July) there can be icy patches or deep snow that are difficult to navigate – projected hut openings offer a good gauge of conditions. In summer some of the rivers can be too deep to cross. Huts are locked out of season, so hiking the trail out of season is decidedly discouraged (and dangerous).

At any time of the year the Landmannalaugar to Þórsmörk hike is not to be undertaken lightly. It is imperative that you pack appropriately (proper footwear, warm and waterproof clothing and gear), as weather conditions change dramatically in an instant. You will be fording rivers, and fog and rain can come up at any time. That means no jeans or cotton clothes next to your skin (which keeps you cool, removes body heat and dries slowly). If you are not a seasoned hiker and don't know what to bring, do your research first. Wardens have reported a huge upswing in unprepared hikers needing intervention. Don't be one of them.

You'll also need to carry sufficient food and water. Light dried foods are recommended. If you are staying at a hut you can fill up your water there. All trash should be disposed of in designated areas at the huts providing this service.

LUGGAGE TRANSPORT

You don't have to schlep all your bags along the Laugavegurinn hike. Guesthouses may store luggage for an extra fee. Or if you are going with a tour company, staff will usually transport your extra bags from the start to the end of the trail, and sometimes even sometimes between huts.

Þórsmörk

Named after the Norse god Thor (Þór), this protected reserve is a hiker's paradise, with scenes seemingly plucked from an enchanting fantasy. The verdant realm is clasped by snowcapped mountain ridges, wild-flower-filled valleys, curling gorges, icy rivers and three looming glaciers (Tindfjallajökull, Eyjafjallajökull and Mýrdalsjökull). The glaciers protect this quiet spot from some of the region's harsher weather; it is often warmer or drier in Þórsmörk than nearby areas.

The higher, northeastern reaches of the area are known as **Goðaland** (Land of the Gods), which is – as the name suggests – divine. Rock formations twist skyward like the stone arches of an ancient cathedral. Fluorescent Arctic flowers burst forth from spongy emerald moss bringing brilliant slashes of colour. At its higher altitudes, Goðaland often has rougher weather than Þórsmörk.

Orientation

Þórsmörk may seem relatively close to the Ring Road on a map, but you'll need to take an amphibious bus or go by high-clearance 4WD (super-Jeep tour) to ford the rivers on the way to the reserve (alternatively, you can hike in from Skógar or Landmannalaugar). As you get close, coming from the south, you must cross the dangerous Krossá river. Regular 4WDs cannot make it. You'll see that they are parked where people have hitched rides with buses or super-Jeeps.

Goðaland is the endpoint for the glorious Fimmvörðuháls trek (p153), which starts in Skógar. The main camping area in Goðaland is Básar (p164); to go between it and Þórsmörk by car you must make the dangerous Krossá river crossing mentioned before. Walkers use footbridges – these are on wheels and tend to move around depending on water levels.

Activities

Hiking is a dream in this dramatically scenic region, and it's possible to go it alone or as part of a guided trip.

It's possible to volunteer to help with the endless task of trail maintenance with Þórsmörk Trail Volunteers (www.trailteam.is), an Iceland Forest Service initiative. No previous experience of trail construction work is necessary, training is provided, plus food and camping.

★Stakkholtsgjá Canyon HIKING

(F249) Stakkholtsgjá is what *Lord of the Rings* movies are made of. It has 100m-deep, ancient moss-covered walls and a dramatic twisting gorge with a hidden waterfall. Walk along the riverbed inside the canyon, when it splits in two veer left down a narrower canyon. Scamper over boulders and spot a crashing cascade (or icicles in winter).

The walk takes around 1½ hours there and back. Stakkholtsgjá Canyon can be difficult to get to unless you are on a private tour with an amphibious vehicle (regular 4WDs cannot cross the nearby rivers). The water levels of the rivers near the canyon change on a daily basis and could be impossible to cross by foot (unless a temporary bridge has been erected). However, you can call the local ranger for water levels or ask one of the daily amphibious buses to stop here (Thule, Reykjavík Excursions, Sterna and Trex often stop at Basar, which is on the F249 – the same road as the canyon). During the day, many tours stop here so it's possible to negotiate a ride for the return. Buses and private vehicles may charge a fee for this.

★Valahnúkur Circle HIKING

(trailhead at Langidalur hut or Húsadalur) A 2½-hour loop takes you up to the brilliant viewpoint at Valahnúkur, which takes in canyons, glaciers and sightlines all the way to the ocean. From Húsadalur, follow the trail up to the viewpoint then down into Langidalur. From there, pass along the ridge between the valleys back to your starting point. Or do it in reverse.

You can hike one way and connect with buses on either side as well.

Útigönguhöfði HIKING

It's a thrilling climb up to the ridge of 850m Mt Útigönguhöfði (around 5.5km, around four to five hours), with spectacular views of the canyon, surreal moonlike landscape below and even the glacier beyond. The trail starts behind the toilet block at Básar's campsite. It can get windy on the summit, and the path up may be unstable and slippery in places – watch your footing and don't proceed beyond your ability.

Réttarfell HIKING

(trailhead at Básar) From Básar (p164), this is a shorter climb (roughly 4km round trip, one to two hours) than up to Mt Útigönguhöfði, but equally as rewarding, with soaring views of the spectacular canyon below. Take the signposted right fork instead of the left one up to Mt Utigonguhofdi. At the peak, retrace your steps to return.

Alternatively, do a loop by taking the path down into the valley and then along the F249. Maps are available at the Básar office.

Tindfjöll Circle HIKING

The longest of the most popular 'short hikes' in the area (around 10km) usually starts in the canyon valley and takes around three to four hours from Básar (p164), 4½ hours from Langidalur (p164) and around six hours from Húsadalur (p164). It will take you along the Tindfjöll gorge and ridge. All of the sleeping huts sell maps of the hike.

Wander through the **Slyppugil Valley** (or follow the like-named ridge), then hike across moraine along the side of a second ridge. You'll then pass through **Tröllakirkja** (Trolls' Church) with its sweeping stone arches. A lush green field appears next before revealing a postcard-worthy viewpoint to the Þórsmörk valley. Follow the top of the sandstone ridge until you find yourself at the coursing Krossá river, which leads you back to Langidalur, or to Húsadalur further on. The trail is well marked all the way along with orange posts; bear in mind that winds can get strong at various points on the trail.

Tours

Coming by guided super-Jeep tour can be a lovely treat, revealing more than what you'll find on your own.

Guides throughout the south, such as Southcoast Adventure (p149), Midgard Adventure (p146) and Icelandic Mountain Guides (p151) are a true luxury – not only do they get you to the region, but they can take you to hidden valleys, waterfalls and glacier approaches that the regular buses do not reach, while sharing local geological and cultural insights. For example, the **Gígjökull** glacial tongue, with its formerly enormous moraine, was one of the main sites of flooding when Eyjafjallajökull erupted. On certain tours you can get close enough to lick it.

Sleeping & Eating

There are three lodging areas in Þórsmörk: Langidalur, with huts and the nearby Slyppugil campsite; Básar (technically in Goðaland); and Húsadalur. All have huts and campsites, cooking facilities and running water. They get busy during summer months, so it's crucial to book space in the huts in advance. We recommend bringing a sleeping bag and your own food. Wild camping is forbidden in the area.

There is one basic buffet-style restaurant at Húsadalur – Volcano Huts Þórsmörk, plus a shop selling very basic groceries at a premium at Langidalur. It's better to bring your own food.

Húsadalur – Volcano Huts Þórsmörk HUT, CAMPGROUND €€
(☎552 8300; www.volcanohuts.com; Húsadalur; sites per person 2600kr, dm/d/cottages/glamping without bathroom 8400/26,600/29,000/32,000kr; 📶) Busy Volcano Huts Þórsmörk fills the Húsadalur area with basic dorm-style huts, private rooms, five-person cottages (sleeping-bag accommodation with kitchenettes, linen costs 3000kr), a campground and heated glamping units (with made-up double beds), all share bathrooms and sauna. There's a cooking area, but you must bring your own stove and utensils.

The good restaurant (breakfast/lunch/dinner 2300/2700/4500kr) offers a lunch of soup, fresh bread, coffee and cake, and a buffet dinner, and has wi-fi. It also sells trail maps and has a small shop with camping supplies and adventure gear. There's also a bar with beer on tap (it's the only place in Þórsmörk to get a pint). Amphibious buses from Reykjavík stop here.

Básar HUT, CAMPGROUND €
(☎893 2910, booking 562 1000; www.utivist.is; F249, N 63°40.559', W 19°29.014'; sites/sleeping-bag huts per person 1500/6000kr) Básar is the choice base for Icelanders, largely due to its beautiful position in the trees. There's hut (mattress only) accommodation for 83 people. Camping space gets extremely crowded on summer weekends. There's a barbecue and good-sized kitchen with large communal wooden benches for eating. Phone charging costs 500kr, showers per person also 500kr.

Básar is at the end of the F249, but not accessible with regular 4WD due to the river crossings en route. Amphibious buses stop here. Booking is advisable in summer.

Slyppugil Campsite CAMPGROUND €
(☎575 6700; www.hostel.is; sites per person 1300kr; ⊙Jun-Aug) The cheapest option in the area is run by Hostelling International, sits within sight (about 500m) of Langidalur, and has showers (500kr per person), toilets and barbecues. The warden can help with information on day hikes.

Langidalur HUT, CAMPGROUND €
(Þórsmörk, Skagfjörðsskáli; ☎893 1191, bookings 568 2533; www.fi.is; N 63°40.960', W 19°30.890'; sites/huts per person 2000/8000kr; ⊙May-Sep) Located at the start/end of the trail to Landmannalaugar, Langidalur is the most rustic accommodation option of the four in Þórsmörk, but it is well maintained. It sleeps 75 and has two kitchens. Campers must bring their own stoves etc. There's a well-tended camping space and large shower block (500kr per person).

Langidalur Shop FOOD & DRINKS
(Langidalur Hut; ⊙May-Sep) A small shop offers hot coffee and tea, plus basic provisions: camping gas, wool socks, maps and limited groceries (soup, noodles and jam etc) at a premium. Hikers like to crack open one of the store's cans of cold beers after a long hike. Opening hours vary; the staff at Langidalur hut may open the shop by request.

Information

Call the **Langidalur Warden** (☎893 1191; Langidalur hut) for river level and weather information or emergencies.

Getting There & Around

BUS

Special all-terrain buses reach all the way to Þórsmörk when the roads are open (see www.road.is). Reykjavík buses to/from Þórsmörk stop in Hveragerði, Selfoss, Hella, Hvolsvöllur and Seljalandsfoss en route. The Reykjavík Excursions schedule is particularly helpful in hopping around the sites within Þórsmörk. The bus rides are an experience in themselves, and are special amphibiously equipped rigs for fording rivers.

Reykjavík Excursions (p429) Bus 9 goes direct (but sells out first) from Reykjavík to Þórsmörk (8000kr, shortest journey four hours, six daily May to mid-October), stopping at Hveragerð, Selfoss, Hella and requiring one change in

Hvolsvöllur. It's also possible to connect on routes 20 and 9 or routes 21 and 9.

Sterna (p430) Bus 14/14a heads from Reykjavík to Þórsmörk (6950kr, four hours, one daily late June to early September).

Trex (p430) Bus T11 from Reykjavík to Þórsmörk (8700kr, 4½ hours, two daily mid-June to mid-September) stops at Hveragerði (7400kr), Selfoss (7400kr), Hella (5400kr), Hvolfsvöllur (5400kr), Seljalandsfoss (5400kr), Gígjökull, Básar and Langidalur).

Thule Travel (p134) Has a hikers bus from Reykjavík to Þórsmörk (7050kr, 4¾ hours, two daily June to mid-September). This service also departs from Hveragerði (6400kr, four hours), Hvolsvöllur and Hella (4650kr, 2¾ hours).

CAR

You cannot drive all the way into Þórsmörk with your rental vehicle. End of story. If you have your own 4WD with excellent clearance, you can plough down Rtes 249 and F249 until you reach the crossroads for Húsadalur and Básar at the Krossá river. It's there that you must leave your vehicle – you will not be able to ford the gushing river unless you're driving a super-Jeep and know what you're doing.

The buses that serve Þórsmörk are special amphibious vehicles outfitted to pass the deep river and boulder-littered ravines. If you park at the crossroads, you can potentially hitch a bus (if the driver is willing and there is space, you may have to pay around 2000kr per person) or a super-Jeep. Super-Jeep tours can get there in winter.

HIKING

Þórsmörk is usually the terminus of the popular Laugavegurinn hike (p158); most choose to begin at Landmannalaugar. It's also popular to reach Þórsmörk from Skógar on the beautiful Fimmvörðuháls hike (p153). If you are planning to reach Þórsmörk by foot, we recommend one of the previously mentioned hikes; walking along Rtes 249 and F249 from Seljalandsfoss is far less scenic.

It takes around 30 minutes to walk between Langidalur and Húsadalur on the shortest path.

Skógar to Vík

As the Ring Road arcs east from Skógar to Vík, the haunches of the foothills rise to the glaciers, mountain tops and volcanoes inland, while rivers descend from mysterious gorges and course across the broad sweep of pastures to black-sand beaches and the crashing ocean. This rural area may be dotted with farmhouses (many of which have guesthouses), but considering the volume of summertime visitors, it still feels alternately dramatic and pastoral.

Sights

The following landmarks are listed from west to east.

★Sólheimajökull GLACIER

(Rte 221) One of the easiest glacial tongues to reach is Sólheimajökull. This icy outlet glacier unfurls from the main Mýrdalsjökull ice cap and is a favourite spot for glacial walks and ice climbing. Rte 221 leads 4.2km off the Ring Road to a small car park and the Arcanum base camp (p166) office, from where you can walk the 800m to the ice along a wide track edging the glacial lagoon. Don't attempt to climb onto the glacier unguided.

Crevasses form often, so to walk on the glacier you should go with any of the area's tour operators; tours depart from the car park.

Mýrdalsjökull GLACIER

This gorgeous glacier is Iceland's fourth-largest ice cap, covering 700 sq km and reaching a thickness of almost 750m in places. The volcano Katla snoozes beneath, periodically blasting up through the ice to drown the coastal plain in a deluge of melt water, sand and tephra. Local operators run tours along the glacial crown as part of longer trips. Don't explore the area on your own; the ice is unstable and the track to the caldera can be impossible to navigate.

Sólheimasandur BEACH

(Rte 1) On 21 November 1973, a US Navy aeroplane was forced to crash-land at Sólheimasandur. The crew all survived, but the wreckage of the militarised Douglas DC-3 remains on the black-sand beach, a lean shell whipped by the wind. There was once a road down to the beach but visitors must now walk from a basic car park. Be aware, it's an easy, but not pretty, walk. It's around 4km each way (roughly three hours to do the round trip).

There is talk of paving a road to the site. Find the Sólheimasandur trail-access car park 8km from Skógar on the right, when travelling towards Vík.

★Dyrhólaey WILDLIFE RESERVE

(Rte 218) One of the South Coast's most recognisable natural formations is the rocky plateau and huge stone sea arch at Dyrhólaey (*deer-lay*), which rises dramatically from the surrounding plain 10km west of Vík, at the end of Rte 218. Visit its crashing black-sand beaches and get awesome views from atop the promontory. The islet is a nature reserve that's rich in bird life, including puffins; some or all of it can be closed during nesting season (15 May to 25 June).

There are two parking areas, one on the top of the cliff near the Dyrhólaey Lighthouse and one at the base. Those without 4WD are best using the bottom car park as the road up is filled with deep potholes and can be tricky in rain. The best view of the archway is from Reynisfjara along the coast.

According to *Njál's Saga*, Kári – the only survivor of the fire that wiped out Njál's clan – had his farm here. Another Viking Age connection is the cave **Loftsalahellir**, reached by a track just before the causeway to Dyrhólaey, which was used for council meetings in Saga times.

★Reynisfjara BEACH

(Rte 215) On the western side of Reynisfjall, the high ridge above Vík, Rte 215 leads 5km down to the black-sand beach Reynisfjara. It's backed by an incredible stack of **basalt columns** that look like a magical church organ, and there are outstanding views west to Dyrhólaey. Surrounding cliffs are pocked with caves formed from twisted basalt, and puffins belly-flop into the crashing sea during summer. Immediately offshore are the towering Reynisdrangur sea stacks. At all times watch for rogue waves: people are regularly swept away.

You may recognise the scene from Bon Iver's 2011 music video *Holocene*, practically an ode to Iceland. The beach can get busy in high season, so try to come early in the day or late in the evening.

Reynisdrangur LANDMARK

(Rte 215) Vík's most iconic cluster of sea stacks is known as Reynisdrangur, which rises from the ocean like ebony towers at the western end of Vík's black-sand beach. Tradition says they're masts of a ship that trolls were stealing when they got caught in the sun. The nearby cliffs are good for puffin watching. A bracing walk up from Vík's western end takes you to the top of **Reynisfjall** ridge (340m), which offers superb views.

Tours

Arcanum ADVENTURE TOUR

(☎487 1500; www.arcanum.is; Rte 221; glacier walks from 9500kr, ATV tours from 19,000kr, snowmobile rides per 2 people from 27,000kr; ⏲9.30am-5pm) This popular tour operator runs daily Sólheimajökull glacier walks, plus snowmobile, quad-bike and other tours geared towards all ages. It has a shop in the car park of Sólheimajökull glacier, with guides offering friendly advice.

Mountain Excursion ADVENTURE TOUR

(☎897 7737; www.mountainexcursion.is; Ketilsstaðaskólavegur, off Rte 1; glacier hikes from 10,500kr, super-Jeep tours from 21,500kr; ⏲9am-5pm) A small outfit offering three-hour Sólheimajökull glacier hikes and a volcano super-Jeep tour. Based at Volcano Hotel.

Sleeping & Eating

Note that camping is prohibited on Dyrhólaey.

★Garðar GUESTHOUSE €€

(☎487 1260; www.reynisfjara-guesthouses.com; Reynisfjara, Rte 215; cottages 16,000-29,000kr) At the end of Rte 215, to the west of Vík, Garðar is a magical, view-blessed place. Friendly farmer Ragnar rents out five self-contained beachside huts: one stone cottage sleeps four, while other timber cottages sleep two to four. Four of them have kitchen facilities, toilets and showers.

★Grand Guesthouse Garðakot B&B €€

(☎894 2877; www.ggg.is; Garðakotsvegur, Garðakot farm; entire house 60,000kr; 📶) Set on a pastoral sheep farm, this small, tidy house is rented out as a whole. It holds four beautiful rooms, two with private bathrooms and two that share. Heated hardwood floors downstairs, sweeping views of volcanoes and sea upstairs, and friendly proprietors, pretty decor, serenity and flat-screen TVs. It's 14km west of Vík, south of the Ring Road on Rte 218. Two-night minimum stay.

Farmhouse Lodge B&B €€

(☎625 8905; www.farmhouse.is; Skeiðflöt; s without bathroom from 20,200kr, d with/without bathroom incl breakfast from 29,500/25,000kr; P📶) Surprisingly sleek and contemporary designer rooms fill this low-key farm lodge on the Ring Road 14km west of Vík. Bedside tables are made from hewn tree trunks, public spaces are tastefully decorated and the buffet breakfast is generous.

Sólheimahjáleiga Guesthouse B&B €€

(☎864 2919; www.solheimahjaleiga.is; Sólheimahjáleiga Farm, Rte 222; d with/without bathroom from 19,900/24,400kr, f from 38,700kr; P📶) A series of cosy renovated farm buildings house

KATLA GEOPARK

In 2011 Iceland formed its first 'geopark' to protect a region of great geological importance, promote local culture and sustainable development, and educate visitors. The **Katla Geopark** (☎862 4066; www.katlageopark.is) extends from Hvolsvöllur northeast to the great Vatnajökull and down to the volcanic black-sand beaches. It includes its namesake Katla volcano, the infamous **Eyjafjallajökull** and the torched earth at Lakagígar. All told, that's about 9% of Iceland. There is no park office, but the geopark website has information.

Of all the volcanoes in Iceland, it is thought that Katla may cause the most trouble to Icelanders over the next few years. This highly active 30km-long volcano, buried deep under the Mýrdalsjökull glacier, has erupted roughly twice per century in the past. Since the last eruption was in 1918, it's now several decades overdue.

It's expected that when Katla does blow, days of ash fall, tephra clouds and lightning strikes will follow the initial explosion, with flash floods caused by the sudden melting of glacial ice. The geological record shows that past eruptions have created tidal waves, which have boomeranged off the Vestmannaeyjar archipelago and deluged the area where the town of Vík stands today.

Local residents receive regular evacuation training for the day when Katla erupts. In the event of an eruption, all mobile phones within range of a tower (including yours) will receive a warning. After the alert, farmers must hang a notice on their front doors to show that they have evacuated, before unplugging their electric fences, opening cattle sheds so that their animals can flee to higher ground, and heading for one of the evacuation centres in Hvolsvöllur, Vík and Kirkjubæjarklaustur.

rooms with private and shared bathrooms, plus a kitchen. The family rooms (sleeping up to five) have private bathrooms. Animal lovers will find some 400 sheep, six horses, a number of hens and two friendly farm dogs on the grounds. The property is 11km east of Skógar, just north of the Ring Road.

Mið-Hvoll Cottages COTTAGE €€
(☎863 3238; https://midhvoll.is; off Rte 1; cottages 27,000kr; P 📶) This stand of seven cosy wooden cottages sits within sight of Dyrhólaey in a pastoral area south of the Ring Road, with mountain and ocean views. Each kitchen-equipped cottage sleeps five. The owners also offer horse riding on nearby beaches and pastures for all ages and skill levels (from 8000kr).

Find it about 12km west of Vík, 3km down a tiny track, just west of the turn-off for Dyrhólaey (Rte 218).

Giljur Gistihús GUESTHOUSE €€
(☎866 0176; Giljavegur, off Rte 1; s/d without bathroom from 16,000/20,000kr, d/tr 25,000/46,600kr; ⏲Jun–mid-Sep; 📶) Just 7km west of Vík and tucked back off the Ring Road at the foot of lush cliffs creased by a waterfall and dotted with grazing horses, this small farm complete with Icelandic turf house has guesthouse rooms with a shared or private bathroom and a hearty breakfast. Book via Icelandic Farm Holidays (www.farmholidays.is).

Gistiheimlilið Reynir GUESTHOUSE €€
(☎894 9788; www.reyni.is; Reynisfjara, Rte 215; d without bathroom 12,500kr, f with/without bathroom 26,200kr; 📶) This family-owned silver strip of rooms looks out over the ocean at Dyrhólaey. The twin bedrooms and one five-person family room share bathrooms and a kitchen; family rooms sleeping four have private bathrooms.

Volcano Hotel HOTEL €€
(☎486 1200; www.volcanohotel.is; Ketilsstaðaskóli, off Rte 1; d/ incl breakfast from 21,900kr; 📶) This seven-room hotel, 11.5km west of Vík, plays with a volcano motif in its decor: floors are made from a mosaic of pebbles, and candles glow throughout. Good breakfast too (eggs, fresh fruits, waffles, coffee, tea and juice). It's a top hotel option in the area and it books up early. Mountain Excursion, a small tour operator, is based here.

Hótel Dyrhólaey HOTEL €€
(☎487 1333; www.dyrholaey.is; Brekknavegur, off Rte 1; d incl breakfast from 30,000kr; @📶) On a hill 10km west of Vík, this 88-room hotel has gorgeous views and is popular with tour groups. Large rooms with basic mod cons sprout off three wings with wide, carpeted hallways and Iceland photographs on the

RESPECTING NATURE

Tantalising as the sights of Iceland may be, with its black-sand beaches and glaciers glinting along the roadside, it is paramount to realise that there are real dangers involved. For example, the famous Reynisfjara beach near Vík is known for rogue waves, and tourists are regularly rescued or drown there. As for glaciers, no one should go onto them without experienced, local guidance. Crevasses form suddenly and are often invisible (beneath snow), gasses can be emitted by volcanic activity, and flooding (sometimes invisible from above) can destabilise the ice even further.

With the growing popularity of tourism in Iceland, the foolhardy behaviour of inexperienced visitors regularly makes the news (one man drove his family onto a glacier in a rental car). Don't be one of them. Always check local conditions and change your plan if it's not safe. Download the 112 Iceland app and log your treks with www.safetravel.is.

walls. The restaurant (7pm to 9pm May to October, 2450kr to 4300kr) serves fish or meat courses, plus veggie mains.

Guesthouse Steig GUESTHOUSE €€€
(487 4660; www.guesthousesteig.is; Steigsvegur; d with/without bathroom incl breakfast from 28,000/21,500kr;) Sixteen kilometres west of Vík and 1.5km north of the Ring Road on a dirt track, sweet Guesthouse Steig is a simple farm building filled with 12 surprisingly spacious, modern and bright rooms. Six of the rooms have washbasins in them and there's a shared kitchen; the staff are friendly, and it feels like a real rural homestay.

Black Beach Restaurant CAFE €€
(Svarta Fjaran; 571 2718; www.svartafjaran.com; Reynisfjara, Rte 215; snacks 990kr, dinner mains 2200-4000kr; 11am-9pm;) Black volcanic cubes, meant to mimic the nearby black-sand beach Reynisfjara with its famous basalt columns, house this contemporary cafe that serves homemade cakes and snacks during the day, plus fish and chips, soups and chicken salads. Plate-glass windows give views to the ocean and Dyrhólaey beyond.

Vík

POP 320

The welcoming little community of Vík (aka Vík í Mýrdal) has become a booming hub for a very beautiful portion of the South Coast. Iceland's southernmost town, it's also the rainiest, but that doesn't stop the madhouse atmosphere in summer, when every room within 100km seems to be booked solid. With loads of services, Vík is a convenient base for the beautiful basalt beach Reynisfjara (p166) just to the west and its puffin cliffs. There's also the rocky plateau Dyrhólaey (p165) and the volcanoes running from Skógar to Jökulsárlón glacier lagoon and beyond. Along the coast, white-capped waves wash up on black sands and the cliffs glow green from all that rain. Put simply, it's pretty special.

Sights & Activities

Víkurkirkja CHURCH
(Hátún) High above town, Vík's 1930s church has stained-glass windows in spiky geometrical shapes and awesome village views.

True Adventure PARAGLIDING
(698 8890; www.trueadventure.is; Suðurvíkurvegur 5; paragliding from 35,000kr; May-Oct) Based at the Vík HI Hostel, this adventure outfit takes groups on thrilling one- to two-hour tandem tours, during which you soar over Vík and Iceland's southern landscape like a puffin.

Tours

Skógar (33km west of Vík) and Hvolsvöllur are the hubs for activity tours on the South Coast. In Vík, you can check with the hostel for tours to Mýrdalsjökull, plus paragliding flights over these rolling pastures. Many Reykjavík tour companies also make the drive out here.

Katla Track DRIVING
(849 4404; www.katlatrack.is; ice cave & volcano tours from 19,900kr) Katla Track runs tours of the area taking in local landmarks and the Mýrdalsjökull glacier.

Sleeping

Whether you prefer a hotel or guesthouse to a cottage or rental house, it all books up solidly around the Vík area during summer. It's vital to reserve well in advance. That said, last-minute camping spots can still be found in town. Note: camping is prohibited on Dyrhólaey.

★Vík HI Hostel HOSTEL €
(Norður-Vík Hostel; ☎487 1106; www.hostel.is; Suðurvíkurvegur 5; dm/s/d incl breakfast without bathroom 6500/10,200/18,000kr, cottages from 40,000kr; @📶) Vík's small, cosy, year-round hostel is in the beige house on the hill behind the village centre. Good facilities include a guest kitchen, and several standalone cottages sleep up to eight people. Staff can arrange local tours like ziplining and paragliding (May to September, 14,900kr and 35,000kr). There's a discount for HI members. Green-certified.

Vík Campsite CAMPGROUND €
(Tjaldsvæðið Vík; ☎487 1345; www.vikcamping.is; Klettsvegur 7; sites per adult/child 1750kr/free; ⏱Jun-Sep; P📶) The campsite sits under a grassy ridge at the eastern end of town, just beyond the Icelandair Hótel Vík. An octagonal building houses cooking facilities, a washing machine, toilets and showers (200kr) and laundry services (500kr). There are also four little cottages (25,000kr).

★Guesthouse Carina B&B €€
(☎699 0961; www.guesthousecarina.is; Mýrarbraut 13, off Rte 1; s/d/t without bathroom from 16,900/21,900/25,900kr; P📶) Friendly Carina and her husband Ingvar run one of the best lodging options in Vík. Neat-as-a-pin, spacious rooms with good light and clean shared bathrooms fill a large converted house near the centre of town.

★Icelandair Hótel Vík HOTEL €€€
(☎487 1480, bookings 444 4000; www.icelandairhotels.com; Klettsvegur 1-5; d economy/regular from 22,000/45,000kr; P📶) This sleek black-window-fronted hotel has merged with the former next-door Hótel Edda. It sits on the eastern edge of town with 88 rooms, some suitably swanky, while the former Hotel Edda rooms are still modern but an economical option. Choose from views to the rear cliffs or the sea. The light, natural decor is inspired by the local environment. Breakfast costs 3000kr.

Eating & Drinking

Ice Cave Restaurant INTERNATIONAL €
(☎788 5070; Austurvegur, Rte 1; mains from 1450kr; ⏱11am-9pm) In the same complex as the Icewear (p170) store, this modern canteen-style dining room has futuristic lighting (with electric tree-like centrepieces) and serves surprisingly satisfying deli-style food from trays. Pick from sandwiches, salads, noodles, marinated chicken legs, lamb chops, chicken curry and burgers.

Víkurskáli INTERNATIONAL €
(☎487 1230; Austurvegur 18; mains 1250-1900kr; ⏱11am-8.30pm) Grab a booth and a burger at the old-school grill inside the N1 petrol station with a view of Reynisdrangur. Daily specials from casserole to traditional Icelandic lamb stew.

Kjarval SUPERMARKET €
(☎487 1325; Austurvegur, Rte 1; ⏱9am-9pm) Groceries. On the main road.

★Suður-Vík ICELANDIC, ASIAN €€
(☎487 1515; www.facebook.com/Sudurvik; Suðurvíkurvegur 1; mains 1300-5350kr; ⏱noon-10pm, shorter hours in winter) The friendly ambience, in a warmly lit building with hardwood floors, exposed beams and interesting artwork, helps to elevate this restaurant beyond its competition. Food is Icelandic hearty, ranging from farm plates and quinoa salad with chicken to pizzas and Asian dishes (think spicy Panang curry with rice). Book ahead in summer. For an nightcap head to the **Man Cave** (☎487 1515; Suðurvíkurvegur 1; beers from 1000kr; ⏱6pm-late) downstairs.

Ströndin Bistro INTERNATIONAL €€
(☎487 1230; www.strondin.is; Austurvegur 18; mains 2000-5000kr; ⏱6-10pm; 📶) Behind the N1 petrol station is this semi-smart wood-panelled option enjoying sea-stack vistas. Go local with lamb soup or fish stew, or global with pizzas and burgers.

Halldórskaffi INTERNATIONAL €€
(☎487 1202; www.halldorskaffi.com; Víkurbraut 28; mains 2000-5000kr; ⏱noon-10pm Jun-Aug, to 9pm Sep-May) Inside Brydebúð museum, this lively timber-lined all-rounder is very popular in high season for its crowd-pleasing menu ranging from burgers and pizza to lamb fillet. Be prepared to wait in summer since it doesn't take reservations. The cakes are too tempting to resist – the Icelandic meringue cake is particularly good.

Smiðjan Brugghús MICROBREWERY
(http://smidjanbrugghus.is; Sunnubraut 15; ⏱11.30am-midnight Sun-Thu, to 1am Fri & Sat) Vík's hippest hang-out is warehouse-style with grey walls, windows looking onto the brewing room and blackboards displaying 10 craft beers on tap. Hop aficionados can try Icelandic India Pale Ales, pale ale, porter and farmhouse ale with a handful of different burgers (including a vegan patty).

Shopping

Icewear GIFTS & SOUVENIRS
(☎487 1250; www.icewear.is; Austurvegur 20; ⏱8am-10pm) The big Icewear souvenir and knitwear shop next to the N1 petrol station is a coach-tour hit. You can peek inside the factory portion to see woollen wear being made and there are Icelandic souvenirs by the bucketload, plus the Ice Cave Restaurant (p169).

Vínbúðin ALCOHOL
(☎486 8660; www.vinbudin.is; Ránarbraut 1; ⏱4-6pm Mon-Thu, 1-7pm Fri, noon-2pm Sat) National liquor chain with limited hours.

Information

Tourist Information Centre (☎487 1395; www.kotlusetur.i; Víkurbraut 28; ⏱10am-8pm May-Sep, noon-6pm Oct-Apr; 📶) Inside the **Brydebúð** (☎487 1395; Víkurbraut 28; adult/child 500kr/free; ⏱10am-6pm Mon-Fri, noon-7pm Sat & Sun Jun-Aug) museum, it has friendly advice about the local area, maps, books and a small gift shop.

Getting There & Away

Vík is a major stop for all Reykjavík–Höfn bus routes; buses stop at the N1 petrol station in the centre of town on Austurvegur/Rte 1.

Strætó (p429) Bus 51 from Reykjavík (1840kr, 2¾ hours, two daily) stops in Vík on the way to Höfn. If you take the early bus you can stop in Vík then continue on to Höfn on the later bus; however, from September to May service is reduced and you can't count on that connection.

Sterna (p430) Bus 12/12a from Reykjavík to Höfn stops in Selfoss and Vík en route. There's one daily service between Selfoss (3800kr, 3¼ hours) and Vík from June to mid-September.

Reykjavík Excursions (p429) Bus 20/20a from Reykjavík (7800kr, four to five hours, one daily June to early September) to Skaftafell stops in Vík.

Vík is an easy self-drive destination. The Ring Road (Rte 1) runs right through the centre; it's 2¼ hours from Reykjavík by car.

East of Vík

Mælifell

On the edge of the Mýrdalsjökull glacier, the 642m-high Mælifell ridge and the countryside around it are spectacular.

You can walk up Mælifell or to the *nunatak* (hill or mountain completely surrounded by a glacier) **Huldufjöll**, if you are properly equipped and experienced. There are also easier walks around the nearby rivers. Check on weather and route conditions before setting out.

There is no public transport to this remote area; you'll need your own wheels (4WD highly recommended for this rough road). Take Rte 214 east of Vík, then drive a further 15km into the mountains.

Sleeping & Eating

Buy groceries and food in Vík – there are no facilities in the isolated Mælifell ridge area.

★ **Þakgil** CAMPGROUND €
(☎893 4889; www.thakgil.is; Höfðarbrekkuafrétti; sites per person 2000kr, cabins 25,000kr; ⏱Jun–mid-Sep) The simple, idyllic campsite at Þakgil, a green bowl among stark mountains and dramatic rock formations, makes a convenient base for exploring the Mælifell ridge area. The simple cottages have bathrooms and kitchenettes. Showers and barbecue on-site.

Hótel Katla – Höfðabrekka HOTEL €€
(☎487 1208; www.hotelkatla.is; Höfðabrekka, Rte 214; d incl breakfast from 23,700kr; @📶) At the start of Rte 214, 5.5km east of Vík, Hótel Katla – Höfðabrekka is a large country hotel with 72 comfy rooms with en suite bathrooms in annexes of varying vintage, ranging from country kitsch to modern. Sauna and geothermal hot tub, plus a good restaurant (6.30pm to 9pm, buffet per person 5900kr).

Mýrdalssandur

The vast black-lava sand flats of Mýrdalssandur, east of Vík, are formed from material washed out from underneath Mýrdalsjökull during Katla eruptions. This 700-sq-km desert is bleak and desolate (some say haunted), but rather awe-inspiring. It looks lifeless, but Arctic foxes and seabirds can be spied here.

South of Rte 1, the small peak of Hjörleifshöfði (221m) rises above the sands and offers good views towards Vestmannaeyjar. On the other side of Rte 1, the green hill of Hafursey (582m) is another option for walks from Vík.

VESTMANNAEYJAR

Jagged and black, the Vestmannaeyjar (sometimes called the Westman Islands) form 15 eye-catching silhouettes off the southern shore. The islands were created by submarine volcanoes around 11,000 years ago, except for Surtsey, the archipelago's newest addition, which rose from the waves in 1963. Surtsey was made a Unesco World Heritage Site in 2008, but its unique scientific status means that it is not possible to land there, except for scientific study.

Heimaey is the only inhabited island. Its little town and sheltered harbour lie between dramatic *klettur* (escarpments) and two ominous volcanoes: blood-red Eldfell and conical Helgafell. These days Heimaey is famous for its puffins (around 10 million birds come here to breed); Þjóðhátíð, Iceland's biggest outdoor festival, held in August; and its state-of-the-art volcano museum.

Heimaey

POP 4500

The small town of Heimaey (*hey*-my) is encased in a fortress of jagged lava; its port sits at the end of a contorted waterway that carves a path between towering cliffs dotted with bird nests. Although only a few kilometres from the mainland, Heimaey feels light years away, lost amid the frigid waters of the North Atlantic.

The volcanoes that formed Heimaey have come close to destroying the island on several occasions. The most famous eruption in modern times began unexpectedly at 1.45am on 23 January 1973, when a vast fissure burst open, gradually mutating into the volcano Eldfell, and prompting the island's evacuation. Visitors can see where the lava flow meets the town's houses.

History

Over the centuries, the island of Heimaey was a marauders' favourite. The English raided the island throughout the 15th century, building the stone fort Skansinn as their HQ. In 1627 Heimaey suffered its most violent attack at the hands of Algerian pirates, who went on a killing spree, murdering 34 islanders and kidnapping more than 230 (almost three-quarters of the population). The rest managed to escape by abseiling down cliffs or hiding in caves along the west coast. Those who were kidnapped were taken as slaves to north Africa; years later, 27 islanders had their freedom bought for them…and had a long journey home.

Sights

The island's sights are clustered in and around the main village, on the point around Skalinn, and in the fascinating fresh lava fields and volcano, plus along puffin-viewing cliffs outside of town. You can download a guide with treasure hunt by searching 'Vestmannaeyjar' in the app store.

Town Centre

★Eldheimar MUSEUM

(Pompeii of the North; ☎488 2700; www.eldheimar.is; Gerðisbraut 10; adult/child 2300/1200kr; ⏲11am-6pm) More than 400 buildings lie buried under lava from the 1973 eruption, and on the edge of the flow 'Pompeii of the North' is a museum revolving around one house excavated from 50m of pumice. It was once home to Gerður Sigurðardóttir and Guðni Ólafsson, their two children and baby. During the eruption the family was forced to leave in the middle of the night with only time to grab one item, a baby bottle.

The modern volcanic-stone building allows a glimpse into the home with its crumbling walls and intact but toppled knick-knacks and is filled with multimedia exhibits on the eruption and its aftermath, from compelling footage and eyewitness accounts to the story of the home owners. An audio guide leads you through it all; upstairs there's a catwalk over the wreckage, a space dedicated to all things Surtsey, and a cafe with broad views across town.

★Skansinn FORT, HISTORIC SITE

This lovely green area by the sea, off Skansvegur, has several unique historical sights. The oldest structure on the island, Skansinn was a 15th-century fort built to defend the harbour (not too successfully, however – when Algerian pirates arrived in 1627 they simply landed on the other side of the island). Its walls were swallowed up by the 1973 lava, but some have been rebuilt. Above them, you can see the remains of the town's old water tanks, which were also crushed by molten rock.

➡ Landlyst MUSEUM

(off Strandvegur; ⏲11am-5pm mid-May–mid-Sep) FREE Shockingly, three out of four of

Heimaey's babies once died of tetanus, due to water deficiency and contaminated soil. In the 1840s an island woman, Sólveig, was sent abroad to be trained as a midwife. The tiny wooden house Landlyst was Sólveig's maternity hospital (and is the second-oldest building on the island). Today it contains a retro medicine cabinet, a small display of her blood-letting equipment and other 19th-century paraphernalia.

➡ **Stafkirkjan** CHURCH

(The Stave Church; Skansinn, off Skansvegur; ⊙11am-5pm mid-May–mid-Sep) The bitumen-coated Stafkirkjan is a reconstruction of a medieval wooden stave church (the exact design of the Holtdalen stave church in Trondheim, Norway). It was presented by the Norwegian government in 2000 to celebrate 1000 years of Christianity.

★ **Sæheimar** AQUARIUM

(☎481 1997; www.saeheimar.is; Heiðarvegur 12; adult/child aged 10-17 yr/child up to 9 yr 1200/500kr/free; ⊙10am-5pm May-Sep, 1-4pm Sat Oct-Apr;) The Aquarium & Natural History Museum has an interesting collection of stuffed birds and animals, videos on puffins and catfish, and fish tanks of Icelandic fish. It's great fun for the family, and there's often a puffin wobbling about. The museum is an informal bird hospital as well.

Sagnheimar Byggðasafn MUSEUM

(Folk Museum; ☎488 2045; www.sagnheimar.is; Raðhústræti; adult/child 1000kr/free; ⊙11am-5pm mid-May–mid-Sep, 1-4pm Sat mid-Sep–mid-May) Housed in the city library, this interactive folk museum tells the story of Heimaey from the era of marauding pirates up to the 1973 eruption and beyond. Displays also shed light on local sports heroes, religion, volcanic activity and native bird life.

Stóraklif & Heimaklettur VIEWPOINT

(Eiðisvegur) The top of the craggy precipice Stóraklif is a treacherous 30-minute climb from behind the N1 petrol station at the harbour. The trail starts on the obvious 4WD track; as it gets steeper you're 'assisted' by ropes and chains (but don't trust them completely). If you can bear the terror, you'll get outstanding views. Further out on the pier, Heimaklettur is more perilous, with wild rickety ladders. Both are top puffin-breeding grounds. When rainy, slick or windy, neither is a good idea.

Out of Town

★ **Eldfellshraun** NATURAL FEATURE

(accesible via Eldfellsvegur) Known as Eldfellshraun, the Mars-like land created by the 1973 lava flow is now criss-crossed with a maze of otherworldly hiking tracks that run down to the Skansinn fort and the area where the lava meets the town's houses, and all around the bulge of the raw, red eastern coast. Here you'll find small black-stone beaches, the Gaujulundur lava garden and a lighthouse.

★ **Eldfell** VOLCANO

(off Fellavegur; P) The 221m-high volcanic cone Eldfell appeared from nowhere in the early hours of 23 January 1973. Once the fireworks finished, heat from the volcano provided Heimaey with geothermal energy from 1976 to 1985. Today the ground is still hot enough in places to bake bread or char wood. Eldfell is an easy climb from town, up the collapsed northern wall of the crater; stick to the path, as the islanders are trying to save their latest volcano from erosion.

It's around a 1.5km hike to the top (taking 30 minutes to one hour), where it can get windy. Limited parking is available at the bottom of the volcano.

Helgafell VOLCANO

(Helgafell Rd) Helgafell (226m) erupted 5000 years ago. Its cinders are grassed over today, and you can scramble up here without much difficulty from the football pitch on the road to the airport.

Activities

Ask at the tourist office for a detailed walking and cycling map of Heimaey. Walks through the lava fields, along puffin-nesting areas and on the island's western shores are particularly ethereal.

★ **Stórhöfði** HIKING, BIRDWATCHING

(Rte 240) A windy **meteorological station** has been built on Stórhöfði (122m), the rocky peninsula at Heimaey's southern end. It's linked to the main island by a narrow isthmus (created by lava from Helgafell's eruption 5000 years ago), and there are good views from the summit. There's also a small **birdwatching hut** for puffin viewing about halfway up the hill; go from the first turnout on the right to the end of a trail across sheep pasture, marked with a hiking sign.

Heimaey

Top Sights

1 Eldheimar D4
2 Sæheimar B2
3 Skansinn D1

Sights

4 Landlyst D1
5 Public Park C3
6 Sagnheimar Byggðasafn C3
7 Stafkirkjan D1
8 Stóraklif & Heimaklettur A1

Activities, Courses & Tours

Eyja Tours .... (see 10)
9 Heilsueyjan Spa C2
Rent A Bike .... (see 10)
10 Ribsafari B1
11 Swimming Pool A3
12 Viking Tours C1

Sleeping

13 Aska Hostel C2
14 B&B Hrafnabjörg B2
15 Gistiheimilið Hreiðrið B2
16 Hótel Eyjar C2
17 Hótel Vestmannaeyjar C2
Sunnuhöll HI Hostel .... (see 17)

Eating

18 Einsi Kaldi C2
Gott .... (see 13)
19 Krónan C2
20 Slippurinn B1
21 Stofan Bakhús C2
22 Tanginn C1

Shopping

23 Útgerðin C2
24 Vínbúðin C2

It's possible to scramble down to the isthmus' boulder beach at **Brimurð** and continue north along the cliffs on the east coast, returning by a road just before the airport. From June to August **Kervíkurfjall** and **Stakkabót** are good places for puffin viewing.

West Coast HIKING, BIRDWATCHING

(Dalvegur) Several perilous tracks climb the steep slopes around Herjólfsdalur, running along the top of Norðklettur to **Stafnsnes**, one of the prime puffin-breeding areas. The ascent is exhilarating, but there are some sheer drops. A gentler walk runs south along the western coast of the island, passing above numerous lava caves where local people hid from the pirates in 1627. At **Ofanleitishamar**, hundreds of puffins nest in the cliffs.

★ **Swimming Pool** SWIMMING

(Sundlaug Vestmannaeyja; ☎488 2400; Brimhólabraut; adult/child 900/300kr; ⏲6.15am-9pm Mon-Fri, 10am-5pm Sat & Sun Jun-Aug, shorter hours Sep-May) Heimaey's got a great sports complex with an indoor saltwater swimming pool, outdoor pools, hot-pots, a Jacuzzi, water slides (one with a trampoline) and a gym.

Rent A Bike CYCLING

(☎896 3340; https://visitwestmanislands.com/tours/rent-a-bike/; Básaskersbryggja 8; 5-/24hr bike rental 3900/5900kr; ⏲hours vary) A good way to get around Heimaey is by bicycle. Rent one at this store near the ferry landing. Book ahead.

Heilsueyjan Spa MASSAGE

(☎481 1513; www.facebook.com/heilsueyjanspa; Vestmannabraut; 30/60min massage from 4500/8000kr, infrared sauna 1500kr; ⏲10am-6pm Mon-Fri, 1-6pm Sat & Sun) Offering various treatments from healing massages to manicures and an infrared sauna experience.

Westman Islands Golf Course GOLF

(☎481 2363; www.gvgolf.is; Hamarsvegur; green fees 7500kr, club rental 3500kr, driving range 350kr; ⏲8am-9pm) Golfers can have a game at this wonderfully windy 18-hole seaside golf course in Herjólfsdalur. Clubs can be hired and there is a driving range (precariously over the road leading into the golf club).

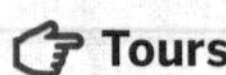

Tours

Most boat tours coincide with ferry departures, which makes them convenient for day-trippers.

THE 1973 ERUPTION

Without warning, at 1.45am on 23 January 1973 a mighty explosion blasted through the winter's night as a 1.5km-long volcanic fissure split the eastern side of the island. The eruption area gradually became concentrated into a growing crater cone, which fountained lava and ash into the sky.

Normally the island's fishing boats would have been out at sea, but a force-12 gale had prevented them from sailing the previous afternoon. Now calm weather and a harbourful of boats allowed all but two to three hundred of the island's 5273 inhabitants to be evacuated to the mainland. Incredibly, there was just a single fatality (from toxic gases).

Over the next five months more than 30 million tonnes of lava poured over Heimaey, destroying 360 houses and creating a brand-new mountain, the red cinder cone Eldfell. One-third of the town was buried beneath the lava flow, and the island increased in size by 2.5 sq km.

As the eruption continued, advancing lava threatened to close the harbour and make the evacuation permanent – without a fishing industry, there would have been little way to survive on the island. In an attempt to slow down the inexorable flow of molten rock, firefighters hosed the lava with more than six million tonnes of cold sea water. The lava halted just 175m short of the harbour mouth – actually improving the harbour by creating extra shelter!

The islanders were billeted with friends and family on the mainland, watching the fireworks and waiting to see if they could ever go home. Finally, the eruption finished, five months after it started, at the end of June. Two-thirds of the islanders returned to face a mighty clean-up operation. Weird lava formations can still be seen dangerously close to some houses around town, and a Mars-like landscape can be explored on the east of the Island.

The fantastic Eldheimar (p171) museum gives a view into the dramatic occurrence.

★ **Ribsafari** BOATING

(☎661 1810; www.ribsafari.is; Básaskersbryggja 8, Harbour; 1hr tour adult/child 11,900/6500kr, 2hr 17,950/9500kr; ⏲mid-Apr–Oct) High-adrenalin tours run daily in a souped-up Zodiac that jets through the archipelago. The small boat allows the captain to navigate through little caves and between rocky outcrops for up-close views of bird colonies. If you're very lucky you might even get to see whales and seals.

Viking Tours BOATING, BUS

(☎488 4884; www.vikingtours.is; Strandvegur 65; adult/child boat trips from 7400/6400kr, bus trips from 6400/5400kr; ⏲10am-6pm May–mid-Sep) Boat trips take in the big bird-nesting sites on the South Coast and sail into the sea cave Klettshellir. Bus trips tour the island.

Eyja Tours BUS

(☎852 6939; www.eyjatours.com; Básaskersbryggja; puffin & volcano tours adult/child 7000/3500kr) Bus tours covering the island's highlights, such as the puffin colonies and volcanoes.

Lyngfell HORSE RIDING

(☎898 1809; www.lyngfell.123.is; off Rte 240; 1hr from 7000k; ⏲Jun-Aug) Lyngfell, on the road to Stórhöfði, offers horse rides along black-sand beaches and along the cliffs when the wind is low. Find it on the left when heading along Rte 240 towards Stórhöfði.

Festivals & Events

★ **Þjóðhátíð** MUSIC

(National Festival Þjódhátíð Vestmannaeyjar; www.dalurinn.is; Dalvegur; 23,900kr, ferry price 1380kr; ⏲Jul or Aug) Three-day Þjóðhátíð is the country's biggest outdoor festival. Held at Herjólfsdalur festival ground over the last weekend in July or the first weekend in August, it involves music, dancing, fireworks, a big bonfire, gallons of alcohol and a light display with an eruption of red torches, a nod to the island's volcanoes. Upwards of 17,000 attend.

Historically, the festival was first celebrated when bad weather prevented Vestmannaeyjar people from joining the mainland celebrations of Iceland's first constitution (1 July 1874). The islanders held their own festival a month later, and it's been an annual tradition ever since.

Extra flights run from Reykjavík, but you must book transport and accommodation months in advance.

Sleeping

It's only a 30-minute ferry ride from the mainland, meaning many people visit Vestmannaeyjar as a day trip, though we highly recommend spending the night. Out of festival season it's usually not hard to find lodging. Visit www.vestmannaeyjar.is for a full list of accommodation options.

B&B Hrafnabjörg B&B €

(☎858 7727; www.facebook.com/BogBGuesthouse; Hásteinsvegur 40; s/d without bathroom incl breakfast 8100/13,400kr; ⏲Apr-Nov; 📶) Welcoming Hrefna and Jónas run this cosy B&B with tidy rooms and a large breakfast room (perfect for the generous breakfast, including homemade waffles).

Aska Hostel HOSTEL €

(☎662 7266; www.askahostel.is; Bárustigur 11; dm/d/t without bathroom 5200/14,000/16,900kr; 📶) This cheery yellow historic building is home to a good hostel in the village centre with bright, modern rooms and welcoming staff. There's also a nice TV lounge, kitchen, free hot showers and towels. Cereal and tea and coffee are available in the morning at no extra charge.

Sunnuhöll HI Hostel HOSTEL €

(☎481 2900; www.hihostels.com; Vestmannabraut 28; d with/without bathroom 13,700/18,600kr; 📶) There's generally a quiet and laid-back vibe at the homey Sunnuhöll hostel, in the same building as the Hótel Vestmannaeyjar, with its handful of prim rooms. Guests get access to the spa and there are laundry and bicycle-rental facilities. HI members get a discount.

Glamping & Camping CAMPGROUND €

(☎846 9111; www.glampingandcamping.is; Dalvegur; sites per adult/child 1500kr/free, huts & barrels 7900-11,000kr; ⏲mid-May–mid-Sep) Cupped in the bowl of an extinct volcano, the Herjólfsdalur campsite has hot showers, a laundry room and cooking facilities. Camping can get windy here, but the owners will point you in the direction of a sheltered spot. There are also A-frame huts and barrel houses to rent. Linen costs 1600kr per person.

Gistiheimilið Hreiðrið GUESTHOUSE €

(☎481 1045; http://tourist.eyjar.is; Faxastígur 33; s/d/q without bathroom 7900/12,500/18,700kr; 📶) This guesthouse looks a little worse for wear on the outside, but the friendly owner ensures it feels like home. Features include a well-stocked kitchen and a cosy TV lounge.

It also runs two- to three-hour walking tours in summer. Sleeping-bag accommodation costs 4300kr. Breakfast is 1600kr per person.

Hótel Eyjar HOTEL €€
(☎481 3636; www.hoteleyjar.is; Bárustíg 2; s/d incl breakfast 23,000/26,000kr; 📶) Spacious, basic rooms are well lit and have private bathrooms; some are extra large with kitchenettes. Rollaway mattresses for children cost 2500kr. The tourist information is on the ground floor.

Hótel Vestmannaeyjar HOTEL €€€
(☎481 2900; www.hotelvestmannaeyjar.is; Vestmannabraut 28; s/d incl breakfast from 18,800/31,200kr; @📶) Iceland's first cinema is now a pleasant hotel, with modern rooms (some with good town and harbour views), friendly staff and the top restaurant Einsi Kaldi downstairs. The spa has two hot tubs and a sauna, plus a snooker room. Book ahead in summer.

Eating & Drinking

Stofan Bakhús BAKERY €
(☎481 2424; www.facebook.com/stofanbakhus; Bárustígur 7; baked goods 300-990kr; ⏱8am-5pm Mon-Fri, 9am-4pm Sat & Sun; 📶) Delicious baked goodies from chocolate cake and fresh bread to pastries. Top-notch coffee drinks, too.

Krónan SUPERMARKET €
(☎585 7000; Strandvegur 48; ⏱9am-9pm Mon-Fri, 10am-7pm Sat & Sun) Groceries.

★ **Slippurinn** ICELANDIC €€
(☎481 1515; www.slippurinn.com; Strandvegur 76; lunch 2400-7200kr, dinner mains 3700-4900kr, set menu 6400-9900kr; ⏱noon-2.30pm & 5-10pm early May–mid-Sep; 📶) Lively Slippurinn fills the upper storey of a beautifully remodelled old machine workshop that once serviced the ships in the harbour and now has great views. The food is delicious Icelandic fare with a level of creativity that sets it above most restaurants in the country. Ingredients are exquisite, and combinations of fish, local produce and locally sourced meats divine.

★ **Gott** FUSION €€
(☎481 3060; www.gott.is; Bárustigur 11; mains 1390-4800kr; ⏱11am-1pm Mon, to 9pm Tue & Sun, 11.30am-9pm Wed-Sat; 🖉) Fresh fusion food is done with care, using organic, healthy ingredients in this jolly wood-floored dining room with coloured chairs. Menu items range from goat cheese and beet salad or avocado, hummus and pesto toast to spelt-wrapped grilled chicken. Plus vegan options.

Tanginn ICELANDIC €€
(☎414 4420; www.facebook.com/tanginn.is; Básaskersbryggja 8; mains 2200-3000kr; ⏱11.30am-9.30pm Sun-Wed, to 1pm Thu, to 2pm Fri & Sat; 📶👪) With giant windows looking onto the harbour and comfortable, modern decor in slate and wood, Tanginn makes for a fun stop for fresh fish, burgers, crêpes, creative salads and the like. Dishes are well presented and there's Icelandic beer on tap.

SURTSEY

In November 1963 the crew on the fishing boat *Ísleifi II* noticed something odd – the sea south of Heimaey appeared to be on fire. Rather than flee, the boat drew up for a closer look – and its crew were the first to set eyes on the world's newest island.

The incredible subsea eruption lasted for 4½ years, throwing up cinders and ash to form a 2.7-sq-km piece of real estate (since eroded to 1.4 sq km). What else could it be called but Surtsey (Surtur's Island), after the Norse fire giant who will burn the world to ashes at Ragnarök.

It was decided that the sterile island would make a perfect laboratory, giving a unique insight into how plants and animals colonise new territory. Surtsey (www.surtsey.is) is therefore totally off limits to visitors (unless you're a scientist specialising in biocolonisation). Just so you know: in the race for the new land, the blue-green algae *Anabaena variabilis* got there first. Another discovery? Fossils were carried up by lava during the eruption and are now part of the island.

Both Ribsafari (p175) and Viking Tours (p175) run boat trips around the island (no entry on the island). You can get a vicarious view of Surtsey's thunderous birth by visiting the display at the museum Eldheimar (p171).

Einsi Kaldi SEAFOOD €€€

(☎481 1415; www.einsikaldi.is; Vestmannabraut 28; mains 2900-7000kr; ⏲5-10pm Jun–mid-Sep, shorter hours mid-Sep–May; 📶) On the ground floor of Hótel Vestmannaeyjar, Einsi Kaldi is Heimaey's highest-end dining experience, with well-crafted seafood recipes and modern mood lighting. The Vestmannaeyjar-born chef creates dishes like monk fish or lobster or beef tenderloin (all usually locally sourced), and *skyr* (Icelandic yoghurt) panna cotta or lava flow chocolate cake to finish.

Shopping

Útgerðin CLOTHING, ARTS & CRAFTS

(☎891 9060; www.facebook.com/utgerdin; Vestmannabraut 30; ⏲11am-6pm Mon-Sat) A good bet for Icelandic crafts and design.

Vínbúðin ALCOHOL

(☎481 1301; www.vinbudin.is; Vesturvegur 50; ⏲11am-6pm Mon-Thu, to 7pm Fri, to 4pm Sat) National liquor chain.

Information

Tourist Information Centre (☎482 3683; www.vestmannaeyjar.is; Strandvegur; ⏲9am-6pm Mon-Fri, 10am-4pm Sat, 1-4pm Sun; 📶) The summer tourist office is staffed by a local cafe-bookstore. Pick up pamphlets and trail maps here.

Getting There & Around

AIR

Vestmannaeyjar Airport (Vestmannaeyjaflugvöllur, VEY; ☎481 1969; www.isavia.is; Dalavegur, off Rte 238) is about 3km south of central Heimaey. Atlantsflug (p75) runs scheduled flights from Bakki (near the ferry port at Landeyjahöfn; one-way adult/child 8500/6900kr).

There are two daily flights between Reykjavík's domestic airport and Vestmannaeyjar (from around 17,000kr one way) on Eagle Air (p428).

BOAT

Eimskip's **Herjólfur** (☎481 2800; www.eimskip.is; Skildingav; per adult/child/bicycle/car 1380/760/690/2220kr) ferry sails from Landeyjahöfn (about 12km off the Ring Road between Hvolsvöllur and Skógar) to **Heimaey** year-round. The journey takes about 30 minutes. You must always reserve ahead for cars, and passengers should book ahead in high season, especially at peak day-tripper hours: the morning to Vestmannaeyjar and the afternoon back. You must arrive at least 30 minutes before departure. Landeyjahöfn ferry terminal has vending machines, bathrooms and water, but no other services.

From 15 May to 14 September five boats depart daily, plus one extra service on Saturday and Sunday. Low-season boats function on a reduced schedule (usually two per day). Fares cost adult/child from 1380/690kr. Bicycles cost 690kr each, cars under 5m cost 2220kr. You can change your ferry time for a fee of 500kr.

In really foul weather (summer or winter), the port at Landeyjahöfn can fill with sand, in which case the ferry may instead sail to/from Þorlákshöfn on a reduced schedule of two per day. The journey takes 2¾ hours, and the fare is substantially more. Changes are posted on the website and Facebook page, and you need to check on your booking. It takes roughly two hours to drive from Landeyjahöfn west to Þorlákshöfn.

To get to/from Landeyjahöfn, you can take Strætó (p429) bus 52 from Reykjavík's Mjódd terminal (4600kr, 2¼ hours, three daily in summer). It stops in Hveragerði, Selfoss, Hella and Hvolsvöllur. There's a local Landeyjahöfn taxi (p146) service.

BICYCLE

Heimaey is a small island. At roughly 8km long, it's easily walkable, taking about 1½ hours to walk from one end to the other. You can bring your own wheels (bikes are allowed on the ferry, and cars can drive onto the ferry with prebooking) or hire a bike (p174) at the ferry landing at Heimaey.

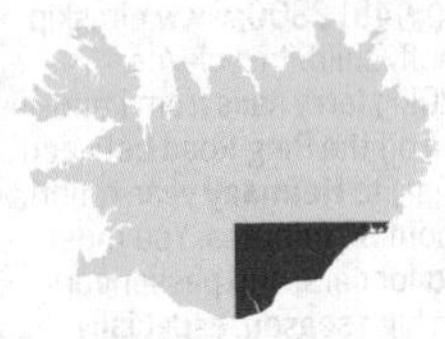

Southeast Iceland

Includes ➡

Best Places to Eat

- Humarhöfnin (p205)
- Pakkhús (p205)
- Jón Ríki (p202)
- Viking Cafe (p205)
- Heimahumar (p198)

Best Places to Stay

- Hrífunes Guesthouse (p179)
- Glacier View Guesthouse (p179)
- Milk Factory (p204)
- Magma Hotel (p182)
- Lækjaborgir Guesthouse (p186)

Why Go?

The 200km stretch of Ring Road from Kirkjubæjarklaustur to Höfn is truly mind-blowing, transporting you across vast deltas of grey glacial sand, past lost-looking farms, around the toes of craggy mountains, and by glacier tongues and ice-filled lagoons. The only thing you won't pass is a town.

The mighty Vatnajökull dominates the region, its huge rivers of frozen ice pouring down steep-sided valleys towards the sea. Jökulsárlón is a photographer's paradise, a glacial lagoon where wind and water sculpt icebergs into fantastical shapes.

The bleak coastal deserts of glacial sand are remnants of calamitous collisions between fire and ice. Further inland is the epicentre of Iceland's worst volcanic event, the Lakagígar fissures. With so much desolation on display, it's not surprising that Skaftafell is so popular. This sheltered enclave between the glaciers and the sands throbs with life and colour, and the footfalls of hikers.

Road Distances (km)

	Höfnt	Reykjavík	Jökulsárlón	Skaftafell
Reykjavík	459			
Jökulsárlón	79	378		
Skaftafell	135	323	57	
Kirkjubæjarklaustur	200	257	122	69

Kirkjubæjarklaustur & Around

POP 195

Many a foreign tongue has been tied in knots trying to say Kirkjubæjarklaustur. It helps to break it into bits: *Kirkju* (church), *bæjar* (farm) and *klaustur* (convent). Otherwise, do as the locals do and call it 'Klaustur' (pronounced like 'cloister').

Klaustur is tiny, even by Icelandic standards – a few houses and farms scattered across a brilliant-green backdrop. Still, it's the only real service town between Vík and Höfn, and it's a major crossroads to several dramatic spots in the interior, including Landmannalaugar and Laki.

History

According to the *Landnámabók* (a comprehensive account of Norse settlement), this tranquil village situated between the cliffs and the river Skaftá was first settled by Irish monks *(papar)* before the Vikings arrived. Originally, it was known as Kirkjubær; the 'klaustur' bit was added in 1186 when a convent of Benedictine nuns was founded (near the modern-day church).

During the devastating Laki eruptions that occurred in the late 18th century, this area suffered greatly – west of Kirkjubæjarklaustur you can see ruins of farms abandoned or destroyed by the lava stream. The lava field, called Eldhraun, averages 12m thick. It contains more than 15 cu km of lava and covers an area of 565 sq km, making it the world's largest recorded lava flow from a single eruption.

Sights & Activities

If you're interested in discovering the forces of nature and the history of the area, pick up the booklet *Klaustur trail* (600kr), which outlines a 20km walking trail that circles the village and takes in many of its natural features. There's also *Hiking Trails In and Around Kirkjubæjarklaustur* (750kr). Maps and good info are available from the Skaftárstofa visitor centre (p183).

Kirkjugólf LANDMARK

The basalt columns of Kirkjugólf (Church Floor), smoothed down and cemented with moss, were once mistaken for an old church floor rather than a work of nature, and it's easy to see why. The honeycombed slab lies in a field about 400m northwest of the N1 petrol station; drive down Rte 203, where there's a small parking area, access gate and sign.

Systrafoss & Systravatn WATERFALL

(Sisters' Falls) At the western end of the village, the lovely double waterfall, Systrafoss, tumbles down the cliffs and a sign outlines three short walks in the pretty wooded area (Iceland's tallest trees grow here!). The lake, Systravatn, reached by a leisurely climb up steps cut into the hill beside the falls, was once a bathing place for nuns. A marked 2.5km **walking path** leads from the lake to descend near Kirkjugólf and takes in glorious views.

Landbrotshólar LANDMARK

West of the village and south of the Ring Road is this vast, dimpled, vivid-green pseudocrater field. Pseudocraters formed when hot lava poured over wetlands; the

WORTH A TRIP

HRÍFUNES

Hrífunes (pronounced something like ri-voo-ness) is a tiny hamlet perfectly placed between Kirkjubæjarklaustur and Vík, in the peaceful and impossibly green surrounds of Skaftártunga. Here you'll find two warm, hospitable guesthouses that are well worth the detour.

Both guesthouses have memorable communal dinner options for around 6000kr per person, and room rates include bumper breakfast spreads. Note that there are no guest-kitchen facilities at either place (except for Hrífunes Guesthouse's apartment).

Glacier View Guesthouse (771 8811; www.glacierviewguesthouse.is; d incl breakfast from 35,600kr;) is run by seasoned travel pros Borgar and Elín. In good weather you can see Vatnajökull and Mýrdalsjökull from the lounge.

Hrífunes Guesthouse (863 5540; www.hrifunesguesthouse.is; d incl breakfast from 31,400kr;), in a community house renovated with flair by owners Haukur and Hadda, is decorated with stunning photos taken by Haukur, who runs photography tours (check out www.phototours.is).

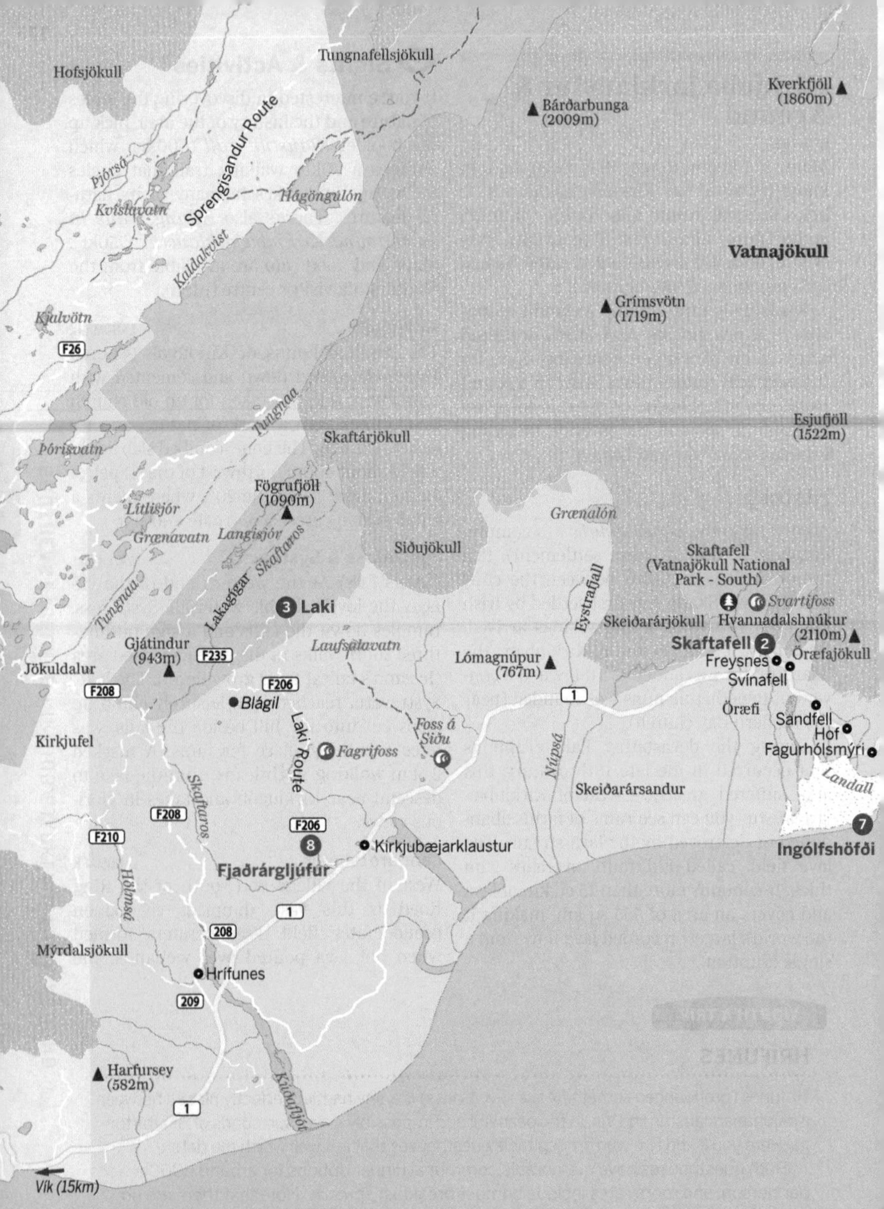

Southeast Iceland Highlights

❶ **Jökulsárlón** (p197) Admiring the ever-changing ice sculptures at this bewitching lagoon.

❷ **Skaftafell** (p187) Visiting Iceland's favourite national-park pocket, an area of green amid icy masses and vast sand deltas.

❸ **Laki** (p184) Striding up Laki for views of three glaciers and an incredible history lesson.

❹ **Heinabergslón** (p199) Joining the IceGuide team to paddle around icebergs on this silent glacier lagoon.

❺ **Skálafellsjökull** (p193) Trying to wipe the smile off

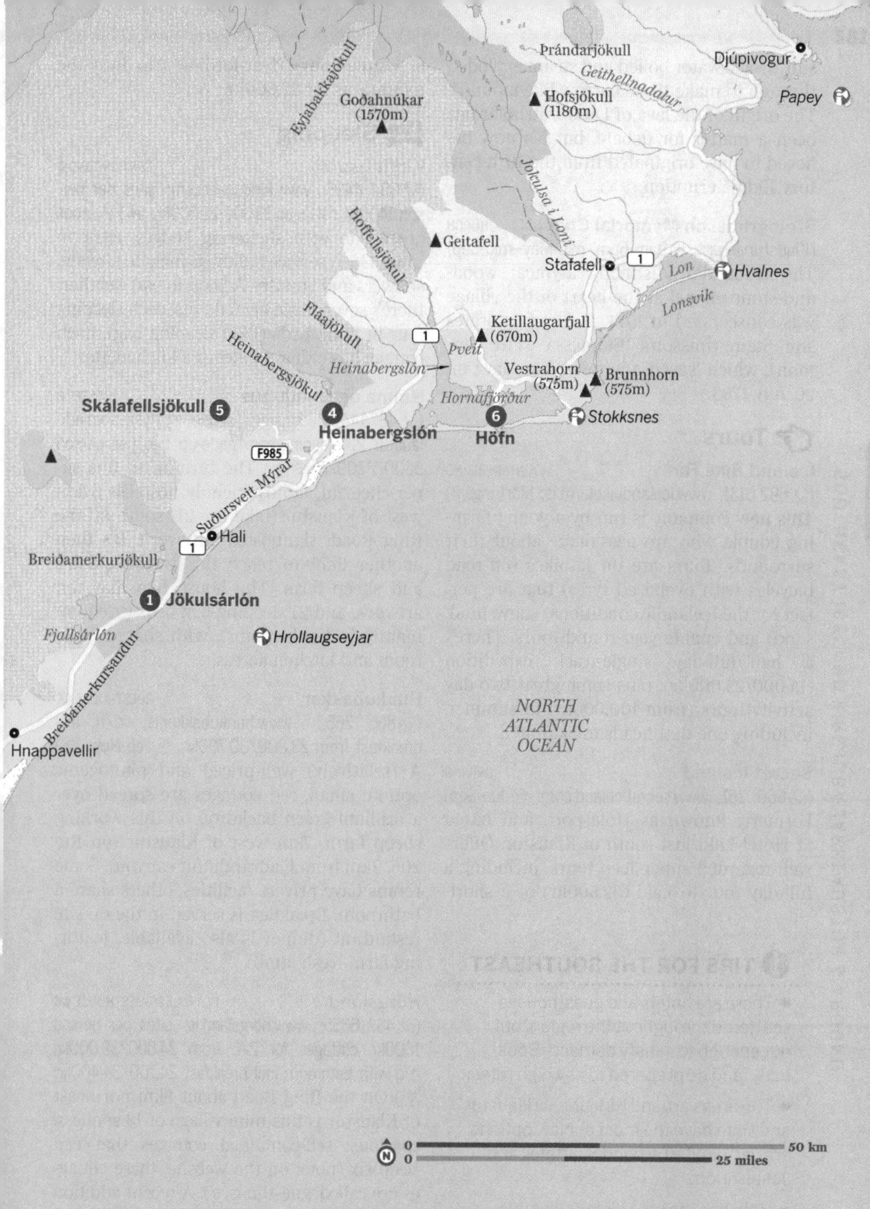

your face as you roar across a glacier on a snowmobile tour.

6 Höfn (p204) Dining in the town's restaurants, sampling delicious seafood treats netted by the local fishing fleet.

7 Ingólfshöfði (p196) Taking a tractor ride and climbing a promontory to check out puffins and dodge dive-bombing skuas.

8 Fjaðrárgljúfur (p183) Peering into the depths from a stunning canyon-edge walking path.

subsurface water boiled and steam exploded through to make these barrow-like mounds. The origin of the lava of Landbrotshólar has been a matter for debate, but it's now believed to have originated from the 10th-century Eldgjá eruption.

Steingrímsson Memorial Chapel CHURCH
(Klausturvegur; ⏲9am-6pm mid-May–mid-Sep) The triangular, distinctly atypical wood-and-stone chapel at the heart of the village was consecrated in 1974. It commemorates Jón Steingrímsson's 'Eldmessa' (Fire Sermon), which 'saved' the town from lava on 20 July 1783.

Tours

Iceland Bike Farm MOUNTAIN BIKING
(☎692 6131; www.icelandbikefarm.is; Mörtunga II) This new company is run by a young farming couple who are passionate about their surrounds. Tours are on fatbikes (off-road bicycles with oversized tyres) that are perfect for the Icelandic conditions (snow, mud, sand) and enable year-round tours. There's a half-/full-day single-track expedition (15,000/25,000kr), plus some great two-day activity tours (from 100,000kr) in summer, including one that heads to Skaftafell.

Secret Iceland DRIVING
(☎660 1151; www.secreticeland.com; ⏲Jun-Sep) Formerly known as Hólasport, and based at Hótel Laki just south of Klaustur. Offers well-regarded super-Jeep tours, including a full-day tour to Laki (32,500kr) or a shorter (three-hour) river-fording trip into the mountains for 22,500kr.

TIPS FOR THE SOUTHEAST

- There are hotels and guesthouses scattered throughout the region, but not enough to satisfy demand. Book early, and be prepared to pay high rates.
- The areas around Kirkjubæjarklaustur and Höfn have the most choice; options are very limited around Skaftafell and Jökulsárlón.
- Höfn has the best dining selection. You'll need to stock up on groceries and supplies in Kirkjubæjarklaustur and/or Höfn.

Good information is online:

- www.south.is
- www.visitvatnajokull.is
- www.vjp.is

Sleeping

Kirkjubær II CAMPGROUND €
(☎894 4495; www.kirkjubaer.com; sites per person 1400kr, cottages 19,000-21,000kr;) A neat green site with sheltering hedges, right in town. Good service buildings include kitchen, showers and laundry. A boon in bad weather; there's seven basic heated huts, each sleeping four in bunk beds (BYO sleeping bag). Each cottage has either a toilet or a kitchenette.

Nonna og Brynjuhús HOSTEL €
(☎487 1446; kiddasiggi@simnet.is; Þykkvabæjarklaustur 2; sleeping-bag/made-up bed per person 5600/8200kr;) The turn-off to this super-cheerful, family-friendly hostel is 37km west of Klaustur (take Rte 211 south off the Ring Road, signposted 'Álftaver'). It's then another 8km to reach this working dairy and sheep farm. The house here has fun artwork, and 21 sleeping-bag beds (predominantly in bunk rooms), with shared bathroom and kitchen access.

Hunkubakkar GUESTHOUSE €€
(☎865 2652; www.hunkubakkar.is; d/tr incl breakfast from 23,800/30,700kr; ⏲Feb-Nov;) A (relatively) well-priced and photogenic option: small, red cottages are spread over a brilliant-green backdrop on this working sheep farm, 7km west of Klaustur (on Rte 206, 2km from Fjaðrárgljúfur canyon). Some rooms have private facilities, others share a bathroom. Breakfast is served in the on-site restaurant (dinner is also available, featuring farm-fresh lamb).

Hörgsland COTTAGES, GUESTHOUSE €€
(☎487 6655; www.horgsland.is; sites per person 1600kr, cottages for 2/6 from 24,800/39,000kr, d/q with bathroom incl breakfast 24,700/34,400kr;) On the Ring Road about 8km northeast of Klaustur is this mini village of 13 spotless, spacious, self-contained cottages that can sleep six (note: on the website, these cottages are called 'guesthouses'). A recent addition is a block of spick-and-span rooms, with and without bathroom. There's also camping, plus outdoor hot-pots, and a simple shop and cafe.

★**Magma Hotel** BOUTIQUE HOTEL €€€
(☎420 0800; www.magmahotel.is; d incl breakfast from 43,000kr;) Winning hearts with its beautiful design, peaceful surrounds and friendly staff, this intimate new hotel is a gem. It's just a few kilometres south of

Klaustur on Rte 204, by a lake and looking onto lush views. Individual turf-roofed chalets (named for volcanoes) are an ode to good taste, and each features a fridge, coffee machine and bluetooth speaker, plus a patio.

Hótel Laki HOTEL €€€
(Efri-Vík; ☎412 4600; www.hotellaki.is; d incl breakfast from 33,800kr;) What started as farmhouse accommodation has grown into a sprawling 65-room hotel on scenic farmland 5km south of Klaustur on Rte 204. As well as comfortable (but extremely pricey) hotel rooms, there are 15 tiny, self-contained cottages (sold online as Efri-Vík Bungalows, and cheaper than the rooms), plus super-Jeep tours, a large restaurant-bar, and lake-fishing opportunities.

The well-regarded restaurant has an à la carte dinner menu (mains 2700kr to 5300kr) that highlights local produce and is open to all; reservations recommended.

Icelandair Hótel Klaustur HOTEL €€€
(☎487 4900; www.icelandairhotels.com; Klausturvegur 6; d from 31,700kr;) There are few surprises here: the Klaustur has friendly staff and attractive decor in its 57 well-equipped rooms (including a new building of superior rooms), plus a sunny enclosed dining terrace and bar-lounge. The restaurant (dinner mains kr2650 to kr5750) is among the town's best and features local produce (grilled Arctic char, slow-cooked lamb shank, langoustine etc).

Eating

Most travellers dine at their accommodation (most lodging eateries are open to nonguests too). If you're looking for a higher-end experience, head to the Icelandair hotel's restaurant.

Look out for local Arctic char (trout) on menus – it comes from pure water directly under the nearby lava field.

Kjarval SUPERMARKET €
(Klausturvegur 13; ⏲9am-9pm Jun-Sep, 10am-6pm Mon-Fri, 10am-2pm Sat Oct-May) For self-caterers. ATM next door.

Systrakaffi INTERNATIONAL €€
(☎487 4848; www.systrakaffi.is; Klausturvegur 12; mains 1100-4700kr; ⏲noon-9pm) The liveliest place in town is this cafe-bar, which can get slammed in summer. Its tasty, wide-ranging menu offers soups, salads, pizzas and burgers – but understandably plays favourites with local char and lamb.

DON'T MISS

FJAÐRÁRGLJÚFUR

The darkly picturesque canyon of **Fjaðrárgljúfur**, carved out by the river Fjaðrá, has been well and truly discovered, thanks to Instagrammers and one Justin Bieber (who filmed a video clip here). A walking trail follows its southern edge for a couple of kilometres, with plenty of places to gaze down into its rocky, writhing depths, and to take in the gorge's gorgeousness and the emerald-green surrounds.

The canyon is not far west of Klaustur, 3km north of the Ring Road via Rte 206.

Kaffi Munkar CAFE €€
(Klausturvegur 1-5; mains 1400-3600kr; ⏲10am-10pm Feb-Nov) At the western end of town, Kaffi Munkar serves as the bright cafe-reception of Klausturhof guesthouse. Pop in for soup, spicy chicken, fish stew or 'Arctic char from next door' (according to the cute blackboard menu).

Vínbúðin ALCOHOL
(Klausturvegur 15; ⏲2-6pm Mon-Thu, 1-7pm Fri, noon-2pm Sat) Government-run liquor store.

Information

The helpful tourist office is inside the **Skaftárstofa Visitor Centre** (☎487 4620; www.visitklaustur.is; Klausturvegur 10; ⏲9am-6pm mid-Jun–mid-Sep, to 5pm mid-May–mid-Jun, 9am-2pm Mon-Fri mid-Sep–mid-May), with good local info plus coverage and exhibitions on Katla Geopark and Vatnajökull National Park. This is the base for the lesser-visited western pocket of the national park, best accessed from the Fjallabak Route (p145), and accessible only by 4WD or summer bus. The visitor centre also screens a short film on the Laki eruption.

Getting There & Away

Klaustur is a stop on the Reykjavík–Vík–Höfn bus routes and also serves as a crossroads to Landmannalaugar and Laki. Buses stop at the N1.

Buses travelling east call at Skaftafell and Jökulsárlón.

Sterna (p430) services include:

- Bus 12 to Skaftafell (2200kr, 1¼ hours, one daily July and August)
- Bus 12 to Jökulsárlón (4200kr, 2¼ hours, one daily July and August)
- Bus 12a to Vík (1800kr, one hour, one daily July and August)

Strætó (p429) services include:

- Bus 51 to Höfn (5980kr, 2¾ hours, two daily)
- Bus 51 to Vík (1380kr, one hour, two daily)
- Bus 51 to Reykjavík (7820kr, 4¼ hours, two daily)

Reykjavík Excursions (p429) services include:

- Bus 10/10a Skaftafell–Klaustur–Eldgjá–Landmannalaugar (three times weekly July and August) Can be used as a day tour or as regular transport. Klaustur to Landmannalaugar one way is 7300kr (4¾ hours).
- Bus 16/16a Klaustur–Lakagígar (3½ hours, six weekly late June to August) Use as a day tour, with four hours at Laki (return 11,000kr).
- Bus 20 to Skaftafell (3400kr, one hour, one daily July and August)
- Bus 20a to Vík (3400kr, one hour, one daily July and August)
- Bus 20a to Reykjavík (9100kr, 5¼ hours, one daily July and August) Stops for 45 minutes at Vík and for 30 minutes at the Lava Centre in Hvolsvöllur.

Lakagígar

It's almost impossible to comprehend the immensity of the Laki eruptions, one of the most catastrophic volcanic events in human history. Nowadays the lava field belies the apocalypse that spawned it some 235 years ago. Its black, twisted lava formations are overgrown with soft green moss. It's a fascinating place to visit, and one that sees relatively few visitors.

History

In the early summer of 1783, a vast set of fissures opened, forming around 135 craters; the Lakagígar (Laki craters) took it in turns to fountain molten rock up to 1km into the air. These Skaftáreldar (River Skaftá Fires) lasted for eight months, spewing out an estimated volume of volcanic material over 15 cu km, with a resulting lava field (known as Eldhraun) covering an area of 565 sq km. Twenty farms in the area were wiped out by lava; another 30 were so badly damaged they had to be temporarily abandoned.

Far more devastating were the hundreds of millions of tonnes of ash and sulphuric acid that poured from the fissures. The sun was blotted out, the grass died off, and around two-thirds of Iceland's livestock died from starvation and poisoning. Some 9000 people – a fifth of the country's population – were killed and the remainder faced the Moðuharðindin ('Hardship of the Mist'), a famine that followed.

The damage wasn't limited to Iceland either. Across the northern hemisphere, clouds of ash blocked out the sun. Temperatures dropped and acid rain fell, causing devastating crop failures in Japan, Alaska and Europe (possibly even helping to spark the French Revolution).

Sights & Activities

Laki — MOUNTAIN

Although the peak called Laki (818m) did not erupt, it has loaned its name to the 25km-long Lakagígar crater row, which stretches northeastwards and southwestwards from its base. Laki can be climbed in about 40 minutes from the parking area. From the top there are boundless 360-degree views of the fissure, vast lava fields and glinting glaciers in the distance.

Lakagígar Crater Row — LANDMARK

The crater row is fascinating to explore, riddled with black sand dunes and lava tubes, many of which contain tiny stalactites. At the foot of Laki, marked walking paths lead you in and out of the two nearest craters, including an interesting lava tunnel.

Visitor Trail — WALKING

An excellent visitor trail has been established along a gentle 500m walk through the crater area; pick up the accompanying brochure (or download it from the national park website) for insight into the history, geology and ecology of the area. Ensure you stick to the marked paths in this ecologically sensitive region.

Fagrifoss — WATERFALL

Fagrifoss (Beautiful Falls) is not a misnomer: this waterfall must be one of Iceland's most bewitching, with rivulets of water pouring over a massive black rock. You'll come to the turn-off on the way to Laki, about 24km along Rte F206. Tours to Lakagígar invariably stop here.

Tours

Visiting the area requires a large, robust Jeep and 4WDing experience (as rivers must be forded). If you don't meet these requirements, it's best to join a tour. Departures to the Laki craters are dependent on road and weather conditions.

Reykjavík Excursions BUS TOUR
(☎580 5400; www.re.is) The full-day tour includes around four hours exploring the crater area. It is in brochures as bus route 16 and departs daily except Tuesday from late June to August, at 9am from the N1 at Kirkjubæjarklaustur (11,000kr return). It stops at Fjaðrárgljúfur canyon on the way to Laki, and Fagrifoss waterfall on the return journey. BYO lunch.

Secret Iceland DRIVING
(☎660 1151; www.secreticeland.com; Hótel Laki) Formerly known as Hólasport, and based at Hótel Laki (p183) just south of Kirkjubæjarklaustur. Offers well-regarded eight-hour super-Jeep day tours to Laki (32,500kr) from June to September. BYO lunch.

Sleeping & Eating

Camping is forbidden within the Laki reserve. The nearest campsite, with hut facilities, toilets and showers, is at **Blágil** (klaustur@vjp.is; bed/site per person 5000/1700kr; mid-Jun–mid-Sep), about 11km from Laki.

There are no facilities for buying food. You will need to bring your own supplies – all tours recommend you BYO lunch.

Information

The Lakagígar area is contained within the boundaries of Vatnajökull National Park (p189). Check the park website (www.vjp.is) for excellent information for travellers. When the access road is open, park rangers are available at the Laki car park from 11am to 3pm.

The Skaftárstofa Visitor Centre (p183) in Kirkjubæjarklaustur is a good port of call for advice before visiting.

Getting There & Away

Rte F206 (just west of Kirkjubæjarklaustur) is generally open from mid-June to mid-September (check at www.road.is). It's a long and very rugged 50km to the Lakagígar crater row. The road is absolutely unsuitable for 2WD cars as there are several rivers to ford. Even low-clearance 4WD vehicles may not be suitable in the spring thaw or after rain, when the rivers tend to run deep.

JÖKULHLAUP! GLACIAL FLOOD!

In late 1996 the devastating Grímsvötn eruption – Iceland's fourth largest of the 20th century, after Katla in 1918, Hekla in 1947 and Surtsey in 1963 – shook Southeast Iceland and caused an awesome *jökulhlaup* (glacial flood) across Skeiðarársandur. The events leading up to it are a sobering reminder of Iceland's volatile fire-and-ice combination.

On the morning of 29 September 1996, a magnitude 5.0 earthquake shook the Vatnajökull ice cap. Magma from a new volcano, in the Grímsvötn region beneath Vatnajökull, had made its way through the earth's crust and into the ice, causing the eruption of a 4km-long subsurface fissure known as Gjálp. The following day the eruption burst through the surface, ejecting a column of steam that rose 10km into the sky.

Scientists became concerned as the subglacial lake in the Grímsvötn caldera began to fill with water from ice melted by the eruption. Initial predictions on 3 October were that the ice would lift and the lake would spill out across Skeiðarársandur, threatening the Ring Road and its bridges. In the hope of diverting floodwaters away from the bridges, massive dyke-building projects were organised on Skeiðarársandur.

On 5 November, more than a month after the eruption started, the ice *did* lift and the Grímsvötn reservoir drained in a massive *jökulhlaup*, releasing up to 3000 billion litres of water within a few hours. The floodwaters – dragging along icebergs the size of three-storey buildings – destroyed the 375m-long Gígjukvísl Bridge and the 900m-long Skeiðará Bridge, both on the Skeiðarársandur. You can see video footage of the eruption and enormous multi-tonne blocks of ice being hurled across Skeiðarársandur at the Gamlabúð (p202) in Höfn.

Some other of Grímsvötn's creations include the Ásbyrgi canyon, gouged out by a cataclysmic flood over just a few days. In 1934 an eruption released a *jökulhlaup* of 40,000 cu metres per second, which swelled the river Skeiðará to 9km in width and laid waste to large areas of farmland.

Grímsvötn erupted again in December 1998, November 2004 and most recently in May 2011, when a huge ash plume was released into the atmosphere, disrupting air traffic (but with nowhere near the disruption caused by 2010's Eyjafjallajökull eruption). There was no *jökulhlaup* on any of these three occasions.

The Sandar

The sandar are soul-destroyingly flat and empty regions sprawling along Iceland's southeastern coast. High in the mountains, glaciers scrape up silt, sand and gravel that is then carried by glacial rivers or (more dramatically) by glacial bursts down to the coast and dumped in huge, desert-like plains. The sandar here are so impressively huge and awful that the Icelandic word (singular: sandur) is used internationally to describe the topographic phenomenon of a glacial outwash plain.

Skeiðarársandur is the most visible and dramatic, stretching some 40km between ice cap and coast from Núpsstaður to Öræfi. Here you'll encounter a flat expanse of grey-black sands, fierce scouring winds (a cyclist's nightmare) and fast-flowing grey-brown glacial rivers.

Note: *do not* drive off-road in these expanses. It is illegal, and hugely destructive to the fragile environment.

Sights

★Lómagnúpur MOUNTAIN

Adding more eye candy to an impressive road trip, a precipitous 767m-tall palisade of cliffs known as Lómagnúpur towers over the landscapes, begging to be photographed. It's the inspiration for many legends, and looks particularly good as a backdrop to the turf-roofed farm at Núpsstaður.

HOW TO AVOID BEING SKUA-ED

The great sandar on Iceland's southern coast are the world's largest breeding ground for great skuas (*Stercorarius skua; skúmur* in Icelandic). These large, meaty, dirty-brown birds tend to build their nests among grassy tufts in the ashy sand. You'll often see them harassing gulls into disgorging their dinner, killing and eating puffins and other little birds, or swooping down on *you* if you get too close to their nests.

Thankfully (unlike feather-brained Arctic terns), skuas will stop plaguing you if you run away from the area they're trying to defend. You can also avoid aerial strikes by wearing a hat or carrying a stick above your head.

Núpsstaður FARM

Lómagnúpur towers over the impossibly photogenic old turf-roofed farm at Núpsstaður. The farm buildings date back to the early 19th century, and the idyllic chapel is one of the last turf churches in Iceland. It was once a museum, but at the time of writing the farm was closed to the public.

You can't drive onto the property, but you can park by the road and walk up to the buildings to check them out and take photos.

Skeiðarársandur LANDMARK

Skeiðarársandur, the largest sandur in the world, covers a 1300-sq-km area and was formed by the mighty Skeiðarárjökull. Since the Settlement Era, Skeiðarársandur has swallowed a considerable amount of farmland and it continues to grow. The area was relatively well populated (for Iceland, anyway), but in 1362 the volcano beneath Öræfajökull (then known as Knappafellsjökull) erupted and the subsequent *jökulhlaup* (flooding caused by volcanic eruption beneath ice) laid waste the entire district. After the 1362 eruption the district became known as Öræfi (Wasteland).

Núpsstaðarskógar FOREST

Inland from Lómagnúpur peak is Núpsstaðarskógar, a beautiful low-growing woodland area on the slopes of the mountain Eystrafjall. Due to the perils of crossing the Núpsá river, this area is best explored on a tour. In July and August, Icelandic Mountain Guides (p190) runs a guided five-day (65km) backpacking hike through Núpsstaðarskógar, over to Grænalón (an ice-dammed marginal lake), across the glacier Skeiðarárjökull and then into Morsárdalur in Skaftafell. The trip costs from 135,000kr.

Sleeping & Eating

This 70km stretch has very little by way of traveller facilities – only a couple of accommodation options in pretty green oases.

★Lækjaborgir Guesthouse COTTAGE €€

(☎833 5500; lækjaborgir@gmail.com; studio from 27,000kr) A cluster of sweet, high-quality studios and cottages is an excellent reason to divert off the Ring Road at Kálfafell, just east of the Fosshotel (about 26km from Klaustur). Another reason: morning **super-Jeep tours** offered by the owners into the epic nature at their back doorstep (15,900kr per adult; open to all, but cottage guests get a discount).

★ Dalshöfði Guesthouse GUESTHOUSE €€
(☎487 4781; http://dalshofdi.is; d/f without bathroom incl breakfast 21,090/33,250kr) An appealing option in this area is Dalshöfði Guesthouse, in a remote and scenic farm setting 5km north of the Ring Road. Rooms are bright and spotless, with access to a kitchen and a sunny, plant-filled outdoor deck. There's a two-bedroom apartment here (37,050kr) too, and some lovely hiking trails in the area.

Hvoll Guesthouse GUESTHOUSE €€
(☎487 4785; www.road201.is; d/f without bathroom from 17,500/25,700kr;) Formerly an HI-affiliated hostel, this well-run guesthouse (also known as Road 201) is on the edge of Skeiðarársandur (3.5km south off the Ring Road via a gravel road) and feels remote despite its large size. There's a busy atmosphere; facilities include several kitchens (bring food – the closest supermarket is 25km away in Klaustur) and a laundry.

Fosshótel Núpar HOTEL €€
(☎517 3060; www.fosshotel.is; d incl breakfast from 21,000kr;) Just west of Hvoll Guesthouse, behind a portacabin-like exterior, this recently expanded chain hotel offers modern, minimalist rooms, many with good views. There's a cosy bar-lounge area, and the only **restaurant** for miles is here, serving a small menu at dinnertime (mains 2890kr to 4590kr).

Skaftafell (Vatnajökull National Park – South)

Skaftafell, the jewel in the crown of Vatnajökull National Park, encompasses a breathtaking collection of peaks and glaciers. It's the country's favourite wilderness: more than 500,000 visitors per year come to marvel at thundering waterfalls, twisted birch woods, the tangled web of rivers threading across the sandar, and brilliant blue-white Vatnajökull with its lurching tongues of ice, dripping down mountainsides like icing on a cake.

Skaftafell deserves its reputation, and few visitors – even those who usually shun the great outdoors – can resist it. In the height of summer it may feel that every traveller in the country is here. However, if you're prepared to get out on the more remote trails and take advantage of the fabulous hiking on the heath and beyond, you'll leave the crowds behind. Shun the crowds by visiting Svartifoss under the midnight sun.

Skaftafell National Park

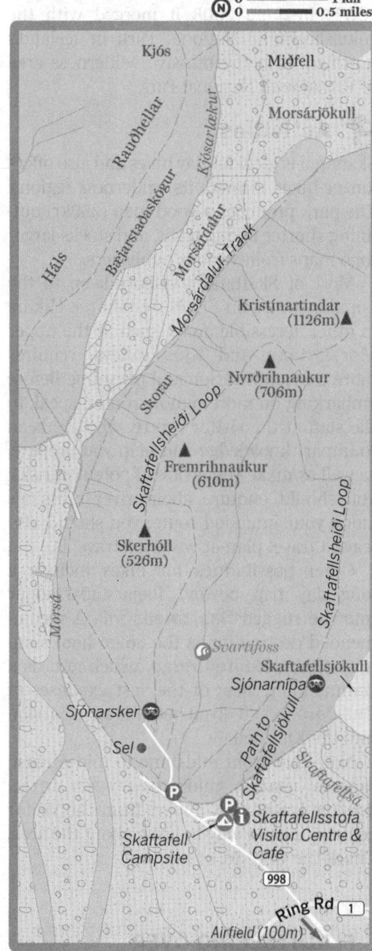

History

The historical Skaftafell was a large farm at the foot of the hills west of the present campground. Shifting glacial sands slowly buried the fields and forced the farm to be moved to a more suitable site, on the heath 100m above the sandur. The district came to be known as Hérað Milli Sandur (Land Between the Sands), but after all the farms were annihilated by the 1362 eruptions the district became the 'land under the sands' and was renamed Öræfi (Wasteland). Once the vegetation returned, however, the Skaftafell farm was rebuilt in its former location.

Skaftafell National Park was founded in 1967 by the Icelandic Government and the WWF. In June 2008 it merged with the Jökulsárgljúfur National Park in Iceland's north to form the massive wilderness area of Vatnajökull National Park.

Activities

Skaftafell is ideal for day hikes and also offers longer hikes through its wilderness regions. The park produces a good map (350kr) outlining shorter hiking trails, and stocks larger topo maps from various publishers.

Most of Skaftafell's visitors keep to the popular routes on **Skaftafellsheiði**. Hiking in other accessible areas, such as the upper **Morsárdalur** and **Kjós** valleys, requires more time, motivation and planning. Before embarking on more remote routes, speak to the staff at the visitor centre, who are keen to impart knowledge and help you prepare, as well as make you aware of potential risks. You should enquire about river crossings along your intended route; you should also leave a travel plan at www.safetravel.is.

Other possibilities for hikes include a long day trip beyond Bæjarstaðarskógur into the rugged **Skaftafellsfjöll**. A recommended destination is the 862m-high summit of the **Jökulfell ridge**, which affords a commanding view of the vast expanses of **Skeiðarárjökull**. Even better is an excursion into the Kjós dell.

Note that from mid-June to mid-August, rangers usually guide **free daily interpretive walks** that depart from the visitor centre – a great way to learn about the area. Check the website, or ask staff.

FLIGHTSEEING OVER SKAFTAFELL

Atlantsflug (☎854 4105; www.flightseeing.is; ⊙May-Sep) sightseeing flights offer a brilliant perspective over all this natural splendour, and leave from the tiny airfield on the Ring Road, just by the turn-off to the Skaftafellsstofa Visitor Centre. Choose between seven tour options, with views over Landmannalaugar, Lakagígar, Skaftafell peaks, Jökulsárlón and Grímsvötn. Prices start from 26,100kr for 20 minutes on the 'pilot special' surprise route (determined by weather and conditions).

Svartifoss

Star of a hundred postcards, Svartifoss (Black Falls) is a stunning, moody-looking waterfall flanked by geometric black basalt columns. It's reached by a relatively easy 1.8km trail leading up from the visitor centre via the campground.

To take pressure off the busy trail to Svartifoss, park staff recommend you take an alternative path back to the visitor centre. From Svartifoss, continue west up the track to **Sjónarsker**, where there's a view disc that names the surrounding landmarks to help you get your bearings, plus an unforgettable vista across Skeiðarársandur. From here you can visit the traditional turf-roofed farmhouse **Sel**; this two-hour, 5.5km return walk (path S2) is classified as easy.

Alternatively, from Svartifoss head east over the heath to the viewpoint at **Sjónarnípa**, looking across Skaftafellsjökull. This walk (path S5/S6) is classified as challenging; allow three hours return (7.4km).

Skaftafellsjökull

A very popular trail is the easy one-hour walk (path S1; 3.7km return) to Skaftafellsjökull. The marked trail begins at the visitor centre and leads to the glacier face, where you can witness the bumps and groans of the ice (although the glacier is pretty grey and gritty here). The glacier has receded greatly in recent decades, meaning land along this trail has been gradually reappearing. Pick up a brochure that describes the trail's geology.

Skaftafellsheiði Loop

On a fine day, the five- to six-hour (path S3; 16.7km) walk around Skaftafellsheiði (Skaftafell Heath) is a hiker's dream. It begins by climbing from the campground to **Sjónarsker**, continuing across the moor to 610m-high **Fremrihnaukur**. From there it follows the edge of the plateau to the next rise, **Nyrðrihnaukur** (706m), which affords a superb view of Morsárdalur, and Morsárjökull and the iceberg-choked lagoon at its base. At this point the track turns southeast to an outlook point, **Gláma**, on the cliff above Skaftafellsjökull. The route continues down to Sjónarnípa and then back to the campground.

For the best view of Skaftafellsjökull, Morsárdalur and the Skeiðarársandur, it's worth scaling the summit of **Kristínartindar** (1126m). The best way follows a well-marked 2km route (classified as difficult)

VATNAJÖKULL NATIONAL PARK

Vast, varied and spectacular, **Vatnajökull National Park** (www.vjp.is) was founded in 2008, when authorities created a giant megapark by joining the Vatnajökull ice cap with two previously established national parks: Skaftafell in Southeast Iceland and Jökulsárgljúfur in the northeast. With recent additions, the park now measures over 14,100 sq km – approximately 14% of the entire country (it's one of the largest national parks in Europe). It has been nominated for inclusion on the Unesco World Heritage list.

The park boundaries encircle a staggering richness of landscapes and some of Iceland's greatest natural treasures, created by the combined forces of rivers, glacial ice, and volcanic and geothermal activity (yes, fire-and-ice cliché alert!). The entirety of the Vatnajökull ice cap is protected, including countless glistening outlet glaciers and glacial rivers. There are incredible waterfalls such as Dettifoss and Svartifoss, the storied Lakagígar crater row, Askja and other volcanoes of the highlands, and an unending variety of areas where geology, ecology and history lessons spring to life.

The park's website (www.vjp.is) is filled with important information – details on trails, campsites, access roads etc, plus it has downloadable maps and brochures. There are useful visitor centres in the Southeast in the towns of Kirkjubæjarklaustur (p183) and Höfn (p205), and at Skaftafell (p191).

Hiking trails and 4WD routes can get you to remote gems, but you don't have to get off the beaten track to sample some of the park's highlights – in fact, quite a few worthy diversions (and awesome vistas) can be accessed from a standard Ring Road journey of the country, and there's a smorgasbord of tour offerings.

up the prominent valley southeast of the Nyrðrihnaukur lookout, and back down near Gláma.

Tours

Glacier Hikes & Ice Climbing

The highlight of a visit to the southern reaches of Vatnajökull is a glacier hike. It's utterly liberating to strap on crampons and crunch your way around a glacier, and there's much to see on the ice: waterfalls, ice caves, glacial mice (moss balls, not actual mice!) and different-coloured ash from ancient explosions. But – take note: as magnetic as the glaciers are, they are also riven with fissures and are potentially dangerous, so don't be tempted to stride out onto one without the right equipment and guiding.

A number of authorised guides operate year-round in the area (and at lesser-visited glacier tongues further east, towards Höfn). The largest companies, Icelandic Mountain Guides (p190) and Arctic Adventures (p190), have info and booking huts beside Skaftafellsstofa Visitor Centre (p191), where you can talk to experts and get kitted out for glacier walks (warm clothes essential; waterproof gear and hiking boots available for hire).

Companies in the area often go further than just easy glacier hikes, offering more challenging options and ice climbs. Some offer combos, such as a glacier hike plus a lagoon boat trip. See the websites for suggestions and for the most up-to-date rates.

Ice Caves

Winter visits to ice caves are in hot demand. These glorious dimpled caverns of exquisite blue light are accessible (usually at glacier edges) only from around November to March – they can be viewed only in cold conditions, and become unstable and unsafe in warmer weather. Temporary ice caves are created anew each season by the forces of nature, and are scouted by local experts. They *must* be visited with guides, who will ensure safety and correct equipment. As with glacier hikes, tours generally involve getting kitted out (crampons, helmets etc), then driving to the glacier edge and taking a walk to reach the destination. Reasonable fitness and mobility are required.

With their rapid growth in popularity, the largest and most accessible ice caves can become busy and crowded when tour groups arrive (from as far afield as Reykjavík). It is often the case that guided groups all visit the same cave – some tourists are disappointed to find queues of visitors waiting to enter. Catering to this, a few tour companies offer private tours to more remote caves: these tours are longer, more expensive, and generally require a higher level of fitness to reach.

WINTER IN SKAFTAFELL

There has been a significant growth in winter travel to the region, with the strong draws of Northern Lights and ice caves (caves that form within the ice of a glacier, which become solid and safe for visiting in the coldest months). You can still do glacier walks in winter – and the glaciers look more pristine, taking on that blue hue so beloved by photographers. In the right conditions, Svartifoss freezes in January–February (on the flip side, in winter the falls are not always accessible, due to slippery, unsafe tracks). Between December and March, access to trails is weather dependent, and some may require crampons. There are also restricted daylight hours, so it pays to talk to park staff about your best options.

There is a growing number of companies offering ice cave visits. Day tours from Reykjavík to this area are not an especially good idea, due to travel time (Reykjavík to Skaftafell is a four-hour drive, one way). We recommend you go with a local company. From Coast to Mountains (p192) and sister company Local Guide are the regional experts on ice caves in the Southeast, and can get you to some more remote, private caves if you have more time, stamina and cash (you can even spend a night in an ice cave, should you dare).

Other good, locally owned companies offering ice-cave exploration include Glacier Adventure (p200), IceGuide (p199), Glacier Journey (p199), Ice Explorers (p200) and Glacier Trips (p200) – spot a trend in the names? Note that some of these companies have cave tours departing from Skaftafell, while most have tours departing from Jökulsárlón (p197) car park (57km east of Skaftafell). Pay attention to the small print when booking.

Tour Companies

★Local Guide ADVENTURE

(☎894 1317; www.localguide.is; Freysnes) Local Guide is a family-owned business – the family has lived in the area for generations, so local knowledge is first-rate. Tours depart from the petrol station in Freysnes, about 5km from Skaftafell. From here, guides run year-round glacier hikes and ice climbs; the shortest tour offers one hour on the ice for adult/child 9490/8900kr (minimum age 10).

Local Guide is also a long-standing expert on ice caves, and runs tours from mid-November to March. The standard ice-cave tour costs 19,900kr, but there longer tours, plus options for private tours to more remote caves. The website outlines all the details.

Icelandic Mountain Guides ADVENTURE

(IMG; ☎Reykjavík 587 9999, Skaftafell 894 2959; www.mountainguides.is) IMG's best-selling walk is the family-friendly 'Blue Ice Experience', with 1½ to two hours spent on the ice (adult/child 10,900/7900kr, minimum age eight years). These tours run from Skaftafell four to eight times daily year-round. There are longer three-hour walks up the same glacier (16,900kr), and an option to combine with an introduction to ice climbing (19,900kr).

Arctic Adventures ADVENTURE

(Glacier Guides; ☎562 7000; www.glacierguides.is) In addition to glacier walks of varying duration and difficulty, Arctic Adventures (formerly Glacier Guides) also offers ice climbing (24,990kr), plus wintertime ice-cave visits (adult/child 19,990/14,993kr) departing from Skaftafell and Jökulsárlón. The company's beginner-level glacier walk is the family-friendly 'Glacier Wonders', a 3½-hour tour with a one-hour walk on Falljökull (adult/child 10,750/5375kr; minimum age 10 years). See the website for schedules.

Sleeping & Eating

Inside the park, the only option is to camp. There's very little accommodation close to the park, and hotels in the Southeast are in huge demand – you'll need either a tent or a firm hotel booking if you're heading this way.

The nearest hotel is at Freysnes (p191), 5km east of the national-park entrance, and there's a handful of options at Hof (p193), a further 15km east.

In summer, there's a cafe inside the park visitor centre, and a food truck nearby, but there are no year-round park options. You can get meals and a few supplies year-round at Söluskálinn Freysnesi (p192), in Freysnes, 5km east of the national-park entrance.

Bring groceries from the supermarkets at Kirkjubæjarklaustur or Höfn.

Skaftafell Campsite CAMPGROUND €
(☎470 8300; www.vjp.is; sites per adult/teen/child 1400/800kr/free; 📶) Most visitors bring a tent (or campervan) to this large, gravelly, panoramic campsite (with laundry facilities, and hot showers for 500kr). It gets very busy in summer, with a capacity of 400 pitches; note that the site is open year-round. Reservations are only required for large groups (40-plus people). No cooking facilities are provided. Wi-fi is available in the visitor centre.

If you're looking for a less-crowded option, consider the campground (p192) at Svínafell, 8km east.

Glacier Goodies FAST FOOD €€
(www.facebook.com/glaciergoodies; mains 2200-2700kr; ⏰11.30am-8pm mid-May–Sep) This food truck close to the visitor centre has a small menu of well-executed dishes made from local ingredients: lobster soup, fish and chips, baby back ribs and chips.

Visitor Centre Cafe CAFE €€
(mains 1490-2290kr; ⏰9am-9pm Jun-Sep, 9am-6pm May, Oct & Nov, 10am-6pm Dec-Apr) A busy cafe beside the visitor centre sells coffee, grilled panini, cake and waffles, plus takeaway hiking snacks (*skyr* etc). Hot food (soup, dish of the day) is served from noon, and there are some vegetarian and vegan options.

ℹ Information

All flora, fauna and natural features of the park are protected, open fires are prohibited and rubbish must be carried out. It's important to stick to the marked paths to avoiding damaging delicate plant life.

Note that drones are prohibited in the national park without official park permission.

Skaftafellsstofa Visitor Centre (☎470 8300; www.vjp.is; ⏰8am-7pm Jun-Sep, 9am-6pm Feb-May & Oct, 10am-6pm Nov-Jan; 📶) The helpful year-round visitor centre has an information desk plus maps for sale, informative exhibitions, a summertime cafe and internet access. The staff here know their stuff, and are keen to impart knowledge and help you prepare for hiking.

ℹ Getting There & Away

Skaftafell is a stop on Reykjavík–Höfn bus route and also a departure point for wilderness areas such as Landmannalaugar. There are regular summer services to Jökulsárlón that can be used as an excursion.

Buses stop in front of the visitor centre.

Sterna (p430) services include:

➡ Bus 12 to Jökulsárlón (2000kr, one hour, one daily July and August) Use as a day trip, with two hours at the lagoon; return 4000kr.

➡ Bus 12a to Vík (4000kr, 2½ hours, one daily July and August)

Strætó (p429) services include:

➡ Bus 51 to Höfn (3680kr, 1¾ hours, two daily) Stops at Freysnes and Jökulsárlón en route.

➡ Bus 51 to Reykjavík (10,120kr, five hours, two daily).

Reykjavík Excursions (p429) services include:

➡ Bus 10/10a to Landmannalaugar (9500kr, five hours, three weekly July and August) Runs via Eldgjá. Can be used as a day tour or as regular transport.

➡ Bus 15 to Jökulsárlón (2800kr, 45 minutes, two daily July and August)

➡ Bus 20a to Reykjavík (11,200kr, 6¼ hours, one daily July and August)

CAR & MOTORCYCLE

All visiting vehicles must pay for parking at Skaftafell. Signs indicate rates and how to pay (you input your licence plate number via a website, app or screens inside the visitor centre). Fees are 600/300kr for a regular car/motorcycle, with increasing fees for larger cars and buses.

The fee is for one day, valid until midnight each day. You can pay for three days in one transaction.

Skaftafell to Jökulsárlón

Glittering glaciers and brooding mountains line the 60km stretch between Skaftafell and the iceberg-filled lagoon Jökulsárlón, and the unfolding landscape makes it difficult to keep your eyes on the road.

Svínafell & Freysnes

The first hamlet you reach east of Skaftafell is Freysnes, home to a hotel, plus petrol station and store. Svínafell is another tiny hamlet just east of Freysnes, with camping opportunities plus a saga connection.

The farm Svínafell was the home of Flosi Þórðarson, the character who burned Njál and his family to death in *Njál's Saga*. It was also the site where Flosi and Njál's family were finally reconciled, thus ending one of the bloodiest feuds in Icelandic history. In the 17th century, Svínafellsjökull nearly engulfed the farm, but it has since retreated.

Svínafellsjökull GLACIER
Heading east on the Ring Road from Skaftafell, a sign points the way to the glacier

Svínafellsjökull. A rough, potholed dirt road leads 2km to a car park, from where it's a short walk to the northern edge of the glacier and some fine photo ops. Don't be tempted to stride out onto the glacier unaccompanied – join a guided walk.

In summer 2018, geologists became concerned over the risk of rock landslide in the region around Svínafellsjökull; at the time of research, guided glacier walks were no longer operating here (companies offering hikes on Svínafellsjökull have moved to other nearby outlet glaciers).

Tours

Glacier Horses HORSE RIDING
(☎847 7170; www.glacierhorses.is; adult/child 11,000/5000kr; ⊙Jun-Oct) Not far past Svínafell (en route to Hof), this operator offers short (one to 1½-hour) horse rides in view-blessed countryside. Bookings are essential, by phone or email.

Sleeping & Eating

Ferðaþjónustan Svínafelli CAMPGROUND €
(☎478 1765; www.svinafell.com; sites per person 1700kr, r & cabins per person 4500-5200kr; ⊙campground May-Sep; 📶) This well-organised place has a campsite and six basic cabins (sleeping four), and a spotless amenities block with a large dining room. With your own vehicle, it's an alternative to the campground at Skaftafell. Note: no powered sites. The owner also offers sleeping-bag beds in apartments and rooms scattered about the hamlet (these are available year-round).

Hótel Skaftafell HOTEL €€€
(☎478 1945; www.hotelskaftafell.is; Freysnes; s/d/tr incl breakfast 30,500/37,250/42,900kr; 📶) This is the closest hotel to Skaftafell; it's 5km east, at Freysnes, and one of very few hotels in the area so it's in hot demand – and prices reflect this. Its 63 rooms are neat and functional (and *very* overpriced) rather than luxurious; staff are helpful. There's a decent restaurant (mains 3750kr to 5750kr) plating up local produce such as Arctic char and lamb fillet.

Söluskálinn Freysnesi ICELANDIC €
(mains 1000-3200kr; ⊙9am-8pm) The petrol station opposite Hótel Skaftafell has a cafeteria serving a well-priced hot dish of the day alongside burgers and pizzas, and it sells a small selection of groceries.

Hvannadalshnúkur

Iceland's highest mountain, Hvannadalshnúkur (2110m), pokes out from **Öræfajökull**, an offshoot of Vatnajökull. This lofty peak is actually the northwestern edge of an immense 5km-wide crater – the biggest active volcano in Europe after Siciliy's Mt Etna. It erupted in 1362, firing out the largest amount of tephra in Iceland's recorded history. The region was utterly devastated – hence its name, Öræfi (Wasteland).

In late 2017 and 2018, scientists detected increased activity in the volcano under Öræfajökull (the glacier and volcano share the same name). The volcano has been dormant for some 250 years, but is recognised as one of Iceland's most powerful.

Tours

The best access for climbing Hvannadalshnúkur is from Sandfellsheiði, about 12km southeast of Skaftafell. Most guided expeditions manage the trip in a very long and taxing day (starting around 5am), and although there are no technical skills required, the trip is both physically and mentally challenging. Total elevation gain is more than 2000m; total distance is around 23km. Independent climbers should carry enough supplies and gear for several days, and must be well versed in glacier travel.

The best time for climbing the mountain is April or May, before the ice bridges melt. Note that each year the ice bridges that make the hike possible are melting earlier and faster, so the climbing season is becoming shorter. Companies may advertise long seasons (April to August, for example), but it is unlikely the conditions will permit ascents beyond June.

Check websites for more details.

Icelandic Mountain Guides and From Coast to Mountains offer guided ascents of Hvannadalshnúkur; briefings are held the night before. Note that prices are always subject to change, as conditions may force the company to hire extra guides per group, raising the costs. Book in advance, and allow yourself extra days in case the weather causes a cancellation.

From Coast to Mountains ADVENTURE TOUR
(Öræfaferðir; ☎894 0894; www.fromcoasttomountains.is; Fagurhólsmýri) Einar, the company owner, holds the record for ascents of Hvannadalshnúkur (around 300!). He offers

private ski-mountaineering ascents from March to May; the price depends on group size (two people costs 80,000kr per person; climbers need their own ski gear). There is also the possibility of ascent in September/ October, under the right conditions. The company's HQ is in Fagurhólsmýri, 26km from Skaftafell.

Icelandic Mountain Guides ADVENTURE TOUR
(☎ Reykjavík office 587 9999, Skaftafell 894 2959; www.mountainguides.is) A guided 10- to 15-hour ascent costs 43,900kr per person (minimum two people). Trips run three times a week in the season (conditions permitting). IMG has a second mountain-climbing option in the park: the Hrútsfjallstindar Peaks (42,900kr), which reach 1875m. The company is based in the car park of Skaftafell National Park.

Hof

At the hamlet of Hof there's a storybook wood-and-peat **church**, built on the foundations of a previous 14th-century building. It was reconstructed in 1884 and now sits pretty in a thicket of birch and ash with flowers growing on the grassy roof.

Hof is about 17km from the turn-off to Skaftafell. You'll need your own transport.

Vesturhús Hostel HOSTEL €
(☎ 854 5585; http://vesturhus.is; d/tr without bathroom 14,000/18,000kr) Basic bedrooms and a cosy kitchen, dining and lounge area are the hallmarks of this six-room hostel. No dorms, but all no-frills bedrooms feature bunks and can sleep up to five. BYO linen, or hire bedding (1800kr per person) and a towel (400kr).

Nónhamar COTTAGES €€
(☎ 620 4000; www.nonhamar.is; d/q 24,900/ 30,900kr; ⏲ Mar-Oct; 📶) Nónhamar has a trio of super-cosy self-contained cabins sleeping four people in bunks (the owner warns that four adults in the 18-sq-metre space will be cramped!). There's a wee kitchenette and bathroom in each.

Adventure Hotel Vatnajökull HOTEL €€€
(☎ 478 2260; www.hof1.is; d with/without bathroom incl breakfast 31,900/25,900kr; 📶) Formerly known as Hof 1 Hotel but now with new owners (the Arctic Adventures tour company), this expanding, renovated hotel has a variety of rooms scattered in various buildings, and a dining area serving dinner (mains 2300kr to 3800kr) that includes vegetarian-frendly options. It's at the foot of the Öræfajökull glacier.

RIDING ON THE VATNAJÖKULL ICE CAP

Vatnajökull ice cap and its attendant glaciers look spectacular from the Ring Road, and most travellers will be seized by a wild desire to get closer. Guided hikes on icy glacial tongues are a wonderful introduction, but access to the serious bulk of Vatnajökull is only for experienced folks set up for a serious polar-style expedition: the ice cap is riven with deep crevasses, which are made invisible by coverings of fresh snow, and there are often sudden, violent blizzards. But don't be disheartened! You can travel way up into the whiteness on organised snowmobile or super-Jeep tours, now offered by a few local companies (including in winter).

These companies utilise the easiest route up to Vatnajökull: the F985 4WD track (p198), about 35km east of Jökulsárlón and 45km west of Höfn, to the broad glacial spur **Skálafellsjökull**. At the end of Rte F985, 840m above sea level and with spectacular 360-degree views, most travellers choose to do an awesome **snowmobile ride**. You are kitted out with overalls, helmets, boots and gloves, then play follow-the-leader along a fixed trail. It's great fun, and although it only gives you the briefest introduction to glacier travel, an hour of noisy bouncing about with the stink of petrol in your nostrils is probably enough for most people! If the skidoo isn't your thing, you can also take a **super-Jeep ride** onto the ice, or do a **glacier hike**.

Glacier Jeeps (p200) and Glacier Journey (p199) both offer snowmobiling and super-Jeep tours; Glacier Jeeps also offers a glacier hike. With the popularity of these tours, it pays to book in advance (online). Children's prices for snowmobile rides are for those aged six to 12 (the rides aren't suitable for younger than six). Snowmobile drivers need a driving licence (passengers don't).

Glacier Journey offers winter snowmobile rides as well as ice cave visits. Check websites for up-to-date rates, schedules and meeting points.

1

SNOMEDIA/SHUTTERSTOCK ©

2

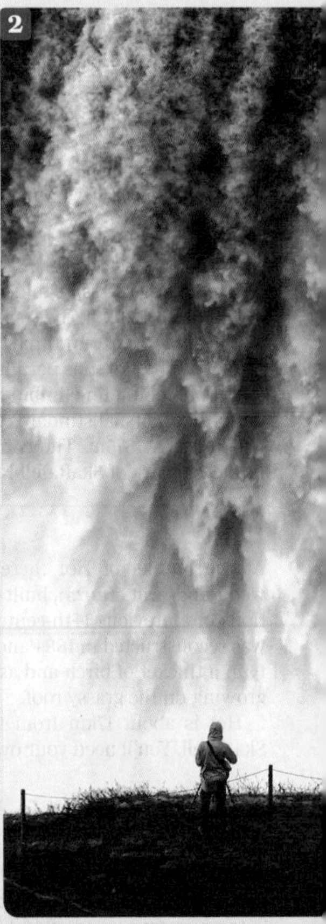

SMIT/SHUTTERSTOCK ©

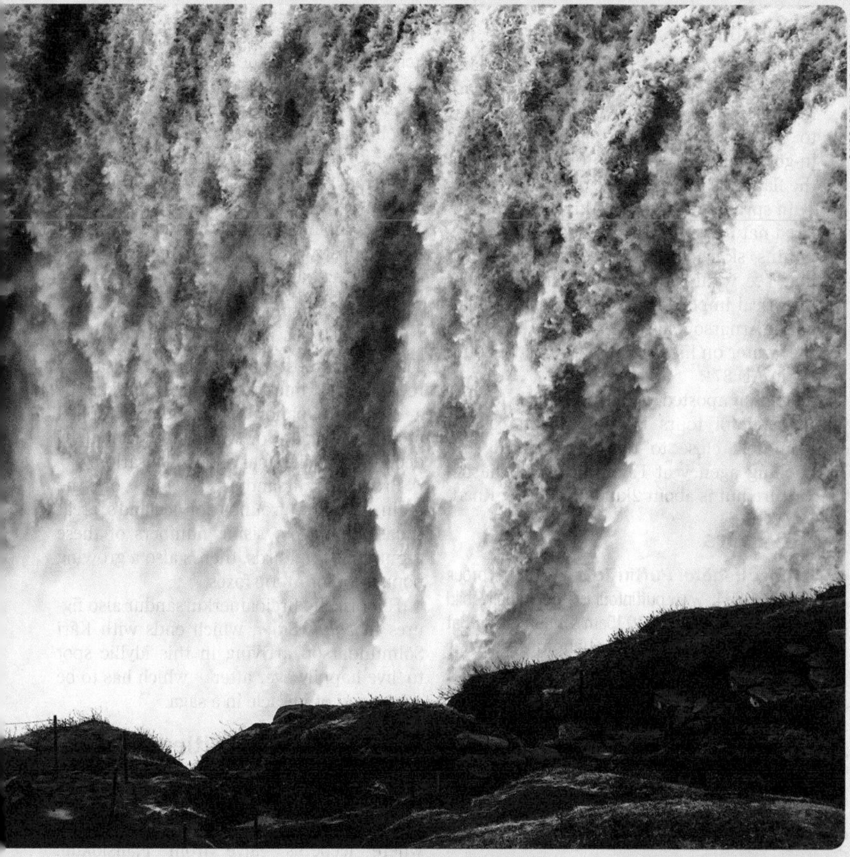

1. Kirkjufellsfoss (p225)
One of the shorter waterfalls, Kirkjufellsfoss is backed by Kirkjufell, said to be one of the most photographed spots in Iceland.

2. Dettifoss (p322)
One of Iceland's most mighty waterfalls, Dettifoss has the greatest volume of any waterfall in Europe.

3. Seljalandsfoss (p149)
A popular stop on the Ring Road, Seljalandsfoss thunders off the lower escarpments of Eyjafjallajökull volcano.

4. Gullfoss (p127)
Situated on the Hvítá River, the mesmerising and voluminous Gullfoss (Golden Falls) is one of the most easily accessible falls.

3

GARY LATHAM/LONELY PLANET ©

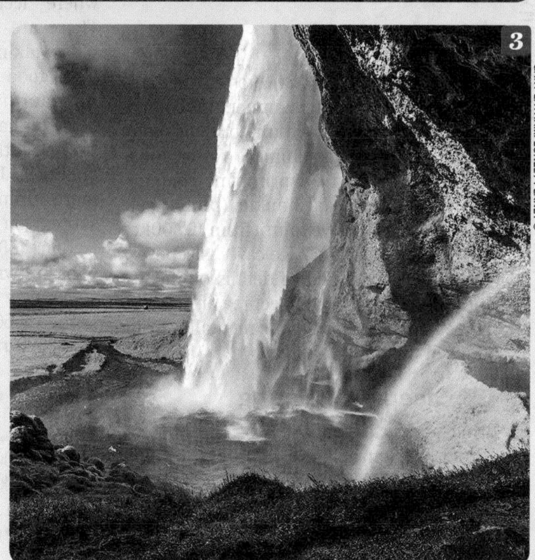

Ingólfshöfði

While everyone's gaze naturally turns inland in this spectacular part of Iceland, there are reasons to look offshore too – in particular to the 76m-high Ingólfshöfði (pronounced in-golvs-hurv-thi) promontory, rising from the flatlands like a strange dream.

In spring and summer, this beautiful, isolated nature reserve is overrun with nesting puffins, skuas and other seabirds, and you may see whales offshore. It's also of great historical importance – it was here that Ingólfur Arnarson, Iceland's first settler, stayed the winter on his original foray to the country in AD 874.

The signposted departure point for the Ingólfshöfði tours is about 25km east of Skaftafell, close to the petrol pump and booking agency at Fagurhólsmýri. The departure hut is about 2km off the Ring Road.

Tours

★Ingólfshöfði Puffin Tour ECOTOUR
(☎894 0894; www.puffintour.is; tours adult/child 7500/2500kr; ⊙tours 10.15am & 1.30pm Mon-Sat mid-May–mid-Aug) The Ingólfshöfði reserve is open to visitors on tours, which begin with a fun ride across 6km of shallow tidal lagoon (in a tractor-drawn wagon). After a short but steep sandy climb, there's a 1½-hour guided walk round the headland. The emphasis is on birdwatching, with stunning mountain backdrops to marvel over. Note that puffins usually leave Iceland around mid-August.

★From Coast to Mountains ADVENTURE TOUR
(Öræfaferðir; ☎894 0894; www.fromcoasttomountains.is; Fagurhólsmýri) In summer, this company operates fun nature tours to Ingólfshöfði reserve. Outside of summer, owner Einar turns his attention to springtime conquering of the Hvannadalshnúkur (p192) peak, and to winter ice cave tours (from 12,500kr). His latest mission: ice-cave sleepovers (125,000kr). Read all the details online, including warnings that sleeping in subzero temperatures is only for the mentally strong and well prepared.

Sleeping & Eating

Bring snacks if you need to. The booking agency at Fagurhólsmýri has a cafe counter selling coffee, sandwiches and cakes. The Fosshotel has a high-end restaurant.

Fosshotel Glacier Lagoon HOTEL €€€
(☎514 8300; www.fosshotel.is; Hnappavellir; r from 39,000kr; 📶) The name is misleading: this large new four-star hotel sits halfway between Skaftafell and Jökulsárlón at Hnappavellir, about 3km east of the departure point for Ingólfshöfði tours. There are *no* lagoon views – Jökulsárlón is a 20-minute drive away. Opened in 2016, the hotel houses 104 simple but stylish rooms (with more under construction), plus a good restaurant and inviting bar area.

Fjallsárlón & Breiðamerkursandur

The easternmost part of the large sandar region, Breiðamerkursandur is backed by a sweeping panorama of glacier-capped mountains, some of which are fronted by deep lagoons like marvelous Fjallsárlón.

Breiðamerkursandur is one of the main breeding grounds for Iceland's great skuas. Thanks to rising numbers of these ground-nesting birds, there's also a growing population of Arctic foxes.

Historically Breiðamerkursandur also figures in *Njál's Saga,* which ends with Kári Sölmundarson arriving in this idyllic spot to 'live happily ever after' – which has to be some kind of miracle in a saga.

Sights & Activities

Fjallsárlón LAGOON
A sign off the Ring Road indicates Fjallsárlón – this is an easily accessible glacier lagoon, where icebergs calve from Fjallsjökull. There are Zodiac tours among the bergs, plus walking trails around the lagoon, and it's a good alternative to busy Jökulsárlón, 10km further east.

If you have the time, we recommend you stop at both lagoons, as they have different qualities: Jökulsárlón is much larger and more dramatic, while from Fjallsárlón's shores you can see the glacier snout. Both lagoons offer boat rides, and Fjallsárlón wins brownie points for building a handsome new visitor centre with a spacious **cafe** (☎666 8006; www.fjallsarlon.is; mains 1700-2500kr; ⊙9.30am-6pm Jun-Sep, 10am-5pm Oct-May).

Fjallsárlón Glacial Lagoon Boat Tours BOAT TOUR
(☎666 8006; www.fjallsarlon.is; adult/child 6900/3500kr; ⊙May-Oct) Meet at the Fjallsárlón visitor centre for 45-minute Zodiac boat trips among lagoon icebergs. You

can book online; tours leave hourly 9.30am to 4.30pm in summer, and less frequently in the shoulder seasons.

Kvíárjökull GLACIER

Kvíárjökull glacier snakes down to the Kvíá river and is easily accessible from the Ring Road; look for the sign for Kvíármýrarkambur just west of the bridge over the river. Leave your car in the small car park and follow the path into the scenic valley.

Breiðármörk Walking Trail WALKING

The Breiðármörk walking trail leads 5km east from Fjallsárlón to Breiðárlón, another lagoon outlet – this one from Breiðamerkurjökull (also the source of Jökulsárlón). From Breiðárlón the trail winds further east to Jökulsárlón – all up, about 15km.

Jökulsárlón

A host of spectacular, luminous-blue icebergs drift through Jökulsárlón (pronounced yokul-sar-lon) glacier lagoon, right beside the Ring Road between Höfn and Skaftafell. It's worth spending a couple of hours here, admiring the wondrous ice sculptures (some of them striped with ash layers from volcanic eruptions), scouting for seals, or taking a boat trip.

The icebergs calve from Breiðamerkurjökull, an offshoot of Vatnajökull, crashing down into the water and drifting towards the Atlantic Ocean. They can spend up to five years floating in the 25-sq-km-plus, 250m-deep lagoon, melting, refreezing and occasionally toppling over with a mighty splash, startling the birds. They then move on via **Jökulsá**, Iceland's shortest river, out to sea.

Although it looks as though it's been here since the last ice age, the lagoon is only about 80 years old. Until the mid-1930s Breiðamerkurjökull reached the Ring Road; it's now retreating rapidly (up to a staggering 500m per year), and the lagoon is consequently growing.

Diamond Beach BEACH

At the Jökulsá river mouth you'll see ice boulders and bergs resting photogenically on the black-sand beach as part of their final journey out to sea. Tourists have dubbed the site 'Diamond Beach', and the name has stuck.

There are car parks on the ocean side of the Ring Road, on both sides of the bridge over the river.

Activities & Tours

The lagoon boat trips are excellent, but you can get almost as close to those cool-blue masterpieces by walking along the shore, and you can taste ancient ice by hauling it out of the shallows. On the Ring Road west of the car park, there are designated parking areas where you can walk over the mounds to visit the lake at less-touristed stretches of shoreline.

Breiðármörk Trail WALKING

A walking trail has been marked from the western car park at Jökulsárlón, leading to the lagoons Breiðárlón (10km one way) and Fjallsárlón (15.3km). It's classified as challenging. There is a plan to eventually build out this walking route from Skaftafell in the west to Lónsöræfi in the east. The visitor centre at Höfn sells a trail map (250kr).

Glacier Lagoon Amphibious Boat Tours BOAT TOUR

(☎478 2222; www.icelagoon.is; adult/child 5700/2000kr; ⏱9am-7pm Jun-Sep, 10am-5pm May & Oct) Take a memorable 40-minute trip in an amphibious boat, which trundles along the shore like a bus before driving into the water. On-board guides regale you with factoids about the lagoon, and you can taste 1000-year-old ice. See the website for timetables, and to prebook tickets. Trips run from the eastern car park (by the cafe) frequently – up to 40 a day in summer.

Note that the last boat tour departs about one hour before closing time. Tours may be available in April and November, depending on demand and weather conditions – contact the operators.

The same company also offers a handful of hour-long **lagoon tours in Zodiacs** (adult/child 9800/5000kr; not recommended for kids under 10). These run on a set schedule, and it's worth booking ahead online.

Ice Lagoon Zodiac Boat Tours BOAT TOUR

(☎860 9996; www.icelagoon.com; adult/child 9700/6200kr; ⏱9am-5.30pm May-Sep) This operator deals exclusively with Zodiac tours of the lagoon. It's a one-hour experience, with a maximum of 20 passengers per boat, and it travels at speed up to the glacier edge (not done by the amphibious boats) before cruising back at a leisurely pace. It pays to book these tours in advance online; minimum age six years.

IceGuide KAYAKING
(☎661 0900; www.iceguide.is; double kayak adult/child 10,900/5900kr) IceGuide has its main base at Flatey, but operates a second base from the Jökulsárlón car park. In winter there are ice cave tours from here, but from mid-May to September it's the chance to get out among the icebergs in a kayak that woos nature-lovers. Prebook online for a one-hour paddle (rated easy); the minimum age is 14.

Festivals & Events

Fireworks FIREWORKS
(www.visitvatnajokull.is; adult/child 1500kr/free; ⏲mid-Aug) If you're in the area in mid-August, don't miss the annual, one-night-only fireworks display held at Jökulsárlón as a fundraiser for the local search-and-rescue team. Buses bring spectators to the event from Höfn, Kirkjubæjarklaustur and Skaftafell.

Sleeping & Eating

The closest accommodation is at the hamlet of Hali, 13km east (no camping at Hali; the next campground east of Jökulsárlón is in Höfn).

To the west, the closest accommodation is the Fosshotel (p201) at Hnappavellir, 28km from Jökulsárlón. Camping is 52km away at Svínafell (p192) or 60km away at Skaftafell National Park (p191).

Accommodation along this stretch of the Ring Road is in hot demand so book early. (Note, however, that there is no need to book campsites.)

There is a small **cafe** (snacks 900-1200kr; ⏲9am-7pm Jun-Sep, to 6pm Mar-May & Oct, to 5pm Nov-Feb) and souvenir shop in the eastern car park, and a couple of toilets, but the dated facilities are woefully inadequate for the number of visitors. There are hopes for new facilities (including a new visitor centre), now that the area is part of the Vatnajökull National Park, but this may take time. In the meantime, you can enjoy good snacks from food trucks, like lobster bisque at excellent **Heimahumar** (lobster roll 1800kr; ⏲11.30am-6pm May-Oct).

Getting There & Away

Sterna (p430) Bus 12/12a between Reykjavík and Jökulsárlón runs daily in July and August. You can take it one way (from Reykjavík, 8¾ hours, 12,000kr) or pick it up at various towns along the south coast. It returns to Vík after two hours at the lagoon; you can stay overnight there and return to Reykjavík the following day (return from Reykjavík 24,000kr).

Strætó (p429) Bus 51 between Reykjavík and Höfn (one way 11,500kr, six hours) runs twice daily and stops here. It simply drops off or picks up passengers, it doesn't linger.

Reykjavík Excursions (p429) Bus 15 runs twice daily between the visitor centre at Skaftafell and Jökulsárlón (2800kr, 45 minutes) in July and August only.

Jökulsárlón to Höfn

The heavenly 80km stretch of Ring Road between Jökulsárlón and Höfn is lined with around 20 rural properties (many with glaciers in their backyards) offering accommodation, activities and occasionally food.

Gentle, family-friendly lures include a petting zoo (p201), an ice-cream producer (p201), a quality museum, bird-filled wetlands and outdoor hot-pots. Those looking for a little more exertion will find walks to (or on) glacier tongues and visits to wintertime ice caves, plus snowmobile safaris, glacier lagoon kayaking, and horse riding taking in natural splendour.

Sights & Activities

Þórbergssetur MUSEUM
(☎478 1078; www.thorbergur.is; Hali; adult/child 1000kr/free; ⏲9am-8pm) This cleverly crafted museum (its inspired exterior looks like a shelf of books) pays tribute to the most famous son of this sparsely populated region – writer Þórbergur Þórðarson (1888–1974). Þórbergur was a real maverick (with interests spanning yoga, Esperanto and astronomy), and his first book *Bréf til Láru* (Letter to Laura) caused huge controversy because of its radical socialist content.

Route F985 SCENIC DRIVE
From the Ring Road, about 35km east of Jökulsárlón and 45km west of Höfn, the F985 4WD track branches off to the broad glacial spur Skálafellsjökull. This 16km-long road is practically vertical in places, with iced-over sections in winter. Glacier Jeeps (p200) and Glacier Journey offer a comfortable ride to the top, where you can explore further (on snowmobile or in a super-Jeep).

Don't even think of attempting to drive Rte F985 in a 2WD car – you'll end up with a huge rescue bill. F roads are *only* for 4WD vehicles. People in small 4WD cars, or inexperienced 4WDers, should likewise not attempt this route.

GET YOUR GLACIER ON

Vatnajökull National Park (p189) authorities are working with a handful of landowners between Jökulsárlón and Höfn to open up public access to some areas of raw natural beauty (and take pressure off the popular Skaftafell region in the face of rising tourist numbers). These areas are signed off the Ring Road – for now, they are not especially well known, so you stand a good chance of finding yourself a tranquil pocket of glaciated wonder.

Uniquely, three glacier tongues (Skálafellsjökull, Heinabergsjökull and Fláajökull) converge on the Hjallanes and Heinaberg area. A fourth glacier tongue, Hoffellsjökull, lies further east, closer to Höfn. These areas boast some remarkable walking trails and scenery (including glacier lakes and moraines where the glaciers once ended).

Heinabergsjökull is 8km off the Ring Road on a gravel road (signposted not far east of Guesthouse Skálafell). Walking trails from Guesthouse Skálafell (p201) include the 8km Hjallanes loop or a 7.5km hike to Heinabergslón (the icy lagoon at the foot of Heinabergsjökull). From Heinabergslón an 8.3km trail leads to Fláajökull. There are also brilliant kayaking trips that operate on Heinabergslón, operated by IceGuide (p199).

Fláajökull is also 8km off the Ring Road on a gravel road signposted just east of Hólmur (p201) guesthouse. A suspension bridge here (which gave walkers front-row views of the glacier) was washed away in 2017 floods, but there are plans to rebuild. Glacier walks are operated on Fláajökull, led by Glacier Trips (p200).

Hoffellsjökull is accessed from the road to Hoffell (p201) guesthouse. A signed, 4km gravel road leads to the glacier, which calves into a small lake. This is a good glacier to walk to from the guesthouse; upon your return, you can soak in the hot-pots here.

The guesthouses mentioned here act as information points (maps are available), or you can stop by the information centre in Höfn to ask about road conditions, and to find out if any other areas have become newly accessible. Pick up the *Heinaberg, Hjallanes, Hoffell* map produced by the national park at the visitor centres at Höfn (p205) or Skaftafellsstofa (p191). Info is also available in the Hornafjörður section of the national park website (www.vjp.is).

Note that access roads are signed off the Ring Road, and are unsealed and often quite rough (they are not F roads). It pays to ask locally about the condition of roads before setting off in a 2WD (the answer will invariably be, 'It's OK, just go slow', but some roads may be better than others (some have maintenance done on them after the winter).

Flatey Farm FARM

The Flatey dairy farm (also known as Flatey á Mýrum) lies almost exactly halfway between Jökulsárlón and Höfn and is hard to miss as you drive along – the shed here is one of the largest structures you'll see in the region. Here you'll find a restaurant (p202) and a couple of tour companies making their summer base camp; namely IceGuide, Glacier Journey and Ice Explorers (p200).

Tours

★IceGuide ADVENTURE

(☎661 0900; www.iceguide.is) Óskar and his team have a brilliant summer offering: kayaking among icebergs on a silent glacier lagoon. The lagoon is the nearby Heinabergslón, at the foot of Heinabergsjökull, and the trip usually includes a short walk on the glacier itself (adult/child from 15,900/8900kr; minimum age 14). Kayaks are 'sit-on-top' style, so experience isn't necessary. The company also has kayaking at Jökulsárlón.

Summer trips to Heinabergslón depart from Flatey. Bookings advised for all tours.

From November to March, IceGuide leads tours to ice caves from a base at Jökulsárlón (29,900kr; minimum age 16). These trips involve a 4WD journey to the glacier edge, then a walk on rough terrain to reach the cave. Participants need a reasonable level of fitness and warm clothes; see the website for more information.

Glacier Journey ADVENTURE

(☎478 1517; www.glacierjourney.is) Glacier Journey offers snowmobile and super-Jeep tours, plus winter ice-cave exploring. In summer (June to September) it operates from a base at Flatey farm and accesses its

DON'T MISS

VATNAJÖKULL BEER

We're a sucker for a good sales pitch, and this beer has it in spades: 'frozen in time' beer brewed from 1000-year-old water (ie Jökulsárlón icebergs), flavoured with locally grown Arctic thyme. It's brewed by Ölvisholt Brugghús (p139) near Selfoss, and sold in restaurants around the Southeast. Give it a try for its fruity, malty flavour.

snow course via Rte F985; in winter the base is at Jökulsárlón. Snowmobile tours cost 24,500/12,250kr per adult/child, with two people to a skidoo; solo riders pay an additional 10,000kr. There's midnight-sun offering in June and July.

Glacier Trips ADVENTURE
(☎779 2919; www.glaciertrips.is; glacier walk 19,900kr) Doing just as its name suggests, this locally owned company leads small-group glacier walks on Fláajökull. The glacier is not visited by other operators, so this is a great chance to get off the beaten track. The meeting point is Lilja Guesthouse.

In winter the focus switches to ice caves (from 19,500kr), including an all-day trip to a more remote spot. Winter trips depart from Jökulsárlón.

Glacier Adventure ADVENTURE
(☎571 4577; www.glacieradventures.is; Hali) The closest guiding company to Jökulsárlón is locally owned Glacier Adventure, based 13km east of the lagoon, operating from Hali Country Hotel. Glacier walks are done on Breiðamerkurjökull, with one to 1½ hours on the ice (adult/child 14,900/7450kr). Half-day ice-climbing excursions (24,900kr) and winter ice-cave visits (from 19,500kr), including a challenging option to a more remote cave, are also available.

Glacier Jeeps ADVENTURE
(☎894 3133, 478 1000; www.glacierjeeps.is; ⊙Mar–mid-Oct) Home base for this long-running snowmobiling company is Vagnsstaðir HI Hostel, which is where its shoulder-season tours meet. From mid-June to mid-October, three-hour tours begin at 9.30am or 2pm from the parking area at the start of Rte F985 (in a small car park by the Ring Road).

Ice Explorers ADVENTURE
(☎866 3490; www.explorers.is) Offers summer super-Jeep tours (18,500kr) up to the ice along the super-scenic Rte F985, and winter-time ice-cave visits (19,900kr) from November to March. Summer base is Flatey; winter departures are from Jökulsárlón.

Sleeping

Many of the properties along this stretch have extended their tourist accommodation in the past couple of years, but even so, in summer demand for rooms far exceeds supply (and prices are *high*). Book well ahead and see websites for up-to-date rates.

We list these options from west to east.

Hali Country Hotel HOTEL €€€
(☎478 1073; www.hali.is; s/d/apt incl breakfast 28,500/36,500/51,900kr; 📶) The Þórbergssetur museum (p198) acts as reception and restaurant for this smart (pricey) option, the closest hotel to Jökulsárlón (and one of a cluster of places at Hali settlement). There are high-standard hotel rooms, plus a couple of excellent two-bedroom self-contained apartments.

★**Skyrhúsið Guesthouse** GUESTHOUSE €€
(☎899 8384; www.facebook.com/skyrhusid; Hali; d/tr without bathroom 19,700/23,000kr; 📶) This cute, petite guesthouse is in Hali, right by Þórbergssetur. It's a cosy place with just nine fresh rooms (limited kitchen facilities), and a tiny, colourful breakfast area.

Gerði Guesthouse GUESTHOUSE €€
(☎478 1905; www.gerdi.is; Hali; d from 28,000kr) Well located for Jökulsárlón explorations, Gerði has a good mix of accommodation: older rooms, a new wing of modern rooms, and a collection of 'bungalows' (motel-style rooms). All come with private bathroom. There's a restaurant on-site.

Vagnsstaðir HI Hostel HOSTEL, HOTEL €
(☎478 1048; www.hostel.is; hostel dm/d without bathroom from 5100/13,500kr, hotel d/f incl breakfast 24,400/38,600kr; 📶) Snowmobiles litter this Ring Road property, HQ of Glacier Jeeps. There's a small, bunk-heavy hostel with a sunny enclosed dining area, plus additional six-bed cottages (each with toilet, but no shower) next to the main building. The common complaint is that the limited bathroom facilities and small kitchen are now inadequate for the number of beds. Non-HI members pay an additional 800kr.

Hótel Smyrlabjörg HOTEL €€€
(☎478 1074; www.smyrlabjorg.is; s/d incl breakfast from 24,400/29,900kr;) A good choice if you're after mod-cons but still want sheep roaming the car park, mountain views, and peace and quiet. This large, welcoming hotel (recently doubled in size) has a restaurant renowned for its good use of local produce (mains 2650kr to 7500kr). It's 34km east of Jökulsárlón.

★ **Guesthouse Skálafell** GUESTHOUSE €€
(☎478 1041; www.skalafell.net; d with/without bathroom incl breakfast 28,500/24,150kr, cottage 38,500kr;) At the foot of Skálafellsjökull, this friendly working farm has a handful of agreeable rooms in the family farmhouse, and also in motel-style units and family-sized cottages. There are no cooking facilities, but dinner is available. In cooperation with the national park, the knowledgeable owners offer information and have set up marked **walking trails** (open to all) in the surrounding glaciated landscapes.

Hólmur GUESTHOUSE €
(☎478 2063; www.holmurinn.is; s/d without bathroom from 10,800/14,000kr;) A perfect pit stop for families about 32km from Höfn, Hólmur offers very well-priced farmhouse accommodation (ask about sleeping-bag rates for extra savings) and a sweet, smile-inducing **farm zoo** (adult/child 900/700kr; open 10am to 5pm June to September) with an abundance of feathered and furry friends. Also here is the standout restaurant, Jón Ríki (p202).

Lambhús COTTAGE €€
(☎662 1029; www.lambhus.is; cottages excl linen 17,000-21,000kr; ⏱Jun–mid-Sep;) Ducks and horses, plus 11 cute, compact self-catering cottages (sleeping four to five and ideal for families with small kids), are scattered about this vista-blessed property, owned by an affable, multilingual family with years of guiding experience. Linen can be hired (1000kr per person). Lambhús is 31km from Höfn.

Brunnhóll HOTEL €€
(☎478 1029; www.brunnholl.is; d incl breakfast from 26,500kr; ⏱Feb-Nov;) The hotel at this friendly dairy farm has simple, decent-sized rooms with big views. There's a simple dinnertime menu served, and the good folk at Brunnhóll are also the makers of delicious Jöklaís (this name means 'Glacier Ice cream'), so stop in any time to buy a scoop/tub. It's about 30km from Höfn.

Lilja Guesthouse GUESTHOUSE €€
(☎892 4088; www.lilja.is; Hólabrekka; d incl breakfast from 27,600kr;) A newcomer to the area, Lilja has a striking, modern building housing smart 'delux' rooms – some with fab glacier views – plus an older building that houses smaller, cheaper rooms (but still with private bathroom). Service is sweet, and there's a quality on-site dining option with a well-priced menu ranging from lobster sandwiches to house-smoked lamb (meals 1290kr to 2990kr).

Hoffell HOTEL €€
(Glacier World; ☎478 1514; www.glacierworld.is; d with/without bathroom incl breakfast 31,100/21,000kr;) The original guesthouse at Hoffell has bright, fresh rooms with a shared bathroom. In mid-2014 a new building opened, housing hotel-style en suite rooms (in a converted cowshed). Prices include access to the outdoor **hot-pots** (per person 1000kr; ⏱10am-8pm) on the property. There's also an on-site restaurant for guests in summer.

Fosshótel Vatnajökull HOTEL €€€
(☎478 2555; www.fosshotel.is; r from 32,000kr;) This upmarket chain hotel, 14km northwest of Höfn, recently grew from 26 to 66 rooms. The modern timber-and-concrete extension was smartly done, with blue-and-grey hues that represent the impressive natural surrounds. Older rooms received a welcome makeover too, but the newer deluxe rooms are a nicer pick. There's a restaurant (dinner mains 3200kr to 6500kr) on-site.

Seljavellir Guesthouse GUESTHOUSE €€
(☎478 1866; www.seljavellir.com; r incl breakfast from 29,700kr;) A newly built complex of 20 smart, minimalist rooms – all with splendid views – and sweet management. Seljavellir is a first-class choice, found opposite Árnanes Country Lodge about 6km from Höfn.

★ **Árnanes Country Lodge** HOTEL €€
(☎478 1550; www.arnanes.is; d with/without bathroom incl breakfast 32,900/26,900kr; ⏱Apr–mid-Oct;) This polished, rural 18-room locale is 6km from Höfn and has motel units and guesthouse rooms. There's an agreeable summertime restaurant (mains 2600kr to 7500kr) showcasing produce from neighbouring farms, and **horse-riding tours** can be arranged for all skill levels (open to nonguests).

Eating

Many of the places along this stretch have in-house restaurants – open to guests, but often also to nonguests. Self-caterers should stock up on groceries in Kirkjubæjarklaustur or Höfn, as there are no shops.

Jöklasel CAFE €
(11am-1pm Jul & Aug) Jöklasel, the base hut for Glacier Jeeps, is situated at the top of Rte F985, 840m above sea level. The cafe at Jöklasel must have the most epic views in Iceland – it's like being on top of the world. There's coffee and snacks on offer.

★ **Jón Ríki** ICELANDIC €€
(478 2063; www.jonriki.is; mains 2600-5900kr; 5-9.30pm) This fabulous farmhouse restaurant at Hólmur (p201) is something of a surprise, with funky decor, a small in-house brewery, and beautifully presented, high-quality dishes: grilled langoustine, avocado chips and panna cotta for dessert. Sourdough pizza also gets a mention – it goes well with super-interesting house brews like the mango IPA or the jalapeno-and-pumpkin ale. It can get busy, so a reservation is advised.

From September to May, the dinner menu is smaller than in summer, and you're advised to make a booking so the owners know you're coming.

Flatey Farm & Restaurant ICELANDIC €€
(620 1070; www.facebook.com/flateyfarm; mains 1650-3500kr; 9am-6pm) At a large dairy farm (p199), this new cafeteria-style restaurant is a decent daytime refuelling stop halfway between Jökulsárlón and Höfn – and it's where a few tour operators have their summer set-up. There's a small menu of soups, hot dishes and sandwiches, plus cakes and apple pie.

Þórbergssetur Restaurant ICELANDIC €€
(478 1078; www.hali.is/restaurant; Hali; mains lunch 1550-3100kr, dinner 3200-5500kr; 11am-9pm) The museum at Hali, Þórbergssetur (p198), is home to a quality cafe-restaurant where the speciality is Arctic char. It's 13km east of Jökulsárlón, and gets very busy.

Höfn

POP 1700

Although it's no bigger than many European villages, the Southeast's main town feels like a sprawling metropolis after driving through the emptiness on either side. Its setting is stunning; on a clear day, wander down to the waterside, find a quiet bench and just gaze at Vatnajökull and its guild of glaciers.

Höfn simply means 'harbour', and is pronounced like an unexpected hiccup (just say 'hup' while inhaling). It's an apt name – this modern town still relies heavily on fishing and fish processing, and is famous for its *humar* (often translated as lobster, but technically it's langoustine).

Most Ring Road travellers stop to use the town's services, so prebook your accommodation, especially in summer. On bus timetables and the like, you may see the town referred to as Höfn í Hornafirði (meaning Höfn in Hornafjörður) to differentiate it from all the other *höfn* (harbours) around the country.

Sights & Activities

Activities that explore Vatnajökull's icy vastness – such as glacier walks, super-Jeep tours, lagoon kayaking and snowmobile safaris – are accessed along the Ring Road west of Höfn.

On the western side of town, a **waterside path** lets you amble and gape at the views.

Gamlabúð NOTABLE BUILDING, MUSEUM
(470 8330; www.vjp.is; Heppuvegur 1; 9am-7pm Jun-Aug, to 6pm May & Sep, to 5pm Oct-Apr) FREE The 1864 warehouse that once served as the regional folk museum has been moved from the outskirts of town to a prime position on the Höfn harbourfront. It's been refurbished to serve as the town's visitor centre, with good exhibits explaining the marvels of the region's flagship national park (including flora and fauna), and also screens documentaries.

Ósland WALKING
This promontory about 1km beyond the harbour – head for the **seamen's monument** (Óslandsvegur) on the rise – boasts a walking path round its marshes and lagoons. The path is great for watching seabirds, but watch out for dive-bombing Arctic terns.

Sundlaug Hafnar SWIMMING
(470 8477; Víkurbraut 9; adult/child 900/200kr; 6.45am-9pm Mon-Fri, 10am-7pm Sat & Sun) The town's popular outdoor swimming pool has water slides, hot-pots and a steam bath.

Festivals & Events

Humarhátíð FOOD & DRINK
Every year in late June or early July, Höfn's langoustine festival honours this tasty crustacean, hauled to shore in abundance by the local fishing fleet. There's usually a fun fair, dancing, music, lots of alcohol and even a few langoustines.

Sleeping

Along with hotels and guesthouses in Höfn itself, there are numerous good options (most with in-house dining) along the Ring Road west of town. Summer rates in this in-demand region are *high;* check online for up-to-date prices, and for sometimes sizeable winter discounts.

There are also a number of apartments rented out around town, accessible via the usual websites.

Höfn Camping & Cottages CAMPGROUND €
(☎478 1606; www.campsite.is; Hafnarbraut 52; campsite per person 1800kr, d cottage excl linen 12,000kr) Lots of travellers stay at the campground on the main road into town. There are 11 decent-value cottages, sleeping up to six; some have private toilet, but all use the amenities block for showers. There's also a playground and laundry, and some camping gear is sold at the reception. The downsides: very few showers for the capacity, and no wi-fi.

HI Hostel HOSTEL €
(☎478 1736; www.hostel.is; Hvannabraut 3; dm/d without bathroom from 8600/19,950kr; wi-fi) Follow the signs from the N1 to find Höfn's sole budget option, hidden away in a residential area. It's a sprawling, dated space (a former aged-care home) that's usually bustling with travellers in summer. It has the requisite facilities (kitchen, laundry) but no lounge areas. Non-members pay an additional fee (800kr); linen is included in prices.

★ **Old Airline Guesthouse** GUESTHOUSE €€
(☎478 1300; www.oldairline.com; Hafnarbraut 24; s/d without bathroom incl breakfast 16,500/21,700kr; wi-fi) This central guesthouse sparkles under the care of friendly host Sigga. On offer are five fresh rooms with shared bathrooms, plus a large lounge and guest kitchen (with self-service breakfast). Big brownie points to free laundry access. It's attached to a small electronics/IT store.

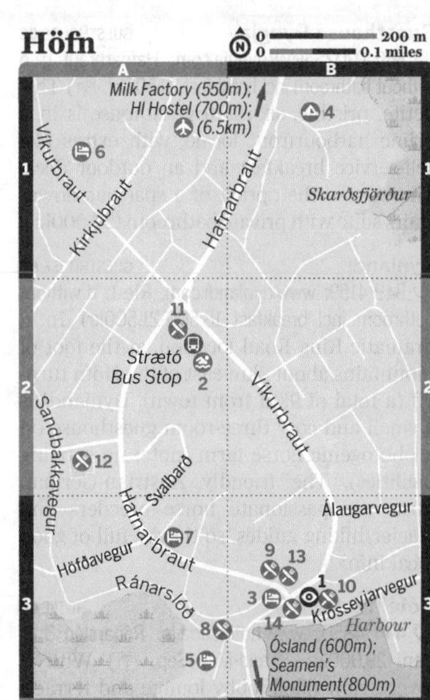

Höfn

Sights
1 Gamlabúð B3

Activities, Courses & Tours
2 Sundlaug Hafnar A2

Sleeping
3 Guesthouse Dyngja B3
4 Höfn Camping & Cottages B1
5 Hótel Edda A3
6 Hótel Höfn A1
7 Old Airline Guesthouse A3

Eating
8 Hafnarbúðin A3
9 Humarhöfnin B3
10 Íshúsið Pizzeria B3
11 Kaffi Hornið A2
12 Nettó A2
Ósinn .... (see 6)
13 Otto Matur & Drykkur B3
14 Pakkhús B3

Shopping
Vínbúðin .... (see 12)

Information
Gamlabúð Visitor Centre .... (see 1)

Guesthouse Dyngja GUESTHOUSE €€
(☎866 0702; www.dyngja.com; Hafnarbraut 1; d without bathroom incl breakfast 19,500kr; 📶) This petite, pristine, six-room guesthouse is in a prime harbourfront locale, with extras like self-service breakfast and an outdoor deck. There's also the option of a spacious downstairs suite with private bathroom (24,000kr).

Dynjandi GUESTHOUSE €€
(☎849 4159; www.dynjandi.com; Rte 1; d without bathroom incl breakfast 18,500-21,500kr) In a dramatic Ring Road location, at the foot of mountains about 3km east of the Höfn turn-off (a total of 9km from town), Dynjandi is a small and cosy three-room guesthouse on a photogenic horse farm (note: no cooking facilities). The friendly Austrian-German hosts are passionate horse breeders and glacier/hiking guides, so they're full of good local info.

Hótel Edda HOTEL €€
(☎444 4850; www.hoteledda.is; Ránarslóð 3; r from 29,000kr; ⏲mid-May–Sep; 📶) With a lovely, view-filled lobby lounge and terrace, the well-located harbourside Edda makes a decent choice. All the neat, no-frills rooms have a bathroo and some have great glacier views. Breakfast is 2400kr.

★**Milk Factory** GUESTHOUSE €€€
(☎478 8900; www.milkfactory.is; Dalbraut 2; d/q incl breakfast 30,000/39,500kr; 📶👪) Full credit to the family – and the designers – behind the restoration of this old dairy factory north of town. There are 17 modern, hotel-standard rooms here, including two with disabled access. The prize allotments are the six spacious mezzanine suites that sleep four – good for families or friends, although they don't have kitchens.

Hótel Höfn HOTEL €€€
(☎478 1240; www.hotelhofn.is; Víkurbraut; s/d incl breakfast from 25,200/35,200kr; 📶) Höfn's business-class hotel is often busy with tour groups in summer. Nicely renovated rooms feature on-trend furnishings, and views are knockout – you'll want one with a glacier outlook (but bear in mind that so does everyone else!). There's also a fresh-faced on-site restaurant, **Ósinn** (mains 2150-6990kr; ⏲4-10pm). Pros: good breakfast. Cons: three storeys and no lift.

✕ Eating & Drinking

Humar (langoustine) is the speciality on Höfn menus – the tails or the whole crustacean grilled with garlic butter is the norm. Prices for main dishes range from 6000kr upwards. You'll find cheaper crustacean-centric options too: bisque, sandwiches or langoustine-studded pizza or pasta.

In peak summer, restaurant bookings are a good idea. In winter, it pays to confirm opening hours.

Look out for the local summertime food truck, Höfn Street Food, down by the harbour, for good-value offerings including burgers, langoustine panini, and fish and chips.

Hafnarbúðin FAST FOOD €
(☎478 1095; Ránarslóð 2; snacks & meals 400-2600kr; ⏲9am-10pm) A fabulous relic, this tiny old-school diner has a cheap-and-cheerful vibe, big breakfasts, a menu of fast-food favourites (hot dogs, burgers, toasted sandwiches) and a fine langoustine baguette – for the (relative) bargain price 2500kr. There's even a drive-up window!

Nettó SUPERMARKET €
(Miðbær; ⏲9am-8pm Mon-Fri, to 7pm Sat & Sun) Supermarket (with bakery) in the central Miðbær shopping centre. Stock up – in either direction, it's miles to the next grocery selection. The bakery sells ready-made meals such as sandwiches and salads. There's an ATM out the front of the shopping centre.

Otto Matur & Drykkur ICELANDIC €€
(☎478 1818; Hafnarbraut 2; mains 2890-5990kr; ⏲noon-10pm) A new incarnation for the oldest house in Höfn (dating from 1897) has turned it into an elegant space high on Nordic style. The small menu spotlights fresh local produce – langoustine is here, of course, as well as simple, elegant dishes of salmon, lamb and more. There's also a cool little bar in the cellar (open until 1am).

Íshúsið Pizzeria PIZZA €€
(☎478 1230; http://ishusidpizzeria.is; Heppuvegur 2a; pizzas 1950-3500kr; ⏲noon-10pm) In an elevated position by the harbour, the family-friendly Ice House doles out thin-crust, stone-baked pizzas with crowd-pleasing toppings, from Hawaiian to the 'lobster festival'.

Kaffi Hornið ICELANDIC €€
(☎478 2600; www.kaffihornid.is; Hafnarbraut 42; mains 2250-6350kr; ⏲11.30am-10pm) This log-cabin affair is an unpretentious bar and restaurant. The atmosphere here is less polished than at fellow Höfn restaurants Humarhöfnin and Pakkhús, and the cheaper

DON'T MISS

STOKKSNES

About 7km east of the turn-off to Höfn, just before the Ring Road enters a tunnel through the Almannaskarð pass, a signposted road heads south to Stokksnes. After 4.5km, in a wild setting under moodily Gothic Vestrahorn mountain, you'll find a cool little outpost: the **Viking Cafe** (☎478 2577; www.vikingcafe.is; snacks & meals 700-1500kr), where coffee, waffles and cake are served. The farm-owner runs the cafe and offers rooms to let, and charges 800kr to explore his incredible property, including a photogenic **Viking village film set** (built by Icelandic movie director Baltasar Kormákur in 2009 but yet to be used for its intended purpose) and miles of **black-sand beaches**, where seals laze and the backdrop of Vestrahorn creates superb photo opportunities. Camping (2000kr per person) includes farm entry.

langoustine dishes are more varied (salad, pizza, pasta). The non-langoustine menu stretches from steak sandwiches to pulled-pork pizza, and there's even a selection of dedicated vegan dishes.

★**Pakkhús** ICELANDIC €€€
(☎478 2280; www.pakkhus.is; Krosseyjarvegur 3; mains 3100-6790kr; ⊙noon-10pm) Hats off to a menu that tells you the name of the boat that delivers its star produce. In a stylish harbourside warehouse, Pakkhús offers a level of kitchen creativity you don't often find in rural Iceland. First-class local langoustine, lamb and duck tempt taste buds, while clever desserts end the meal in style; who can resist a dish called '*skyr* volcano'?

Unlike its competitors, Pakkhús doesn't have a selection of budget-friendly langoustine dishes. Also, no reservations are taken. You may have to wait for a table, but there is a bar area downstairs.

★**Humarhöfnin** ICELANDIC €€€
(☎478 1200; www.humarhofnin.is; Hafnarbraut 4; mains 2900-7900kr; ⊙noon-10pm May-Sep, to 9pm Oct-Nov) Humarhöfnin offers 'Gastronomy Langoustine' in a cute, cheerfully Frenchified space with great attention to detail: chequerboard tiled floor and herb pots on the windowsills. Mains that centre on pincer-waving critters cost around 7000kr, but there are also more budget-friendly dishes including a fine langoustine baguette (3900kr) or pizza (2900kr).

Vínbúðin ALCOHOL
(Miðbær; ⊙11am-6pm Mon-Thu, to 7pm Fri, to 4pm Sat) Government-run liquor store.

ℹ Information

Gamlabúð Visitor Centre (☎470 8330; www.visitvatnajokull.is; Heppuvegur 1; ⊙9am-7pm Jun-Aug, to 6pm May & Sep, to 5pm Oct-Apr) Harbourfront Gamlabúð houses a national-park visitor centre with excellent exhibits, plus local tourist information. Ask about activities and hiking trails in the area.

ℹ Getting There & Away

AIR

Höfn's **airport** (www.isavia.is; Hwy 1) is 6.5km northwest of town. Eagle Air (www.eagleair.is) flies year-round between Höfn and Reykjavík Domestic Airport (ie not Keflavík International Airport). One-way fare from 20,000kr.

BUS

In summer 2018, Höfn's bus connections were dramatically reduced compared with previous summers, and there was no easy bus connection between Höfn and Egilsstaðir. This situation may change; it's best to refer to www.publictransport.is.

Travelling to/from East Iceland is tricky but not impossible. SVAust (www.svaust.is) bus route 4 connects Höfn with Breiðdalsvík; bus 2 runs from Breiðdalsvík to Reyðarfjörður; and bus 1 connects Reyðarfjörður to Egilsstaðir. But it's not seamless. Timetables are also found on www.straeto.is. We suggest you check carpooling websites (eg www.samferda.is) or ask around at your accommodation to try to get a lift if your goal is Egilsstaðir.

Strætó (☎540 2700; www.straeto.is) services pick-up and drop-off from a **bus stop** (Vikurbraut 9) out the front of the swimming pool. Its bus 51 to/from Reykjavík (13,340kr, seven hours, two daily) stops at Jökulsárlón, Skaftafell, Kirkjubæjarklaustur, Vík, Skógar, Hvolsvöllur, Hella and Selfoss.

Höfn to Djúpivogur

The 105km stretch around Iceland's southeast corner, between Höfn and Djúpivogur, is another impossibly scenic stretch, the road curving past only a handful of farms backed by precipitous peaks. There are black-sand beaches and bird-filled wetlands to add plenty of 'oooh' moments.

Stafafell

In the middle of nowhere, Stafafell is a lonely farm, lost under the mountains. It's a good hiking base for exploring Lónsöræfi.

There are a number of day hikes in the hills and valleys north of Stafafell. Perhaps the best day hike is a well-marked, 14.3km, four- to five-hour return walk from Stafafell to **Hvannagil**, a colourful rhyolite canyon on the eastern bank of the river Jökulsá í Lóni; pick up a route description from the farmhouse or see online at www.stafafell.is.

A trio of brothers owns the farm; one operates a **hostel** (☎478 1717; www.stafafell.is; d without bathroom 11,300kr, cottages incl linen 18,000-22,000kr) and has a couple of simple cottages for rent, while another runs a basic **campsite** (☎699 6684; site per person 1500kr).

Hrafnavellir Guest House GUESTHOUSE €€
(☎892 1527; hrafnavellir@hrafnavellir.is; d incl breakfast 27,600kr; 📶) Brand new for summer 2018, this row of seven small cabins sits about 25km east of Höfn on a super-peaceful patch of turf. Views look across the river delta, with peaks looming behind. Each cabin offers a modern, hotel-style room with private bathroom and terrace. The website www.stafafell.is is rich in local information.

Lónsöræfi

If you're in Iceland to get in touch with your inner hermit, the remote, rugged nature reserve Lónsöræfi could be on your hit list. This protected wilderness, inland from Stafafell, contains some colourful rhyolite mountains and, at 320 sq km, is one of Iceland's largest conservation areas.

Hiking in this region is challenging and only for experienced hikers (some trails require substantial river crossings). Longer treks range towards the eastern part of Vatnajökull, and northwest to Snæfell. Although Lónsöræfi isn't part of Vatnajökull National Park, the park's website (www.vjp.is) has details of hiking trails, and the visitor centres at Skaftafell, Höfn and Skríðuklaustur (in the east, covering the Snæfell region of the national park) can advise on options and sell topo maps, which you will certainly require.

You need your own transport to reach this area. Note that the only road into the reserve is the F980, a rough track off the Ring Road that ends after 25km at Illikambur. It's only suitable for super-Jeeps and experienced drivers – there is a deep, fast-flowing river to cross (small 4WDs will simply not cut it).

The rest of the reserve is only accessible on foot.

South East ehf DRIVING
(☎846 6313; www.southeasticeland.is) Siggi offers well-reviewed customised super-Jeep tours in the southeast, including a five-hour tour from Höfn into the Lónsöræfi area (25,000kr per person) from mid-June to September. Prebooking is required.

Icelandic Mountain Guides HIKING
(IMG; ☎587 9999; www.mountainguides.is) In July and August, IMG offers a four-day, 50km backpacking tour through Lónsöræfi (from 139,900kr), staying in mountain huts (travelling north to south, beginning near Snæfell). It's in its program under the name 'In the Shadow of Vatnajökull'.

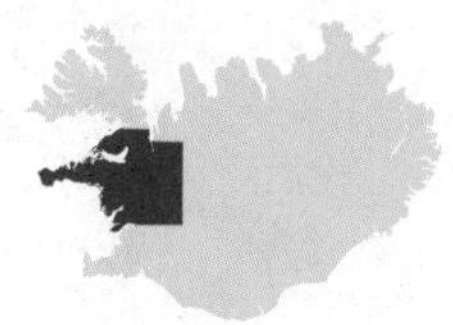

West Iceland

Includes ➡

Best Places to Eat

- Bjargarsteinn Mathús (p226)
- Hótel Húsafell (p218)
- Settlement Centre Restaurant (p214)
- Narfeyrarstofa (p223)

Best Places to Stay

- Guesthouse Nýp (p229)
- Hótel Egilsen (p223)
- Hótel Flatey (p221)
- Hótel Húsafell (p218)
- Bjarg (p214)

Why Go?

Geographically close to Reykjavík, yet far, far away in sentiment, West Iceland (known as Vesturland) is a splendid microcosm of what Iceland has to offer. Yet many tourists have missed the memo, and you're likely to have remote parts of this wonderful region to yourself.

The long arm of Snæfellsnes Peninsula is a favourite for its glacier, Snæfellsjökull, and the area around its national park is tops for birding, whale watching, lava-field hikes and horse riding. Inland beyond Reykholt you'll encounter lava tubes and remote highland glaciers, including enormous Langjökull with its unusual ice cave. Icelanders honour West Iceland for its local sagas: two of the best known, *Laxdæla Saga* and *Egil's Saga,* took place along the region's brooding waters, marked today by haunting cairns and an exceptional museum in lively Borgarnes. West Iceland offers everything from windswept beaches to historic villages and awe-inspiring terrain in one neat little package.

Road Distances (km)

	Borgarnes	Húsafell	Stykkishólmur	Hellnar	Buðardalur
Húsafell	65				
Stykkishólmur	99	158			
Hellnar	122	179	90		
Buðardalur	79	103	86	145	
Reykjavík	74	129	173	194	152

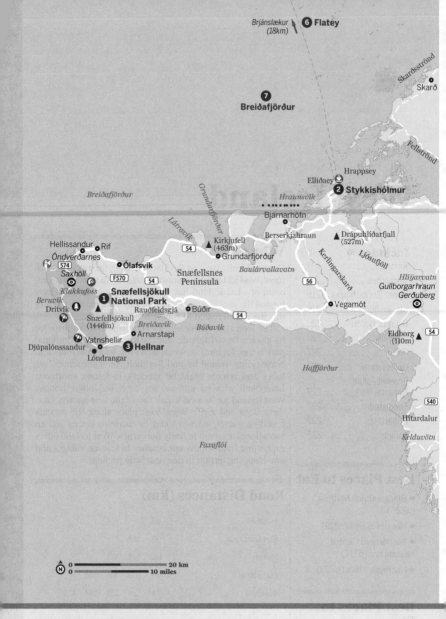

West Iceland Highlights

1 Snæfellsjökull National Park (p227) Tramping through crunchy lava fields, along windswept coastlines, and over Snæfellsjökull, the icy heart of this magical park.

2 Stykkishólmur (p219) Wandering past charming chocolate-box houses in this buzzy harbour town.

3 Hellnar (p234) Following seabirds past trailside crags on the slender trail east from Hellnar to Arnarstapi.

4 Langjökull (p218) Exploring deep inside this glacier's ice cave and dining at base camp in Húsafell.

5 Borgarnes (p211) Stepping back into Saga times at the impressive Settlement Centre in this fun-loving town.

6 Flatey (p221) Casting away all of your cares and spending a night (or six) on this tiny island.

7 Breiðafjörður (p219) Sailing past swooping puffins and searching for whales on a boat ride on this beautiful fjord.

8 Viðgelmir (p218) Discovering the fascinating subterranean remains of a violent volcanic eruption in this huge lava tube.

HVALFJÖRÐUR

Hvalfjörður (pronounced *kval*-fyur-thur) and the surrounding area feels suddenly pastoral despite being a mere 30-minute drive from the capital. Although lacking the majesty of the Snæfellsnes Peninsula further on, the sparkling fjord offers excellent day-trip fodder. Those in a hurry to get to Borgarnes and beyond should instead head straight through the 5.7km-long tunnel beneath the fjord. Cyclists aren't permitted in the tunnel.

Sights

★Glymur WATERFALL

At the head of Hvalfjörður, and up Botnsdalur valley, lies Glymur, Iceland's highest waterfall (198m). From the trailhead, it'll take a couple of hours to reach the cascade's viewpoints on rough, slippery trails. A log is placed to bridge the river only in summer. At the trailhead there's a good map with instructions. Reach the trailhead by following the turn-off on Rte 47 to Botnsdalur.

Bring water shoes for fording the river, if you plan to cross and return on the west side, or retrace your steps on the east side. Try to visit after heavy rains or snow-melt for full effect. Note: there is no camping allowed around the trailhead.

Mt Esja HIKING

On the southern side of Hvalfjörður you'll find dramatic Mt Esja (914m), a great spot for wilderness hiking. The most popular trail to the summit begins at Esjustofa Hiking Center (with a cafe), just north of Mosfellsbær. There are several routes up the mountain, but most people hike 2.8km to the viewpoint at Steinn. The trail gets much more technical after that.

To reach the trailhead by bus, take bus 15 from Reykjavík towards Mosfellsbær, get off in Háholt and change to bus 57 to the Esjustofa Hiking Centre.

War & Peace Museum MUSEUM

(Hernámssetrið; ☎433 8877; www.warandpeace.is; Hlaðir, Hvalfjarðarströnd; adult/child 1250kr/free; ⊙1-5pm Wed-Fri, from 10am Sat & Sun late May-Aug) During WWII Hvalfjörður contained a submarine and warship station and over 20,000 American and British soldiers passed through. This museum houses artefacts from that time and a small cafe, and has a **campground** (1500kr per person) with a swimming pool.

Saurbæjarkirkja CHURCH

(Hallgrímskirkja í Saurbæ; Rte 47) The church at the Saurbær farmstead is worth a look for its beautiful stained-glass work by Gerður Helgadóttir. It is named for Reverend Hallgrímur Pétursson, who served here from 1651 to 1669, and composed Iceland's most popular religious work, *Passion Hymns*.

Sleeping & Eating

Hvalfjörður has a hotel and a handful of country guesthouses as well as good campgrounds on area farms.

There are no grocery stores.

Hótel Glymur HOTEL €€

(☎430 3100; www.hotelglymur.is; Rte 47; d incl breakfast from 19,000kr; @☎) This hotel on the northern side of Hvalfjörður, near Saurbær, is a cache of contemporary amenities, from double-decker 'executive doubles' with giant picture windows to a hot-pot named one of the 'top five hot tubs in the world' by the *New York Times*. There's also a good restaurant (two-course menu 5900kr, mains 4300kr to 5000kr; open 6.30pm to 9pm) with spectacular views.

Hotel Laxárbakki HOTEL €€

(☎551 2783; www.laxarbakki.is; Rte 1, Hvalfjarðarsveit; d without bathroom 12,800kr, apt/cottage from 19,200/23,000kr; ☎⊕) A friendly family has taken over this cluster of cottages just 6km north of Hvalfjörður. Tidy, well-kitted-out apartments sleep from two to six, cottages sleep four, and standard rooms share bathrooms. The restaurant offers standard fare (burgers, lamb, fish; mains 2000kr to 4000kr; open daily 9am to 9pm).

Kaffi Kjós CAFE €

(☎566 8099; www.kaffikjos.is; Meðalfellsvegi (Rte 461); mains 1500-4000kr; ⊙noon-8pm May, 11am-10pm Jun & Jul; ☎⊘) Tucked into a verdant valley winding southeast off Hvalfjörður (Rte 461), this welcoming roadside cafe overlooking glittering Meðalfellsvatn offers a welcome break with a menu of local fare, burgers, sandwiches and vegetarian options. They also have **camping** (2000/1000kr per adult/child) with showers, and a **cottage** (double 18,000kr) just up the road.

Getting Around

Bring your own wheels. The buses between Reykjavík and points north bypass the fjord by taking the tunnel.

Akranes

Set under striking **Akrafjall** (572m), the town of Akranes (www.visitakranes.is) lies at the tip of the peninsula separating Hvalfjörður from Borgarfjörður. Largely an administrative and factory town, it's mainly worth a stop for its **lighthouse** and its sprawling **Folk Museum** (Byggðasafnið í Görðum Akranesi; ☎431 5566; www.museum.is; Garðaholti 3; adult/child 800kr/free; ⏲10am-5pm mid-May–mid-Sep, by appointment mid-Sep–mid-May), with a restored boathouse, drying shed, church and fishing boats.

BORGARBYGGÐ

Buzzy Borgarnes and its broad Borgarfjörður were the landing zone for several famous Icelandic settlers. Inland, up the river-twined valley, you'll find fecund farms with deep history leading to powerful stone-strewn lava tubes and highlands, the gateway to the ice caps beyond.

Borgarnes

POP 1962

Unassuming Borgarnes has got it going on. For such a tiny place, it bubbles with local life. One of the original settlement areas for the first Icelanders, it's loaded with history, and sits on a scenic promontory along the broad waters of Borgarfjörður. Zip past the busy petrol stations and go into the old quarter to encounter the fun small-town vibe and one of Iceland's best museums.

Sights

★Settlement Centre MUSEUM

(Landnámssetur Íslands; ☎437 1600; www.settlementcentre.is; Brákarbraut 13-15; adult/child 2500kr/free; ⏲10am-9pm; 📶) Housed in an imaginatively restored warehouse by the harbour, the must-see Settlement Centre offers fascinating insights into the history of Icelandic settlement and the Saga era. The museum is divided into two exhibitions; each takes about 30 minutes to visit. The Settlement Exhibition covers the discovery and settlement of Iceland. Egil's Saga Exhibition recounts the amazing adventures of Egil Skallagrímsson (the man behind *Egil's Saga*) and his family. A detailed multilingual audio guide is included.

This is not your run-of-the-mill Icelandic folk museum: the Settlement Centre offers deep background into Iceland's history and flora and fauna, and a firm context in which to place your Icelandic visit. Egil's Saga is one of the most nuanced and action-packed of the sagas and the centre has placed cairns throughout town marking key sites from it. It also has a top-notch restaurant.

Borgarfjördur Museum MUSEUM

(Safnahús; ☎433 7200; www.safnahus.is; Bjarnarbraut 4-6; adult/child 1000kr/free; ⏲1-5pm May-Aug, 1-4pm Mon-Fri Sep-Apr) This small municipal museum has an engaging exhibit on children in Iceland over the last 100 years. It's told through myriad photographs and found items, and though it's accompanied by English translations, don't be shy about having museum staff show you through. The story behind each photograph is captivating and stays with you long after you've left.

EGIL'S SAGA

Egil's Saga starts by recounting the tale of Kveldúlfur, grandfather of the warrior-poet Egil Skallagrímsson, who fled to Iceland during the 9th century after a falling out with the king of Norway. Kveldúlfur grew gravely ill on the journey, and instructed his son, Skallagrímur Kveldúlfsson, to throw his coffin overboard after he died and build the family farm wherever it washed ashore – this happened to be at Borg á Mýrum (p215). Egil Skallagrímsson grew up to be a fierce and creative individual who killed his first adversary at the age of seven, went on to carry out numerous raids on Ireland, England and Denmark, and saved his skin many a time by composing eloquent poetry. Learn about him at Borgarnes' excellent Settlement Centre.

For those who'd like to go deep into how the saga ties to the landscape around Borgarnes, download the detailed Locatify SmartGuide smartphone or iPad app and load the 'Egils Saga, Borg on the Moors' tour, which tells the stories of local landmarks from the tale. The Settlement Centre has marked eight of the sites with cairns, including Brákin (p213), Borg á Mýrum and Skallagrímsgarður (p213), the burial mound of Skallagrímsson's father and son.

Borgarnes

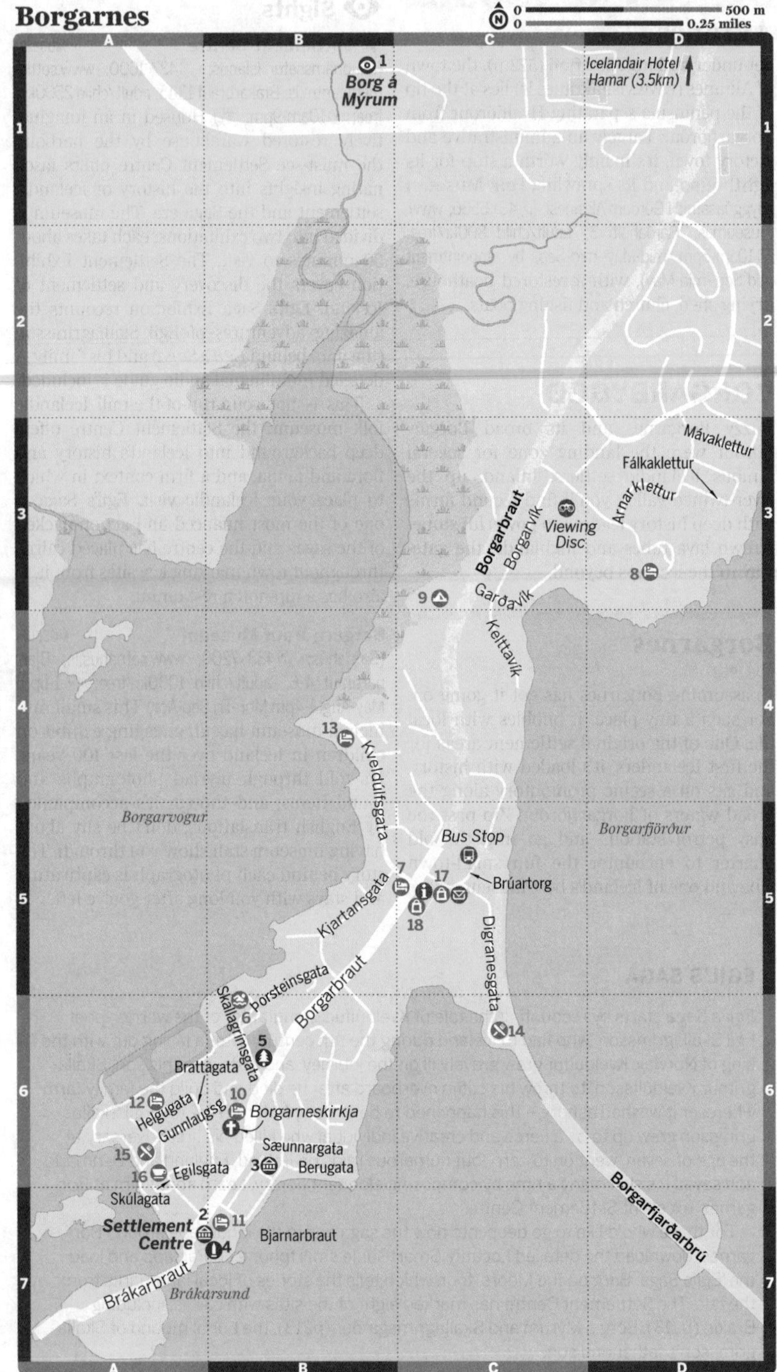

0 500 m
0 0.25 miles
Borg á Mýrum
Icelandair Hotel Hamar (3.5km)
Mávaklettur
Fálkaklettur
Arnarklettur
Viewing Disc
Borgarbraut
Borgarvík
Garðavík
Kelttavík
Kveldúlfsgata
Borgarvogur
Borgarfjörður
Bus Stop
Brúartorg
Kjartansgata
Digranesgata
Þorsteinsgata
Skallagrímsgata
Brattagata
Helgugata
Gunnlaugsg
Borgarneskirkja
Sæunnargata
Berugata
Egilsgata
Skúlagata
Settlement Centre
Bjarnarbraut
Brákarbraut
Brákarsund
Borgarfjarðarbrú

Brákin SCULPTURE

Þorgerður Brák was Egil's nursemaid, thought to be a Celtic slave. In one of the more dramatic moments in *Egil's Saga,* she heroically saves Egil's life (from an attempted crime of passion, by his own father, Skallagrímur Kveldúlfsson), and jumps into the sea to escape the enraged Skallagrímur. Today a sculpture marks a spot near where she leapt, ultimately to her death: Skallagrímur hit her with a stone, and she never emerged from the water again.

Skallagrímsgarður PARK

The Settlement Museum has marked sites featured in *Egil's Saga* with cairns, including Skallagrímsgarður, the burial mound of the father and son of saga hero Egil Skallagrímsson. Find it in this small park.

Activities & Tours

Swimming Pool GEOTHERMAL POOL

(www.borgarbyggd.is; Þorsteinsgata; adult/child 900/300kr; 6am-10pm Mon-Fri, 9am-6pm Sat & Sun) Borgarnes' beautiful pool, hot-pots and steam room are part of a large fjordside sports complex, and are a wonderful place to relax.

Hestaland HORSE RIDING

(Staðarhús; 435 1444; www.hestaland.net; Staðarhús farm; 1½hr trail ride 10,000kr; Mon-Sat Jun–mid-Sep) Ride through fields and along fjord shores with this top-notch horse farm. They give a short lesson in the arena before heading out. Find Staðarhús farm 14km northeast of Borgarnes, 2km off Rte 1.

They also have a lovely **guesthouse** (www.stadarhus.com; double 19,900kr).

A FOODIE TOUR OF THE WEST

Crisscross Food Tour (897 6140; www.crisscross.is) offers food tours across West Iceland, with farm stops, snacks and a meal (half/full day 24,900/39,500kr), while taking in local natural sites, from waterfalls to lava fields. Pick-up in Reykjavík or Borgarnes.

Oddsstaðir HORSE RIDING

(435 1413; www.oddsstadir.is; Rte 512, Oddsstaðir farm) Multiday riding tours throughout West Iceland with a large team of horses.

Festivals & Events

Brákarhátíð CULTURAL

(www.brakarhatid.is; late Jun) A festival in honour of Þorgerður Brák, a heroine from *Egil's Saga.* Expect town decorations, parades, a concert and a lively, offshore, mud-football match.

Sleeping

Borgarnes HI Hostel HOSTEL €

(695 3366; www.hostel.is; Borgarbraut 11-13; dm 5900kr, d with/without bathroom 18,200/16,300kr; @) This recently updated hostel has a sleek well-lit look in its public spaces, and clean, comfortable rooms. There's a 10% discount for HI members.

Borgarnes Campsite CAMPGROUND €

(www.facebook.com/campinborgarnes; Borgarbraut; sites per adult/child 1200kr/free) This basic fjordside campground is on the main road running up Borgarnes' peninsula.

Borgarnes

Top Sights

1 Borg á Mýrum B1
2 Settlement Centre A7

Sights

3 Borgarfjördur Museum B6
4 Brákin B7
5 Skallagrímsgarður B6

Activities, Courses & Tours

6 Swimming Pool B6

Sleeping

7 B59 Hotel & Hostel C5
8 Bjarg D3
9 Borgarnes Campsite C3
10 Borgarnes HI Hostel B6
11 Egils Guesthouse & Apartments B7
12 Helgugata Guesthouse A6
13 Kría Guesthouse B4

Eating

14 Bónus C6
15 Englendingavík A6
Settlement Centre Restaurant .... (see 2)

Drinking & Nightlife

16 Blómasetrið–Kaffi Kyrrð A6

Shopping

17 Ljómalind C5
18 Vínbúðin C5

★**Bjarg** GUESTHOUSE €€
(☎437 1925; www.facebook.com/bjargborgarnes; Bjarg farm; d with/without bathroom incl breakfast 20,700/17,300kr; 📶) One of the most beautifully situated places to stay in the area, this attractive series of linked cottages 1.5km north of Borgarnes overlooks the fjord and mountains. It has warm, cosy rooms with tasteful wood panelling and crisp white linens. There are shared guest kitchens, a good buffet breakfast, a BBQ, spotless bathrooms, and a turf-roofed cottage that sleeps four.

Helgugata Guesthouse GUESTHOUSE €€
(☎431 4442; www.booking.com/hotel/is/helgugata.html; Helgugata 5; s/d incl breakfast from 12,000/19,000kr) Friendly Ludmila keeps this tidy guesthouse, perched on the cliff overlooking the football pitch and the twinkling fjord beyond. All rooms have shared bathrooms, except for one on the top floor with a private toilet. Public spaces are welcoming, and breakfast is downright sumptuous.

Egils Guesthouse & Apartments GUESTHOUSE €€
(☎860 6655; www.egilsguesthouse.is; Brákarbraut 11; d with/without bathroom incl breakfast 22,000/18,000kr, studios from 19,125kr; P📶👪) Choose from pristine tasteful guest rooms with fjord views in the Kaupangur Guesthouse to full studios and apartments nearby in the centre of town. The guesthouse also has a small cafe.

Kría Guesthouse GUESTHOUSE €€
(☎845 4126; www.kriaguesthouse.is; Kveldúlfsgata 27; s/d without bathroom incl breakfast 13,600/18,600kr; 📶) Kría offers two rooms with great water views in a private home on a quiet residential street. There's a pleasant shared kitchen and a large wheelchair-accessible bathroom, plus outdoor seating with views and a hot-pot.

B59 Hotel & Hostel HOTEL €€€
(☎419 5959; www.b59hotel.is; Borgarbraut 59; dm from 3500kr, d incl breakfast from 34,000kr; 📶) Lines are clean at this brand-new outfit with private rooms with ensuite bathrooms and Sóley Organics products in the hotel side, and snappy dormitory beds in the hostel.

BORGARNES' BREWS

The little family-run **Steðji Brugghús** (☎896 5001; www.stedji.com; tasting 1500kr; ⏲1-5pm Mon-Sat), 25km north of Borgarnes off Rte 50, has a good range of local beers, from strawberry beer to lager and seasonal beers. Try them all in the microbrewery's tasting room.

Eating & Drinking

Have a coffee or drink at any of the town's restaurants. There's also a **Vínbúðin** (☎431 3858; www.vinbudin.is; Borgarbraut 58-60, Hyrnu Torg centre; ⏲11am-6pm Mon-Thu, to 7pm Fri, to 4pm Sat Jun-Aug, reduced hours Sep-May) for stocking up on alcholic drinks.

Bónus SUPERMARKET €
(Digranesgata 6; ⏲11am-6.30pm Mon-Thu, 10am-7.30pm Fri, to 6pm Sat, noon-6pm Sun) Bónus sits at the edge of the fjord bridge coming into town.

★**Settlement Centre Restaurant** INTERNATIONAL €€
(☎437 1600; www.landnam.is; Brákarbraut 13; lunch buffet 2200kr, mains 2200-4600kr; ⏲10am-9pm; 📶) The Settlement Centre's restaurant, set in a light-filled room built into the rock face, is airy, upbeat and one of the region's best bets for food. Choose from traditional Icelandic and international eats (lamb, fish stew etc). The lunch buffet (11.30am to 3pm) is very popular. Book ahead for dinner.

Englendingavík CAFE €€
(☎555 1400; www.englendingavik.is; Skúlagata 17; mains 2500-5100kr; ⏲11.30am-11pm May-Sep, reduced hours Apr & Oct; 📶🍷) Casual and friendly, with a wonderful waterfront deck, Englendingavík serves good homemade dishes, from cakes to full meals of roast lamb or fresh fish. They have an attached **guesthouse** (doubles with shared bathroom from 27,400kr) in a restored building with good bay views.

Blómasetrið–Kaffi Kyrrð CAFE
(☎437 1878; www.blomasetrid.is; Skúlagata 13; ⏲9am-9pm Mon-Fri, 11am-7pm Sat & Sun; 📶) This quaint flower and gift shop is also a cosy cafe with hot drinks, beer and snacks. Relax in overstuffed chairs.

Shopping

★**Ljómalind** MARKET
(Farmers Market; ☎437 1400; www.ljomalind.is; Brúartorg 4; ⏲10am-6pm May-Sep, noon-5pm Oct-Apr) 🍃 A long-standing collaboration between local producers, this packed farmers market sits at the edge of town near the roundabout. It stocks everything from fresh dairy products from Erpsstaðir (p238) and

organic meat to locally made bath products, handmade wool sweaters, jewellery and all manner of imaginative collectables.

Information

Tourist Information Centre (437 2214; www.west.is; Borgarbraut 58-60; 9am-5pm Mon-Fri, 10am-4pm Sat, noon-4pm Sun Jun-Aug, 9am-5pm Mon-Fri Sep-May;) West Iceland's main tourist information centre; in the big shopping centre.

Getting There & Away

Borgarnes is the major transfer point between Reykjavík and Akureyri, Snæfellsnes and the Westfjords. The **bus stop** (Borgarbraut) is at the cluster of petrol stations (N1, Orkan). All services are reduced in winter.

Strætó (p429) bus services:

- Bus 57 to Reykjavík (1840kr, 1½ hours, seven Monday to Friday, three Saturday, four Sunday)
- Bus 57 to Akureyri (8740kr, five hours, two daily Monday to Friday, one Saturday, two Sunday)
- Bus 58 to Stykkishólmur (2760kr, 80 minutes, one or two daily; can change to bus 82 at the Vatnaleið crossroads for buses to Hellissandur and from early May to mid-September to Arnarstapi)
- Bus 59 to Holmavík (5520kr, 2¼ hours, one Monday, Wednesday, Friday and Sunday)
- Bus 81 to Reykholt (920kr, 40 minutes, one Monday, Tuesday and Thursday), loops back to Borgarnes.

Around Borgarnes

There is lots of great-value accommodation around Borgarnes; the Borgarnes tourist information centre can supply more, as can Hey Iceland (www.heyiceland.is).

Sights & Activities

★Borg á Mýrum LANDMARK

(Rock in the Marshes; Rte 54) FREE The Borg á Mýrum farm, just northwest of Borgarnes on Rte 54, is the site where Skallagrímur Kveldúlfsson, Egil's father, made his farm at settlement. The farm is named for the large rock *(borg)* behind the farmstead (private property); you can walk up to the cairn for views all around. You can also visit the small cemetery, which includes an ancient gravestone marked by runes.

Hafnarfjall HIKING

The dramatically sheer mountain Hafnarfjall (844m) rises south across the fjord from Borgarnes. You can climb it (7km) from the trailhead on Rte 1, near the southern base of the causeway into Borgarnes. Be careful of slippery scree cliffs once you ascend. You'll get sweeping views from the top.

Sleeping & Eating

Ensku Húsin GUESTHOUSE €€

(437 1826; http://enskuhusin.is; Rte 54; d with/without bathroom incl breakfast 24,900/20,500kr;) Located 8km northwest of central Borgarnes off Rte 54, this former fishing lodge with a dramatic riverside setting has been refitted with generous amounts of old-school charm. Upstairs rooms retain much of the long-ago feel, and there's a newer block with additional rooms. The friendly owners also offer accommodation in a restored farmhouse 2km away.

Hotel Varmaland HOTEL €€

(690 4220; www.hotelvarmaland.is; Rte 527, Grenihlíð;) Out in the open country of West Iceland, the nice and spacious Hotel Varmaland is perfect if you'd like to relax in the midst of pastures, rivers and crags. Rooms all have private baths and there's a pool and hot-pot nearby.

Fossatún HOTEL €€

(433 5800; www.fossatun.is; Rte 50; hut/cottage 8700/31,000kr, d with/without bathroom from 22,000/14,800kr;) This family-friendly spot has a guesthouse, hotel, full cottage and camping huts next to a beautiful roaring waterfall. The spacious **restaurant** (mains 1600kr to 3000kr) overlooks the falls and themed walking paths. It's located on the southern branch of Rte 50, about 23km east of Borgarnes and 18km southwest of Reykholt.

Icelandair Hotel Hamar HOTEL, GUESTHOUSE €€

(433 6600; www.icehotels.is; Rte 1, Golfvöllurinn; d from 18,800kr;) Hotel Hamar sits on a popular golf course 4km north of Borgarnes. We found the silver prefab exterior to be slightly off-putting, but surprisingly sleek decor and a cache of mod cons hide within. On-site restaurants.

Skemma Cafe CAFE €

(Skemman Kaffihús; 868 8626; www.facebook.com/skemmancafe; Agricultural Museum of Iceland complex, Havnneyri; snacks 900-1350kr; noon-5pm Tue-Sun Jun–mid-Aug) Tucked away in the village of Havnneyri, 12km east of Borgarnes, in a renovated building that dates from 1896, this small cafe has a sunny deck and soups, waffles, cakes and coffees.

Shopping

★Ullarselið CLOTHING, ARTS & CRAFTS

(☎437 0077; www.ull.is; Hvanneyri; ⏰11am-5pm Jun-Aug, 1-5pm Thu-Sat Sep-May) Find your way to off-the-beaten-path village Hvanneyri, 12km east of Borgarnes, and in among fjordside homes you'll find this fantastic wool centre. Handmade sweaters, scarves, hats and blankets share space with skeins of beautiful hand-spun yarn, and interesting bone and shell buttons. Plus there are needles and patterns to get you started.

Upper Borgarfjörður

Reykholt

Incredibly unassuming, Reykholt is a sleepy outpost (just a few farmsteads really) that on first glance offers few clues to its past as a major medieval settlement. It was home to one of the most important medieval chieftains and scholars, Snorri Sturluson, who was killed here, and today the main sights revolve around him.

Sights & Activities

Krauma GEOTHERMAL BATHS

(☎555 6066; www.krauma.is; Deildartunguhver, Rte 50; adult/child 3800kr/free; ⏰11am-11pm mid-Jun–mid-Aug, to 9pm rest of year) Water from neighbouring **Deildartunguhver** – Iceland's largest hot spring – heats this modern outdoor bathing complex with five multi-temperature hot-pots and two steam baths. Guests also enjoy a relaxation room and the brave can get their circulation going with a cold tub dip. Attached is a bistro with Icelandic cuisine (mains 2700kr to 3800kr).

Snorrastofa MUSEUM

(☎433 8000; www.snorrastofa.is; 1200kr; ⏰10am-6pm Apr-Sep, to 5pm Mon-Fri Oct-Mar) The interesting medieval study centre Snorrastofa is devoted to celebrated medieval poet, historian and statesman Snorri Sturluson, and is built on his old farm, where he was brutally slain. The centre houses displays explaining Snorri's life and accomplishments, including a 1599 edition of his *Heimskringla* (sagas of the Norse kings). There's also material on the laws, literature and society of medieval Iceland, and on the excavations of the site. You can ask to see the modern church and reading room upstairs.

Snorralaug SPRING

FREE The most important relic of Snorri Sturluson's farm is Snorralaug (Snorri's Pool), a circular, stone-lined pool fed by a hot spring. The stones at the base of the pool are original (10th century), and it is believed that this is where Snorri bathed. A wood-panelled tunnel beside the spring (closed to the public) leads to the old farmhouse – the site of Snorri's gruesome murder. The pool may be the oldest handmade structure in Iceland.

Reykholt Old Church CHURCH

FREE Among the more modern buildings found on the ancient farm of Snorri Sturluson is a quaint church dating from 1896, which is open to the public. A 1040–1260 cistern for a smithy was found beneath it in 2001; look for the viewing glass in the floor.

Icelandic Goat Centre FARM

(☎435 1448; www.geitur.is; Rte 523, Háafell; tour per adult/child 1500/750kr; ⏰1-6pm Jun-Aug) Farm workers walk you through pretty fields with endangered Icelandic goats. The farm's most famous resident is Casanova, a bright-eyed goat who had a starring turn in *Game of Thrones* (running from a dragon). Find the farm on dirt-road Rte 523, northeast of Reykholt. Coffee or tea included.

Sleeping & Eating

Reykholt has a simple restaurant at its hotel. Head to Borgarnes for much better choice and to stock up on groceries, or to Húsafell for fine dining.

Steindórsstaðir GUESTHOUSE €€

(☎435 1227; www.heyiceland.is; Rte 517, Reykholtsdalur; s/d/tr without bathroom 11,300/16,300/20,000kr; 📶) Set on a farm in the rolling fields about 2km from Reykholt proper, this sweet guesthouse offers clean, cosy rooms with countryside views. There's a shared kitchen, a hot tub (with views too) and friendly owners.

Fosshótel Reykholt HOTEL €€

(☎562 4000, 435 1260; www.fosshotel.is; d incl breakfast from 22,000kr; P@📶) The only hotel in Reykholt proper, the Fosshótel is a bland block with recently updated business-style rooms, a couple of hot-pots and a restaurant. It's expanding and the new wing should open in 2019.

SNORRI STURLUSON

The chieftain and historian Snorri Sturluson (1179–1241) is one of the most important figures in medieval Icelandic history, and he was one of the main chroniclers of Norse sagas and histories. Snorri was born at Hvammur near Búðardalur (further north), was raised and educated at the theological centre of Oddi near Hella, and later married the heir to the historic farm Borg á Mýrum (p215) near Borgarnes. He eventually left Borg and retreated to the wealthy church estate at Reykholt. At the time, Reykholt was home to 60,000 to 80,000 people and was an important trade centre at the crossroads of major routes across the country. Snorri composed many of his most famous works at Reykholt, including *Prose Edda* (a textbook of medieval Norse poetry) and *Heimskringla* (a history of the kings of Norway). Snorri is also widely believed to be the hand behind *Egil's Saga*, a family history of Viking *skald* (court poet) Egil Skallagrímsson.

At the age of 36, Snorri was appointed *lögsögumaður* (law speaker) of the Alþingi (Icelandic parliament). In the following decades he endured heavy pressure from the Norwegian king to promote the ruler's private interests but, instead, Snorri busied himself with his writing until the unhappy Norwegian king Hákon finally snapped and issued a warrant for his capture – dead or alive. Snorri's political rival and former son-in-law Gissur Þorvaldsson saw his chance to impress the king and possibly snag the position of governor of Iceland in return. He arrived in Reykholt with 70 armed men on the night of 23 September 1241 and hacked the historian to death in the basement of his farmhouse.

Hverinn Restaurant INTERNATIONAL €
(☎571 4433; www.hverinn.is; Rte 50, Kleppjámsreykir; mains 1600-4000kr; ⏲10.30am-9pm May-Oct) Simple eats from daily soups to burgers are on offer at this large roadside restaurant with friendly staff. Also has basic groceries and a campground (1500kr per adult) and guesthouse (double with shared bathroom 14,500kr). Find it about 5km west of Reykholt near the junction of Rtes 518 and 50.

Getting There & Away

Strætó (p429) runs bus 81 to Borgarnes (920kr, 50 minutes, one Monday, Tuesday and Thursday), also stopping in Kleppjárnsreykir.

Húsafell

Tucked into an emerald, river-crossed valley, with the Kaldá River on one side and a dramatic lava field on the other, Húsafell, with its encampment of summer cottages, campground, chic hotel, bistro and geothermal swimming pool, is a popular outdoor retreat for Reykjavík residents, and the main access point for nearby Langjökull glacier.

Sights

★Hraunfossar WATERFALL
(Rte 518) The name of this spectacular waterfall translates to 'Lava Field Waterfall' because the crystalline water streams out from below the lava field all around. Walk a little further on the marked trail to reach Barnafoss, another churning chute. Find the turn-off on the north side of Rte 518, 6.5km west of Húsafell.

Sundlaugin á Húsafelli GEOTHERMAL POOL
(Húsafell Swimming Pool; ☎435 1552; www.husafell.is; Rte 518; adult/child 1300/300kr; ⏲10am-8pm Mon-Thu, to 10pm Fri & Sat Jun-Aug, 1-7pm Mon-Fri, noon-8pm Sat & Sun Sep-May) Beautiful outdoor geothermal swimming pool and two hot-pots.

Sleeping & Eating

The Húsafell complex has a recently renovated bistro (open 11am to 9pm June to August, mains 2000kr to 5000kr, dinner buffet 2700kr) with a mini-mart (open 9am to 9pm in summer), and there's a gourmet restaurant in the hotel. Borgarnes is the largest nearby city for more choices.

Gamli Bær GUESTHOUSE €
(Old Farmhouse; ☎895 1342; sveitasetrid@simnet.is; Rte 518; d with/without bathroom from 14,000/10,000kr; ⏲mid-May–Sep) Quaint, renovated 1908 farmhouse full of charm and with country views and a hot-pot, run by jovial Sæmi.

Húsafell CAMPGROUND €
(Ferðaþjónustan Húsafelli; ☎435 1556; www.husafell.is; Rte 518; sites per adult/child 1500/800kr; ⏲May-Sep) The Húsafell holiday resort's verdant campsites have showers, a mini-market, bistro and geothermal swimming pool.

★**Hótel Húsafell** HOTEL €€€

(☎435 1551; www.hotelhusafell.com; Rte 518; d incl breakfast from 34,200kr; P 📶) The star of the show in the Húsafell holiday village is this chic and contemporary hotel, offering spacious, comfortable rooms. Top-notch bathrooms feature organic Icelandic toiletries. Art is the original work of local artist Páll Guðmundsson, and the **restaurant** (☎435 1551; www.hotelhusafell.com; Rte 518; mains lunch 2600-5400kr, dinner 4800-7600kr; P) is one of the best in the region.

Hraunfossar Cafe CAFE €€

(☎435 1155; www.hraunfossar.is; Rte 518; mains 1900-2700kr; ⏲10am-8pm Jun-Aug, reduced hours rest of year) This welcoming cafe just back from the waterfalls of the same name has wide decks and a solid menu of basic soup, burgers, salads and snacks.

Getting There & Away

You'll need your own wheels to reach Húsafell.

Hallmundarhraun

East of Húsafell, along Rte 518, the vast, barren lava flows of Hallmundarhraun make up a wonderful eerie landscape dotted with gigantic lava tubes. These long, tunnel-like caves are formed by flows of molten lava beneath a solid lava crust, and it's possible to visit several of them.

If you've got a 4WD, it's also possible to continue into the interior along Rte F578 beyond Surtshellir, through the lakes at **Arnarvatnsheiði**, and on to **Hvammstangi**. Note that Rte F578 is usually only open seven weeks a year; see www.road.is.

Sights

★**Viðgelmir – the Cave** CAVE

(☎783 3600; www.thecave.is; off Rte 518; tour per adult/child from 6500kr/free) The easiest lava tube to visit, and the largest in Iceland, 1100-year-old, 1.5km-long Viðgelmir is located on private property near the farmstead Fljótstunga. It sparkles with ever-changing rock formations and has a stable walkway within it on which tours are conducted. Check the website for tour times; helmet and torch included.

Surtshellir NATURAL FEATURE

(Rte F578) FREE Just a bit to the southeast of Fljótstunga on Rte 518, a bright yellow sign marks the turn-off to Arnarvatnsheiði along Rte F578 (rental cars not allowed). Follow the bumpy track for 7km to reach Surtshellir, a dramatic, 2km-long lava tube connected to Stefánshellir, a second tunnel about half the size. You can explore Surtshellir on your own if you have caving gear (helmet, torch etc).

Langjökull & Kaldidalur Corridor

Southeast of Húsafell, the extraordinary Kaldidalur valley skirts the edge of a series of glaciers, offering incredible views of the Langjökull ice cap (the second largest glacier in Iceland) and, in clear weather, Eiríksjökull, Okjökull and Þórisjökull.

The Kaldidalur Corridor, also simply known as unsurfaced Rte 550, is slow but dramatic going (mountain ice, barren rock), and is often fogged in in summer. It links south to the Golden Circle, offering the option to create an extended loop from Reykjavík. Access to Rte 550 is limited to sanctioned vehicles – ask your rental outfit before setting off.

Tours are available on Langjökull and of the glacier's ice cave, departing from Reykjavík or Húsafell. Do not attempt to drive up onto the glacier yourself.

Sights

★**Langjökull** GLACIER

The Langjökull ice cap is the second largest glacier in Iceland, and the closest major glacier to Reykjavík. It's accessed from the 4WD Kaldidalur or Kjölur tracks, and its closest access village in West Iceland is Húsafell. Tours depart from Reykjavík or Húsafell: the Into the Glacier ice cave is a major tourist attraction, Mountaineers of Iceland (p73) offers snowmobiling, and Dog Sledding (p73) sometimes has summertime tours.

★**Into the Glacier** CAVE

(Langjökull Ice Cave; ☎578 2550; www.intotheglacier.is) This enormous (300m-long) human-made tunnel and series of caves head into Langjökull glacier at 1260m above sea level. The glistening, LED-lit tunnel and caves opened in 2015 and contain exhibitions, a cafe and even a small chapel for those who want to tie the knot inside a glacier. Tours leave from Húsafell (shuttle adult/child 2000kr/free) or the glacier edge (tour adult/child 19,500kr/free) in summer if you have a 4WD. Tours also leave from Reykjavík (29,900kr), and there are many combo tours (snowmobiling, helicopter).

A maximum of 80 visitors at a time can travel up the glacier by monster truck, then have about 45 minutes touring the glacier – which will continue to creep down the mountain in the years to come.

Sleeping & Eating

You'll find food and lodging in Húsafell (p217), Reykholt (p216) or Borgarnes (p211); the Ice Cave base camp has just a tiny cafe.

Getting There & Away

Come on a tour. Note: while you can drive the roads with a sanctioned vehicle (check with your rental company), never go up on the glacier without a guide.

SNÆFELLSNES PENINSULA

Sparkling fjords, dramatic volcanic peaks, sheer sea cliffs, sweeping golden beaches and crunchy lava flows make up the diverse and fascinating landscape of the 100km-long Snæfellsnes Peninsula. The area is crowned by the glistening ice cap Snæfellsjökull, immortalised in Jules Verne's *Journey to the Centre of the Earth*. Good roads and regular buses mean that it's an easy trip from Reykjavík, offering a cross-section of the best Iceland has to offer in a very compact region.

Stykkishólmur, on the populated northern coast, is the region's largest town and a logical base. Moving west along the northern coast, you'll pass smaller townships. On the western part of the peninsula, Snæfellsjökull National Park encompasses not only its glacier but also bird sanctuaries and lava fields. The quiet southern coast has several good horse farms beneath towering crags.

Stykkishólmur

POP 1173

The charming town of Stykkishólmur (www.visitstykkisholmur.is), the largest on the Snæfellsnes Peninsula, is built up around a natural harbour tipped by a basalt islet. It's a picturesque place with a laid-back attitude and a sprinkling of brightly coloured buildings from the late 19th century. With a comparatively good choice of accommodation and restaurants, and handy transport links, Stykkishólmur makes an excellent base for exploring the region. There's free wi-fi throughout the whole town.

Sights & Activities

★Breiðafjörður NATURAL FEATURE

Stykkishólmur's jagged peninsula pushes north into stunning Breiðafjörður, a broad waterway separating the Snæfellsnes from the looming cliffs of the distant Westfjords. According to local legend, there are only two things in the world that cannot be counted: the stars in the night sky and the craggy islets in the bay. You *can* count on epic vistas and a menagerie of wild birds (puffins, eagles, guillemots). Boat trips, including whale watching and puffin viewing, are available from Stykkishólmur, Grundarfjörður and Ólafsvík.

★Norska Húsið MUSEUM

(Norwegian House; ☎433 8114; www.norskahusid.is; Hafnargata 5; adult/child 1000kr/free; ⊙11am-6pm May-Aug, 2-5pm Tue-Thu Sep-Apr; 📶) Stykkishólmur's quaint maritime charm comes from the cluster of wooden warehouses, shops and homes around the town's harbour. Most date back about 150 years. One of the most interesting (and oldest) is the Norska Húsið, now the regional museum. Built by trader and amateur astronomer Árni Thorlacius in 1832, the house has been skilfully restored and displays a wonderfully eclectic selection of local antiquities. On the 2nd floor you visit Árni's home, an upper-class 19th-century residence decked out with his original wares.

★Súgandisey ISLAND

The basalt island Súgandisey features a scenic **lighthouse** and grand views across Breiðafjörður. Reach it via the causeway at Stykkishólmur harbour.

Volcano Museum MUSEUM

(Eldfjallasafn; ☎433 8154; www.eldfjallasafn.is; Aðalgata 8; adult/child 1000kr/free; ⊙10am-5pm Jun-Aug, 11am-5pm Tue-Sat Sep-May) The Volcano Museum, housed in the town's old cinema, is the brainchild of vulcanologist Haraldur Sigurðsson, and features art depicting volcanoes, plus a small collection of interesting lava ('magma bombs') and artefacts from eruptions. A film screens upstairs.

Library of Water GALLERY

(Vatnasafn; ☎865 4516; www.facebook.com/vatnasafn; Bókhlöðustígur 17; adult/child 650kr/free; ⊙10am-5pm May-Sep, Tue-Sat Oct-Apr) For relaxing views of town and bay, head up the hill to the Library of Water. This window-lined space showcases an installation by American artist Roni Horn (b 1955). Light reflects and refracts through

Snæfellsnes Peninsula

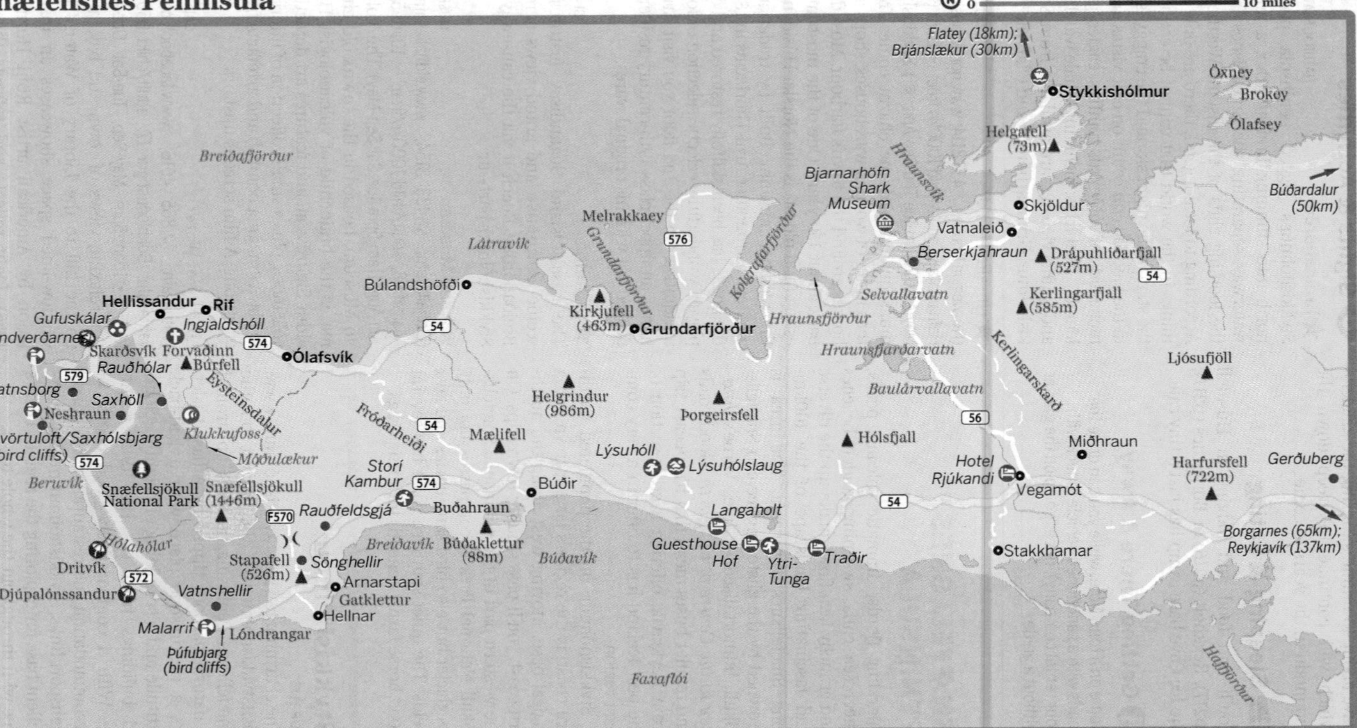

WORTH A TRIP

FLATEY

Of Breiðafjörður's innumerable islands, little Flatey (literally 'Flat Island') is the only one with year-round inhabitants. In the 11th century Flatey (www.flatey.com) was home to a monastery, and today the appealing island is a popular stopover for travellers heading to (or from) the Westfjords, as well as filmmakers: several movies and series have been shot here. Push the slow-mo button on life, and enjoy a windswept afternoon amid brightly coloured houses and swooping Arctic terns.

Sleeping & Eating

Krákuvör (☎438 1451; sites per person 1200kr; ⏱Jun-Aug) One of the island's farms, about 300m from the pier, Krákuvör offers camping on a meadow sweeping to the shore.

Læknishús (☎438 1476; s without bathroom 10,000kr; ⏱Jun-Aug, by reservation only Sep-May) Læknishús is about 400m from the pier and offers simple accommodation in the former doctor's house in summer. Sleeping-bag accommodation costs 4000kr. Outside of summer, when there is no restaurant on the island, bring supplies and use the kitchen.

Hótel Flatey (☎555 7788; www.hotelflatey.is; s/d/tr without bathroom incl breakfast 25,900/29,900/38,900kr; ⏱Jun-Aug) Hótel Flatey has some of the most charming, nook-like vintage rooms in Iceland, and the on-site **restaurant** (mains lunch 2400kr to 3200kr, dinner 4300kr to 6100kr, three-course menu 9500kr; open noon to 5pm and 6pm to 9pm) is fantastic as well. On some evenings, slip down into the basement bar for live music.

Getting There & Away

The Baldur Ferry (p224) crosses Breiðafjörður with a stop in Flatey, only pausing on the island for around five minutes. In summer, when there are two boats per day, it is possible to take some time on the island and then continue on to the Westfjords/Stykkishólmur all in the same day: take the first ferry of the day, have your time on Flatey, and then catch the second ferry the rest of the way across. No cars are allowed on Flatey, so for those travelling with a car, it is possible to send it on across (no additional charge) while you stay behind in Flatey.

To visit Flatey as a day trip from Stykkishólmur, take either boat during summer, disembark at Flatey and catch the ferry as it returns to Stykkishólmur.

Note that the twice-per-day ferry service only runs from June to August; the rest of the year there is one per day. You can also visit with local tour companies.

24 glass pillars filled with Icelandic glacier water. There's also a chess set if you feel like lingering.

Stykkishólmskirkja CHURCH
(☎438 1560; www.stykkisholmskirkja.is; ⏱10am-5pm) Stykkishólmur's futuristic church, designed by Jón Haraldsson, has a sweeping bell tower that looks like a whale vertebra. The interior features hundreds of suspended lights and a painting of the Madonna and child floating in the night sky.

Stykkishólmur Swimming Pool GEOTHERMAL POOL, HOT-POT
(Sundlaug Stykkishólms; ☎433 8150; Borgarbraut 4; adult/child 900/300kr; ⏱7am-10pm Mon-Thu, to 7pm Fri, 10am-6pm Sat & Sun Jun-Aug, reduced hours rest of year) Water slides and hot-pots are the highlights at the town's geothermal swimming pool in the municipal sports complex.

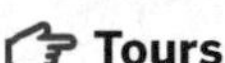

Tours

Seatours BOATING
(Sæferðir; ☎433 2254; www.seatours.is; Smiðjustígur 3; ⏱8am-8pm mid-May–mid-Sep, 9am-5pm rest of year) Various boat tours are on offer, including the much-touted 'Viking Sushi', a one-/two-hour boat ride (6220/7700kr) taking in islands, bird colonies (puffins until August) and basalt formations. A net brings up shellfish to devour raw. Also offers dinner cruises and runs the Baldur Ferry (p224) to Flatey. Partners with Reykjavík Excursions for Reykjavík pick-up. On-site shop and cafe. Children under 15 travel free.

Ocean Adventures FISHING, WILDLIFE TOUR
(☎898 2028; www.oceanadventures.is; Sæbraut; ⏱9am-6pm) Try your hand at angling (adult/child 11,000/9000kr) or go on a puffin viewing tour (adult/child 7000/4500kr) with this popular outfit with a kiosk on the harbour.

Stykkishólmur

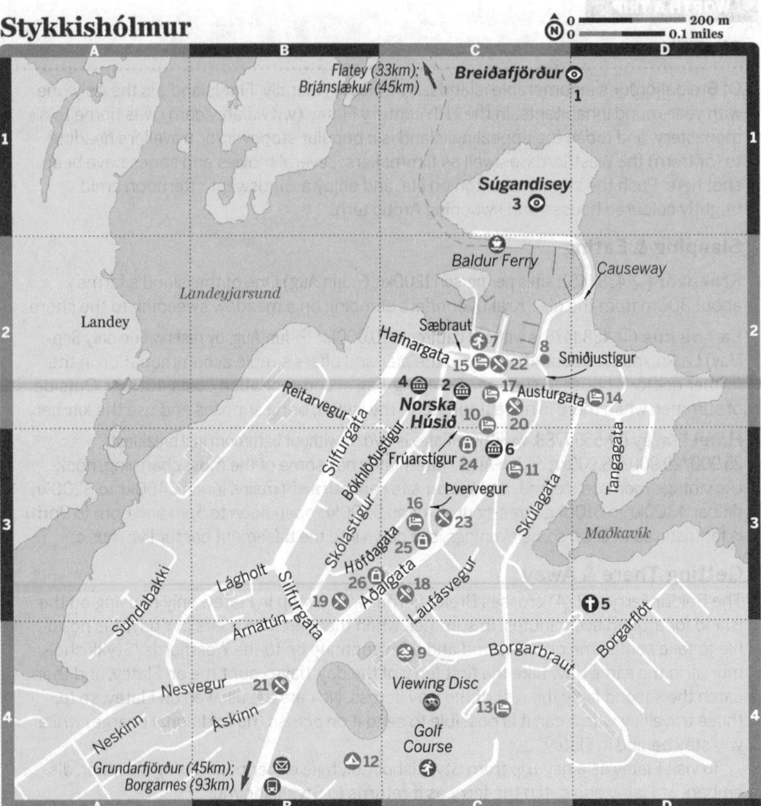

Stykkishólmur

Top Sights
1 Breiðafjörður ... D1
2 Norska Húsið ... C2
3 Súgandisey ... C1

Sights
4 Library of Water ... C2
5 Stykkishólmskirkja ... D3
6 Volcano Museum ... C3

Activities, Courses & Tours
7 Ocean Adventures ... C2
8 Seatours ... C2
9 Stykkishólmur Swimming Pool ... C4

Sleeping
10 Akkeri ... C2
11 Bænir og Brauð ... C3
12 Campground ... B4
13 Fosshotel Stykkishólmur ... C4
14 Fransiskus Hotel ... D2
15 Harbour Hostel ... C2
16 Höfðagata Guesthouse ... C3
17 Hótel Egilsen ... C2

Eating
18 Bónus ... C3
19 Meistarinn ... B3
20 Narfeyrarstofa ... C2
21 Nesbrauð ... B4
22 Sjávarpakkhúsið ... C2
23 Skúrinn ... C3

Shopping
24 Gallerí Lundi ... C3
25 Leir 7 ... C3
26 Vínbúðin ... B3

Sleeping

Harbour Hostel HOSTEL €

(📞517 5353; www.harbourhostel.is; Hafnargata 4; dm/d/q without bathroom from 4500/14,800/21,400kr; 📶👪) This simple harbourside hostel offers some of the town's best cheap lodging, with dorm rooms (four, eight- and 12-bed), doubles and family rooms.

Campground CAMPGROUND €

(📞438 1075; Aðalgata 27; sites per adult/child 1500kr/free; 🕒late May-Sep; 📶) Basic with a new bathroom block; managed by the golf course nearby.

Akkeri GUESTHOUSE €€

(📞844 1050; www.facebook.com/Akkeri-Guesthouse-390669541439953; Frúarstígur 1; d incl breakfast from 19,700kr; 📶) This sparkling new family-run guesthouse smack in the centre of town offers minimalist, cool-toned, comfortable rooms with swanky bathrooms, and one has a balcony. Note: no guest kitchen.

Bænir og Brauð GUESTHOUSE €€

(📞554 7700; www.baenirogbraud.is; Aðalgata 7; d with/without bathroom 24,800/20,500kr; 📶) This snug, immaculate house dates from 1896. Greta, the kindly owner, also owns Hótel Egilsen across the road. Breakfast is not included, but there is a grand shared kitchen. Prices drop drastically in the low season.

Höfðagata Guesthouse GUESTHOUSE €€

(📞831 1806; www.hofdagata.is; Höfðagata 11; d with/without bathroom incl breakfast from 22,100/16,500kr, apt 25,500kr; 📶) This tidy, well-run guesthouse offers five small but well-appointed double rooms with a shared refrigerator and one fully equipped apartment.

★**Hótel Egilsen** BOUTIQUE HOTEL €€€

(📞554 7700; www.egilsen.is; Aðalgata 2; s/d from 26,320/31,900kr; @📶) One of our favourite little inns in Iceland, this boutique hotel fills a lovingly restored timber house that creaks in the most charming way when winds howl off the fjord. The friendly owner has outfitted cosy (tiny!) rooms with traditional woollen blankets, original artwork and organic Coco-Mat mattresses. IPads and a homemade breakfast (2500kr) sweeten the deal.

Fransiskus Hotel HOTEL €€€

(📞422 1101; www.fransiskus.is; Austurgata 7; s with/without bathroom incl breakfast from 19,000/13,100kr, d/f incl breakfast from 32,700/38,000kr; P📶👪) This hotel in a renovated wing of a Catholic monastery and hospital complex offers well-maintained modern rooms, some with private bathrooms and flat-screen TVs. Breakfast is excellent.

Fosshotel Stykkishólmur HOTEL €€€

(📞430 2100; www.fosshotel.is; Borgarbraut 8; s/d/tr 30,100/32,800/36,700kr; @📶) The best rooms in this jarring silver box up on a hill have super bay and island views. Rooms are motel-basic and favoured by groups.

Eating & Drinking

There's a **Vínbúðin** (📞430 1414; www.vinbudin.is; Aðalgata 24; 🕒2-6pm Mon-Thu, 1-7pm Fri, 11am-2pm Sat Jun-Aug, reduced hours rest of year) for stocking up on liquor, or have a drink at one of the local restaurants, such as Sjávarpakkhúsið which has Icelandic beer on tap.

Nesbrauð BAKERY €

(📞438 1830; www.facebook.com/nesbraudehf; Nesvegur 1; snacks 400-1200kr; 🕒7.30am-5pm Mon-Fri, from 8am Sat & Sun) On the road into town, this bakery is a good choice for a quick breakfast or lunch. Stock up on sugary confections such as *kleinur* (traditional twisty doughnuts) or *ástar pungur* (literally 'love balls'; fried balls of dough and raisins).

Meistarinn FAST FOOD €

(📞848 0153; www.facebook.com/meistarinnsth; Aðalgata; hot dogs 540-600kr, sub sandwiches 1400-1600kr; 🕒noon-8pm Jun-Aug) This friendly *pýlsuvagninn* (hot-dog wagon) has the best hot dogs in town. Each menu item is named after someone from Stykkishólmur.

Bónus SUPERMARKET €

(Borgarbraut 1; 🕒11am-6.30pm Mon-Thu, 10am-7.30pm Fri, to 6pm Sat, noon-6pm Sun) Groceries; near the swimming pool.

★**Narfeyrarstofa** ICELANDIC €€

(📞533 1119; www.narfeyrarstofa.is; Aðalgata 3; mains 2000-5000kr; 🕒11.30am-10pm May-Sep, reduced hours Oct-Apr; 🖉) This charming restaurant is the Snæfellsnes' darling fine-dining destination. Book a table on the 2nd floor for the romantic lighting of antique lamps and harbour views. Ask your waiter about the portraits on the wall – the building has an interesting history.

Sjávarpakkhúsið ICELANDIC €€

(📞438 1800; www.sjavarpakkhusid.is; Hafnargata 2; mains 2800-3500kr; 🕒noon-10pm; 📶) This old fish-packing house has been transformed into a wood-lined cafe-bar with harbourfront outdoor seating. The speciality is blue-shell mussels straight from the bay. It's a great daytime hang-out too, and on weekend evenings it turns into a popular bar where locals come to jam.

Skúrinn INTERNATIONAL €€
(☎544 4004; Þvervegur 2; mains 1900-3200kr; ⊙noon-2pm & 6-9pm; 📶) Casual spot for grabbing a pizza, burger, nachos, fish and chips, and beer, with a nice deck for sunny days.

Shopping

Leir 7 ARTS & CRAFTS
(☎894 0425; www.leir7.is; Aðalgata 20; ⊙2-5pm Mon-Fri, to 4pm Sat) Artist Sigríður Erla produces beautiful ceramics from the fjord's dark clay at this pottery studio in the heart of town. There's also woodcraft by Lára Gunnarsdóttir (www.smavinir.is).

Gallerí Lundi ARTS & CRAFTS
(☎893 5588; Aðalgata 4a; ⊙12.30-6pm May-Sep) Local handicrafts sold by friendly villagers. Also offers coffee.

Getting There & Away

BOAT

The **Baldur Ferry** (☎433 2254; www.seatours.is) runs between Stykkishólmur and Brjánslækur in the Westfjords (2½ hours) via Flatey (1½ hours). From June to August there are daily departures from Stykkishólmur at 9am and 3.45pm, returning from Brjánslækur at 12.15pm and 7pm. During the rest of the year there is only one ferry per day, leaving Stykkishólmur at 3pm (no boats on Fridays and Saturdays), returning at 6pm.

Adult/child fares to Brjánslækur are 5760kr/free in summer. Reserve ahead for vehicles (additional 5760/8340kr per car/small camper).

> **WISHING AT HELGAFELL**
>
> It is commonly believed that those who ascend humble mountain Helgafell will be granted three wishes, provided that the requests are made with a pure heart. However, you must follow three important steps to make your wishes come true:
>
> **Step 1** Start at the grave of Guðrún Ósvífursdóttir, heroine of an ancient local saga.
>
> **Step 2** Walk up to the Tótt (the chapel ruins), not uttering a single word, and (like Orpheus leaving Hades), never looking back.
>
> **Step 3** Once at the chapel ruins, you must face east while wishing. And never tell your wishes to anyone or they won't come true.

Return trip from Stykkishólmur to Flatey costs 7840kr. Check online for concession and winter fares.

BUS

You can get to Reykjavík (4140kr, 2½ hours) by changing in Borgarnes. All services are greatly reduced in winter.

Strætó (p429) services from the bus stop (Aðalgata) at the Olís petrol station:

- Bus 58 to Borgarnes (2760kr, 80 minutes, one or two daily).
- Bus 82 to Hellissandur via Vatnaleið (crossroads of Rtes 54 and 56), Grundarfjörður, Ólafsvík and Rif (1840kr, 1¼ hours, two daily mid-May to mid-September, continuing on to Arnarstapi once per day). The rest of the year it only goes from Stykkishólmur to Hellissandur four days per week.

Stykkishólmur to Grundarfjörður

The scenic stretch between Stykkishólmur and Grundarfjörður is filled with myth and mystique, from spiritual mountains to saga-storied lava fields, with the bright water just offshore.

Sights

Helgafell MOUNTAIN
About 5km south of Stykkishólmur, the holy mountain Helgafell (73m) was once venerated by worshippers of the god Þór. Although quite small, the mountain was so sacred in Saga times that elderly Icelanders would seek it out near the time of their death. Today locals believe that wishes are granted to those who climb the mount.

In the late 10th century, Snorri Goði, a prominent Þor worshipper, converted to Christianity and built a church at the top of the hill; its ruins still remain. The nearby farm of the same name was where the conniving Guðrun Ósvífursdóttir of *Laxdæla Saga* lived out her later years in isolation. Her grave marks the base of the mount.

Berserkjahraun NATURAL FEATURE
About 15km west of the intersection of Rte 54 and Rte 56 lies the dramatic, spiky lava field at Berserkjahraun (Berserkers' lava field). Crowned by looming mountains, this lunar landscape gets its name from the Eyrbyggja Saga, minor saga set around the Snæfellsnes Peninsula, where ghosts are taken to court over their hauntings.

Bjarnarhöfn Shark Museum MUSEUM
(☎438 1581; www.bjarnarhofn.is; Bjarnarhöfn farm; adult/child 1200kr/free; ⏰9am-6pm Jun-Aug, reduced hours Sep-May) The farmstead at Bjarnarhöfn is the region's leading producer of *hákarl* (fermented shark meat), a traditional Icelandic dish. The museum has exhibits on the history of this culinary curiosity, along with the family's fishing boats and processing tools. A video explains the butchering and fermenting procedure.

Find the museum off Rte 54 on a turnout from Rte 577, on the fjordside, northeastern edge of **Bjarnarhafnarfjall** (575m).

Greenland shark, which is used to make *hákarl,* is poisonous if eaten fresh; fermentation neutralises the toxin. Note that Greenland shark is classified as near threatened, and is the longest-living vertebrate on the planet, with some living over 500 years.

Each visit to the museum comes with a bracing nibble of *hákarl,* accompanied by Brennivín (aka 'black death') schnapps. Ask about the drying house out the back. You might find hundreds of dangling shark slices drying, the last step in the process.

Grundarfjörður

POP 834

Spectacularly set on a dramatic bay, little Grundarfjörður is backed by waterfalls and surrounded by ice-capped peaks often shrouded in cottony fog. More prefab than wooden, the town feels like a typical Icelandic fishing community, but the tourist facilities are good and the surrounding landscape can't be beat, with its iconic Kirkjufell.

Sights & Tours

★**Kirkjufell** MOUNTAIN
Kirkjufell (463m), guardian of Grundarfjörður's northwestern vista, is said to be one of the most photographed spots in Iceland, appearing in *Game of Thrones* and on everyone's instagram. Ask staff at the Saga Centre if you want to climb it; they may be able to find you a guide. Two spots involving a rope climb make it dangerous to scale when wet or without local knowledge.

Kirkjufell is backed by the roaring waterfalls, **Kirkjufellsfoss**; more camera fodder.

Saga Centre MUSEUM
(Eyrbyggja Heritage Centre; ☎438 1881; www.grundarfjordur.is; Grundargata 35; ⏰9am-5pm; 📶) FREE The Saga Centre is a tourist information centre, cafe (p226), library, internet point and small museum rolled into one. The museum displays an old fishing boat and gear, plus a children's toy collection. It sells national park maps, and has a free walking map of the area.

★**Láki Tours** WHALE WATCHING, WILDLIFE
(☎546 6808; www.lakitours.com; Nesvegur 5) Láki Tours has excellent fishing, puffin-spotting and whale-watching trips from Grundarfjörður or Ólafsvík. Puffin tours (adult/child 5900kr/free; June to August) from Grundarfjörður go to the wonderful basalt island **Melrakkaey**, with puffins, kittiwakes and other seabirds. Whale-watching tours (adult/child 9900kr/free, no tours mid-October to mid-December) cover the area's best whale habitat; orca, fin, sperm, blue, minke and humpback are all possibilities.

Check online for tours and departure points. Its Grundarfjörður office has a **cafe** (mains 1300kr to 2500kr; open 9am to 4pm) serving pizza and panini, and a shop.

Snæfellsnes Excursions BUS TOUR
(☎616 9090; www.sfn.is; Sólvellir 5; tours from 10,000kr) Private day trips around the major sites of Snæfellsnes Peninsula, from Stykkishólmur, Grundarfjörður and Ólafsvík. Also offers a Snæfellsjökull glacier tour (7900kr) departing from Arnarstapi.

Sleeping

Grundarfjörður has a broad collection of guesthouses, excellent rental apartments and a basic campground. Check www.grundarfjordur.is for a full list and Hey Iceland (www.heyiceland.is) for accommodation on nearby headlands, such as Suður-Bár.

Grundarfjörður HI Hostel HOSTEL €
(☎562 6533; www.hostel.is; Hlíðarvegur 15; dm/s from 6800/9700kr, d with/without bathroom from 18,000/13,000kr, q 32,000kr; @📶👪) This outfit features everything from prim dorm rooms to smart, apartment-style lodging. Reception is in the red house (at the listed address), while accommodation is spread across several buildings in town. HI members get a discount of 10%.

Hamrahlíð 9 Guesthouse GUESTHOUSE €€
(☎824 3000; hamrahlid9@gmail.com; Hamrahlíð 9; d without bathroom 18,700kr; 📶) Central and well-maintained, Hamrahlíð 9 has tidy, small rooms with a well-equipped shared kitchen and living room.

H5 Apartments APARTMENT €€
(898 0325; Hrannarstígur 5; apt 28,800kr;) Large modern apartments in the centre of town.

Eating

Café Emil CAFE €
(Kaffi Emil; 897 0124; www.facebook.com/pg/KaffiEmil; Grundargata 35, Saga Centre; mains 1200-2000kr; 9am-6pm;) In the Saga Centre (p225), this cheery cafe is tops for cappuccinos, hot soup and sandwiches.

Meistarinn FAST FOOD €
(Grundargata; hot dogs 540-600kr, sandwiches 700-1600kr; noon-8pm Jun-Sep) The Meistarinn hot-dog and sandwich wagon has menu items named after members of the Danish royal family.

Kjörbúðin SUPERMARKET €
(438 6700; www.samkaup.is; Grundargata 38; 9am-7pm Mon-Fri, 10am-6pm Sat, noon-6pm Sun) Small supermarket and N1 petrol station with a grill.

★ **Bjargarsteinn Mathús** SEAFOOD €€
(438 6770; www.facebook.com/Bjargarsteinnrestaurant; Sólvellir 15; mains 2800-4900kr; 4-10pm Jun-Aug, 5-9pm Sep–mid-Dec & mid-Jan–May;) This superb waterfront restaurant on the point in Grundarfjörður is operated by seasoned restaurateurs who have created a lively menu of Icelandic dishes, with an emphasis on seafood and everything fresh. Desserts are delicious, and pretty too. The seasonal menu is always changing, the decor is quaint, and views to Kirkjufell are stupendous.

Information

Saga Centre (p225) has tourist information and local maps.

Getting There & Away

Strætó (p429) services runs Bus 82 Stykkishólmur–Hellissandur (920kr to Stykkishólmur, two daily mid-May to mid-September, continuing on to Arnarstapi once per day; the rest of the year it only goes from Stykkishólmur to Hellissandur four days per week). It runs via Vatnaleið (crossroads Rtes 54 and 56) and Ólafsvík–Rif–Hellissandur; stops at the N1 station in Grundarfjörður.

Ólafsvík

POP 970

Quiet, workaday Ólafsvík won't win any hearts with its fish-processing plant. Although it's the oldest trading town in the country (it was granted a trading licence in 1687), few of the original buildings survive. For visitors it's best as a jumping-off point for whale watching.

The Pakkhúsið (Packhouse; 433 6930; Ólafsbraut; adult/child 500kr/free; noon-5pm Jun–mid-Sep) has a mildly interesting display telling the story of the town's development as a trading centre, and has an on-site handicraft shop and cafe (coffee included in your admission).

Sleeping & Eating

Við Hafið Guesthouse GUESTHOUSE €
(436 1166; vid.hafid@hotmail.com; Ólafsbraut 55; dm/d/q without bathroom incl breakfast 5500/16,400/21,500kr;) Clean, simple rooms with shared bathrooms and kitchen facilities are the order of the day in this large guesthouse.

Campground CAMPGROUND €
(433 6929; www.snb.is; Dalbraut; sites per adult/child 1500kr/free; Jun-Sep) Local campground with showers and playground.

Welcome Apartments HOTEL €€
(487 1212; www.welcome.is; Ólafsbraut 19; studio from 17,500kr;) Good studios with kitchenettes, some with sea views. Popular with tour groups. Avoid its partner North Star Hotel that has merely functional rooms.

Hraun INTERNATIONAL €€
(431 1030; www.facebook.com/hraun.veitingahus; Grundarbraut 2; mains 2900-5900kr; 11.30am-9pm Mon-Fri, noon-9pm Sat & Sun Jun-Aug, some weekends Sep-May;) This upbeat establishment on the main road cheerfully fills a blond-wood building with a broad front deck. The only gig in town besides fast food, it does excellent fresh mussels and lamb, burgers and fish, and has beer on tap.

Information

Ólafsvík is the largest settlement in the Snæfellsbær district – the region's **tourist information centre** (433 6929; www.snb.is; Kirkjutún 2; 9am-5pm Mon-Fri Jun-Aug, reduced hours rest of year) is located in a white building behind Pakkhúsið.

Getting There & Away

Strætó (p429) services run bus 82 Stykkishólmur–Hellissandur (1380kr to Stykkishólmur, two daily mid-May to mid-September, continuing on to Arnarstapi once per day); the rest of the year it only goes from Stykkishólmur to Hellissandur four days per week.

Rif

POP 135

Blink-and-you'll-miss-it Rif is a harbour hamlet that makes the nearby village of Ólafsvík look like a teeming metropolis. Dramatic waterfall **Svödufoss**, with its barrelling cascades and dramatic hexagonal basalt, can be seen in the distance.

Between Rif and Hellissandur, spot the lonely **church** (built 1903) at **Ingjaldshóll**, the setting of *Víglundar Saga*. If the church doors are open, you can see a painting depicting Christopher Columbus' possible visit to Iceland in 1477; it's thought he came with the merchant marine and enquired about Viking trips to Vinland.

Sleeping

Freezer Hostel HOSTEL €
(☎833 8200; www.thefreezerhostel.com; Hafnargata 16; dm/apt from 6100/21,200kr; ☎) This quirky joint in a former fish factory combines austere four-, six-, and eight-bed dorms with a cool theatre and live-music venue. In summer there's an active program of plays, storytelling and music. Check online for the schedule. It also lets two apartments in Hellissandur.

Gamla Rif GUESTHOUSE €€
(Háarifi 3; d without bathroom from 14,000kr; ☎) Formerly a popular cafe, Gamla Rif has been made over into a handful of wood-panelled rooms with views to the mountains or the sea, and a shared living area and kitchen.

Getting There & Away

Strætó (p429) runs Bus 82 Stykkishólmur–Hellissandur (1840kr to Stykkishólmur, two daily mid-May to mid-September). Also serves Arnarstapi once per day in summer.

Hellissandur

Hellissandur is the original fishing village in this area. There's not much to it any more, except great views of the glacier and fjord. **Sjóminjasafnið** (Maritime Museum; ☎436 6619; www.facebook.com/sjominjasafnhellissandi; Útnesvegur (Rte 574); adult/child 1300kr/free; ⏲10am-5pm Jun-Sep) houses *Bliki*, the oldest fishing boat in Iceland, and a cool replica of a fisher's turf house, plus loads of old photos and memorabilia. Look for the lifting stones once used to test the strength of prospective fishermen.

There's a basic hotel and campground in town and food at the petrol station. The folks at Freezer Hostel in Rif let two apartments in Hellissandur.

Snæfellsjökull National Park

Snæfellsjökull National Park (☎436 6860; www.snaefellsjokull.is) encompasses much of the western tip of Snæfellsnes Peninsula and wraps around the rugged slopes of the glacier Snæfellsjökull (pronounced *sneye*-fells-yo-kutl), the icy fist at the end of the long Snæfellsnes arm. Around its flanks lie lava tubes, protected lava fields, which are home to native Icelandic fauna, and prime hiking and coastal bird- and whale-watching spots.

When the fog swirling around the glacier lifts, you'll see the mammoth ice cap, which was made famous by Jules Verne in *Journey to the Centre of the Earth*.

Sights

★Snæfellsjökull GLACIER
It's easy to see why Jules Verne selected Snæfell for his adventure *Journey to the*

ÖNDVERÐARNES

At the westernmost tip of Snæfellsnes, Rte 574 cuts south, while Rte 579, a tiny gravel and occasionally surfaced track, heads further west across an ancient lava flow to the tip of the Öndverðarnes (pronounced *und*-ver-thar-nes) peninsula, which is great for whale watching.

As the paved road winds through charcoal lava cliffs you'll pass **Skarðsvík**, a golden beach with basalt cubes alongside. A Viking grave was discovered here in the 1960s and it's easy to understand why this stunning spot would have been a favoured final resting place.

After Skarðsvík the track is unpaved and bumpier (though still manageable for a 2WD). Park at the turn-off (left side) to walk through craggy lava flows to the imposing volcanic crater **Vatnsborg**, or continue driving straight on until you reach a T-intersection. One kilometre to the left lie the dramatic **Svörtuloft bird cliffs** (Saxhólsbjarg), with excellent walkways, and a tall, orange **lighthouse**. To the right, a bumpy track runs parallel to the sea 1.9km to a squat, orange **lighthouse**. From its parking area, you can walk to the very tip of the peninsula, for **whale watching**, or walk 200m northeast to **Fálkí**, an ancient stone well that was thought to have three waters: fresh, holy and ale!

Centre of the Earth: the peak was torn apart when the volcano beneath it exploded and then collapsed back into its own magma chamber, forming a huge caldera. Among certain New Age groups, Snæfellsjökull is considered one of the world's great 'power centres'. Today the crater is filled with the ice cap (highest point 1446m) and is a popular summer destination.

The best way to reach the glacial summit is to take a tour with Summit Adventure Guides (p229), Snæfellsjökull Glacier Tours (p229) or Go West! (p234). These companies approach the peak from the south, on Rte F570; Rte F570's northern approach (near Ólafsvík) is frustratingly rutty (4WD needed) and frequently closed due to weather-inflicted damage. Even the well trained and outfitted are not allowed to ascend the glacier without a local guide; contact the National Park Visitor Centre (p229) in Malarrif for more information.

Saxhöll Crater VOLCANO

(Rte 574) Southeast of the Öndverðarnes area, on Rte 574, follow the marked turn-off to the roadside scoria crater Saxhöll, which was responsible for some of the lava in the area. There's a drivable track leading to the base, from where it's an uneven 300m climb for magnificent views over the Neshraun lava flows.

GUÐRIÐUR ÞORBJARNARDÓTTIR: THE FAR TRAVELLER

Guðriður Þorbjarnardóttir was among Iceland's most celebrated explorers, and surely earned her nickname the 'Far Traveller'. Born in Hellnar before the year 1000 (a small sculpture marks the site of her family's farm at Laugarbrekka), Guðriður had a serious case of wanderlust. Not only was she one of the first Europeans to reach Vinland (thought to be Canada's Newfoundland), she bore a child while she was there: the first European born in North America! Later, Guðriður converted to Christianity and embarked on an epic pilgrimage to Rome, where some say she met the pope and recounted her experiences.

For more about Guðriður, read *Saga of Erik the Red* and *Saga of the Greenlanders*, or *The Far Traveler* by Nancy Marie Brown and *The Sea Road* by Margaret Elphinstone.

★ **Djúpalón Beach** BEACH

(Djúpalónssandur; Rte 572) On the southwest coast, Rte 572 leads off Rte 574 to wild black-sand beach Djúpalónssandur. It's a dramatic place to walk, with rock formations (an elf church, and a **kerling** – a troll woman), two brackish pools (for which the beach was named) and the rock-arch **Gatklettur**. Some of the black sands are covered in pieces of rusted metal from the English trawler *Eding,* which was shipwrecked here in 1948. An asphalt car park and public toilets allow tour-bus access, and crowds.

Down on the beach you can still see four **lifting stones** where fishing-boat crews would test the strength of aspiring fishermen. The smallest stone is Amloði (Bungler) at 23kg, followed by Hálfdrættingur (Weak) at 54kg, Hálfsterkur (Half-Strong) at 100kg, and the largest, Fullsterker (Fully Strong), at 154kg. Hálfdrættingur marked the frontier of wimphood, and any man who couldn't heft it was deemed unsuitable for a life at sea.

A series of rocky sea stacks, some of which are thought to be a troll church, emerge from the ocean up the coast as you tramp north over the craggy headland to reach the black-sand beach at **Dritvík**. From the 16th to the 19th century Dritvík was the largest fishing station in Iceland, with up to 60 fishing boats, but now there are only ruins near the edge of the lava field.

Vatnshellir NATURAL FEATURE

(Rte 574) This 8000-year-old lava tube with multiple caverns lies 32m below the earth's surface, 1km north of Malarrif. The pull-out is visible from Rte 574, and the tube can only be visited by guided tour with Summit Adventure Guides.

Malarrif LIGHTHOUSE

FREE About 2km south of Djúpalónssandur, a paved road leads down to the rocket-shaped lighthouse at Malarrif, from where you can walk 1km east along the cliffs to the rock pillars at **Lóndrangar** (an eroded crater; it also has its own parking off Rte 574), which surge up into the air in surprising pinnacles. Locals say that elves use the lava formations as a church. A bit further to the east lie the **Þúfubjarg bird cliffs**, also accessible from Rte 574. The National Park Visitor Centre – Gestastofa is here.

OFF THE BEATEN TRACK

DETOUR: RTE 590

The dramatic coastline of the oft-forgotten peninsula between the Snæfellsnes Peninsula and the Westfjords is traced by this 85km track (OK for 2WD; along Rte 60 look for the turn-off at Fellströnd). Windswept farmsteads lie frozen in time, and boulder-strewn hills, crowned with flattened granite, roll skyward. Keep a lookout for white-tailed eagles.

Near the beginning of the track, the farm at **Hvammur** produced a whole line of prominent Icelanders, including Snorri Sturluson of *Prose Edda* fame. It was settled in around 895 by Auður the Deep-Minded, the wife of the Irish king Olaf Godfraidh, who has a bit part in *Laxdæla Saga*. Árni Magnússon, who rescued most of the Icelandic sagas from a fire in Copenhagen in 1728, was also raised at Hvammur.

You can spend the night at well-renovated **Vogur Country Lodge** (435 0002; www.vogur.org; Rte 590, Fellsströnd; d/tr from 12,500/28,800kr; restaurant 6-9pm;) or remote, lovely **Guesthouse Nýp** (896 1930; www.nyp.is; Rte 590, Skarðsströnd; d without bathroom incl breakfast 13,800kr;). There's also a campground, **Á** (663 1420, 434 1420; traustibjarnason@gmail.com; Rte 590, Skarðsströnd; sites per tent or camper 3000kr; Jun-Aug), just before **Skarð** – a lonely farm that has remained in the hands of the same family for over 1000 years.

Tours

★Summit Adventure Guides ADVENTURE
(787 0001; www.summitguides.is) Offers much-loved 45-minute tours of the Vatnshellir lava tube (adult/child 3750kr/free). Guides shed light on the fascinating geological phenomenon and the region's troll-filled lore. Helmet and torch included. Dress warmly, wear hiking boots, and preferably gloves too. The outfit also runs myriad Snæfellsjökull glacier tours (13,900kr to 22,900kr) with a skiing option. They also have challenging fatbiking tours up Rauðhóll volcano (25,900kr).

Snæfellsjökull Glacier Tours SNOWMOBILE TOUR
(865 0061; www.theglacier.is; Litli-Kambur; snowcat tour adult/child 7900/5000kr, snowmobile tour 18,000kr; May-Aug) Two-hour snowcat (truck with chain wheels) and snowmobile tours ascend the glacier to about 1410m.

Sleeping & Eating

Most of the small towns just outside of the park have rental houses, campgrounds or guesthouses, which are an easy drive away. Summit Adventure Guides operates Westpark Guesthouse, just inside the north edge of the park.

Stock up on groceries in Borgarnes or Stykkishólmur; provisions and restaurants are few and far between in the park.

Westpark Guesthouse GUESTHOUSE €
(837 7700; www.westpark.is; Rte 574; s/d without bathroom from 8700/12,400kr, 4-bedroom house 34,000kr;) This large, simple guesthouse makes a handy base for exploring Snæfellsjökull National Park – it's the only lodging actually in the park, albeit on the edge, near a large TV antenna. It has shared bathrooms and kitchens.

Information

National Park Visitor Centre – Gestastofa
(Snæfellsjökull National Park Visitor Centre; 591 2000, 436 6888; www.snaefellsjokull.is; Malarrif; 10am-5pm late Apr-Oct, 11am-4pm Mon-Fri rest of year;) This visitor centre in Malarrif is the go-to spot for information on Snæfellsjökull National Park, with maps and brochures, as well as displays on local geology, history, flora, fauna and customs. Rangers have an active summer program of free park **guided tours**; check online or email. NB: the park office in Hellissandur is administrative only and not open to the public.

Getting There & Away

Having your own wheels is the best way to see the park.

Strætó (p429) runs bus 82 Stykkishólmur–Hellissandur runs twice daily mid-May to mid-September, continuing on to Arnarstapi once per day; the rest of the year it only goes from Stykkishólmur to Hellissandur four days per week.

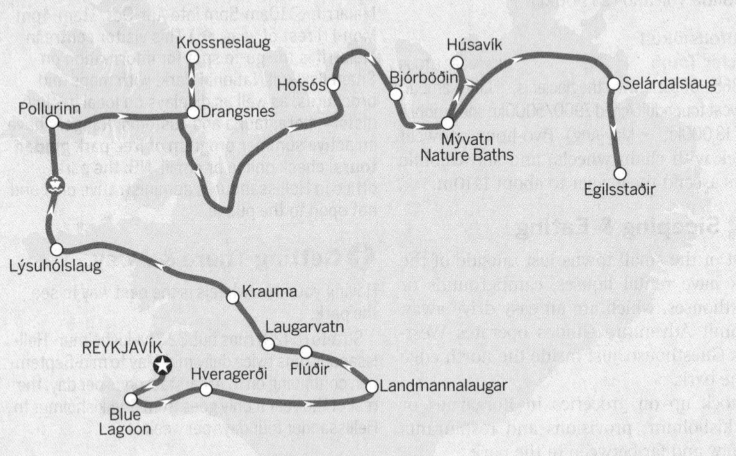

Krossneslaug
Húsavík
Hofsós
Bjórböðin
Selárdalslaug
Pollurinn
Drangsnes
Mývatn
Nature Baths
Egilsstaðir
Lýsuhólslaug
Krauma
Laugarvatn
REYKJAVÍK
Flúðir
Hveragerði
Landmannalaugar
Blue
Lagoon

VERVERIDIS VASILIS/SHUTTERSTOCK ©

2 WEEKS Hot-Pot Hop

Slap on those swimsuits and enjoy Iceland's favourite pastime: wading in warm, mineral-rich hot springs that soothe both the body and the mind. Hop across this geothermic kingdom, dipping your toes in at each source.

➡ Start in **Reykjavík** and do as the locals do – bring your backstroke and some gossip to share at the public pools.

➡ Next, try the **Blue Lagoon**, the Disneyland of swimming spots, and slather rich silica over your face.

➡ Pause in **Hveragerði**, one of Iceland's most geothermally active areas – bubbling water abounds.

➡ Head to **Landmannalaugar**, where a steaming stream is the perfect cure-all after some serious hiking.

➡ Cruise by **Flúðir** and see who else is in the natural, meadow-surrounded lagoon.

➡ Swing through mod Fontana, in **Laugarvatn**, for its naturally occurring geyser-sauna (you'll see!).

➡ Be drawn in by **Krauma**, a sleek new complex near Reykholt that harnesses the energy from Europe's biggest hot spring.

➡ Soak in **Lýsuhólslaug** and emerge from the algae soup with baby-soft skin.

➡ Scout out **Pollurinn**, just outside of Tálknafjörður – a favourite local hang-out.

➡ Blink and you'll miss the roadside hot-pots in **Drangsnes**, built into a sea wall.

➡ Bask in the otherworldly beauty at **Krossneslaug**, set along the wild, pebble-strewn shore.

➡ Check out stunning **Hofsós**, with near-infinity views from its fjord-side pool.

➡ Drop by Árskógssandur to quench your thirst at **Bjórböðin**, where wooden tubs are filled with beer, water, hops and yeast.

➡ The north's mellower version of the Blue Lagoon is found at **Mývatn Nature Baths**.

➡ Reenergise after a whale-watch tour at **GeoSea**, Húsavík's hot new attraction.

➡ Finish up at **Selárdalslaug**, tucked between two hillocks near Vopnafjörður.

➡ Fly back to Reykjavík from Egilsstaðir – but first check if **Vök Baths**, the new lakeside spa complex outside town, is ready for action.

SAM SPICER/GETTY IMAGES ©

Top: Mývatn Nature Baths (p311)
Bottom: Bather floats in a hot spring at Hveragerði (p131)

1

2

1. Drangsnes Hot-Pot (p267)
Drangsnes' free, geothermal, waterfront hot-pots are built into the sea wall.

2. Seljavallalaug (p150)
The Seljavallalaug geothermal pool, near Skogar, has become very popular with bathers.

3. Landmannalaugar (p156)
Home to mind-blowing multi-hued mountains, Landmannalaugar also offers hot-spring bathing.

4. Gamla Laugin (p129)
The 'secret lagoon' gets packed by mid-afternoon so it's best to visit earlier or later.

4

KOVOP58 / SHUTTERSTOCK ©

JEAFISH PING/SHUTTERSTOCK ©

3

GORODISSKIJ/SHUTTERSTOCK ©

Southern Snæfellsnes

To the east of Snæfellsjökull National Park, coastal Rte 574 passes the hamlets of Hellnar and Arnarstapi, with their glacier tour companies and interesting sea-sculpted rock formations. It continues east along the broad southern coastal plain, hugging huge sandy bays such as Breiðavík on one side, and towering peaks with waterfalls on the other. This stretch has some super horse riding.

Hellnar

Bárður, the subject of *Bárðar saga Snæfellsáss,* was part giant, part troll and part human. He chose an area near Hellnar, a picturesque spot overlooking a rocky bay, as his home (called Laugarbrekka). Towards the end of his intense saga, he became the guardian spirit of Snæfell. Today Hellnar is a tiny fishing village (once huge) where the shriek of seabirds fills the air and whales are regularly sighted.

Sights

Bárðarlaug, up near the main road, was supposedly Bárður's bathing pool, though the pond is no longer hot. Down on the shore, the cave **Baðstofa** is chock-a-block with nesting birds. Nearby is the head of the trail to Arnarstapi. Ancient, velvety moss-cloaked lava flows tumble east through the **Hellnahraun**.

Sleeping & Eating

★Fosshotel Hellnar HOTEL €€€
(☎435 6820; www.fosshotel.is; Brekkubær; d from 31,200kr; ⏲Mar-Nov; P 📶) Fosshotel Hellnar, with its sun-filled, comfortable rooms, is the area's choice sleeping option (and thus often booked solid). Even if you're not overnighting, we highly recommend having dinner at the **restaurant** (mains 3800-5000kr; ⏲6-10pm Mar-Nov; P 📶), which sources local organic produce for its Icelandic menu, plus offers heavenly *skyr* (yoghurt-like dessert). Reserve ahead. It's all run with sustainability in mind.

Primus Café CAFE €
(☎865 6740; www.facebook.com/primuskaffi; Hellnavegur; mains 1600-2600kr; ⏲10am-9pm May–mid-Sep, 11am-4pm mid-Sep–Apr) Welcoming spot for cakes, soups and simple meals.

★Fjöruhúsið SEAFOOD €€
(☎435 6844; www.facebook.com/FjoruhusidHellnum; cakes & quiches 950kr, mains 2500-2800kr; ⏲11am-10pm Jun-Aug, reduced hours Mar-May & Sep-Nov) It's well worth following the stone path down to the ocean's edge for the renowned fish soup at beautifully situated, quaint Fjöruhúsið, which is located by the bird cliffs at the trailhead of the scenic Hellnar–Arnarstapi path, it also serves coffee in sweet, old-fashioned china.

Getting There & Away

There's no public transport in Hellnar. You can catch Strætó (p429) bus 82 Stykkishólmur–Anarstapi (one daily mid-May to mid-September only) in nearby Arnarstapi.

HIKING THE COAST BETWEEN HELLNAR & ARNARSTAPI

Local maps detail myriad hiking trails connecting the sights of the Snæfellsnes Peninsula (www.snaefellsjokull.is). One of the most popular (and scenic) is the 2.5km coastal walk (around 40 minutes) between Hellnar and Arnarstapi. This slender trail follows the jagged coastline through a nature reserve, passing lava flows and eroded stone caves. During tumultuous weather, waves spray through the rocky arches; when it's fine, look for nesting seabirds.

Arnarstapi

Linked to Hellnar by both the main road and a wonderful coastal hike, this hamlet of summer cottages is nestled between the churning Arctic waters and the gnarled pillars of two neighbouring lava fields. A monument pays tribute to Jules Verne and a comical signpost measures distances to major cities via the earth's core. A second, enormous troll-like monument stands as a tribute to Bárður, the region's guardian spirit, and the leading character in a local saga.

Tours to ascend the Snæfellsjökull glacial crown usually start from near Arnarstapi.

Tours

★Go West! ADVENTURE TOUR, CYCLING TOUR
(☎695 9995; www.gowest.is) Friendly couple Jón Joel and Maggy run ecofriendly cycling, hiking, boating, hot-spring and glacier tours. Some focus on cultural aspects, others on landscape. Snæfellsjökull

glacier tours (from 22,000kr) are hikes, with crampons, ice axe etc included. Also runs tours in southern Iceland, or with Reykjavík pick-up.

Sleeping & Eating

There are summer cottages for rent in Arnarstapi. Buy groceries in Borgarnes or Stykkishólmur before arriving; there are no shops in town.

Arnarstapi Center Hotel & Cottages HOTEL, COTTAGES €€€
(Snjófell; ☎435 6783; www.arnarstapicenter.is; Arnarstapavegur; d/tr/q incl breakfast from 30,000/35,800/50,500kr, cottages from 33,700kr; ⌚Mar-Oct;) This brand-new hotel and cluster of cottages sprawls in the centre of Arnarstapi. Modern rooms have sleek bathrooms, and cottages are equipped with a coffee maker, microwave and fridge. There's also more basic shared-bathroom accommodation in an older guesthouse. The light-filled **restaurant** (mains 3600kr to 5200kr; open 9.30am to 10pm) serves fish, lamb and burgers. They may institute a campground.

Stapinn Café CAFE €
(☎766 7229; Arnarstapavegur; dishes 500-2400kr; ⌚noon-8pm or 9pm;) This small but welcoming cafe along the main road serves coffee drinks and a range of snacks, from cake to lamb schnitzel and burgers (including a vegan version).

Getting There & Away

There is no public transport going east. To get to Reykjavík, in summer take bus 82 to the Vatnaleið crossroads (at Rtes 56 and 55) and change for bus 58 to Borgarnes, where you must change once more.

Strætó (p429) runs bus 82 Stykkishólmur–Anarstapi (2300kr, one daily mid-May to mid-September); note it does not serve Arnarstapi in winter.

FROM ARNARSTAPI TOWARDS THE GLACIER

If you drive up the F570 from Arnarstapi, you'll pass **Stapafell** (526m), legendary home to the local little people, and you'll see miniature house gables painted onto rocks in their honour. Further along you'll pass a collapsed crater, which created a series of lava caves about 1.5km from the main road. The largest cave is **Sönghellir** (Song Cave), which is full of 18th-century graffiti and is rumoured to resound with the songs of dwarfs. Bring a torch to read the various markings and don't be shy about belting out your favourite melody.

Rauðfeldsgjá

Rauðfeldsgjá CANYON
Just north of Arnarstapi and Stapafell, on Rte 574, a small track branches off to the stunning Rauðfeldsgjá (pronounced *roith*-felds-gyow), a steep, narrow cleft that mysteriously disappears into the cliff wall. Birds wheel overhead, a stream runs along the bottom of the gorge, and you can slink between the sheer walls for quite a distance. The gorge figures in a dramatic part of the local saga of Bárður, described on a sign at the parking area.

Breiðavík

East of Rauðfeldsgjá, Rte 574 skirts the edges of an enormous sandy bay at Breiðavík (pronounced *bray*-tha-veek). The windswept coast, with its yellow expanse of sand, is wonderfully peaceful, though tricky to access. The pasture-filled region running along the coastal mountains from here east to Vegamót is considered one of the best places in Iceland for horse riding, and there are several stables of international repute.

On the eastern edge of Breiðavík, look for the placard telling the grisly tale of Axlar-Björn, Iceland's notorious 16th-century serial killer, who made his living in lean times by murdering travellers here.

Tours

Stóri Kambur HORSE RIDING
(☎852 7028; www.storikambur.is; Rte 574; ⌚late May–mid-Sep) A family-run operation offering one-/two-hour rides on the beach (from 8000/14,000kr), some with an historical saga them, and all with glacier views when it's clear. Short kids' rides costs 3500kr. They have cottages to let (for two people from 20,000kr).

Búðir & Búðahraun

Búðir has a lonely church and a hotel, but there is no sign of its former fishing village along its craggy, mossy inlets. A walking trail leads across the elf-infested nature preserve, Buðahraun lava field. The ancient lava field is protected; if you look down into its hollows and cracks you'll find flourishing flowers and ferns, many of them protected native Icelandic species. The path also leads to the crater Búðaklettur. According to local legend, a lava tube beneath Buðahraun, paved with gold and precious stones, leads all the way to Surtshellir in upper Borgarfjörður. It takes about three hours to walk to the crater and back.

Sleeping & Eating

Hótel Buðir HOTEL €€€

(☎435 6700; www.hotelbudir.is; Buðir; d 39,900-54,500kr, ste 72,000kr; @ 📶) Windswept and on a gorgeous, remote coastline, Hótel Buðir tries to be stylish, though it's besieged by tour groups and prices are stiff for what you get. Room 28 has the best views (and a teeny balcony). The restaurant (mains 4700kr to 6000kr) is sometimes closed to those not in prebooked tour groups.

> **HJARÐARHOLT & THE SAGAS**
>
> Although the Dalir is central to several of the best-loved Icelandic sagas, little remains of the original farms. For example no trace remains of **Hjarðarholt**, the one-time home of Kjartan Ólafsson and his father, Ólaf the Peacock. Their farmstead was said to be one of the wonders of the Norse world, with scenes from the sagas carved into the walls, and a huge dining hall that could seat 1100. You will find, however, a beautiful **church** on the site with great views over the valley where the region's history unfurled.
>
> Nearby, and also on the Laxá River, **Höskuldsstaðir** was the birthplace of Hallgerður Longlegs (also called Longtresses), wife of Gunnar of Hlíðarendi, who starred in *Njál's Saga*. Other important residents of the farm include Bolli and his foster brother Kjartan from *Laxdæla Saga*.

Lýsuhóll to Gerðuberg

Horse ranches dot this area (several offering accommodation). Grassy fields and sandy beaches alternate with lava fields and mountain backdrops, making for great riding country.

Sights & Activities

★**Lýsuhólslaug** GEOTHERMAL POOL

(☎433 9917; lysuholslaug@gmail.com; adult/child 1000/300kr; ⏲11am-8.30pm Jun–mid-Aug) The geothermal source for Lýsuhólslaug pumps carbonated, mineral-filled waters in at a perfect 37°C to 39°C. Don't be alarmed that the pool is a murky green: the iron-rich water attracts some serious algae. Find it just beyond the horse ranch at Lýsuhóll.

Gerðuberg LANDMARK

Just where Rte 54 curves between the Snæfellsnes Peninsula and the mainland, you'll find the dramatic basalt towers of Gerðuberg rising from the plain.

★**Lýsuhóll** HORSE RIDING, COTTAGES

(☎435 6716; www.lysuholl.is) Equine enthusiasts should look no further than this friendly horse farm. Even if you're not riding, the farm and its guesthouse and cottages (single/double/quad including breakfast 16,500/20,000/35,000kr, cottage 27,000kr) are a fun place to stay. Guides will show you around the stables, and there are both short excursions (one hour 7000kr) and multiday tours (eight days €1850).

Ytri-Tunga WILDLIFE WATCHING

The deserted farmstead at Ytri-Tunga, just east of Hof, occasionally has a colony of seals offshore, best seen in June and July.

Sleeping & Eating

Traðir Guesthouse GUESTHOUSE €€

(☎431 5353; www.tradirguesthouse.net; Rte 54, Traðir farm; sites per adult/child 1500kr/free, d without bathroom from 18,600kr, cottage from 26,500kr; 📶) Comfortable guest rooms, cottages and a campsite are set on the shore of the southern Snæfellsnes Peninsula, and there's a small cafe serving simple meals. It also offers horse riding, and fishing licences for the nearby Staðará River.

Hotel Rjúkandi HOTEL €€

(☎788 9100; www.rjukandi.com; cnr Rtes 54 & 56, Vegamót; d/q incl breakfast 20,200/36,600kr; ⏲cafe 10am-6pm, restaurant 6-10pm Jun-Aug, to 8pm Sep-May; 📶👪) 🌿 Vegamót means 'crossroads', and that's exactly where you'll find this sustainably operated hotel, cafe and restaurant. Simple, clean rooms have private bathrooms. You'll probably spot its cafe, Rjúkandi Kaffi (snacks 450kr to 1700kr), first. It's next to the N1 station, and is loaded with homemade cakes, daily soups and happy locals. The hotel's restaurant serves well-presented Icelandic fare.

Guesthouse Hof GUESTHOUSE, COTTAGE €€
(☎846 3897; www.gistihof.is; Rte 54, Hof farmstead; d with/without bathroom 17,500/14,900kr, 2-bedroom houses from 28,000kr; 📶👪) Friendly Hof has a varied selection of basic apartment-style accommodation, each with its own hot tub and beautiful views, as well as free-standing cabins with private bathrooms, and their own shared kitchen cabin. There is also sleeping-bag accommodation. Wi-fi in public areas only.

DALIR

The scenic corridor of rolling fields and craggy river-carved buttes between West Iceland and the Westfjords is known as Dalir. It served as the setting for the *Laxdæla Saga,* the most popular of the Icelandic sagas. The story revolves around a love triangle between Guðrun Ósvífursdóttir, said to be the most beautiful woman in Iceland, and the foster brothers Kjartan Ólafsson and Bolli Þorleiksson. In typical saga fashion, Guðrun had both men wrapped around her little finger and schemed and connived until both were dead – Kjartan at the hands of Bolli, and Bolli at the hands of Kjartan's brothers. Most Icelanders know the stories and characters by heart and hold the area in which the story took place in great historic esteem.

Eiríksstaðir

Eiríksstaðir Reconstruction LANDMARK
(☎434 1118; www.leif.is; Rte 586; adult/child 1500kr/free; ⏰9am-6pm Jun-Aug) The farm Eiríksstaðir was home to Eiríkur Rauðe (Erik the Red), father of Leifur Eiríksson, the first European to visit America. Although only a faint outline of the original farm remains, a reconstructed turf house was built using only the tools and materials available at the time. Period-dressed guides show visitors around and tell the story of Erik the Red, who went on to found the first European settlement in Greenland.

Find Eiríksstaðir 8km inland on gravel and paved Rte 586, east of Stóra-Vatnshorn's church, on Haukadalsá River.

OFF THE BEATEN TRACK

COUNTRY LIVING

Part of the charm of the Dalir is its vast, rolling expanses of farmland and river valleys. Soak up the mood in the peaceful countryside by sleeping over at renovated farmhouse **Sauðafell Guesthouse** (☎846 6012; www.facebook.com/Saudafell-Guesthouse-1289366557754710/; Rte 60, Sauðafell farm; d without bathroom incl breakfast 23,300kr; 📶). Or explore remote Hörðudal valley (Rte 581), where the Snaefellsnes Peninsula joins the Dalir, and stay in a cottage at **Dalahyttur** (☎586 1025; www.dalahyttur.is; Rte 581, Hlíð; cottage 22,700kr), with sweeping views of Hólsfjall mountain, or at its neighbour **Seljaland Guesthouse** (☎434 1116; www.seljaland.is; Rte 581; d/tr 15,000/16,000kr; ⏰mid-May–mid-Sep; 📶).

Búðardalur

POP 272

Founded as a cargo depot in Saga times, the pin-sized town of Búðardalur (pronounced *boo*-thar-dalur) occupies a pleasant position looking out over Hvammsfjörður, at the mouth of the Laxá River. A current claim to fame is its dairy, which produces most of the cheese in Iceland. The local supermarket carries a good sampling.

Sleeping & Eating

Búðardalur Campground CAMPGROUND €
(☎434 1644; www.visitdalir.is; sites per adult/child 1500kr/free) This simple roadside campsite has showers (included) and laundry.

Dalakot GUESTHOUSE €€
(☎434 1644; www.dalakot.is; Dalbraut 2; d with/without bathroom 17,500/12,300kr; 📶) Guesthouse Dalakot has simple rooms, and a restaurant (open noon to 9pm) specialising in pizza and burgers (mains 1700kr to 3000kr).

Leifsbúð Café & Restaurant CAFE €€
(☎434 1441; www.leifsbud.is; Búðarbraut 1; 11am-4pm & 6-9pm Wed-Mon May-Sep; ⏰snacks

WORTH A TRIP

ERPSSTAÐIR DAIRY FARM

When the peanut gallery starts moaning, 'Are we there yet?', you know it's time to head to **Erpsstaðir** (☎868 0357; www.erpsstadir.is; Rte 60; cowshed tour adult/child 600kr/free; ⊙11am-6pm mid-Jun–mid-Aug, 1-5pm mid-May–mid-Jun & mid-Aug–mid-Sep;), the perfect place to stretch your legs. Like a mirage for sweet-toothed wanderers, this dairy farm on the gorgeous Rte 60 (between Búðardalur and the Ring Road; with high mountain valleys, streams and waterfalls) specialises in delicious homemade ice cream (400kr). You can tour the farm, greet the buxom bovines, chickens, rabbits and even guinea pigs, then gorge on a scoop. The farm also sells *skyr* (yoghurt-like dessert) and cheese ; try the rocket-shaped skyr-konfekt (meant to look like an udder), a delicious dessert made with a hard white chocolate shell encasing thick skyr. It'll blow you away..

Erpsstaðir also offers a **rental house** (from 26,000kr; linen 1000kr per person) for those contemplating ice cream for breakfast

800-1800kr, mains 1800-3200kr;) This little eatery near the water offers cakes, soup and salad, as well as full seafood and pasta meals.

Veiðistaðurinn SEAFOOD €€
(☎434 1110; www.facebook.com/pg/veidistadurinn; Vesturbraut 12a (Rte 60); mains 2500-5000kr; ⊙noon-3pm & 6-9.30pm Mon-Thu, noon-9.30pm Fri-Sun) This simple shopfront houses a seafood joint run by a friendly family serving dishes from fish-and-chips to mussels.

Shopping

Bolli Craft ARTS & CRAFTS
(☎434 1410; www.facebook.com/bollicraft; Vesterbraut 12; ⊙10am-6pm May-Sep, Fri-Sun Oct) Cool local arts and crafts include handmade sweaters, sheep-horn buttons and charming elves.

Getting There & Away

Strætó (p429) runs bus 59 Borgarnes–Bifröst–Búðardalur–Skriðuland–Króksfjarðarnes–Hólmavík (to Hólmavík 3220kr, one hour, one Monday, Wednesday, Friday and Sunday, reduced in winter). It stops in Búðardalur at the N1 petrol station.

Laugar

Just north of the spot where Rte 590 heads west off Rte 60 you'll find the encampment at Laugar, the birthplace of *Laxdæla Saga* beauty Guðrun Ósvífursdóttir. Historians believe they've found **Guðrun's bathing pool (Guðrúnarlaug)**: the hot pool is well marked above the entrance to Hótel Edda, and has a small changing kiosk. **Tungustapi**, in the distance, is a large elf cathedral.

Sights

Dalir Heritage Museum MUSEUM
(☎434 1328; www.dalir.is/thjonusta/byggdasafn/; Hótel Edda; adult/child 1000kr/free; ⊙10am-4pm Jun-Aug, by appointment Sep-May) This neat museum's curator is a wonderful character who knows a great deal about Dalir's brilliant history, and if you make your way through the innumerable artefacts, there's an unexpected 1883 traditional **baðstofa** (living/sleeping room). The museum is in the basement of the hotel.

Sleeping & Eating

Hótel Edda HOTEL, CAMPGROUND €€
(☎444 4930; www.hoteledda.is; Sælingsdalur; sites per person 1200kr, d with/without bathroom 20,325/11,700kr; ⊙early Jun–late Aug;) The Hótel Edda has a newer wing with surprisingly modern rooms, an older hospital-style annexe with shared bathrooms, and sleeping-bag space in converted classrooms. The **restaurant** (mains 2200-4400kr; ⊙6-9pm early Jun–late Aug) gets good reviews – it serves the delicious ice cream from Erpsstaðir, plus there's a large swimming pool.

The Westfjords

Includes ➡

Best Places to Eat

- Tjöruhúsið (p256)
- Dunhagi (p248)
- Fisherman Kitchen (p252)
- Litlibær (p261)
- Stúkuhúsið (p247)

Best Places to Stay

- Hótel Djúpavík (p268)
- Hótel Laugarhóll (p268)
- Camping in Hornstrandir Nature Reserve (p262)
- Stekkaból (p246)
- Guesthouse Kirkjuból í Bjarnardal (p251)

Why Go?

The Westfjords is where Iceland's dramatic landscapes come to a riveting climax and where mass tourism disappears – only about 10% of Iceland's visitors ever see the region. Jagged bird cliffs and broad multihued dream beaches flank the south. Rutted dirt roads snake north along jaw-dropping coastal fjords and over immense central mountains, revealing tiny fishing villages embracing traditional ways of life. In the far north, the Hornstrandir hiking reserve crowns the quiet region, and is home to cairn-marked walking paths revealing bird life, Arctic foxes and ocean vistas. The Strandir coast is less visited still, with an end-of-the-line, mystical feel, geothermal springs and minuscule oceanside hamlets.

Leave plenty of time: unpaved roads weave around fjords and over pothole-pitted mountain passes, but the scenery is never short of breathtaking. Once you get used to it, you may not want to leave.

Road Distances (km)

	Patreksfjörður	Þingeyri	Ísafjörður	Holmavík	Norðurfjörður
Þingeyri	129				
Ísafjörður	175	47			
Holmavík	234	265	221		
Norðurfjörður	333	348	303	105	
Reykjavík	397	405	450	230	334

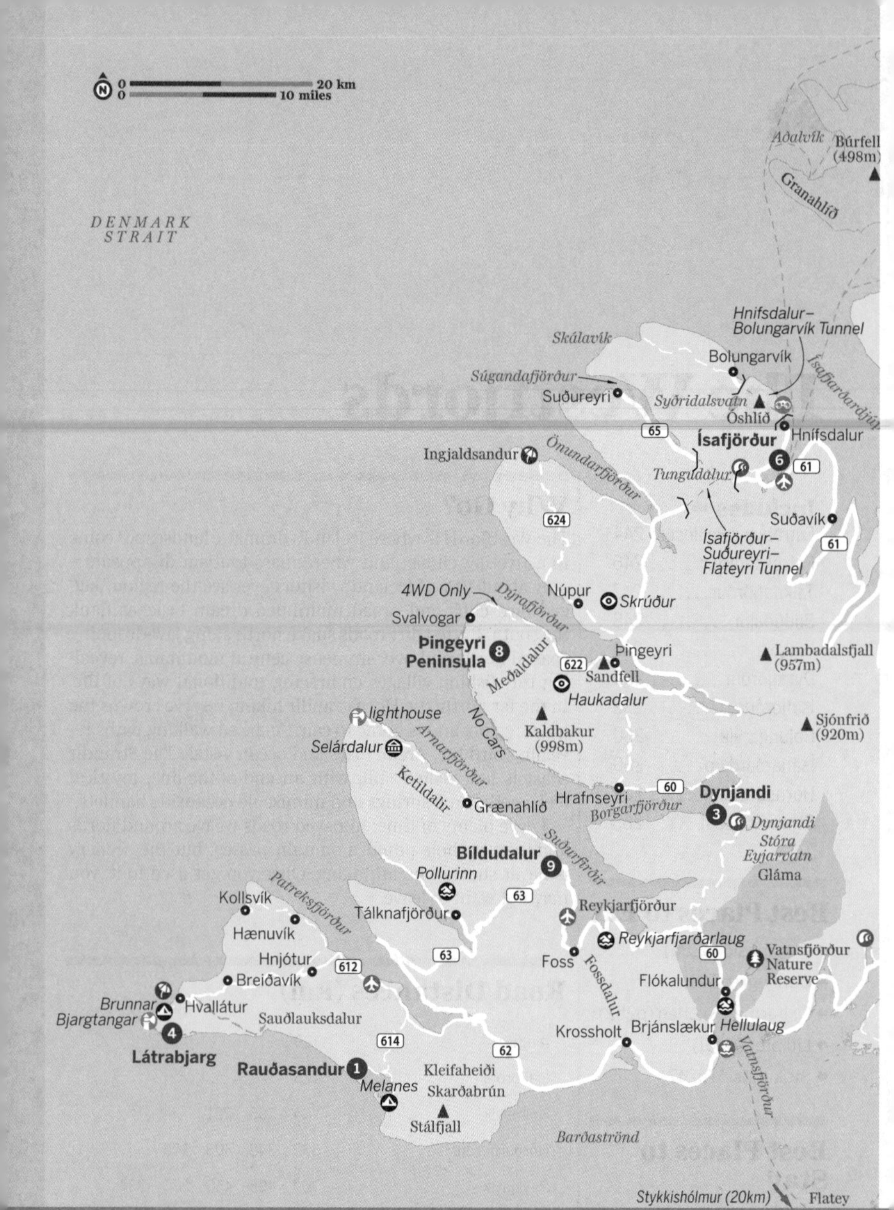

0 20 km
0 10 miles

DENMARK STRAIT

Aðalvík
Búrfell (498m)
Granahlíð
Skálavík
Hnífsdalur–Bolungarvík Tunnel
Bolungarvík
Ísafjarðardjúp
Súgandafjörður
Suðureyri
Syðridalsvatn
Óshlíð
65
Ísafjörður
Hnífsdalur
Ingjaldsandur
Önundarfjörður
Tungudalur
6
61
624
Suðavík
Ísafjörður–Suðureyri–Flateyri Tunnel
61
4WD Only
Dýrafjörður
Núpur
Skrúður
Svalvogar
Þingeyri Peninsula
8
Meðaldalur
Þingeyri
622
Sandfell
Lambadalsfjall (957m)
Haukadalur
lighthouse
No Cars
Kaldbakur (998m)
Sjónfrið (920m)
Selárdalur
Arnarfjörður
Ketildalir
Grænahlíð
Hrafnseyri
60
Borgarfjörður
Dynjandi
3
Dynjandi
Stóra Eyjarvatn
Gláma
Bíldudalur
9
Suðurfirðir
Pollurinn
Patreksfjörður
Kollsvík
63
Reykjarfjörður
Hænuvík
Tálknafjörður
Reykjarfjarðarlaug
Hnjótur
63
60
Vatnsfjörður Nature Reserve
612
Foss
Fossdalur
Breiðavík
Flókalundur
Brunnar
Hvallátur
Bjargtangar
Sauðlauksdalur
Hellulaug
4
Krossholt
Brjánslækur
Látrabjarg
614
62
Vatnsfjörður
Rauðasandur
1
Kleifaheiði
Melanes
Skarðabrún
Stálfjall
Barðaströnd
Stykkishólmur (20km)
Flatey

The Westfjords Highlights

1 Rauðasandur (p245) Exploring an ethereal rosy beach and azure lagoon while looking for basking seals.

2 Hornstrandir Nature Reserve (p262) Roving saw-cliffs and spying on Arctic foxes.

3 Dynjandi (p249) Letting the mists of this majestic waterfall swirl around you as you climb its dizzying cascades.

4 Látrabjarg (p245) Watching tilting puffins swoop around gigantic sheer bird cliffs.

5 Reykjarfjörður (p268) Delighting in the cutting-edge art at a former herring factory.

6 Ísafjörður (p254) Discovering the region's compelling past in its cosmopolitan capital.

7 Strandir coast (p265) Exploring a magical, mystical coast then soaking in Krossneslaug – a geothermal infinity pool.

8 Þingeyri Peninsula (p249) Fat biking along remote coastal tracks to the lighthouse at Svalvogar.

9 Bíldudalur (p248) Spooking yourself with sea-monster lore then heading out to the tip of breathtaking Arnarfjörður.

10 Ísafjarðardjúp (p260) Duelling with Arctic terns on Vigur island and kayaking in a vast, seal-studded fjord.

SOUTH COAST

The sparsely populated south coast of the Westfjords is a tiny version of what's to come on the wild and wonderful peninsulas further north. Remote fjords (in a smaller version here) twist into the coastline, and though there's been a new road built to cut across their desolate isolation, it's still a bare and dramatic place. It's the primary breeding area for the endangered white-tailed eagle.

Reykhólar

Tiny Reykhólar sits on the southern edge of the Reykjanes Peninsula, a minor geothermal area and gateway to the southernmost section of the Westfjords. To the east Gilsfjörður is an eagle breeding ground, and west along the coast, the key inlets for eagle spotting are Þorskafjörður, Djúpifjörður and Vatnsfjörður.

Sights & Activities

Reykhólar Tourist Office Museum MUSEUM
(☎894 1011; www.visitreykholahreppur.is; museum adult/child 750/500kr; ⏲11am-5pm early-Jun–Aug; 📶) The well-managed tourist office has a little museum with antique boats, stuffed birds and a movie of local life in the 1950s and '60s. There's a small on-site cafe (snacks from 600kr), plus lots of Westfjords information.

Grettislaug GEOTHERMAL POOL, HOT-POT
(☎434 7738; www.visitreykholahreppur.is; Grettiströð; adult/child 570/250kr; ⏲9am-9pm mid-June–Aug, shorter hours rest of year) The outdoor pool at Grettislaug is a magnet for local families and the two soothing hot-pots alongside have views over the plains leading to the sea.

There's a small campground just behind (per person 1700kr).

White-Tailed Eagle Centre MUSEUM
(☎894 1011; www.visitreykholahreppur.is; Króksfjarðarnes; adult/child 600kr/free; ⏲11am-6pm mid-Jun–mid-Aug) The White-Tailed Eagle Centre highlights the attempts to increase the population of the struggling species, which peaked in 2011 at 66 nests. It also has a handicraft market. The centre is just north of the causeway on Rte 60 that crosses Gilsfjörður.

Strætó (p67) bus 59 Hólmavík–Búðardalur–Borgarnes stops outside.

Reykhólar Sea Baths HOT-POT
(Sjávarsmiðjan; ☎577 4800; www.sjavarsmidjan.is; Vesturbraut; adult/child 3900kr/free; ⏲variable) In windswept Reykhólar, the seaweed baths give you soft skin and a view of the coastal plain, rimmed by salt bays. It tends to be open 1pm to 7pm from early June to August, but hours can vary, so call to check.

Norður Salt LANDMARK
(☎537 9095; www.nordursalt.com; Hafnarslóð 1) Norður Salt, on the point in Reykhólar, processes sea salt from the local salt bays. You can peek in its windows.

Sleeping & Eating

There are no restaurants in Reykhólar, just a minuscule cafe at the tourist office. There's a small grocery store at the two-pump petrol station (open 10am to 6pm); Hótel Bjarkalundur, 15km northeast on Rte 60, serves food.

Miðjanes GUESTHOUSE $
(☎690 3825; ⏲s/d without bathroom 6100/11,100kr) There's a tranquil feel at this cattle and sheep farm at the foot of a steep ridge near a rushing waterfall. Here unfussy rooms have wide views of the shore and Breiðafjörður beyond. Miðjanes is set just back from Rte 607, 5km west of Reykhólar.

Reykhólar HI Hostel HOSTEL $
(Álftaland; ☎863 2362, 892 7558; www.hostel.is; Maríutröð; dm/s/d/q without bathroom 6100/10,600/15,200/23,300kr; ⏲May-Sep; 📶👪) A well-equipped kitchen, cosy lounge, luxury bathroom and pristine bedrooms make for a comfortable stay here. The dorms and their showers are simpler but still good quality, and everyone can use the free coffee and hot-pot out back.

Hótel Bjarkalundur HOTEL $$
(☎519 2626; www.hotelbjarkalundur.is; d with/without bathroom 15,100/11,600kr, cabins from 16,600kr; ⏲May-Oct; 📶) A heritage-themed revamp of Bjarkalundur's public rooms reflect its status as the oldest summer hotel in Iceland. Now dark green walls frame polished wood furniture, well-worn books and wing-backed chairs. Bedrooms are styled more plainly and overall the hotel hasn't quite shaken off a motel feel. Bjarkalundur also offers cabins, camping (per person 1500kr) and has a decent restaurant.

Getting There & Away

Strætó (p429) bus 59 Hólmavík–Búðardalur–Borgarnes stops at Króksfjarðarnes' White-Tailed Eagle Centre, but doesn't go into Reykhólar.

TRANSPORT & THE WESTFJORDS

Getting There & Away

From Reykjavík's domestic airport, **Air Iceland Connect** (☎570 3030; www.airicelandconnect.is; Reykjavík Domestic Airport) has twice-daily flights to Ísafjörður; Eagle Air (p428) flies from Reykjavík to Bíldudalur and Gjögur.

You can take Baldur Car Ferry (p244) between West Iceland at Stykkishólmur and Brjánslækur in the Westfjords. Coming from Reykjavík, take Strætó (p429) bus 57 to Borgarnes then take bus 58 to Stykkishólmur. The Westfjords ferry terminal in Brjánslækur is served in summer only by **Westfjords Adventures** (☎456 5006; www.westfjordsadventures.com) bus.

From Hólmavík on the Westfjord's Strandir Coast, year-round Strætó bus 59 runs to Borgarnes; there are connections to Reykjavík, Akureyri and Staðarskáli from Borgarnes. En route, it stops at Króksfjarðarnes' White-Tailed Eagle Centre, too.

Getting Around

Bus service in the Westfjords can change from year to year. Check www.westfjords.is or www.publictransport.is for the latest info.

Hólmavík is connected by regional bus Hópferðamiðstöð Vestfjarða (p257) to Ísafjörður, mid-May to mid-September.

Ísafjörður **municipal buses** (☎456 5518; www.isafjordur.is) go to Bolungarvík, Suðureyri, Flateyri and Þingeyri.

From June to August Westfjords Adventures has a bus that connects Patreksfjörður–Brjánslækur–Flókalundur–Dynjandi–Þingeyri–Ísafjörður (one daily each direction Monday, Wednesday and Friday).You can also pre-book for services in late-May and early-September.

From June to August, a bus (14,500kr regardless of destination) runs from Brjánslækur to Patreksfjörður, Látrabjarg and Rauðasandur, then back to Brjánslækur, which returns in time for the ferry back to Stykkishólmur.

A **Flybus** (☎893 0809, 456 2336, 893 2636; flat rate 2000kr) runs by request from Patreksfjörður to meet flights into Bíldudalur Airport.

Petrol & Driving

There is car rental in Ísafjörður and Patreksfjörður and at Bíldudalur Airport. NOTE: The road between Hrafnseyri and Þingeyri is closed for six to eight months in winter. Check www.road.is.

- Throughout the Westfjords, petrol stations can be few and far between; fill up whenever you have the chance.
- The Westfjords official tourist map shows the N1 petrol stations.
- Many of the stations have unstaffed pumps; using these requires a credit card with a PIN.
- You can also buy N1 cards stocked with credit when you do find someone at a full-service station. We recommend it, just in case your own credit card does not work in a pinch.
- Expect lots of unpaved, often rugged, but universally beautiful roads; most are accessible with a 2WD.
- For ride-sharing, consult www.samferda.net.

DON'T MISS

HELLULAUG

The memorable natural hot-pot **Hellulaug** (Rte 62; by donation) lies about 500m east of Hótel Flókalundur on Rte 62 and in among the rocks near the seashore. At high tide, do as the locals do and jump in the frigid sea, then run back to the big toasty rockpool to warm up (38°C).

Flókalundur

Flókalundur, on the junction between the road up to Arnarfjörður and Ísafjörður, and Rte 62 to the southwestern peninsulas, sits at the head of Vatnsfjörður. The two-house encampment at Flókalundur was named after the Viking explorer Hrafna-Flóki Vilgerðarson, who gave Iceland its name in AD 860.

Today, the most interesting thing in the area is a wonderful natural hot spring and the **Vatnsfjörður Nature Reserve**, established to protect the area around Lake Vatnsdalsvatn, a nesting site for harlequin ducks and great northern divers (loons). Various hiking trails run around the lake and into the hills beyond. Pick up a hiking brochure at Hótel Flókalundur.

Sleeping

Hótel Flókalundur HOTEL **$$**
(☎456 2011; www.flokalundur.is; sites per person 1500kr, d incl breakfast 24,500kr; ⊗mid-May–mid-Sep;) Hótel Flókalundur, a recently updated bungalow-style hotel, features small, tidy wood-panelled rooms with renovated bathrooms. Its **restaurant** (lunch mains 1500-3500kr, dinner mains 3000-5000kr; ⊗7.30-10am & 11am-9pm;) has plate-glass windows overlooking the fjord. There's camping too, and a petrol pump. Only hotel guests can use the wi-fi.

Brjánslækur

Brjánslækur is nothing more than the terminus for the *Baldur* ferry from Stykkishólmur and Flatey. West of the ferry terminal, rugged Rte 62 follows the coast until it reaches the top of scenic Patreksfjörður, marking the beginning of the southwest peninsulas.

A simple **cafe** (☎860 0220; Rte 62; snacks 450-1300kr; ⊗10am-7pm Jun-Aug) that serves soup, sandwiches and hot dogs during summer; also sells ferry tickets and has brochures.

Getting There & Away

Brjánslækur is the terminus for the **Baldur Car Ferry** (☎433 2254; www.seatours.is; Rte 62). To get to Reykjavík, catch the ferry from Brjánslækur to Stykkishólmur, then take Strætó (p429) bus 58 to Borgarnes and transfer to bus 57 to Reykjavík.

From June to August Westfjords Adventures (p243) runs a bus along the route Patreksfjörður–Brjánslækur–Flókalundur–Ísafjörður, stopping in Brjánslækur (to Patreksfjörður 3000kr, to Ísafjörður 8400kr, one daily each direction Monday, Wednesday and Friday). You can also pre-book for services in late May and early September.

With pre-booking, Westfjords Adventures also runs a summer-time bus from Brjánslækur to Patreksfjörður, Látrabjarg and Rauðasandur, then back to Brjánslækur (14,500kr for the circuit, no matter where you get on), which returns in time for the ferry back to Stykkishólmur.

The closest car rental is in Patreksfjörður.

SOUTHWEST PENINSULAS

The trident-shaped peninsulas in the southwest of the Westfjords are spectacularly scenic. It's a truly wild-feeling area, where white, black, red and pink beaches meet shimmering blue water, and towering cliffs and stunning mountains cleave the fjords. The region's most popular destination is Látrabjarg, a 12km stretch of cliffs that is home to thousands of nesting seabirds in summer. The pitted roads in this sparsely populated region are rough and driving is slow – take a deep breath, you'll get there!

Látrabjarg Peninsula

Best known for its dramatic cliffs and abundant bird life, the remote Látrabjarg Peninsula also has wonderful, deserted, multihued beaches, such as the exquisite Rauðasandur, and plenty of long, leisurely walks. Roads are sandy, pitted and bumpy, but you really won't mind.

Sights

Joining Rte 612 from Rte 62, you'll pass the rusting hulk of the fishing boat *Garðar* near the head of the fjord. From there you'll start encountering empty, golden beaches, the airstrip at Sauðlauksdalur and sights dotted around the peninsula.

★Rauðasandur BEACH

Stunning Rauðasandur beach stretches out in shades of pink and red sands on the southern edge of the peninsula. Pounded by surf and backed by a huge azure lagoon, it's an exceptionally beautiful, serene place. You can walk out to the lagoon edge at low tide; keep a lookout for seals. A coastal path (about 20km) runs between Rauðasandur and the Látrabjarg bird cliffs. Approach Rauðasandur by car from Rte 612 by taking steep, winding Rte 614 for about 10km.

★Breiðavík BEACH

An enormous and stunning golden-sand beach, framed by rocky cliffs and the turquoise waters of the bay. Certainly one of Iceland's best beaches, the idyllic spot is usually deserted. The large Hotel Breiðavík (p246) is here.

Bjargtangar Lighthouse LIGHTHOUSE

At the tip of the Látrabjarg Peninsula, the Bjargtangar Lighthouse, Europe's westernmost point (if you don't count the Azores), comes into view. Just up the slope you'll find the renowned Látrabjarg bird cliffs.

Hvallátur BEACH

Eight kilometres west of Breiðavík, the tiny hamlet of Hvallátur has a gorgeous white-sand beach, but no services.

Minjasafn Egils Ólafssonar Museum MUSEUM

(Hnjótur Museum; ☎456 1511; www.hnjotur.is; Hnjótur, Örlygshöfn; adult/child 1000kr/free; ⏲10am-6pm May-Sep; Wi-Fi) In Hnjótur, about 10km west of Sauðlauksdalur, it's worth stopping at tthis museum. The eclectic collection includes salvaged fishing boats and displays on regional history, from whaling and farming to 1947 footage of a trawler wreck. There's a basic cafe (cake 500kr).

Activities

★Látrabjarg Bird Cliffs BIRDWATCHING

These renowned, dramatic cliffs on the headland beside Bjargtangar Lighthouse extend for 12km. Ranging from 40m to 400m they're mobbed by nesting seabirds in early summer. Unbelievable numbers of puffins, razorbills, guillemots, cormorants, fulmars, gulls and kittiwakes nest here from June to mid-August. It's best to visit in the evening, when the birds return to their nests.

On calm days, seals are often seen basking on the skerries around the lighthouse. Beware: the cliffs are prone to erosion and there are few railings – use extreme caution, especially when winds are high. There are no facilities (the nearest toilet is at Brunnar campsite, 2km east, on the road in); camping at the cliffs is prohibited.

Tours

Patreksfjörður tour operator Westfjord Adventures (p246) offers hiking and guided trips to view birds and seals; guides can meet you on the peninsula or take you out there.

Sleeping & Eating

The few camping and accommodation options are remote, rather basic and usually in gorgeous settings.

★Melanes Camping CAMPGROUND $

(☎783 6600; www.melanes.com; Rauðasandur; sites per adult/child 1500kr/free, pods 9900kr; ⏲mid-May–mid-Sep) Melanes is one of the Westfjords most spectacularly sited campsites – sitting as it does right beside sweeping Rauðasandur cove. The grassy site has new flush toilets, showers, a kitchen and a laundry, and best of all a clutch of adorable hobbit-sized, two-person wooden pods.

Melanes is 4km southeast of the turn-off from Rte 614 to Rauðasandur.

Brunnar Camping CAMPGROUND

FREE You can camp right beside the beach at Brunnar, about 2km before (northeast of) the Látrabjarg bird cliffs. There are basic toilets but no reliable running water. Camping at the bird cliffs themselves is prohibited.

Hnjótur Guesthouse GUESTHOUSE, CAMPGROUND $$

(☎456 1596, 893 8024; www.hnjoturtravel.is; Hnjótur, Örlygshöfn; site per person 2000kr, d with/without bathroom 23,000/18,000kr, f 28,000kr; Wi-Fi) It's not super-fancy, but the bedrooms at Hnjótur are comfy and owner Kristen is warmly welcoming – he'll even cook up a fish supper on request. The upstairs rooms are smarter, and there's a kitchen, a deck and a cluster of new wooden cabins outside.

Hótel Látrabjarg HOTEL $$$

(☎456 1500; www.latrabjarg.com; Örlygshöfn; s/d/tr from 24,160/36,600/46,500kr; ⏲mid-May–mid-Sep) This former boarding school has been converted into an appealing hotel with tasteful, modern rooms decked out in bright colours. To get to the hotel, turn right onto

Rte 615 just after the museum at Hnjótur and drive about 3km.

Hotel Breiðavík GUESTHOUSE $$$
(☎456 1575; www.breidavik.is; Breiðavík Bay; sites per adult/child 2200kr/free, d with/without bathroom incl breakfast 33,000/22,600kr; ⊙mid-May–mid-Sep;) Located behind the incredible cream-coloured beach (p245) of the same name, Hotel Breiðavík has a bit of a lock on the area's accommodation market. Prices are stiff for what is offered: simple rooms, sleeping-bag accommodation (16,500kr) and camping. But the setting is sublime, and it sure is nice to overnight on the peninsula. Facilities include a laundry, restaurant, guest kitchen and barbecue.

★**French Café** CAFE
(Franska kaffihúsið; ☎770 2161; www.facebook.com/FranskaKaffihusid; Rauðasandur; snacks 750-950kr; ⊙noon-6pm mid-Jun–Aug) This wonderful small cafe serves delicious cake and coffee or beer and wine (1300kr) on a farm called Kirkjuhvammur, just back from Rauðasandur (p245). At low tide you can walk right down to the reef.

Getting There & Away

From June to August Westfjords Adventures (p243) runs a bus (14,500kr) from Brjánslækur to Patreksfjörður, Látrabjarg and Rauðasandur – it then returns to Brjánslækur in time for the ferry back to Stykkishólmur. Note, it has to be booked in advance.

Two-wheel-drive cars can traverse the rutted tracks slowly, but there is no petrol on the peninsula. Fuel up in Patreksfjörður to the north or Flókalundur to the east.

Patreksfjörður

POP 677

The largest village in this part of the Westfjords, zippy little Patreksfjörður on the fjord of the same name is a convenient jumping-off point for visits to the Látrabjarg Peninsula. The no-frills town has dramatic views to the bluffs and good services for those preparing to head out to more remote fjords. The town was named after St Patrick of Ireland, who was the spiritual guide of Örlygur Hrappson, the first settler in the area.

Activities

Patreksfjörður Pool SWIMMING
(☎456 1301; Aðalstræti 55; adult/child 700kr/free; ⊙8am-9.30pm Mon-Fri, 10am-6pm Sat & Sun mid-May–mid-Sep, reduced hours winter) Patreksfjörður's swim spot is an absolute beauty – the infinity pool sits on a 2nd-storey terrace overlooking the fjord. There's a sauna and two hot-pots too.

Tours

★**Westfjords Adventures** HIKING TOUR, JEEP TOUR
(☎456 5006; www.wa.is; Þórsgata 8a; ⊙8.15am-5pm Mon-Fri, 10am-noon Sat & Sun mid-May–mid-Sep, 9am-noon mid-Sep–mid-May) The area's top tour provider offers everything from birdwatching and hikes on the Látrabjarg Peninsula (eight hours 29,500kr) to day-long jeep tours around the fjords (34,000kr) or along the remote Kjaran's Ave (39,900kr), a rough gravel track hewn into the fjord. There's a menu of boat, whale-watching and fishing tours (from 13,900kr) on Patreksfjörður, as well as tours further afield.

Bikes are also available for rent (per four hours/day 4200/7200kr) and staff sell maps, give advice and book accommodation. Westfjords Adventures also runs bus services (p243) around the region.

Sleeping

Patreksfjörður Camping CAMPGROUND $
(☎849 8502; Aðalstræti 107; sites per adult/child 1700kr/free; ⊙Jun–mid-Sep;) Municipal campground in a grassy field. Has excellent new showers, laundry (per load 1000kr) and kitchen.

Stekkaból GUESTHOUSE $$
(☎864 9675; www.stekkabol.net; Stekkar 14; s/d/q without bathrooms, incl breakfast 14,600/18,700/33,200kr;) A playful exuberance pervades fjord-view Stekkaból, from the up-cycled wood furniture, to the barbecue deck built into the hillside and the alfresco showers. It's welcoming, warm and fun.

Ráðagerði Guesthouse GUESTHOUSE $$
(☎456 1560; www.radagerdi.net; Aðalstræti 31; d with/without bathroom 24,000/19,000kr, q without bathroom 30,500kr;) Many of the rooms at this stylish guesthouse have sweeping fjord views. Decor is modern, the owners are friendly and breakfast (included in the price) is hearty.

Fosshótel Westfjords HOTEL $$
(Fosshótel Vestfirðir; ☎456 2004; www.fosshotel.is; Aðalstræti 100; s/d/ste incl breakfast from 24,500/28,700/44,500kr; ⊙May-Sep;) One of the town's historic buildings has been

WORTH A TRIP

ARNARFJÖRÐUR & SELÁRDALUR

The drive out to the tip of Arnarfjörður, along Rte 619 beyond Bíldudalur (p248), is absolutely magnificent. The tiny track rims soaring mountains, lush pastured valleys and untouched beaches, and looks onto the churning fjord and the incredible landscape on its northern side. Towards sunset and on partly cloudy days, the light shifts continually, and rainbows often form.

At the tip of the fjord (24km), local artist Samúel Jónsson lived out his remaining years at a remote farm in Selárdalur, and filled his days by creating a series of 'naive', cartoonlike sculptures. Visitors can peruse the surreal remains of his farm, now called **Samúel Jónsson's Art Museum** (698 7533; www.samueljonssonmuseum.jimdo.com; Brautarholt, Selárdalur; adult/child 500kr/free; 24hr). There's a flamboyant house, a circle of lions (created from a postcard Samúel saw of the Alhambra), an ornate church and Samúel's home.

well renovated into this super-sleek, stylish hotel with modern rooms offering private bathrooms, flat-screen TVs and views to either the fjord or the mountain. There's a restaurant and bar too.

Hotel West HOTEL $$
(456 5020; www.hotelwest.is; Aðalstræti 62; s/d from 20,000/26,000kr;) A former co-op building has been transformed into a smart hotel with sunny bedrooms decked out like a Nordic design magazine; many overlook glittering Patreksfjörður.

Eating & Drinking

Patreksfjörður is the best place to stock up on groceries or eat out before heading to more remote fjords – try delightful Stúkuhúsið or the Fosshótel restaurant.

Albína SUPERMARKET $
(456 1667; Aðalstræti 89; 8am-10pm, from 9am Sat & Sun) Supermarket, which also sells fresh bread, cakes and pastries.

★**Stúkuhúsið** BISTRO $$
(456 1404; www.stukuhusid.is; Aðalstræti 50; mains 1300-4990kr; 11am-11pm mid-May–Aug, noon-4pm Wed-Sat rest of year;) In this cool eatery, friendly staff serve up filling salads, chicken soup, Icelandic lamb and their speciality: succulent fish fresh from the fjord outside the window – the cod with hints of wasabi is superb.

Vínbúðin ALCOHOL
(456 244; www.vinbudin.is; Þórsgata 10; 11am-6pm Mon-Thu, to 7pm Fri, to 2pm Sat) National liquor-store chain.

Getting There & Away

Use the Westfjords Adventures bus services to get around (see p243).

A Flybus (p243) runs by request from Patreksfjörður to meet flights into Bíldudalur Airport (p249).

Westfjords Adventures is also a Europcar rental outlet and rents bikes (four hours 4200kr).

Tálknafjörður

POP 231

Set amid rolling green hills, rocky peaks and a wide fjord, sleepy Tálknafjörður village is a bit bland, but it's surrounded by truly magnificent scenery.

Activities

Ask at the town swimming pool for the detailed hiking map *Vestfirðir & Dalir 4* (1200kr) and head out on the gorgeous 10km cairn-marked hike to Bíldudalur.

★**Pollurinn** GEOTHERMAL POOL, HOT-POT
(24hr) FREE The cement-lined natural hot-pots (46°C) at Pollurinn (literally, 'The Puddle'), are a Westfjords hot-pot highlight. Backed by the mountains, the shallow pools have a wilderness setting and look out on the broad sweep of the fjord. You'll find them 3.8km beyond the Tálknafjörður Swimming Pool along Rte 617 – they're signposted with a tiny white sign with black lettering.

Tálknafjörður Swimming Pool GEOTHERMAL POOL, HOT-POT
(456 2639; www.talknafjordur.is; Sveinseyri; adult/child 900/370kr; 9am-9pm Jun-Aug, reduced hours rest of year) Fed by one of the few geothermal fields in the area, the Tálknafjörður Swimming Pool is the town's main hang-out. In summer pool staffers provide tourist information.

DON'T MISS

NATURAL SPRINGS

At the head of tiny Reykjarfjörður, plan to stop at the glorious geothermal pools of **Reykjarfjarðarlaug**. Up front there's a freshly refinished concrete pool (32°C), but the real treat is 30 paces out back – a piping hot (45°C), natural, turf-fringed pool. And all around are soaring seabirds, mountains and fjord views.

The pools are 23km southeast of Bíldudalur and 17km west of the junction with Rte 60.

Sleeping & Eating

Tálknafjörður Campground CAMPGROUND $
(456 2639; www.talknafjordur.is; sites per adult/child 1500kr/free; Jun-Aug;) This campground beside the swimming pool (p247) has laundry, cooking facilities and showers.

Guesthouse Bjarmaland GUESTHOUSE $$
(891 8038; www.guesthousebjarmaland.is; Bugatún 8; d with/without bathroom 22,800/17,800kr;) Spotless accommodation awaits at Guesthouse Bjarmaland, where the friendly owners also offer sleeping-bag space (4000kr).

★**Dunhagi** ICELANDIC $
(662 0463; www.cafedunhagi.is; Sveinseyri; mains 1900-3900kr; 2-10pm late May–Aug;) Dunhagi delivers a true taste of the Westfjords. A beautifully restored historic house, with rough-hewn wood floors, comfy booths and vintage photographs, sets the scene for Icelandic lamb, trout fresh from the fjord, and seaweeds and salads picked from the neighbouring beach by the affable owner, Dagný herself.

Hópið INTERNATIONAL $
(456 2777; Hrafnardalsvegur 3; mains 1300-4400kr; noon-1pm & 6-9pm Mon-Fri, 6-9pm Sat & Sun;) Hópið is a low-key joint with a pool table. It serves burgers and basic Icelandic mains.

Shopping

★**Villimey** COSMETICS
(892 8273; www.villimey.is; Strandagata 44; hours vary mid-May–mid-Aug) This renowned Icelandic company is family run, and makes a line of excellent organic balms and ointments from wild-gathered Icelandic herbs. There are no set opening hours, so call if the shop is closed and someone from the family will come open it up. Also has an online shop.

Getting There & Away

The Patreksfjörður–Bíldudalur Flybus (p243) stops in Tálknafjörður, but it only runs in conjunction with flights. Ask at the town's swimming pool (p247) for details.

Bíldudalur

POP 225

Set on a gloriously calm bay on grand Arnarfjörður, and surrounded by towering peaks, the attractive fishing village Bíldudalur (www.bildudalur.is) has one of the finest fjord-side positions in the country. Arriving by road from either direction, you're treated to spectacular views. Bíldudalur was founded in the 16th century and today is a major supplier of prawns and salmon.

Sights

Skrímslasetur Icelandic Sea Monster Museum MUSEUM
(456 6666; www.skrimsli.is; Strandgata 7; adult/child 1200kr/free; 10am-6pm mid-May–mid-Sep;) Moody, fun, elaborate and dramatic exhibits about Icelandic and foreign monster legends fill the rooms here. The interactive multimedia table tells 180 stories of local sightings. You won't look at Arnarfjörður in quite the same way again.

While it's great for larger kids, wee ones might get freaked out by some of the giant models. The museum also has a small cafe.

Tours

Eagle Fjord Tours TOURS
(694 8057; www.eaglefjord.is; Gilsbakka 8; Jun-Sep) This small company runs tours in the central and southern Westfjords (adult/child from 20,700/9590kr), including birdwatching cruises, fishing in Arnarfjörður and evening meals aboard their boat.

Sleeping & Eating

Bíldudalur Campground CAMPGROUND $
(867 3768; www.vesturbyggd.is; Hafnarbraut 3; per tent 1450kr;) Pitch a tent on this grassy, level, fjord-side campsite and you'll wake up to mountain views. It's right beside the town swimming pool, which means you get to use their showers, hot-pot and sauna too.

Harbour Inn B&B $$
(☎898 2563; info@harbourinn.is; Dalbraut 1; s/d 16,800/22,800kr, without bathroom 12,800/17,800kr, all incl breakfast; 📶) The decor in the 12 cosy rooms in this excellent little B&B is smart and modern, but is rather upstaged by the gorgeous fjord and mountain views. There's a guest kitchen and comfortable dining room.

Vegamót CAFE $
(☎456 2232; Tjarnarbraut 2; mains 1650-2570kr; ⏰10am-10pm, from noon Sat & Sun) On sunny days head straight for the sheltered deck of this cheery little grill, look down onto the harbour and tuck into burgers, garlic-laced prawn crêpes or succulent, locally landed fish with chips. It's got a great mini-market too.

Getting There & Away

Eagle Air runs flights to/from Reykjavík (from 20,200kr, 45 minutes, one daily) and **Bíldudalur Airport** (BIU; ☎456 2266), 8km south of town.

Flybus (p243) Runs on request to/from Patreksfjörður via Tálknafjörður to connect with flights.

Hertz (☎522 4400; www.hertz.is; Bíldudalur Airport) Rents cars at Bíldudalur Airport; there are other car-hire outfits in Patreksfjörður and Ísafjörður.

CENTRAL PENINSULAS

The central peninsulas of the Westfjords range from Ísafjarðardjúp in the north, with its bustling city of Ísafjörður; west to the teeny fjord at Súgandafjörður; and the broad blue Önundarfjörður with its hamlet, Flateyri. These three fjords are connected by an elaborate tunnel (p252).

Further south, spectacular Dýrafjörður is worth exploring from its village at Þingeyri. A rutted track leads over the mountains to the Westfjords' mightiest waterfall, Dynjandi, in a branch fjord off enormous Arnarfjörður.

Dynjandi & Around

★**Dynjandi** WATERFALL
(Fjallfoss) Tumbling in a broad sweep over a 100m-rocky scarp at the head of Dynjandivogur bay, Dynjandi is the most dramatic waterfall in the Westfjords. The bumpy drive to it is famous for incredible views; you'll see how the falls are the catchment area for run-off from the peaks and inland valleys all around. On Monday, Wednesday and Friday from June to August a Westfjords Adventures bus (p243) linking Ísafjörður, Brjánslækur and Patreksfjörður stops at Dynjandi twice a day.

Climbing up from the car park you'll pass many smaller falls until you reach the thundering main chute. You're allowed to approach the massive cascade as it plunges over the mountainside, and the views over the broad fjord are spectacular.

The surrounding area is a protected nature reserve. There is a campsite (free) but it is for cyclists and hikers only (you can't park a car overnight) and then only for one night. There are basic toilets (200kr) and – fittingly – running water.

Jón Sigurðsson Memorial Museum MUSEUM
(Hrafnseyri; ☎456 8260; www.hrafnseyri.is; Hrafnseyri, Arnarfjörður; ⏰11am-6pm Jun–early Sep) FREE Farmstead Hrafnseyri is the birthplace (on 17 June 1811) of Jón Sigurðsson, the architect of Iceland's independence. The interesting, modern Jón Sigurðsson Memorial Museum outlines his life and has a reconstruction of his turf house, a 19th-century church and a small cafe. It's on a beautiful point with fjord views.

The museum is signed off rutted Rte 60, which runs along the north side of Arnarfjörður. The road between Hrafnseyri and Þingeyri is closed for six to eight months in winter. Check www.road.is.

Þingeyri

POP 281

A tiny village on the southern side of beautiful Dýrafjörður, Þingeyri sits on the fringes of an important Viking site and celebrates that connection with a Viking-themed festival and replica sailing ship. The town (www.thingeyri.is) is also a good jumping-off point for hiking, cycling and horse riding on the Þingeyri Peninsula, just to the west.

Sights & Activities

★**Þingeyri Peninsula** HIKING, CYCLING
West of Þingeyri, the peninsula and its dramatic peaks offer spectacular hiking and cycling. You can rent fat bikes and mountain bikes at Simbahöllin (p250) cafe and follow the dirt road that runs northwest

along the northern edge of the peninsula and along Dýrafjörður to the scenic valley at **Haukadalur**, an important Viking site.

If landslides don't block the road (check locally), you can continue around the peninsula, passing cliffs where birds perch and the remote lighthouse at **Svalvogar**. Do not attempt this track with a 2WD car – you will not make it. Local tour operators, and those in Ísafjörður, also offer tours here.

Inland, the Westfjords' highest peak, **Kaldbakur** (998m), is a good hiking spot. The steep trail to the summit begins from the road about 2km west of Þingeyri town.

Þingeyri Tourist Office can provide maps and advice.

Old Blacksmith's Workshop MUSEUM
(Gamla Smiðjan Þingeyri; ☎456 3291; www.nedsti.is; Hafnarstræti 14; adult/child 1200/950kr; ⏲9am-5pm mid-May–Aug) It was the first of its kind in Iceland when it was created in 1913, and today Þingeyri's atmospheric Old Blacksmith's Workshop is still crammed with original machinery and tools. It's part of Ísafjörður's Westfjords Heritage Museum (p254); the ticket includes admission to both sights.

Sleeping & Eating

Þingeyri Campsite CAMPGROUND $
(☎450 8470; tjald@isafjordur.is; Hafnarstræti; sites per tent 1500kr; ⏲mid-May–mid-Sep; 📶) Bijou Þingeyri campground has excellent facilities: a laundry, luxury showers and a smart new kitchen and dining room. Find it behind the town swimming pool.

Hotel Sandafell HOTEL $$
(☎456 1600; www.hotelsandafell.com; Hafnarstræti 7; s without bathroom 14,400kr, d with/without bathroom 25,700/18,300kr, all incl breakfast; ⏲mid-May–mid-Sep; P📶) The friendly, simply styled Sandafell hotel has immaculate rooms in the village centre. Dinner (served daily 6pm to 9pm) might feature chilli (3200kr), pizza (2300kr) or a flavourful fish soup (2800kr).

Við Fjörðinn GUESTHOUSE $$
(☎456 8172; vidfjordinn@vidfjordinn.is; Aðalstræti 26; s/d without bathroom from 9500/20,500kr, apt from 21,000kr; ⏲mid-May–Sep; 📶👪) The comfortable, traditional rooms of this welcoming guesthouse feature homey decor. Bathrooms are shared, and there's a TV lounge, barbecue and good guest kitchen.

Wi-fi can be patchy.

★**Simbahöllin** CAFE $$
(☎899 6659; www.simbahollin.is; Fjarðargata 5; mains 1400-3100kr; ⏲10am-10pm mid-Jun–Aug, noon-6pm mid-May–mid-Jun & early-Sep; 📶) Simbahöllin is a cool cafe in a restored 1915 general store with friendly staff serving tasty Belgian waffles during the day and hearty lamb tagines at night. Outdoor seating, fjord views and a cosy vibe ensure this is one of the Westfjords best boltholes.

Simbahöllin also arranges top-quality horse-riding tours, and mountain and fat-bike rental.

EXPLORING ÞINGEYRI

You will get deep into the remote Þingeyri Peninsula on the high-quality, small-group horse-riding tours run by **Simba Horses & Bike Rental** (Simbahöllin Cafe; ☎869 5654; www.westfjords-horseriding.com; Fjarðargata 5; ⏲mid-May–mid-Sep). Choose from a two-hour meander through the tranquil Sandar valley (9900kr) or trek across rivers to black sand beaches (12,900kr). Or rent a classic mountain bike (from 7500kr) or all-terrain fat bike (from 9000kr) for self-guided explorations of rugged trails.

Information

Þingeyri Tourist Office (☎456 8304; www.thingeyri.is; Hafnarstræti 6; ⏲10am-6pm mid-May–early-Sep) On the main road.

Getting There & Away

Municipal bus (p243) services:

- Flateyri (350kr, 30 minutes, three to four daily Monday to Friday)
- Ísafjörður (350kr, one hour, three to four daily Monday to Friday)

Westfjords Adventures bus services (p243) also run to Þingeyri.

Dýrafjörður

A series of gorgeous broad valleys stretch across the northern shore of Dýrafjörður. The gentle town of Þingeyri is on its south shore, and has great walks and cycling routes. On bumpy track Rte 624, on the northern edge of the fjord, there's a lovely weatherboard **church** and one of Iceland's oldest botanic gardens.

Skrúður GARDENS
(⏲24hr) FREE One of Iceland's oldest botanic gardens sits on the lower slopes

of the fjordside valleys on Dýrafjörður's northern edge. Teeny Skrúður was established as a teaching garden in 1909. You'll see arched whalebones at one entrance, just off Rte 624.

Ingjaldssandur BEACH

On the northern edge of Dýrafjörður, Rte 624 forks off west from Rte 60. It turns into a dirt road and passes an abandoned farmhouse before swerving inland to head over the top of the rugged peninsula. It takes about 20 minutes to reach Ingjaldssandur at the mouth of Önundarfjörður. Set in a picturesque valley, this isolated beach is a fantastic spot to watch the midnight sun as it flirts with the sea before rising back up into the sky.

Núpur Sólvellir RENTAL HOUSE $$

(Rte 624, Nupur; house 30,500kr;) The clean cube-like lines of Núpur Sólvellir are set slightly back from the shore of Dýrafjörður. Contemporary, open-plan rooms have expansive mountain and fjord views. With three bedrooms, a fully kitted-out kitchen and all the home comforts, it's a charismatic, get-away-from-it-all retreat.

No website/email but can be booked through third-party booking websites.

Önundarfjörður

Azure Önundarfjörður has sheer mountain walls on either side, with cod drying racks arranged along the shores. The tiny village of Flateyri looks across the fjord onto beautiful sand bars, and you'll notice an unusual avalanche-blocking wall above the town to keep it from being inundated with snow, built after a tragic avalanche in 1995.

Sleeping

Korpudalur HI Hostel GUESTHOUSE, HOSTEL $

(Korpudalur Kirkjuból; 456 7808; www.korpudalur.is; Rte 627; sites per tent 1600kr, dm from 5400kr, d without bathroom from 13,800kr; mid-May–mid-Sep;) At the head of Önundarfjörður, a turn-off marked Kirkjuból (not to be confused with a nearby guesthouse of the same name) leads 5km down rough Rte 627 to the popular Korpudalur HI Hostel. The stunning location at the fjordhead and generous breakfasts (2000kr) make this 100-year-old farmhouse worth visiting. Only drawback: rooms are tiny. HI members get a 750kr discount.

★ Guesthouse Kirkjuból í Bjarnardal GUESTHOUSE $$

(456 7679; www.kirkjubol.is; Rte 60, Bjarnardalur; d with/without bathroom, incl breakfast 22,000/15,800kr; Jun-Aug;) Just south of Önundarfjörður, lying on the east side of Rte 60, a marked turn-off for Kirkjuból leads to this remote white-and-green farmstead. It's squeaky-clean inside, with lovely rooms sporting antiques, a guest kitchen and a living room. It's a serene spot with friendly owners and good views down the fjord.

Flateyri

POP 177

Once a giant support base for Norwegian whalers, Flateyri (www.flateyri.is) is now a quiet little place set on a striking gravel spit sticking out into sparkling Önundarfjörður. There's a quaint museum and geothermal pool, but kayaking, fishing and the beautiful scenery are the main draws.

Sights & Activities

Old Bookstore in Flateyri MUSEUM

(Gamla Bókabúðin Flateyri; 840 0600; www.facebook.com/bokabudinflateyri; Hafnarstræti 3; by donation; 11am-5pm mid-May–mid-Sep) Peruse Iceland's oldest original store – a well-preserved historic bookshop and its attached apartment, which feel wonderfully trapped in amber.

Kayak Flateyri KAYAKING

(863 7662; www.facebook.com/kajakleiga; Ólafstúni 7; trips from 7000kr) Paddle out on gorgeous Önundarfjörður, with or without a guide.

Iceland ProFishing FISHING

(861 7442; www.icelandprofishing.com; Melagata 3; Apr-Sep) Rents boats for angling trips around the fjords (guides can be hired), and offers week-long trips (from 158,100kr) with lodging in Flateyri and Suðureyri.

Sleeping & Eating

Síma Hostel GUESTHOUSE $

(897 8700; www.icelandwestfjords.com; Ránargata 1; d/f without bathroom from 11,300/19,200kr, apt 29,400kr; mid-May–early Sep;) Many of these tidy, simple rooms and cosy apartments have good fjord views.

Litlabyli Guesthouse GUESTHOUSE $$

(848 0920; www.litlabyli.com; Ránargata 2; d with/without bathroom 19,200/15,400kr;) The odd hurricane lamp, stack of old books

BRACE YOURSELF!

Completed in 1996, the 9km-long **Ísafjörður–Suðureyri–Flateyri Tunnel** (Vestfjarðagöng) beneath the mountains becomes an unusual one-lane tunnel in parts of the 6km stretch from Ísafjörður to Flateyri. In the middle of the mountain it branches, and a 3km section of tunnel shoots off to Suðureyri. Worry not: pull-outs throughout allow oncoming traffic to alternate as it rides through the damp chutes.

and vintage typewriter help reinforce this historic guesthouse's traditional feel. Light, painted walls and stripped floors help bring things up to date. Breakfasts are likely to include homemade cake. They also run a basic **campground** (per person 1300kr).

Bryggjukaffi CAFE $

(Harbor Café; ☎861 8976; www.facebook.com/bryggjukaffi; Hafnarstræti 4; cake 350-900kr, soup 1700kr; ⏰11am-6pm, to 8pm Sat-Mon Jun-Aug, 11am-6pm Sat & Sun rest of year; 📶) A friendly local woman serves up delicious daily soup (the fish stew is outstanding) with excellent fresh bread, and bakes cakes and irresistible waffles. There are simple guest rooms upstairs (double/family with shared bathroom 12,200/18,200kr).

ℹ Getting There & Away

Municipal bus (p243) services:

- Buses connect Þingeyri, Flateyri and Ísafjörður (350kr, three to four daily Monday to Friday).
- The bus stops in Flateyri at Ránargata 1 (in front of the Síma Hostel p251).

Suðureyri

POP 257

Perched on the tip of 13km-long Súgandafjörður, the fishing community of Suðureyri (www.isafjordur.is) was isolated for decades by the forbidding mountains. Now connected with Ísafjörður and Flateyri by a 9km tunnel network, the village's main draws are its fishing heritage, angling and superb seafood eateries.

Geothermal Swimming Pool GEOTHERMAL POOL, HOT-POT

(☎450 8490; ithrottamidstod@isafjordur.is; Túngata 8; adult/child 750/350kr; ⏰11am-7pm Jun-Aug, reduced hours rest of year) Locals congregate at the geothermal swimming pool, with its indoor and outdoor bathing, sauna and hot-pots.

Tours

Iceland ProFishing (p251) in Flateyri also operates from Suðureyri. The Fisherman hotel-restaurant promotes the life of the fishing village with seafood-themed **tours** (☎450 9000; www.fisherman.is; per person 5000kr; ⏰tours 11am May-Sep), which include a visit to the local fish factory.

Sleeping & Eating

Fisherman HOTEL $$

(☎450 9000; www.fisherman.is; Aðalgata 14; d with/without bathroom, incl breakfast 26,000/19,700kr; ⏰May-Sep; @📶) Hardwood floors, white linen and modern, pared-down designs define the rooms at this small hotel. It's pretty much the hub of the town, thanks to a smart **cafe** (mains 1490-1990kr; ⏰10am-10pm) and superb **restaurant** (mains 3900-5000kr; ⏰6-9pm).

Shopping

Á Milli Fjalla ARTS & CRAFTS

(☎450 9000; sui@simnet.is; Aðalgata 14; ⏰1-6pm Jul & Aug) This teeny, summer-only, pop-up sells locally crafted knits, ceramics and unique trinkets.

ℹ Getting There & Away

Municipal bus (p243) service goes to Ísafjörður (350kr, 25 minutes, three to four daily Monday to Friday).

Ísafjörður

POP 2620

Hub of Westfjords adventure tours, and by far the region's largest town, Ísafjörður (www.isafjordur.is) is a pleasant and prosperous place and an excellent base for travellers. The town is set on an arcing spit that extends out into Skutulsfjörður, and is hemmed in on all sides by towering peaks and the dark waters of the fjord.

The centre of Ísafjörður is a charming grid of old timber and tin-clad buildings, many unchanged since the 18th century, when the harbour was full of tall ships and Norwegian whaling crews. Today it is a surprisingly cosmopolitan place, and after some time spent travelling in the Westfjords, it'll feel like a bustling metropolis with its tempting cafes and fine choice of restaurants.

Ísafjörður

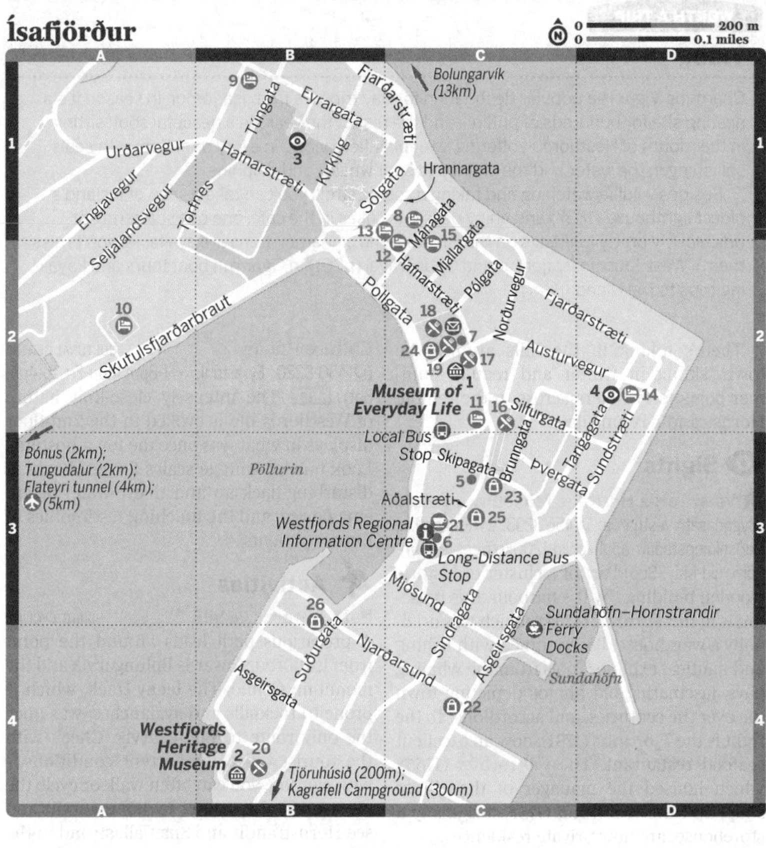

Ísafjörður

Top Sights
1 Museum of Everyday Life....C2
2 Westfjords Heritage Museum....B4

Sights
3 Culture House....B1
4 Old Town....D2

Activities, Courses & Tours
5 Borea....C3
6 West Tours....C3
7 Wild Westfjords....C2

Sleeping
8 Gamla Gistihúsið....C1
9 GentleSpace Guesthouse & Apartments....B1
10 Hótel Edda....A2
11 Hótel Ísafjörður....C2
12 Ísafjörður Hostel....C2
13 Koddinn....B1
14 Litla....D2
15 Mánagisting Guesthouse....C2

Eating
16 Gamla Bakaríð....C2
17 Hamraborg....C2
Húsið....(see 13)
18 Netto....C2
19 Thai Koon....C2
20 Tjöruhúsið....B4
Við Pollinn....(see 11)

Drinking & Nightlife
21 Edinborg....C3

Shopping
22 Fiskbúð Sjávarfangs....C4
23 Karitas....C3
24 Neisti Centre....C2
25 Rammagerð Ísafjarðar....C3
26 Vínbúðin....B3

WORTH A TRIP

VIGUR

Charming Vigur is a popular destination for day trippers from Ísafjörður. In season it's a nesting site for hundreds of puffins, and the rest of the year it's a peaceful spot, sitting in the mouth of Hestfjörður, offering sweeping fjord views in every direction, with seals splashing in the water and the chance to spot whales and dolphins.

Besides wildlife watching and taking a scenic stroll, you can take a snap of Iceland's oldest lighthouse (1837) and enjoy delicious cakes in the cafe, one of a scattering of ridiculously pretty buildings on the island (if the cinnamon buns are available, don't miss them). West Tours in Ísafjörður and Ögur Travel (p261) in Ögur run boat tours and kayaking trips to the island.

There's hiking in the hills around the town, skiing in winter and regular summer boats ferry hikers across to the remote Hornstrandir Peninsula.

Sights

★Westfjords Heritage Museum MUSEUM
(Byggðasafn Vestfjarða; ☎456 3293; www.nedsti.is; Neðstikaupstaður; adult/child 1200kr/free; ⏱9am-5pm mid-May–Sep) Part of a cluster of historic wooden buildings by the harbour, this museum is in the **Turnhús** (1784), which was originally a warehouse. It's crammed with fishing and nautical exhibits, tools from the whaling days, fascinating old photos depicting town life over the centuries, and accordions. To the right is the **Tjöruhús** (1781), now an excellent seafood restaurant. The **Faktorhús** (1765), which housed the manager of the village shop, and the **Krambúd** (1757), originally a storehouse, are now private residences.

The museum ticket is also good for the Old Blacksmith's Workshop (p250) in Þingeyri.

★Museum of Everyday Life MUSEUM
(Hversdagssafn; ☎694 4266; www.everydaylife.is; Hafnarstræti 5; 10am-5pm Mon-Fri, 11am-2pm Sat; ⏱adult/child 700kr/free) Celebrating the magic of the mundane is the aim of the powerful, creative displays here, where shoes, books and mini-movies each come with personal narratives and story fragments. As an intriguing insight into life in the Westfjords it's poetic, thought-provoking and beautifully done.

Old Town AREA
(Tangagata) Ísafjörður's historic quarter borders it's eastern edges. Start explorations in Tangagata to see gabled, tin-clad homes, often brightly painted in patriotic russet red or blue, trimmed with white. Look out for the dates from the late 1890s and early 1900s above the doors.

Culture House CULTURAL CENTRE
(☎450 8220; Eyrartúni; ⏱1-6pm Mon-Fri, to 4pm Sat) FREE The intensely close-knit nature of Westfjords life is evoked in the 2nd-floor displays in what was once the town hospital. Look out for vintage scales for newborns, a disturbing hacksaw and an eye-watering enema device, and the touching testimonies of former patients.

Activities

Path Towards Óshlíð HIKING, CYCLING
A precarious path leads around the point from Ísafjörður towards Bolungarvík and the mountain Óshlíð. The teeny track, which is prone to rockfalls and avalanches, was once the only route to Bolungarvík. Check with the tourist office for current conditions – with caution, you can often walk or cycle the bit nearest the tunnel to Bolungarvík and see Hornstrandir and Snæfjallaströnd in the distance.

Tours

★West Tours ADVENTURE TOUR
(Vesturferðir; ☎456 5111; www.westtours.is; Aðalstræti 7; ⏱8am-6pm Mon-Fri, 8.30am-4.30pm Sat, 10am-3pm Sun Jun-Aug, 8am-4pm Mon-Fri Sep-May) Popular, professional West Tours organises a mind-boggling array of trips throughout the Westfjords including tours of Vigur island (11,000kr), hiking in Hornstrandir (from 32,900kr) and kayaking trips (from 7000kr), plus cycling, horse riding, boat and angling tours, birdwatching and cultural excursions. Kids are generally half-price.

Housed in the same building as the tourist information centre (p257), it also runs ferries to Hornstrandir and rents bicycles (per four/12 hours 7500/10,000kr).

★Borea ADVENTURE
(☎456 3322; www.borea.is; Aðalstræti 18; ⏱8am-6pm Mon-Fri, 9am-7pm Sat, 10am-4pm

Sun Jun-Aug, reduced hours rest of year) Adventure outfitter offering fjord kayaking (from 13,900kr), excellent hiking in Hornstrandir (from 41,900kr) and mountain biking (from 13,900kr). It also runs ferry services to Hornstrandir and operates Kviar, its private cabin in the reserve.

Wild Westfjords ADVENTURE TOUR
(☎456 3300; www.wildwestfjords.com; Hafnarstræti 9; ⏱9am-5.30pm May-Sep, reduced hours rest of year) Operates multiday guided or self-drive tours around the fjords and Iceland, as well as day tours, including trips to Dynjandi waterfall (adult/child 28,000/14,000kr), kayaking tours (from 12,800kr), hiking in Hornstrandir (from 33,000kr), and more challenging, adult-only treks to the iconic Hornbjarg cliffs (44,000kr).

Fosshestar HORSE RIDING
(☎842 6969; www.fosshestar.is) Short riding tours (from 15,000kr) for all skill levels in the nearby Engidalur Valley. Also offers horse feeding and petting (3500kr). Book ahead; cash only. The price includes pick-up and drop-off from Ísafjörður.

Sleeping

★Ísafjörður Hostel HOSTEL $
(☎456 4611; www.isafjordurhotels.is; Mánagata 1; dm 5500kr) A luxury hostel with pristine four-bed dorms, hotel-standard shower rooms, a well-equipped kitchen and a spacious lounge in which to share travellers' tales.

★Tungudalur Campground CAMPGROUND $
(☎864 8592; www.gih.is; Tungudal; sites per adult/child 1800kr/free; ⏱mid-Jun–mid-Sep; 📶) The rushing river that tumbles from the Bunarfoss waterfall bisects this peaceful, picturesque site. There's a laundry (900kr), decent showers and a toasty kitchen-dining room, where an acoustic guitar waits for guests to play.

It's 5km out of Ísafjörður; buses run nearby.

Mánagisting Guesthouse GUESTHOUSE, APARTMENT $
(Gistiheimilið Mánagisting; ☎615 2014; Mánagata 4; dm/d without bathroom 6000/12,000kr, studio 16,800kr; 📶) The hallway and corridors of this rambling, four-storey guesthouse are decidedly scruffy, but the simple rooms are Ok, if not pristine. The mattresses can be a bit thin.

GentleSpace Guesthouse & Apartments APARTMENT $$
(☎892 9282; www.gentlespace.is; Hlíðarvegur 14; d/apt from 13,200/20,500kr; 📶) Small touches combine to make these lodgings a big hit: soothing natural colour schemes, hardwood floors, underfloor heating in the (shared) bathroom, free coffee and biscuits, and Robert, a hugely welcoming host.

Gamla Gistihúsið GUESTHOUSE $$
(☎456 4146; www.gistihus.is; Mánagata 5; d/tr without bathroom, incl breakfast 23,200/29,800kr; @📶) Bright, cheerful and well kept, this excellent guesthouse has simple but comfortable rooms with plenty of cosy touches. The bathrooms are shared, but each double room has a telephone, washbasin and bathrobes. It's owned by Hotel Ísafjörður so check-in is often there.

Koddinn GUESTHOUSE $$
(☎456 5555; lovisa@snerpa.is; Hrannargata 2; s/d 7000/17000kr;) In the five cosy rooms set above the buzzing Húsið cafe-bar (p256), old-style furnishings are teamed with a kitchen and all the mod cons. Bathrooms are shared. If you're not a night owl avoid Friday and Saturday when the bar stays open till 3am. Ask about sleeping-bag rates to save some money.

Hótel Edda HOTEL, CAMPGROUND $$
(☎444 4960; www.hoteledda.is; Mantaskólinn; d/tr with bathroom 20,000/23,000kr; ⏱early Jun–mid-Aug) Summer-only accommodation is available at the town's secondary school, where you'll find 33 simple but smart en-suite bedrooms, along with more basic sleeping bag accommodation (2700kr) and a tents-only campsite (from 1200kr).

Litla GUESTHOUSE $$
(☎474 1455; Sundstræti 43; d/tr without bathroom 16,000/17,800kr; 📶) The colour scheme is a sludgy olive green and the rooms are homely rather than fancy, but this snug guesthouse is set on one of Ísafjörður's most characterful historic streets.

Hótel Ísafjörður BUSINESS HOTEL $$
(☎456 4111; www.hotelisafjordur.is; Silfurtorg 2; d/tr incl breakfast 25,800/43,300kr; @📶) The rooms on the higher floors of this central, classic business hotel favoured by tour groups have great views over the tin-roofed town and the waters beyond.

Eating

Hamraborg FAST FOOD $
(☎456 3166; www.facebook.com/pg/hamraborgehf; Hafnarstraeti 7; mains from 1200kr; ⏰9am-11.30pm; 📶) Voted Iceland's best fast-food joint by national radio polls, this outpost attracts locals who gossip over Béarnaise burgers and pizza. Sport frequently plays on the TV.

Thai Koon THAI $
(☎456 0123; Hafnarstræti 9, Neisti Centre; mains from 1800kr; ⏰11.30am-8pm Mon-Sat, 5-8pm Sun) After a stretch of limited food options in remote Iceland, this small Thai canteen seems decidedly exotic. There's no grand ambience but the curries and noodles are reliably tasty and served up in heaping portions.

★**Tjöruhúsið** SEAFOOD $$
(☎456 4419; www.facebook.com/tjoruhusid; Neðstakaupstaður 1; mains 2600-5700kr; ⏰noon-2pm & 7-9pm Jun-Sep) Set in a building from 1781, warm, rustic Tjöruhúsið offers some of the best seafood around. The set-course, serve-yourself dinner includes soup, catches of the day (fresh off the boat from the nearby harbour), and dessert such as chocolate mousse. There's outdoor seating on benches when it's sunny. Dinner starts promptly at 7pm and they're deservedly popular, so book in advance.

★**Húsið** INTERNATIONAL $$
(☎456 5555; Hrannargata 2; mains 1890-3590kr; ⏰kitchen 11am-10pm; 📶) Sidle up to the rough-hewn wood tables inside this tin-clad house, or kick back on the sunny terrace for flavourful, relaxed meals and local beer on tap. Groovy tunes play as staff serve fish, burgers, pizza and Icelandic lamb. It's a fun hang-out with regular live music and DJs.

Við Pollinn ICELANDIC, SEAFOOD $$$
(☎456 3360; www.vidpollinn.is; Silfurtorg 2; mains 2700-5900kr; ⏰11am-9pm May-Sep, reduced hours rest of year) Although the minimalist decor at Hótel Ísafjörður's restaurant lacks pizzazz, the food more than makes up for it. The strong selection of local cuisine, especially fish, is prepared with flair and the windows offer great views over the fjord – you might even see your next meal getting hauled into the harbour.

Self-Catering

Ísafjörður is ideal for stocking up before heading to remote areas.

Gamla Bakaríð BAKERY $
(☎456 3226; www.facebook.com/gamlabakariid; Aðalstræti 24; ⏰7am-6pm Mon-Fri, 8am-4pm Sat & Sun) For breakfast, lunch or a mid-morning sugar fix, Gamla is the best bakery in town and is usually packed for its full range of sweet treats (cookies, doughnuts and cakes) as well as fresh bread.

Bónus SUPERMARKET $
(☎527 9000; www.bonus.is; Skeiði 1; ⏰11am-6.30pm Mon-Thu, 10am-7.30pm Fri, 10am-6pm Sat, noon-6pm Sun) Moderately priced supermarket on the main road into town.

Netto SUPERMARKET $
(www.netto.is; Hafnarstræti 9, Neisti Centre; ⏰10am-7pm) On Hafnarstræti.

Vínbúðin ALCOHOL
(☎456 3455; www.vinbudin.is; Suðurgötu 8; ⏰11am-6pm, to 7pm Sat, to 4pm Sun) National liquor chain.

Drinking & Nightlife

Edinborg CAFE, BAR
(☎456 8335; Aðalstræti 7; ⏰noon-11pm Mon-Thu, to 3am Fri, 4pm-3am Sat, 4-11pm Sun; 📶) There's a mellow feel to Edinborg, where a relaxed bar with a pool table sits side by side with a restaurant serving great burgers and fish. That makes it popular, as does occasional live music and having the local brew – zesty, amber-coloured Dokkan – on tap. It's in the same building as the tourist office, which dates from 1907.

Shopping

Fiskbúð Sjávarfangs FOOD & DRINKS
(☎869 2429; kari10@simnet.is; Sindragata 11; ⏰11am-6pm Mon- Fri) Trays packed with fish landed yards away fill the counters of this friendly fishmongers. Owner Kári points out cooked prawns, smoked rainbow trout and Arctic char, plus haddock, halibut and catfish *harðfiskur* (dried fish) and leather made from salmon skin in a dazzling array of colours – buy it in whole strips (from 4300kr) or transformed into purses and bow ties.

Karitas CLOTHING
(Aðalstræti 20; ⏰11am-6pm Mon-Thu, to 4pm Fri & Sat) A small seasonal pop-up selling traditional, handcrafted Icelandic jumpers, plus knitted socks, hats, shawls and jewellery.

Rammagerð Ísafjarðar ARTS & CRAFTS
(☎456 3041; Aðalstræti 14; ⊙1-6pm Mon-Fri, noon-2pm Sat) Sells quality knitting and other local crafts.

Neisti Centre SHOPPING CENTRE
(Hafnarstræti 9; ⊙10am-8pm, from noon Sat & Sun) Ísafjörður's central shopping centre houses the post office, a supermarket and the canteen Thai Koon.

Information

Hospital (Heilbrigðisstofnun Vestfjarða Ísafirði; ☎450 4500; www.fsi.is; Torfnes) Ísafjörður has a full-service hospital, which also operates clinics around the Westfjords.

Post Office (☎580 1000; www.postur.is; Hafnarstræti 9; ⊙9am-4.30pm Mon-Fri)

Westfjords Regional Information Centre (☎450 8060; www.isafjordur.is; Aðalstræti 7, Edinborgarhús; ⊙8am-6pm Mon-Fri, 8am-3pm Sat & Sun Jun-Aug, 8am-4pm Mon-Fri Sep-May) By the harbour in the Edinborgarhús (1907). Helpful staff have loads of info on the Westfjords and Hornstrandir Nature Reserve. Internet terminal with free 10-minute session; luggage storage 200kr per day.

Getting There & Away

AIR

Air Iceland Connect (p243) flies between **Ísafjörður Airport** (IFJ; ☎570 3000; www.airicelandconnect.com), 5km south on the fjord, and Reykjavík's domestic airport twice daily. It also offers day tours.

A Flybus, timed to meet flights, runs between Ísafjörður and the airport (1000kr); it stops near Hótel Ísafjörður. The bus also goes onto Bolungarvík (1500kr).

BOAT

In summer, West Tours (p254) and Borea (p254) ferries to Hornstrandir depart from the Sundahöfn docks on the eastern side of the town promontory.

BUS

Ísafjörður is the major bus hub in the Westfjords. The long-distance bus stop is at the tourist information centre.

Westfjords Adventures (p243) services:

- From June to August there's a bus to Patreksfjörður (9900kr) and Brjánslækur (the terminal for the Stykkishólmur ferry; 8400kr) via Þingeyri, Dynjandi and Flókalundur (one daily each direction Monday, Wednesday and Friday).
- You must pre-book in late May and early September.
- There are no buses from mid-September to late-May.

The following buses run from Ísafjörður from around mid-May to early-September (services are reduced in the winter):

- **Bus to Hólmavík** (7000kr, three hours, three per week) Operated by **Hópferðamiðstöð Vestfjarða** (☎893 1058; vidfjordinn@vidfjordinn.is). Book the day before.
- **Bus to Reykjavík** (13,900kr, seven hours, three per week) Catch a bus to either Hólmavík or Brjánslækur then transfer. From Hólmavík, catch Strætó (p429) bus 59 to Borgarnes, where you transfer again. From Brjánslækur, take the ferry to Stykkishólmur then catch Strætó bus 58 to Borgarnes and onto Reykjavík from there.
- **Bus to Akureyri** Take the bus to Brjánslækur, ferry to Stykkishólmur, overnight there, then continue by bus the next morning, transferring in Borgarnes (25,500kr, 24 hours, three per week). Or go via Hólmavík to Borgarnes and transfer onto Akureyri from there (19,400kr, 12 hours, three per week). Do note though that the latter option is only completed in one day on Sunday – on Wednesday and Friday you need to overnight in either Borgarnes or Bifröst. This route is operated by Hópferðamiðstöð Vestfjarða and Strætó buses.

Municipal buses (p243) stop at Pollgata on the waterfront:

- Flateyri and Þingeyri (350kr, three to four daily Monday to Friday)
- Suðureyri (350kr, 20 minutes, three to four daily Monday to Friday)
- A bus for Bolungarvík (1000kr, 15 minutes, five daily Monday to Friday) leaves from the kiosk at Hamraborg, near the Netto supermarket.

Check with the information centre or www.westfjords.is for current schedules.

CAR

For ride-sharing check www.samferda.net.

Avis (☎591 4000; www.avis.com; Ísafjörður Airport)

Europcar (☎840 6074; www.holdur.is; Ísafjörður Airport)

Hertz (☎522 4400; www.hertz.is; Ísafjörður Airport)

Getting Around

City buses (350kr) operate from 7.30am to 6.15pm and connect the town centre with Hnífsdalur and Holtahverfi on the town's edges; the bus stop is along the waterfront.

West Tours (p254) rents bikes (per four/12 hours 75000/10,000kr).

Icelandic Culture

Weather not conducive for hiking? Never fear – let Iceland's rich culture and creativity take you places. There's a storytelling heritage forged by sagas; music and design that channel nature in inspiring ways; and a celebration of both tradition and experimentation. Above all, it's a willingness to wear your Icelandic identity on your sleeve (or in your knitwear).

1

DARIA MEDVEDEVA/SHUTTERSTOCK ©

ARCTIC-IMAGES/GETTY IMAGES ©

1. Saga Museum (p59)
Battle of Örlygsstaðir reenactment at Saga Museum.

2. Sculpture
Outdoor sculpture *Waiting*, by artist Aðalheiður S. Eysteinsdóttir, in Siglufjörður (p285).

3. Reykjavík Pride (p26)
A pedestrian street decorated for the gay pride parade.

4. Hallgrímskirkja (p59)
A laser light show on Hallgrímskirkja at the annual Winter Lights festival.

5. Reykjavík Culture Night (p26)
Reykjavikers turn out in force for a day and night of art, music, dance and fireworks.

5

KONDRUKHOV/SHUTTERSTOCK ©

Bolungarvík

POP 924

Despite a dramatic position at the end of the fjord, Bolungarvík itself is rather dull and uninspiring, although its Maritime Museum is well worth a visit. Bolungarvík used to be connected to Ísafjörður by a perilous track (p254) around the mountain Óshlíð, but now there is a 5.4km tunnel connecting the two, and the track is used only for walking.

Sights

★Ósvör Maritime Museum MUSEUM
(Ósvör Sjóminjasafn; ☎892 5744; www.osvor.is; adult/child 1000kr/free; ⏲9am-5pm, from 10am Sat & Sun Jun–mid-Aug, by appointment rest of year) The old turf-and-stone fishing shacks of the Ósvör Maritime Museum powerfully evoke a past age. A guide in a typical lambskin fisher's outfit shows you around the shore-side settlement, outlining its history and traditional seafaring life from the Settlement Era to the present day. There's also a cramped fishers' hut full of relics and a rowing boat.

The museum is down a turning to the right, just after you emerge from the tunnel heading into Bolungarvík from Ísafjörður.

Natural History Museum MUSEUM
(☎456 7507; www.nabo.is; Vitastígur 3; adult/child 1000kr/free; ⏲9am-5pm, from 10am Sat & Sun Jun–mid-Aug, by appointment rest of year) Features a comprehensive collection of minerals (lignite from when Iceland was covered in forests) and taxidermied animals – including a giant blue whalebone more than 100 years old and a polar bear shot by local fishers while swimming off the Hornstrandir coast.

Sleeping & Eating

There's really only one eatery in Bolungarvík, quaint Einarshúsið; head to Ísafjörður for more choice and large grocery stores.

Einarshúsið GUESTHOUSE $$
(☎456 7901; info@einarshusid.is; Hafnargata 41; d/ste without bathroom 15,300/20,300kr; ⏲May-Sep; 📶) Einarshúsið is a turn-of-the-century heritage home near the harbour, and the best place to eat and sleep rolled into one. The eight lovely rooms are decorated in the house's original style, but boast modern bathrooms (avoid the basement room). The restaurant (open 10am to 8pm; mains 1900kr to 3900kr) serves breakfasts, burgers, soup, etc and an excellent fish of the day.

Shopping

O-Design ARTS & CRAFTS
(☎692 5607; www.facebook.com/odesigniceland; Vitastígur 1; ⏲4-6.30pm Thu & Fri, noon-4pm Sat) This small, bright shop sells Icelandic-design, artworks and homewares. Hours can be erratic – check ahead for times.

Getting There & Away

Buses (p243) serve Ísafjörður (1000kr, five daily Monday to Friday) and leave from the corner of Vitastígur and Aðalstræti.

Flybuses to Ísafjörður Airport (p257) cost 1500kr and are timed to coincide with flights.

Ísafjarðardjúp

The largest of the fjords in the region, 75km-long Ísafjarðardjúp takes a massive swath out of the Westfjords' landmass. Circuitous Rte 61 winds in and out of a series of smaller fjords on the southern side, making the drive from the bustling city of Ísafjörður (the largest in the Westfjords) to Hólmavík on the Strandir coast like sliding along each tooth of a fine comb.

Across the fjord lies the enormous Drangajökull glacier. The remote Hornstrandir Nature Reserve (p262) lies further north still.

Súðavík

Just east of Ísafjörður, the small fishing community of Súðavík (www.sudavik.is) commands an imposing view across the fjord to Snæfjallaströnd peninsula. Although the township is nothing more than a string of bright, box-shaped houses, it is definitely worth stopping to visit the **Arctic Fox Center** (Melrakkasetur; ☎456 4922; www.arcticfoxcenter.com; Eyrardalur; adult/child 1200kr/free; ⏲9am-6pm Jun-Aug, 10am-4pm Sep & May, 10am-2pm Mon-Fri Oct-Apr; 📶). The study of the Arctic fox has been underway on nearby Hornstrandir for years, and this locally loved exhibition details the life of the creatures, their relationship with humans and their habitat. It also has a wealth of stuffed foxes in realistic poses plus some cute-looking live ones, who were orphaned, in a pen outside. The centre sits inside the renovated farmstead of **Eyrardalur** – one of the oldest buildings in the area. The on-site cafe is a great place to hang with welcoming locals – try the daily soup (1600kr), which comes with homemade bread. See their website for volunteering opportunities.

Skötufjörður

★ Litlibær CAFE $

(☎456 4809; Skötufjörður; waffles & coffee 1200kr; ⊙10am-5pm mid-May–mid-Sep) One of the Westfjord's most atmospheric eateries, Litlibær is a 19th century, turf-roofed hut that's crammed with family photos and memorabilia. The owners were born and raised on this Skötufjörður farmstead and today rustle up tasty heart-shaped waffles with whipped cream and homemade blueberry and raspberry jam.

Look out for the seal **viewpoint** (Rte 61; ⊙24hr) FREE 1km north.

Ögur

Ögur Travel TOURS

(☎857 1840; www.ogurtravel.com; Rte 61, Ögur; ⊙May-Sep) Book ahead to join Ögur Travel on kayaking or hiking trips (from 5500kr) for a few hours or a few days. A popular kayak is the four-hour tour of Vigur island (p253) (24,500kr) which takes in the incredible scenery and local bird life. Tours run from their cute, welcoming **cafe** (snacks 700-1400kr; ⊙10am-6pm Jun–early-Aug) on the point just east of Skötufjörður.

Mjóifjörður

Heydalur GUESTHOUSE, CAMPGROUND $$

(☎456 4824; www.heydalur.is; Mjóifjörður; sites per adult 1300kr, s/d/cabins from 15,500/17,200/25,600kr; 🛜🏊) It's worth detouring 11km off Rte 61 to hunt out Heydalur, tucked away at the head of Mjóifjörður. Here cabins cluster around a converted barn, the campground stretches beside the river, and indoor and outdoor hot-pots and a geothermal pool are dotted around. The **restaurant** (mains 1800kr to 3600kr; open 10am to 9pm June to August) serves hearty food.

Local activities include guided **horse riding** (per hour 8000kr), and **kayaking** (per two hours 7000kr).

Reykjarfjörður

★ Saltverk Reykjanes FOOD

(☎519 6510; www.saltverk.com; Reykjarfjörður; adult/child 2000kr/free) Some of world's best restaurants buy the crunchy salt produced at this tiny, artisan plant, set on a land spit at Reykjanes. You'll see the steamy, sauna-like tank house and flaky salt crystals being scooped from huge vats. You can buy jars at the end; flavours include seaweed, liquorice and smoked birch. Call ahead to be sure of a tour.

Hótel Reykjanes HOTEL, CAMPGROUND $$

(☎456 4844; www.hotelreykjanes.is; Reykjarfjörður; sites per tent 2900kr, dm/d/q without bathroom 5500/20,200/33,700kr; @🛜🏊) At the end of tiny Reykjarfjörður, well-weathered Hótel Reykjanes is housed in a huge white complex that was once the district's school. Best only if you can't drive any further: rooms are basic (most bathrooms shared), but there's a grassy campground and a 50m outdoor geothermal pool (adult/child 750/400kr) fed by a steamy spring. Simple meals cost 1700kr to 5500kr.

Snæfjallaströnd

On the northeastern shore of Ísafjarðardjúp, the unsurfaced Rte 635 leads north to **Kaldalón**, where a beautiful green valley runs up to the receding **Drangajökull** ice cap. It's possible to hike up to the snow line, but don't venture any further without a local guide, as dangerous crevasses form in the ice and are often invisible under the snow pack.

Further northwest, **Snæfjallaströnd** was abandoned in 1995, but well-prepared walkers can embark on the two-day (30km) hike along the 'Postal Road' from the church at Unaðsdalur along the coast to the bunkhouse at **Grunnavík**, from where you can catch boats to Ísafjörður.

Just before the church at Unaðsdalur, **Dalbær** (☎893 6405; www.snjafjallasetur.is/tourism.html; Rte 635; dm 4000kr, sites per person 1500kr; ⊙mid-Jun–late-Aug) is a great wilderness outpost on the edge of Hornstrandir with sleeping-bag accommodation and camping.

Steinshús MUSEUM

(☎822 1508; www.steinnsteinarr.is; Rte 635, Nauteyri; ⊙10am-8pm Jun-Sep) FREE One of Iceland's most famous poets, Steinn Steinarr (1908–58), is commemorated at this museum set in his former homestead. It details, in Icelandic and English, his wretched childhood, during which his family was split up, and his discovery of poetry and blossoming as a writer. Find it about 3km north of Rte 61 on unpaved Rte 635.

HORNSTRANDIR

Craggy mountains, precarious sea cliffs and plunging waterfalls ring this barely inhabited peninsula, at the northern end of the Westfjords. This is one of Europe's last true wilderness areas, covering some of the most inhospitable parts of the country. It's a fantastic destination for hiking, with challenging terrain and excellent opportunities for spotting Arctic foxes, seals, whales and teeming bird life.

A handful of hardy farmers lived in Hornstrandir until the 1950s, but since 1975 the 580 sq km of tundra, fjord, glacier and alpine upland have been protected as **Hornstrandir Nature Reserve** (☎591 2000; www.ust.is/hornstrandir) with some of the strictest preservation rules in Iceland, thanks to its incredibly rich, but fragile, vegetation. Descendants of some of the old farmers have recently returned and rebuilt their old houses; much of the land is privately owned (so be respectful of landowners' privacy). Keep to marked trails, stick to designated campgrounds and carry out all rubbish.

Weather, Safety & Gear

There are no services available in Hornstrandir and hikers must be fully prepared to tackle all eventualities. The passes are steep, heavy rains will make rivers impassable, fog can be dense and you'll need to carry all your gear, so hiking can be slower than you might expect. In addition, most trails are unmarked, primitive and uneven, so it's essential to carry a good map (eg *Vestfirðir & Dalir: 1*), a compass and a GPS. Rangers stress the need for high-quality, completely weatherproof gear as you will often be hiking in rain, without any way to get dry. Don't force a rescue operation due to ill preparation.

Although scheduled ferries run June to August, and the visitor season runs from late-June to mid-August, the best time to visit Hornstrandir is July. Outside the summer season there are even fewer people around and the weather is even more unpredictable. Between September and 15 June it's mandatory to register with a ranger.

Even in the summer it's smart to register your plans with www.safetravel.is. It's also always essential to plan ahead and get local advice, as vast snow drifts with near-vertical faces can develop on the mountain passes, rivers can be unfordable, and occasionally polar bears arrive on Hornstrandir having been transported by ice floes.

At various points in the park there are emergency huts with VHF radios preset to the Icelandic Coast Guard in case of emergency. Emergency huts are often located near campsites.

You always need to book your return boat in advance; this serves as a safety measure, in case you don't turn up for it. Be aware ferries don't run every day to all pick-up points – you need to schedule your arrival to be in good time to meet the boat.

Be sure to ask rangers about current conditions before setting off. Guided trips can also be easily arranged with operators in Ísafjörður.

Tours

The main operators running tours (boating, hiking, kayaking, skiing etc) into Hornstrandir are West Tours (p254), Borea (p254) and Wild Westfjords (p255), all based in Ísafjörður.

Sleeping

Camping is the main way to stay in Hornstrandir. There are also three options for sleeping-bag accommodation in the main part of Hornstrandir: Hesteyri village, Hornbjargsviti and Grunnavík. Two additional options are in the far-eastern part of the reserve at Reykjarfjörður and Bolungarvík.

Camping in Hornstrandir is free. Carry out all rubbish, and stick to designated campgrounds: wild camping is prohibited in the nature reserve. All campsites have dry latrines. Latrine doors are weighed down with heavy timber to prevent near-certain wind damage if they are left open, so be sure to secure the door after use.

Camping on private grounds with facilities costs from around 1500kr per person. Expect to pay upwards of 5000kr for sleeping-bag space, which must be reserved well in advance, especially in Hesteyri.

Old Doctor's House HOSTEL $

(☎845 5075, Jun-Aug 899 7661; www.hesteyri.net; Hesteyri; d incl breakfast & dinner 16,000kr; ⏲mid-Jun–late-Aug) By far the most developed lodging in Hornstrandir. A stay at this cafe-guesthouse involves dinner, bed and a buffet breakfast. Book well ahead.

Hornbjargsviti HOSTEL $

(☎852 0333, Ferðafélag Íslands 568 2533; www.fi.is; sites per person 2100kr, dm 8500kr; ⏲Jul–early-Aug) Run by Ferðafélag Íslands (FI), and attached to the lighthouse of the same name on the east coast, this hostel sleeps 40 and has a kitchen, drying room and coin-operated showers.

Grunnavík HOSTEL $

(☎866 5491, 456 4664; www.facebook.com/thjonustagrunnavik; Jökulfjirðir; sites per person 1500kr, dm

HIKING HORNSTRANDIR

How is one supposed to choose from the array of trails that zigzag across Hornstrandir's peninsula? Locals and tourists agree: the Royal Horn (or 'Hornsleið') is, hands down, your best option for getting a taste of all that the reserve has to offer. This four- to five-day hike from Veiðileysufjörður to Hesteyri can also be easily modified if you run into bad weather. The trail is partially marked with cairns, but there are very few tourists, so keep track of the route. It's a great way to experience this remote land. Make sure you're fully prepared, pre-book your return boat, and check with the rangers for the latest conditions before setting out.

The Royal Horn

Day 1 Sail from Ísafjörður to Veiðileysufjörður, one of the local *jökulfirðir* (glacier fjords). The hike begins on a street near the bottom of the fjord and follows a cairn-marked trail up the slope and through the mountain pass. From the pass you can descend the mountain on either side until you reach the campground at Höfn in Hornvík. The hike from Veiðileysufjörður to Hornvík can take anywhere between four and eight hours. There's a ranger station at the campground at Höfn in Hornvík, so feel free to get the latest weather forecast and information about trail conditions.

Day 2 Stay in Hornvík for a second night and use your second day to visit **Hornbjarg**, one of Iceland's most beautiful bird cliffs with diverse flora and fauna.

Day 3 Hike from Hornvík to Hlöðuvík. The partly marked trail goes through a mountain pass and is relatively easy to find. At Hlöðuvík, the campsite is situated next to **Hlöðuvíkurós** (the mouth of the Hlöðuvík river). Like Hornvík, Hlöðuvík faces north – it's the perfect place to watch the spectacular midnight sun. Figure around six hours to reach Hlöðuvík.

Day 4 Hike through **Kjarnsvíkurskarð** (a mountain pass) and **Hesteyrarbrúnir** pass to Hesteyri (figure around eight hours). **Hesteyri** is an old village that was abandoned around the middle of the 20th century. There are still several well-kept houses amid the fields of angelica. Ruins of a turn-of-the-century whaling station are found near the village. The coffee shop in Hesteyri is a good place to stop at the end of your hike – you can wait here for your pre-booked ferry back to Ísafjörður.

Day 5 Or enjoy a night in Hesteyri and spend one more day exploring the area before catching the boat. Pitch your tent at the campground, or book in advance to stay at the Old Doctor's House.

Abridged Hikes

You can take the ferry to Veiðileysufjörður, hike up to Hornvík and spend a couple of nights there, ensuring there's time to explore Hornbjarg. From there you can backtrack to Veiðileysufjörður to link up with the boat, *but only if you've pre-booked it*.

Alternatively, just sail in and use Hesteyri as a day-hike base. (Pre-book at the Old Doctor's House if you want sleeping-bag accommodation.)

5000kr; ⏲Jul–mid-Aug) Grunnavík, outside the boundaries of Hornstrandir Nature Reserve, has camping and space for around 20 in sleeping-bag accommodation.

Bolungarvík á Ströndum HUT $

(☎861 1425, 893 6926; hut per person 4000kr; ⏲Jul, rest of year by appointment) Bolungarvík's basic hut sits on the southeast coast of Hornstrandir and is usually used by hikers walking in or out.

Reykjarfjörður HUT $

(☎892 1545, Reykjarfjörður 853 1615; www.reykjarfjordur.is; sites per adult/child 1500kr/free, dm 4700kr, cottage from 15,600kr; ⏲Jun & Jul;) Choose from camping, a sleeping-bag bed (no electricity) or a small cottage that sleeps five. There's also a 20m geothermal pool and hot-pot. The hut is located in the Hornstrandir Nature Reserve, not to be confused with Reykjarfjörður further south on the Strandir coast.

Hornstrandir

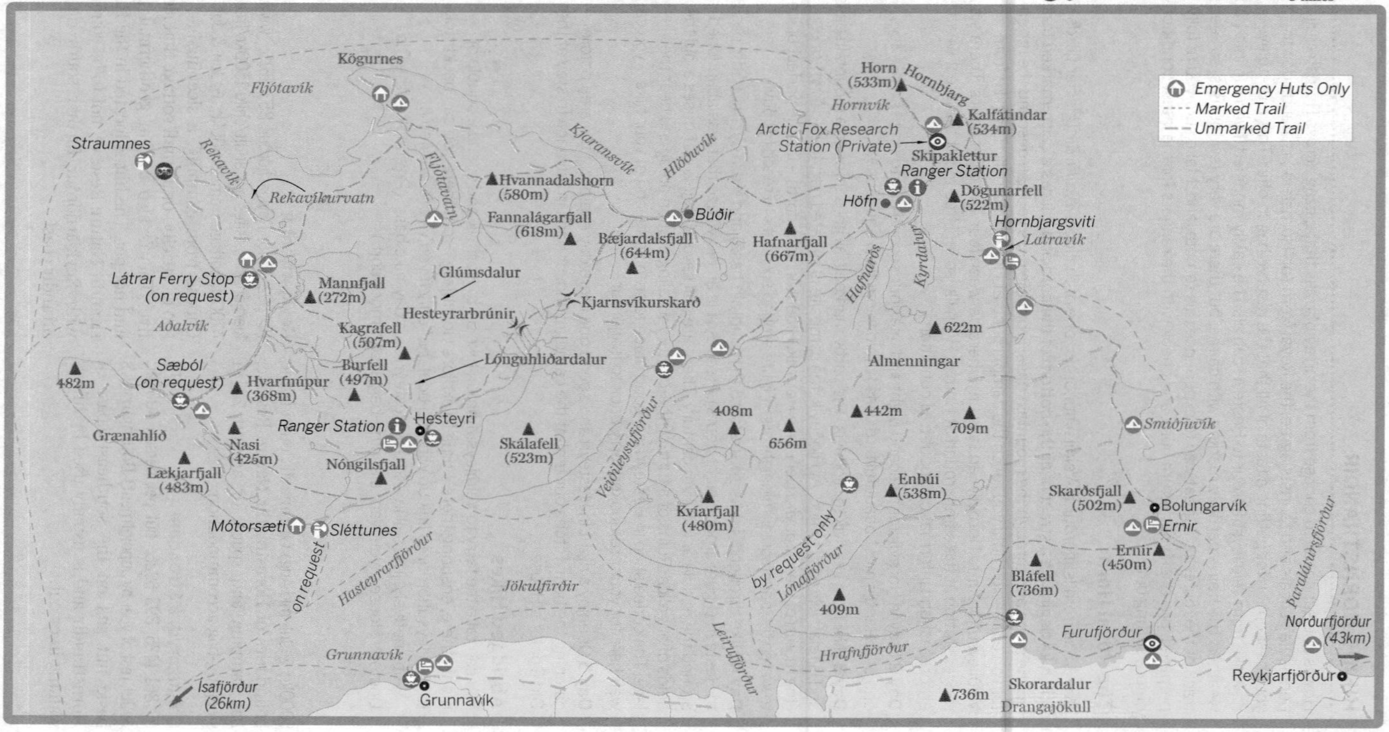

Eating

Besides the basic meals available at the Old Doctor's House (p262) in Hesteyri, you'll need to bring in all food and supplies.

Campfires are prohibited in the reserve, and stoves should be used with caution.

Information

Hornstrandir Park Rangers (Environmental Agency of Iceland; ☎591 2000; www.ust.is/hornstrandir) If entering Hornstrandir Nature Reserve (p262) between September and 15 June it is mandatory to register with a ranger.

Getting There & Away

Take a ferry from Ísafjörður (at the Sundahöfn (p257) docks on the eastern side of the town promontory) or Norðurfjörður (on the Strandir Coast) to Hornstrandir from June to August. One-way rides cost 9500kr to 15,700kr, depending on your destination; children are half-price. You must book your return boat ticket, for safety reasons.

From Ísafjörður, West Tours (p254) books *Sjóferðir* boats to:

Aðalvík (10,700kr, two weekly)
Grunnavík (10,300kr, one weekly)
Hesteyri (10,300kr, six weekly)
Hornvík (6800kr, one weekly)
Hrafnfjörður (15,700kr, one weekly)
Veiðileysufjörður (2700kr, two weekly)

Also from Ísafjörður, Borea (p254) runs *Bjarnarnes* boats to:

Aðalvík (11,500kr, two weekly)
Grunnavík (9500kr, two weekly)
Hesteyri (10,500kr, four weekly)
Hornvík (14,500kr, two weekly)
Veiðileysufjörður (11,500kr, six weekly)

Hornbjargsviti, Hlöðuvík, Fljótavík, Slétta (Sléttunes) and Lónafjörðurare by request only. Early June and late August there is an eight-person minimum.

From Norðurfjörður on the Strandir coast, *Strandferðir* boats run on a schedule (or can be chartered) from June to mid-August to Drangar (9000kr), Reykjarfjörður (10,000kr), Þaralátursfjörður/Furufjörður (13,000kr), Látravík/Hornbjargsviti (15,000kr) and Hornvík (kr16,000kr). Prices are one-way, children travel half-price.

HIKING

It is possible to hike into the reserve from Dalbær in the south, Grunnavík in the southwest or Norðurfjörður on the Strandir coast, but don't underestimate the distances or terrain. The map *Vestfirðir & Dalir: 1* shows estimated durations for different sections of the trails.

STRANDIR COAST

Sparsely populated, magnificently peaceful and all but ignored by travellers, the Westfjords' eastern spine is one of the most dramatic places in all of Iceland. Indented by a series of bristle-like fjords and lined with towering crags, the drive north of Hólmavík, the region's only sizeable settlement, is rough, wild and incredibly rewarding. The end of the line in Iceland, Strandir was thought to be the home of the island's great, persecuted sorcerers. South of here, gently rolling hills stretch along the isolated coastline as far as Staðarskáli, where the sudden rush of traffic tells you that you've returned to the Ring Road and the travelling masses.

Staðarskáli to Hólmavík

Although lacking the natural drama on show further north, the long drive along Rte 68 from Staðarskáli (formerly Brú) to Hólmavík hugs the edge of vast fjords. It's a pleasantly pastoral route, with rolling hills dotted by small farmhouses and lonely churches.

The small **Sheep Farming Museum** (Sauðfjársetur á Ströndum; ☎693 3474, 451 3324; www.strandir.is/saudfjarsetur; adult/child 1000kr/free; ⏲10am-6pm Jun-Aug; 📶), 12km south of Hólmavík, details the region's farming history through photos and artefacts, and offers an inviting **cafe**. For lodging try the basic rooms at **Kirkjuból guesthouse** (☎451 3474; www.strandir.is/kirkjubol; Rte 68; s/d without bathroom incl breakfast 10,500/16,200kr), or the dorms at the modern **Broddanes HI Hostel** (☎618 1830; www.hostel.is; dm/d without bathroom 5800/15,300kr; ⏲mid-May–mid-Sep; 📶) on the point south of Kollafjörður.

There is no public transit on Rte 68, although Strætó (p429) buses do link Staðarskáli with Reykjavík and Akureyri (bus 57), and Hólmavík with Borgarnes (bus 59).

Hólmavík

POP 320

Fishing town Hólmavík offers sweeping views over the still waters of Steingrímsfjörður and has a quirky witchcraft museum (p266). The no-frills village is the best place to stock up on supplies before venturing off into the more rugged territory further north.

Sights & Activities

★Museum of Icelandic Sorcery & Witchcraft
MUSEUM

(Strandagaldur; ☎897 6525; www.galdrasyning.is; Höfðagata 8; adult/child 950kr/free; ⏲9am-7pm May-Sep, reduced hours rest of year; 📶) The multilingual displays at this award-winning museum brilliantly convey dark, dramatic tales. Unlike the witches of New England's Salem trials, most of Iceland's convicted witches were men. Often 'occult practices' were simply old Viking traditions or superstitions, but hidden *grimoires* (magic books) full of puzzling runic designs were proof enough for the local witch hunters (the area's elite) to burn around 20 souls (mostly peasants) at the stake. Don't miss the detailed descriptions of the spells, and the startling 'necropants'.

The tourist information centre is located here, as is Restaurant Galdur.

Another part of the museum, a turf-roofed Sorcerer's Cottage (p268), lies up the coast in Bjarnarfjörður.

Láki Tours
WHALE WATCHING

(☎546 6808; www.lakitours.com; Hafnarbraut 14; adult/child 7300/3650kr; ⏲mid-Jun–Aug) You've a good chance of spotting playful humpbacked wales on these trips onto sheltered Steingrímsfjörður, run by a responsible, small-scale operator. Also look out for minke and pilot whales, white-beaked dolphins, and even orcas and sperm whales.

Tours

Strandahestar
HORSE RIDING

(☎862 3263; www.strandahestar.is; Víðidalsá; per hr 6000kr; ⏲Jun-Aug) Horse riding for all levels in the tranquil valleys near Hólmavík. Book by phone or at the tourist information centre.

Sleeping

Iceland Visit Hostel
HOSTEL $

(☎860 6670; info@hotjoomlatemplates.com; Hafnarbraut 25; dm 6500kr; 📶) Every bunk bed here (yes, every bed) has its own smart TV, plus curtains and lights. Dorms have four beds, while showers and kitchen are sleek and modern.

Holmavík Campsite
CAMPGROUND $

(☎451 3560; www.strandabyggd.is; sites per adult/child 1290kr/free; ⏲mid-May–mid-Sep) Grassy site beside the town swimming pool (pay there), with laundry.

Kríukot
GUESTHOUSE $$

(☎892 6737; Hafnarbraut 17; d without bathrooms from 16,150kr; 📶) Behind a well-weathered exterior sit stylish rooms that blend heritage beds, slender modern chairs and eastern influences. The guest kitchen is roomy and the comfy lounge has sea views.

No email or website, but you can book through third-party websites.

Finna Hótel
HOTEL $$

(☎451 3136; www.finnahotel.is; Borgarbraut 4; d with/without bathroom, incl breakfast 22,500/15,500kr; 📶) At this hillside mini-hotel a corridor of chequerboard tiles leads to cherry-red doors opening into smart, modern rooms, half of them with sea views. The sunny breakfast room overlooks the fjord.

Eating & Drinking

Kaupfélag
SUPERMARKET $

(☎455 3107; www.ksholm.is; Höfðatúni 4; ⏲9am-10.30pm Jun-Aug, closed Sun rest of year) The biggest grocery shop in the area is by the N1 petrol station. Also has a small cafe.

NECROPANTS

Of all the mystical displays at the Museum of Icelandic Sorcery & Witchcraft, perhaps the most bizarre is a plastic replica of legendary 'necropants' – trousers made from the skin of a dead man's legs and groin. It was commonly believed that if a donor made a verbal agreement that his corpse could be skinned upon his death, the resulting necropants would produce money when worn (with the scrotum always full of coins). In order for this to work, the skinned portion of the corpse had to be without holes; the sorcerer had to put the necropants on immediately; then a coin stolen from a poor widow had to be placed in the necropants' scrotum.

Though the boundless scrotum loot was a boon, there was a catch: if the sorcerer didn't get someone else to put on the pants before he himself died, he would be infested with lice for eternity.

Restaurant Galdur CAFE $$
(☎897 6525; www.galdrasyning.is; Höfðagata 10; mains 1800-3500kr; ⊙9am-9pm;) The menu changes daily at this friendly restaurant: look for fish fresh from the fjord, crispy pizzas and rhubarb with cream for dessert. Great outdoor tables when sunny.

Café Riis INTERNATIONAL $$
(☎451 3567; www.caferiis.is; Hafnarbraut 39; mains 2000-3650kr; ⊙11.30am-9pm, bar to 10pm;) The town's welcoming pub and restaurant is set in a historic wooden building with carved magic symbols on the bar. The nutty, sesame-crusted chicken is delicious.

Vínbúðin ALCOHOL
(☎461 2114; www.vinbudin.is; Höfðatúni 4; ⊙4-6pm Mon-Fri, 1-7pm Sat, 2-4pm Sun) National liquor chain.

Information

The **Tourist Information Centre** (☎451 3111; www.holmavik.is/info; Höfðagata 10; ⊙9am-6pm;), in the witchcraft museum; has internet access, lots of info and hiking maps (1500kr).

Getting There & Away

Buses stop at the supermarket near the N1 petrol station.

Reykjavík Take Strætó (www.bus.is; ☎540 2700) bus 59 from Hólmavík to Borgarnes then catch connecting bus 57 to Reykjavík from there (6900kr, four hours, four weekly mid-May to mid-September, two weekly mid-September to mid-May).

Akureyri On Sundays between June and August catch Strætó bus 59 to Bifröst or Borgarnes and transfer onto bus 57 to Akureyri from there (14,200kr, eight hours). On Wednesday and Friday the same route requires an overnight stay in Bifröst or Borgarnes.

Ísafjörður Operated by Hópferðamiðstöð Vestfjarða (p257), a bus (7000kr, three hours, three per week) runs from mid-May to mid-September. Book the day before.

Note that purchasing petrol in Hólmavík requires an N1 card (not available on-site), chip card or card with PIN.

Drangsnes

POP 77

Across Steingrímsfjörður from Hólmavík, Drangsnes (*drowngs*-ness) is a remote little town with views across to North Iceland and the small uninhabited island of Grímsey. The town is well worth a detour for a memorable waterside hot-pot, a rock stack linked to troll legends and birdwatching boat trips.

North of Drangsnes, rough Rte 645 winds around a series of gorgeous crumbling escarpments and tiny driftwood-filled bays. There are no services on this route, but if you've got your own vehicle, the utter tranquillity, incredible views and sheer sense of isolation are truly remarkable. For those interested in the sagas, you'll be keen to know that *Njál's Saga* starts here.

Sights & Activities

The **town's swimming pool** (☎451 3201; sundlaug@drangsnes.is; Grundargata 15; adult/child 600kr/free; ⊙10am-9pm Mon-Fri, 11am-6pm Sat & Sun early-Jun–late-Aug, reduced hours rest of year) has two sparkling hot-pots – handy when the seaside weather is too tumultuous for using the famous hot-pots.

★**Drangsnes Hot-Pot** HOT-POT
(Aðalbraut; by donation) One not to miss: Drangsnes's free, waterfront, geothermal hot-pots are built into the sea wall along the shore road. You'll need eagle eyes to spot a small swimming sign and, over the road, the white building with blue trim containing showers and toilets. Remember to do as Icelanders do and shower thoroughly before crossing to the three geometric pools.

Kerling LANDMARK
Legend has it that this stumpy rock stack is the remains of a petrified troll and Uxi, her bull, is the formation out at sea near the island of Grímsey. The trolls were said to have been digging a trench to sever the Westfjords from the mainland. So absorbed were they in their evil task that they failed to notice the rising sun, its rays struck and they were turned to stone on the spot.

Malhorn Boat Tours BOATING
(☎899 4238, 451 3238; www.malarhorn.is; Grundargata 17; adult/child from 8000/4000kr; ⊙mid-Jun–mid-Aug) Hop aboard snub-nosed *Sundhani ST3* and you might see seals, puffins or even whales as you cruise Steingrímsfjörður. In fine weather the four-hour boat trip to Grímsey Island sails at 2pm on Thursday and Sunday.

Sleeping & Eating

Malarhorn GUESTHOUSE $$
(☎853 6520; www.malarhorn.is; Grundargata 17; d with/without bathroom from 28,400/22,800kr, apt from 38,600kr;) Malarhorn's peaceful row of crisp pine cabins feel thoroughly modern yet remarkably cosy; there's a smart

four-bedroom cottage as well. Breakfast, served in the bright **cafe** (mains 1950-5900kr; ⏲8am-9pm Jun-Aug, by appointment rest of year;), is included in the summer-time guesthouse rates; if you book in winter or for the apartment it costs 2000kr per person.

Bjarnarfjörður

Peaceful Bjarnarfjörður's attractions provide an insight into this coast's magical past – a recreation of a sorcerer's cottage and a scenic hot-pot fed by a sacred spring. It's also the gateway to the dramatic drive north, which reveals fine views across to the rugged Skagi Peninsula in North Iceland. This road often closes with the first snows in autumn and may not reopen until spring; ask locally for information on conditions.

At **Kaldbaksvík** the steep sides of a broad fjord sweep down to a small fishing lake that serenely reflects the surrounding mountains. Just beyond the lake, a 4km trail runs up to the summit of craggy **Lambatindur** (854m). You'll notice copious amounts of enormous driftwood piled up along the shore on this coast – most of it has arrived from Siberia across the Arctic Ocean.

★Geothermal Pool GEOTHERMAL POOL
(adult/child 500/250kr; ⏲8am-10pm May-Sep) Hótel Laugarhóll has a beautifully situated, hot geothermal pool (32°C to 35°C). Don't miss the tiny hot-pot (41°C) tucked in alongside. Only really big enough for one person, it's a deep, natural hollow in the rock, and is fed by **Gvenderlaug** FREE, the sacred pool set just up the hill.

Sorcerer's Cottage MUSEUM
(www.galdrasyning.is; Bjarnarfjörður; ⏲8am-10pm Jun-Aug) FREE The three-room turf-roofed Sorcerer's Cottage is part of the Museum of Icelandic Sorcery & Witchcraft (p266) in Hólmavík and shows what living conditions were like for the purported sorcerers. It's dim, cramped, cluttered interior is intensely atmospheric – look out too for the magic staves carved into the woodwork; designed to deter evil, cast spells or bring good luck. The cottage is signposted behind Hótel Laugarhóll.

★Hótel Laugarhóll HOTEL $$
(☎451 3380; www.laugarholl.is; s with/without bathroom 18,600/14,100kr, d with/without bathroom 25,700/20,000kr; ⏲May-Sep;) Welcome to one of the Westfjords most appealing retreats. Amid mountain-framed plains, an old school has been converted into a smart but relaxed hotel that's run by two of the former teachers. Bedrooms feature crisp white duvets and original art; a generous breakfast buffet is included in the price. There's also a gorgeous geothermal hot-pot and **pool**.

The hotel's **restaurant** (open noon to 5pm and 7pm to 9pm) serves a superb dinner buffet (4900kr), featuring traditional Icelandic dishes such as slow-roast pork with rhubarb jam, pan-fried cod with buttery onions and a rich rye bread and sultana pudding.

Reykjarfjörður

Tucked beneath a looming rock wall and an enormous waterfall at Reykjarfjörður, and approached by way of incredible mountain roads and fjord views, is the strangely enchanting **factory** (☎451 4037; www.djupavik.is; Reykjarfjörður; ⏲9am-6.30pm Jun-Aug) FREE at **Djúpavík**. Once a thriving centre for herring processing, the area was all but abandoned when the plant closed in 1950. The derelict factory (now home to cutting-edge art exhibits) and a beached trawler dominate this hamlet of quaint dorms and houses, and create a magical, memorable mood on this enormous, remote, deep fjord.

Factory Tour WALKING
(☎451 4037; www.djupavik.is; Reykjarfjörður; per person 2000kr; ⏲tours at 10am & 2pm Jun-Aug) The immense abandoned herring factory on the shore at Reykjarfjörður found fame in Sigur Rós' 2007 concert video *Heima*. Tours of the site start at nearby Hótel Djúpavík and guide you through the derelict spaces and the building's past.

Keen photographers can book ahead for an exclusive opportunity to take in the building at their own pace (6000kr, plus 2000kr for any additional people).

★Hótel Djúpavík INN $$
(☎451 4037; www.djupavik.com; s/d/tr without bathroom, incl breakfast 16,200/22,600/29,00kr;) This charming inn decorated with antiques is set on one of the most stunning bays in Iceland in a defunct herring factory's former women's dormitory. The vibe is warmly welcoming from the moment you step into its bustling ground-floor restaurant (mains 2000kr to 5000kr).

Norðurfjörður

Clinging to life at the end of the bumpy road up the Strandir Coast is the tiny fishing hamlet Norðurfjörður (also the name of the fjord). The bustling hamlet has a cafe, a petrol pump and a few guesthouses, and it's the last place to stock up before heading off to Hornstrandir Nature Reserve (p262) on foot or by boat.

As you drive north of Djúpavík to Norðurfjörður, there are two interesting churches at **Árnes** – one is a traditional wooden structure, and the other (virtually across the street) is dramatically futuristic. The small museum, **Kört** (☎451 4025; Árnes 2; adult/child 800kr/free; ⏲10am-6pm Jun-Aug, by appointment rest of year), has displays on fishing and farming, and sells handicrafts.

Kistan (meaning 'the coffin'), an area of craggy rocks, served as the region's main site for witch executions. Iceland's last documented case of witch burning took place here. It's marked on the main road, but is easier to find if you ask for directions.

Sleeping & Eating

There's one good harbourside restaurant and a small minimart near the petrol pumps.

Norðurfjörður Hut HUT $
(☎655 0368; www.fi.is; dm 7000kr; ⏲Jun-Sep) Run by Ferðafélag Íslands (FI), this simple hostel by the beach on Norðurfjörður bay sleeps 22 and has a kitchen.

There's also a basic campsite 2500kr.

Bergistangi GUESTHOUSE $
(☎842 5779; www.bergistangi.is; d 11,400kr,) One of the unfussy rooms of this old-fashioned hostel has wide fjord and mountain views. Save money by requesting sleeping-bag accommodation (4700kr).

The same people also run a hostel at the harbour itself (dm 4000kr).

★Urðartindur GUESTHOUSE $$
(☎843 8110; www.urdartindur.is; Norðurfjörður; d 18,900kr; ⏲May-Sep) Unobstructed fjord views grace these simple, modern guesthouses with private bathrooms and refrigerators – the best have balconies looking onto a black-sand beach. Two cottages (from 23,400kr) each sleep up to four; camping (sites per adult/child 1350kr/free) is possible here too.

Ask the owners about a secret hiking path that leads to a hidden lake.

★Kaffi Norðurfjörður ICELANDIC $$
(☎862 3944; www.facebook.com/KaffiNordurfjordur; Norðurfjörður Harbour; mains 1390-4850kr; ⏲noon-9pm Jun-Aug) Settle at a table overlooking the tiny harbour and let a pair of friendly women transform produce from the fjords and hills – the Icelandic lamb with Béarnaise sauce and local cod with capes are renowned. Be sure to pre-order breakfast, it includes American pancakes, Icelandic cinnamon-scented oatmeal, bacon and eggs.

DON'T MISS

KROSSNESLAUG

Krossneslaug (adult/child 650/200kr; ⏲24hr) is a geothermal (infinity) pool and hot-pot that shouldn't be missed. Up a dirt track about 3km beyond Norðurfjörður, you'll park, then walk down to where it sits at the edge of the universe on a wild black-pebble beach. It's an incredible place to watch the midnight sun flirt with the roaring waves.

Getting There & Away

AIR

Eagle Air (p428) flies between Reykjavík's domestic airport and the airstrip at Gjögur (22,300kr, 50 minutes, one weekly), 16km southeast of Norðurfjörður.

BOAT

Strandferðir (☎849 4079, 859 9570; www.strandferdir.is; Norðurfjörðurr Harbour) boats to Hornstrandir Nature Reserve (p262) operate on a schedule (or can be chartered) between June and mid-August. They run from Norðurfjörður to Drangar (9000kr), Reykjarfjörður (10,000kr), Þaralátursfjörður/Furufjörður (13,000kr), Látravík/Hornbjargsviti (15,000kr) and Hornvík (kr16,000kr). Prices are one-way, children travel half-price.

North Iceland

Includes ➡

Best Places to Eat

- ➡ Vogafjós (p307)
- ➡ Gísli, Eiríkur, Helgi (p288)
- ➡ Siglunes Guesthouse Restaurant (p286)
- ➡ Sjávarborg (p274)
- ➡ Naustið (p317)

Best Places to Stay

- ➡ Tungulending (p318)
- ➡ Deplar Farm (p285)
- ➡ Halllandsnes (p302)
- ➡ Kaldbaks-Kot (p316)
- ➡ Nordic Natura (p321)

Why Go?

Iceland's mammoth and magnificent north is a geologist's heaven. A wonderland of moonlike lava fields, belching mud-pots, epic waterfalls, snowcapped peaks and whale-filled bays – this is Iceland at its best. The region's top sights are variations on a couple of themes: the grumbling, volcanically active earth, and water and ice coursing towards the broad coast.

There are endless treats to discover: little Akureyri, with its surprising moments of big-city living; windy fjordside pastures full of stout Viking horses; and fishing villages clinging tenaciously to life at the end of unsealed roads.

Prepare to be enticed by offshore islands populated by colonies of seabirds and a few hardy locals; lonely peninsulas stretching out towards the Arctic Circle; white-water rapids ready to deliver an adrenaline kick; national-park walking trails to reach unparalleled views; unhyped and underpopulated ski fields; and underwater marvels that woo divers into frigid depths.

Road Distances (km)

	Reykjavík	Akureyri	Siglufjörður	Húsavík	Reykjahlíð (Mývatn)
Akureyri	389				
Siglufjörður	384	76			
Húsavík	476	92	168		
Reykjahlíð (Mývatn)	478	100	176	54	
Þorshöfn	613	235	311	142	172

EASTERN HÚNAFLÓI

Sparsely populated and scattered with only a handful of tiny settlements, the bay of Húnaflói is rich in wildlife. It's known as Bear Bay, named after the polar bears that have occasionally drifted on sea ice from Greenland and come ashore here. The scenery of the area is far gentler than that of the Westfjords, and the low, treeless hills provide nesting sites for rich bird life. Add some neatly manicured towns, seals, horse-riding opportunities and a cluster of museums, and there's plenty to keep you occupied.

Hrútafjörður

The inlet of little Hrútafjörður marks the divide between Northwest Iceland and the Westfjords. As you follow Rte 1 (the Ring Road), you'll encounter **Staðarskáli** (once known as Brú). No more than a road junction with a big, busy N1 petrol station and cafeteria, Staðarskáli acts as a popular leg-stretching spot for motorists.

Sæberg HI Hostel HOSTEL €
(☎894 5504; www.hostel.is; Reykjaskóli; dm/d without bathroom 3800/10,000kr, cottage from 16,000kr; ⏲Mar-Oct; 📶) At Reykjaskóli, barely a cluster of houses 13km north of Staðarskáli, Sæberg HI Hostel is a peaceful little place with hot-pots, cottages and sprawling views. Campers are welcome; bring supplies, as the nearest shop is at Staðarskáli.

Staðarskáli N1 FAST FOOD €
(☎440 1336; www.n1.is; Staðarskáli; ⏲8am-11.30pm; 📶) Petrol, bathrooms, wi-fi, a shop and a grill bar – stop in, as there's not much else along this stretch of Ring Road for a while (until Blönduós, if you're heading east).

Hvammstangi

POP 578

Six kilometres north of the Ring Road, sweet, slow-paced Hvammstangi builds its appeal around its local seal colonies. Many visitors are here to take a seal-watching cruise, go horse riding in the area, or drive the scenic loop around the Vatnsnes Peninsula.

Sights & Activities

Selasetur Íslands MUSEUM
(☎451 2345; www.selasetur.is; Strandgata 1; adult/child 1100kr/free; ⏲9am-7pm Jun-Aug, to 4pm May & Sep, noon-3pm Mon-Fri Apr-Oct) The town's prime attraction is the prominent Icelandic Seal Centre on the harbourfront, where you can learn about conservation of seals, historical seal products and traditional folk tales involving seals. There's also a helpful **tourist information desk** located here; staff are happy to explain where to find the best seal-watching locations in the area.

Selasigling WILDLIFE
(☎897 9900; www.sealwatching.is; Höfðabraut 13; 1¾hr tour adult/child 8500/4500kr; ⏲mid-May–Sep) Seal- and nature-watching trips leave from the harbour on a traditional wooden fishing boat. Scheduled tours leave at 10am, 1pm and 4pm (weather permitting). Midnight-sun sailings are possible by arrangement. Tickets are sold at Selasetur Íslands and include admission to the centre.

Sleeping

Kirkjuhvammur Campsite CAMPGROUND €
(☎899 0008; hvammur.camping@gmail.com; Kirkjuhvammi; sites per person 1200kr, campsite tax 333kr; ⏲early May–mid-Oct; 📶) The excellent, well-maintained Kirkjuhvammur campsite is up the hill near the photogenic old church. Find the turn-off near the town pool. The site has good facilities including a handy service building – with a large dining area where campers can eat – and there are nice walks in the area.

Hvammstangi Cottages & Hostel COTTAGE €€
(☎860 7700; www.stayinhvammstangi.is; Kirkjuhvammsvegur; cottages incl linen 18,200kr; 📶) A cluster of nine cookie-cutter cottages found by the campground. Each is petite but fully self-contained with bathroom, kitchenette and TV, and can sleep up to four (three beds, plus sofa bed) – although that would be snug. Their brand-new hostel is on the waterfront road (Norðurbraut 22a/Rte 711) and is a good deal with sleek rooms with shared baths and kitchen.

Mörk Homestay GUESTHOUSE €€
(☎862 5466; Rte 711; d 25,000kr) Just north of town, this delightful waterfront property offers a modern, stylish fjordside cottage – your room's terrace is the perfect place to enjoy a cuppa and a water view. Breakfast (2500kr per person) is delivered to your room. Reserve on booking.com.

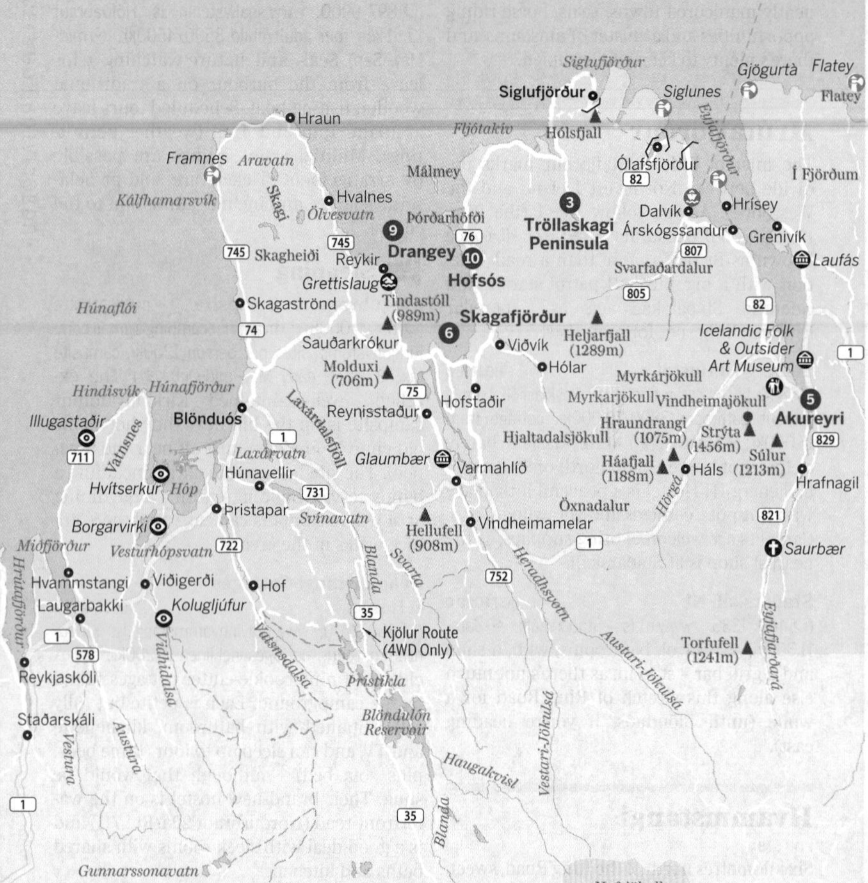

North Iceland Highlights

❶ **Húsavík** (p313) Watching whales emerge from the deep on a trip from this picture-perfect village.

❷ **Jökulsárgljúfur** (p319) Savouring waterfalls, hypnotic rock forms and a storied canyon in this national park.

❸ **Tröllaskagi** (p281) Revelling in vast vistas and rugged mountainscapes between perfect pit stops.

❹ **Mývatn** (p303) Exploring lava castles, pseudo-craters and bubbling fissures before a soak at the Nature Baths.

❺ **Akureyri** (p290) Discovering northern Iceland's

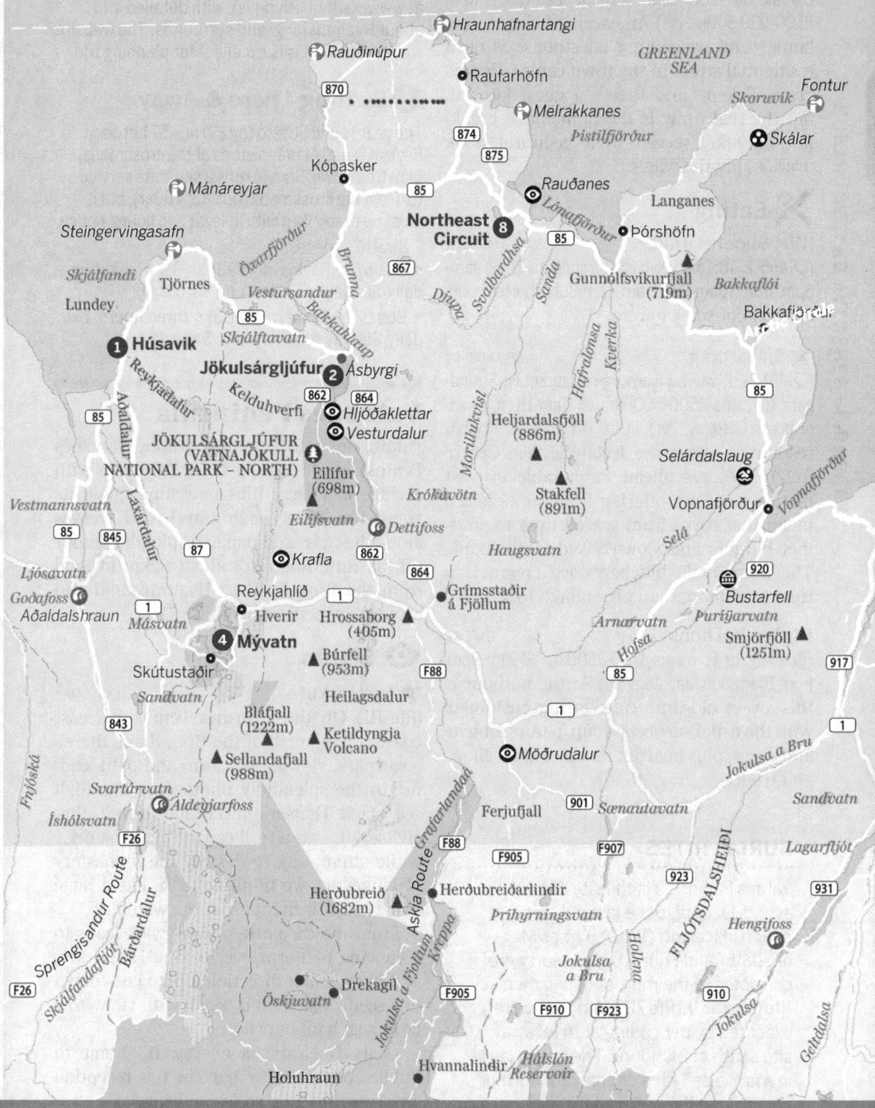

version of urban living in the country's second city.

❻ **Skagafjörður** (p276) Combining river rafting with hot-pot soaks and horse rides.

❼ **Grímsey** (p300) Crossing Iceland's only slice of the Arctic Circle on this bird-filled and troll-packed island.

❽ **Northeast Circuit** (p324) Getting lost amid coastal crags, ponds and rural hamlets.

❾ **Drangey** (p280) Summiting this tiny, puffin-filled outpost.

❿ **Hofsós** (p281) Soaking up infinity views in its perfect fjordside swimming pool.

Guesthouse Hanna Sigga GUESTHOUSE €€
(☎451 2407; www.facebook.com/hannasigg; Garðavegur 26; d/tr without bathroom from 16,000/19,800kr;) An excellent choice, this homey and welcoming guesthouse is on a residential street in the town centre. Rooms are well kept, and there's a guest kitchen, but the real draw is the homemade breakfast (1800kr) served in a beautiful nook overlooking the water.

Eating

KVH Supermarket SUPERMARKET €
(☎455 2310; www.kvh.is; Strandgata 1; 9am-6pm, from 10am Sat, 11am-4pm Sun, shorter hours Apr-Oct) For self-caterers.

★ **Sjávarborg** ICELANDIC €€
(☎451 3131; www.sjavarborg-restaurant.is; Strandgata 1; mains 2500-5000kr; 11am-11pm, shorter hours Oct-May;) Hats off to this stylish restaurant above the Icelandic Seal Centre (p271). Reserve ahead for a table by vast picture windows offering fjord views and a menu that roves from seared tuna to gourmet burgers and slow-cooked lamb shank. The homemade blueberry ice cream is a treat (and more than big enough to share).

Hlaðan Kaffihús CAFE €€
(Brekkugata 2; meals 1700-3500kr; 9am-9pm, from 10am Sun May-Aug;) At the harbour is this sweet old-time cafe, luring customers with the usual suspects: soup, panini, quiche and cakes, plus heartier meals of lamb chops and trout.

BURIAL RITES

Vatnes Peninsula is the site of the events leading to the last public execution in Iceland (1830). Agnes Magnúsdóttir and Friðrik Sigurðsson were convicted of the murder of two men at **Illugastaðir** (Rte 711), and they were executed by beheading at **Þrístapar**, a site south of Blönduós. Their remains lie in a grave at **Tjörn** churchyard, further north along the peninsula.

The story of the crime and executions was the basis for a 1995 Icelandic film *Agnes*, and acclaimed novel *Burial Rites*, by Australian writer Hannah Kent, plus a forthcoming film starring Jennifer Lawrence. The brochure *Burial Rites: The Story of Agnes* maps the sites. Or take a tour with **Seal Travel** (www.sealtravel.is).

Information

Pick up the *Húnaþing vestra* booklet (also online at www.visithunathing.is), with detailed info about Hvammstangi and surrounds. The website www.northwest.is is excellent for planning too.

Getting There & Away

The year-round Strætó (p429) bus 57 between Reykjavík and Akureyri stops at the crossroads, 6km from town. Strætó runs a separate service to/from the crossroads (bus 83; 460kr), but it must be prebooked with at least two hours' notice.

Strætó services:

- Bus 57 to Reykjavík (5980kr, 3½ hours, two daily Sunday to Friday, one Saturday).
- Bus 57 to Akureyri (4600kr, three hours, two daily Sunday to Friday, one Saturday).

Vatnsnes Peninsula

Poking out into Húnaflói, stubby Vatnsnes Peninsula is a starkly beautiful place with a ridge of craggy hills marching down its spine. Rte 711, a rough gravel road, weaves along the coast and makes a splendid detour off the Ring Road (it's about 82km in total from the Ring Road to Hvammstangi and around the peninsula on Rte 711).

Sights

★ **Hvítserkur** LANDMARK
(Rte 711) On the Vatnsnes Peninsula's east coast, 30km north of the Ring Road, there's a car park, viewing platform and path leading to the splendidly photogenic 15m-high sea stack Hvítserkur. Legend has it that Hvítserkur was a troll caught by the sunrise while attempting to destroy the monastery at Þingeyrar; we think he looks like a huge stone beast drinking from the water.

From the car park, a short walk leads to a viewing platform overlooking Hvítserkur, and in the other direction a path goes down to a scenic black-sand beach with views to a large seal haul-out site.

Ósar HI Hostel is nearby. It's home to public toilets and a bar (in the reception area) serving beer, coffee and snacks.

Sleeping & Eating

Ósar HI Hostel HOSTEL €
(☎862 2778; www.hostel.is; Rte 711; dm/d without bathroom 5400/17,000kr; by appointment only Nov-Apr;) Just south of Hvítserkur, or 30km north of the Ring Road on gravel, is Ósar, one of Iceland's most serene farm hostels thanks

to friendly owner Knútur, sweeping views and nearby wildlife. The simple accommodation is in various buildings on a working sheep and horse farm, with rooms, cottages, guest kitchen and laundry.

Geitafell ICELANDIC €€
(☎861 2503; www.geitafell.is; Rte 711; fish soup 3200kr; ⏲11am-10pm early May-Sep) Roughly 25km from Hvammstangi – 3km north of Illugastaðir – is the wonderfully unique Geitafell, a restaurant in a converted barn where fish soup is the star, served with salad and home-baked bread (*skyr* – a yoghurt-like dessert – is another highlight on the short menu). The property owners, Sigrún and Robert, are long-time locals with fascinating stories.

Hvammstangi to Blönduós

If you're following the Ring Road (Rte 1) between Hvammstangi and Blönduós, you can be tempted off the main road with some nice little diversions, from horse farms to photogenic stone churches.

Sights & Tours

Kolugljúfur CANYON
(Rte 715) Take Rte 715 south off the Ring Road to reach the scenic waterfalls at Kolugljúfur, an enchanting canyon that legend has it was once home to a beautiful female troll. It's a 6km drive if you take the turn-off 7km past Gauksmýri horse farm.

Þingeyrar CHURCH
(http://thingeyraklausturskirkja.is/en; Rte 721; adult/child 500kr/free; ⏲10am-5pm Jun-Aug) Around 19km west of Blönduós, a 6km detour along Rte 721 leads you to a precious stone church, Þingeyrar, sitting quietly and photogenically beside Hóp lagoon. The current structure was erected in the 1860s, but 800 years earlier the site hosted a district *þing* (assembly) and a Benedictine monastery. There's a small visitor centre here too, with exhibits and a few refreshments for sale. The church's entrance fee gets you a guided tour.

Gauksmýri Lodge HORSE RIDING
(☎451 2927; www.gauksmyri.is; Rte 1) As well as its lovely accommodation and restaurant, Gauksmýri is well known for guided horse-riding tours. The most popular is the 90-minute tour (adult/child 9500/7000kr), which runs daily, weather permitting. Bookings advised. There are longer tours, stable visits (800kr) and horse shows (1800kr).

Brekkulækur HORSE RIDING
(☎451 2938; www.abbi-island.is; Rte 704) Serious horse riders should book ahead with Brekkulækur, which offers adventurous and acclaimed multiday trips (from €1520 for eight days). The farm (with guesthouse) is 9km south of the Hvammstangi turn-off on Rte 704. There's also a rich program of multiday hiking tours, plus the opportunity to join the annual *réttir* (sheep and round-up) on horseback in September (€1740). Has lodging.

Sleeping & Eating

Gauksmýri Lodge HOTEL €€
(☎451 2927; www.gauksmyri.is; Rte 1; d with/without bathroom incl breakfast 24,050/16,500kr; @🛜👪) Horse-lovers will be in heaven at Gauksmýri, a highly regarded horse farm with tours and a lodge on the Ring Road 3.5km east of the turn-off to Hvammstangi. Rooms are comfy, with equine accents in the decor, and the lodge has lovely grounds, restaurant and lounge.

The restaurant is open to nonguests and does a full lunch/dinner buffet (2900/5900kr; open June to mid-September) where the variety of meats may rankle (it includes foal, but also local char and lamb) and has a broad menu.

Blönduós

POP 821

A couple of museums, an unusual modern church and an island nature walk – the service town Blönduós is about as simple as that. Except for an incredible foodie retreat (p276), there isn't much to woo you off the road, but the town makes a fine place to refuel and stretch your legs.

The churning Blanda River divides the town in half; the N1 station marks the northern entrance.

Sights

The small island, **Hrútey**, in the middle of the Blanda River and connected to town by a small footbridge, makes for a pleasant stroll to take in the bird life, including harlequin ducks. Wear solid footwear – trails can be slippery.

Textile Museum MUSEUM
(Heimilisiðnaðarsafnið; www.textile.is; Árbraut 29; adult/child 1200kr/free; ⏲10am-5pm Jun-Aug)

Set in a head-turning modern building on the north bank of the Blanda River, this small, attractive museum displays local handicrafts, painstakingly intricate embroideries and early Icelandic costumes.

It hosts a knitting festival in June.

Sleeping & Eating

There are a couple of basic eateries along the main road, and a **supermarket** (☎455 9020; Húnabraut 4; ⏲9am-7pm Mon-Fri, 10am-6pm Sat, noon-6pm Sun) and cafe just off it.

★ **Brimslóð Atelier** GUESTHOUSE €€
(☎820 0998; www.brimslod.is; Brimslóð 10; d/tr without bathroom incl breakfast 22,400/31,100kr; ⏲Mar-Nov; 📶) This fabulous seaside guesthouse is hands down Blönduós' finest option. It's a stylish retreat run by welcoming locals with a fine food pedigree (including publishing cookbooks and running food workshops). Four rooms share two bathrooms and a chic lounge. As you might expect, breakfast is a highlight. With prior notice, guests can also enjoy a three-course dinner showcasing local ingredients (7500kr). Workshops delve into Icelandic food heritage.

Retro Guesthouse GUESTHOUSE €€
(☎5194445; www.facebook.com/Retroguesthouse; Blöndubyggð 9; d 19,700kr; 📶) Serene and seafront: what's not to love? Two beautifully tranquil cottages, one standard-house shaped and one shaped like a wooden barrel, perch on the shore, each one a private retreat, perfect for two.

Glaðheimar CAMPGROUND, COTTAGES €€
(☎820 1300; www.gladheimar.is; Rte 1; camping per person 1350kr, cottages from 15,500kr) In an appealing setting near the river, Glaðheimar has camping and an assortment of self-contained cottages sleeping up to six people (larger cottages have the bonus of a hot tub, and a few also have sauna). Linen costs extra.

Getting There & Away

Strætó (p429) services:

- Bus 57 to Reykjavík (7360kr, four hours, two daily Sunday to Friday, one Saturday).
- Bus 57 to Akureyri (3220kr, 2¼ hours, two daily Sunday to Friday, one Saturday).

If you call 540 2700 two hours ahead of the scheduled service, bus 84 serves Skagaströnd (920kr, 30 minutes, three daily Sunday to Friday, two Saturday).

WESTERN SKAGAFJÖRÐUR

Skagafjörður is renowned for horse breeding and wild landscapes – this, plus its historical remains and adrenaline-infused activities, make it one of Iceland's lesser-known but most fabulous stops.

Note that settlements on the western half of Tröllaskagi Peninsula (Hólar í Hjaltadalur, Hofsós, Lónkot) sit on the Skagafjörður shoreline, and there are a couple of fjord islands – Drangey (p280) in particular is well worth a visit. For online information, see www.visitskagafjordur.is.

Varmahlíð

POP 127

This Ring Road service centre is slightly more than a road junction and yet not quite a town, and it's a great base for white-water rafting and horse riding. Access to most activity operators is along the sealed Rte 752, south of the township.

Varmahlíð (pronounced *var*-ma-leeth) is also a convenient 'doorway' into the highlands: the Kjölur route (Rte 35) leaves the Ring Road about 25km west of town (note that 2WD rental cars are prohibited to drive it – you need a 4WD). A bus runs this route daily in summer.

Activities

Horse farms in the area often host hour-long shows that showcase the five gaits of the Icelandic horse, and detail the breed's history. Shows are usually scheduled for groups, and individuals can then attend. Ask at the tourist information centre (p278) or contact the farms directly.

The summertime weekly 'Horses & Heritage' evening program (2000kr) at Lýtingsstaðir encompasses facts and stories in a beautifully crafted turf house known as the Old Stable. Or just check out its Old Stable exhibition (adult/child 1000kr/free; open daily).

Tours

Horse Riding

There are half a dozen companies in and around Varmahlíð offering one to two hours rides for beginners, plus longer day rides. A few plan week-long expeditions into the highlands, or offer the chance to participate in the annual sheep roundup *(réttir)* in September.

★**Lýtingsstaðir** HORSE RIDING
(☎453 8064; www.lythorse.com; Rte 752; 1/2hr horse ride 6000/9000kr) The lovely farm Lýtingsstaðir, 20km south of Varmahlíð, has a great program of short and long horse rides. There's a fantastic 'Stop and Ride' package including one night in a self-contained cottage and a two-hour ride for 32,000kr (two people, including linen). Multiday tours (from €1400 for six days) include a highlands expedition, or sheep roundup participation. Good cottage accommodation.

Hestasport HORSE RIDING
(☎453 8383; www.riding.is; Rte 752) One of Iceland's most respected horse-riding outfits, with its helpful office just off the Ring Road on Rte 752. It offers one-/two-hour tours along the Svartá River for 8500/12,000kr (no experience required), and full-day rides for 22,000kr. Multi-day trips (book well in advance) start at 117,000kr. Short winter rides are available (10,000kr).

Rafting

The area around Varmahlíð is home to northern Iceland's best white-water rafting. Trips run from about May to September on the high-octane Austari-Jökulsá (East Glacial River; Class 4+ rapids) and the more placid, family-friendly Vestari-Jökulsá (West Glacial River; Class 2+ rapids). Drysuits are provided.

Bakkaflöt RAFTING
(☎453 8245; www.bakkaflot.com) Run by a local family, Bakkaflöt offers family-friendly rafting on beautiful Vestari-Jökulsá (14,500kr), and an adrenaline-pumping five hours on churning Austari-Jökulsá (24,500kr; minimum age 18). There's also guided white-water kayaking or sedate evening kayaking (9900kr). Good **accommodation** includes camping, a comfortable guesthouse and tidy cottages, plus there's a tasty **restaurant**. They also offer packages including horse riding and sailing. Find the farm 11km south of Varmahlíð, off Rte 752.

Viking Rafting RAFTING
(☎823 8300; www.vikingrafting.com; Rte 752) Options include a family-friendly four-hour float on the Vestari-Jökulsá (adult/child 14,990/9990kr; minimum age six); a challenging six-hour adventure on the Austari-Jökulsá (24,990kr; minimum age 18); and the ultimate rafting expedition, a three-day trip (189,990kr) that starts from the Sprengisandur highlands. Also possible: guided white-water kayaking trips.

WORTH A TRIP

GLAUMBÆR

The 18th-century turf-farm museum **Glaumbær** (www.glaumbaer.is; Rte 75; adult/child 1700kr/free; ⌚9am-6pm mid-May–mid-Sep, 10am-4pm Mon-Fri early May & mid-Sep–mid-Oct) is the best museum of its type in northern Iceland and worth the easy 8km detour off the Ring Road, following Rte 75 north from Varmahlíð.

The traditional Icelandic turf farm was a complex of small separate buildings, connected by a central passageway. Here you can see this style of construction, with some building compartments stuffed full of period furniture, equipment and utensils. It gives a fascinating insight into the cramped living conditions of the era.

The company's base camp is at Hafgrímsstaðir, 15km south of Varmahlíð on Rte 752. Camping is possible here. Pick-ups for the longer trips can be arranged from Akureyri.

Sleeping & Eating

There are plenty of rural places to crash in the area; ask at the tourist information centre (p278). If you're doing rafting or riding tours with Bakkaflöt or Lýtingsstaðir, note that they both have good sleeping options. These are open to all; see their websites for details.

There's a busy grill-bar in the petrol station that marks the hub of town; the **supermarket** (☎455 4680; Rte 1; ⌚9am-10pm), is also here. The restaurant at **Hótel Varmahlíð** (☎453 8170; www.hotelvarmahlid.is; Laugavegur 1; d/tr incl breakfast from 20,000/23,000kr; @ 📶) has a decent reputation, but the best place for a bite is Áskaffi at Glaumbær (you can visit the cafe without paying the museum entrance fee).

Campsite CAMPGROUND €
(☎899 3231; http://tjoldumiskagafirdi.is; sites per person 1300kr, campsite tax 333kr; ⌚mid-May–mid-Sep) Follow the signs from Hotel Varmahlíð to reach this secluded, sheltered campground above the town, near hiking trails.

★**Hestasport Cottages** COTTAGE €€
(☎453 8383; www.riding.is/cottages; cottages for 2/4/6 people 25,000/35,000/40,000kr; 📶 👪) Perched on the hill above Varmahlíð, this

cluster of seven high-quality self-contained timber cottages has good views, comfy rooms and a very inviting stone hot-pot. Some sleep six and all include kitchen facilities and linen. They're excellent value, especially for families and groups.

Shopping

Alþýðulist ARTS & CRAFTS
(453 7000; Rte 1; 10am-6pm) In a sweet turf-roofed house just next door to the N1, this shop is crammed full of colourful knitwear and handicrafts made in the Skagafjörður area. Look for the horse motif in the *lopapeysur* (traditional Icelandic sweaters). The info centre is here too.

Information

Tourist Information Centre (455 6161; www.visitskagafjordur.is; Rte 1; 9am-6pm mid-May–Sep, 10am-4pm Mon-Fri rest of year;) In a turf house next to the service station, they have brochures and maps.

Getting There & Away

All buses stop at the N1.

SBA-Norðurleið (p429) services:

- Bus 610a to Reykjavík via the Kjölur route (13,700kr, nine hours, one daily mid-June to mid-September).

Strætó (p429) services (two daily Sunday to Friday, one Saturday):

- Bus 57 to Reykjavík (7820kr, 5¼ hours).
- Bus 57 to Akureyri (2760kr, 1¼ hours).
- Bus 57 to Sauðárkrókur (920kr, 20 minutes).

Öxnadalur

If you haven't the time to explore scenic Skagafjörður or magnificent Tröllaskagi, never fear: you'll still be treated to incredible vistas courtesy of Öxnadalur, a magnificent, narrow, 30km-long valley on the Ring Road between Varmahlíð and Akureyri. Stunning peaks and thin pinnacles of rock flank the mountain pass; the imposing 1075m spire of **Hraundrangi** and the surrounding peaks of **Háafjall** are among the most dramatic in Iceland.

Rent a room or the whole house on **Auðnir** (%847 9309; http://audnir1.wixsite.com/audnir; Rte 1; d without bathroom 10,400kr), a lush farm beautifully situated under Hraundrangi. Shared kitchen and living room.

Sauðárkrókur

POP 2574

As the winding Jókulsá River collides with the marshy delta of upper Skagafjörður (pronounced *sow*-thowr-kroak-ur), you'll find scenic Sauðárkrókur sitting quietly at the edge of the waterway.

Economically, Sauðárkrókur is doing quite nicely, thank you, with fishing, tanning and trading keeping the community afloat and the population vibrant. The town has all the services you'll need, plus good sleeping and eating options; tourist information is dispensed by the town museum. Sauðárkrókur is also the gateway to treasures around Tin-

WINTER WONDERS

You're probably aware that the number of visitors to Iceland has skyrocketed in recent years. You may well be asking: what if there was a way to experience Iceland's awesome outdoors, but with smaller crowds? There is: visit in winter. For the Northern Lights, yes, but so much more. And don't feel you need to be confined to Reykjavík and surrounds – domestic flights to Akureyri operate year-round, and there's a growing number of winter activities and operators in the country's north to help you experience the snowy-mountain magic.

Akureyri, the Tröllaskagi Peninsula and Mývatn are all winter wonderlands. Akureyri has winter festivals and easy access to Iceland's biggest ski field at Hlíðarfjall (p294). Tröllaskagi offers smaller ski fields (at Dalvík, Ólafsfjörður and Siglufjörður), plus great heliskiing (peak months: March and April); get info on skiing and great passes at www.skiiceland.is. Mývatn has activities like snowshoe and cross-country ski tours, snowmobiling on the frozen lake and dog sledding in the hills. Tip: travel from February on, when daylight hours are increasing, or Christmas–New Year, a festive time to visit.

If you're not experienced in winter driving, it's a good idea to leave that to the kitted-out professionals with their super-Jeeps and local expertise. Operators such as Saga Travel (p295), based in Akureyri and Mývatn, are a sure bet – and check out Bergmenn Mountain Guides (p288), Viking Heliskiing (p287), and Mývatn's Geo Travel (p305), Hike&Bike (p305) and Sel-Hótel (p309), to see what else appeals.

dastóll (p280), and brilliant excursions to offshore Drangey (p280).

Sights

Tannery Visitor Centre FACTORY
(Gestastofa Sútarans; ☎512 8025; www.facebook.com/tanneryvisitorcenter; Borgarmýri 5; ⏰8am-4pm, to noon Sat & Sun mid-May–mid-Sep, 11am-4pm Mon-Fri rest of year) At 9am and 2pm weekdays (from mid-May to mid-September) you can tour Iceland's only tannery (500kr), or stop by the visitor centre anytime to admire (and purchase) the products: gorgeous long-hair sheepskins, colourful leather goods, and unique products made from fish skin processed at the tannery.

Puffins & Friends MUSEUM
(☎845 1590; www.puffinandfriends.com; Aðalgata 24; adult/child 1500/500kr; ⏰9am-5pm, from noon Sat & Sun) Learn about puffins, whales and their seal friends, and watch a 360-degree movie of puffins and the Northern Lights.

Minjahúsið MUSEUM
(Aðalgata 16b; ⏰noon-7pm Jun-Aug) FREE There's a quirky ensemble of exhibits at the excellent 'heritage house', including a series of restored craftsmen's workshops, a pristine A-model Ford from 1930, and a stuffed polar bear caught locally in 2008.

Sleeping

Grand-Inn Bar & Bed GUESTHOUSE €
(☎844 5616; www.facebook.com/GrandinnBarandBed; Aðalgata 19; s/d without bathroom 10,500/12,400kr; 📶) At the Grand-Inn Bar (p280) on the main street, the '& Bed' part of the equation is 10 budget beds in five rooms in the building adjacent to the bar. There's a small guest kitchen and lounge, and decent-sized rooms.

Campsite CAMPGROUND €
(☎899 3231; http://tjoldumiskagafirdi.is; Skagfirðingabraut; sites per person 1300kr, campsite tax 333kr; ⏰mid-May–mid-Sep) The campsite beside the swimming pool is a bit barren and treeless, but has decent facilities.

★**Gamla Posthúsið** APARTMENT €€
(☎892 3375; www.ausis.is; Kirkjutorg 5; apt 23,000-25,500kr; 📶) Australian Vicki moved to town in 2010 and took it upon herself to restore the old post office opposite the church. The two resulting one-bedroom apartments make a superb home away from home. Each boasts a full modern kitchen, a welcome pack of food, oodles of room and Scandi-chic decor. Winter prices drop by around 40%, making them a great bargain.

★**Guesthouse Hofsstaðir** GUESTHOUSE €€
(☎453 7300; www.hofsstadir.is; Rte 76; d/tr incl breakfast 21,400/27,400kr; 📶) In a unique position at the head of Skagafjörður, roughly equidistant (20km to 25km) from Sauðárkrókur, Varmahlíð and Hofsós, this high-end guesthouse offers warm hospitality, first-class rooms and a cosy restaurant (open April to October). The panoramas are pretty cool, and easily enjoyed from your terrace.

Helluland Guesthouse GUESTHOUSE €€
(☎853 3220; www.helluland.is; Helluland 1; d without bathroom incl breakfast 15,500kr) Sweeping views down the fjord and out to sea makes these tidy rural rooms on a horse farm a relaxing option. Guest kitchen and modern shared bathroom. Arranges horse tours too.

Keldudalur Farm Cottages CABIN €€
(☎453 6233; www.keldudalur.is; Rte 754; apt/cottages from 19,300/24,300kr; 📶) Gorgeous sweeps of river and pastures surround Keldudalur and its batch of apartments and small houses kitted out with TVs, fully equipped kitchens and a shared hot-pot.

Eating & Drinking

Sauðárkróksbakarí BAKERY, CAFE €
(Aðalgata 5; ⏰7am-6pm Mon-Fri, 9am-4pm Sat & Sun) This main-street bakery is the heartbeat of the town. Stop in to stock up on supplies for your drive – everything from fresh-baked bread to soup to iced doughnuts, and some fine choc-chip cookies.

Hard Wok Cafe INTERNATIONAL €
(☎453 5355; www.facebook.com/Hard.Wok.Cafe.Island; Aðalgata 8; mains 1800-3000kr; ⏰11.30am-9.30pm Jun-Aug, shorter hours rest of year; 📶) The newest entry on Sauðárkrókur's food scene, this casual restaurant specialises in noodles and Asian fusion, but also offers popular pizza, fish-and-chips and other classics. Warm staff and homemade ice cream too!

Skagfirðingabúð SUPERMARKET €
(☎455 4530; Ástorg 1; ⏰9am-7pm Mon-Fri, 10am-4pm Sat) South of town, close to the N1.

Kaffi Krókur ICELANDIC €€
(☎453 6454; www.kaffikrokur.is; Aðalgata 16; mains 1700-7000kr; ⏰11.45am-9pm, to 10pm Fri & Sat; 📶) This restaurant has a welcoming yellow exterior and a crowd-pleasing menu. It's known for its lobster and shrimp sandwich, burgers, pizza and lamb.

DON'T MISS

DRANGEY

The tiny rocky islet of **Drangey** (*drown*-gay), in the middle of Skagafjörður, is a dramatic flat-topped mass of volcanic tuff with 180m-high sheer cliffsides rising abruptly from the water. The cliffs serve as nesting sites for around a million seabirds (puffins, guillemots, gannets, kittiwakes, fulmar, shearwaters and predatory gyrfalcons), and have been used throughout Iceland's history as 'nature's grocery store' (for locals seeking birds and eggs).

Grettir's Saga recounts that both outlaw hero Grettir and his brother Illugi lived on the island for three years and were slain there. Brave (foolhardy?) saga fans come to the area to recreate Grettir's feat, swimming the 7km between Drangey and Reykir.

Drangey Tours (☎821 0090; www.drangey.net; tours adult/child 13,500/7000kr) offers fabulous three-hour boat trips to Drangey. The tour (bookings required), departing from a small harbour beside Grettislaug, involves a boat trip and guided hike up the steep cliff-face – this is challenging for people with height phobias or mobility issues, as it involves ropes and ladders. You can stay in the boat.

Note that puffins have usually departed Drangey by mid-August.

Grand-Inn Bar BAR
(Aðalgata 19; ⏲4-10pm Mon-Wed, to midnight Thu, to 3am Fri & Sat, 3-6pm Sun) Cool mountain-peak graphics and vintage sofas set the scene at this end-of-week bar on Sauðárkrókur's main drag, where local brews are on tap, plus loads more in bottles. Gæðingur is the local draught pick: Indian Pale Ale, wheat beer or stout.

Vínbúðin ALCOHOL
(Smáragrund 2; ⏲11am-6pm Mon-Thu, to 7pm Fri, to 4pm Sat) Government-run liquor store.

Getting There & Away

The bus stop is at the N1, about 1.3km south of the town centre along Aðalgata.

Strætó (p429) services:

- Bus 57 to Reykjavík (7820kr, five hours, two daily Sunday to Friday, one Saturday).
- Bus 57 to Akureyri (2760kr, 1½ hours, two daily Sunday to Friday, one Saturday).
- Bus 57 to Varmahlíð (920kr, 20 minutes, two daily Sunday to Friday, one Saturday).
- Bus 85 to Hólar and Hofsós (920kr to either destination, two daily Wednesday, Friday and Sunday). These services only operate if prebooked. Call Strætó at least two hours before departure.

Tindastóll & Grettislaug

North of Sauðárkrókur, Skagafjörður's western coast is a stunningly silent place capped by scenic mountains. Tindastóll is the most prominent peak, and at its northern end is a geothermal area and storied waterfront bathing pool known as Grettislaug.

Offshore, guarding the mouth of Skagafjörður, are the uninhabited islands of Drangey and Málmey, both tranquil havens for nesting seabirds. Summertime boat tours of Drangey depart from a small harbour beside Grettislaug.

At Grettislaug is a campground (1500kr per person) and no-frills **guesthouse** (☎841 7313; fagranesgisting@gmail.com; Rte 748, Reykir; d without bathroom 16,800kr) with a cafe, or you can visit from a base in Sauðárkrókur.

Sights & Activities

Grettislaug GEOTHERMAL POOL
(Grettir's Bath; Rte 748; adult/child 1000kr/free) At the northern end of Tindastóll is a geothermal area, Reykir, that was mentioned in *Grettir's Saga*. Grettir supposedly swam ashore from the island of Drangey and soothed his aching bones in an inviting spring. Today Grettislaug is a popular natural bathing hole, alongside a second hot-pot.

Tindastóll MOUNTAIN
Tindastóll (989m) is a prominent Skagafjörður landmark, extending for 18km along the coast. The mountain and its caves are believed to be inhabited by an array of sea monsters, trolls and giants. The summit of Tindastóll affords a spectacular view across all of Skagafjörður. The easiest way to the top is along the marked trail that starts from the high ground along Rte 745 west of the mountain (it's a strenuous hike). There's **skiing** here in winter (see http://skitindastoll.is).

TRÖLLASKAGI

Tröllaskagi (Troll Peninsula) rests its vast mountainous bulk between Skagafjörður and Eyjafjörður. Here the craggy mountains, deep valleys and gushing rivers are reminiscent of the Westfjords, but bigger. Tunnels link the northern townships of Siglufjörður and Ólafsfjörður, once dead-end towns that saw little tourist traffic.

Having your own wheels makes exploring this region easier. The journey from Varmahlið to Akureyri along the Ring Road (Rte 1) is a very scenic 95km, but if you have time up your sleeve and a penchant for getting off the beaten track, the 186km journey between those two towns following the Tröllaskagi coastline (Rtes 76 and 82) conjures up magical scenery, and plenty of excuses to pull over and explore.

Hólar í Hjaltadalur

POP 94

With its prominent church dwarfed by looming mountains, tiny Hólar (www.holar.is), in the scenic valley of Hjaltadalur, makes an interesting historical detour. The bishopric of Hólar was the ecumenical and educational capital of northern Iceland between 1106 and the Reformation, and it continued as a religious centre and the home of the northern bishops until 1798, when the bishop's seat was abolished.

Hólar then became a vicarage until 1861, when the vicarage was shifted west to Viðvík. In 1882 the present agricultural college was established – it's now known as Hólar University College, specialising in equine science, aquaculture and rural tourism. In 1952 the vicarage returned to Hólar. Another attraction is the **Icelandic Craft Beer Festival** (⏲ Jun), which is held here.

A historical-trail brochure (available at Hólar's accommodation information desk) guides you round some of the buildings at Hólar. **Nýibær** is a historical turf farm dating from the mid-19th century and inhabited until 1945. Also worth seeing is **Auðunarstofa**, a replica of the 14th-century bishop's residence, built using traditional tools and methods.

There's some basic accommodation in the college buildings at Hólar, plus an appealing campground.

Hólar is 11km off Rte 76; the turn-off is signed 20km east of Sauðárkrókur, and 15km south of Hofsós.

Cathedral CHURCH

(Hóladómkirkja; www.kirkjan.is/holadomkirkja; ⏲ 10am-6pm Jun–mid-Sep) Completed in 1763, Hólar's red-sandstone cathedral is the oldest stone church in Iceland and brims with historical works of art, including a 1674 baptismal font carved from a piece of soapstone that washed in from Greenland on an ice floe. Check online for summer concert series.

Icelandic Horse History Centre MUSEUM

(Sögusetur Íslenska Hestsins; ☎ 455 6345; www.sogusetur.is; adult/child 900kr/free; ⏲ 10am-6pm Tue-Sun Jun-Aug) The admission price gets you a personalised tour around this comprehensive exhibit on Iceland's unique horse breed and its role in Iceland's history. It's fittingly located in an old stable at the heart of the Hólar estate.

Hofsós

POP 147

The sleepy fishing village of Hofsós has been a trading centre since the 1500s, but is now on the map for its spectacular fjord-front swimming pool.

Sights & Activities

★ **Hofsós Swimming Pool** SWIMMING

(Sundlaugin á Hofsósi; ☎ 455 6070; www.facebook.com/sundlauginhofsosi; Suðurbraut; adult/child 900/300kr; ⏲ 7am-9pm Jun-Aug, shorter hours rest of year) The village's magnificent outdoor swimming pool (with adjacent hot-pot) has placed Hofsós firmly in the country's collective consciousness. It was opened in 2010 thanks to donations from two local women, and its fjordside design, integrated into the landscape and offering infinity views, is close to perfect.

Infinity Blue (www.infinityblue.is) offers a relaxing late-night 'float therapy' session at the pool (4900kr), available nightly from 10pm to midnight (under the midnight sun or even Northern Lights, if conditions are right). Bookings essential.

SKI PASS

Love to ski or snowboard? The 5x5 Ski Pass (www.skiiceland.is; adult/child €140/45, for snowboarding €190/100) gives you five days of skiing at the five major resorts in North Iceland: Akureyri, Sauðárkrókur, Siglufjörður, Ólafsfjörður and Dalvík.

The Northern Lights

Topping myriad bucket lists and filling Instagram feeds, the Northern Lights (or aurora borealis) are a magnet drawing countless cool-weather visitors, who arrive with fingers crossed for good viewing conditions, their necks craned skywards.

What Are They?

The Inuit thought the Northern Lights were the souls of the dead; Scandinavian folklore describes them as the spirits of unmarried women; and the Japanese believed that a child conceived under the dancing rays would be fortunate in life. Modern science, however, has a different take on the aurora borealis.

The magical curtains of colour that streak across the northern night sky are the result of solar wind – a stream of particles from the sun that collides with oxygen, nitrogen and hydrogen in the upper atmosphere. These collisions produce haunting greens and magentas as the earth's magnetic field draws the wind towards the polar regions.

Where & How to See Them

Catching a glimpse of the Northern Lights requires nothing more than a dark, partly clear night (ie few clouds) and a pinch of luck. It's as simple as that.

Many tour companies offer 'Northern Lights tours' (by boat, jeep or bus) – they are essentially taking you to an area with less light pollution and cloud cover to increase your viewing odds. You can do this yourself, too, though we don't recommend inexperienced winter drivers chase clear skies in remote, snowy areas.

Head to recommended viewing spots on the outskirts of Reykjavík (these include Grótta lighthouse at

KRISSANAPONG WONGSAWARNG/SHUTTERSTOCK ©

ARIET/SHUTTERSTOCK ©

COOLKENGZZ/SHUTTERSTOCK ©

1. Jökulsárlón (p197)
2. Snæfellsnes Peninsula (p219)
3. Skaftafell (p187)

Seltjarnarnes, or Öskjuhlíð hill), or book a few nights at a rural inn and wait for the light show in the evening. Many hotels offer viewing wake-up calls should the lights appear in the middle of the night while you're asleep.

Recent winters have been excellent for Northern Lights, with viewings beginning as early as late August. Mid-September to mid-April is the 'official' season, but it can be longer, in the right conditions. Peak winter months enjoy the most darkness (an important factor for viewing), but also heavier weather conditions, storms and cloud cover.

And note you don't always need to be away from the city to enjoy a show – when the aurora is strong, even the lights of Reykjavík can't hide them.

Predicting Activity

Predicting the likelihood of an aurora is close to impossible, but there are various tools, apps and alerts that report factors such as solar activity and therefore the probability of seeing one in the short term.

The comprehensive website of the Icelandic Met Office details aurora activity, cloud cover, sunlight and moonlight, in order to provide an aurora forecast (generally for the week ahead, from September to mid-April). Check it out at http://en.vedur.is/weather/forecasts/aurora. More resources are outlined at www.easyaurora.com.

Icelandic Emigration Center MUSEUM
(Vesturfarasetrið; ☎453 7935; www.hofsos.is; adult/child 1700kr/free; ⊙11am-6pm Jun-Aug) Several restored harbourside buildings have been turned into a museum exploring the reasons behind Icelanders' emigration to North America, their hopes for a new life and the reality of conditions when they arrived. Incredibly, this small country lost 16,000 emigrants from 1870 to 1914, leaving behind a 1914 population of only 88,000.

The main exhibition, 'New Land, New Life', follows the lives of emigrating Icelanders through carefully curated photographs, letters and displays.

Sailing in Skagafjörður BOAT TOUR
(☎861 9803; www.hafogland.is; tours adult/child from 9000/6000kr; ⊙May-Oct) This operator runs boat trips from the small harbour taking in the scenery and bird life around the tiny island of Málmey and the bizarre promontory Þórðarhöfði (tethered to the mainland by a delicate spit). There's also the possibility of arranging sea-angling and birdwatching tours.

Sleeping & Eating

There are simple lodgings in town, a small and basic campsite on Skólagata (1300kr per person) and a few options in the surrounds.

For somewhere quite special, drive 25km south to Guesthouse Hofsstaðir (p279).

Sunnuberg GUESTHOUSE €
(☎893 0220; www.sunnuberg.is; Suðurbraut 8; s/d 11,800/15,700kr;) Cosy rooms with bathroom are available at homey Sunnuberg, 200m past the pool (p281), opposite the petrol pump and grocery store. (Note: there's no kitchen.)

KS Hofsósi SUPERMARKET €
(☎455 4692; www.ks.is; Suðurbraut 9; ⊙9.30am-9.30pm Mon-Fri, 11am-8pm Sat & Sun Jun-Aug, 9.30am-6pm Mon-Fri, 11am-4pm Sat Sep-May) Pick up supplies here, where you can also get simple grill-bar food. There's a petrol pump out the front.

Sólvík ICELANDIC €€
(☎861 3463; www.facebook.com/solvikhofsos; Harbour; mains 1250-3500kr; ⊙10am-10pm May-Aug, noon-9pm Sep;) Down at the small harbour, Sólvík is a sweet country-style restaurant with a short, simple menu of local classics (cod, lamb, burgers, fish and chips). Traditional pancakes too.

Getting There & Away

Hofsós is difficult to reach without your own wheels, but not impossible.

Strætó (p429) runs bus 85 between Sauðárkrókur and Hofsós (920kr to either destination, two daily Wednesday, Friday and Sunday). Only operates if prebooked. Call Strætó at least two hours before departure. It's scheduled to meet bus 57 between Akureyri and Reykjavík.

Northwest Tröllaskagi

The 60km stretch between Hofsós and Siglufjörður is full of scenic eye candy. Offshore the panorama is of the wee islet of **Málmey** and the promontory **Þórðarhöfði**, and lakes in the north. Inland are a few farms and fields dotted among valleys and peaks – the latter attract heliskiers in winter and spring. There are also rivers that lure fishers.

You need your own transport to get here – there is no bus service covering this route.

Sleeping & Eating

★ **Brúnastaðir** COTTAGE €€
(☎467 1020; www.brunastadir.is; Rte 76, Fljótsdalur; house from 29,000kr;) Brúnastaðir is run by a big friendly family, for big families (or groups). Two fully equipped three-bedroom cottages each sleep 10 people). Views are stupendous, and there's a flower-filled garden, access to kayaks and boats, and loads of animals – kids will love it. Price excludes linen (2000kr per person).

The farm's petting zoo is open to passers-by from 10am to 6pm daily in summer, for a small fee. It's on Rte 76, 22km from Siglufjörður.

Lónkot GUESTHOUSE €€
(☎453 7432; www.lonkot.is; Rte 76; d with/without bathroom incl breakfast from 26,900/21,900kr; ⊙May-Sep;) Wonderfully blustery Lónkot is a gourmet pit stop along the rugged coast, 13km north of Hofsós. Billed as a 'rural resort' it has boutique accommodation (including a big family suite) with super sea views, and an indoor hot-pot. The output from its restaurant (mains 4300kr to 5200kr; open noon to 9.30pm mid-May to August) is inspired by local produce and slow-cooking principles.

Lunch is served too, or drop by for coffee and cake. Campers are also welcome (1000kr per person), though facilities for them are limited.

★**Deplar Farm** CHALET €€€

(☎349 7761; www.elevenexperience.com; Rte 82, Fljótsdalur; d from 257,250kr;) Northwest Tröllaskagi is so scenic that the Fljót valley is home to Iceland's most exclusive accommodation, the ultra-luxe Deplar Farm, a secluded new hideout for celebs and tycoons. Modern with every conceivable amenity, top-notch service and all the activity gear you can imagine, these are turf houses like you've never seen before. No drop-ins.

Siglufjörður

POP 1182

Sigló (as the locals call it) sits precariously at the foot of a steep slope overlooking a beautiful fjord. In its heyday it was home to 10,000 workers, and fishing boats crammed into the small harbour to unload their catch for the waiting women to gut and salt.

After the herring abruptly disappeared from Iceland's north coast in the late 1960s, Siglufjörður declined and never fully recovered. Tunnels now link the town with Ólafsfjörður and points further south, and these days Sigló is receiving warranted attention from travellers smitten by its hiking, marina and excellent diversions (and its role as the sordid small town in the Icelandic TV series *Trapped,* which was filmed here, and in the Ragnar Jónasson's crime novels). Just reaching the town (from either direction) involves a journey that will take your breath away.

Sights

★**Herring Era Museum** MUSEUM

(Síldarminjasafnið; ☎467 1604; www.sild.is; Snorragata 10; adult/child 1800kr/free; 10am-6pm Jun-Aug, 1-5pm May & Sep, by appointment rest of year) Lovingly created over 16 years, this award-winning museum does a stunning job of recreating Siglufjörður's boom days between 1903 and 1968, when it was the herring-fishing capital of Iceland. Set in three buildings that were part of an old Norwegian herring station, the museum brings the work and lives of the town's inhabitants vividly to life.

Icelandic Folk Music Centre MUSEUM

(Þjóðlagasetur; ☎467 2300; www.folkmusik.is; Norðurgata 1; adult/child 800kr/free; noon-6pm Jun-Aug) Traditional-music enthusiasts may be interested in this sweet little museum that displays 19th-century instruments and offers recordings of Icelandic songs and chants. Admission free with a ticket to the Herring Era Museum.

Segull 67 Brugghús BREWERY

(☎863 2120; www.segull67.is; Vetrarbraut 8-10) Sample tasty local brews at this microbrewery that's open for two visitors or more for a tour and tasting (2500kr). Usually open on Friday and Saturday, it pays to call first to double-check.

Activities

Siglufjörður is a great base for hikers and in summer you can opt for an ultra-scenic round of golf at the nine-hole course.

In winter, ski lifts operate at popular **Skarðsdalur** (☎878 3399; www.skardsdalur.is) above the head of the fjord. Check www.skiiceland.is for info on good ski passes. Heliskiing operators work around Tröllaskagi; contact Viking Heliskiing (p287) based out of Ólafsfjörður for info.

Hiking

Interesting hikes in the area include some 19km of paths marked along the avalanche-repelling fence above town, with numerous access points. There's a worthwhile information panel on the northern outskirts of town, beside a parking area, detailing these **avalanche defences**.

Another popular option is over the passes of Hólsskarð and Hestsskarð into the beautiful, uninhabited **Héðinsfjörður**, the next fjord to the east. This is where the tunnels connecting Siglufjörður and Ólafsfjörður see the light.

There's a large amount of hiking-trail info at www.fjallabyggd.is.

Festivals & Events

Folk Music Festival MUSIC

(www.folkmusik.is; Jul) Folk-music aficionados will enjoy this relaxed five-day affair in early July.

Herring Festival CULTURAL

(Aug) Siglufjörður's biggest shindig takes place on the bank-holiday weekend in early August and recreates the gold-rush atmosphere of the town's glory days. The week leading up to it is full of events: singing, dancing and fishy feasting.

Sleeping

Campsite CAMPGROUND €

(Snorragata; sites per person 1200kr; mid-May–mid-Sep) Oddly placed in the middle of town near the harbour, it has a small block housing showers and laundry (800kr). There's a second patch of grass beyond the city limits; follow Suðurgata (or take Norðurtún, signed off Snorragata).

★ Siglunes Guesthouse GUESTHOUSE €€
(467 1222; www.hotelsiglunes.is; Lækjargata 10; d with/without bathroom from 23,000/19,1000kr, q 30,100kr; restaurant 6-9pm Tue-Thu, to 10pm Fri-Sun;) Personality shines through in this cool guesthouse, where vintage furniture is paired with contemporary art and ultra-modern bathrooms in the hotel wing. There are equally appealing guesthouse rooms (shared bathrooms, no kitchen), but the highlight may be the restaurant run by excellent Moroccan chef Jaouad Hbib.

Herring Guesthouse GUESTHOUSE €€
(868 4200; www.theherringhouse.com; Hávegur 5; s/d without bathroom 14,700/19,200kr, 4-person apt 48,200kr;) Þorir and Erla are charming, knowledgeable hosts (he's a former town mayor) offering personalised service at their stylish, view-blessed guesthouse with two locations (the second is at Hlíðarvegur 1, behind the church). There is a guest kitchen at the main house, and a lovely breakfast spread (2500kr). Families will appreciate the two-bedroom apartment.

Siglo Harbour Hostel & Apartments GUESTHOUSE, APARTMENT €€
(897 1394; www.sigloharbourhostel.is; Tjarnargata 14; d without bathroom 13,500kr, apt 32,000kr;) The 'hostel' element of this establishment is more like a decent-value guesthouse: five double rooms with linen, shared bathroom, kitchen access and laundry. The two spacious apartments each sleep six and are good for families and groups. There's a multinight discount.

★ Sigló Hótel HOTEL €€€
(461 7730; www.siglohotel.is; Snorragata 3; d/ste incl breakfast from 40,140/70,900kr) This upmarket, 68-room harbourside hotel is part of a local empire, including several restaurants. Rooms are smart and well fitted out, but it's the public areas that shine brightest: the elegant restaurant and bar, suspended over the water, the stylish lounge and waterside hot-pot.

Eating & Drinking

The street opposite the supermarket is Aðalgata; it's home to a busy **bakery** (467 1720; Aðalgata 28; snacks 200-900kr; 7am-5pm Mon-Fri, 8am-5pm Sat, 9am-4pm Sun) and pizzeria, but come mealtime many appetites focus on the primary-coloured marina.

Frida Chocolate CAFE €
(Frida Súkkulaðikaffihús; www.facebook.com/Fridachocolate; Túngata 40a; 1-6pm) Handmade artisanal chocolate in a local artist's gallery – what's not to like? Look for the unique facade on the main street in the northern part of town. Once inside, admire the kooky chairs, the bathroom wallpapered in cartoons, and the cranberry-sea-salt chocolate.

Kjörbúðin SUPERMARKET €
(467 1987; www.samkaup.is; Túngata 2-4; 9am-7pm Mon-Fri, 11am-6pm Sat, noon-6pm Sun) Well stocked for self-caterers. ATM inside.

★ Siglunes Guesthouse Restaurant MOROCCAN €€
(467 1222; www.hotelsiglunes.is; Lækjargata 10; mains 3000-4000kr; 6-9pm Tue-Thu, to 10pm Fri-Sun) A refreshing surprise in this remote village, Moroccan chef Jaouad Hbib prepares delicious, from-scratch Moroccan cuisine for the wood-lined restaurant at Siglunes Guesthouse. Tajines sizzle with heat, both in the temperature and flavour sense, and starters are a well-conceived blend of delicate salads and exquisite homemade cheeses. Top it off with crème brûlée for dessert. Book ahead.

Kaffi Rauðka ICELANDIC €€
(461 7730; www.raudka.is; Gránugata 19; mains 1900-2500kr; noon-5pm, to 10pm Fri & Sat Jun-Aug;) Ruby-red Rauðka has an informal atmosphere, with an all-day menu of sandwiches, salads and tasty mains like the catch of the day.

Hannes Boy ICELANDIC €€
(461 7734; www.hannesboy.is; Gránugata 23; mains 2300-4200kr, buffet adult/child 6600kr/3300kr; 11.30am-9.30pm Jun-Aug) Dressed in sunny yellow, this stylish, light-filled space is furnished with cool seats made from old herring barrels. It's under the same ownership as Sigló Hótel and offers a good selection of seafood, meat and local desserts.

Vínbúðin ALCOHOL
(467 1262; www.vinbudin.is; Eyrargata 25; 11am-6pm Mon-Thu, to 7pm Fri, 11am-2pm Sat May-Aug, closed Sat rest of year) Government-run liquor store.

Information

The town has services such as a bank, pharmacy, post office etc.

Tourist Information Centre (☎467 1555; www.visittrollaskagi.is; Gránugata 24; ⊙9am-5pm Mon-Fri, 11am-3pm Sat & Sun Jun-Aug, shorter hours rest of year; 📶) Helpful desk inside the library.

Getting There & Away

Strætó (p429) runs bus 78 Akureyri–Dalvík–Ólafsfjörður–Siglufjörður (to Akureyri 2760kr, 70 minutes, three daily Monday to Friday, one daily Sunday).

Ólafsfjörður

POP 792

Beautifully locked between sheer mountain slopes and dark fjord waters, fishing town Ólafsfjörður still retains a sense of isolation, even with tunnels now linking it with Siglufjörður, its sister settlement further north.

From Akureyri, you have to pass through a thin 3km tunnel just to make your way into town, which makes for a cinematic entrance.

Activities & Tours

Ólafsfjörður receives good snow in winter. Check www.skiiceland.is for info on good ski passes for the slopes. A few companies are ramping up winter activities in the pristine peaks of Tröllaskagi, with bases in and around Ólafsfjörður.

There's also an excellent **swimming pool**, and nine-hole **golf course**. Brimnes Hotel offers boat and kayak rentals; check their website for local activities.

Viking Heliskiing SKIING
(☎846 1674; www.vikingheliskiing.com; 3-day guided package from €4900) Expert local guides (former Winter Olympians) offer heliskiing trips exploring the peaks of the peninsula (vertical drop is up to 1500m), operating from about mid-March to mid-June (conditions permitting). There are package-tour options that include transfers from Akureyri and lodge accommodation with meals.

Arctic Freeride ADVENTURE
(☎859 8800; www.facebook.com/arcticfreeride; 2hr tour adult/child 9000/5500kr; ⊙Jan-May) A local father-son team operates tours aboard a snowcat. Take a sightseeing tour up the 984m peak Múlakolla, or a longer evening tour to view the Northern Lights in season. There's the option of a one-way ride too (snowcat up, ski down).

Sleeping & Eating

At mealtimes, consider a jaunt up the road to Siglufjörður, where options are better.

Campsite CAMPGROUND €
(☎466 4044; www.fjallabyggd.is; Aðalgata; sites per person 1200kr, campsite tax 333kr; ⊙mid-May–mid-Sep) Toilets, water and electricity are available; guests use the showers inside the neighbouring swimming-pool complex.

Brimnes Hotel & Bungalows HOTEL, COTTAGES €€
(☎466 2400; www.brimnes.is; Bylgjubyggð 2; s/d incl breakfast from 9900/12,400kr, cottages from 19,800kr; 📶) The real draws at the town's primary accommodation are the fabulous lakeshore log cabins (varying sizes, sleeping up to seven), with hot tubs built into the verandah and views over the water. There are also 11 bright, fresh en suite rooms, plus a decent restaurant serving the usual soup, fish and burgers (open 6.30pm to 9.30pm June to August).

Gistihús Jóa GUESTHOUSE €€
(Joe's Guesthouse; ☎847 4331; www.kaffiklara.is; Strandgata 2; d/q without bathroom incl breakfast from 12,300/24,400kr; 📶👪) Joe's handsome six-room guesthouse is part of Kaffi Klara downstairs, where breakfast is served. Compact rooms in a restored old post office have hand basins, quirky flooring and modern earth-toned decor.

Kaffi Klara CAFE €
(☎466 4044; www.kaffiklara.is; Strandgata 2; dishes 950-2000kr; ⊙10am-5.30pm, to 9pm Fri & Sat) This sweet cafe in a former post office has info about the area, plus a selection of soups, sandwiches, cakes and wine. There are books and board games to help pass rainy days.

Kjörbúðin SUPERMARKET €
(☎466 2200; www.samkaup.is; Aðalgata 2-4; ⊙9am-7pm Mon-Fri, 10am-6pm Sat, noon-6pm Sun) For self-catering.

Information

Tourist Information Centre (☎464 9215; www.visittrollaskagi.is; Ólafsvegur 4; ⊙1-5pm Mon-Fri) Helpful desk inside the local library, just off the main road through town.

Getting There & Away

Strætó (p429) services:

- Bus 78 to Siglufjörður (920kr, 15 minutes, three daily Monday to Friday, one daily Sunday).

➡ Bus 78 to Akureyri (2300kr, 55 minutes, three daily Monday to Friday, one daily Sunday). Runs via Dalvík.

Dalvík

POP 1367

Sleepy Dalvík is in a snug, scenic spot between breezy Eyjafjörður and the rolling hills of Svarfaðardalur. Most tourists come here to catch the Grímsey (p300) ferry, but if you've got some time there are plenty of reasons to linger, including great activities in the area, plus interesting museums and quality accommodation.

Sights & Tours

Byggðasafnið Hvoll MUSEUM

(☎460 4928; www.dalvik.is/byggdasafn; Karlsbraut; adult/child 800kr/free; ⏰11am-6pm early Jun–mid-Aug, 2-5pm Sat rest of year) Dalvík's quality folk museum is high on oddball factor. Skip the usual taxidermic characters (yes, another polar bear) and find the rooms dedicated to the poignant story of local giant Jóhan Pétursson. At 2.34m (almost 7ft 7in), Jóhan was Iceland's (and some say the world's) tallest man.

Arctic Sea Tours WILDLIFE

(☎771 7600; www.arcticseatours.is; Hafnarbraut 22; 3hr tour adult/child 9900/4950kr; ⏰Mar-Nov) This professional outfit operates three-hour tours up to four times a day in high summer (it has scheduled whale-watching tours from March to November). All tours include a short sea-angling stint, and your catch is grilled on the barbecue as soon as the boat docks. Meet at its office on the main road through town, by the N1 petrol pumps.

Bergmenn Mountain Guides ADVENTURE

(☎858 3000; www.bergmenn.com) Based outside Dalvík, this pioneering company specialises in ski touring, ski mountaineering, heliskiing, ice climbing, alpine climbing and other mountain-related activities. Fun fact: the name of the company's owner, Jökull Bergmann, translates as 'Glacier Mountainman' – so you know he found his calling. The company runs Arctic Heli Skiing (www.arcticheliskiing.com) and has four lodges dotted around the peninsula.

Sleeping & Eating

★**Dalvík HI Hostel** HOSTEL €

(☎699 6616, 865 8391; www.dalvikhostel.com; Hafnarbraut 4; dm/d/tr without bathroom 5700/15,200/18,900kr; 📶👪) This is, for our money, one of Iceland's best hostels, and certainly its prettiest – it's more like a boutique guesthouse than a budgeteer's bunkhouse. Heiða, one of the friendly owners, has a creative streak put to good use in quirky, vintage-inspired decor. The seven-room hostel is in the town centre, in a white building called Gimli.

Campground CAMPGROUND €

(www.dalvik.is; Svarfaðarbraut; per campervan/tent 2500/1700kr, campsite tax 333kr; ⏰Jun-Aug) Large camping area by the town pool; follow the signs to Hotel Dalvík to access it (pay at the pool).

Vegamót COTTAGE €€

(☎699 6616, 865 8391; www.dalvikhostel.com; Skiðarbraut; cottages 19,900-29,500kr; 📶) Heiða and Bjarni, the friendly owners of the town's excellent hostel, also offer three wooden cabins and Gamli Bærinn (the 'Old Farmhouse'), a gorgeously romantic self-contained cottage. These are at their property opposite the Olís petrol station at the southern entrance to town.

★**Gísli, Eiríkur, Helgi** ICELANDIC €

(Kaffihús Bakkabræðra; ☎666 3399; www.facebook.com/bakkabraedurkaffi; Grundargata 1; soup & salad buffet 1990kr; ⏰10am-10pm, to 1am Fri & Sat, to 7pm Sun) Named after three brothers from a folk tale, this might just be the perfect small-town cafe. It's decked out in timber, full of vintage bric-a-brac and mismatched china – it's owned by the folks behind the town's retro-chic hostel – and serves delicious fish soup and homemade cakes. The locals love it (understandably), and there's a bar area and small theatre out the back.

Kjörbúðin SUPERMARKET €

(☎466 3211; www.samkaup.is; Hafnarbraut; ⏰9am-7pm Mon-Fri, 10am-6pm Sat, 2-6pm Sun) Central supermarket.

Information

Tourist Information Desk (☎846 4928; www.dalvikurbyggd.is; Goðabraut; ⏰9am-5pm Mon-Fri, noon-5pm Sat) This helpful info desk is at Menningarhúsið Berg, the modern cultural centre that houses the library and a cafe. Staff can help with information on activities in the region, including horse riding, skiing, golf, hiking and birdwatching.

Getting There & Away

Dalvík is the jumping-off point for ferries to Grímsey (p300) and has some services to Hrísey (p290) (though Árskógssandur is the main ferry hub for Hrísey).

Strætó (p429) bus services:

➡ Bus 78 to Siglufjörður (1380kr, 35 minutes, three daily Monday to Friday, one daily Sunday).

➡ Bus 78 to Akureyri (1840kr, 40 minutes, three daily Monday to Friday, one daily Sunday).

GREATER AKUREYRI

Akureyri sits on the longest fjord in Iceland, Eyjafjörður, where it's not uncommon to see whales cavorting across the glittering waters. In addition to visiting jaunty Akureyri itself, if you have time and wheels, it's well worth getting off the Ring Road to explore the gorgeous region around Akureyri. Ferries run frequently to the little island Hrísey in the middle of the fjord.

Akureryi is packed with lodgings of all types, and there is a good deal of rural guesthouse accommodation in the Eyjafjarðará Valley and around the fjord. For other options, including camping, consult Akureyri's tourist office (p300).

Dalvík to Akureyri

A rich agricultural region runs north from Akureyri to Dalvík along Rte 82, punctuated by side roads to tiny fishing villages on the western shore of Eyjafjörður – from south to north these are Hjalteyri, Hauganes and Árskógssandur. Árskógssandur is the main jumping-off point for exploring little Hrísey island, out in the middle of the fjord.

Sights & Activities

Bjórböðin SPA

(☎414 2828; www.bjorbodin.is; Ægisgata 31, Árskógssandur; beer bath 7900kr; ⊙noon-8pm Mon-Thu, 11am-9pm Fri & Sat) Launched by Iceland's first microbrewery, Bruggsmiðjan – Kaldi, this spa and its restaurant are focused on the benefits of beer. Key to the experience is a private 25-minute beer bath in a huge, handcrafted wooden tub. Poured fresh for each guest, the baths are rich in Vitamin B, antioxidants and alpha acids. There's also an outdoor hot-pot with spectacular fjord views.

Whale Watching Hauganes WILDLIFE

(☎867 0000; www.whales.is; Hafnargata 2, Hauganes; 3hr tour adult/child 9900/4500kr; ⊙May-mid-Nov) From the hamlet of Hauganes, climb aboard one of two oak former fishing boats for a carbon-neutral adventure that includes fishing and whale watching (this is Iceland's oldest whale-watch operator).

Bruggsmiðjan – Kaldi BREWERY

(Kaldi Beer; ☎466 2505; www.bruggsmidjan.is; Öldugata 22, Árskógssandur; tour 2000kr; ⊙tours by appointment) Árskógssandur is home to Bruggsmiðjan microbrewery, producing excellent, in-demand Kaldi brews using Czech techniques. The brewery welcomes visitors, but call ahead to arrange a tour time. Akureyri-based Saga Travel (p295), also has some tours (from 15,900kr) that come here.

Hjalteyri VILLAGE

Hjalteyri (population 43) was once a major herring harbour, and its old fish factory was Iceland's largest herring-processing plant when it was built in 1937. The herring disappeared in the 1960s and the factory was closed. These days, it's a cool place to wander around, with a few surprises; summertime art exhibitions, craftspeople, diver operator Stryten Divecentre (p291), and whale-watching outfit North Sailing (p315). It's 20km north of Akureyri.

Sleeping & Eating

★Hótel Hjalteyri BOUTIQUE HOTEL €€

(☎897 7070, 462 2770; www.hotelhjalteyri.is; Hjalteyri; d/apt incl breakfast from 21,400/26,000kr;) The wow factor delights at this former school en route to Hjalteyri's harbour. It's been renovated to house three double rooms and four apartments of varying sizes (including a delightful penthouse with hot-pot and terrace), and it's dripping with good taste: big proportions, loads of artworks and books, and stylish decor.

★Skjaldarvík GUESTHOUSE €€

(☎552 5200; www.skjaldarvik.is; Rte 816; s/d without bathroom incl breakfast 20,900/22,600kr; @) A slice of guesthouse nirvana, Skjaldarvík lies in a bucolic farm setting 6km north of Akureyri. It's owned by a young family and features quirky design details (plants sprouting from shoes, vintage typewriters as artwork on the walls). Plus: bumper breakfast buffet, horse-riding and buggy tours (p295), mountain-bike rental, a hot-pot, and an honesty bar in the comfy lounge.

The pretty-as-a-picture restaurant (open 6.30pm to 8.30pm May to September) prepares a small but well-executed menu (buffet 4900kr); it's open to nonguests,

WORTH A TRIP

HRÍSEY

Iceland's second-largest off shore island (after Heimaey) is the peaceful, low-lying Hrísey (population 151), easily reached from the mainland. Thrust out into the middle of Eyjafjörður, the island enjoys spectacular panoramas and is especially noted as a breeding ground and protected area for ptarmigan, as well as being home to an enormous colony of Arctic terns. Tame ptarmigan frequent the village streets. From here, three marked nature trails loop around the southeastern part of the island and lead to some good viewpoints.

There's a small **information office** (☎695 0077; www.hrisey.is; Norðurvegur 3; ⏲1-5pm Jun-Aug) inside Hús Hákarla-Jörundur, a small museum (admission 500kr) on shark-fishing beside the church in the picturesque village where the boat docks. Pick up the handy Hrísey brochure here or in Akureyri, or visit www.hrisey.is.

While a leisurely half-day is enough to explore the island, consider staying overnight for a more authentic glimpse of island life. The website www.visithrisey.is outlines a couple of houses for rent on the island.

There's a simple **campground** (☎461 2255; Austurvegur; sites per person 1500kr; ⏲Jun-Aug) with its reception and amenities at the modern swimming-pool complex. Like staying in a comfy share-house, **Wave Guesthouse** (☎695 2277; www.waveguesthouse.is; Austurvegur 9; d without bathroom 12,400kr; 📶) offers three doubles and one twin room. All share a kitchen, lounge and bathroom. **Verbúðin 66** (☎467 1166; www.facebook.com/verbudin66; Sjávargata 2; meals 2000-3600kr; ⏲11am-10pm Jun-Aug) is a small, cosy restaurant is close to the boat dock and has a simple lunchtime menu of soup and sandwiches, plus burgers and catch of the day. Super-sweet wee cafe **Eyjakaffi** (☎864 5901; www.facebook.com/pg/Eyjakaffi.Brynjolfshus; Austurvegur 12; ⏲noon-7pm Jul & Aug) opens for a short burst in peak summer, in the kitchen and lounge of a local house. It serves soup, coffee and wine, plus excellent home-baked cakes. For self-caterers the village store **Hríseyjarbúðin** (Norðurvegur 7; ⏲11.30am-6pm Mon-Fri, 1-4pm Sat & Sun) sells supplies.

Passenger ferry **Sævar** (☎695 5544; www.hrisey.is) runs between Árskógssandur and Hrísey (15 minutes; adult/child 1500/750kr) at least seven times daily year-round. Bus 78 from Akureyri doesn't drive into the village at Árskógssandur – it stops about 1km from the ferry harbour. Ferry Sæfari (p301) serves Dalvík (30 minutes; adult/child 1500kr/free), once or twice weekly.

but bookings are essential. Consider the excellent 'Ride & Bite' or 'Buggy & Bite' options to combine dining and activities.

Eyri Restaurant SEAFOOD €€
(☎618 3716; www.facebook.com/taleofawhale; Hjalteyri; mains 2600-4000kr; ⏲10am-9pm Jun-Aug) Relax in a cosy log cabin while sampling fish straight from the fjord, or other local lamb and beef dishes.

Baccalá Bar FISH & CHIPS €€
(☎620 1035; www.ektafiskur.is; Hafnargata 6, Hauganes; mains 1900-3200kr; ⏲11am-9pm mid-May–Sep) Beside the whale-watching (p289) office in Hauganes, the local company Ektafiskur, known for its traditional *bacalao* (salted codfish), operates this fun, kitschy place (sit in a Viking longboat out the front). The menu is short, simple and offers fishy favourites (fish soup, fish and chips etc), plus drinks and ice cream.

Akureyri

POP 18,600

Akureyri (pronounced *ah*-koo-rare-ee) stands strong as Iceland's second city, but a Melbourne, Manchester or Montréal it is not. And how could it be with only 18,600 residents? It's a wonder the city (which would be a 'town' anywhere else) generates this much buzz. Expect cool cafes, quality restaurants, a handful of art galleries and even some late-night bustle – a far cry from other rural Icelandic towns.

Akureyri nestles at the head of Eyjafjörður, Iceland's longest (60km) fjord, at the base of snowcapped peaks. In summer flowering gardens belie the location, just a stone's throw from the Arctic Circle. Lively winter festivals and some of Iceland's best skiing provide plenty of off-peak (and off-piste) appeal. With its relaxed attitude and extensive food and accommodation choices, it's the natural base for exploring Eyjafjörður and around, and it's seeing a growing number of cruise ships calling by (passenger numbers can sometimes overwhelm the town).

Sights

Akureyri has several museums, and the most interesting of these, the Akureyri Art Museum, has just undergone a major expansion. The *Akureyri Art Trail* brochure (available at the tourist office) maps public art around town. There are also museums dedicated to aviation, local industry, antique toys and motorbikes. Many visitors use Akureryi as a base for visiting Tröllaskagi, Mývatn and Húsavík.

★Lystigarðurinn GARDENS
(☎462 7487; www.lystigardur.akureyri.is; Eyrarlandsholt; ⏲8am-10pm Mon-Fri, from 9am Sat & Sun Jun-Sep) FREE The most northerly botanical garden in the world makes a delightful spot for a fragrant wander on sunny days. The wealth of plant life on display is truly astonishing considering the gardens' proximity to the Arctic Circle. You'll find examples of every species native to Iceland, as well as a host of high-latitude and high-altitude plants from around the world. There's also a beautifully situated cafe.

Akureyrarkirkja CHURCH
(☎462 7700; www.akureyrarkirkja.is; Eyrarlandsvegur; ⏲generally 10am-4pm Mon-Fri) Dominating the town from high on a hill, Akureyri's landmark church was designed by Guðjón Samúelsson, the architect responsible for Reykjavík's Hallgrímskirkja. Although the basalt theme connects them, Akureyrarkirkja looks more like a stylised 1920s US skyscraper than its big-city sibling.

Built in 1940, the church contains a large 3200-pipe organ and a series of rather untraditional reliefs of the life of Christ. There's also a suspended ship hanging from the ceiling, reflecting an old Nordic tradition of votive offerings for the protection of loved ones at sea. Perhaps the most striking feature is the beautiful central stained-glass window above the altar, which originally graced Coventry Cathedral in England.

The church admits visitors most days; check the board outside for opening times, as they change frequently.

Akureyri Art Museum MUSEUM
(Listasafnið á Akureyri; ☎461 2610; www.listak.is; Kaupvangsstræti 8; 1500kr; ⏲10am-5pm Jun-Aug, noon-5pm Tue-Sun Sep-May) Stimulate your senses at the Akureyri Art Museum, which hosts eclectic, innovative exhibitions – from

DIVING IN EYJAFJÖRÐUR

Thoughts of scuba diving usually involve sun-kissed beaches and tropical fish, so perhaps it's surprising that some of the world's most fascinating diving lies within Iceland's frigid waters. Most divers flock to crystalline Silfra near Þingvellir in the south, but the real diving dynamo, known as **Strýtan**, lurks beneath Eyjafjörður.

Strýtan, a giant cone (55m) soaring up from the ocean floor, commands a striking presence as it spews out gushing hot water. This geothermal chimney – made from deposits of magnesium silicate – is truly an anomaly. The only other Strýtan-like structures ever discovered were found at depths of 2000m or more; Strýtan's peak is a mere 15m below the surface.

In addition to Strýtan, there are smaller steam cones on the other side of Eyjafjörður. Known as **Arnanesstrýtur**, these smaller formations aren't as spectacular, but the water bubbling out of the vents is estimated to be 11,000 years old. The water is completely devoid of salt, so you can put a thermos over a vent, bottle the boiling water, and use it to make hot chocolate when you get back to the surface!

Diving around the island of Grímsey (p300) is also memorable. The water is surprisingly clear here, but the main draw is the bird life: guillemots dive down deep as they search for food. Swimming with birds is definitely a strange experience – when the visibility is particularly good it can feel like you're flying.

To check out these and other underwater curiosities in the north (including fissures and geothermal rivers), contact Erlendur Bogason at **Strytan Divecentre** (☎862 2949; www.strytan.is; Hjalteyri; 2 guided dives 40,000kr), based at Hjalteyri, about 20km north of Akureryri. Erlendur discovered Strýtan in 1997, and now officially protects it. Check the website for the diving experience required; note that there is also the opportunity for drysuit snorkelling in some locales.

Akureyri

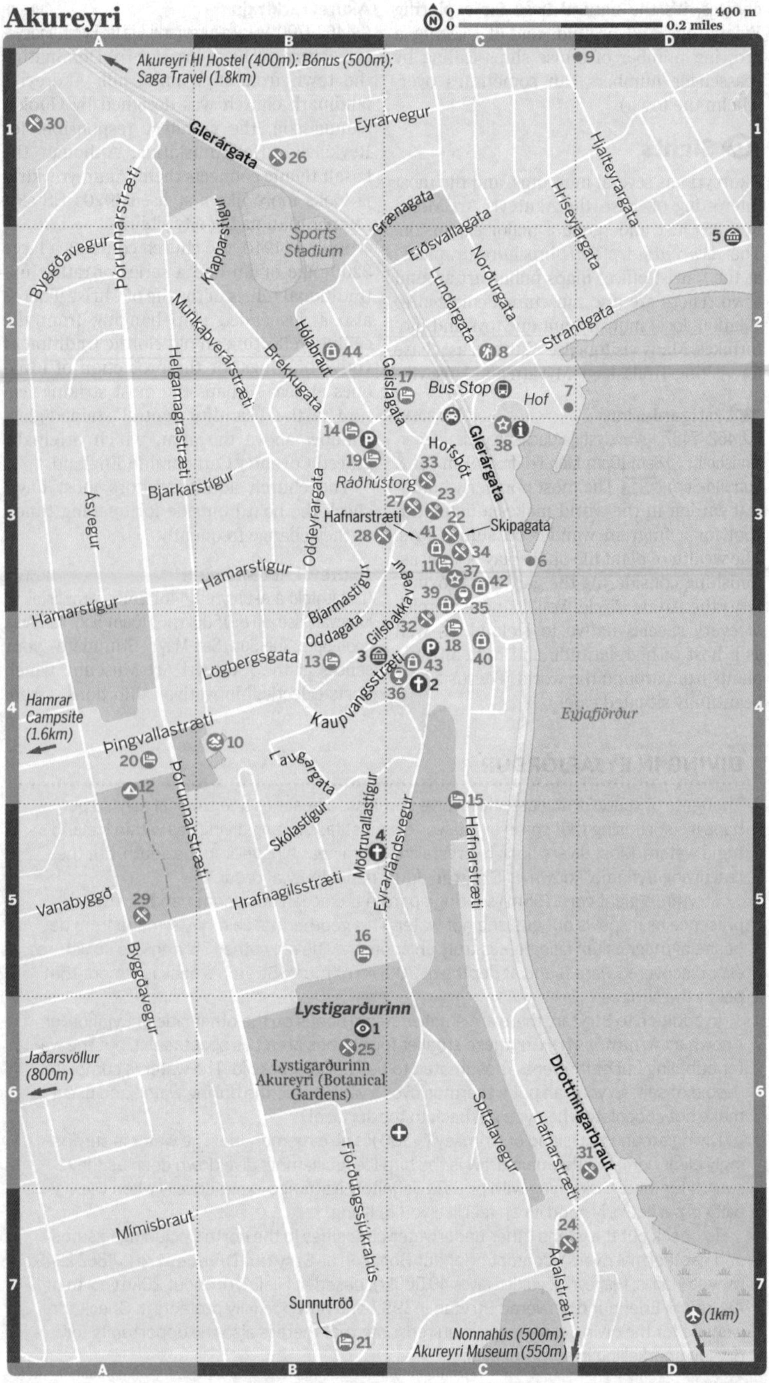

0 — 400 m
0 — 0.2 miles

A B C D

Akureyri HI Hostel (400m); Bónus (500m); Saga Travel (1.8km)

9

30

Glerárgata

26

Eyrarvegur

Hjalteyrargata

Þórunnarstræti

Klapparstígur

Sports Stadium

Grænagata

Eiðsvallagata

Hríseyjargata

5

Byggðavegur

Norðurgata

Lundargata

Munkaþverárstræti

Strandgata

Hólabraut

44

8

Helgamagrastræti

Brekkugata

Geislagata

17

Bus Stop

Hof

7

14

38

19

Hofsbót

Glerárgata

33

Oddeyrargata

Ráðhústorg

Bjarkarstígur

27

23

Ásvegur

Hafnarstræti

22

41

Skipagata

28

34

6

11

37

Hamarstígur

42

Bjarmastígur

39

35

Hamarstígur

Gilsbakkavegur

Oddagata

32

18

Lögbergsgata

13

3

40

43

Kaupvangsstræti

36

2

Hamrar Campsite (1.6km)

Eyjafjörður

Þingvallastræti

10

20

Laugargata

12

Þórunnarstræti

Skólastígur

Möðruvallastígur

Eyrarlandsvegur

15

Hafnarstræti

4

Hrafnagilsstræti

Vanabyggð

29

16

Byggðavegur

Lystigarðurinn

1

25

Jaðarsvöllur (800m)

Lystigarðurinn Akureyri (Botanical Gardens)

Drottningarbraut

Spítalavegur

Hafnarstræti

31

Fjórðungssjúkrahús

Mímisbraut

24

Aðalstræti

Sunnutröð

21

Nonnahús (500m); Akureyri Museum (550m)

(1km)

1 2 3 4 5 6 7

NORTH ICELAND AKUREYRI

Akureyri

Top Sights
1 Lystigarðurinn....B6

Sights
2 Akureyrarkirkja....C4
3 Akureyri Art Museum....B4
4 Catholic Church....B5
5 Into the Arctic....D2

Activities, Courses & Tours
6 Ambassador....C3
7 Elding....C2
8 Ferðafélag Akureyrar....C2
9 SBA-Norðurleið....D1
10 Sundlaug Akureyrar....B4

Sleeping
11 Akureyri Backpackers....C3
12 City Campsite....A4
13 Guesthouse Hvítahúsið....B4
14 Gula Villan....B3
15 Hótel Akureyri....C4
16 Hótel Edda....B5
17 Hótel Íbúðir....C2
18 Hótel Kea....C4
19 Hrafninn....B3
20 Icelandair Hotel Akureyri....A4
21 Sæluhús....B7

Eating
22 Akureyri Fish Restaurant....C3
23 Berlin....C3
Blaá Kannan....(see 35)
24 Brynja....C7
25 Café Laut....B6
26 Greifinn....B1
Icelandair Hotel Akureyri....(see 20)
27 Indian Curry House....C3
28 Kaffi Ilmur....B3
29 Krambúð....A5
30 Nettó....A1
31 Noa Seafood Restaurant....D6
32 Rub23....C4
33 Serrano....C3
34 Strikið....C3

Drinking & Nightlife
Akureyri Backpackers....(see 11)
35 Götubarinn....C3
36 Ölstofa Akureyrar....C4

Entertainment
37 Græni Hatturinn....C3
38 Hof....C3

Shopping
39 Eymundsson....C3
40 Flora....C4
41 Fold-Anna....C3
Geysir....(see 11)
42 Hornið....C3
43 Sjoppan....C4
44 Vínbúðin....B2

graphic design to portraiture – and is surrounded by a handful of local galleries. At the time of research, it was undergoing a major extension and renovation, including a museum shop and cafe.

Into the Arctic MUSEUM
(Norðurslóð; ☎588 9050; www.nordurslod.is; Strandgata 53; adult/child 1500kr/free; ⏲11am-6pm Mon-Fri, to 5pm Sat & Sun) Akureyri's newest entry on the exhibition scene, Into the Arctic displays cover the great north's wildlife, settlement, explorers and culture, from dog sledding and aviation to handicrafts. The founders' extensive map collection is on display as well.

Akureyri Museum MUSEUM
(Minjasafnið á Akureyri; ☎462 4162; www.akmus.is; Aðalstræti 58; adult/child 1500kr/free; ⏲10am-5pm Jun-Sep, 1-4pm Oct-May) This sweet, well-curated museum houses art and historical items relating to town life, including maps, photos and recreations of early Icelandic homes. The **museum garden** became the first place in Iceland to cultivate trees when a nursery was established here in 1899. Next door is a tiny, black-tarred timber **church** dating from 1846. A combined ticket including neighbouring Nonnahús and several town museums costs 2000kr.

Nonnahús MUSEUM
(☎462 4162; www.nonni.is; Aðalstræti 54; adult/child 1400kr/free; ⏲10am-5pm Jun-Aug, Thu-Sun Sep &Oct) The most interesting of the artists' residences in Akureyri, Nonnahús was the childhood home of renowned children's writer Reverend Jón Sveinsson (1857–1944), known to most as Nonni. His old-fashioned tales of derring-do have a rich local flavour. The house dates from 1850; its cramped rooms and simple furnishings provide a poignant insight into life in 19th-century Iceland.

Activities

A seafront path fronts the fjord from the town centre to the airport. In winter snowfields draw skiers, while independent summertime activities include hiking, golf and hot-pot-hopping. Akureryi is also the base for tours and guided activities all over Iceland's North.

Sundlaug Akureyrar SWIMMING
(☎461 4455; www.visitakureyri.is; Þingvallastræti 21; adult/child 950/250kr; ⏰6.45am-9pm Mon-Fri, 8am-9pm Sat, 8am-7.30pm Sun; 👪) The hub of local life, Akureyri's outdoor swimming pool is one of Iceland's finest. It has three recently refurbished heated pools, plus hot-pots, water slides, saunas and steam rooms.

Hlíðarfjall Ski Centre SKIING
(☎462 2280; www.hlidarfjall.is; Rte 837; day pass adult/child 4900/1400kr; 👪) Iceland's premier downhill ski slope is 5km west of town. The resort has a vertical drop of 537m, and a recently added lift has increased the longest trail to over 2.6km. There are eight lifts, 23 alpine slopes and also cross-country ski routes.

The season usually runs from November to May, with best conditions in February and March (Easter is particularly busy).

In the long hours of winter darkness, all of the main runs are floodlit.

There's ski and snowboard rental, two restaurants and a ski school. In season, buses usually connect the site with Akureyri; check the website for details and www.skiiceland.is for great passes.

Kjarnaskógur OUTDOORS
(👪) About 3km south of town is Iceland's most visited 'forest', the 600-hectare Kjarnaskógur woods. This bushland area has walking and mountain-bike trails, picnic areas and barbecues, and kids' playgrounds. In winter the area is good for cross-country skiing (there's a 7km trail with lighting). The campground (p296) at Hamrar has easy access to the woods.

LONG WEEKEND REMIX: THE DIAMOND CIRCLE

Perfectly positioned between North America and Europe, Iceland has become the *it* destination for a cool weekend getaway. The constant stream of tourists has turned the three-day Reykjavík–Golden Circle–Blue Lagoon trip into a well-worn circuit, so why not blaze a new trail and tackle Iceland's stunning Diamond Circle, a circa-260km route taking in the headlining acts of Húsavík, Ásbyrgi, Dettifoss and Mývatn (check out coverage at www.diamondcircle.is).

It's less legwork than you think if you fly into Akureyri, or when you land at Keflavík International Airport, catch a bus or connecting flight to Akureyri (you will need to travel to the capital's domestic airport).

Day 1: Akureyri

Jump-start your visit to the north with something quintessentially Icelandic: horse riding, preferably with grand panoramas to enjoy. Then, a half-day is plenty of time to bop around the streets of the city centre. Or for those who can withstand another plane ride, spend the afternoon on Grímsey (p300), Iceland's only slice of the Arctic Circle. For dinner, a good option is Strikið (p298) or Rub23 (p298), followed by a night out on the town.

Day 2: Húsavík & Around

In the morning, head to Húsavík. First swing by the Húsavík Whale Museum (p313) for a bit of background info, then hop aboard a whale-watching tour. Consider heading east for a walk among the canyon walls of Ásbyrgi (p320), check out the roar of thunderous Dettifoss (p323), then recount your whale tales over dinner back at Naustið (p317) in Húsavík. Wrap up with an evening session at GeoSea (p314) saltwater baths.

Day 3: Mývatn

For those who have been drooling over photos of Iceland's turquoise-tinted spa springs, fret not. Mývatn has its very own version of the Blue Lagoon: the Mývatn Nature Baths (p311). After a leisurely soak, it's time to get the blood flowing again. A three-hour hike around eastern Mývatn takes in a smorgasbord of geological anomalies. A stop at stinky Hverir (p311) is a must, and, if time permits, have a wander around the steam vents and turquoise Víti (p312) crater at Krafla. Then zip back to Akureyri to catch your flight, but not before visiting the heavenly waterfall Goðafoss (p303), and if you have a 4WD, Aldeyjarfoss (p303).

Ferðafélag Akureyrar HIKING
(☎462 2720; www.ffa.is; Strandgata 23; ⊙2-5pm Mon-Fri May-Aug, 11am-1pm Mon-Fri Sep-Apr) For information on hiking in the area, contact Ferðafélag Akureyrar. Its helpful website details (in English) the huts it operates in northern Iceland and the highlands, and has notes on the Askja Trail and its program of hiking and skiing tours that travellers can join.

Mt Súlur HIKING
A pleasant but demanding day hike leads up the Glerárdalur valley to the summit of Mt Súlur (1213m). The trail begins on Súluvegur, a left turn off Þingvallastræti just before the Glerá bridge. Give yourself at least six hours to complete the return journey.

Tours

★**Saga Travel** ADVENTURE TOUR
(☎558 8888; www.sagatravel.is; Fjölnisgata 6a; ⊙booking office 8am-4pm Mon-Fri, to 2pm Sat & Sun) Saga offers a rich and diverse year-round program of excursions and activities throughout the north. It includes obvious spots such as Mývatn (from 17,900kr), Húsavík (for whale watching) and Askja in the highlands, but also offers innovative tours along themes such as food or art and design.

Winter tours include snowmobiling, snowshoeing and Northern Lights viewing (of course, weather dependent, but includes a lesson in photographing them). Private itineraries can be arranged; guides are local and well connected. Tours have a maximum of 19 participants (and minimum of two).

Traveling Viking ADVENTURE TOUR
(☎896 3569; www.ttv.is; 👪) Plenty of tours, from the expected (Mývatn, Dettifoss, Húsavík) to the offbeat, including a four-hour family-friendly option focusing on the 'hidden people', plus winter ice-fishing, a *Game of Thrones* tour of the Mývatn region and kayaking.

★**Skjaldarvík** HORSE RIDING, ADVENTURE TOUR
(☎552 5200; www.skjaldarvik.is; horse rides from 11,900kr, buggy tours s/d 23,900/38,800kr) Skjaldarvík offers a couple of top-notch activities from its scenic fjordside locale 6km north of town: horse-riding tours, plus fun adrenaline-pumping buggy rides. These buggies are golf carts on steroids; you'll drive along trails on the surrounding farm (driving licence required; helmet and overalls supplied). Their base has a superb guesthouse (p289) and restaurant.

Elding WILDLIFE
(☎519 5000; www.elding.is; Akureyri harbour; 3hr tour adult/child 10,990/5495kr) From a base on the harbour behind the Hof cultural centre, Reykjavík company Elding operates a three-hour whale-watching cruise, with year-round sailings, plus an 'express tour' on a RIB (per person 20,000kr; no children under 10) from April to September. They also have a Northern Lights tour in winter.

Ambassador WHALE WATCHING, BOAT TOUR
(☎462 6800; www.ambassador.is; Torfunefsbryggja dock; 3hr tour adult/child 10,990/5495kr) Ambassador has a growing range of tours on Eyjafjörður, from three-hour whale-watching cruises to fast-paced explorations on RIBs (two hours, adult 19,990kr). Also runs winter Northern Lights cruises, though sightings cannot be guaranteed.

Circle Air FLIGHT TOUR
(☎588 4000; www.circleair.is) Operating out of Akureyri Airport, this company offers flightseeing starting at 42,000kr for an 1½-hour flight over Dettifoss and Mývatn, plus the central highlands (52,000kr) or a one-hour stop on Grímsey (54,000kr).

SBA-Norðurleið BUS TOUR
(☎550 0700; www.sba.is; Hjalteyrargata 10) This bus company runs a range of sightseeing tours in North Iceland, with popular destinations including Mývatn, Dettifoss, Ásbyrgi and Húsavík.

Festivals & Events

The Calendar page at www.visitakureyri.is lists events.

Iceland Winter Games SPORTS
(www.icelandwintergames.com; ⊙Mar) Snowy activities take centre stage in Iceland's winter-sports capital, including international freeski and snowboard competitions.

Summer Arts Festival CULTURAL
(Listasumar; www.listasumar.is; ⊙mid-Jul–Aug) Over six weeks from mid-July into August, Akureyri celebrates the arts with exhibitions, events and concerts.

Akureyri Town Festival CULTURAL
(⊙Aug) Akureyri's biggest summertime fiesta, celebrating the city's birthday on the last weekend of August with concerts, exhibitions and events.

Sleeping

Akureyri Backpackers HOSTEL €

(☎571 9050; www.akureyribackpackers.com; Hafnarstræti 98; dm from 4900kr, d without bathroom 14,300kr;) Supremely placed in the town's heart, this backpackers has a chilled travellers' vibe and a popular bar. Rooms spread over three floors: four- to eight-bed dorms, plus private rooms (on the top floor). Minor gripe: there are toilets and sinks on all levels but showers are in the basement, as is the free sauna. There's a small kitchen and a laundry. Breakfast 1215kr.

Hamrar Campsite CAMPGROUND €

(☎461 2264; www.hamrar.is; sites per person 1500kr; mid-May–late Sep) This huge site, 1.5km south of town in a leafy setting in Kjarnaskógur woods, has newer facilities than the city campsite, and mountain views. There's a hostel-style building here that has the cheapest beds in town: mattresses on the floor in a sleeping loft for 2000kr.

Akureyri HI Hostel HOSTEL €

(Stórholt; ☎462 3657; www.hostel.is; Stórholt 1; dm 5400kr, d with/without bathroom 20,350/14,600kr;) This friendly, well-run hostel is a 15-minute walk north of the centre and has a TV lounge and two kitchens in the main house (rooms all have TV), a barbecue deck and two self-contained cottages sleeping up to eight. The owner happily imparts local knowledge. Check-in time (from 3pm) is strictly enforced. HI members get a 10% discount.

AKUREYRI ACCOMMODATION

- Akureyri fills up in summer – book ahead.
- There are plenty of options outside the centre, including excellent rural farmstays (you'll need your own car for these). Consult Hey Iceland (www.heyiceland.is).
- Most accommodation is open year-round (winter weekends are especially busy with skiers).
- The tourist office (p300) website lists most options in the area.
- Check accommodation websites for up-to-date rates and low-season discounts.

City Campsite CAMPGROUND €

(☎462 3379; www.hamrar.is; Þórunnarstræti 23; sites per adult 1500kr; early Jun–mid-Sep) This central site is popular for its location, not its charm. It has a washing machine, small dining area and showers (500kr), plus a car-free policy (except for loading and unloading; campervans accepted). Note: no kitchen. Handily, it's close to the swimming pool (p294) and a supermarket.

★Icelandair Hotel Akureyri HOTEL €€

(☎518 1000; www.icelandairhotels.com; Þingvallastræti 23; d from 22,100kr;) This high-class hotel showcases Icelandic designers and artists within its fresh, white-and-caramel-toned decor; rooms are compact but well designed. Added extras: outdoor terrace, good on-site restaurant, and a lounge (p298) serving high tea in the afternoon and happy-hour cocktails in the early evening.

Guesthouse Hvítahúsið GUESTHOUSE €€

(☎869 9890; www.guesthousenorth.is; Gilsbakkavegur 13; d without bathroom from 16,400kr;) In an elevated, hidden residential pocket behind Kaupvangsstræti, the 'White House' shines with the personal touch of its stylish owner, Guðrún. There are five rooms, plus a kitchen with free tea and coffee. (Note: no breakfast served.) Attic rooms are the pick – one has a balcony.

Hrafninn GUESTHOUSE €€

(☎462 5600; www.hrafninn.is; Brekkugata 4; s/d from 20,000/24,700kr;) Branding itself as a 'boutique guesthouse', central Hrafninn (the Raven) feels like an elegant manor house without being pretentious or stuffy. Over three floors, all rooms have bathroom and TV; the common areas feature some cool artworks. There is a small communal kitchenette for guests. Note: no breakfast served.

Hótel Íbúðir APARTMENT €€

(☎892 9838; Geislagata 10; studio 21,500kr, apt 19,400-37,600kr;) Íbúðir has a choice of six quite luxurious apartments ranging in size (the largest sleeping eight). With a central location and balconies with town views, they make a fine choice for families and groups.

Hótel Akureyri HOTEL €€

(☎462 5600; www.hotelakureyri.is; Hafnarstræti 67; d incl breakfast from 19,200kr;) Compact, well-equipped rooms are found at this boutique-style hotel, under friendly, service-minded family ownership. Front rooms have water views, back rooms have an outlook on lush greenery. (It's worth paying a little extra for fjord views.)

Gula Villan GUESTHOUSE €€
(☎896 8464; www.gulavillan.is; Brekkugata 8; s/d/q without bathroom from 12,100/17,400/26,290kr;) Bright, well-maintained rooms at this cheerful yellow-and-white villa are in a good central location, and the prices are reasonable. There is a second building, Gula Villan II, and both locations have guest kitchens and serve breakfast (2000kr). BYO sleeping bag to reduce the price.

Hótel Edda HOTEL €€
(☎444 4900; www.hoteledda.is; entry at Þórunnarstræti 14; d with/without bathroom from 16,575/9,775kr; ⊙mid-Jun–mid-Aug; @) With 200-plus rooms, this vast summer hotel in the local boarding school is not somewhere you'll feel the personal touch. The newer wing is modern with bright, well-equipped rooms (bathroom, TV); the cheaper old wing has shared bathrooms and a dated feel. Communal lounge areas are lovely. It's a short walk to the pool (p294) and botanical gardens (p291).

★**Sæluhús** APARTMENT €€€
(☎412 0800; www.saeluhus.is; Sunnutröð; studios/houses from 26,750/32,250kr;) This awesome mini-village of modern studios and houses is perfect for a few days' R&R. The houses may be better equipped than your own back home: three bedrooms (sleeping seven), kitchen, washing machine and verandah with hot tub and barbecue. Smaller studios are ideal for couples, with kitchen and access to a laundry (some have a hot tub, but these cost extra).

Hótel Kea HOTEL €€€
(☎460 2000; www.keahotels.is; Hafnarstræti 87-89; d incl breakfast from 34,500kr; @) Akureyri's largest year-round hotel (104 rooms) and popular with groups, super-central Kea has business-style rooms with good facilities (including minibar and tea-/coffee-making gear). There's little local character about it, but some rooms have balconies and fjord views. Its smart restaurant, Múlaberg, is also a cosy lounge.

Eating

There's a surprising array of options, and they get busy – in summer, it pays to make dinner reservations. Fast-food-style places cluster around the east side of Ráðhústorg.

Kaffi Ilmur CAFE €
(☎571 6444; www.kaffiilmur.com; Hafnarstræti 107b; dishes 1500-2500kr, lunch buffet 2400kr; ⊙8am-11pm, to 7pm Fri-Sun) In a charming historical building painted butter yellow (and once a saddlery), this welcoming cafe offers a tasty range of bodacious breakfast and lunch options and a substantial lunch buffet. Kitchen closes at 3.30pm, and then cakes, snacks and drinks are served.

Berlin CAFE €
(☎772 5061; www.facebook.com/berlinakureyri; Skipagata 4; breakfast 800-1700kr; ⊙8am-6pm;) Breakfast served all day? Hello Berlin! If you need a fix of bacon and eggs or avocado on toast, this cosy timber-lined cafe is your spot. Good coffee is a bonus, and you can linger over waffles with caramel sauce too. From 11.30am the menu adds lunch-y offerings such as vegetable dhal and chicken wings.

Blaá Kannan CAFE €
(☎461 4600; www.facebook.com/blaakannan; Hafnarstræti 96; lunchtime buffet 1800kr; ⊙9am-10.30pm, from 10am Sat & Sun) Prime people-watching is on offer at this much-loved cafe (the Blue Teapot, in the dark-blue Cafe Paris building) on the main drag. The interior is timber-lined and blinged up with chandeliers; the menu offers panini and bagels, and there's a cabinet full of sweet treats. It's a popular spot for late-night coffee or wine.

Café Laut CAFE €
(☎461 4601; www.facebook.com/cafelaut; Eyrarlandsvegur 30; dishes 1000-2600kr; ⊙10am-10pm Jun-Sep) What could be better than a designer cafe in a botanical garden (p291)? This cafe has gorgeous picture windows, good coffee, a big sun terrace and a lunchtime soup-and-bread buffet (1590kr), as well as bagels, salads and panini.

Brynja ICE CREAM €
(www.facebook.com/Brynjuis; Aðalstræti 3; ice cream from 500kr; ⊙10am-11.30pm;) This legendary ice-cream shop is known across Iceland for one of the best ice creams in the country (it's made with milk, not cream). It's 500m downhill from the botanical garden (p291).

Serrano FAST FOOD €
(www.serrano.is; Ráðhústorg 7; meals 1500-1800kr; ⊙11am-9pm, from noon Sun) Like your food fast, but fresher than you've been encountering at all those N1 grill-bars? Hit up

Serrano for a delish burrito, made to order; you can also nosh on tacos and quesadillas, or go green with salads.

★Strikið INTERNATIONAL €€
(☎462 7100; www.strikid.is; Skipagata 14; mains lunch 2000-3200kr, dinner 4000-5500kr; ⏲11.30am-10pm) Huge windows with fjord views lend a magical glitz to this 5th-floor restaurant, and the cool cocktails help things along. The menu showcases prime Icelandic produce (reindeer burgers, super-fresh sushi, lamb shoulder, shellfish soup). Crème brûlée makes for a sweet ending. The four-course signature menu is 9000kr. Reserve ahead.

Noa Seafood Restaurant SEAFOOD €€
(Örkin hans Nóa; ☎461 2100; www.noa.is; Hafnarstræti 22; mains 3800-7400kr; ⏲4-9pm) Part gallery, part furniture store, part restaurant – 'Noah's Ark' is certainly unique, and offers a simple food concept done well. The menu features a selection of fresh fish options, which are pan-fried and served with vegetables, with the pan brought to the table. Classic, effective and tasty. There are quality beef and lamb dishes for non-fish-fans. Bookings recommended.

Akureyri Fish Restaurant FISH & CHIPS €€
(☎414 6050; www.facebook.com/pg/Akureyri-fish-and-chips; Skipagata 12; mains 1500-2500kr; ⏲11.30am-10pm; 📶) The short blackboard at this bustling, casual place highlights piscatorial pleasures: fish and chips is the bestseller, or there's oven-baked salmon, crumbed cod, fish soup, fish burger, mussels (in season) and *plokkfiskur* (a tasty, traditional, creamy mashed-fish stew served with rye bread). All good washed down with local beers.

Icelandair Hotel Akureyri DESSERTS €€
(www.icelandairhotels.com; Þingvallastræti 23; high tea 2750kr; ⏲high tea 2-5pm) Suffering afternoon sluggishness? Get your sugar rush courtesy of the great-value high tea served every afternoon in the smart lounge of the Icelandair Hotel (p296). You'll be served a three-tiered tray of delights: savoury, sweet and more sweet. Coffee or tea included, champagne optional. You're welcome.

Greifinn INTERNATIONAL €€
(☎460 1600; www.greifinn.is; Glerárgata 20; mains 1700-5000kr; ⏲11.30am-10pm; 👪) Family-friendly and *always* full to bursting, Greifinn is one of the most popular spots in town. The menu favours comfort food above all: ribs and wings, juicy burgers, pizzas, pastas, milkshakes and devilish ice-cream desserts. Takeaway available.

Indian Curry House INDIAN €€
(☎461 4242; www.facebook.com/IndianCurryHutAkureyri; Ráðhústorg 3; dishes 1900-2500kr; ⏲11.30am-1.30pm & 5.30-9pm Tue-Fri, 5.30-9pm Sat & Sun) Add a little heat to a chilly evening with a flavourful curry from this family-run restaurant.

Rub23 INTERNATIONAL €€€
(☎462 2223; www.rub23.is; Kaupvangsstræti 6; mains lunch 2600-3200kr, dinner 5000-5900kr; ⏲11.30am-2pm & 5.30-10pm Mon-Fri, 5.30-10pm Sat & Sun) This sleek, seafood-showcasing restaurant has a decidedly Japanese flavour, but also promotes its use of 'rubs' or marinades (along the lines of sweet mango chilli or citrus rosemary). The food is first-rate, and at dinner there's an array of menus (including a sushi menu and tasting menus). Bookings advised.

Self-Catering

Nettó SUPERMARKET €
(Glerárgata; ⏲10am-7pm) In the Glerártorg shopping mall.

Bónus SUPERMARKET €
(Langholt 1; ⏲11am-6.30pm Mon-Thu, 10am-7.30pm Fri, 10am-6pm Sat, noon-6pm Sun) Bargain supermarket.

Krambúð SUPERMARKET €
(www.samkaup.is; Byggðavegur 98; ⏲8am-10.30pm, from 9am Sat & Sun) Near the campsite (p296) west of the centre.

Drinking & Nightlife

An evening stroll down Hafnarstræti will present you with a few good options, and a chance to see where the crowds are.

★Ölstofa Akureyrar BAR
(☎663 8886; www.facebook.com/olstofak; Kaupvangsstræti 23; ⏲6pm-1am Mon-Thu, to 3am Fri & Sat, to 10pm Sun) *The* place in town for draught and local beers, this convivial spot has recently partnered with local (and well-loved) brewery Einstök to create a brewer's lounge (www.brewerslounge.is) where you sample their delicious wares, fresh from the brewery.

Akureyri Backpackers BAR
(☎571 9050; www.akureyribackpackers.com; Hafnarstræti 98; ⏲reception 7.30am-11pm Sun-Thu, to 1am Fri & Sat) Always a hub of convivial main-street activity, the fun timber-clad bar at Akureyri Backpackers (p296) is beloved of both travellers and locals for its occasional live music, good-value burgers and weekend brunches, and a wide beer selection – this is a fine spot to sample local microbrews Kaldi and Einstök.

Götubarinn BAR
(☎462 4747; www.facebook.com/gotubarinn; Hafnarstræti 96; ⏲1.30-9pm Tue, 5pm-1am Thu, 5pm-3am Fri & Sat) The locals' favourite drinking spot, fun and central Götubarinn (Street Bar) has a surprising amount of cosiness and charm for a place that closes so late. It's all timber, mirrors and couches, and there's even a downstairs piano for late-night singalongs.

Vínbúðin ALCOHOL
(☎462 1655; www.vinbudin.is; Hólabraut 16; ⏲11am-6pm Mon-Thu & Sat, to 7pm Fri) Government-run liquor store.

☆ Entertainment

★Græni Hatturinn LIVE MUSIC
(☎461 4646; http://graenihatturinn.is; Hafnarstræti 96) Tucked down a lane beside Blaá Kannan (p297), this intimate venue is the best place in town to see live music – and one of the best in the country. If you get the chance, buy a ticket to anything going.

Hof MUSIC, PERFORMING ARTS
(☎450 1000; www.mak.is; Strandgata 12) Modern Hof is a cultural centre designed for music and other performing arts. Along with conference and exhibition facilities and a good daytime restaurant (1862 Nordic Bistro), it's also home to Akureyri's tourist office (p300); ask here about any scheduled performances or check the website.

Shopping

Several shops on Hafnarstræti sell traditional *lopapeysur* Icelandic woollen sweaters, books, knick-knacks and souvenirs. Remember to look for Icelandic-made knitwear (some is now mass-produced in China) and ask about the tax-free scheme.

The Glerártorg shopping mall (http://www.glerartorg.is), on Rte 1 about 1km north of the town centre, is home to a large Nettó supermarket and other shops and services.

★Flora DESIGN
(☎661 0168; www.facebook.com/flora.akureyri; Hafnarstræti 90; ⏲10am-7pm, from noon Sun) This artist-run collective selling creative designware and handicrafts strives for sustainability and reuse in the materials in its goods.

★Geysir CLOTHING
(☎519 6040; www.geysir.com; Hafnarstræti 98; ⏲10am-6pm, noon-5pm Sun) We covet everything in this unique shop, from the woollen blankets to the hipster-chic *lopapeysur* (traditional Icelandic sweaters) and the old Iceland maps. It looks like it dresses all the stylish lumbersexuals in town.

Sjoppan DESIGN
(☎864 0710; www.facebook.com/sjoppanvoruhus; Kaupvangsstræti 21; ⏲hours vary) Cute as a button, this tiny shop dispenses cool design items and gifts from a hutch out the front (ring the bell for service). It's across from the art museum (p291). Check out its Facebook page for hours and other details.

Eymundsson BOOKS, SOUVENIRS
(☎540 2180; www.eymundsson.is; Hafnarstræti 91-93; ⏲9am-10pm, from 10am Sat & Sun; 📶) First-rate bookshop selling maps, souvenir books and a wide selection of international magazines. There's a tasty cafe on-site with wi-fi for customers.

Hornið SPORTS & OUTDOORS
(☎461 1516; www.utivistogveidi.is; Kaupvangsstræti 4; ⏲10am-6pm Mon-Fri, to 4pm Sat) Forget your long johns? Here's the shop for outfitting for backcountry travel and sport.

Fold-Anna CLOTHING
(Hafnarstræti 100; ⏲9.30am-6.30pm Mon-Fri, 10am-4pm Sat & Sun) Staff can be seen knitting behind the counter as you browse this outlet loaded with *lopapeysur* (traditional Icelandic sweaters) and assorted crafty items.

ℹ Information

EMERGENCY

Police (☎464 7700; Þórunnarstræti 138)

MEDICAL SERVICES

Akureyri Hospital (☎463 0100; www.sak.is; Eyrarlandsvegur) Just south of the botanical gardens.

GRÍMSEY

Best known as Iceland's only true piece of the Arctic Circle, the remote island of Grímsey, 40km from the mainland, is a serene little place where birds outnumber people by about 10,000 to one. The island is small (5 sq km) but the welcome is big and the relaxation deep.

Scenic coastal cliffs and dramatic basalt formations make a popular home for dozens of species of seabirds, including loads of puffins, plus the kamikaze Arctic tern. We're particularly fond of the anecdote that the airport runway has to be cleared of the terns a few minutes before aircraft arrive.

Dive or snorkel with the bird life – puffins and guillemots dive deep as they search for food – with local company Arctic Trip. Birders: note that puffins are not guaranteed beyond early August (viewing is best from May to July); terns (May to September) are pretty aggressive in July, when their chicks begin to be active. Take care walking around cliff edges. The Akureyri tourist office helps with information for a visit; see also www.grimsey.is, or ask at the island shop.

The Arctic Circle

Grímsey's appeal to many lies in what it represents. Tourists flock here to snap up their 'I visited the Arctic Circle' certificate and appreciate its windswept setting. Though the Arctic Circle is shown on maps at a fixed 66.5°, it actually moves with the wobble of the Earth's tilt (2.4° every 40,000 years). As of 2017, a 7980kg concrete sphere marks the actual spot on the island, currently about a 45-minute hike north of the airstrip. So unless you are a runner, the best way to ensure you actually get to the real Arctic Circle is by coming by boat (longer layover) or staying the night.

Sleeping & Eating

To soak up Grímsey's Arctic Circle relaxation and fresh air, there's two guesthouses and a small **campground** (800kr per person) by the community centre with very basic facilities – enquire at the town's shop.

Básar (☎467 3103; www.gistiheimilidbasar.is; s/d without bathroom incl breakfast 14,900/19,200kr; 📶) Homey Básar is right next to the air strip and has peaceful views of the bluffs and wide open ocean. Sleeping-bag accommodation is possible, and there is a guest kitchen and comfy lounge area.

Gullsól (☎467 3190; www.gullsol.is; s/d without bathroom from 7500/13,000kr; 📶) Follow the stairs up through the trapdoor at cosy Gullsól to find teeny-tiny rooms perched above the

Apótekarinn (www.apotekarinn.is; Hafnarstræti 95; ⏱9am-5.30pm Mon-Fri) Central pharmacy.

On-Call Doctor Service (☎1700; ⏱24hr) Twenty-four-hour number; only for urgent issues.

Primary Health Care Clinic (Heilsugæslustöðin; ☎460 4600; 3rd fl, Hafnarstræti 99; ⏱8am-4pm Mon-Fri)

TOURIST INFORMATION

The friendly and efficient **Tourist Office** (☎450 1050; www.visitakureyri.is; Hof, Strandgata 12; ⏱8am-6.30pm Jun–mid-Sep, 8am-4pm Mon-Fri mid-Sep–Apr, 8am-4pm May; 📶) inside Hof (p299) offers loads of brochures, maps, internet access and a great design store. Knowledgeable staff advise on tours and transport.

ℹ Getting There & Away

AIR

Akureyri Airport (www.isavia.is; Rte 821) is 3km south of the city centre.

Air Iceland Connect (☎460 7000; www.airicelandconnect.is) Runs flights up to eight times daily between Akureyri and Reykjavík's domestic airport (45 minutes). They sometimes have a flight to/from Keflavík, for connecting international travellers only – thus you don't need to travel to Reykjavík's domestic airport to connect to Akureyri. These flights are only bookable as part of an international flight to and from Iceland with Icelandair.

Norlandair (www.norlandair.is) Has flights from Akureyri to Grímsey island (30 minutes) and to Greenland. There's also a weekday link with Vopnafjörður and Þórshöfn in Northeast Iceland.

island's gift shop-cafe (which opens in conjunction with ferry arrivals and serves waffles). The full kitchen is handy for self-caterers.

Krían (☎467 3112; ⏲noon-9pm mid-May–early Sep, hours vary rest of year) The island's only restaurant (named after the Arctic tern, *kría* in Icelandic) is an agreeable place with an outdoor deck that enjoys views over the harbour. Soups and fish dishes are generally available.

Búðin (☎898 2058; ⏲open daily) Small but well-stocked supermarket. If it's closed when you need it, it's usually just a matter of letting a local know and they'll arrange for it to be opened. (It's that kind of island!) Has info about camping and geothermal pool.

Getting There & Away

Reach Grímsey by ferry or flight – guided tours to the island are usually available in summer months.

Air

Norlandair (www.norlandair.is) operates flights to/from Akureyri (daily in June; five weekly July and August; three weekly September to May). The 25-minute journey takes in the full length of Eyjafjörður and is an experience in itself. Ticketing is handled by Air Iceland Connect; one-way fares start at around 10,300kr. Flights from Reykjavík to Akureyri can connect to the Grímsey flights. If you book the 'daytour' option (additional €40), instead of the basic airline ticket on the website, it comes with a guided tour. Flightseeing operators offering one-hour landings on the island include Mýflug Air (p305; 48,000kr) in Mývatn and Circle Air (p295; 54,000kr) in Akureyri.

Boat

There is year-round ferry service between Dalvík and Grímsey. The **Sæfari** (☎458 8970; www.saefari.is; three hours; adult/child 3500kr/free) departs from Dalvík at 9am Monday, Wednesday, Thursday and Friday, returning from Grímsey at different hours (giving you two to five hours on the island). June to August there is also a service on Sunday.

If you're coming from Akureyri, Strætó's (p429) bus 78 won't get you to Dalvík in good time for the ferry. Without your own wheels you'll need to spend the night before in Dalvík.

From Dalvík, and utilising the Sæfari ferry, island outfit **Arctic Trip** (☎848 1696; www.arctictrip.is) has a day tour for 26,000kr, or Dalvík's Arctic Sea Tours (p288) organises a 10-hour tour with four guided hours on Grímsey for 25,200kr. In Húsavík, Gentle Giants (p315) offers rigid inflatable boat (RIB) day trips to Grímsey (72,300kr).

Super Break (www.superbreak.com) Has winter flights serving the UK.

BUS

Bus services are ever-changing in Iceland, so it pays to get up-to-date information on schedules and fares from bus company websites or tourist information centres. Winter services are reduced.

Akureyri is the hub for bus travel in the North, provided by Strætó (p429) from a **bus stop** (Strandgata 12) in front of Hof (p299), with one summer route by SBA-Norðurleið.

Strætó services generally run year-round:

- Bus 56 to Egilsstaðir (8280kr, 3½ hours), via Mývatn (2760kr, 1½ hours) one daily; drops to four weekly services in winter.
- Bus 57 to Reykjavík via Rte 1 (10,120kr, 6½ hours, two daily, except one on Saturday).
- Bus 78 Akureyri–Dalvík–Ólafsfjörður–Siglufjörður (2760kr, 70 minutes, three daily Monday to Friday, one Sunday).
- Bus 79 to Húsavík (2760kr, 1½ hours, three Monday to Friday, one Saturday, two Sunday).

SBA-Norðurleið (p295) service:

- Bus 610a to Reykjavík via the Kjölur route (17,900kr, 10½ hours, one daily mid-June to mid-September).

CAR

After Reykjavík, Akureyri is Iceland's second transport hub. All the major car-hire firms have representation at the airport. For a fee, most will let you pick up a car in Akureyri and drop it off in Reykjavík or vice versa.

Check out www.samferda.is for information about car-pooling, or check hostel noticeboards.

Getting Around

Central Akureyri is quite compact and easy to get around on foot.

BUS

There's a free town bus service on six routes, running regularly from 7am to 8pm weekdays and 1pm to 6pm weekends – look for the yellow buses. No route serves the airport. The tourist office has a printed bus map and schedule.

CAR

Akureyri has a unique parking system for Iceland (one that many northern Europeans will be familiar with). When parking in the town centre, you must set a plastic parking clock indicating the time you parked, and display it on the dashboard of your car (so as to be seen through the windshield).

Parking is free, but spaces are signposted with maximum parking times (from 15 minutes to two hours, enforced from 10am to 4pm weekdays). Note: '1 klst' means one hour. You'll be fined if your car overstays the advertised time limit. Pick up a parking clock (free) at the tourist office (p300), banks and petrol stations.

TAXI

The **BSO** (461 1010; www.bso.is; Strandgata) taxi stand is opposite Hof (p299). Taxis may be booked 24 hours a day. Their website (and a board at the taxi stand) outlines the cost for rides to nearby sightseeing destinations.

South of Akureyri

Eyjafjarðarsveit is the valley south of Akureyri, accessed by Rtes 821 and 829. The Eyjafjarðará River runs through fertile farmland with idyllic pastoral views and mountain backdrops. At **Kaffi Kú** (867 3826; www.kaffiku.is; Rte 829; dishes 500-2500kr; 10am-6pm, from noon Sat & Sun;) dine above a high-tech cowshed (you can watch the cows queue to be milked by a 'robot') on excellent beef goulash or roast-beef bagels, plus waffles that pair perfectly with farm-fresh cream. **Christmas Garden** (Jólagarðurinn; 463 1433; Rte 821; 10am-9pm Jun-Aug, 2-9pm Sep-Dec, 2-6pm Jan-May) fills a multilevel gingerbread house with a super-festive selection of locally made decorations and traditional Icelandic Christmas foods for sale.

Eastern Eyjafjörður

Eyjafjörður's eastern shore is much quieter than its western counterpart, and offers a few good places to pause among the sweeping vistas, including the eclectic **Icelandic Folk & Outsider Art Museum** (Safnasafnið; 461 4066; www.safnasafnid.is; Rte 1 (Svalbarðsströnd); adult/child 1000kr/free; 10am-5pm mid-May–Sep), 12km from Akureyri on Rte 1.

Further north, Rte 83 branches off the Ring Road to lead you 20km north to the tiny, tidy fishing village of **Grenivík**, which has a spectacular outlook and good facilities: campground and pool, a small maritime museum, and a small supermarket with attached restaurant. En route (along Rte 83) are the photogenic turf roofs at **Laufás** (462 4162; www.minjasafnid.is; Rte 83; adult/child 1500kr/free; 9am-5pm Jun-Aug) and the acclaimed stables of **Pólar Hestar** (463 3179; www.polarhestar.is; Rte 83, Grýtubakki II; 1/2hr horse rides 6000/10,000kr).

Near and in Grenivík, Nollur (www.nollur.is) rents out architect-designed holiday houses by the week in high season (minimum two nights from September to May; all bookings done online). Most enjoy outstanding views and plenty of creature comforts (including hot-pots).

★ **Halllandsnes** APARTMENT €€

(895 6029; www.halllandsnes.is; Rte 1; apt from 18,900kr;) There's an unexpected touch of the Mediterranean at this outstanding property 6km east of Akureyri along Rte 1. Its whitewashed buildings and delightful outdoor area enjoy sweeping fjord views, while inside are impeccable, well-furnished apartments with quality appliances, full kitchens including dishwasher, and washer-dryers – you may not want to leave. Each apartment sleeps four or six in comfort.

Hotel Natur HOTEL €€

(467 1070; www.hotelnatur.com; Þórisstaðir; s/d incl breakfast 20,500/29,400kr;) About 15km east of Akureyri along Rte 1, this family-run property offers Nordic simplicity in its minimalist rooms, a huge dining space and breathtaking fjord views. The main accommodation is housed in the farm's old cow barn – but you'd never guess! Nice attention is given to recreation facilities, including a cool 'sightseeing tower', walking trails, hotpot and billiard table.

Goðafoss

Travellers on the Ring Road between Akureyri and Mývatn will happen across heavenly waterfall Goðafoss (pronounced *go*-tha-foss), a magnet that pulls most motorists off the road for a closer look.

★**Goðafoss** WATERFALL

(Rte 1) Goðafoss (Waterfall of the Gods) rips straight through the Bárðardalur lava field along Rte 1. Although smaller and less powerful than some of Iceland's other chutes, it's definitely one of the most beautiful. There are two car parks: one on the Ring Road, the other down the road beside the petrol station. Take the path behind the falls for a less-crowded viewpoint.

The falls play an important part in Icelandic history. At the Alþingi (National Assembly) in the year 1000, the *lögsögumaður* (law speaker), Þorgeir, was forced to make a decision on Iceland's religion. After 24 hours' meditation, he declared the country a Christian nation. On his way home he passed the waterfall near his farm, and tossed in his pagan carvings of the Norse gods, thus bestowing the falls' present name.

Sleeping & Eating

Kiðagil GUESTHOUSE, CAMPGROUND €€

(☎464 3290; www.kidagil.is; Rte 842; site per tent 1800kr, d incl breakfast with/without bathroom 23,200/14,400kr; ⊙early May-Sep; 📶👪) A friendly family operates this simple guesthouse with tidy rooms and good food. A welcome respite, it's the inn closest to the northern access of the Sprengisandur route, 24km south of Goðafoss. Has family rooms and campground.

Fosshóll GUESTHOUSE €€

(☎464 3108; www.godafoss.is; Rte 1; d with/without bathroom incl breakfast 26,000/21,500kr; ⊙May–mid-Oct; 📶) If the sound of pounding water puts you to sleep, a night in the (overpriced) rooms of sunny yellow Fosshóll, next to Goðafoss falls, might be for you. Ask about sleeping-bag rates to save money. There's a restaurant here too.

Tourist Complex CAFETERIA €

(Rte 1; ⊙8am-10pm; 📶) Right beside Goðafoss is a complex with information, free wi-fi, a few groceries, a souvenir shop, public toilets, a petrol pump and a decent cafeteria. The simple menu has soups, burgers, pizza etc.

Getting There & Away

Goðafoss' access is right on the Ring Road, just east of the Rte 85 turn-off to Húsavík. There are N1 petrol pumps here.

Buses between Akureyri and Mývatn stop here; some buses between Akureyri and Húsavík also stop (others travel Rte 85).

OFF THE BEATEN TRACK

ALDEYJARFOSS

Spectacular waterfall **Aldeyjarfoss** (F26) , 41km south of Goðafoss, is well worth the journey. The Skjálfandafljót river churns through a narrow passage and into a deep pool in a canyon lined with intriguing basalt column formations.

Take unsealed Rte 842 to the northern entrance/exit of the long, lonely 4WD Sprengisandur route (p364) (Rte F26) across the interior highlands. Note: only 4WD permitted on F26, which is the last 3.5km to Aldeyjarfoss' small parking area, as you drive south.

You can park your 2WD near the gate for F26 and walk the 3.5km if you don't have a 4WD.

MÝVATN REGION

Undisputed gem of the northeast, Mývatn (pronounced *mee*-vaht) lake and the surrounding area are starkly beautiful, an otherworldly terrain of spluttering mudpots, weird lava formations, steaming fumaroles and volcanic craters, set around a bird-filled lake.

The Mývatn basin sits squarely on the Mid-Atlantic Ridge and the violent geological character of the area has produced a jam-packed landscape unlike anywhere else in the country.

History & Geology

Ten thousand years ago the Mývatn basin was covered by an ice cap, which was destroyed by fierce volcanic eruptions that also obliterated the lake at its base. The explosions formed the symmetrical *móberg* peaks (flat-topped mountains formed by subglacial volcanic eruptions) south of today's lake, while volcanic activity to the east formed the Lúdent tephra complex (tephra is solid matter ejected into the air by an erupting volcano).

Another cycle of violent activity more than 6000 years later created the Ketildyngja volcano, 25km southeast of Mývatn. The lava from that crater flowed northwest along the Laxárdalur valley, and created a lava dam and a new, improved lake. After another millennium or so a volcanic explosion along the same fissure spewed out Hverfjall, the classic tephra crater that dominates the modern landscape. Over the next 200 years, activity escalated along the eastern shore and craters were thrown up across a wide region, providing a steady stream of molten material flowing towards Öxarfjörður. The lava dam formed during the end of this cycle created the present Mývatn shoreline.

Between 1724 and 1729 the Mývatnseldar (Mývatn Fires) eruptions began at Leirhnjúkur, close to Krafla, northeast of the lake. This dramatic and sporadically active fissure erupted again in the 1970s (the Kröflueldar or Krafla Fires), with that episode lasting nine years.

In 1974 the area around Mývatn was set aside as the **Mývatn-Laxá Nature Conservation Area**, and Hverfjall and the pseudo-crater field at Skútustaðir, at the southern end of the lake, are preserved as national natural monuments.

Orientation

Mývatn lake is encircled by a 36km sealed road (Rte 1 on the western and northern shores, and Rte 848 on the southern and eastern shoreline). The main settlement is Reykjahlíð, in the north-east corner – an information centre is here, as are many sleeping and eating options.

Most of the points of interest are linked by the lake's looping road, including the diverse lava formations in eastern Mývatn, the cluster of pseudocraters near southern Mývatn, and the bird-friendly marsh plains around western Mývatn.

In northern Mývatn, the Ring Road (Rte 1) veers east, away from Reykjahlíð, and takes you over the Námaskarð pass to the Hverir geothermal area. Then, a turn-off to the north (Rte 863) leads to Krafla, 14km from Reykjahlíð. Continue along the Ring Road and after another 20km you'll reach the turn-off (sealed Rte 862) to Dettifoss waterfall.

With your own vehicle this whole area can be explored in a day, but if you're using the bus or a bike allow two days. If you want to hike and explore more distant mountains and lava fields, allow at least three days.

Activities

Tourism reigns supreme at Reykjahlíð, and for travellers without transport there are

Mývatn & Krafla

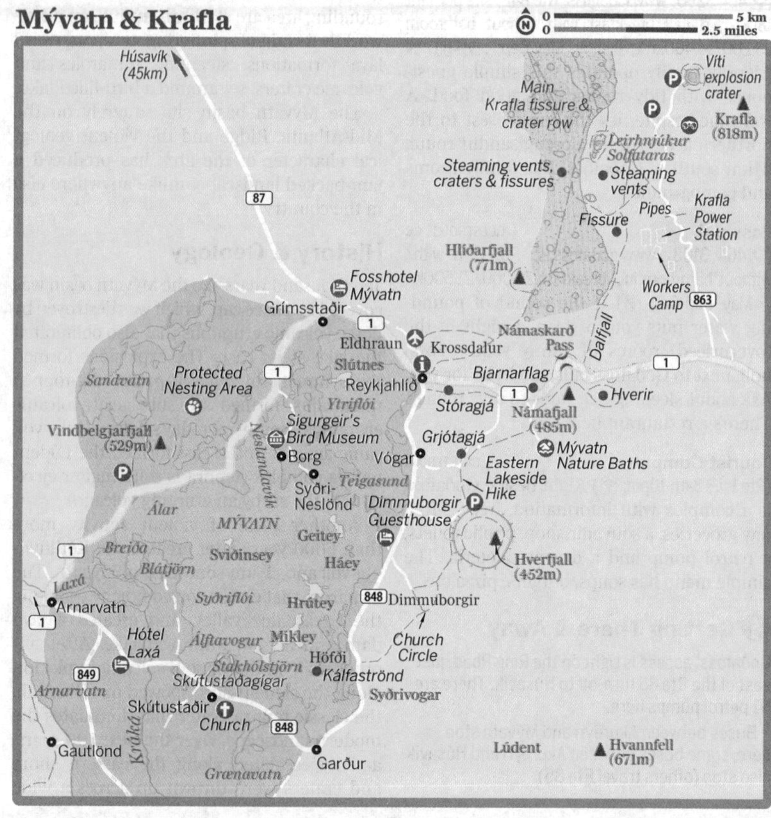

sightseeing tours in the area (some originate in Akureyri). Tours fill up fast during summer, so try to book at least a day before.

A number of operators run super-Jeep tours into the highlands, to Askja and surrounds, from mid-June (when the route opens) until as late into September if the weather permits. From Akureyri it makes for a long day tour (up to 15 hours); 12-hour tours leave from Reykjahlíð. Tour companies pick up and drop off at the car park by the visitor centre.

Saga Travel (p295) operates an array of fabulous year-round tours in the Mývatn area, including sightseeing, caving, birdwatching and lava walks (see website for full selection). Northern Lights tours offer photography tips. There is often the option of joining tours from Akureyri or Reykjahlíð.

★Geo Travel ADVENTURE TOUR
(☎464 4442; www.geotravel.is) A small company owned by two well-connected local guys who plant trees to carbon offset their tours. They offer excellent year-round small-group trips, from tours of lava and ice cave Lofthellir (17,500kr) to super-Jeep excursions to Askja and Holuhraun (34,900kr), Northern Lights tours (17,500kr) and half-hour snowmobile trips (14,900kr). They're also birdwatching specialists.

Mývatn Activity – Hike&Bike ADVENTURE TOUR
(☎899 4845; www.hikeandbike.is) Hike&Bike has a booth by the Gamli Bærinn (p307) tavern in Reykjahlíð that offers tour bookings and mountain-bike rental (adult/child 5000/4000kr per day). A vast program of cycling and hiking tours includes a fatbike ride to Lofthellir lava and ice cave (24,900kr), a one-hour ATV-ride (22,500kr) and an evening sightseeing cycle that ends with a soak at the Nature Baths (p311), costing 13,500kr including baths admission.

Mýflug Air SCENIC FLIGHT
(☎464 4400; www.myflug.is; Reykjahlíð Airport) Mýflug Air operates daily flightseeing excursions (weather permitting) including a 20-minute trip over Mývatn and Krafla (19,000kr). A two-hour 'super tour' (57,000kr) also includes Dettifoss, Ásbyrgi, Kverkfjöll, Herðubreið and Askja. Or fly north for a one-hour stop in Grímsey (48,000kr).

Snowdogs DOG SLEDDING
(☎847 7199; www.snowdogs.is; off Rte 849; sled tour adult/child 30,000/10,000kr) Sæmi and his family run winter dog-sledding tours across wilderness on remote farm Heiði, about 8km off Rte 848 in southern Mývatn (take Rte 849 west of Skútustaðir). Tours vary depending on the dogs, people, weather and trail conditions, but guests are generally on the snow for 45 to 60 minutes and cover around 8km. Dog cart rides in summer (19,000kr). The family also runs kennel visits (3500kr).

Saltvík HORSE RIDING
(☎847 6515; www.saltvik.is; Rte 848; 2hr tour 9900kr) Just south of Reykjahlíð, Saltvík operates horseback sightseeing tours around Mývatn (suitable for all skill levels, including beginners) from June to August. They also have a larger operation in Húsavík (p316).

Safarí Hestar HORSE RIDING
(☎464 4203; www.safarihorserental.com; Rte 848, Álftagerði III; 1/2hr tour 7000/11,000kr) Scenic horse tours operate from Álftagerði III farm on the south side of the lake, 400m west of Sel-Hótel (p309), and take in the lakeshore and pseudocraters.

SBA-Norðurleið BUS TOUR
(☎550 0700; www.sba.is) SBA has one tour from Reykjahlíð (15,300kr; late June to August) to Dettifoss and Asbyrgi, ending in Akureyri. Plus other sightseeing trips in the northeast.

Sleeping & Eating

Mývatn's popularity means that room rates soar in summer when demand far outstrips supply, so be sure to book ahead. Most prices are very inflated, with €275 being the norm for a run-of-the-mill hotel double in summer's peak. Off-season rates drop considerably. To save money at guesthouses, ask about sleeping-bag options.

Most places to stay and eat are located in Reykjahlíð, Vógar and Dimmuborgir (along the lake's northeastern shore) or Skútustaðir (southern shore). Several large hotels dot the lakeshore, and all have restaurants – Hótel Gígur's (p309) is one of the best. Note that wine and beer are only available in restaurants; the closest Vínbúðin (p299) is in Húsavík.

The local food speciality is the moist, cakelike rye bread called *hverabrauð* (often translated as 'geysir bread'), which is slow-baked underground using geothermal heat.

Information

Mývatnsstofa Visitor Centre (☎464 4390; www.visitmyvatn.is; Hraunvegur 8; ⌚8.30am-

6pm Jun-Aug, shorter hours rest of year) This well-informed centre in Reykjahlíð (by the supermarket) has good displays on the local geology and park rangers to advise on local sights. Pick up a copy of the useful *Mývatn* map, which gives a decent overview of hiking trails in the area (though it's not to scale).

Getting There & Away

All buses pick up and drop off passengers at the visitor centre (p305) in Reykjahlíð; buses also stop in Skútustaðir, by the Sel-Hótel (p309).

Strætó (p429) services (reduced in winter):

- Bus 56 to Akureryi (2760kr, 1½ hours, one daily).
- Bus 56 to Egilsstaðir (5980kr, two hours, one daily).

Reykjavík Excursions (p429) services:

- Bus 14/14a to Landmannalaugar along the highland Sprengisandur route (16,100kr, 10 hours, one weekly July to August).

Getting Around

There are wonderful hiking trails around Mývatn, but they're not all connected. Without wheels you may find yourself on long walks along the lakeshore road.

You can rent a car in Akureyri or, during calmer weather, hire a mountain bike from Hike&Bike (p305). The 36km ride around the lake can be done in a day.

If you need a taxi (June to August), call ☎893 4389.

Reykjahlíð

POP 208

Reykjahlíð (pronounced *rey*-kya-leeth), on the northeastern shore of Mývatn lake, is the main village and Mývatn's obvious base. There's little to it beyond a collection of guesthouses and hotels, a supermarket, petrol station and information centre (p305).

Sights

Reykjahlíð Church CHURCH

(Reykjahlíðarkirkja) During the Krafla eruption of 1727, the Leirhnjúkur (p311) crater, 11km northeast of Reykjahlíð, kicked off a two-year period of volcanic activity, sending streams of lava along old glacial moraines towards the lakeshore. On 27 August 1729 the flow ploughed through the village, destroying farms and buildings, but amazingly (some would say miraculously) the wooden church was spared when the flow parted, missing the church by only metres. It was rebuilt on its original foundation in 1876, then again in 1962.

Sleeping

Bjarg CAMPGROUND €

(☎464 4240; ferdabjarg@simnet.is; Rte 1; site per person 2000kr; ⊙mid-May–Sep) This campsite has a gorgeous, peaceful location on the Reykjahlíð lakeshore (though it gets packed and noisy in summer) almost opposite the supermarket. There is a cooking area (no stoves or utensils, so bring everything), laundry service (1200kr per wash or dry), tour-booking desk and bike hire. Note: no wi-fi.

Hlíð CAMPGROUND, GUESTHOUSE €

(☎464 4103; www.myvatnaccommodation.is; off Rte 1, Hraunbrún; sites per person 2000kr, dm 5600kr, d incl breakfast 26,000kr, 2-bedroom cottage 40,000kr; @) Sprawling, well-run Hlíð is 300m uphill from the church and offers a full spectrum of accommodation: camping, sleeping-bag dorms and rooms with kitchen access, no-frills huts, self-contained cottages sleeping six, and en suite guesthouse rooms. There's also a laundry, playground and bike hire.

Icelandair Hotel Mývatn HOTEL €€

(☎444 4000; www.icelandairhotels.com; Rte 1; s/d incl breakfast from 20,000/23,800kr; @) Bought by Icelandair and renovated in 2018, Hotel Reynihlíð, the grand dame of Mývatn hotels, is now a smartly dressed 50-room affair. Sleek guestrooms have all the top mod-cons and brand-new bathrooms plus a welcoming bar. We also like the nine rooms at its cosy 'economy' annexe, the pretty, lakeside **Hótel Reykjahlíð**.

Helluhraun 13 B&B €€

(☎464 4132; www.helluhraun13.blogspot.com; Helluhraun 13; d without bathroom incl breakfast 19,000kr; ⊙Jun-Aug;) Ásdis is the sunny host at this small, homely guesthouse with lava-field views. There are just three rooms and one bathroom, but they're bright, spotless and tastefully decorated.

Vógar GUESTHOUSE, CAMPGROUND €€

(☎464 4399; www.vogahraun.is; Rte 1, Vógar; sites per person/tent 1500/500kr, guesthouse d with/without bathroom from 27,700/18,100kr;) There's a range of options here, 2.5km south of Reykjahlíð: camping, basic accommodation in utilitarian prefab huts and a newer block of compact guesthouse rooms, with and without bathroom. Sleeping bags reduce the price, as do longer stays. All rooms have kitchen access; rooms with private bathroom include breakfast.

Vogafjós Guesthouse GUESTHOUSE €€
(☎464 3800; www.vogafjos.net; Rte 1, Vógar; d incl breakfast from 25,600kr;) Fresh scents of pine and cedar fill the air in these log-cabin rooms (cosy with underfloor heating), set in a lava field 2.5km south of Reykjahlíð and a few minutes' walk from the Cowshed restaurant, where breakfast is served. Most rooms sleep two, with family rooms also available.

Eldá GUESTHOUSE €€
(☎464 4220; www.elda.is; Helluhraun 9; s/d without bathroom incl breakfast 16,400/21,300kr;) This friendly operation owns three basic properties along Helluhraun and offers no-frills accommodation. There are guest kitchens and TV lounges, and buffet breakfast is included. All guests check in at Helluhraun 9.

Eating

Kjörbúðin SUPERMARKET €
(☎464 4466; www.samkaup.is; Rte 1; 9am-7pm Mon-Fri, 10am-6pm Sat, noon-6pm Sun) Busy, well-stocked supermarket (with petrol pumps) next to the visitor centre (p305). Has a grill and outdoor picnic tables.

★**Vogafjós** ICELANDIC €€
(☎464 3800; www.vogafjos.net; Rte 848; dishes 2000-5900kr; 10am-11pm Jun-Aug, shorter hours rest of year;) The 'Cowshed', 2.5km south of Reykjahlíð, is a memorable restaurant where you can enjoy views of the lush surrounds, or of the dairy shed of this working farm (cows are milked at 7.30am and 5.30pm). The menu is an ode to local produce: smoked lamb, house-made mozzarella, dill-cured Arctic char, geysir bread, home-baked cakes and homemade ice cream. It's all delicious. Kitchen closes at 10pm in summer.

Gamli Bærinn ICELANDIC €€
(☎464 4270; www.myvatnhotel.is; Rte 1; mains 2100-4000kr; 10am-11pm;) The cheerfully busy 'Old Farm' tavern beside Hótel Reynihlíð serves up good-quality pub-style meals all day, ranging from lamb soup, burgers and grilled trout to pizzas. In the evening it becomes a local hang-out – opening hours may be extended at weekends, but the kitchen closes at 10pm.

EASTERN LAKESIDE HIKE

Although easily accessible by car, the sights along Mývatn's eastern lakeshore can also be tackled on a pleasant half-day hike. A well-marked track runs from Reykjahlíð village to Hverfjall (p308) (4km), passing Grjótagjá along the way. Then it's on to Dimmuborgir (p308) (another 3km) with its collection of gnarled statuesque lava. If you start in the late afternoon and time your hike correctly, you'll finish the day with a meal at Dimmuborgir while sunset shadows dance along the alien landscape. As an alternative, the walk from Hverfjall's northwest corner to the Nature Baths (p311) is 2.3km – and the sunsets here are pretty special too.

Daddi's Pizza PIZZERIA €€
(☎773 6060; www.vogahraun.is; Rte 848, Vógar; small pizza 1720-2900kr; noon-11pm;) At Vogár campground, this small space cranks out tasty pizzas to eat in or take away. Try the house speciality: smoked trout, nuts and cream cheese (tastier than it sounds).

Eastern Mývatn

If you're short on time, make this beautiful, sight-packed area your first stop in the Mývatn region. The features along Mývatn's eastern lakeshore can be linked together on an enjoyable half-day hike.

Sights

Grjótagjá CAVE
(Rte 860) *Game of Thrones* fans may recognise this as the place where Jon Snow is, ahem, deflowered by Ygritte. Grjótagjá is a gaping fissure with a 45°C water-filled cave. It's on private property – it's prohibited to bathe here, but the owners allow the public to visit and photograph. This is a beautiful spot, particularly when the sun filters through the cracks in the roof and illuminates the interior. There is easy road access.

★**Hverfjall** NATURAL FEATURE
(off Rte 848) Dominating the lava fields on the eastern edge of Mývatn is the classic tephra ring Hverfjall (also called Hverfell). This near-symmetrical crater appeared 2700 years ago in a cataclysmic eruption. Rising 452m from the ground and stretching

OFF THE BEATEN TRACK

LOFTHELLIR

The dramatic lava cave at Lofthellir is a stunning destination, with magnificent natural ice sculptures dominating the interior. Although it's one of Mývatn's highlights, the cave is on private property and can only be accessed on a half-day tour with Geo Travel (p305). The tour involves a one-hour 4WD journey and a 25-minute walk across gorgeous lava fields to reach the cave, and then the donning of special equipment (headlamps, studded boots etc) and intensely physical wriggling through tight spaces. Wear warm, waterproof gear.

Winter tours cross snowfields. In summer, you can cycle to the cave with Mývatn Activity – Hike&Bike (p305). While Geo travel runs the tours, they can also be booked via Saga Travel (p295).

1040m across, it is a massive and awe-inspiring landmark in Mývatn.

The crater is composed of loose gravel, but an easy track leads from the northwestern end (toilets here) to the summit and offers stunning views of the crater itself and the surrounding landscape. A path runs along the western rim of the crater to a lookout at the southern end before descending steeply towards Dimmuborgir.

Access the walking track via a signed gravel road – it's about 2.5km from the main road to the car park.

★Dimmuborgir NATURAL FEATURE

(Rte 884) The giant jagged lava field at Dimmuborgir (literally 'Dark Castles') is one of the most fascinating flows in the country. A series of nontaxing, colour-coded walking trails runs through the easily anthropomorphised landscape. The most popular path is the easy Church Circle (2.3km). Check with the visitor centre (p305) in Reykjahlíð or at the cafe at Dimmuborgir about free guided ranger walks in summer.

It's commonly believed that Dimmuborgir's strange pillars and crags were created about 2000 years ago when a lake of lava from the Þrengslaborgir and Lúdentarborgir crater rows formed here, over marshland or a small lake. The water of the marsh started to boil, and steam jets rose through the molten lava and cooled it, creating the pillars. As the lava continued flowing towards lower ground, the hollow pillars of solidified lava remained.

Höfði PARK

(Rte 848) One of the area's gentlest landscapes is on the forested lava headland at Höfði. Wildflowers, birch and spruce trees cover the bluffs, while the tiny islands and crystal-clear waters attract migratory birds.

From footpaths along the shore you'll see small caves and stunning *klasar* (lava pillars), the most famous of which rise from the water at **Kálfaströnd** on the southern shore of the Höfði Peninsula. The peninsula is another *Game of Thrones* shooting location.

Sleeping & Eating

★Dimmuborgir Guesthouse GUESTHOUSE €€

(☎464 4210; www.dimmuborgir.is; Geiteyjarströnd 1, off Rte 848; d/cottages from 23,300/37,200kr; 📶👪) This lakeside complex close to Dimmuborgir lava field has a block of simple en suite rooms (with shared kitchen-dining area), plus a smattering of timber cottages, which include modern, well-equipped, family sized options. Breakfast is served in the main house behind big picture windows overlooking the lake.

Birkilauf GUESTHOUSE €€

(☎554 0618; off Rte 860; d 27,900kr) This brand-new guesthouse in the lava fields and forests on the eastern shore of Mývatn may be constructed from cinderblock, but the rooms are comfortable with spanking new decor and bathrooms, plus spacious shared areas, including a guest kitchen and deck.

Kaffi Borgir ICELANDIC €€

(☎464 1144; www.kaffiborgir.is; Rte 884; mains 1950-3950kr; ⏱10am-9.30pm Jun-Aug, reduced hours rest of year) Kaffi Borgir is a cafe-souvenir shop at the top of the ridge overlooking the Dimmuborgir lava field. Grab a table on the outside terrace, sample the house speciality (grilled trout), and watch the sun dance its shadows across the jagged lava bursts. The soup buffet (11.30am to 4pm) is 1950kr; the summertime two-course dinner special (3500kr) is excellent value.

Southern Mývatn

Eastern Mývatn may be a treasure trove of geological anomalies, but the south side of the lake lures with its epic cache of pseudocraters.

The hamlet of **Skútustaðir** is the only settlement around the lake apart from Reykjahlíð. There's a cluster of tourist infrastructure here, including a couple of hotels, a guesthouse, petrol pump and bus stop.

Sights

★ Skútustaðagígar NATURAL FEATURE

The Skútustaðagígar pseudocraters were formed when molten lava flowed into Mývatn lake, triggering a series of gas explosions. These dramatic green dimples then came into being when trapped subsurface water boiled and popped, forming small scoria cones and craters.

The most accessible pseudocrater swarm is located along a short path just across from Skútustaðir, which also takes in the nearby pond, **Stakhólstjörn**, a haven for nesting waterfowl.

Sleeping & Eating

Skútustaðir Farmhouse GUESTHOUSE €€

(464 4212; www.skutustadir.is; Rte 848, Skútustaðir; d with/without bathroom incl breakfast 31,200/23,700kr, f 34,200kr; closed Dec) Friendly owners and spotless facilities are found at this recommended year-round guesthouse. Rooms in the homey farmhouse share bathroom, but there's also an annexe of five en suite rooms, plus a two-bedroom cottage (53,500kr), and a newer block of rooms and large guest kitchen.

Hótel Gígur HOTEL €€

(464 4455; www.keahotels.is; Rte 848, Skútustaðir; d incl breakfast from 22,300kr; @) Gígur's stylish contemporary look doesn't hide the fact that rooms are small, even by Icelandic standards. To compensate, there's friendly service, a prime lakeside location in Skútustaðir and ace views. Easily the hotel's best feature is its superb **restaurant** (mains 2800kr to 5500kr), one of the area's best. Regional fare includes perfect pan-fried trout and grilled lamb fillet; finish with rhubarb crumble and blueberry ice cream.

Hótel Laxá HOTEL €€€

(464 1900; www.hotellaxa.is; Rte 848; d incl breakfast from 41,400kr;) This architecturally arresting, sustainably designed hotel opened in mid-2014 about 2km east of Skútustaðir. There are 80 modern, simple rooms – comfy, with colour schemes complementing the surrounds. The big windows and green sofas of the bar-lounge area invite contemplation. There's also stylish, well-regarded Eldey Restaurant (mains 3200kr to 5900kr; open 6pm to 9pm).

Sel-Hótel Mývatn HOTEL €€€

(464 4164; www.myvatn.is; Rte 848, Skútustaðir; s/d incl breakfast 28,700/35,000kr; @) Solid midrange rooms and lobby area plus good facilities and friendly service make this a safe bet. The hotel's best feature, though, is its winter discount. The hotel's simple **restaurant** offers buffets (lunch/dinner 3900/6900kr) favoured by tour groups, but there are also à la carte choices. They also offer tours (super-Jeep explorations, snowmobile, horse riding etc).

Kaffi Sel CAFETERIA €

(Rte 848, Skútustaðir; snacks 350-1800kr; 8am-9pm Jun-Aug, 10am-5pm Sep-May) If you're just after a quick bite, grab a hot dog, soup or prepackaged sandwich at this combined souvenir shop-cafeteria next door to the Sel-Hótel.

Western Mývatn

Travellers flock to the quieter, less-developed western Mývatn shore for its bumper birdwatching.

The Ring Road (Rte 1) actually travels the western shore of the lake, rather than the more-populous eastern shore.

Buses travel the south and east shore, rather than the west.

Sights & Activities

Western Mývatn offers some of the best **birdwatching** in Iceland, with more than 115 species recorded in the area – including 28 species of ducks. Most species of Icelandic waterfowl are found here in great numbers. Three duck species – the scoter, the gadwall and the Barrow's goldeneye – breed nowhere else in Iceland.

Other species frequenting the area include harlequin and tufted ducks, mallards, scaup, whooper swans, great northern divers, Arctic terns and golden plovers. The area's bogs, marshes, ponds and wet tundra are a high-density waterfowl nesting zone. Off-trail hiking in defined (and signposted) nesting areas on the western shore is restricted between 15 May and 20 July (when the chicks hatch), but hides near Sigurgeir's Bird Museum (p310) allow for birding.

Vindbelgjarfjall HIKING

(Rte 1) The steep but relatively straightforward climb up 529m-high Vindbelgjarfjall (also known as Vindbelgur), on Mývatn lake's western shore, offers one of the best views across the lake and its alien pseudocraters.

The trail to the summit starts at a car park south of the peak, near the farm Vagnbrekka. Reckon on at least a half-hour to reach the mount, and another half-hour to climb to the summit.

★ Sigurgeir's Bird Museum MUSEUM

(Fuglasafn Sigurgeirs; ☎464 4477; www.fuglasafn.is; off Rte 1, Ytri-Neslönd farm; adult/child 1500/800kr; ⊙noon-5pm mid-May–Oct, reduced hours rest of year) For superb birdwatching background, visit Sigurgeir's Bird Museum, housed in a beautiful lakeside building that fuses modern design with traditional turf house. Inside you'll find an impressive collection of taxidermic avians (more than 180 types from around the world), including every species of bird that calls Iceland home (except one – the grey phalarope). Detailed captions, designer lighting and a small cafe further enhance the experience.

The menagerie of stuffed squawkers started as the private collection of a local named Sigurgeir Stefansson. Tragically, Sigurgeir drowned in the lake at the age of 37 – the museum was erected in his honour. The museum also lends out high-tech telescopes to ornithological enthusiasts, plus it has hides for rent.

Laxá RIVER

The clear and turbulent Laxá (Salmon River), one of the many Icelandic rivers so named, cuts the western division of Mývatn, rolling straight across the tundra towards Skjálfandi (Húsavík's whale-filled bay). The Laxá is one of the best (and most expensive) salmon-fishing spots in the country. More affordable brown-trout fishing is also available.

MARIMO BALLS

Marimo balls are bizarre little spheres of green algae that are thought to grow naturally in colonies in only a handful of places in the world (including Mývatn and Lake Akan in Japan). The name *marimo* is the Japanese word for 'algae ball' – around Mývatn, the locals call 'em *kúluskítur*, which literally means 'ball of shit'. Swing by Sigurgeir's Bird Museum to check them out – they live in the small pool of lake water in the exhibition space – ask for assistance to locate them. Recent studies marked the rapid decline of *marimo* in Mývatn, but they seemed to stage a slight comeback in the summers of 2016 and 2017.

Northern Mývatn

The Ring Road (Rte 1) zips along the northern shore of Mývatn through signature stretches of crispy lava dotted with pastoral farmsteads.

Eldhraun NATURAL FEATURE

The lava field along Mývatn's northern lakeshore includes the flow that nearly engulfed the Reykjahlíð Church (p306). It was belched out of Leirhnjúkur during the Mývatn Fires in 1729, and flowed down the channel Eldá. With some slow scrambling, it can be explored on foot from Reykjahlíð.

Hlíðarfjall HIKING

If you're hiking directly to the Krafla area from Mývatn's northern edge at Reykjahlíð, you'll pass the prominent 771m-high rhyolite mountain Hlíðarfjall just before the halfway mark. Around 5km from Reykjahlíð, the mount can also be enjoyed as a pleasant day hike from the village, affording spectacular views over the lake on one side and the Krafla lava fields on the other.

★ Fosshotel Mývatn HOTEL €€€

(☎453 0000; www.fosshotel.is; Rte 1, Grímsstaðir; d/ste from 25,000/62,000kr; @📶) The magnificent dining area (mains 4000kr to 5000kr; dinner 6pm to 9.45pm) with broad windows overlooking the lava field and lake is one of the first things you see when you enter this spanking-new hotel. Guestrooms are modern, using ecologically minded components, and it's worth plumping for a room enjoying those lava and lake views.

East of Reykjahlíð

Northern Mývatn's collection of geological gems lie along the Ring Road (Rte 1) as it weaves through the harsh terrain between the north end of the lake and the turn-off to Krafla. There are plenty of paths for exploring the area on foot.

Bjarnarflag GEOTHERMAL AREA

(Rte 1) Bjarnarflag, 3km east of Reykjahlíð, is an active geothermal area where the earth hisses and bubbles, and steaming vents line the valley. Historically the area has been home to a number of economic ventures attempting to harness the earth's powers. (Early on, farmers tried growing potatoes here, but these often emerged from the ground already boiled.)

In the 1960s, 25 test holes were bored at Bjarnarflag to ascertain the feasibility of a proposed geothermal power station. One is 2300m deep and the steam still roars out of the pipe at a whopping 200°C.

Later a diatomite plant was set up, but all that remains of the processing plant is the shimmering turquoise pond that the locals have dubbed the 'Blue Lagoon'. This inviting puddle is actually quite toxic and should not be confused with nearby Mývatn Nature Baths (sometimes called the 'Blue Lagoon of the North').

★Mývatn Nature Baths SPA

(Jarðböðin; ☎464 4411; www.myvatnnaturebaths.is; off Rte 1; adult/child 4700kr/free; ⏲9am-midnight May-Sep, noon-10pm Oct-Apr) Northern Iceland's answer to the Blue Lagoon is blessedly smaller and more low-key than its southern counterpart. It's also less hyped (a good thing) and a gorgeous place to soak in powder-blue, mineral-rich waters while enjoying the panorama. Also try one of two natural steam baths or grab a bite at the simple cafeteria (soup 1700kr). Arrive early or late to avoid tour groups. It's 3km east of Reykjahlíð.

Námafjall MOUNTAIN

(Rte 1) Vaporous vents cover the pinky-orange Námafjall ridge, which lies 3km east of Bjarnarflag on the south side of the Ring Road. Produced by a fissure eruption, the ridge sits squarely on the spreading zone of the Mid-Atlantic Ridge. As you travel east through the Námaskarð pass and tumble down its far side, you enter the alien world of Hverir.

★Hverir HOT SPRINGS

(Rte 1) The magical, ochre-toned world of Hverir (also called Hveraröndin) is a lunar-like landscape of mud cauldrons, steaming vents, radiant mineral deposits and piping fumaroles. Belching mudpots and the powerful stench of sulphur may not sound enticing, but Hverir's ethereal allure grips every passer-by.

Safe trails through the features have been delineated by ropes; to avoid risk of serious injury and damage to the natural features, avoid any lighter-coloured soil and respect the ropes. A walking trail loops from Hverir up Námafjall ridge. This 30-minute climb provides a grand vista over the steamy surroundings.

Krafla

Steaming vents and craters await at Krafla, an active volcanic region 7km north of the Ring Road. Technically Krafla is just the 818m-high mountain, but the name is now used for the entire area as well as a geothermal power station and the series of eruptions that created one of Iceland's most awesome lava fields. The so-called Mývatn Fires occurred 1724–29, when many of the fissure vents opened up. The Krafla Fires (1975–84) were very similar: fissure eruptions and magma movements that occurred on and off for nine years.

Sights & Activities

From Reykjahlíð, a reasonably straightforward hike of around 13km (three to five hours) leads to Hlíðarfjall and Leirhnjúkur along a marked path from near the airstrip. Another walking route (difficult; estimate three to five hours) leads from the Námaskarð pass – opposite Námafjall – along the Dalfjall ridge to Leirhnjúkur.

Krafla Power Station NOTABLE BUILDING

(www.landsvirkjun.com; Rte 863; ⏲visitor centre 10am-5pm Jun–mid-Sep) The idea of constructing a geothermal power station at Krafla was conceived in 1973, and preliminary work commenced with the drilling of holes to determine project feasibility. In 1975, however, after a long rest period, the Krafla fissure burst into activity. The project went ahead regardless and has been expanded since. The power plant's visitor centre explains how it all works.

The viewpoint over the area (continue up Rte 863 to reach it) is impressive.

★Leirhnjúkur NATURAL FEATURE

Krafla's most impressive, and potentially most dangerous, attraction is the Leirhnjúkur crater and its solfataras, which originally appeared in 1727, starting out as a lava fountain and spouting molten material for two years before subsiding.

A well-defined track leads northwest to Leirhnjúkur from the Krafla parking area (which has toilets); with all the volcanic activity, high temperatures, bubbling mudpots and steaming vents, it's best not to stray from the marked paths.

In 1975 the Krafla Fires began with a small lava eruption by Leirhnjúkur, and after nine years of on-and-off action Leirhnjúkur became the ominous-looking, sulphur-encrusted mudhole that tourists love today. The earth's crust here is extremely thin and in places the ground is ferociously hot.

★Víti VOLCANO

(Rte 863) The ochre crater of Víti reveals a secret when you reach its rim – a cerulean pool of floodwater at its heart. The 300m-wide explosion crater was created in 1724 at the beginning of the destructive Mývatn Fires. There is a circular path from the car park around the rim.

Note: don't confuse this Víti crater with the Víti crater beside the Askja caldera (you can bathe inside the latter, but not the former). Fun fact: Víti means 'hell' in Icelandic.

Getting There & Away

Hike or cycle here from Reykjahlíð or drive; it's 15km by road (via the Ring Road and Rte 863).

MÝVATN TO EGILSSTAÐIR

Travelling east from Reykjahlíð towards Egilsstaðir, the Ring Road crests Námafjall (p311) ridge, passes Hverir (p311) (mind the stench!) and offers a turn-off to Krafla (p311). After another 20km you'll encounter the turn-off north to mighty Dettifoss (p322) via Rte 862 (sealed), and then the 4WD-only Rte F88 turn-off south to Askja in the highlands.

Soon you'll cross the bridge over the glacial river Jökulsá á Fjöllum; Rte 864 is signposted north from just east of the bridge; this rough gravel road is generally open June to October, and arrives at Dettifoss (eastern vantage point) after 31km, and Ásbyrgi after 60km.

From the bridge, the Ring Road takes a short cut inland across the stark highlands of the northeast interior. If you won't be travelling into the highlands proper, you'll glimpse their start here. The ostensibly barren, grey-toned landscape is dotted with low hills, small lakes caused by melting snowfields, and wandering streams and rivers.

Möðrudalur

This area has always been a difficult place to eke out a living, and farms here are few and far between. Isolated Möðrudalur (pronounced *muh*-thru-dalur), a storied oasis in the desert, is the highest farm in Iceland at 469m. Here you'll find a popular mini-village catering to tourists and bustling in summer.

They have a new volcanic highlands film (500kr) and information centre, offering advice to people travelling in the area and into the highlands. After visiting Möðrudalur, many folks head into the central highlands (p358) via nearby Rte F905 (note you'll need to be well set up for highland exploration, and a 4WD vehicle is essential).

Sights & Activities

Volcano Heli SCENIC FLIGHT

(☎647 3300; www.volcanoheli.is; Rte 901, Möðrudalur) Liechtenstein-born heli-pilot Matthias and his team work from a summer base on Möðrudalur farm, and have epic highland landscapes in their backyard: Askja, Holuhraun, Mývatn and Kverkfjöll are all within a short flying time. The helicopter can carry three passengers, and rates are given for the entire trip (not per person). Prices start at 95,700kr for 30 minutes.

Sænautasel MUSEUM

(☎853 6491; www.facebook.com/Saenautasel; off Rte 907; 500kr; ⏰10am-6.30pm Jun–mid-Sep) The remote, reconstructed turf farmhouse Sænautasel, dating from 1843, brings the past to life…plus it sells pancakes and coffee. This is one of several old farms on Jökuldalsheiði heath that were originally abandoned when Askja erupted in 1875. The area was a source of inspiration for Halldór Laxness' master work, *Independent People;* notice that many farm names here match the fictional farms in the book. The farm is in a lovely lakeside spot, about 35km southeast of Möðrudalur and has a basic camping area. It's signposted 5km south of Rte 901, on Rte 907.

Sleeping & Eating

★Fjalladýrð GUESTHOUSE, CAMPGROUND €€

(☎471 1858; www.fjalladyrd.is; Rte 901, Möðrudalur; sites per person 1450kr, d with/without bathroom 35,000/15,900kr;) Fjalladýrð is the name of the tourist service at Möðrudalur farm, and it has a wide array of excellent accommodation spread over various buildings and budgets: camping, sleeping-bag beds (7800kr), guesthouse rooms, button-cute turf-roofed cottages (45,000kr), family-sized suites, and luxe, brand-new en suite rooms (which include a lavish breakfast) with peaceful views of Herðubreið. Outside summer, rates drop by around 30%.

It's worth spending the night if you're interested in tackling some of Iceland's interior – Fjalladýrð runs excellent super-Jeep trips to Askja and Kverkfjöll.

★Fjallakaffi ICELANDIC €€
(☎471 1858; www.fjalladyrd.is; Rte 901, Möðrudalur; mains 2150-7490kr; ⏲7am-10pm May-Sep, shorter hours rest of year; 📶) Folks simply passing through Möðrudalur should stop at Fjallakaffi for coffee and homemade *kleina* (traditional twisted doughnut) or *ástarpungur* (love ball), or try the true farm-to-table dishes. Specialities range from fillet of mountain lamb to goose breast, pan-fried Arctic char and reindeer steak. You can also get a simple soup (or Icelandic moss soup!) or toasted sandwich.

ℹ Getting There & Away

Möðrudalur is 8km south of the Ring Road on Rte 901, with the turn-off about 63km east of Reykjahlíð and 104km west of Egilsstaðir. Petrol is available here. After visiting Möðrudalur, many people head into the central highlands via Rte F905 (a 4WD-only route that usually opens in late June). For another diversion, take gravel Rte 901 east (this is the old Rte 1, and in summer is rough but passable in a 2WD).

HÚSAVÍK

POP 2307

Húsavík, Iceland's whale-watching capital, has become a firm favourite on travellers' itineraries – and with its colourful houses, unique museums and stunning snowcapped peaks across the bay, it's easily the northeast's prettiest fishing town.

Sights

★Húsavík Whale Museum MUSEUM
(Hvalasafnið; ☎414 2800; www.whalemuseum.is; Hafnarstétt 1; adult/child 1900/500kr; ⏲9am-6pm May-Sep, reduced hours rest of year) This excellent museum provides all you need to know about the impressive creatures that visit Skjálfandi bay. Housed in an old harbourside slaughterhouse, the museum interprets the ecology and habits of whales, conservation and the history of whaling in Iceland through beautifully curated displays, including several huge skeletons (they're real) soaring high above and a mind-blowing blue whale skeleton.

★Húsavíkurkirkja CHURCH
(☎464 1317; www.husavikurkirkja.is; Garðarsbraut 9a; ⏲9am-5pm) Húsavík's beloved church is quite different from anything else seen in Iceland. Constructed in 1907 from Norwegian timber, the delicately proportioned red-and-white church would look more at home in the Alps. Its cruciform shape becomes apparent inside and is dominated by a depiction of the resurrection of Lazarus (made from lava) on the altarpiece. It's open most days in summer.

Skrúðgarður GARDENS
A walk along the duck-filled stream of the endearing town park, which is as scenic as the waterfront area, offers a serene break. Access is via a footbridge on Ásgarðsvegur, or beside Árból (p316) guesthouse.

Flatey ISLAND
Flatey (pronounced *Flat*-eh) is a serene 2.5km-long island 9km from Húsavík, on the northwest edge of Skjálfandi Bay. The name simply means flat island (highest point: 20m). Today the island is home to a teeny hamlet with a church, lighthouse and summer houses, which are far outnumbered by the 30 types of birds that visit, including dive-bombing Arctic terns and large squads of puffins (May to August). Gentle Giants (p315) offers a tour and a summer yoga package.

Exploration Museum MUSEUM
(☎464 2328; www.explorationmuseum.com; Héðinsbraut 3; adult/child 1000/500kr; ⏲2-6pm Jun-Aug, noon-3pm Sep, by appointment rest of year) Opened in 2014, this museum salutes the history of human exploration, covering Viking voyages and polar expeditions, but its most nootable exhibition focuses on the Apollo astronauts in Iceland in the 1960s, who received geology training in the lunar-like landscapes near Askja. There are some great photos from this era, and museum operators organised a return of some of the astronauts in 2015.

Culture House MUSEUM
(Safnahúsið; ☎464 1860; www.husmus.is; Stórigarður 17; adult/child 1000kr/free; ⏲10am-6pm Jun–mid-Sep, to 4pm Mon-Fri mid-Sep–May; 📶) A folk, maritime and natural-history museum rolled into one, the Culture House is one of the North's most interesting regional museums. 'Man and Nature' nicely outlines a century of life in the region, from 1850 to 1950 (lots of local flavour), while the stuffed animals include a frightening-looking hooded seal, and a polar bear that was welcomed to Grímsey in 1969 with both barrels of a gun.

Húsavík

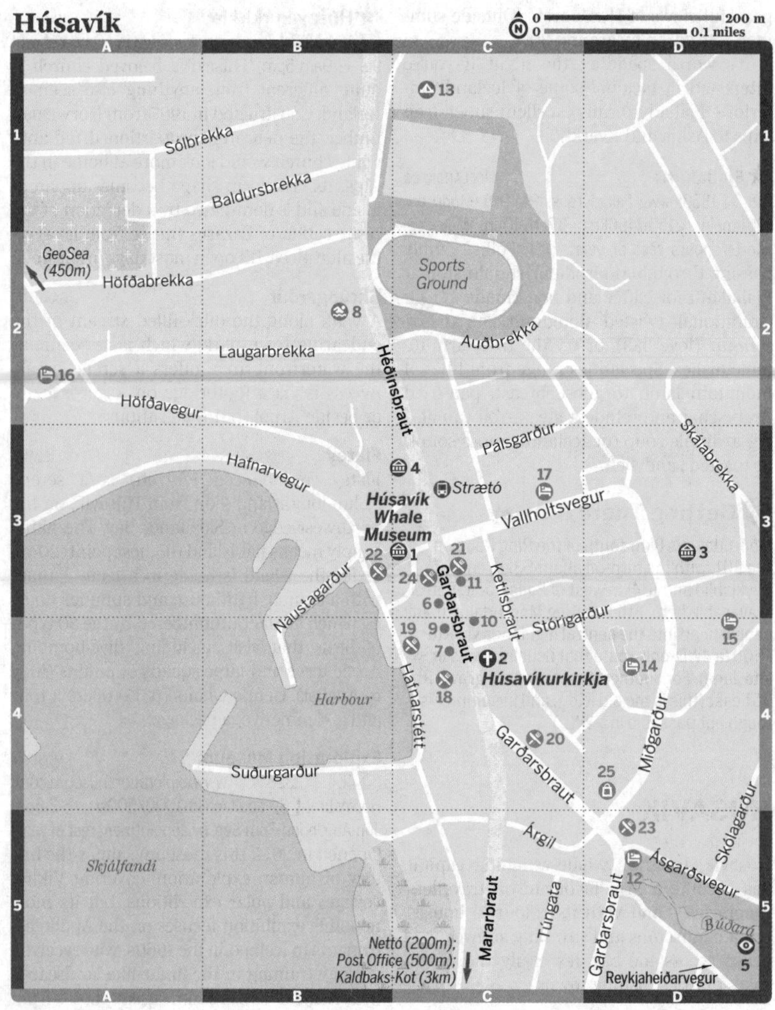

Activities

GeoSea SPA

(☎860 0202; www.geosea.is; Vitaslóð 1; adult/child 4300/1800kr; ⏰9am-midnight May-Sep, noon-10pm Oct-Apr) Brand-new salt-water spa GeoSea fills the point near the lighthouse on the north edge of town, looking over the broad bay and the snow-capped peaks across the way. Geothermally heated sea water fills pools with perfectly warm (38° to 39°C) soaking waters. The modern cafe allows for ocean-view dining.

Húsavík Swimming Pool SWIMMING

(Sundlaug Húsavíkur; ☎464 6190; Laugarbrekka 2; adult/child 700/300kr; ⏰6.45am-9pm Mon-Fri, 10am-6pm Sat & Sun Jun-Aug, shorter hours rest of year; 👪) The local swimming pool has hot-pots, and water slides for kids.

Tours

Whale Watching

This is why you came to Húsavík. Although there are other Iceland locales where you can do whale-watching tours (eg Reykjavík and Eyjafjörður, north of Akureyri), this area has become Iceland's premier whale-watching

Húsavík

destination, with up to 11 species coming here to feed in summer. The best time to see them is between June and August (the height of tourist season) when you'll have a near-certain chance of a sighting.

Four whale-watching companies operate from Húsavík harbour. Don't stress *too* much over picking an operator; prices are similar and services comparable for standard three-hour tours (warm overalls supplied). When puffins are nesting (roughly mid-April to mid-August), all companies offer tours combining whale watching with a sail by puffin-thronged Lundey.

Where the differences are clear, however, is in the excursions that go beyond the standard. North Sailing has an atmospheric old schooner and hoists sails when conditions are right. Gentle Giants has a high-speed rigid inflatable boat (RIB), and a tour that takes in idyllic Flatey.

Trips depart throughout the day (June to August) from around 8am to 8pm, and large signs at the ticket booths advertise the next departure time. Boats also also run frequently in April, May, September and October, but drop way off in March, November and December. In winter, boats operate as Northern Lights cruises. You can't miss the offices on the waterfront.

When booking, it's worth enquiring about how big the boat is and how many passengers might be on it. Consider taking an early-morning or evening cruise (bus groups visit in the middle of the day). Note that RIB tours are not suitable for children under about seven years.

Gentle Giants WILDLIFE
(☎464 1500; www.gentlegiants.is; Garðarsbraut; 3hr tours adult/child 10,400/4400kr) Owner Stefán, whose family has lived on the bay for generations, has a flotilla of wooden fishing vessels for standard three-hour tours, plus high-speed rigid inflatable boats (RIBs) for covering more of the bay (from 19,000kr). Also runs special trips to idyllic Flatey (p313) for birdwatching (29,900kr), sea angling trips, and fast RIB day trips to Grímsey (72,300kr).

North Sailing WILDLIFE
(☎464 7272; www.northsailing.is; Garðarsbraut; 3hr tours adult/child 10,500/3500kr) The original whale-watching operator has a fleet of lovingly restored traditional boats. Some tours are advertised as carbon-neutral using electricity instead of fossil fuel. The tour aboard their old schooner (adult/child 12,500/4000kr) is special: when conditions are right, sails are hoisted and engines cut. Northern Lights tours (10,500kr) in winter. They also offer ski combo tours and Greenland sailing trips.

Salka WILDLIFE
(☎464 3999; www.salkawhalewatching.is; Garðarsbraut 7; 3hr tours adult/child 9950/4200kr; ⊙May-Sep) A relatively new player on the whale-watching scene, taking on the long-established companies with two, compact oak boats, slightly cheaper prices and a tighter menu of offerings. Adding puffins to the tour costs a bit more (adult/child 11,500/4200kr). Its base is its light-filled cafe on the main street. Horse riding combos, too.

Húsavík Adventures WILDLIFE
(☎853 4205; www.husavikadventures.is; Garðarsbraut 5; 2hr RIB tours adult/child 17,900/11,900kr) This company offers racy two-hour RIB tours, three to seven times a day from May to September and partners with Mývatn Activity – Hike&Bike (p305) to offer ATV tours year-round.

Other Tours

The two largest whale-watching operators offer combo tours that involve cruises plus a horse ride at Saltvík. Gentle Giants (p315) also offers sea angling expeditions, yoga on Flatey, and a two-day hiking trip; North Sailing (p315) offers a unique 'Ski to the Sea' multiday package in April and May, working with ski guides. North Sailing also has week-long sailing trips to Greenland each summer. See websites for full details.

Fjallasýn ADVENTURE TOUR
(☎464 3941; www.fjallasyn.is) This well-established Húsavík-based company does tours in the area – day or multiday, 4WD, hiking, birdwatching etc – both in Húsavík and further afield to various parts of northeast Iceland and the highlands.

Saltvík Horse Farm HORSE RIDING
(☎847 9515; www.saltvik.is; Rte 85; 2hr tours 9900kr) Two-hour coastal rides with glorious views over Skjálfandi bay are available at Saltvík Horse Farm, 5km south of Húsavík. No special riding experience is required. Saltvík also offers week-long rides (around Mývatn, into the more-remote northeast, or along the highland Sprengisandur route), plus farmhouse accommodation.

Travel North WALKING TOUR
(☎894 1470; www.travelnorth.is; Garðarsbraut 5; tours from 4000kr) Local tourist agency Travel North offers guided walks in and around Húsavík, a sweet, low-key way to learn more about the area. Loads of other tours and packages too.

Sleeping

Guesthouses and hotels are in high demand – book in advance.

Húsavík Hostel HOSTEL €
(☎858 5848; www.husavikhostel.com; Vallholtsvegur 9; dm 6600kr, d with/without bathroom 21,000/15,840kr;) This is the only in-town budget option, and its 21 beds are popular. There are bunk-filled dorm rooms and a couple of private rooms (which include linen), plus a kitchen but no real lounge space. Management is friendly and offers good local information.

Árbót HOSTEL €
(☎464 3677; www.hostel.is; off Rte 85, Aðaldalur; dm/d without bathroom 5600/15,300kr; Apr-Sep; @) One of two HI hostels on tranquil, remote rural properties in the area (owned by the same family; the other is called Berg and is well-liked) – both are about 20km south of Húsavík off Rte 85. You'll need your own transport and will have to BYO food. There are decent facilities and comfy common areas. HI members get a 10% discount.

Campground CAMPGROUND €
(camping@nordurthing.is; Héðinsbraut; site per person 1650kr; mid-May–Sep;) Next to the sports ground at the north end of town, this well-maintained spot has washing machines and limited cooking facilities, but not nearly enough to cope with summertime demand. Pay at the swimming pool (p314), or to the warden who visits nightly.

★ **Kaldbaks-Kot** COTTAGES €€
(☎892 1744; www.husavikcottages.com; Rte 85; 2-/4-person cottages from 22,000/26,000kr; May–late Sep; @) Located 3km south of Húsavík is this spectacular spread-out settlement of cosy timber cottages that all feel like grandpa's log cabin in the woods (but with considerably more comfort). Choose your level of service: BYO linen or hire it (1900kr per person); and bring supplies or buy breakfast here (1850kr), served in the magnificent converted cowshed.

Minimum stay is two nights – perfect for enjoying the grounds, the hot-pots, the views, the serenity and the prolific bird life. Options include larger houses sleeping up to 10.

★ **Árból** GUESTHOUSE €€
(☎464 2220; www.arbol.is; Ásgarðsvegur 2; s/d/q without bathroom incl breakfast 12,400/21,100/36,500kr;) This 1903 heritage house has a pretty stream and the town park as neighbours. Spacious, spotless rooms are spread over three levels – those on the ground and top floors are loveliest (the pine-lined attic rooms are particularly sweet). Note: no kitchen.

Gamli Skólinn GUESTHOUSE €€€
(☎847 5722; www.husavikapartments.is; Stórigarður 6; apt from 50,000kr;) Grand, new two- and three-bedroom apartments fill the 'Old School' and fully equipped kitchens

make it easy to self-cater. The perfect chance to pretend your family are Húsavík locals.

Fosshótel Húsavík HOTEL €€€
(☎464 1220; www.fosshotel.is; Ketilsbraut 22; d incl breakfast from 30,000kr; 📶) Fosshótel has put its stylish, contemporary stamp on these 110 rooms with charcoal tones, bright colour accents etc. Deluxe rooms are a good step up from standard rooms. The airy lobby creates a great first impression, and the bar and bistro have a subtle whale theme.

Húsavík Cape Hotel HOTEL €€€
(☎463 3399; www.husavikhotel.com; Laugarbrekka 16; s/d incl breakfast 28,400/35,500kr; 📶) A boutique-y option in a former fish factory above the harbour. Fresh, modern rooms are a good size (some come with bunks, for families), but summer prices are steep.

Eating

Fish & Chips FAST FOOD €
(☎464 2099; Hafnarstétt 19; fish & chips 1800kr; ⏲11.30am-10pm May-Oct) Doing exactly what it says on the label, this small window-front on the harbour doles out good-value fish (usually cod) and chips, with a few picnic tables out the front and a broad deck above. Access it from the harbour; or from town, walk down the stairs opposite the church and turn left.

Café Hvalbakur CAFE €
(☎464 7278; www.gamlibaukur.is; Hafnarstétt 9; snacks & meals 400-1700kr; ⏲8am-9pm) With a sun-trap terrace overlooking the waterfront, this friendly cafe – owned by North Sailing (p315) – has a big cabinet full of baguettes, wraps, muffins and cakes. Good coffee, too. It's just down the stairs from the North Sailing ticket office.

Lókal CAFE €
(www.facebook.com/Lókal-Bistró-183696185798864; Hafnarstétt 1; snacks 300-1600kr; ⏲8am-8pm; 📶) Grab a quick bite or check your email in this little cafe where they home-make the fillings for their wraps (from chilli to stir-fry) and homebake their muffins and cakes. Find it beneath the Húsavík Whale Museum (p313).

Heimabakarí Konditori BAKERY, CAFE €
(☎464 2901; www.heimabakari.is; Garðarsbraut 15; ⏲7am-6pm Mon-Fri, 8am-4pm Sat & Sun) Sells fresh bread, sandwiches and a cabinet full of sugary cakes and pastries.

★**Naustið** SEAFOOD €€
(☎464 1520; www.facebook.com/naustid; Ásgarðsvegur 1; mains 2000-4000kr; ⏲11.45am-10pm; 📶) Buttercup-yellow Naustið wins wide praise for its super-fresh fish and a simple concept that's well executed: skewers of fish and vegetables, grilled to order. There's also a top-tier fish soup (natch), fish tacos and langoustine, plus home-baked rhubarb cake for dessert.

Gamli Baukur ICELANDIC €€
(☎464 2442; www.gamlibaukur.is; Hafnarstétt 9; mains 3400-4700kr; ⏲11.30am-midnight Jun-Aug, shorter hours rest of year) Among shiny nautical relics, this timber-framed restaurant-bar serves high-quality food (spaghetti with shellfish, wild mushroom barley, organic lamb). Occasional live music and a sweeping terrace make it one of the most happening summertime places in northeast Iceland. Kitchen closes at 10pm in summer.

Salka Restaurant INTERNATIONAL €€
(☎464 2551; www.salkarestaurant.is; Garðarsbraut 6; mains 2100-4500kr; ⏲11.30am-10pm) Once home to Iceland's first cooperative, this historical building houses an easy-breezy, crowd-pleasing restaurant serving a diverse menu: everything from veggie patties to pizza, by way of langoustine, burgers, club sandwiches and salted cod.

Self-Catering

Nettó SUPERMARKET €
(☎464 1750; www.netto.is; Garðarsbraut 64; ⏲10am-7pm) South of town, Nettó is located by the Olís service station.

Krambúð SUPERMARKET €
(☎464 1779; www.samkaup.is; Garðarsbraut 5; ⏲8am-10pm, from 10am Sat & Sun) Central supermarket.

Vínbúðin ALCOHOL
(☎464 2230; Garðarsbraut 21; ⏲11am-6pm Mon-Thu, to 7pm Fri, to 4pm Sat May-Aug, shorter hours rest of year) Government-run liquor store.

Information

Check www.visithusavik.is for info.

Getting There & Away

Húsavík's airport is 12km south of town. Eagle Air (www.eagleair.is) flies year-round between Reykjavík and Húsavík.

Strætó (☎540 2700; www.straeto.is) runs bus 79 to Akureyri (2760kr, 1¼ hours, three daily

Monday to Friday, one Saturday, two Sunday), departing from the N1 service station.

Check local tourist offices or www.publictransport.is for the latest.

CAR

Húsavík Car Rental Service (☎464 1888; www.bilaleigahusavikur.is; Garðarsbraut 66) allows drop-off in Akureyri, Mývatn and Keflavík Airport.

TJÖRNES PENINSULA & VESTURSANDUR

Heading north from Húsavík along Rte 85 you'll sweep along the coast of the broad, fractured **Tjörnes Peninsula**. The area is known for its fossil-rich coastal cliffs (the oldest layers dating back about two million years). **Mánárbakki Museum** (☎464 1957; Rte 85; adult/child 1000kr/free; ⊙9am-6pm early Jun–Aug), at the tip of the peninsula, is worth checking out.

Giant cracks, fissures and grabens (depressions between geological faults) scar the earth at low-lying **Kelduhverfi**, where the Mid-Atlantic Ridge enters the Arctic Ocean. Like the rift valley at the ancient parliament site Þingvellir, the area reveals some of the most visible evidence that Iceland is being ripped apart from its core.

There's a great coastal viewpoint about 12km east of Mánárbakki Museum, with information boards giving details of earth movements.

The road then drops down to the bird-packed lagoons and deltas of **Vestursandur**.

Sleeping & Eating

Tungulending is a special offering about 13km northeast of Húsavík, and there's a handful of lodgings within 12km of Ásbyrgi in the Vestursandur area.

There's a restaurant at Hótel Skúlagarður, and food can be arranged at Tungulending and Keldunes. The closest supermarket is in Húsavík, or the smaller shop in Ásbyrgi.

River Guesthouse GUESTHOUSE €

(☎463 3390; www.skulagardur.com; Rte 85; s/d without bathroom 6900/12,400kr;) This huge blue portacabin offers 30 *very* basic budget rooms with shared bathroom and kitchen. There's little by way of atmosphere or charm. Sleeping-bag beds available (s/d 5100/9500kr). It's owned by (and next door to) Hótel Skúlagarður.

★**Tungulending** GUESTHOUSE €€

(☎896 6948; www.tungulending.is; off Rte 85; d/tr without bathroom incl breakfast from 17,000/23,900kr;) Soak up the tranquil seafront ambience at this unique, well-hidden guesthouse. The turn-off is about 11km northeast of Húsavík; you then travel 2.5km through farmland (leave gates as you found them) to reach the handcrafted, waterfront, view-enriched outpost. There's no kitchen, but there's a cafe (open to all) serving delicious dinner. There's a two-night minimum stay – linger and enjoy.

Hótel Skúlagarður HOTEL €€

(☎465 2280; www.skulagardur.com; Rte 85; s/d incl breakfast 14,100/21,200kr;) A country hotel behind an unpromising exterior (in a former boarding school), Skúlagarður offers a warm welcome, plus compact, modern, overpriced en suite rooms, and a no-frills restaurant serving good home cooking (oven-baked Arctic char or lamb fillet; mains 3200kr to 4500kr). It's 13km west of Ásbyrgi. There's a budget wing here too, the River Guesthouse.

Keldunes GUESTHOUSE €€

(☎465 2275; www.keldunes.is; Rte 85, Keldunes II; s/d without bathroom incl breakfast 14,900/20,900kr;) Modern guesthouse with good kitchen-dining area, a hot-pot, and large balconies for birdwatching; dinner is available on request. There are decent cottages with bathroom (20,900kr), plus some basic cabins with sleeping-bag beds (4000kr per person). It's 11km west of Ásbyrgi.

Getting There & Away

Rte 85 covers the 65 scenic kilometres from Húsavík to Ásbyrgi.

In summer 2018, buses were cut between Húsavík and Ásbyrgi. Check local tourist offices or www.publictransport.is for the latest.

JÖKULSÁRGLJÚFUR (VATNAJÖKULL NATIONAL PARK – NORTH)

In 2008 the Vatnajökull National Park – one of Europe's largest protected reserves – was formed when Jökulsárgljúfur National Park merged with Skaftafell National Park to the south. The idea was to protect the Vatnajökull ice cap and all of its glacial run-off under one super-sized preserve.

The Jökulsárgljúfur (pronounced *yu-kul-sour-glyoo-vur*) portion of the park protects a unique subglacial eruptive ridge and a 25km-long canyon carved out by the formidable Jökulsá á Fjöllum (Iceland's second-longest river) – the name Jökulsárgljúfur literally means 'Glacier River Canyon'.

Jökulsá á Fjöllum starts in the Vatnajökull ice cap and flows just over 200km to the Arctic Ocean at Öxarfjörður. *Jökulhlaup* (floods from volcanic eruptions beneath the ice cap) formed the canyon and have carved out a chasm that averages 100m deep and 500m wide. The canyon is well known for its waterfalls – Dettifoss is of course the most famous, but there are others.

Vatnajökull National Park's northern section can be roughly divided into three parts.

Ásbyrgi The northern entry: a verdant, forested plain enclosed by vertical canyon walls. The visitor centre (p320) is here.

Vesturdalur The middle section, with caves and fascinating geological anomalies.

Dettifoss This mighty waterfall anchors the park's southern entrance.

A wonderful two-day hike (p323) weaves along the canyon, taking in all of the major sights en route. If you're not so keen on hiking, the big attractions, such as horseshoe-shaped Ásbyrgi canyon at the northern end of the park and the waterfalls at the southern end, are accessible by drivable roads. The road between Ásbyrgi and Dettifoss on the western side of the canyon (Rte 862) is being paved in stages.

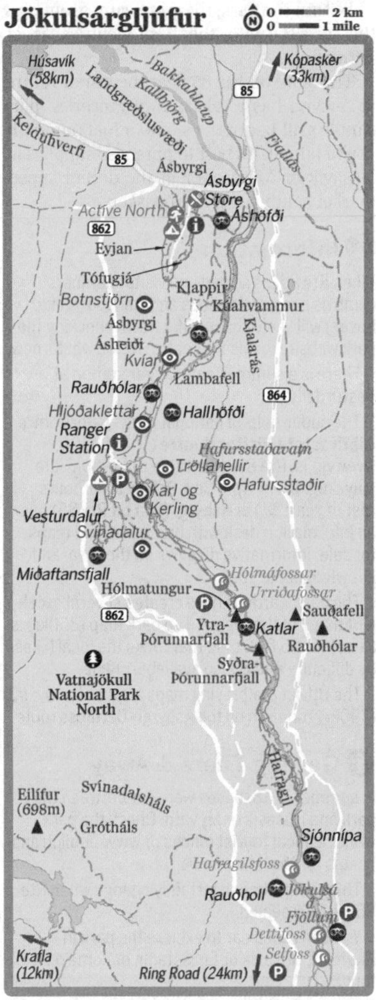

Tours

Several companies in Mývatn (eg Geo Travel; p305), Akureyri (eg Saga Travel; p295) and Húsavík (eg Fjallasýn; p316) offer guided tours.

From mid-June to mid-August, rangers guide free daily interpretive walks that depart from the parking place closest to Ásbyrgi canyon. Check the national-park website, or ask staff.

Active North ADVENTURE TOUR

(☎858 7080; www.activenorth.is; 2hr horse ride 10,900kr) Fancy horse-riding around a canyon said to be formed by a mythical hoofprint? Headquartered opposite the visitor centre (p320), Active North offers easy, scenic two-hour horse-riding trips around the Ásbyrgi canyon. Other trips on horseback, mountain bike or via super-Jeep are also available, inside the park but also beyond its borders. Mountain bikes can also be hired (990kr per hour).

Jeep tours operate year-round (and include a Northern Lights option); horse riding and biking are generally available June to September.

Jökulsárgljúfur

Sleeping & Eating

Several accommodation providers are within 15km of the park: Nordic Natura (p321) is perched just on its edge, and others lie between Húsavík and Ásbyrgi; there are also options north of Ásbyrgi towards Kópasker and a couple south of Dettifoss.

Within the park, there are campgrounds – the largest, with the best facilities, is at Ásbyrgi.

The store on Rte 85 near the visitor centre at Ásbyrgi has a selection of groceries, plus simple grill-bar options (and a fuel pump). If you're hiking, it's best to purchase supplies in Húsavík or Mývatn, or at the decent supermarket 35km north in Kópasker.

Information

When Rte 862 is sealed and visitor numbers climb as a result, facilities and transport (like buses) will likely change. It's worth checking the park website (or visitor centre) to see what's new.

There is a summer-only ranger station at Vesturdalur.

The super-helpful national-park visitor centre **Gljúfrastofa Visitor Centre** (☎470 7100; www.vjp.is; Rte 85, Ásbyrgi; ⏲9am-6pm late May-Aug, 10am-4pm Sep-Oct, shorter hours rest of year; 📶) at Ásbyrgi (just off Rte 85) has an information desk with brochures and maps for sale, informative displays on the area, and knowledgeable staff.

The park wardens have created several excellent maps of the region. The park map (350kr) is a useful 1:55,000 plan that ranks the local hikes by difficulty and is also available online.

The Útivist & afþreying maps are also handy; #3 (790kr) zooms in on the Ásbyrgi–Dettifoss route.

Getting There & Away

In summer 2018, buses were cut between the park and Húsavík or Mývatn. Check the park website, local tourist offices or www.publictransport.is for the latest news.

Things will almost certainly change when Rte 862 is fully sealed.

You can rent a car to explore the park in Akureyri, Húsavík or Egilsstaðir, or come on a tour.

CAR

Rte 85 (sealed) takes you smoothly to the northern section of the park and the visitor centre at Ásbyrgi (from Húsavík it's 65km).

There are two north–south roads running parallel on each side of the canyon. Although the national park is open all year, the gravel roads only open from about late May to early October (weather dependent; check www.road.is).

Rte 862 (west) From the Ring Road to Dettifoss (24km), the road is sealed. North of Dettifoss, the road is gravel for about 29km past turn-offs to Hólmatungur and Vesturdalur, then sealed for the final 8km to reach Rte 85 and Ásbyrgi. This route is being sealed in stages; enquire locally about its condition.

Rte 864 (east) This is a gravel road (narrower than Rte 862) for its 60km length; it's passable by 2WD vehicles, but it's rutted and potholed, so drive slowly. There are no plans to improve this road's condition.

The sealed portion of Rte 862 from the Ring Road to Dettifoss is open all year, however Dettifoss access is not guaranteed in winter, when weather conditions may close the road for a few days or more. During this time, you may still be able to visit the falls on a super-Jeep tour from Mývatn.

Wherever you are, make sure you stick to roads and marked trails. Off-road driving is hugely destructive to the country's fragile environment, and illegal.

> **NO DRONES**
>
> Drones are prohibited in the Jökulsárgljúfur national park, except with permission from park authorities.

Ásbyrgi

At the northern end of Vatnajökull National Park, the lush canyon Ásbyrgi (pronounced *ows*-beerg-ee) extends in a massive horseshoe shape, measuring 3.5km from north to south and averaging 1km in width. From the car park at the end of the access road, 3.5km south of the visitor centre, several easy short tracks lead through the forest to viewpoints of the canyon. Heading east the track leads to a spring near the canyon wall, while the western track climbs to a good view across the valley floor. The trail leading straight ahead ends at **Botnstjörn**, a small bird-friendly pond at the head of Ásbyrgi. There's also a signposted loop trail showcasing the area's flora.

You can climb to the summit of Eyjan (p322), the prominent outcrop at the centre of the canyon, from the Ásbyrgi campsite (4.5km return), or take a trail from the visitor centre – from where it's easiest to take the route east along the golf course and turn south at the junction.

Sleeping & Eating

Dettifoss Guesthouse GUESTHOUSE €
(☎869 7672; www.facebook.com/dettifossguesthouse; Rte 85, Lundur; s/d/q without bathroom 6600/13,600/18,800kr; 📶) Don't be misled by the name: this reasonably priced guesthouse is actually 7km north of Ásbyrgi en route to Kópasker (not south, towards Dettifoss). It's a comfy spot with 11 rooms of varying sizes,

guest kitchen and flash shared bathrooms. Campers also welcome (per person 1200kr).

Ásbyrgi Campsite CAMPGROUND €
(☎470 7100; www.vjp.is; site per adult/teen/child 1900/800kr/free; ⊙mid-May–Sep;) Camping inside the park boundaries is strictly limited to the official campsites at Ásbyrgi and Vesturdalur, plus Dettifoss for hikers only. The large, easily accessible campsite at Ásbyrgi has a good service building containing showers (500kr) and washing machine (500kr). There are powered sites, but no cooking facilities. No reservations are taken.

★**Nordic Natura** COTTAGE €€
(☎862 7708; www.nordicnatura.is; Rte 85, Meiðavellir; cottage 26,000kr;) Three brand-new cute-as-a-button cottages share fabulous views over the canyon at Ásbyrgi. A charming local family has built them on their farm on the edge of the national park, and they welcome visitors with open arms. Cottages are completely modern, with fully equipped kitchenette, flat-screen TV and wi-fi – though you might not use them if you're out on the deck, taking in the beauty.

Ásbyrgi Store FAST FOOD €€
(☎465 2260; Rte 85; mains 900-2950kr; ⊙9am-10pm Jun-Aug, 10am-6pm Sep-May) This store on Rte 85, close to the visitor centre, has a selection of groceries, plus simple grill-bar options (soup, lamb, fish, burgers). There's also a petrol pump. The grill sometimes closes in winter.

Vesturdalur

Off the beaten track and home to diverse scenery, Vesturdalur is a favourite destination for hikers. A series of weaving trails leads from the scrub around the campsite to the cave-dotted pinnacles and rock formations of Hljóðaklettar, the Rauðhólar crater row, the ponds of Eyjan (not to be confused with the Eyjan at Ásbyrgi) and the Jökulsárgljúfur canyon itself.

There is a summer ranger stationed at Vesturdalur.

Vesturdalur Campsite CAMPGROUND €
(☎470 7100; www.vjp.is; off Rte 862; site per adult/teen/child 1900/800kr/free; ⊙early Jun–mid-Sep) Camping inside the park boundaries is strictly limited to the official campsites at Ásbyrgi and Vesturdalur (plus Dettifoss for hikers only). Vesturdalur's campsite is near the ranger station and has no powered sites, showers or hot water – toilets and running water are the only luxuries here.

THE CREATION OF THE CANYON

There are two stories about the creation of Ásbyrgi. The early Norse settlers believed that Óðinn's normally airborne eight-legged horse, Slættur (known in literature as Sleipnir), accidentally touched down on earth and left one hell of a hoof-print to prove it. The other theory, though more scientific, is also incredible. Geologists believe that the canyon was created by an enormous eruption of the Grímsvötn caldera beneath distant Vatnajökull. It released a catastrophic *jökulhlaup* (glacial flood), which ploughed northward down the Jökulsá á Fjöllum and gouged out the canyon in a matter of days. The river then flowed through Ásbyrgi for about 100 years before shifting eastward to its present course.

Vesturdalur is 14km south of Ásbyrgi off Rte 862. At the time of research, it was 8km from Rte 85 on newly sealed road, a further 4km on gravel to the Vesturdalur turn-off, then 2km to the area.

★**Hljóðaklettar** NATURAL FEATURE
The bizarre swirls, spirals, rosettes, honeycombs and basalt columns at Hljóðaklettar (Echo Rocks) are a highlight of any hike around Vesturdalur and a puzzling place for amateur geologists. It's difficult to imagine what sort of volcanic activity produced these twisted rock forms. Dazzling concertina formations and repeat patterns occur throughout, and the normally vertical basalt columns (formed by rapidly cooling lava) show up on the horizontal here.

These strange forms and patterns create an acoustic effect that makes it impossible to determine the direction of the roaring river, a curiosity that gave the area its name.

A circular **walking trail** (3km) from the parking area takes around an hour to explore. The best formations, which are also riddled with lava caves, are found along the river, northeast of the parking area.

Rauðhólar NATURAL FEATURE
The Rauðhólar (Red Hills) crater row, just north of Hljóðaklettar, displays a vivid array of colours in the cinder-like gravel on the

remaining cones. The craters can be explored on foot during a 5km loop walk from the Vesturdalur parking area.

Karl og Kerling NATURAL FEATURE

Karl og Kerling ('Old Man' and 'Old Woman'), two rock pillars, believed to be petrified trolls, stand on a gravel bank west of the river, a 2km return walk from the Vesturdalur car park. Across the river is **Tröllahellir**, the gorge's largest cave, but it's reached only on a 5km cross-country hike from Rte 864 on the eastern side.

Eyjan NATURAL FEATURE

Eyjan is an island-like mesa covered with low, scrubby forests and small ponds.You can walk a 7km trail around Eyjan from Karl og Kerling to Vesturdalur. From Karl og Kerling, follow the river south to Kallbjarg, then turn west along the track to the abandoned site of **Svínadalur**, where the canyon widens into a broad valley, and follow the western base of the Eyjan cliffs back to the Vesturdalur parking area.

★ **Hólmatungur** OUTDOORS

(Rte 887) South of Vesturdalur, lush vegetation, tumbling waterfalls and an air of utter tranquillity make the Hólmatungur area one of the most beautiful in the park. Underground springs bubble up to form a series of short rivers that twist, turn and cascade their way to Jökulsárgljúfur canyon.

For the best overall view of Hólmatungur, hike to the hill **Ytra-Þórunnarfjall**, just south of the car park.

The most popular walk here is the 4.5km loop from the parking area, which leads north along the Hólmá River to Hólmáfossar, where the harsh lines of the canyon soften and produce several pretty waterfalls.

From here you head south again on the Jökulsá to its confluence with the Melbugsá River, where the river tumbles over a ledge, forming the **Urriðafossar** waterfalls. To see the falls, you need to walk along the (challenging) 2km trail spur to Katlar.

Hólmatungur is accessed by turning off Rte 862 onto Rte 887. A 4WD is not essential but is helpful (you need good ground clearance to travel the 1km of Rte 887). Or, park at Vesturdalur and do a long round-trip day hike. Camping is prohibited at Hólmatungur, but it's a great spot for a picnic.

Dettifoss

The power of nature can be seen in all its glory at mighty Dettifoss, one of Iceland's most impressive waterfalls.

Although Dettifoss is 'only' 45m high and 100m wide, a massive 400 cu metres of water thunders over its edge every second in summer, creating a plume of spray that can be seen 1km away. With the greatest volume of any waterfall in Europe, this truly is nature at its most spectacular. On sunny days, brilliant double rainbows form above the churning milky-grey glacial waters, and you'll have to jostle with the other visitors for the best views.

The falls can be seen from either side of the canyon, but there is no link (ie no bridge) between the sides at the site itself.

HOW TO REACH DETTIFOSS

Loads of tours visit the falls, but in summer 2018 public buses were cut completely. Check the park website, local tourist offices or www.publictransport.is for the latest news. Things will almost certainly change when Rte 862 is fully sealed.

Dettifoss can be reached three ways in summer by car – and only one way in winter (with no guarantee of access). Verify road openings at www.road.is.

Rte 862 north from the Ring Road The turn-off to Dettifoss is 27km east of Reykjahlíð (Mývatn); it's then an easy 24km on sealed road to reach the falls. Note that snowfall may close this road in winter, thus winter road access is not guaranteed. You can join a super-Jeep tour from Mývatn to see the falls when the road is closed.

Rte 862 south from Ásbyrgi (37km) At the time of writing this route was slowly being sealed, in stages (the northern 16km are expected to be sealed by the end of summer 2019). Check locally about its condition. It's open from about June to early October (weather dependent).

Rte 864 on the eastern side of the river It's gravel for its 60km length, from the Ring Road to Ásbyrgi. It's not an F road (ie for 4WDs only), but it can be tough going in a 2WD. Rte 864 is open from about June to early October (weather dependent).

OFF THE BEATEN TRACK

DETTIFOSS TO ÁSBYRGI HIKE

The most popular hike in Jökulsárgljúfur is the two-day trip (roughly 30km) between Dettifoss and Ásbyrgi, which moves through birch forests, striking rock formations, lush valleys and commanding perpendicular cliffs while taking in all of the region's major sights and offering awesome canyon views.

The hike can be done in both directions; however, the park rangers recommend starting in Dettifoss and heading north. Pick up information and a map from the visitor centre (p320) in Ásbyrgi, or download the map from the website and consult with them over the phone.

The Dettifoss to Vesturdalur hike takes an estimated six to eight hours. There are two options on this stretch: the considerably more difficult route involves a steep trail and a spectacular walk via the Hafragil lowlands (18km); the easier option takes a route north of Hafragil (19.5km). The lowland trail is not suitable for untrained hikers or people afraid of heights.

On the second day of your walk, take some trails around Vesturdalur's highlights, then enjoy a leisurely hike to Ásbyrgi (12km, three to four hours), opting for either the rim of Ásbyrgi or walking along the Jökulsá River. You'll return to hot showers at the Ásbyrgi campsite.

Since no buses currently serve Ásbyrgi, you'll need to arrange for pick-up locally. Remember to log your hike with safetravel.is.

Both viewpoints are grand and have pros and cons, and both require a walk from the respective car park of around 15 to 20 minutes to reach the falls. Many photographers rate the east side as their preferred side, especially in winter: road access is easier on the west side (making it busier with tour buses). Consider visiting either side under the summertime midnight sun for smaller crowds. Take care on the paths, made wet and slippery from the spray.

A sealed road, Rte 862, links the Ring Road with the **western bank of Dettifoss**, ending in a large car park and toilet facilities. From the car park, it's 1km to the falls, or a 2.5km loop walk takes in the dramatic, canyon-edge viewpoint of Dettifoss plus views of a smaller cataract, **Selfoss**. Bring waterproof gear to keep the spray at bay.

If you visit the **eastern side of the falls** via unsealed Rte 864, be sure, also, to drive 2km north of the Dettifoss car park and look for the sign to **Hafragilsfoss** – smaller, photogenic falls downriver from Dettifoss with a brilliant viewpoint over the canyon.

Sleeping & Eating

There is nowhere to overnight here, but there are a couple of guesthouses on the east side (Rte 864) near the Ring Road. Visitors drop in to view Dettifoss from various points, but the closest major settlement is at Reykjahlíð (Mývatn), 52km away.

There is a tiny, basic campsite north of Dettifoss on Rte 862, strictly reserved for hikers.

Grímsstaðir GUESTHOUSE, CAMPGROUND €€
(☎464 4292; www.grimsstadir.is; Rte 864, Grímsstaðir á Fjöllum; campsite per person 750kr, d without bath incl breakfast 19,900kr; ⊙late Jun–mid-Sep) Highland farm Grímsstaðir lies 28km south of Dettifoss near the junction with the Ring Road. An old farmhouse contains sleeping-bag accommodation (per person 6000kr), and the farmer's own house offers three double rooms with made-up beds. There's camping in the fields by a brook.

Grímstunga Cafe & Guesthouse GUESTHOUSE €€
(☎464 4294; www.grimstunga.is; Rte 864, Grímstunga 1 at Grímsstaðir a Fjöllum; d with/without bathroom from 24,500/17,500kr; 📶) Welcoming Grímstunga, 28km south of Dettifoss near the junction with the Ring Road, offers basic cosy rooms with shared bathrooms and a guest kitchen. The cafe (open 9am to 7pm) sells cake and coffee during the day and buffet dinners (4800kr). They also have a house with en suite rooms at Hólssel, 6km north on Rte 864.

NORTHEAST CIRCUIT

Bypassed by the tourist hordes who whiz around the Ring Road, this wild, sparsely populated coastal route around Iceland's remote northeast peninsulas is an interesting alternative to the direct road from Mývatn to Egilsstaðir. It's an area of desolate moors and beautiful scenery, stretching to within a few kilometres of the Arctic Circle. If you're looking for brilliantly unspoilt, untouristed, unhyped Iceland – well, you've found it.

Information

For information on the northeast, visit www.edgeofthearctic.is. Birdwatchers should get their hands on the *Birding Trail* map (see www.birdingtrail.is).

Getting There & Around

In summer 2018, bus services to this area were cut. Check www.bus.is and www.publictransport.is to see the latest news.

Mostly sealed Rte 85 links Vopnafjörður, Þórshöfn, Raufarhöfn and Kópasker. Rough tracks lead further afield.

Air Iceland Connect (p428) has a weekday air link connecting Akureyri with Þórshöfn and Vopnafjörður.

Kópasker

POP 122

Tiny Kópasker is the westernmost town on the edges of the wilds of Iceland's far northeast. It's a prime place to stock up on groceries if you'll be camping when you travel to more remote spots, like Melrakkaslétta.

Kópasker HI Hostel HOSTEL €

(☎465 2314; www.hostel.is; Akurgerði 7; dm/d without bathroom 5000/12,700kr; ⊙May–mid-Oct; 📶) Your best bet for a bed is the homely Kópasker HI Hostel, run by Benni. Rooms are spread across a couple of houses; everything is well maintained, and there's good birdwatching (and sometimes seal-watching) in the neighbourhood. HI members receive a 10% discount. Cash only.

Campsite CAMPGROUND €

(☎864 3013; www.nordurthing.is; Austurtröð 4; site per adult/child 1200kr/free; ⊙Jun-Aug) Neat little campground at the southern entrance to town.

Skerjakolla SUPERMARKET, CAFE €

(☎465 1150; www.facebook.com/budinaskerinu.skerjakolla; Bakkagata 10; snacks & pizza 300-2200kr; ⊙10am-8pm, from noon Sat, noon-6pm Sun Jun-Aug, shorter hours Sep-May) Skerjakolla is a sweet surprise: a decent grocery store, with a small and simple cafe serving pizza, sandwiches, coffee and cake. There's even a **Vínbúðin** (☎465 1118; www.vinbudin.is; Bakkagata 10; ⊙4-6pm Mon-Thu, 1-6pm Fri) here too, and a petrol pump out the front.

Raufarhöfn

POP 186

Distant Raufarhöfn (*roy*-ver-hup), Iceland's northernmost mainland township, is a quiet place with a jaunty orange lighthouse on the point. The port has functioned since the Saga Age, but the town's economic peak came early in the 20th century during the herring boom, when it was second to Siglufjörður in volume. Today Raufarhöfn's rows of dull prefab housing give few clues to its illustrious past. You feel a long way from the gloss and glamour of Iceland's well-oiled tourist machine here. It's best known for the Arctic Henge project.

Sights

Arctic Henge MONUMENT

(www.arctichenge.com; Rte 870; ⊙24hr) FREE The striking stone arches of Arctic Henge are the darling of many a brochure, and in real life they live up to the exalted mood. The massive stone circle on the hill just north of Raufarhöfn is 50m in diameter with four giant gates (representing the seasons) up to 7m in height. The goal: a finely tuned sundial to celebrate the solstices, view the midnight sun, and explain the strong local beliefs in the mythology of the Edda poem *Völuspá* (Wise Woman's Prophecy).

This ambitious long-term building project is still underway.

Sleeping & Eating

There's a **campground** (☎465 2254; www.nordurthing.is; Rte 870; site per adult/child 1200kr/free, campsite tax 333kr; ⊙Jun–mid-Sep), a simple hotel and a couple of OK guesthouses.

Nest GUESTHOUSE €

(Gistiheimilið Hreiðrið; ☎472 9930; www.nesthouse.is; Aðalbraut 16; s/d/apt without bathroom 8900/14,000/23,900kr; 📶👪) This main-street guesthouse has bright, appealing rooms, plus guest lounge and kitchen.

Hótel Norðurljós HOTEL €€

(☎465 1233; www.hotelnordurljos.is; Aðalbraut 2; d with/without bathroom 24,800/18,100kr; ⊙Jun-Sep; 📶) Hótel Norðurljós is the town's 'fanciest' accommodation (ie it's the only one with private bathrooms). Under new management, the rather bland hotel is pulling off a comeback. It has a dining area (one of Raufarhöfn's few eating options) and seafront deck.

★Kaupfélagið Raufarhöfn CAFE €
(☎849 3536; www.facebook.com/kaupfelagidRaufarhofn; Aðalbraut 24; soup & coffee 1500kr; ⌚10.30am-9pm, to 7pm Fri, to 5pm Sun) Easily the brightest spark in town, this charming cafe and handicrafts gallery has bags of personality (driftwood, artworks, coffee pots). It's a welcome addition to the town, and opens for a breakfast buffet, afternoon cake and coffee, and simple evening meals.

Rauðanes

★Rauðanes NATURE RESERVE
There's excellent hiking on Þistilfjörður at Rauðanes headland, where a 7km marked walking trail leads to bizarre rock formations, natural arches, caves and secluded beaches, plus great bird life (including puffins). The turn-off to Rauðanes is between Raufarhöfn (42km) and Þórshöfn (32km). Look for a small sign – the road leads 1.5km to an information board (with walking trail details) and small car park.

Þórshöfn

POP 352

Þórshöfn (pronounced *thors*-hup) has served as a busy port since Saga times and saw its heyday when a herring-salting station was established here in the early 20th century. Today it's a very modest place, but makes a good base for the remote Langanes peninsula.

Sights & Activities

Sauðaneshús MUSEUM
(☎464 1860; Rte 869; adult/child 800kr/free; ⌚11am-5pm mid-Jun–Aug) Sauðaneshús, the old vicarage on the church estate 7km north of town (en route to Langanes), provides insights into how locals lived a century ago, and houses a cafe.

Sports Complex SWIMMING
(Íþróttahús; ☎468 1515; Langanesvegur 18b; adult/child 800/400kr; ⌚8am-8pm Mon-Fri, 11am-5pm Sat & Sun Jun-Aug, shorter hours rest of year) Large swimming-pool/gym complex with tourist info.

Þórshöfn Kayak KAYAKING
(☎468 1250; www.baranrestaurant.is; Eyrarvegur 3; ⌚May-Sep) Operating out of Báran restaurant by the harbour, this outfit offers kayaking tours, from a short and sweet taster (one hour, 4000kr) to coastal paddling checking out low cliffs, a lighthouse and lots of seabirds (three hours, 9700kr). There's a midnight sun tour, too, in June and July. Prices include drysuits.

> OFF THE BEATEN TRACK
>
> **DETOUR: RTE 870**
>
> The unsealed but magnificent old coastal road (Rte 870) around the wildlife-rich and little-visited **Melrakkaslétta** (Arctic Fox Plain) bumps along for 55km between Kópasker and Raufarhöfn. It passes by driftwood, rolling fields, ponds and marshes of this birder's paradise. There are trails and turn-offs to lonely lighthouses on remote headlands. The road sees little maintenance – 4WDs will face few problems, but it's best to ask locally whether Rte 870 is in a suitable state for 2WDs.

Sleeping & Eating

Lyngholt Guesthouse GUESTHOUSE €
(☎897 5064; www.lyngholt.is; Langanesvegur 12; s/d without bathroom 9900/15,500kr, cottage 21,000kr; 📶👪) This handsome timber guesthouse is situated near the pool. It has good facilities, including kitchen and lounge. They also operate two other guesthouse locations and let a holiday home.

Þórshöfn Campsite CAMPGROUND €
(☎468 1220; Miðholt; sites per person 1200kr; ⌚Jun–mid-Sep) Neat, grassy campsite close to the heart of town.

★Grásteinn Guesthouse GUESTHOUSE €€
(☎895 0834; www.grasteinnguesthouse.is; Rte 868, Holt; cottages 20,500kr; 📶) Get away from it all at these boutique cottages on a remote sheep farm 14km southwest of Þórshöfn. Farmers Siggi and Hildur have kitted out the rooms in understated, comfortable style – all have kitchenettes and some have balconies. The family will serve a breakfast of farm produce directly to the cottage. Perfect for lazing the day away, or preparing for a day out birding.

Kjörbúðin SUPERMARKET €
(☎468 1100; Langanesvegur 2; ⌚9am-7pm Mon-Fri, 10am-6pm Sat, noon-6pm Sun) For self-catering.

Báran ICELANDIC €€
(☎468 1250; www.baranrestaurant.is; Eyrarvegur 3; mains 2900-4300kr; ⌚10am-10pm, to 1am Fri, to 3am Sat May-Sep, shorter hours Oct-Apr) Behind

the N1 is a harbourside restaurant – and it's a cool surprise to find a loungey area, wide-ranging menu, high-quality food and some excellent local beer choices. Pizza, pasta and burgers are well-done standards, but there's also good local lamb and fish. Some may be offended by the minke whale on the menu. Drop by for a late-night drink with the locals on weekends.

Vinbúðin ALCOHOL
(☎560 7883; www.vinbudin.is; Langanesvegur 2; ⏲4-6pm Mon-Thu, 1-6pm Fri) Government-run liquor store.

Langanes

Shaped like a goose with a very large head, foggy Langanes peninsula is one of the loneliest corners of Iceland. The peninsula's flat terrain, cushioned by mossy meadows and studded with crumbling remains, is an excellent place to break in your hiking shoes and find solitude.

Sealed Rte 869 ends just north of Þórshöfn. The rutted track continues 50km along the Langanes peninsula, and although it's possible to continue to the tip at Fontur lighthouse in a 4WD, parts of the road can be difficult to navigate.

If you don't have your own vehicle, you can arrange a transfer to Ytra Lón Farm Lodge from Þórshöfn (for a fee).

Ytra Lón Farm Lodge APARTMENT €€
(☎846 6448; www.ytralon.is; Rte 869; s/d incl breakfast 22,000/24,500kr; 📶) For Langanes exploration, base yourself at excellent Ytra Lón, 14km northeast of Þórshöfn and just off Rte 869. It's part of a working sheep farm run by a welcoming Dutch-Icelandic family. Here, colourful studio apartments, each with bathroom and kitchenette, are housed in cargo containers and lined up under a greenhouse-style roof. There's a breakfast buffet of local produce, and a hot-pot.

SAGA OF THE PEOPLE OF VOPNAFJÖÐUR

Vopnafjöður figures prominently in a dramatic saga of AD960–990. Written in the 13th century, the *Saga of the People of Vopnafjöður* details the high jinks of local chieftan Helgi Þorgilsson (known as Brodd-Helgi) and Geitir Lytingsson and their kin, featuring fierce alliances, violent feuds and eventual reconciliations. At the tourist information centre, look for the pamphlet detailing the story; guided tours of remaining sites around today's fjord can be booked (one day in advance).

Vopnafjörður & Around

POP 526

Legend has it 'Weapon Fjord' was once the notorious home of a fearsome dragon that protected Northeast Iceland from harm. Today, there are no dragons, and the town is an agreeably sleepy place; it's well known for the superlative salmon rivers in the area (Prince Charles and George Bush Sr have fished here; James Ratcliffe is buying property on them).

Note that, officially, Vopnafjörður is considered to be part of East Iceland and online information is found at www.east.is. We have covered it under North Iceland due to the logistics of travelling the Northeast Circuit along Rte 85.

Sights & Activities

★**Selárdalslaug** SWIMMING
(off Rte 85; adult/child 700/350kr; ⏲10am-10pm mid-May–Sep, shorter hours rest of year) This exquisite swimming pool lies on the edge of roaring Selá River, with open skies, in the middle of nowhere – it's signed 8km north of Vopnafjörður off Rte 85, just south of the river. Stop for a quick soak in the geothermal waters of the hot-pot, cold plunge pool, and standard pool.

Kaupvangur CULTURAL CENTRE
(☎473 1200; Hafnarbyggð 4a) FREE The town's most significant building is Kaupvangur, a restored customs house. You'll find an excellent cafe and information centre on the ground floor, and a handicrafts shop. Upstairs there's a well-curated exhibit about two locals, Iceland's version of the Gershwin brothers. Also on the 2nd floor is a small display about East Iceland émigrés: from 1850 to 1914, a wave of locals purchased boat tickets to North America from this very building.

The **East Iceland Emigration Center** (www.vesturfarinn.is) is based here, and can help 'Western Icelanders' (ie North Americans with Icelandic heritage) reconnect with their heritage.

Bustarfell MUSEUM
(☎471 2211; off Rte 920; adult/child 900/200kr; ⏲10am-5pm Jun-Sep) This high-quality folk museum is set in a photogenic 18th-century turf-roofed manor house southwest of Vopnafjörður township. The on-site Cafe Croft serves home-baked cake and coffee. It's 8km off Rte 85 about 19km from Vopnafjörður (just off the sealed Rte 920).

Sleeping & Eating

There are some excellent rural guesthouses in the valleys around Vopnafjörður.

Campsite CAMPGROUND €
(☎473 1330; www.vopnafjardarhreppur.is; Hamrahlíð 9-15; sites per person 1300kr; ⏲May–mid-Oct) Good campsite with views of the fjord and town below. Follow Miðbraut north and turn left at the school.

★**Hvammsgerði** GUESTHOUSE €€
(☎588 1298; www.hvammsgerdi.is; Rte 85; s/d/f without bathroom incl breakfast from 9900/12,900/18,900kr;) Just north of the turn-off to Selárdalslaug, about 9km north of Vopnafjörður township, is this welcoming riverside option. It's a cosy, family-friendly guesthouse with agreeable rooms, sweet pets to play with, and farm-fresh eggs at the breakfast table (breakfast 1800kr). Sleeping-bag beds are available (3900kr).

Hótel Tangi HOTEL €€
(☎473 1203; www.hoteltangi.com; Hafnarbyggð 17; d with/without bathroom incl breakfast 21,600/16,200kr;) A friendly in-town hotel open year-round with an on-site restaurant (open to all), a pleasant lounge area, and rooms with and without private bathroom. The smartest accommodation is the studio, which sleeps four.

★**Kaupvangskaffi** CAFE €
(☎473 1331; www.kaupvangskaffi.com; Hafnarbyggð 4a; soup buffet 1390kr, pizza 1360-4620kr; ⏲11am-9pm Jun-Sep, shorter hours rest of year;) It seems everyone passing through town stops here – and with excellent reason. Inside Kaupvangur, you'll find sofas to relax on, plus delicious coffee, a big lunchtime soup buffet, homemade pizzas (eat in or take away; the langoustine and garlic pizza is to die for) and a tempting array of sweet treats.

Kauptún SUPERMARKET €
(☎473 1403; www.facebook.com/Kauptun; Hafnarbyggð 4; ⏲9.30am-6pm Mon-Fri, noon-4pm Sat) The supermarket shares a car park with **Vínbúðin** (☎471 2200; www.vinbudin.is⏲4-6pm Mon-Thu, 1-6pm Fri Jun-Aug, shorter hours rest of year).

WORTH A TRIP

ROUTE 917

East of Vopnafjörður, the truly spectacular 73km mountain drive along mostly unpaved Rte 917 takes you over 655m **Hellisheiði** and down to the east coast. The road may be impassable in bad weather, but in summer is generally doable in a small car. It climbs up a series of switchbacks and hairpin bends before dropping down to the striking glacial river deltas on the **Héraðssandur**.

Information

Tourist Information Centre (☎473 1331; www.visitvopnafjordur.com; Hafnarbyggð 4a; ⏲11am-5pm Mon-Fri) Good information, inside Kaupvangur. Outside of office opening hours you can still get brochures and local info – look for the handy, free guides to local walking routes and the brochure on the *Saga of the People of Vopnafjöður*; tours possible with one-day advance booking).

You can also find information at www.vopnafjordur.com and www.east.is.

Getting There & Away

There is no bus service to Vopnafjörður.

From Vopnafjörður it's 137km to Reykjahlíð and 136km to Egilsstaðir (via Rte 85 and the Ring Road), so check fuel levels before you leave town.

It's a shorter, more majestic (and more hair-raising) route to Egilsstaðir (95km) via the gravel mountain road Rte 917.

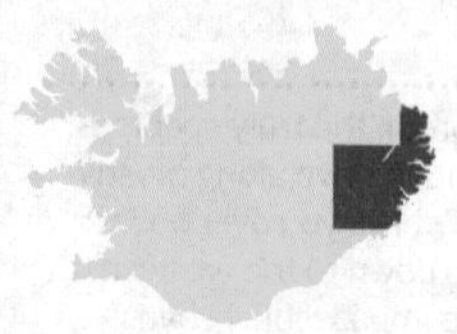

East Iceland

Includes ➡

Best Places to Eat

- ➡ Klausturkaffi (p337)
- ➡ Norð Austur Sushi & Bar (p345)
- ➡ Beituskúrinn (p352)
- ➡ Havarí (p356)
- ➡ Randulffs-sjóhús (p350)

Best Places to Stay

- ➡ Hafaldan Old Hospital Hostel (p344)
- ➡ Fosshotel Eastfjords (p353)
- ➡ Silfurberg (p355)
- ➡ Wilderness Center (p336)
- ➡ Blábjörg Guesthouse (p340)

Why Go?

Iceland's impressively varied and sparsely populated east (called Austurland) doesn't announce itself as loudly as other parts of the country, preferring subtle charms over big-ticket attractions. The Eastfjords is the area's most wondrous destination – the scenery is particularly spectacular around the northern fjord villages, backed by sheer-sided mountains etched with waterfalls. If the weather's fine, days spent hiking here may be some of your most memorable in Iceland.

Away from the convoluted coast, the country's longest lake stretches southwest from Egilsstaðir, its shores lined with perfect diversions. Further inland are the forgotten farms, fells and reindeer-roamed heathlands of the empty east, and Snæfell, one of Iceland's prime peaks. Ring Road motorists often simply overnight in Egilsstaðir then speed out of the east. Lunacy! The east's spectacular fjords, scenic hiking trails, fascinating geology and friendly villages are some of Iceland's unsung treasures.

Road Distances (km)

	Djúpivogur	Reykjavík	Egilsstaðir	Borgarfjörður Eystri	Seyðisfjörður	Neskaupstaður
Reykjavík	552					
Egilsstaðir	85	698				
Borgarfjörður Eystri	155	702	70			
Seyðisfjörður	111	660	27	92		
Neskaupstaður	164	703	72	140	96	
Breiðdalsvík	64	612	84	153	109	100

Getting There & Away

The Visit East Iceland website (www.east.is) outlines transport to/from and within the region.

AIR

Egilsstaðir's airport is 1km north of town. Air Iceland Connect (www.airicelandconnect.is) flies three times daily year-round between Egilsstaðir and Reykjavík Domestic Airport (ie **not** Keflavík International Airport). Flights are popular (and in peak winter may offer the only transport connection).

BUS

Egilsstaðir is a major stop on the Ring Road, but at the time of writing there was no longer a direct bus service linking Egilsstaðir with Höfn.

It is possible, though hard work, to find a way to travel this route to the southeast using local buses operated by **SVAust** (☎471 2320; www.svaust.is), but at the time of research it involved three separate bus journeys – local bus 1 from Egilsstaðir to Reyðarfjörður, bus 2 from Reyðarfjörður to Breiðdalsvík, then bus 4 from Breiðdalsvík to Höfn. We suggest you check carpooling sites or ask around at your accommodation to try to get a lift.

Strætó (☎540 2700; www.straeto.is) is the only busline linking Egilsstaði with Akureyri and Mývatn in the north. Pick-up and drop-off is at the campground:

- Bus 56 to Reykjahlíð, Mývatn (5980kr, two hours, one daily)
- Bus 56 to Akureyri (8280kr, 3½ hours, one daily)

Getting Around

BUS

Local buses run from Egilsstaðir to villages around the fjords (as far south as Höfn), under the SVAust umbrella. Note that these buses don't carry bikes (except for the service linking Egilsstaðir with Seyðisfjörður).

As well as handy direct services to Borgarfjörður Eystri and Seyðisfjörður, SVAust runs year-round buses geared to service the needs of Alcoa commuters. Buses 1 and 2 run every day (fewer services on weekends); route 4 is not a daily service.

Bus 1 Egilsstaðir–Reyðarfjörður–Eskifjörður–Neskaupstaður (Nordfjörður)

Bus 2 Reyðarfjörður–Fáskrúðsfjörður–Stöðvarfjörður–Breiðdalsvík

Bus 3 Egilsstaðir-Seyðisfjörður

Bus 4 Breiðdalsvík–Djúpivogur–Höfn

Bus 5 Egilsstaðir-Borgarfjörður Eystri

Check online for schedule and fare details (ticket price depends on distance travelled, eg 720kr for a journey of 16km to 30km), or ask at tourist information centres in the area.

CAR

The Ring Road (Rte 1) steams through Egilsstaðir, and was re-routed in 2017 to travel south through the southern fjords of Reyðarfjörður, Fáskrúðsfjörður and Stöðvarfjörður.

ROUTE OPTIONS

Driving between Egilsstaðir and Djúpivogur, there are three options: two mountain roads and one fjordside route – the fjordside road is now the official Rte 1 (Ring Road), after authorities re-routed the highway in November 2017.

All three options are incredibly panoramic. In winter, Route 1 is often the only option – any closures are outlined on www.road.is. Note that many GPS units and Google maps automatically follow Rte 939 as it's the shortest option, but do give some consideration as to whether it's the best route for you (and *do not* attempt it when signs say 'Impassable').

Note that routes here are described heading south from Egilsstaðir; for motorists heading north from Djúpivogur, read these directions in reverse.

Rte 1 The Ring Road now travels via the fjords Reyðarfjörður, Fáskrúðsfjörður and Stöðvarfjörður.

Rte 95 From Egilsstaðir, Rte 95 (the former Ring Road) heads south, descending steeply from the empty moors of Breiðdalsheiði heath and travelling east through the scenic Breiðdalur valley to Breiðdalsvík, then weaving along the coast to Djúpivogur. Some 25km of this route is gravel (Breiðdalsheiði and Breiðdalur). In winter, bad weather and snowfall often closes the mountain road at Breiðdalsheiði.

Rte 939 A summer-only, gravel short cut off Rte 95 which runs via the **Öxi mountain pass** (this is not a great option in bad weather or fog, and is closed in winter). This road turns off Rte 95 about 45km south of Egilsstaðir, connecting with the head of Berufjörður after 19km. It's steep, and not for novice drivers.

East Iceland Highlights

❶ Seyðisfjörður (p341) Arriving in Iceland in style by sailing up a lovely, long fjord to this bohemian village.

❷ Borgarfjörður Eystri (p339) Hiking magical trails, looking for the hidden people, and snapping photos of puffin posses in this tiny hamlet.

❸ Lagarfljót (p335) Touring Lagarfljót's forested lake shores while looking for sea monsters.

❹ Mjóifjörður (p348) Learning the definition of tranquil isolation in this ruin-strewn fjord.

❺ Stöðvarfjörður (p353) Marvelling over the magnificent mineral collection in this tiny town.

❻ Wilderness Center (p336) Exploring highland life and ace walking trails at a remote, unique farm.

❼ Húsey Horse Farm (p339) Watching birds, seals and spectacular scenery on horseback.

❽ Havarí (p356) Checking out live music and vegetarian food at this fabulous venue on Berufjörður.

❾ Breiðdalur (p354) Seeking serenity in this under-the-radar valley of colourful peaks and braided rivers.

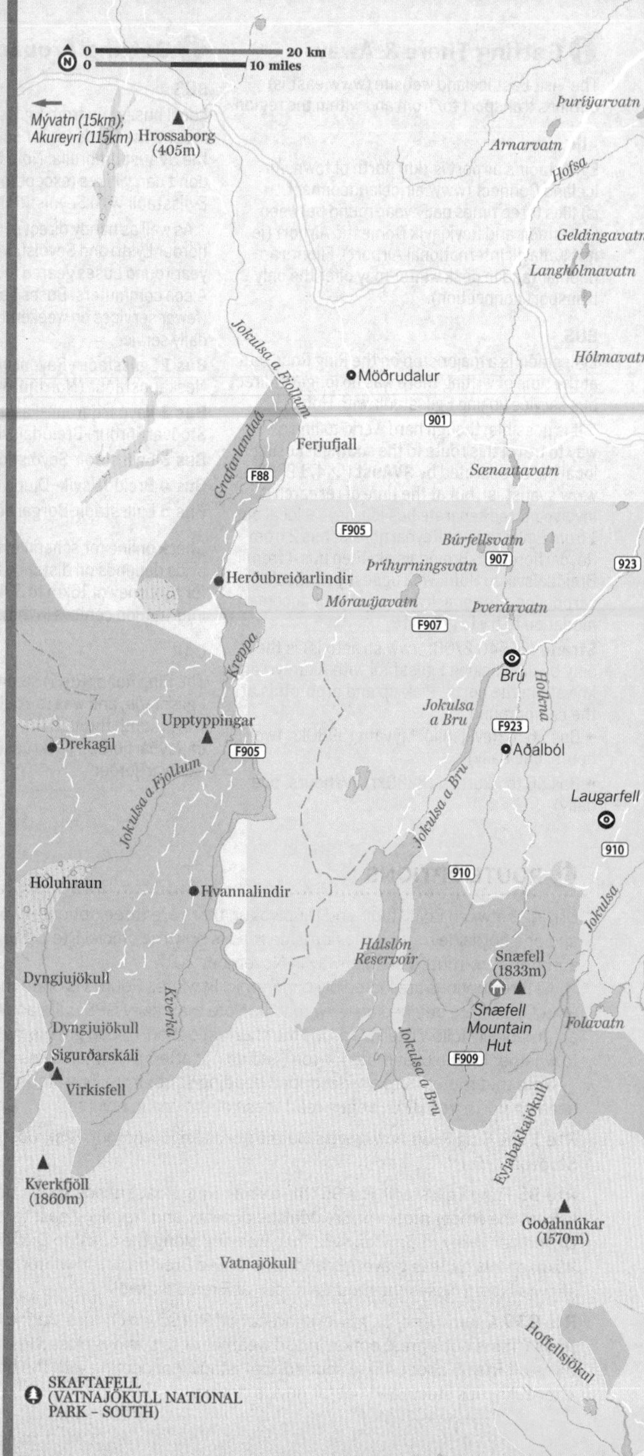

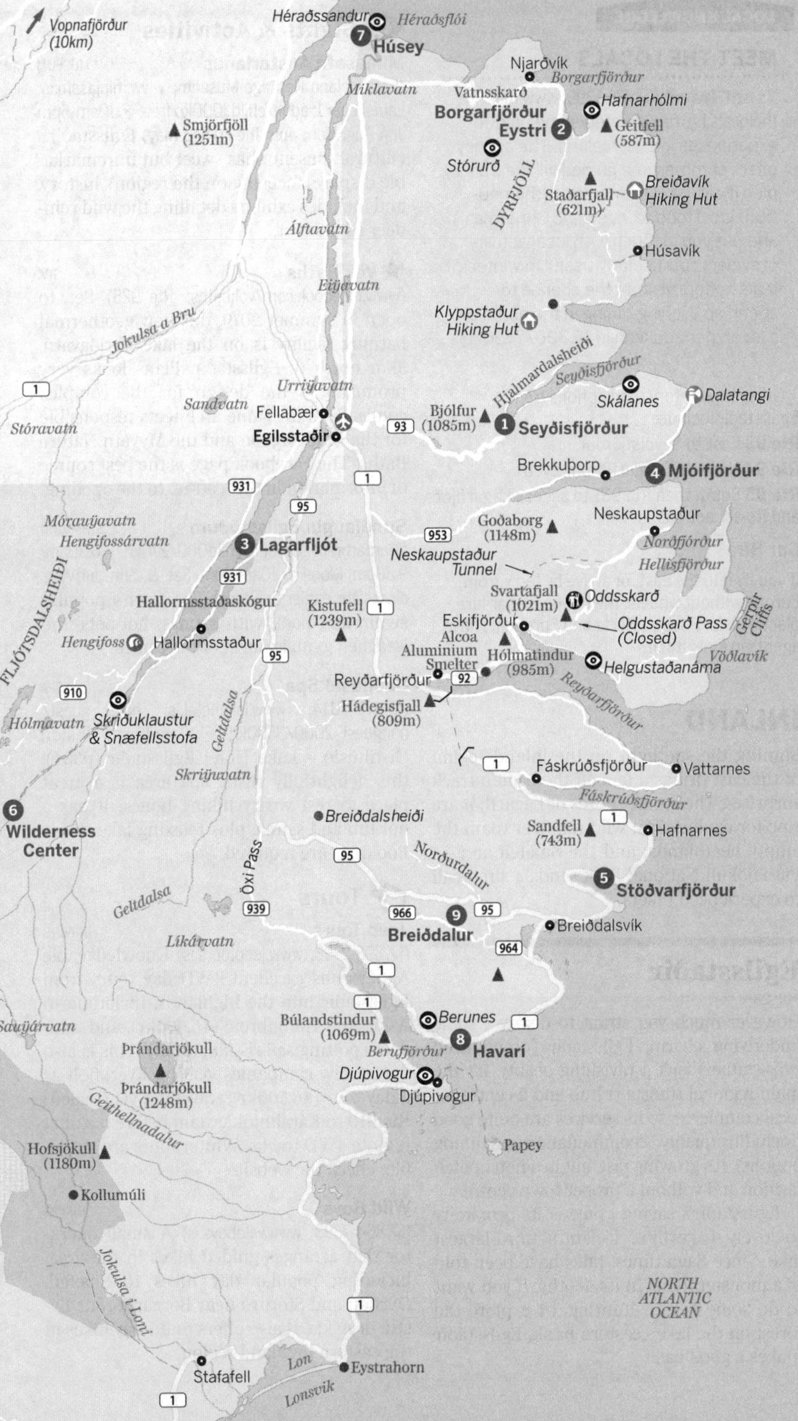

Vopnafjörður (10km)
Héraðssandur
Héraðsflói
7 Húsey
Njarðvík
Borgarfjörður
Miklavatn
Vatnsskarð
Hafnarhólmi
Borgarfjörður Eystri 2
Geitfell (587m)
Smjörfjöll (1251m)
Stórurð
DYRFJÖLL
Staðarfjall (621m)
Breiðavík Hiking Hut
Álftavatn
Húsavík
Eiríjavatn
Klyppstaður Hiking Hut
Jokulsa a Bru
Hjalmardalsheiði
Seyðisfjörður
Skálanes
Dalatangi
Urriðavatn
Sandvatn
Fellabær
Bjólfur (1085m)
1 Seyðisfjörður
Stóravatn
Egilsstaðir
Brekkuþorp
4 Mjóifjörður
Móraujavatn
Goðaborg (1148m)
Neskaupstaður
Hengifossárvatn
3 Lagarfljót
Norðfjörður
Neskaupstaður Tunnel
Hellisfjörður
FLJÓTSDALSHEIÐI
Svartafjall (1021m)
Oddsskarð
Hallormsstaðaskógur
Kistufell (1239m)
Gerpir Cliffs
Eskifjörður
Oddsskarð Pass (Closed)
Hengifoss
Hallormsstaður
Alcoa Aluminium Smelter
Hólmatindur (985m)
Helgustaðanáma
Vöðlavík
Reyðarfjörður
Hádegisfjall (809m)
Skriðuklaustur & Snæfellsstofa
Geitdalsa
Hólmavatn
Fáskrúðsfjörður
Vattarnes
Skriðuvatn
6 Wilderness Center
Breiðdalsheiði
Sandfell (743m)
Hafnarnes
Öxi Pass
Norðurdalur
5 Stöðvarfjörður
Geitdalsa
9 Breiðdalur
Breiðdalsvík
Líkárvatn
Búlandstindur (1069m)
Berunes
8 Havarí
Sauðjárvatn
Berufjörður
Þrándarjökull
Djúpivogur
Þrándarjökull (1248m)
Geithellnadalur
Papey
Hofsjökull (1180m)
Kollumúli
Jokulsa i Loni
NORTH ATLANTIC OCEAN
Stafafell
Lon
Eystrahorn
Lonsvik
1
93
931
95
953
910
92
939
966
964

LOCAL KNOWLEDGE

MEET THE LOCALS

Tanni Travel (☎476 1399; www.meet-thelocals.is) has created some unique experiences in East Iceland. The agency offers summertime guided village walks, plus it can devise itineraries (themed from local food to 'nostalgic Christmas') and put you in touch with local activity providers (particularly useful in winter). It also offers visitors the chance to spend an evening dining in the home of a local (per adult/child 15,300/7650kr).

Other exploratory road options from Egilsstaðir include:

Rte 93 East to Seyðisfjörður.

Rte 94 North to Borgarfjörður Eystri.

Rte 95 South then Rte 931 to access Lagarfljót and its attractions.

Car Hire

If you fly into the east, or arrive by ferry from Europe without wheels, the big-name car-hire places (Avis, Budget, Hertz and Europcar) have agents in Egilsstaðir.

INLAND

Shining the spotlight on the inland region of the east brings a few off-the-beaten-track surprises. The scenic shores of Lagarfljót are ripe for exploration; wild reindeer roam the empty heathlands; and the Snæfell area of Vatnajökull National Park sends a siren-call to experienced hikers.

Egilsstaðir

POP 2875

However much you strain to discover some underlying charm, Egilsstaðir (pronounced eyils-stather) isn't a ravishing beauty. It's the main regional transport hub and a centre for local commerce, so its services are quite good (including quality accommodation and dining options). It's growing fast, but in a hotchpotch fashion and without a proper town centre.

Egilsstaðir's saving grace is its proximity to lovely Lagarfljót, Iceland's third-largest lake. Since Saga times, tales have been told of a monster living in its depths. If you want to do some beastie-hunting, or explore the forest on the lake's eastern bank, Egilsstaðir makes a good base.

Sights & Activities

Minjasafn Austurlands MUSEUM

(East Iceland Heritage Museum; www.minjasafn.is; Laufskógar 1; adult/child 1000kr/free; ⌚10am-6pm Jun-Aug, 11am-4pm Tue-Fri Sep-May) Egilsstaðir's cultural museum has sweet but unremarkable displays focusing on the region's history, and includes exhibits detailing the wild reindeer of the east.

★**Vök Baths** SPA

(www.facebook.com/vokbaths; Rte 925) Set to open in summer 2019, this new geothermal bathing facility is on the lake Urriðavatn, 5km north of Egilsstaðir. Plans looks very promising – the design for the complex comes from the same architects responsible for the Blue Lagoon and the Mývatn Nature Baths. The Facebook page is the best source of information in the lead-up to the opening.

Sundlaugin Egilsstöðum SWIMMING

(Tjarnarbraut 26; adult/child 900/270kr; ⌚6.30am-9.30pm Mon-Fri, 10am-6pm Sat & Sun Jun-Aug, closes 1hr earlier Sep-May) The town's popular swimming pool, with saunas, hot-pots and attached gym, is north of the centre.

Baðhúsið Spa SPA

(☎471 1114; www.lakehotel.is; hotel guest/nonguest 2000/3500kr; ⌚10am-10pm) Inside Gistihúsið – Lake Hotel Egilsstaðir (p334), this delightfully rustic spa area is a great place to rest weary hiking bones; it has a hot tub and sauna, plus relaxing lake views. Bookings are required.

Tours

Jeep Tours DRIVING

(☎898 2798; www.jeeptours.is) Knowledgeable Agnar runs excellent 4WD day tours from Egilsstaðir into the highlands, including to Askja and Herðubreið (46,500kr), and reindeer-spotting safaris (38,000kr). This is also one of few companies visiting Kverkfjöll as a day tour (46,500kr), travelling via (sealed) Rte 910 to Kárahnjúkar dam before tackling remote 4WD tracks. Winter tours are available; check the website.

Wild Boys HIKING

(☎864 7393; www.wildboys.is) A small operator that arranges guided hikes in the area, including popular day hikes to Snæfell, Dyrfjöll and Stórurð near Borgarfjörður Eystri, or Askja. It also offers multi-day hikes in the eastern highland region.

Egilsstaðir

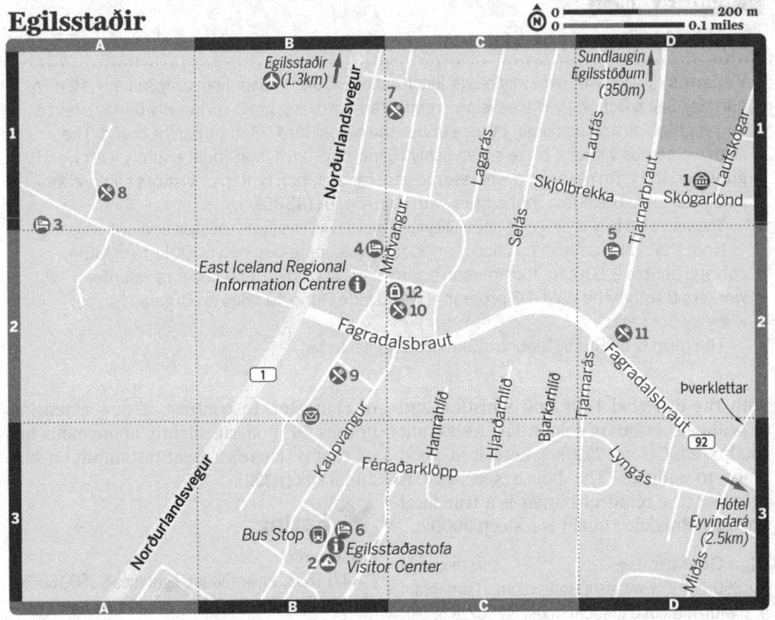

Egilsstaðir

Sights

1 Minjasafn Austurlands D1

Activities, Courses & Tours

Baðhúsið Spa .... (see 3)

Sleeping

2 Egilsstaðir Camping B3
3 Gistihúsið – Lake Hotel Egilsstaðir A1
4 Icelandair Hótel Hérað B2
5 Olga Guesthouse D2
6 Tehúsið Hostel B3

Eating

7 Bónus C1
Eldhúsið .... (see 3)
8 Fjóshornið A1
9 Nettó B2
10 Salt C2
11 Skálinn Diner D2

Shopping

12 Vínbúðin C2

Sleeping

Rooms and campsites in the area are in hot demand on Wednesday nights in summer, as the ferry to Europe sails from Seyðisfjörður (27km away) on Thursday mornings. If you are taking the ferry, book your accommodation well ahead. Refer to accommodation websites for up-to-date rates.

Tehúsið Hostel HOSTEL €

(☎471 2450; www.tehusidhostel.is; Kaupvangur 17; dm/d without bathroom from 6850/19,000kr; 📶) A welcome addition to the local scene, the Teahouse has six bunk-filled rooms – the spaces are tight, but the price is reasonable (rooms can be booked as doubles or family rooms). There's a communal kitchen, but the best feature is the chilled cafe-bar, filled with character and a fine place to relax over a beer.

Egilsstaðir Camping CAMPGROUND €

(☎470 0750; camping@egilsstadir.is; Kaupvangur 17; sites per adult/child 1900kr/free; @📶👪) Camping pitches are in utilitarian rows, but it's central and facilities are reasonable; there's a laundry, but no camper kitchen. At reception you can rent bikes (3000kr for 24 hours) and book tours.

Icelandair Hótel Hérað HOTEL €€

(☎471 1500; www.icelandairhotels.is; Miðvangur 1-7; r from 25,400kr; @📶) This stylish, friendly, business-standard hotel is kitted out

WORTH A TRIP

FARM-TO-TABLE TREATS

Vallanes (☎471 1747; www.vallanes.is; lunch buffet 2500kr; ⏲9am-6pm daily Jun-Aug, Mon-Fri Apr, May, Sep & Oct;) Vallanes is an organic farm growing grain (primarily barley), herbs and vegetables and packaging these under the Móðir Jörð (Mother Earth) brand. The farm welcomes visitors; there's a stylishly rustic cafe-farmshop (built entirely with wood grown on the farm) serving a wholesome vegetarian lunch buffet, or visitors can prebook a field-to-table breakfast that comes with a farm tour (4500kr).

You can also buy a range of speciality products such as jams, pestos and crispbreads.

Note that Vallanes also has accommodation (sleeping-bag bed 5000kr to 6000kr, cottage double 22,000kr, four-person apartment 34,000kr), and accepts volunteer workers through the WWOOF program (Worldwide Opportunities on Organic Farms; www.wwoof.net).

The farm is on Rte 931, about 13km from Egilsstaðir.

with the expected bells and whistles, and appealing splashes of colour. The restaurant (mains 2390kr to 7550kr) here is a good place to indulge. The house speciality is reindeer (the reindeer burger is a true local flavour). Breakfast buffet is a steep 3000kr.

Olga Guesthouse GUESTHOUSE €€
(☎860 2999; www.gistihusolgu.com; Tjarnabraut 3; d with/without bathroom from 23,260/18,660kr;) In a good central location, dressed-in-red Olga offers five rooms that share three bathrooms and a small kitchen – all rooms come with tea- and coffee-making facilities, TV and fridge. Two doors down is Olga's sister, yellow **Birta Guesthouse**, under the same friendly ownership and with similar high-quality facilities. Birta has an additional annexe containing en-suite rooms.

Hótel Eyvindará HOTEL, COTTAGES €€
(☎471 1200; www.eyvindara.is; Eyvindará II; s/d incl breakfast from 21,900/25,200kr; ⏲Apr-Nov;) Set 4km out of town (on Rte 94), Eyvindará is a handsome, family-run collection of new hotel rooms, plus good motel-style units and cute timber cottages. The cottages sit hidden among fir trees, while motel rooms enjoy verandahs and views. It's known for friendly staff, and there's a decent restaurant (open June to August), a stylish lounge area, plus new hot-pots.

Gistihúsið – Lake Hotel Egilsstaðir HOTEL €€€
(☎471 1114; www.lakehotel.is; Egilsstöðum 1-2; d incl breakfast from 29,400kr;) The town was named after this farm and splendid heritage guesthouse (now big enough to warrant the 'hotel' label) on the banks of Lagarfljót, 300m west of the crossroads. In its old wing, en-suite rooms retain a sense of character. In contrast, a new extension houses 30 modern, slightly anonymous hotel rooms. There's a great restaurant on-site, and a spa (p332).

Eating

Fjóshornið CAFE €
(☎471 1508; Egilsstöðum; light meals 750-1600kr; ⏲noon-6pm Tue-Sun) For a taste of local produce stop by 'Cowshed Corner', beside Gistihúsið – Lake Hotel Egilsstaðir, where you can buy beef and dairy products (such as *skyr*, a yoghurt-like dessert, and feta) direct from the farm. Bagels, soup, waffles and cakes are also available.

Bókakaffi Hlöðum CAFE €€
(☎471 2255; www.bokakaffi.is; Helgafelli 2; meals 1750-2500kr; ⏲9am-6pm Mon-Fri, noon-6pm Sat;) In Fellabær, at the western end of the bridge across the river from Egilsstaðir, is this sweet, low-key cafe with quality coffee, retro furniture, vinyl records, secondhand books, great crêpes and soups, and top-notch baked treats.

Salt INTERNATIONAL €€
(☎471 1700; www.saltbistro.is; Miðvangur 2; snacks & meals 990-3900kr; ⏲10am-10pm Mon-Sat, noon-10pm Sun;) We understand the appeal of this cool cafe-bistro, which offers one of the most diverse menus in regional Iceland. Service can be slow but the food is good: try the gourmet-topped flatbread pizza made with local barley, or opt for a burger, salad, kebab or tandoori-baked Indian dish. There are lots of veg options, and a kids' menu too.

Skálinn Diner AMERICAN €€
(☎471 1899; Fagradalsbraut; mains 990-2800kr; ⏲8am-11pm) A little slice of Americana in the East, this gas-station restaurant had a fun

makeover in 2018 and now has a retro 1950s feel, complete with leather booths, jukebox, milkshakes, pancake breakfasts, and southern fried chicken. You can still get Icelandic staples (hot dog, lamb chops, fish stew), and food is served until 11pm.

★**Eldhúsið** ICELANDIC €€€
(☎471 1114; www.lakehotel.is; Egilsstöðum 1-2; lunch 1490-3990kr, dinner mains 3390-64390kr; ⊙11.30am-10pm; 📶☎) Some of the east's most creative cooking happens at the restaurant inside Gistihúsið – Lake Hotel Egilsstaðir. The menu is an ode to locally sourced produce (lamb, fish and game), and the speciality is the beef, raised right here on the farm. Try a rib-eye with Béarnaise, or fjord-fresh fish with grape salad and dill mayonnaise. Desserts are pretty, polished affairs. Bookings advised.

Self-Catering

Nettó SUPERMARKET
(⊙9am-8pm) Behind the N1 petrol station.

Bónus SUPERMARKET
(⊙11am-6.30pm Mon-Thu, 10am-7.30pm Fri, 10am-6pm Sat, noon-6pm Sun) On the Ring Road north of the N1.

Vínbúðin ALCOHOL
(Miðvangur 2-4; ⊙11am-6pm Mon-Thu, to 7pm Fri, to 4pm Sat) Government-run liquor store.

Information

East Iceland Regional Information Centre
(☎471 2320; www.east.is; Miðvangur 1-3; ⊙8.30am-6pm Mon-Fri, 10am-4pm Sat, 1-6pm Sun Jun-Aug, shorter hours Sep-May; 📶) Maps and brochures are plentiful here – you'll find everything you need to explore the eastern region. It shares the space with an excellent art and design store.

Egilsstaðastofa Visitor Center (☎470 0750; www.visitegilsstadir.is; Kaupvangur 17; ⊙7am-11pm Jun-Aug, 8am-3pm Mon-Fri May & Sep, 8am-noon Mon-Fri Oct-Apr; 📶) From its info desk at the campground reception, this place focuses on Egilsstaðir and surrounds and can hook you up with bus tickets and various activity tours: hiking, super-Jeep tours, sea-angling etc. Bike hire is available (2000kr for up to four hours, 3000kr for 24 hours).

Getting There & Away

Egilsstaðir is the transport hub of East Iceland. There's an airport, and most bus services (p329) pass through or originate here. The main **bus stop** is at the campground.

Lagarfljót

The grey-brown waters of the river-lake Lagarfljót are reputed to harbour a fearsome monster, **Lagarfljótsormur**, which has allegedly been spotted since Viking times. The most recent 'sighting' of the serpentine beast (also called the Worm/Wyrm) caused quite a stir – in 2012 a local farmer released footage of a large creature moving in the river. The clip has attracted more than five million hits on YouTube, and garnered international news coverage. Read more at www.lagarfljotsormur.com.

Real or imagined, the poor beast must be pretty chilly – Lagarfljót starts its journey in the Vatnajökull ice cap and its glacial waters flow north to the Arctic Ocean, widening into a 38km-long, 50m-deep lake, often called Lögurinn, south of Egilsstaðir. Whether you see a monster or not, it's a lovely stretch of water to circumnavigate by car.

Rte 931, a mixture of sealed surfaces and gravel (gravel on the less-trafficked western shore), turns off Rte 95 about 10km south of Egilsstaðir and runs around the lake to Fellabær – a circuit of around 70km. This is an area you need your own wheels to explore.

There's useful information about the area at www.hengifoss.is.

Hallormsstaðaskógur

One of Iceland's largest forests, 740-hectare Hallormsstaðaskógur (www.skogur.is) is king of the woods and venerated by the arboreally challenged nation. Although it's small by most countries' standards, it's a leafy reprieve after the stark, bare mountainsides to the north and south of Egilsstaðir. Common species include native dwarf birch and mountain ash, as well as 85 tree species gathered from around the world.

The forest (pronounced roughly 'hatlorm-statha-skoh-er') is a popular recreation area, with marked trails and footpaths. Pick up a free hiking map around the area, or at visitor centres in Egilsstaðir.

Tours

East Highlanders ADVENTURE
(☎852 5450; www.easthighlanders.is; 1hr tour from 17,000kr) East Highlanders offers fun summertime 4WD quad-bike tours through Hallormsstaðaskógur – cross streams and get a little muddy while taking in the sights

DON'T MISS

WILDERNESS CENTER

The brilliant **Wilderness Center** (Óbyggðasetur Íslands; ☎440 8822; www.wilderness.is; museum adult/child 2500kr/free) opened in 2016 and defies easy classification. It's a remote farm that offers museum exhibits, unique accommodation, local food, horse riding and hiking trails, and the opportunity for tailor-made tours, all year-round. It's 12km past Skriðuklaustur on Rte 934, at the end of Norðudalur valley, on the edge of the eastern highlands. The historic exhibits here were designed by the farm's owners (a filmmaker and historian) so are of superb quality – as is the entire farm concept.

Accommodation is offered in simple farmhouse rooms with shared bathroom (double 18,600kr) or – more intriguingly – in a dormitory room styled as a *baðstofa*, the traditional living/sleeping room on old Icelandic farms (bed for two 14,100kr to 15,100kr). Food is available all day (mid-May to September). There are new hot-pots, and a glorious Northern Lights–viewing hut for winter. Guided tours range from three-hour horse rides (15,000kr) to exploration of an abandoned nearby farm (8500kr). You can rent a mountain bike, or join a super-Jeep tour. Multiday activities are also possible; see the website for information.

If you're staying, give yourself a couple of nights here, and consider walking the **Waterfall Trail**, an easy six-hour riverside hike (one-way transfer possible) to Laugarfell.

and history of the forest. Tours range from one to three hours; a driver's licence is required for drivers, but two people can ride on one vehicle. Super-Jeep tours are also available.

Sleeping

Bring a picnic to enjoy at one of the picnic sites in the forest or beside the lake, or stop for a meal at Hótel Hallormsstaður.

Atlavík Campsite CAMPGROUND €
(sites per person 1500kr; ⊙mid-May–Sep) In a wooded cove on the lakeshore, idyllic Atlavík is a popular campsite, often the scene of summer weekend parties. In July, pedal boats, rowing boats and canoes can be hired for watery pursuits.

Höfðavík Campsite CAMPGROUND €
(sites per person 1500kr; ⊙mid-May–Sep) A second campsite on the lakeshore small and quiet Höfðavík is just north of the petrol station. Powered sites available.

Hótel Hallormsstaður HOTEL €€
(☎471 2400; www.hotel701.is; hotel d from 31,600kr, guesthouse s/d without bathroom 16,900/22,700kr, all incl breakfast; 📶) A campus of buildings among the trees, this bucolic country retreat offers modern hotel rooms, cottages and the small Grái Hundurinn guesthouse, plus two restaurants (a renowned dinner buffet and an Indian restaurant), spa and inviting outdoor area. There are nearby forest walks, mountain bikes for rent, and tours can be arranged.

Hengifoss

★Hengifoss WATERFALL
Crossing the bridge across Lagarfljót on Rte 931, you'll reach the parking area for lovely Hengifoss, Iceland's second-highest waterfall. The falls plummet 128m into a photogenic brown-and-red-striped boulder-strewn gorge.

Getting to Hengifoss requires a return walk of one to two hours (2.5km each way). From the car park, a staircase and path lead up the hillside – Hengifoss is soon visible in the distance. It's a steep climb in places but flattens out as you enter the canyon.

Halfway to Hengifoss is a noteworthy smaller waterfall, **Litlanesfoss**, surrounded by vertical basalt columns in a honeycomb formation.

Skriðuklaustur

Head south from Hengifoss waterfall for 5km to reach historic Skriðuklaustur (pronounced roughly 'skri-the-cloister'), where you can investigate medieval and 20th-century history, plus indulge in excellent local produce. Neighbouring the cultural centre at Skriðuklaustur is the worthwhile visitor centre for the eastern territory of Vatnajökull National Park.

Skriðuklaustur MUSEUM
(☎471 2990; www.skriduklaustur.is; adult/child 1100kr/free; ⊙10am-6pm Jun-Aug, 11am-5pm May & Sep, noon-4pm Apr & Oct) Skriðuklaustur is the site of both an excavated, late-15th-

century monastery and the photogenic home of an Icelandic author feted by the Third Reich. The unusual black-and-white turf-roofed building was built in 1939 by Gunnar Gunnarsson (1889–1975), and now holds a cultural centre dedicated to him. This prolific writer achieved phenomenal popularity in Denmark and Germany – at the height of his fame only Goethe outsold him.

Snæfellsstofa – National Park Visitor Centre TOURIST INFORMATION
(☎ 470 0840; www.vjp.is; ⏲ 9am-5pm Jun-Aug, 10am-3pm May & Sep) FREE This stylish centre covers the eastern territory of the behemoth that is Vatnajökull National Park. Excellent displays highlight the nature of Snæfell mountain and the eastern highlands, and staff sell maps and offer advice to travellers wishing to hike or otherwise experience the park.

★ Klausturkaffi CAFE €€
(☎ 471 2990; www.skriduklaustur.is; lunch buffet adult/child 3490/1745kr; ⏲ 10am-6pm Jun-Aug, 11am-5pm May & Sep, noon-4pm Apr & Oct) Klausturkaffi, inside Skriðuklaustur, serves an impeccable lunch buffet showcasing local ingredients (seafood soup, reindeer pie, brambleberry *skyr* cake). Perhaps more tantalising, however, is every sweet-tooth's dream: the brilliant all-you-can-eat cake buffet (adult/child 2290/1145kr), served from 3pm. Kids welcome. Note that you don't have to pay to enter Skriðuklaustur if you are only visiting the cafe.

Eastern Highlands

The Snæfell peak (at 1833m, Iceland's highest outside the Vatnajökull massif) looms over the southern end of Fljótsdalsheiði, an expanse of wet tundra, boulder fields, perennial snow patches and alpine lakes, stretching westwards from Lagarfljót into the highlands.

Work on the controversial Kárahnjúkar dam and Fljótsdalur hydroelectric power plant brought improved roads around Snæfell, with the paved Rte 910 from Fljótsdalur being the best way up. Along Rte 910, watch for wild reindeer, and bring your swimsuit to stop at the hot springs of Laugarfell. If you want to tour the area with someone else behind the wheel, check offerings from companies such as Egilsstaðir-based Jeep Tours (p332).

The Rte 910 turn-off is just north of Skriðuklaustur (on Rte 934), and the road climbs *fast* but then levels out; it's suitable for 2WDs in summer. Note the road is often closed in winter. No public transport travels here, but a few tours do (largely from Egilsstaðir).

To travel south beyond the Kárahnjúkar-dam viewpoint (to Askja or Kverkfjöll, for example), a large, high-clearance 4WD is required, and a GPS – this area is well off the beaten path.

Kárahnjúkar Dam VIEWPOINT
A scenic 60km drive from the Rte 910 turn-off takes you to the Kárahnjúkar dam and Hálslón reservoir, where information boards and viewing areas allow you to appreciate this vast feat of engineering, as well as observe the incredible **Hafrahvammagljúfur canyon**, below the dam.

Aðalból HISTORIC SITE
Rte F923 (off Rte 910, for 4WDs only) leads you to the valley of **Hrafnkelsdalur**, full of sites relating to Hrafnkell's Saga, which tells of struggles between chieftains and farmers in the east of Iceland in the 10th century. The remote farm Aðalból was the home of the saga's hero, Hrafnkell Freysgoði, and his burial mound is here. There's a marked saga trail, threading together places mentioned in the story. There's a **guesthouse** (☎ 471 2788; www.samurbondi.com; Aðalból II; sites per person 1800kr, s/d without bathroom incl breakfast 10,600/19,900kr; ⏲ Jul & Aug) and campground here.

You can also access Aðalból from the Ring Road – it's 43km on unsealed Rte 923 (which becomes an F road south of the farm, where there is a river to ford).

★ Laugarfell GUESTHOUSE, CAMPGROUND €€
(☎ 773 3323; www.laugarfell.is; d/f without bathroom 17,000/30,000kr; ⏲ Jun-Sep; 👪) Laugarfell is 2km off Rte 910 (OK for 2WD cars) and beckons with **hot springs** (adult/child 1500/500kr) and a cosy guesthouse. Formerly a hostel, the place has moved more upmarket with twin and family rooms (sleeping up to six) and all linen supplied. Note: there's no kitchen, but breakfast (1900kr) and dinner (3500kr) are available, and daytime sandwiches and cakes offered.

Snæfell

No one seems to know whether 1833m-high Snæfell (pronounced snye-fetl) is an extinct volcano, or if it's just having a rest. Iceland's highest peak outside the Vatnajökull massif is relatively accessible, making it popular with hikers and mountaineers.

Snæfell is part of the vast Vatnajökull National Park; the park website www.vjp.is has useful information, and the national-park visitor centre, Snæfellsstofa (p337), has info, maps and displays, plus staff ready to answer questions and give guidance.

A 4WD is required to travel Rte F909 (off Rte 910) to reach Snæfell mountain hut at the base of the Snæfell peak. It's 12km from Rte 910 to the hut.

No public transport serves the area.

Bring all of your own supplies – the closest supermarket is in Egilsstaðir.

Activities

Although climbing the mountain itself is not difficult for experienced, well-prepared hikers, the weather can be a concern and crampons are advisable. Ascending from the west is most common – it's a hike of six to nine hours, depending on ice conditions. Discuss your route with the hut warden.

One of Iceland's most challenging and rewarding hikes takes you from Snæfell to the Lónsöræfi district in Southeast Iceland. The three- to five-day, 45km route begins at the Snæfell hut and heads across the glacier Eyjabakkajökull (an arm of Vatnajökull) to Geldingafell, Egilssel and Múlaskáli huts before dropping down to the coast at Stafafell.

This route should not be approached lightly – it's for experienced trekkers only. You'll need a GPS and, for the glacier crossing, you must be skilled at using a rope, crampons and an ice axe. If you're unsure of your skills, you'd be wiser doing the trip commercially with the likes of **Icelandic Mountain Guides** (IMG; ☎587 9999; www.mountainguides.is) – although IMG's four-day, 50km backpacking tour through Lónsöræfi (139,900kr), called 'In the Shadow of Vatnajökull', begins at Eyjabakkar wetlands east of Snæfell and avoids the glacier traverse.

Snæfell Mountain Hut HUT €

(Snæfellsskáli; ☎842 4367; snaefellsstofa@vjp.is; N 64°48.223', W 15°38.479'; sites/dm per person 1700/6500kr) The Snæfell mountain hut is run by the national park and can accommodate up to 45 people. It has a kitchen, a camping area and showers. A 4WD is required to reach it. Rangers are based here in summer.

THE EASTFJORDS

The fjords are the true highlight of East Iceland. Despite (mostly) good surfaced roads and the Alcoa-related activity, the Eastfjords still seem remote – a feeling enhanced by immense, dramatic mountainsides and the tiny working fishing villages that nestle under them.

There are some superb hiking trails, you can kayak to far-off headlands, and thousands of seabirds nest along the cliffs. In a Finest Fjord competition it would be hard to pick a winner: Borgarfjörður has ethereal rhyolite cliffs and well-organised hiking; Seyðisfjörður fosters a cheery bohemian vibe; Mjóifjörður is riddled with waterfalls; and Neskaupstaður has regular whale visi-

OFF THE BEATEN TRACK

HIKING IN DYRFJÖLL

One of Iceland's most dramatic ranges, the Dyrfjöll mountains rise precipitously to an altitude of 1136m between the marshy Héraðssandur plains and Borgarfjörður Eystri. The name Dyrfjöll means 'Door Mountain' and is due to the large and conspicuous notch in the highest peak – an Icelandic counterpart to Sweden's famous Lapporten.

There are walking tracks crossing the range, which allow for plentiful day hikes from Borgarfjörður Eystri. The prime drawcard in the range is the boulder-strewn oasis known as **Stórurð**.

To plan your hikes, pick up the *Borgarfjörður Eystri & Víknaslóðir Hiking Map – Trails of the Deserted Inlets* (1000kr), or contact Travel East Iceland (p339) in Borgarfjörður Eystri (based out of Álfheimar (p340)) if you're looking for a guide or possible transfers to trailheads.

There are companies that can arrange guided day hikes of Dyrfjöll mountain and Stórurð from Egilsstaðir, including Wild Boys (p332).

Trail access is from points along Rte 94 en route to Borgarfjörður Eystri, or from the village of Borgarfjörður Eystri itself.

tors to its fjord. You'll just have to visit and choose your own favourite.

Stand by too for possible development in some of the smaller towns, with the recent rerouting of the Ring Road to take in Reyðarfjörður, Fáskrúðsfjörður and Stöðvarfjörður.

Borgarfjörður Eystri

POP 110

This wee hamlet (pronounced 'borgar-fjur-ther esstri') sits in a stunning location, framed by a backdrop of rugged rhyolite peaks on one side and the spectacular Dyrfjöll mountains on the other; the hiking in the area is outstanding. There's very little in the village itself (which is less commonly known as Bakkagerði), although driftwood sculptures, hidden elves and crying seabirds exude a magical charm. As a bonus, this is one of Iceland's most accessible places for up-close viewing of nesting puffins.

For local information, check out www.borgarfjordureystri.is.

Sights

★Hafnarhólmi ISLAND

(www.puffins.is) Five kilometres past the wee church is the photogenic small-boat harbour and islet of Hafnarhólmi, home to a large **puffin colony**. A staircase and viewing platforms allow you to get close to these cute, clumsy creatures (and other seabirds). The puffins arrive by mid-April and are gone by early to mid-August, but other species (including kittiwakes, fulmars and common eiders) may linger longer.

Bakkagerðiskirkja CHURCH

Jóhannes Sveinsson Kjarval (1885–1972), Iceland's best-known artist, was brought up nearby and took much of his inspiration from Borgarfjörður Eystri and surrounds. His unusual altarpiece in this small church depicts the Sermon on the Mount and is directly aimed at this village: Jesus is preaching from Álfaborg, with the mountain Dyrfjöll in the background.

Álfaborg NATURE RESERVE

Álfaborg (Elf Rock), the small mound and nature reserve near the campsite (p340), is the 'borg' that gave Borgarfjörður Eystri its name. Some locals believe that the queen of Icelandic elves lives here. From the top of the rock there's a fabulous vista of the surrounding fields.

WORTH A TRIP

HÚSEY

Reaching **Húsey Horse Farm** (☎471 3010; www.husey.de; 2/4hr tour 9000/19,365kr) involves a long but scenic drive, 30km off the Ring Road along the rough, unsealed Rtes 925 and 926 beside the Jökulsá á Brú river (all up, about 60km from Egilsstaðir). Venture out to this isolated farm for seafront birdwatching trails and seals cavorting in the riverine backdrop. Húsey (pronounced hoo-say) has a unique offering: seal-watching on horseback. Two-hour rides (9000kr) leave daily at 10am and 5pm; bookings are required. It's worth staying a few days to enjoy the natural surrounds and the homey atmosphere of the cosy, no-frills **Húsey HI Hostel** (☎471 3010; www.husey.de; dm/d without bathroom 4000/8500kr; ⊙mid-Mar–mid-Nov; 📶👪). Linen is available (1300kr) but you will need to bring other supplies – the closest supermarket is in Egilsstaðir.

Lindarbakki HOUSE

You can't miss the village's hairiest and most photogenic house: bright-red Lindarbakki (1899) is completely cocooned by whiskery green grass, with only a few windows and a giant pair of antlers sticking out. It's a private home (not open to the public); an information board outside outlines its history.

Activities

There are loads of well-marked trails criss-crossing the area around Borgarfjörður – everything from easy one-hour strolls to serious mountain hiking. For a full array, get your hands on the *Borgarfjörður Eystri & Víknaslóðir Hiking Map – Trails of the Deserted Inlets* (1000kr). It's sold at most places in town, and also in Egilsstaðir visitor centres.

A good source of hiking information is the website of the Touring Club of Fljótsdalshérað (www.ferdaf.is). It has a summer program of walks and welcomes participants.

If you prefer to plan guided day or multiday hikes, there are a few options; most companies can help with transfers from Egilsstaðir. Contact **Travel East Iceland** (☎471 3060; www.traveleast.is), Borg Guesthouse (p340) or Wild Boys (p332).

Musterið Spa SPA

(The Temple; 861 1792; www.blabjorg.com; adult/child 3000/1000kr; 3-10pm or by appointment) Underneath Blábjörg Guesthouse and enjoying supreme views, this spa features both indoor and outdoor hot tubs and saunas (the brave can take a dip in the sea). It's perfect for a post-hike soak. Note: admission is free for people staying at Blábjörg.

Festivals & Events

Bræðslan MUSIC

(www.braedslan.is; late Jul) Held in an old herring plant over a weekend in late July, Bræðslan is one of Iceland's best summer concert festivals, earning itself a reputation for great music as well as its intimate atmosphere. Some big local names (and a few international ones) come to play.

Sleeping

Borg Guesthouse GUESTHOUSE €

(894 4470, 472 9870; gistingborg@simnet.is; s/d/tr without bathroom 11,000/18,000/23,000kr;) Borg is a solid bet for a budget bed. Rooms are OK if old-fashioned, with cooking and lounge facilities; breakfast costs 1250kr. Cheaper sleeping-bag options are better value (eg a double room excluding linen is 14,000kr). Hiking, guiding and luggage transfers can be arranged.

Campsite CAMPGROUND €

(sites per person 1200kr; mid-May–mid-Oct) This popular, well-kept site has free kitchen access, plus washing machine and showers.

★ **Blábjörg Guesthouse** GUESTHOUSE €€

(861 1792; www.blabjorg.com; s/d without bathroom incl breakfast from 12,500/16,200kr;) In a cleverly converted fish factory, this well-run, year-round guesthouse houses 11 pristine white rooms (you'll pay a little extra for a sea view), plus guest kitchen and small lounge area. There is also a handful of excellent studio and family-sized apartments (from 38,600kr). The standout features are the downstairs spa, Musterið which is free for guests, and the new cafe-bar.

Álfheimar HOTEL €€

(471 2010; www.alfheimar.com; s/d/f incl breakfast 22,200/28,900/40,800kr; Apr-Oct;) Álfheimar has 32 motel-style units in long annexes (the only rooms in town with private bathrooms!). The timber-lined rooms have more atmosphere than the newer building, but all are spotless and well equipped. The affable owners are a font of local knowledge – they are part of Travel East Iceland (p339); hiking tours and packages can be arranged.

There's a **restaurant** (two/three courses 4800/6200kr; open 7pm to 9pm) open to all and offering the dish of the day from the fjord's fishers and farmers.

PIT STOP!

Halfway between Egilsstaðir and Borgarfjörður on Rte 94 sits one of East Iceland's quirkier roadside wonders: a pea-green-coloured hut surrounded by miles of nothingness. Built by a local eccentric, the structure is simply a hut to house a solar-powered refrigerated vending machine. If the power is off, flick the 'on' switch (we're not kidding) and wait two minutes (you can sign the guestbook while waiting). Then, voila: a refreshingly cold beverage or snack. Note: Icelandic coins required.

Eating

Village Store SUPERMARKET €

The small supermarket by Fjarðarborg (the community centre) closed in 2017, but at the time of research the locals were banding together to create a much-needed village store. It's great to support it if you can. It's worth checking with your accommodation before you arrive to find out if the store has opened and what hours it keeps.

Frystiklefinn INTERNATIONAL €€

(846 0085; www.blabjorg.com; mains 1690-3200kr; noon-10pm May-Sep, shorter hours winter;) At Blábjörg Guesthouse, this stylish, airy space is an inviting cafe-bar, with a small but pleasing menu that runs from traditional Icelandic *plokkfiskur* (fish stew) to chicken burgers, supplemented by daily specials and appealing desserts. If you're visiting Borgarfjörður Eystri in winter, it's worth enquiring about the opening hours here, as this is likely your only dining option.

Já Sæll Fjarðarborg ICELANDIC €€

(472 9920; meals 1500-3700kr; 11.30am-midnight Jun-Aug;) The menu is simple and the decor uninspiring at this option inside Fjarðarborg (the community centre), but it's well worth a visit for its bumper burgers or lamb chops, and a beer among the locals. Ask about the weekly live music held in summer.

BORGARFJÖRÐUR TO SEYÐISFJÖRÐUR HIKE

Wildly wonderful and unexplored, the rugged country between Borgarfjörður and Seyðisfjörður makes for one of the best multi-day hikes in the region.

To plan your journey, pick up a copy of the *Borgarfjörður Eystri & Víknaslóðir Hiking Map – Trails of the Deserted Inlets* (1000kr), and contact Travel East Iceland (p339) or Wild Boys (p332) if you're looking for a guide. For hiker huts along this route, see www.ferdaf.is.

In summer, Icelandic Mountain Guides (www.mountainguides.is) offers both a guided and a self-guided six-day package of this walk (called 'Hiking at the End of the World') and they arrange transfers and hut bookings etc.

Day 1 Start at Kolbeinsfjara, 4km outside the township of Borgarfjörður Eystri, and venture up into the mountains along the Brúnavíkurskarð pass (trail #19 on the map). Turn south (along trail #21) at the emergency hut in Brúnavík, passing beautiful Kerlingarfjall further on. After your five- to six-hour hike (12.5km), settle in for the night at the outfitted farmhouse/campsite in Breiðavík.

Day 2 Next day features another stunning five hours of hiking (13.5km along trail #30). You'll first walk through the grassy leas below Hvítafjall, then link up with the 4WD track heading south to the Húsavík lodge, where you'll spend the second night. The land between Breiðavík and Húsavík is infested with hidden people – the elf sheriff lives at Sólarfjall and the elf bishop lives at Blábjörg further south along the coast.

Day 3 Another 14km of trails are tackled in five hours of hiking (along trail #37) as the path reunites with the sea at silent Loðmundarfjörður. The 4WD track ends at the Klyppstaður lodge on the Norðdalsá river delta at the uppermost point of the fjord.

Day 4 The last day links Loðmundarfjörður to Seyðisfjörður over 12km (trail #41). At the highest point of the mountain pass you'll find a logbook signed by previous hikers. As you venture down into Seyðisfjörður, you'll be treated to a watery fanfare of gushing chutes.

Getting There & Away

The village is 70km from Egilsstaðir along Rte 94, about half of which is sealed (accessible by 2WD in summer). It winds steeply up over the Dyrfjöll mountains before dropping down to the coast.

There's a petrol pump close to the entry to the village. A year-round weekday **bus service** (☎ 894 8305; www.svaust.is; 1800kr, one hour) operates between the Fjarðarborg community centre (departs 8am) and Egilsstaðir (departs from the Egilsstaðir campground at noon).

Seyðisfjörður

POP 650

If you visit only one town in the Eastfjords, this should be it. Made up of multicoloured wooden houses and surrounded by snowcapped mountains and cascading waterfalls, super-picturesque Seyðisfjörður (pronounced 'say-this-fjurther') is the most historically and architecturally interesting town in East Iceland. It's also a friendly place with an international community of artists, musicians, craftspeople and students.

If the weather's good, the scenic Rte 93 drive from Egilsstaðir is a delight, climbing to a high pass then descending along the waterfall-filled river Fjarðará.

Summer is the liveliest time to visit, particularly when Smyril Line's ferry sails majestically up the 17km-long fjord to town – a perfect way to arrive in Iceland. Note: you may wish to avoid Seyðisfjörður on Wednesday nights in summer, as the ferry to Europe sails on Thursday mornings and accommodation and meals in town are in hot demand. If you are taking the ferry, book accommodation well ahead.

History

Seyðisfjörður started as a trading centre in 1848, but its later wealth came from the 'silver of the sea' – herring. Its long, sheltering fjord gave it an advantage over other fishing villages, and it grew into the largest and most prosperous town in East Iceland. Most of the unique wooden buildings here were built by Norwegian merchants, attracted by the herring industry.

During WWII Seyðisfjörður was a base for British and American forces. The only attack was on an oil tanker (the *El Grillo*) that was bombed by three German warplanes. The bombs missed their target, but one exploded so near that the ship sank to the bottom of the fjord, where it remains today (a good dive spot).

Seyðisfjörður

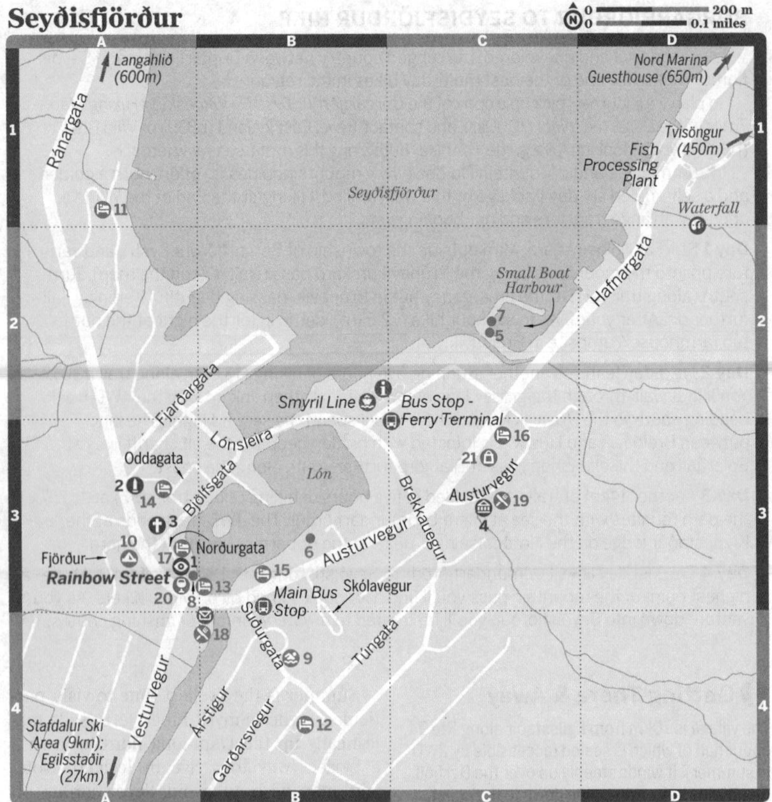

Seyðisfjörður

Top Sights
1 Rainbow Street ... A3

Sights
2 Avalanche Monument ... A3
3 Bláa Kirkjan ... A3
4 Skaftfell – Center for Visual Art ... C3

Activities, Courses & Tours
5 Austursigling ... C2
6 Hlynur Oddsson ... B3
7 Sea Fishing Seyðisfjörður ... C2
8 Seyðisfjörður Tours ... A3
9 Sundhöll Seyðisfjarðar ... B4

Sleeping
10 Campsite ... A3
11 Hafaldan Harbour Hostel ... A1
12 Hafaldan Old Hospital Hostel ... B4
13 Hótel Aldan ... B3
14 Hótel Aldan (Old Bank) ... A3
15 Hótel Aldan (Snæfell) ... B3
16 Post-Hostel ... C3
17 Við Lónið ... A3

Eating
18 Kjörbúðin ... B4
Norð Austur Sushi & Bar ... (see 13)
Nordic Restaurant ... (see 13)
19 Skaftfell Bistro ... C3

Drinking & Nightlife
20 Kaffi Lára – El Grilló Bar ... A3

Entertainment
Blue Church Summer Concerts ... (see 3)

Shopping
21 Vínbúðin ... C3

Seyðisfjörður's steep-sided valley has made it prone to avalanches. In 1885 an avalanche from Bjólfur killed 24 people and pushed several houses straight into the fjord. A more recent avalanche in 1996 flattened a local factory, but no lives were lost.

Sights

Seyðisfjörður is stuffed with 19th-century timber buildings, brought in kit form from Norway; several of these have been transformed into cosy ateliers where local artisans work on various projects. A quick loop around town will reveal half a dozen places to drop some krónur, on art, handicrafts, knitwear and designer homewares.

★ Rainbow Street STREET

(Norðurgata) This street is supremely photogenic: a rainbow is painted on the pavement, and the Blue Church serves as a sweet backdrop. It features in many advertising campaigns and is a popular tourist photo opp.

Bláa Kirkjan CHURCH

(Blue Church; www.blaakirkjan.is; Bjólfsgata 10) The star of many a tourist photo, the Blue Church has a dramatic mountain backdrop to add to its highly photogenic exterior. It's often locked, but opens for weekly summer concerts (p345).

Tvisöngur LANDMARK

A favourite walk takes explorers from a parking area south of Tækniminjasafn Austurlands about 15 or 20 minutes uphill to the 'sound sculpture' Tvísöngur, a concrete installation created by German artist Lukas Kühne. The piece comprises five interconnected domes of different sizes, and each is designed to resonate at a different harmony.

Avalanche Monument MONUMENT

(Ránargata) The monument near the church dates from the 1996 avalanche, and is made from twisted girders from the factory demolished by the event. The girders were painted white and erected as they were found.

Skaftfell – Center for Visual Art GALLERY

(472 1632; www.skaftfell.is; Austurvegur 42; noon-6pm Jun-Aug, hrs vary Sep-May) It's well worth a look in this gallery space above the Skaftfell Bistro (p345). Skaftfell is a visual art centre with a focus on contemporary art, and it stages exhibitions and events, hosts workshops, and facilitates artist residencies. See the website for more.

Activities

Short walking trails lead from the museum area uphill to waterfalls, and to the 'sound sculpture' **Tvísöngur** – five interconnected concrete domes. Another short walk leads from the road on the north shore of the fjord (about 6km beyond the Bláa Kirkjan) to the signposted **Dvergasteinn** (Dwarf Rock) – according to folklore, this is a dwarf church that followed the people's church across the fjord.

The hills above Seyðisfjörður are the perfect spot for longer hiking. **Vestdalur** is a grassy valley north of town renowned for its glorious waterfalls. The hike begins just before the Langahlið cottages. Following the Vestdalsá river, after two to three scenic hours you'll arrive at a small lake, **Vestdalsvatn**, which remains frozen most of the year (it's generally covered by snow until July).

Trails are marked on the widely available *Borgarfjörður Eystri & Víknaslóðir Hiking Map – Trails of the Deserted Inlets* map (1000kr), and the www.visitseydisfjordur.com website outlines some options, including the Seven Peaks Hike (trails climbing seven of the 1000m-plus peaks surrounding the town).

Stafdalur Ski Area SKIING

(www.stafdalur.is; 5-8pm Tue-Fri, 11am-4pm Sat, 10am-4pm Sun Dec-May) From about December to May there's downhill and cross-country skiing (and gear rental) at Stafdalur, 9km from Seyðisfjörður on the road to Egilsstaðir. Opening hours depend on the day's weather, with weekends being especially popular. Contact the tourist office (p345) for more details.

Sundhöll Seyðisfjarðar SWIMMING

(Suðurgata 5; adult/child 950/300kr; 7-11am & 3-8pm Mon-Fri, 1-4pm Sat Jun-Aug, shorter hours Sep-May) Seyðisfjörður's indoor pool has a sauna and hot-pots.

Tours

Seyðisfjörður Tours TOURS

(785 4737; www.seydisfjordurtours.com; Norðurgata 6; Jun-mid-Sep) From a central base, this friendly outfit offers bike rental and guided walking and hiking tours of the town and surrounds (varying lengths; 75 minutes 'Stories of Seyðisfjörður' is 4500kr; a two-hour easy scenic hike is 6000kr). Tailored biking and boating can be arranged.

Hlynur Oddsson KAYAKING

(865 3741; hlynur@hotmail.de; Austurvegur 15b; Jun-Aug) For a sublime outdoor experience,

contact Hlynur, a charming Robert Redford–esque character who spends his summers around town and offers tailor-made tours. Options on the fjord range from one to six hours, visiting a shipwreck or waterfalls (one/three hours 4000/8000kr). Experienced kayakers can choose longer trips (full day 25,000kr, minimum two people).

Sea Fishing Seyðisfjörður BOAT, FISHING
(785 4737; www.seydisfjordurtours.com; 1hr 30,000kr; Jun-Aug, plus Sep by request) From the small boat harbour, experienced fisherman Halli can take up to seven people in his boat, for fishing and/or guided sightseeing around the fjord. Great options include a spin to neighbouring Loðmundarfjörður. There's a one-hour minimum, but two hours gets you more options and time for fishing. Bookings are handled by Seyðisfjörður Tours (p343). Bonus: your fishing catch can be cooked by Nordic Restaurant.

Austursigling BOATING
(899 2409; www.austursigling.is) From the docks off Austurvegur, Beggi takes passengers out on his 12-passenger boat. Standard tours are three hours (but shorter or longer trips can easily be arranged), and can take in sea angling, birdwatching, sunset, or Northern Lights hunting in winter. Contact Beggi to make arrangements – the price varies with numbers and trip duration (minimum is 15,000kr per hour for a small group).

Sleeping

Accommodation in town is of a high standard. Book well ahead for Wednesday nights in summer (the ferry to continental Europe leaves on Thursday mornings).

★Hafaldan Old Hospital Hostel HOSTEL €
(611 4410; www.halfadan.is; Suðurgata 8; dm 5400kr, d with/without bathroom 16,300/14,700kr; Apr–mid-Sep;) Seyðisfjörður's first-class HI budget digs are housed in two locations: the Harbour Hostel is a little out of town, and this is the more central option (and the reception for both venues). The Old Hospital houses dorms, a handful of en-suite rooms, a basement 'spa' (great bathrooms and sauna), and a beautiful kitchen-dining facility. Linen is included in prices.

Hafaldan Harbour Hostel HOSTEL €
(611 4410; www.hafaldan.is; Ránargata 9; dm/d/q without bathroom 5400/12,930/23,100kr; Apr-Oct;) Cosy, view-enriched dining and lounge areas are the standout feature of Harbour Hostel, found a little out of town past the Bláa Kirkjan (p343). The thin-walled rooms are small and unremarkable but pleasant, and all share bathrooms. Linen is included in prices.

Campsite CAMPGROUND €
(Ránargata 5; campsites per person 1600kr; May-Sep;) There are two areas for camping – one sheltered, grassy site for tents opposite the Bláa Kirkjan (p343), and another nearby area for vans. The service building houses kitchen, showers and laundry facilities.

★Hótel Aldan HOTEL €€
(472 1277; www.hotelaldan.com; Norðurgata 2;) This wonderful hotel is shared across three old wooden buildings: reception and a bar-restaurant (where breakfast is served) are at the Norðurgata location. Guest rooms are in two other buildings: Snæfell and the Old Bank. Ask about the hotel's central apartments (from 35,000kr), with full kitchens, washing machines, lots of space (two and three bedrooms) and some fun retro styling.

➡ Hótel Aldan (Snæfell) HOTEL €€
(472 1277; www.hotelaldan.com; Austurvegur 3; s/d incl breakfast from 14,300/18,000kr;) Snæfell is a creaky, characterful three-storey place with the cheapest rooms, fresh white paintwork and Indian bedspreads. The ground-floor has family suites (from 32,000kr).

➡ Hótel Aldan (Old Bank) HOTEL €€€
(472 1277; www.hotelaldan.com; Oddagata 6; d incl breakfast from 33,900kr;) The Old Bank building of Hótel Aldan houses a boutique guesthouse with antique furnishings and a refined air.

Við Lónið GUESTHOUSE €€
(899 9429; http://vidlonidguesthouse.com; Norðurgata 8; r from 24,000kr;) A 21st-century makeover has transformed a 1907 kit home into a black-clad, eight-room beauty in the heart of the village. 'By the Lagoon' is a new boutique guesthouse that's decorated with Nordic minimalist flair. The top choices have lagoon view and balcony.

Nord Marina Guesthouse GUESTHOUSE €€
(787 0701; nordmarina1@gmail.com; Strandarvegur 21; d with/without bathroom 16,800/11,600kr; Apr-Oct;) Two kilometres northeast of the supermarket, this unassuming guesthouse enjoys splendid views from its waterfront position and is home to 13 good-value rooms spread over two buildings; there's kitchen access and a comfy lounge area. It

also has two apartments (one sleeps up to seven people for 37,300kr).

Post-Hostel GUESTHOUSE €€
(☎898 6242; info@posthostel.com; Hafnargata 4; d with/without bathroom from 19,100/16,600kr;) The name is a little misleading – this high-quality 11-room guesthouse (in yet another old post office) has fresh, renovated rooms, including some family-friendly ones (with bunks for kids), plus smart kitchen and laundry facilities.

★**Langahlið** COTTAGES €€€
(☎897 1524; www.langahlid.com; cottages sleeping 4/6 from 32,300/37,400kr;) Book *very* early for these three-bedroom cottages, sleeping up to six in a whole lot of comfort, including a kitchen, lounge, and barbecue and hot-pot on the deck enjoying astounding views. They're about 2km north of Hótel Aldan. The friendly Italian owners will take care of you; do yourself a favour and book two nights.

Eating & Drinking

Kjörbúðin SUPERMARKET €
(Vesturvegur 1; ⊙9am-7pm Mon-Fri, 10am-6pm Sat, noon-6pm Sun) For self-caterers. ATM out the front.

★**Norð Austur Sushi & Bar** SUSHI €€
(☎787 4000; www.nordaustur.is; 2nd fl, Norðurgata 2; small dishes 690-2190kr, maki rolls 2190-2690kr; ⊙5-10pm Sun-Thu, to 11pm Fri & Sat Jun-early Sep) Locals rave about this place – and with good reason: the salmon, trout and char come straight off the fishers' boats and into the hands of accomplished sushi chefs with international pedigree. Set tasting menus offer excellent value (five/seven courses for 6300/7500kr); the decor is cool, as are the cocktails and sake. Bookings recommended.

★**Skaftfell Bistro** INTERNATIONAL €€
(☎472 1633; http://skaftfell.is/en/bistro; Austurvegur 42; pizzas 1600-3500kr; ⊙3-10pm;) This fabulous bistro-bar and cultural centre is perfect for chilling, snacking and/or meeting locals and artists. There's a short menu that changes weekly, plus popular pizza options (including 'reindeer bliss' and 'langoustine feast'). Be sure to check out the exhibitions in the gallery (p343) upstairs. Kitchen closes at 9pm. Bookings recommended for larger groups.

Nordic Restaurant ICELANDIC €€
(☎472 1277; www.hotelaldan.is; Norðurgata 2; lunch 1250-2650kr, dinner mains 2900-4600kr; ⊙noon-9pm) At the reception building for Hótel Aldan, coffee and cakes are served all day in a country-chic setting, and lunches feature the likes of goat's-cheese salad or burger and fries. In the evening, flickering candles prettify the tables, and the menu showcases fine local ingredients (lamb, fish) with a contemporary touch. Dinner reservations advised.

Kaffi Lára – El Grilló Bar BAR
(☎472 1703; Norðurgata 3; ⊙11am-1.30am Sun-Thu, to 3.30am Fri & Sat;) When you can't get a table elsewhere in town, there's usually space at this friendly, two-storey cafe-bar offering supremely tasty barbecue dishes and more than 20 different Icelandic beers. The must-try: El Grillo beer, brewed according to a recipe with a great backstory, and named after the bombed British tanker at the bottom of the fjord.

Vínbúðin ALCOHOL
(Hafnargata 4a; ⊙4-6pm Mon-Thu, 1-6pm Fri) Government-run liquor store.

Entertainment

Blue Church Summer Concerts LIVE MUSIC
(www.blaakirkjan.is; Bjólfsgata 10; adult/child 2800kr/free; ⊙8.30pm Wed Jul–mid-Aug) On Wednesday evenings from July to mid-August, the Bláa Kirkjan (p343) is the setting for a popular series of jazz, classical- and folk-music concerts; see the website for the program. If you're leaving on the Thursday ferry, this is a lovely way to spend your final night in Iceland.

Information

There's an ATM outside the supermarket.

The website www.visitseydisfjordur.com is invaluable.

The **Tourist office** (☎472 1551; www.visitseydisfjordur.com; Ferjuleira 1; ⊙9am-5pm Mon-Fri May-Sep, 1-5pm Mon-Fri Oct-Apr), in the ferry terminal building, stocks local brochures, plus info on the entire country. Also open Tuesday mornings in winter (8am to noon) when the Smyril Line ferry docks, and during cruise-ship visits.

Getting There & Away

BOAT

Smyril Line (☎Faroe Islands +298 345900; www.smyrilline.com; Ferjuleira 1) operates a weekly car ferry, the *Norröna*, on a convoluted year-round schedule from Hirsthals (Denmark) through Tórshavn (Faroe Islands) to Seyðisfjörður.

BECKI SCOTT/GETTY IMAGES ©

1. Malamut husky sled dogs 2. Hlíðarfjall Ski Centre (p294)
3. Gígjökull glacier ice cave (p163) 4. Skógafoss (p151)

DARIA MEDVEDEVA/SHUTTERSTOCK ©

Winter Travel

Winter travel to Iceland is surging in popularity, and it's not hard to figure out the appeal: Northern Lights dance across the sky, nature is at its most raw, and night-owls have the chance to experience crazy diurnal rhythms. It's also a great option if summer crowds don't appeal – but beware, those winter crowds are growing...

Tours from Reykjavík

Despite shortened daylight hours, city life goes on as normal in the capital, and opportunities for outdoor adventure are great: frozen waterfalls, snowy peaks, and skating, skiing and snowshoeing. Seek out the experts to travel safely during this time – day tours from Reykjavík (p52) are ideal, and locals know the best winter secrets.

Skiing & Snowsports

Bláfjoll outside Reykjavík draws skiers from November to April, but North Iceland is where serious snow bunnies should head: Akureyri is home to Hlíðarfjall (p294), Iceland's biggest ski field, while just north of here are smaller local ski fields and top-shelf heliskiing on the Tröllaskagi peninsula (p281). Time your visit for the Iceland Winter Games (p24) in Akureyri in late March.

Ice Caves

The southeast is a winter magnet, thanks to the frozen blue wonder of ice caves. The caves are accessible (usually at glacier edges) from around November to March. You'll need a guide: there are local experts leading the way from points between Skaftafell and Höfn. Bonus: the glaciated landscapes often take on a gleaming blue hue in the winter.

Snowshoeing & Dog Sledding

Snowmobiling, ice climbing, glacier hikes and even dog sledding can be done year-round in Iceland (those ice caps come in handy!), but if you're seeking the full fairy-tale experience, Mývatn makes a fine choice, for its snowshoe and cross-country ski tours, snowmobiling on the frozen lake, and dog sledding in the hills.

From mid-June to late August, the *Norröna* sails into town at 8.30am on Thursday, departing for Scandinavia two hours later. The rest of the year, the boat pulls in at 9am on Tuesday, leaving Wednesday at 8pm. Winter passage is possible (from October to March, departures are weather-dependent); see the website for more.

BUS

SVAust (☎893 2669, 472 1515) runs a bus service between Egilsstaðir and Seyðisfjörður (1080kr, around 45 minutes). Services operate year-round, one to three times daily from Monday to Saturday. An up-to-date schedule can be found on www.visitseydisfjordur.com.

The bus picks up from the **ferry terminal** only on ferry day; the main stop is outside the library on **Austurvegur**. In Egilsstaðir, the bus services the airport and campground.

Mjóifjörður

The fjord south of Seyðisfjörður is Mjóifjörður ('Narrow Fjord', pronounced 'myoh-ee-fjurther'), flanked by spectacular cliffs and rows of cascading waterfalls. The gravel road leading into the fjord is very slow-going for 2WDs (summer only), but once you make it in you'll be surrounded by lush hills peppered with fascinating ruins and schools of farmed fish in the frigid fjord water. A rusted herring vessel sits beached, the perfect photographic prop.

Note: come here for peace and isolation (and reputedly excellent berry-picking), but don't come looking for a buzz – the permanent population of Mjóifjörður is 14.

There's some wonderful **hiking** around Mjóifjörður. For a fee, the folks at Sólbrekka can ferry you across the fjord, from where it's a four-hour hike to Neskaupstaður, or you can climb over northern mountains to reach Seyðisfjörður on a six- to seven-hour trek (it's best to hike in late summer, from mid-July or later, when the high-altitude snow has finally melted).

From the head of Mjóifjörður it's 12km to the settlement at **Brekkuþorp** (often labelled Iceland's smallest village), then the road continues 14km east to the **Dalatangi light**, Iceland's first lighthouse, dating from 1895 (next to it is the 'modern' one, dating from 1908 and still in use). Beyond Brekkuþorp a 4WD is advisable.

Coffee and light snacks are available at **Sólbrekka Cafe** (snacks & sandwiches 350-650kr; ⊙11am-7pm Jul–mid-Aug), and breakfast and dinner can be arranged for overnight guests. Bring supplies from Egilsstaðir or Reyðarfjörður.

Sólbrekka GUESTHOUSE, COTTAGES €€
(☎476 0007; http://mjoifjordur.weebly.com; cottages excl linen 18,500kr; ⊙guesthouse Jul–mid-Aug, cottages Jun-Sep) On the north side of Mjóifjörður, Sólbrekka is the only place to stay. There's a schoolhouse near the sea, offering camping (per person 1200kr) and no-frills rooms with shared bathroom (single/double 9850/12,300kr), but the real treat lies up the hill; two self-contained pine cottages sleeping four (one bedroom plus small sleeping loft and a sofa bed).

Getting There & Away

It's 30km from Egilsstaðir to the head of Mjóifjörður (on Rtes 1 and 953), then a further 12km to Brekkuþorp. No transport runs here.

The road into and out of Mjóifjörður is impassable from October to sometime in May – during this time, access is by boat twice a week from Neskaupstaður.

Reyðarfjörður

POP 1270

In the Prettiest Fjord pageant, Reyðarfjörður (pronounced 'ray-thar-fjurther') wouldn't be in the running to take home the crown. It's a relatively new settlement that only came into existence – as a trading port – in the 20th century.

More recently, Reyðarfjörður garnered attention when Alcoa installed a giant 2km-long aluminium smelter just beyond the town along the fjord. Conservationists were up in arms, but the infusion of foreign workers has added a small splash of international flavour in Reyðarfjörður and surrounding towns. Alcoa jobs (the company employs approximately 450 people) have also brought a prosperity to the region best evidenced by the homes being built by new residents.

And if you feel the fabulous scenery is familiar? You may have seen Reyðarfjörður feature in the British TV series *Fortitude*.

Sights

Íslenska Stríðsárasafnið MUSEUM
(http://stridsarasafn.fjardabyggd.is; Spítalakampu; adult/child 1500kr/free; ⊙1-5pm Jun-Aug) During WWII around 3000 Allied soldiers (10 times the local population) were based in Reyðarfjörður. At the top end of Heiðarvegur you'll find the excellent (but pricey) Icelandic Wartime Museum, which details these strange few years. The building is surrounded by mines, Jeeps and aeroplane propellers,

and holds other war relics. Photographs and tableaux provide a background to Iceland's wartime involvement.

Sleeping

Reyðarfjörður HI Hostel HOSTEL €
(Hjá Marlín; ☎474 1220, 892 0336; www.hjamarlin.is; Vallargerði 9; dm 6500kr, d with/without bathroom 21,000/15,600kr, q with bathroom 32,000kr; @📶👪) Multilingual Marlín (Belgian, but resident in Iceland for more than 20 years) is a warm host at this expanding spot. The primary house has en-suite rooms and a breakfast (2000kr) area; a large second house down the street has simple rooms, a barbecue and a sauna. Nearby on Austurvegur, a newly converted furniture store (!) has 12 four-bed rooms with private bathroom.

Campsite CAMPGROUND €
(sites per person 1200kr; ⏱mid-Apr–mid-Oct) At the entrance to town on Rte 92, this neat campground sits beside a duck pond, with decent facilities (including washing machine).

Tærgesen GUESTHOUSE €€
(☎470 5555; www.taergesen.com; Búðargata 4; d with/without bathroom, incl breakfast 24,300/16,200kr; 📶👪) Timber-lined and dressed with white window shutters, the cosy rooms above Tærgesen restaurant have loads of cottagey character (and shared bathrooms). They're inside a black corrugated-iron building from 1870. A newer addition to the complex is an annex of 22 spacious motel-style units with bathroom.

Eating & Drinking

Sesam Brauðhús BAKERY, CAFE €
(www.sesam.is; Hafnargata 1; snacks from 300kr; ⏱7.30am-5pm Mon-Fri, 9am-4pm Sat) Stop by this first-rate bakery-cafe and choose from a cabinet full of sandwiches, salads and pastries.

Krónan Supermarket SUPERMARKET €
(Hafnargata 2; ⏱11am-6pm Mon-Thu, to 7pm Fri, to 5pm Sat, noon-4pm Sun) Central option for self-caterers.

Tærgesen ICELANDIC €€
(☎470 5555; www.taergesen.com; Búðargata 4; mains 1480-5540kr; ⏱10am-10pm) Tærgesen makes much of its connection to the British TV series *Fortitude*. It's known for its pizzas, and for hearty traditional fare that ranges from steak sandwiches to butter-fried trout.

Next door and under the same management is Kaffi Kósý, a popular locals' bar open Friday and Saturday nights.

Vínbúðin ALCOHOL
(Hafnargata 2; ⏱11am-6pm Mon-Thu, to 7pm Fri, to 4pm Sat) Government-run liquor store.

Information

You may see reference on maps and info boards to Fjarðabyggð – this is the municipality that centres on Reyðarfjörður and encompasses fjords from Mjóifjörður south to Stöðvarfjörður. There is comprehensive info online at www.visitfjardabyggd.is.

Getting There & Away

Daily SVAust buses (p329) connect Reyðarfjörður with Egilsstaðir and its neighbouring fjords.

Eskifjörður

POP 1015

This friendly, prospering little town is stretched out along a dimple in the main fjord of Reyðarfjörður. Its setting is magnificent: it looks directly onto the mighty mountain Hólmatindur (985m), rising sheer from the shining blue water.

Sights

Helgustaðanáma MINE
The remains of the world's largest spar quarry lie east of Eskifjörður. Iceland spar (*silfurberg* in Icelandic) is a type of calcite crystal that is completely transparent and can split light into two parallel beams. It was a vital component in early microscopes.

To reach the quarry, follow the gravel road past Mjóeyri, driving 7km along the coastline until you reach an information panel and public toilet; the quarry is then a 500m walk uphill.

Sjóminjasafn Austurlands MUSEUM
(Strandgata 39b; adult/child 1500kr/free; ⏱1-5pm Jun-Aug) Inside the 1816 black timber warehouse 'Gamlabuð', the East Iceland Maritime Museum illustrates two centuries of the east coast's historic herring, shark and whaling industry. For more salty-dog stories, be sure to check out Randulffs-sjóhús (p350).

Activities

There are plenty of hiking routes up the nearby mountains. Multi-day hikes around the peninsulas east of Eskifjörður abound – particularly popular is the area known as Gerpir. At the time of writing it was tough to obtain a hiking map locally, so ask around for local advice. The owners of Ferðaþjónustan Mjóeyri) are good for hooking you up with guides and activities (and have motorboats for hire if you want to head off to explore).

Gönguvikan (Hiking Week) is a big event on the district's annual calendar, falling the week after the summer solstice.

★Hólmanes Peninsula HIKING

The southern shore of the Hólmanes Peninsula, below the peak **Hólmatindur**, is a nature reserve. Hiking in the area offers superb maritime views (look out for pods of dolphins). The Hólmaborgir hike, south of the main road, is a popular loop that takes but an hour or two.

Oddsskarð SKIING

Given the right conditions, from December to April skiing is possible on slopes near Oddsskarð, the mountain pass above town. See www.visitfjardabyggd.is for details.

Sundlaug Eskifjarðar SWIMMING

(Eskifjarðarvegur; adult/child 900/250kr; ⌚6am-9pm Mon-Fri, 10am-6pm Sat & Sun) This swimming pool has water slides, hot-pots and a sauna; it's on the main road into town.

Sleeping

Guesthouse Askja GUESTHOUSE €

(☎476 1150; www.kaffihusid.is/guesthouse-askja; Strandgata 86; d/tr without bathroom from 12,150/16,650kr;) In 2018, new owners took on this guesthouse by the water and freshened it up, and have even opened a small Thai restaurant downstairs. Good-value, comfortable rooms share bathrooms, and there's a guest kitchen and nice lounge area. It's also a member of the HI hostelling network, so ask about discounts if you have a membership.

Campsite CAMPGROUND €

(Strandgata; sites per person 1200kr; ⌚mid-May–mid-Sep) A simple site in a pretty treed setting not far from the entrance to town.

★Ferðaþjónustan Mjóeyri GUESTHOUSE, COTTAGES €€

(☎696 0809, 477 1247; www.mjoeyri.is; Strandgata 120; s/d without bathroom 15,400/20,100kr, cottages from 31,900kr;) On the eastern edge of town, this view-blessed complex juts into the waterway at the tip of a teeny peninsula. There are guesthouse rooms in the main building, but it's the excellent, family-sized cottages spread around the property that make Mjóeyri a great choice. There are also camper amenities, and one of the funkiest hot-pots we've seen (in a converted boat).

Hotel Eskifjörður HOTEL €€

(☎476 0099; www.hoteleskifjordur.is; Strandgata 47; d 27,000-29,000kr;) In the centre of town, this hotel has transformed an old bank into a fresh, stylish place to stay, with sweet puffin themes to set the scene. Room prices vary with size and view – the most expensive have a balcony. Breakfast is 1500kr.

Eating & Drinking

There are not a lot of places to eat in town, and options shrink outside of summer. In winter you may need to drive to neighbouring towns for a good meal. Quick-eat options include a petrol station with a grill. If you're after a surprise, seek out Thai restaurant **Hús Fílsins - Ban Chang** (☎476 1150; Strandgata 86; dishes 2000-2800kr; ⌚noon-2pm & 6-9.30pm Wed-Mon).

Kjörbúðin SUPERMARKET €

(Strandgata 50; ⌚9am-7pm Mon-Fri, 10am-6pm Sat, noon-6pm Sun) For picnic supplies and self-catering. There's an ATM out front, too.

★Randulffs-sjóhús ICELANDIC €€

(☎477 1247; www.mjoeyri.is; Strandgata 96; mains 3290-6790kr; ⌚5-9pm Jun-Aug or by appointment) This extraordinary boathouse dates from 1890, and when new owners entered it in 2008, they found it untouched for 80-odd years. The upstairs sleeping quarters of the fishermen have remained as they were found; downstairs is an atmospheric restaurant among the maritime memorabilia. Unsurprisingly, the tasty, upmarket menu is heavy on fish (including local specialities shark and dried fish).

Kaffihúsið BAR

(☎476 1150; www.kaffihusid.is; Strandgata 10; ⌚6-11pm Tue-Thu, 6pm-3am Fri, noon-3am Sat, noon-11pm Sun;) You can't miss the oversized coffee cup announcing this place, primarily a restaurant-bar (kitchen closes at 9.30pm) and pub hang-out for locals. There's also a cluster of rooms (single/double 9000/13,600kr) in the back; they're decent, basic affairs, with shared bathroom (but noisy at the end of the week).

Getting There & Away

Eskifjörður is 15km northeast of Reyðarfjörður on Rte 92. A new 8km tunnel opened in 2017 to connect Eskifjörður with Neskaupstaður, further east.

A scenic mountain road over Oddsskarð pass was previously the only road access to Neskaupstaður. The road from Eskifjörður to Oddsskarð remains open in summer (but not from Oddsskarð to Neskaupstaður); it's worth a drive up to Oddsskarð to enjoy the steep climb and panoramic views.

Neskaupstaður

POP 1460

Although it's one of the largest of the fjord towns, the dramatic end-of-the-line location makes Neskaupstaður (nes-coop-stathur, also known as Norðfjörður) feel small and far away from the rest of the world. Attempt to drive further east and you simply run out of road.

As with most towns in the Eastfjords, Neskaupstaður began life as a 19th-century trading centre and prospered during the herring boom in the early 20th century. Its future was assured by the building of the biggest fish-processing and freezing plant in Iceland, Síldarvinnslan (SNV), at the head of the fjord. The east's main regional hospital is located here.

Sights & Activities

★Fólkvangur Neskaupstaðar NATURE RESERVE

At the eastern end of town, where the road runs out, is this lovely nature reserve perfect for short strolls. Various paths run over boardwalks and past boulders, peat pits, cliffs and the sea, with a soundtrack of crying seabirds. You may see whales offshore.

Safnahúsið MUSEUM

(Egilsbraut 2; adult/child 1500kr/free; 1-9pm Mon-Sat, 1-5pm Sun Jun-Aug) Three collections are clustered together in one bright-red harbour front warehouse, known as 'Museum House'. **Tryggvasafn** showcases a collection of striking paintings by prominent modern artist Tryggvi Ólafsson, born in Neskaupstaður in 1940. Upstairs, the **Maritime Museum** is one man's collection of artefacts relating to the sea; on the top floor, the **Museum of Natural History** has a big collection of local stones (including spar from the Helgustaðanáma (p349) mine), plus an array of stuffed animals, birds, fish and pinned insects.

Stefánslaug SWIMMING

(Miðstræti 15; adult/child 900/250kr; 6am-8pm Mon-Fri, 10am-6pm Sat & Sun Jun-Aug, shorter hours Sep-May) The town's pride and joy, this pool has hot-pots and water slides and an ace view.

Tours

★Skorrahestar HORSE RIDING, HIKING

(477 1736; www.skorrahestar.is; Skorrastaður; 30min ride 8500/19,500kr; short riding tours mid-May–mid-Oct) Based on a farm west of town, Skorrahestar offers longer treks for experienced riders, including weeklong trips to uninhabited fjords led by Doddi, a storytelling, guitar-playing guide who is a former biologist and teacher (the perfect guide?). A brilliant taster involves two hours of guided riding or hiking in the local landscapes, followed by pancakes and coffee. Good guesthouse accommodation, too.

★Neskaupstaður Sailing BOATING

(477 1950; www.hildibrandhotel.com/neskaupstadur-sailing; 2½hr tour adult/child 8900/4450kr) Take in the dramatic scenery while hearing about local history and scouting for whales from an old sailing vessel as it tours Neskaupstaður. Tours last 2½ hours and are scheduled in the evenings. There's a gorgeous weekly trip that sails to serene Mjóifjörður (11,900kr). Sea-angling and customised trips can also be arranged. See options online.

Festivals & Events

Eistnaflug MUSIC

(www.eistnaflug.is; Jul) A beloved metal and punk festival, Eistnaflug ('Flying Testicles') is held every summer in town on the second weekend in July. Sixty bands plus friendly metalheads plus long daylight equals a great summer party.

Sleeping

Campsite CAMPGROUND €

(sites per person 1200kr; mid-May–mid-Sep) High above the town, near the avalanche barriers (worth a visit for the great views). It's signposted from the hospital.

Tónspil GUESTHOUSE €

(894 1580; www.tonspil.is; Hafnarbraut 22; s/d/tr without bathroom from 5900/9900/14,900kr;) Like an extra in the film *High Fidelity*, you need to ask the dude in the music shop about the rooms above. They're simple and cheap, and there's a handy TV room and kitchen area with a washing machine.

★**Hildibrand Hotel** HOTEL €€
(☎477 1950; www.hildibrand.com; Hafnarbraut 2; d/apt from 18,500/28,700kr) The biggest thing to happen to Neskaupstaður in years, this complex of 15 super-spacious, fully equipped apartments is plumb in the town centre. Each apartment has one to three bedrooms (sleeping up to eight), full kitchen, balcony (those views!) and custom-made furniture – you may be persuaded to move in. In a neighbouring building are standard hotel rooms – small but bright and well equipped.

Hótel Edda HOTEL €€
(☎444 4860; www.hoteledda.is; Nesgata 40; d from 16,575kr; ⊙early Jun–mid-Aug; @ 🛜) On the waterfront at the eastern end of town, this friendly, well-run summer hotel has brilliant views; neat, no-frills rooms (all with bathroom); and a quality dinnertime restaurant (mains 2500kr to 3200kr). Breakfast is available for 2400kr.

Eating & Drinking

Nesbær Kaffihus CAFE €
(Egilsbraut 5; lunch 890-2290kr; ⊙9am-6pm Mon-Wed & Fri, to 10pm Thu, 10am-6pm Sat; 🛜) This cafe-bakery and craft shop has a quintessential small-town vibe and offers excellent crêpes, cakes, sandwiches and soup.

Kjörbúðin SUPERMARKET €
(Hafnarbraut 13; ⊙9am-7pm Mon-Fri, 10am-6pm Sat, noon-6pm Sun) Supermarket in the centre of town, opposite Hildibrand Hotel.

★**Beituskúrinn** SEAFOOD €€
(Bait Shack; ☎477 1950; www.facebook.com/beituskurinn; Egilsbraut 26; mains 1300-3600kr; ⊙noon-10pm Sun-Thu, to 2am Fri & Sat) A touch of New England in the Eastfjords: this photogenic waterfront shed has been reborn as a cheerfully rustic eatery-bar, with a deck boasting million-dollar views. The menu roves from toasted foccaccia to pizza, but the headliners are the *plokkfiskur* (traditional fish stew) and the *fiskipanna* – a simple, flavourful skillet of fresh fish cooked with potatoes and served with salad.

Kaupfélagsbarinn ICELANDIC €€
(☎477 1950; www.hildibrand.com; Hafnarbraut 2; mains 1990-5690kr; ⊙5-9pm; 🛜) Part of the Hildibrand complex, this is easily the most upmarket restaurant in this neck of the woods. In its large, mid-century-modern space, say hello to a menu that showcases local produce. Choose between a langoustine sub, lamb burger, a build-your-own salad, or a fab tasting plate 'Of farmers and fishermen'.

Vínbúðin ALCOHOL
(Hafnarbraut 15; ⊙2-6pm Mon-Thu, 11am-7pm Fri, 11am-2pm Sat) Government-run liquor store.

Getting There & Away

A new 8km-long tunnel opened in 2017 to connect the fjord with Eskifjörður. Prior to that the only road access was via the highest highway pass (632m) in Iceland and a nerve-wracking, single-lane, 630m-long tunnel. The old tunnel is now closed to traffic.

There are limited bus services (p329) but most travellers rely on their own wheels in this region.

Fáskrúðsfjörður

POP 710

The sleepy village of Fáskrúðsfjörður (pronounced 'fouw-skruths-fjurther; sometimes known as Búðir) was originally settled by French seamen who came to fish the Icelandic coast between the late 19th century and 1914. In a gesture to the local heritage, street signs are in both Icelandic and French.

The full story about the French in Fáskrúðsfjörður can be found at Fosshotel Eastfjords, a new development inside the sensitively renovated former French hospital and other buildings from the era.

Sights & Activities

Frakkar á Íslandsmiðum MUSEUM
(☎475 1170; Hafnargata 12; adult/child 2000kr/free; ⊙10am-6pm mid-May–Sep, other times by appointment) Accessed through the lobby of Fosshotel Eastfjords, this quality museum (with very pricey admission) paints a detailed portrait of the French connection to the fjord. The hotel's reception is in the old doctor's house, and a walkway under Hafnargata links it to the old hospital (now home to hotel rooms). Check out the recreated sailors' quarters in the walkway. Museum entry is free for hotel guests.

Sandfell HIKING
Geologists may get a buzz from the laccolithic mountain Sandfell (743m), above the fjord's southern shore, which was formed by molten rhyolite bursting through older lava layers. It's one of the world's finest examples of this sort of igneous mountain. It's a four-hour return hike to the peak.

Sleeping & Eating

Guesthouse Elín Helga GUESTHOUSE €
(☎868 2687; elinhelgak99@gmail.com; Stekkholt 20; d without bathroom from 9800kr; 📶) This four-room guesthouse, high above town (take Skólavegur then Holtavegur), is recommended for its pine-fresh cosiness, sweet host, fab breakfast spread (1120kr), and great views (note: no kitchen, but laundry access is available).

Campsite CAMPGROUND €
(Óseyri; sites per person 1200kr; ⏲mid-May–mid-Sep) Small and simple, at the west end of the village.

★**Fosshotel Eastfjords** HOTEL €€
(☎470 4070; www.fosshotel.is; Hafnargata 11-14; d incl breakfast from 27,200kr; 📶) This acclaimed hotel opened in 2014 inside the relocated and restored French hospital. It's all class: 56 high-quality rooms (featuring lovely decor in stylish blues and greys, and a clever mix of old and new), plus a restaurant and lounge-bar with majestic views.

Kjörbúðin SUPERMARKET €
(Skólavegur 59; ⏲9am-7pm Mon-Fri, 10am-6pm Sat, noon-6pm Sun) For food supplies; has a Vínbúðin inside.

L'Abri ICELANDIC €€
(☎470 4070; www.fosshotel.is; Hafnargata 9; dinner mains 3290-7990kr; ⏲noon-11pm) As befits its location, L'Abri has a slight French accent, showcasing local produce (seafood soup, beef fillet) plus offering lighter, cheaper bistro dishes (salads and pizzas around 2500kr). It's part of the Fosshotel complex, sitting inside the old French hospital and enjoying a splendid fjord view. A good pit stop for coffee and cake.

Vínbúðin ALCOHOL
(⏲4-6pm Mon-Thu, 1-6pm Fri) Government-run liquor store.

Getting There & Away

Fáskrúðsfjörður sits just off the Ring Road (Rte 1). There are limited bus services (p329) but most travellers rely on their own wheels in this region.

Stöðvarfjörður

POP 185

If you think geology is boring, it's worth challenging that notion in this tiny village (pronounced sturth-var-fjurther), which the Ring Road now cruises right through. It's a small place, but it has built a sizeable reputation for both its stone collection and its creativity. Look out for what may be the country's cutest bird hide just west of town, at the head of the fjord.

You might see references on maps and info boards to Fjarðabyggð – this is the municipality that encompasses the fjords from Stöðvarfjörður north through to Mjóifjörður. There is excellent info online at www.visitfjardabyggd.is.

Sights

★**Steinasafn Petru** MUSEUM
(☎475 8834; www.steinapetra.is; Fjarðarbraut 21; adult/child 1500kr/free; ⏲9am-6pm May–mid-Oct) The wondrous assemblage at Petra's Stone Collection was a lifelong labour of love for Petra Sveinsdóttir (1922–2012). Inside her house, stones and minerals are piled from floor to ceiling – 70% of them are from the local area. They include beautiful cubes of jasper, polished agate, purple amethyst, glowing creamy 'ghost stone', glittering quartz crystals...it's like opening a treasure chest.

Creative Centre ARTS CENTRE
(☎537 0711; www.inhere.is; Bankastræti 1) Going by various names (Fish Factory, Sköpunarmiðstöð, 'In Here'), this once-abandoned fish factory by the harbour is a hive of creativity; it's a collaborative space that's home to artists' studios, a recording studio, workshops and concerts. Keep an eye out for events, or drop by, preferably with advance notice (it's a work space, without fixed opening times, but visitors are generally welcome, and a donation of 500kr is appreciated).

Sleeping & Eating

Campsite CAMPGROUND €
(sites per person 1200kr; ⏲mid-May–mid-Sep) Small, neat, basic campsite just east of the village; it's signed off the main road. Note: no showers, but the local swimming pool is close by.

Saxa GUESTHOUSE €€
(☎511 3055; www.saxa.is; Fjarðarbraut 41; s/d/tr from 10,100/16,800/21,300; 📶) The town's best option demonstrates that Icelanders have yet to find a building they couldn't convert into a guesthouse! This was a supermarket, and now houses fresh well-priced rooms (all with bathroom); note, there's no kitchen.

There's a pleasant all-day **cafe** (snacks and meals 400kr to 3900kr) serving homemade fare (great cakes), and a small selection of dishes of an evening.

Kaffi Sunnó CAFE €

(Fjarðarbraut 21; soup 1300kr; ⏱10am-5pm Jun–mid-Sep) Good road-tripping fare: out front of Steinasafn Petru (p353) a small kiosk sells takeaway soup, coffee and baked treats.

Shopping

Salthússmarkaður ARTS & CRAFTS

(Fjarðarbraut 43; ⏱11am-5pm mid-May–mid-Sep) This market in the community hall sells a variety of charming products (carvings, stones, ceramics etc) from crafty locals. The knitwear selection is top-notch.

Getting There & Away

Stöðvarfjörður now sits directly on the Ring Road (Rte 1), thanks to the rerouting of the highway that took place in late 2017.

There are limited bus services (p329) but most travellers rely on their own wheels in this region.

Breiðdalsvík

POP 135

Fishing village Breiðdalsvík is beautifully sited at the end of Breiðdalur. It's a quiet place – more a base for walking in the nearby hills and fishing the rivers and lakes than an attraction in itself. The newest addition to town is a microbrewery, and it's a sweet place drawing curious travellers.

Information is available online at www.breiddalsvik.is.

Tinna Adventure ADVENTURE

(☎832 3500; www.tinna-adventure.is; Selnes 28-30) This agency can arrange local tours and activities, from fishing to guided 'yoga hikes'. There's a good menu of year-round jeep-tours options, including a half-day summer tour of Breiðdalur highlights (24,900kr).

Sleeping & Eating

Campsite CAMPGROUND €

(sites per person 1000kr; ⏱May-Sep) Campers will find a small campsite behind Hótel Bláfell.

Hótel Bláfell HOTEL €€

(☎470 0000; www.hotelblafell.is; Sólvellir 14; s/d incl breakfast from 12,800/17,100;) Located in the centre of 'town' (we use that term lightly), Hótel Bláfell has smart monochrome rooms (some timber-lined), a sauna and a superb guest lounge with open fire. The hotel also has quality two-bedroom apartments in town, and owns Hotel Post next door.

Hamar GUESTHOUSE €€

(☎846 5547; www.facebook.com/hamarkaffihus; Rte 1; d incl breakfast from 23,700kr) There's a new incarnation for this cosy five-room lodge, on Rte 1 heading towards Stöðvarfjörður. Rooms are simple and modern (some have a balcony), and the **cafe** (mains 1590-2990kr; ⏱11am-9pm) downstairs is first-rate.

Kaupfjélagið CAFE €

(☎475 6670; www.facebook.com/kaupfjelagid; Sólvellir 23; light meals 370-1650kr; ⏱10am-7pm Mon-Thu, to 8pm Fri & Sat, to 5pm Sun) Kaupfjélagið stocks groceries and serves up coffee and light meals to passing travellers. Its best feature is the fun displays of vintage general-store items (some for sale) that were discovered in the attic during renovations.

Frystihúsið ICELANDIC €

(www.breiddalsvik.is; Sólvellir; mains 1250-1950kr; ⏱hrs vary) The old fish factory is a big, bright community centre and event space opposite Hótel Bláfell. It opens most days in summer with a cafeteria-style lunch, catering to groups and tourists passing through. There's also an interesting free exhibit of a large relief map of Iceland, made in concrete in the 1930s by artist Axel Helgason.

Getting There & Away

Breiðdalsvík sits down a 1km access road off the Ring Road. There are limited bus services (p329) but most travellers rely on their own wheels in this region.

Breiðdalur

Inland from Breiðdalsvík is Breiðdalur ('Wide Valley'). It's a quiet, panoramic place to explore, with the broad valley nestled beneath colourful rhyolite peaks and cut by a popular fishing river, the Breiðdalsá.

Rte 95 travels through the valley – this road was part of the Ring Road (Rte 1), but in 2017 the Ring Road was rerouted via the coast. That change makes this part of the east extra secluded – there are few tourists out this way, meaning you can have parts of it all to yourself.

LOCAL BREWS

Maybe every tiny town should have a microbrewery. Especially when it's as genial as **Beljandi Brugghús** (☎860 9905; www.facebook.com/beljandibrugghus; Sólvellir 23; ⏰11am-11.45pm Fri-Wed Jun-Aug, shorter hrs rest of year) . Opened in 2016, this brewery and bar has free samples of its concoctions: the signature Beljandi is a pale ale, but there's also Skuggi, a porter, and Spaði, an IPA. The bar area hosts occasional events (live music, big-screen sports) and the chance to imbibe more options.

Flögufoss WATERFALL
From Rte 966 take the turn-off to Flögufoss, which is a 60m-high waterfall (19km west of Breiðdalsvík), if you feel like a scenic leg-stretch.

Tours

Strengir Angling Service FISHING
(☎660 6890; www.strengir.com) Strengir brings anglers to the region's salmon-rich waters and runs Eyjar Fishing Lodge.

Odin Tours Iceland HORSE RIDING
(☎475 8088, 849 2009; www.odintoursiceland.com; Höskuldsstaðir) Odin Tours operates year-round horse-riding and hiking tours in Breiðdalur, plus has a cottage for rent. It's about 24km from Breiðdalsvík.

Sleeping & Eating

Eyjar Fishing Lodge GUESTHOUSE €€
(☎567 5204; www.strengir.com; r incl breakfast 25,000kr; 📶) Operated by Strengir, a Reykjavík-based company that brings anglers to the region's salmon-rich waters, this high-end, year-round accommodation option is open to all. There's a Jacuzzi and sauna, a fabulous lounge area, and dinner is available. It's on Rte 964, off Rte 1.

Hótel Staðarborg HOTEL €€
(☎475 6760; www.stadarborg.is; s/d incl breakfast from 13,600/20,200kr; 📶) Once a school, cheerful, plant-filled Hótel Staðarborg has neat, updated rooms, plus lake-fishing and horse-riding opportunities. There's a handful of sweet one-bedroom cottages, plus a Jacuzzi and sauna. Dinner is offered (mains around 4000kr). It lies 6km west of Breiðdalsvík.

★**Silfurberg** GUESTHOUSE €€€
(☎475 1515; www.silfurberg.com; Þorgrímsstaðir; d incl breakfast from 48,000kr; ⏰Jun-Aug; 📶) Silfurberg is a stunning boutique guesthouse on a secluded rural property about 50km south of Egilsstaðir (30km from Breiðdalsvík). Style, humour and artisanship have been used to convert a barn into first-class accommodation containing four rooms, one suite and delightful, deluxe common areas. The outdoor sauna and dome-enclosed hot-pot are the icing on the cake. Meals by arrangement.

Berufjörður

Between Djúpivogur and Breiðdalsvík the Ring Road meanders around panoramic Berufjörður, a long, steep-sided fjord flanked by rhyolite peaks. There is no village, just a handful of farms strung along the scenic shores. The southwestern shore is dominated by the obtrusive, pyramid-shaped mountain **Búlandstindur**, rising 1069m above the water.

Teigarhorn NATURE RESERVE
(☎869 6550; www.teigarhorn.is; ⏰9am-5pm Jun-Aug) Rockhounds will love the display of zeolites at this farm, now a natural monument and nature reserve 5km northwest of Djúpivogur. It's renowned for its zeolite crystals, and the caretaker can open the small **museum** here on request (it's best to contact him beforehand). The farm has also developed short walking trails around its coast, good for a leg-stretch and birdwatching.

Öxi Pass (Route 939) LANDMARK
At the head of Berufjörður, the 19km Öxi mountain pass (Rte 939) offers a summer short cut to drivers en route to or from Egilsstaðir. The pass cuts about 70km off the Djúpivogur–Egilsstaðir journey (compared with following the coastal Ring Road) and gives some gorgeous views, but it's a narrow gravel road and isn't advised in bad weather or fog, or for nervous drivers. Note: the road is closed in winter.

Google Maps and GPS systems may give Öxi pass as the shortest option – which it is, in summer – but it's best to think about the options and not blindly follow directions.

Sleeping & Eating

★Berunes HI Hostel HOSTEL €€

(☎478 8988, 869 7227; www.berunes.is; dm/d without bathroom 6600/16,200kr, cottages from 22,620kr; ⏱Apr-Oct; @📶👨‍👩‍👧) 🌿 Berunes hostel is on a century-old farm run by affable Ólafur and his family. The wonderfully creaky old farmhouse has rooms and alcoves, plus kitchen and lounge; there are also rooms in the newer farmhouse, plus a campsite (1750kr per person) and ensuite cottages. Breakfast includes homemade bread and cakes; there's also a summer restaurant (or BYO food supplies).

Non-HI members pay a little extra, or can purchase membership at the hostel.

The hostel is 22km along the Ring Road south of Breiðdalsvík, and 40km from Djúpivogur. There are excellent hiking trails from the farm.

★Havarí CAFE, HOSTEL €

(☎663 5520; www.havari.is; Karlsstaðir; meals 800-2000kr; ⏱8am-9pm May-Sep, shorter hrs Oct-Apr; 📶🌱) Continuing the wonderful Icelandic tradition of live music in unlikely places, this warm, creative farm (1km east of Berunes HI Hostel is owned by a young family that includes acclaimed musician Prins Póló. A converted barn is now a cafe and music venue; look out for events on Havarí's Facebook page, or stop by to try the tasty farm-made *bulsur* (vegan sausages).

You can also order great coffee, soup and waffles. Also here: a small, excellent new hostel, with communal kitchen and bathrooms (dorm/double from 5860/17,300kr).

Outside summer, hours for the cafe are less concrete – call, or check Facebook.

The farm is 21km along the Ring Road south of Breiðdalsvík, and 41km from Djúpivogur.

Djúpivogur

POP 350

Djúpivogur's neat historic buildings and small harbour are worth a look, and there's a low-key creative vibe to the town, but the main reason to visit this friendly fishing village at the mouth of Berufjörður is to catch the boat to Papey. At the time of writing, the Papey tours were on hold due to boat-licensing arrangements. Hopefully by the time you read this they will have been reinstated.

Djúpivogur (*dyoo*-pi-vor) is actually one of the oldest ports in the country – it's been around since the 16th century, when German merchants brought goods to trade. The last major excitement was in 1627: pirates from North Africa rowed ashore, plundering the village and nearby farms, and carrying away dozens of slaves.

These days the town has embraced the Cittaslow movement ('Slow Cities'; www.cittaslow.org), an offshoot of the Slow Food initiative. Djúpivogur is the only Icelandic member of the Cittaslow network, whose objectives are to promote and spread the culture of good living.

Sights

There's a low-key, creative vibe in the town, and a few quirky artisans work with local stones and driftwood to create jewellery or artful objects. Workshops are open when the artists are around (generally daily in summer).

Eggin í Gleðivík PUBLIC ART

Walk or drive down to the waterfront behind Langabúð and follow the road west to reach this intriguing public artwork: 34 oversized eggs along the jetty, each one representing a local bird. While you're there, check out the old fish factory (Bræðsla) nearby, which hosts contemporary-art exhibitions in summer.

JFS Handcraft & Stone Garden GALLERY

(Hammersminni 10; ⏱10am-6pm) FREE A small place with a big reputation thanks to its owner. Jón is a welcoming local character with a great stonework collection; he makes beautiful jewellery and souvenirs.

Langabúð Museum MUSEUM

(adult/child 500/300kr; ⏱10am-6pm Jun-Aug) Djúpivogur's oldest building is the long, bright-red **Langabúð**, a harbourside log warehouse dating from 1790. It now houses a **cafe** (☎899 7600; www.langabud.is; lunch 550-1750kr; ⏱10am-6pm Sun-Thu, to 11.30pm Fri & Sat May-Sep) and an unusual local museum. Downstairs is a collection of works by sculptor Rikarður Jónsson (1888–1977), ranging from lifelike busts of worthy Icelanders to mermaid-decorated mirrors and reliefs depicting saga characters. Upstairs, in the tar-smelling attic, is a collection of local-history artefacts.

Activities

For exploration of the surrounding mountains and fjords, buy a copy of the *Göngu-*

leiðir í Djúpavogshreppi (Hiking Routes in Djúpavogur Municipality) map (1000kr).

Bird life in the area is prolific; twitchers should check out www.birds.is (good general info, despite not being up to date).

Sleeping

Klif Hostel HOSTEL €
(☎478 8802; klifhostel@simnet.is; Kambur 1; d/q without bathroom 12,000/24,000kr; ⊙May-Oct; 📶) Klif is a new-ish addition to town, a small, homey, five-room hostel in the old post office. The very reasonable prices include linen; breakfast is available.

Campsite CAMPGROUND €
(sites per person 1750kr; 📶) Behind Við Voginn, this campground is run by Hótel Framtíð; pay at the hotel's reception or the information booth. There are cooking facilities, plus coin showers and a laundry. A newer addition: cool wooden 'barrel' huts, housing three beds and little else (from 16,800kr, linen not included).

★ **Bragðavellir Cottages** COTTAGE €€
(☎787 2121; www.bragdavellir.is; 1-/2-bedroom cottage 25,000/36,000kr; 📶👪) Some 13km from Djúpivogur, this pristine property is rich in views and wildlife (including ducks and chickens; possibly reindeer in winter), and there are great walking trails. A cluster of cosy self-contained cottages come in two sizes – one or two bedroom. There's an on-site 'barn restaurant', too.

Hótel Framtíð HOTEL €€€
(☎478 8887; www.hotelframtid.com; Vogaland 4; d with/without bathroom 34,900/21,000kr; 📶) This friendly hotel is impressive for a village of this size. It's been around awhile (the original building was brought in pieces from Copenhagen in 1906), and there's an assortment of beds (and budgets) in various buildings. The hotel includes timber-lined hotel rooms, four cute cottages and five apartments (including two sleek, modern options).

Eating & Drinking

Kjörbúðin SUPERMARKET €
(Búland 2; ⊙9am-7pm Mon-Fri, 10am-6pm Sat, noon-6pm Sun) On the main road, with a Vínbúðin attached.

Við Voginn FAST FOOD €€
(☎478 8860; Vogaland 2; meals 1000-2100kr; ⊙9am-9pm Mon-Fri, 10am-9pm Sat & Sun) Come to this popular, central grill bar for cracker fish and chips, burgers, hot dogs and pitas, or to start the day with eggs and bacon.

Hótel Framtíð Restaurant ICELANDIC €€€
(☎478 8887; www.hotelframtid.com; Vogaland 4; dinner mains 3860-6400kr; ⊙10am-9pm) The elegant restaurant at Hótel Framtíð is easily the nicest option in town. Dinner of lobster tails or roast lamb fillet hits the top end of the price scale and palate, but there are all-day pizzas too (from 1830kr), and coffee and cake.

Vínbúðin ALCOHOL
(Búland 1; ⊙4-6pm Mon-Thu, 1-6pm Fri Jun-Aug) Government-run liquor store.

Information

Pick up a map of the town – which has decent facilities (bank, post office etc) – from the season **Information Centre** (☎470 8740; ⊙9am-5pm Mon-Fri, 10am-2pm Sat & Sun mid-May–mid-Sep) by the camping area.

Getting There & Away

At the time of writing, there was no longer a direct summer bus connecting Egilsstaðir with Höfn via Djúpivogur.

SVAust (www.svaust.is; ☎471 2320) operates a network of local buses in East Iceland, and bus 4 runs between Breiðdalsvík, Djúpivogur and Höfn, but not daily. Check timetables online, and pay attention to the notes that indicate days of operation.

Buses leave town from outside Hótel Framtíð. Djúpivogur to Breiðdalsvík is one hour (1800kr); to Höfn is 80 minutes (2520kr).

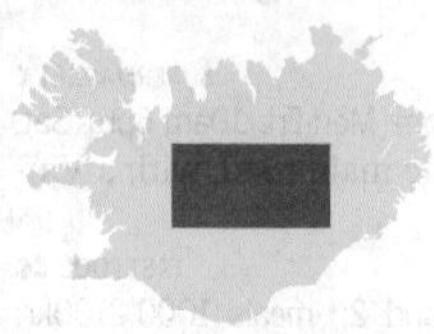

The Highlands

Includes ➡

Best Places to Eat

➡ Highland Center Hrauneyjar (p366)

➡ Hveravellir (p364)

➡ Kerlingarfjöll Highland Centre (p364)

➡ Árbúðir (p362)

Best Places to Stay

➡ Kerlingarfjöll Highland Centre (p364)

➡ Þorsteinsskáli Hut (p369)

➡ Laugafell Hut (p365)

➡ Sigurðarskáli Hut (p372)

➡ Hveravellir (p364)

➡ Gíslaskáli (p362)

Why Go?

The interior highlands' undulating multi-coloured lava flows, creeping glaciers, seething volcanos, and vast, unbroken horizons of sand, rock and mountain feel like another world. Gazing across the unspoilt, remote expanses, you could imagine yourself, as many have noted, on the moon or Mars. Those aren't overactive imaginations – Apollo astronauts trained here before their lunar landing.

The highlands are home to Iceland's King and Queen of the Mountains, and the only sign of life you'll see (besides other homo sapiens) is an occasional delicate moss or flower, or the vibrant ripple of bright green where vegetation grows along a hot river. The isolation and the humbling scale of the natural world in its rawest form are the reasons people visit. The solitude is exhilarating, the views unending. But there are practically no services, accommodation, bridges over rivers – or guarantees if something goes wrong. Be prepared with logistics and your spirit of adventure.

Good to Know

➡ Access to the highlands is not year-round – it is dependent on opening dates for mountain roads. These are determined by weather conditions, and not all roads open at the same time. Openings occur any time from early June to early July. Roads become impassable and are closed again in September or October.

➡ Check www.road.is or phone 1777 for info.

➡ Winter access is possible to some highland areas, but only on guided tours by snowmobile or in large, modified super-Jeeps driven by experienced locals.

KJÖLUR ROUTE

If you want to sample Iceland's central deserts but don't like the idea of ford crossings, the 200km Kjölur (pronounced *kyu*-loor) route has had all of its rivers bridged. In summer there are even scheduled daily buses that use it as a 'short cut' between Reykjavík and Akureyri.

From the south, Rte 35 starts just past Gullfoss, passing between two large glaciers before emerging near Blönduós on the northwest coast. It reaches its highest point (around 700m) between the Langjökull and Hofsjökull ice caps, near the mountain Kjalfell (1000m). Its northern section cruises scenically past Blöndulón, a large reservoir used by the Blanda hydroelectric power station. Road conditions in the north are better than those in the south.

The Kjölur route usually opens in mid-June, and closes sometime in September, depending on weather conditions.

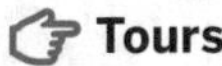

Tours

Hiking and horse-riding tours follow the Kjölur route (eg Eldhestar (p74), or look online and also search the term 'Kjalvegur') and there are a few super-Jeep tours (eg Saga Travel. You can use the scheduled summertime buses as a day tour, or as a regular bus service.

Saga Travel DRIVING
(☎558 888; www.sagatravel.is) From July to September (weather permitting), Saga Travel does a one-day cross-country guided tour from Reykjavík to Akureyri (215,900kr for a 4-person vehicle), visiting the Golden Circle highlights before taking the Kjölur route

TRAVELLING TO & AROUND THE HIGHLANDS

Before you embark on your highlands journey, take note:

Weather conditions Can be fickle and snow isn't uncommon, even in midsummer. Check www.vedur.is (and its app) for forecasts.

Road-opening dates Depend on weather conditions, and usually occur any time from early June to early July. Check www.road.is, or phone 1777.

Safety Do your homework – read up on alerts and advice on www.safetravel.is. Log a travel plan online, and when you stop into huts write your plan in the guestbook. Have good maps and GPS gear. Consider your level of driving experience and type of vehicle when choosing a route (see p431 for information on F Roads).

4WD vehicles Highlands routes are strictly for robust, high-clearance 4WD vehicles (not 4WD passenger cars), as jagged terrain and treacherous river crossings are common. Know how to cross a river before setting out – this is not the place to learn – and ask locals about current river conditions before setting out.

Convoy It's recommended that vehicles travel in pairs, so if one gets bogged or breaks down, the other can drag it out, fetch help or transport passengers to shelter. There is increased traffic in July and August on the most popular routes, so this is not an absolutely necessary precaution during summer, but is recommended if you are heading onto less-travelled tracks.

Fill up before setting out There are no petrol stations in the highlands, except at Hrauneyjar, south of the Sprengisandur route. Möðrudalur, close to one of the northern entrances to the Askja route, also sells fuel. Despite some websites' advice, there is no petrol available at Hveravellir on the Kjölur route.

Supplies Depending on your itinerary you may need additional fuel. You will certainly need food supplies – there are very few places in the highlands selling food.

Buses and/or tours These make a good alternative to driving yourself. You can use the 4WD summer buses on the Kjölur and Sprengisandur routes as a day tour (travelling between, say, Reykjavík and Akureyri in one burst), or as a regular bus, hopping on and off along the route. Tour operators offer comfortable super-Jeep vehicles and experienced drivers/guides.

No off-road driving In the highlands, as with everywhere in Iceland, stick to numbered roads and marked trails. Off-road driving is hugely destructive to the country's fragile environment, and illegal. There are now police in the highlands enforcing the law.

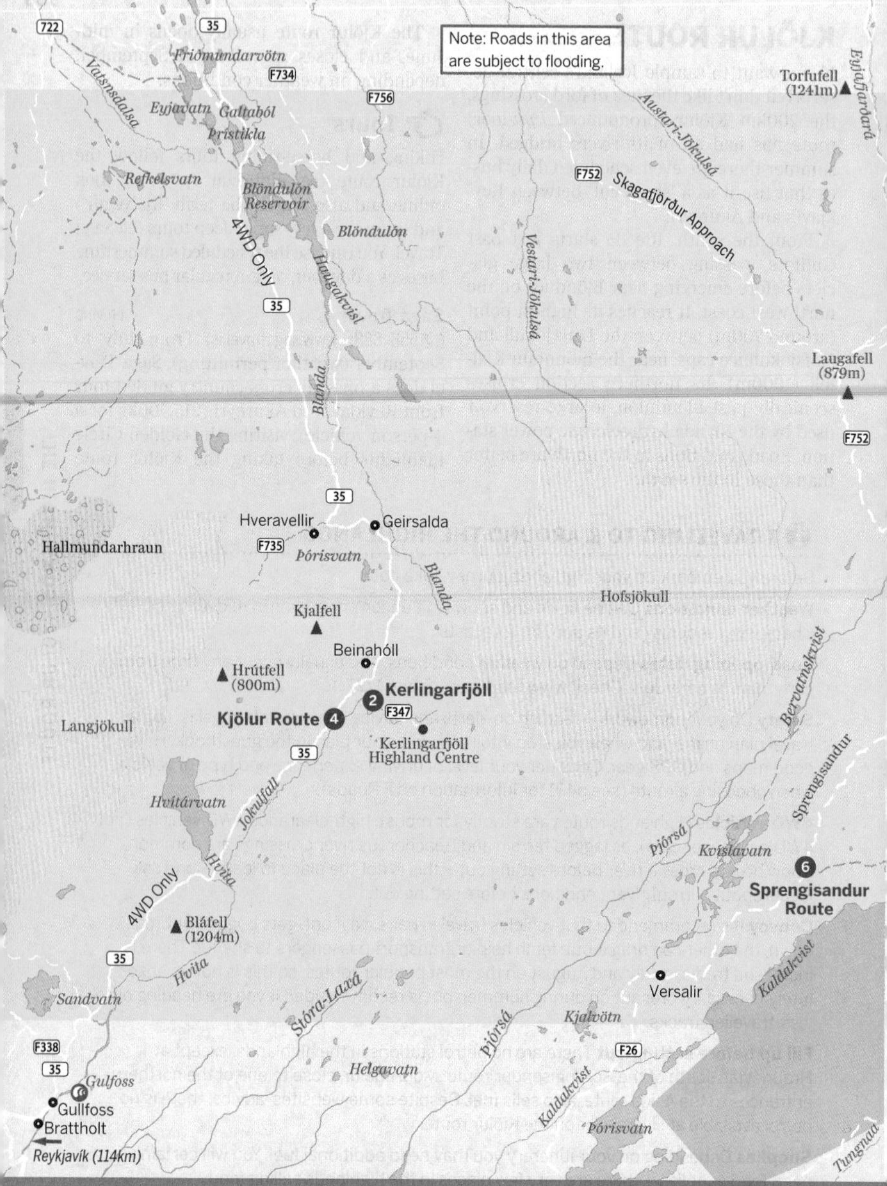

The Highlands Highlights

1 Askja (p370) Hiking across the lava field, drinking in the caldera views, then soaking in the waters of Víti crater.

2 Kerlingarfjöll (p363) Investigating hiking trails around the majestic massif and its striated geothermal valley.

3 Herðubreið (p369) Paying homage to the Queen of the Mountains.

4 Kjölur route (p359) Spicing up the endless vistas of

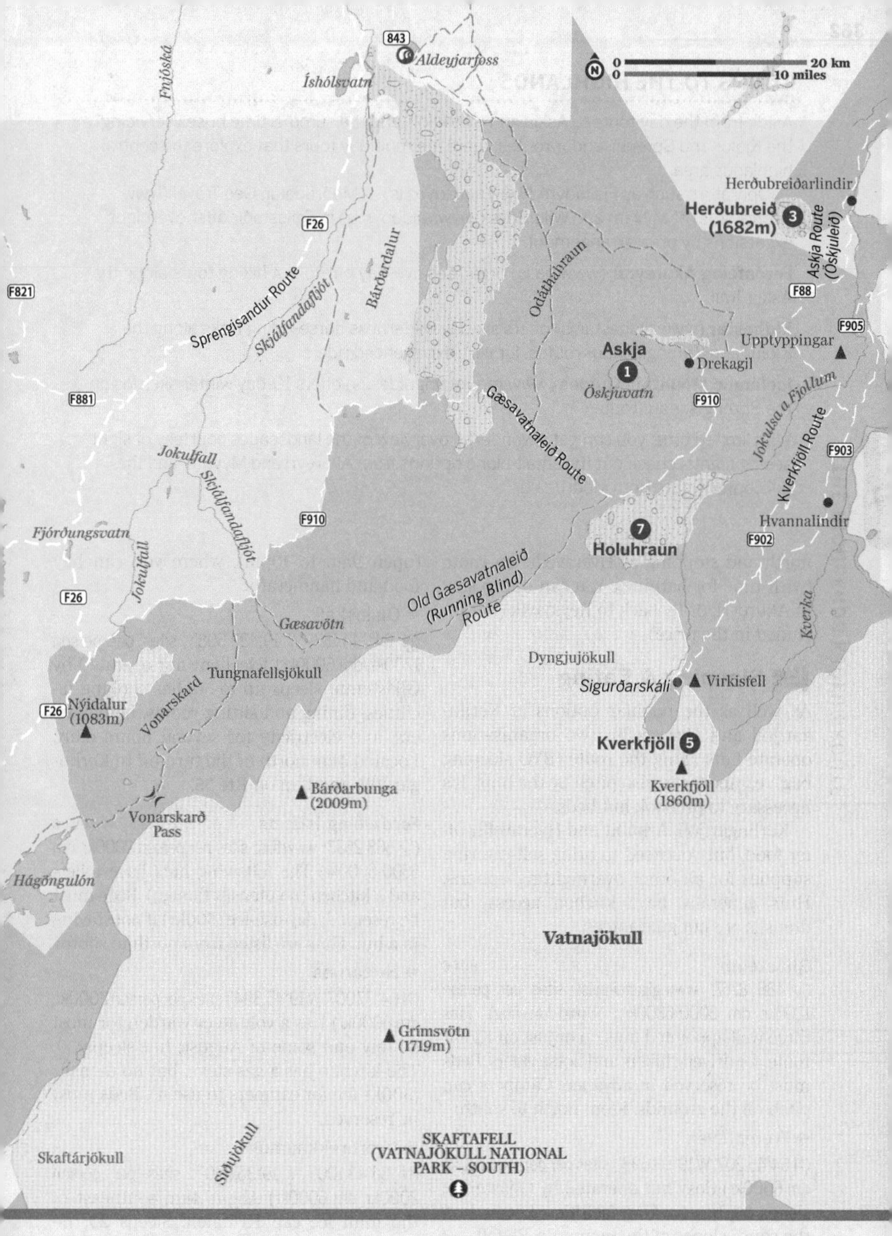

rock and ice with stops at hot springs and climbable crags.

5 Kverkfjöll (p372) Marvelling at the openings of geothermal caves in a vast glacier.

6 Sprengisandur route (p364) Pitying the melancholy ghosts and outlaws on Iceland's longest, loneliest north–south track.

7 Holuhraun (p371) Getting an impressive geology lesson and treading gingerly on Iceland's newest lava field.

TOURS TO THE HIGHLANDS

Aside from the day tours to Askja and Kverkfjöll, and the summertime buses servicing the Kjölur and Sprengisandur routes, there are multiday tours that explore the central highlands area.

Operators such as Fjalladýrð (www.fjalladyrd.is) at Möðrudalur, Geo Travel (www.geotravel.is) at Mývatn and Wild Boys (www.wildboys.is) in Egilsstaðir offer overnight excursions by prior arrangement.

Ferðafélag Akureyrar (www.ffa.is) organises five-day hut-to-hut hiking tours along the Askja Trail.

Eldhestar (www.eldhestar.is) offers six-day wilderness horse-riding treks along the Kjölur and Sprengisandur routes, for very experienced riders.

Icelandic Mountain Guides (www.mountainguides.is) offers 10-day winter ski trips on the Sprengisandur route.

With limited time, you can get a wonderful overview of the landscapes courtesy of sightseeing flights; check out the small-plane options from Akureyri and Mývatn, and the helicopter flights from Möðrudalur.

north and stopping at Hveravellir en route (with time for bathing). You can opt to stay in Akureyri, or fly back to Reykjavík (not included in the price).

Sleeping & Eating

As well as the popular options at Kerlingarfjöll and Hveravellir, two organisations operate huts along the route (BYO sleeping bag); campers can also pitch by the huts. It's necessary to prebook hut beds.

Kerlingarfjöll, Árbúðir and Hveravellir offer food, but you need to bring self-catering supplies for all other overnighting options. Huts generally have kitchen access, but utensils are not guaranteed.

Gljásteinn — HUT €

(☎486 8757; www.gljasteinn.is; sites per person 1200kr, dm 6000-6800kr; ⏲mid-Jun–Aug) Has three well-appointed huts on or just off Kjölur route, for drivers, hikers and horse riders. Beds must be reserved in advance. Campers can pitch on the grounds. From north to south:

➡ **Fremstaver**

(N 64°45.207', W 19°93.699'; sites per person 1200kr, dm 6000kr) Cosy hut operated by Gljásteinn; sleeps 25, has cooking facilities. Located on the south slopes of the mountain Bláfell.

➡ **Árbúðir**

(N 64°609.036', W 19°702.947'; sites per person 1000kr, dm 6800kr) Good hut operated by Gljásteinn; sleeps 30, has cooking facilities and hot shower (750kr). Located on the banks of the Svartá river, right on Rte 35 about 42km north of Gullfoss. There's a small cafe here (open 9am to 10pm), where you can buy food and handicrafts.

➡ **Gíslaskáli**

(N 64°744.187', W 19°432.508'; sites per person 1200kr, dm 6000kr) Excellent hut operated by Gljásteinn; sleeps up to 50, has cooking facilities, dining and sitting rooms, hot showers, and electricity for several hours daily. Located 4km north of the turn-off to Kerlingarfjöll, and 1km off Rte 35.

Ferðafélag Íslands — HUT €

(☎568 2533; www.fi.is; sites per person 2000kr, dm 5500-6000kr) The following huts have toilets and a kitchen (no utensils though). Beds must be reserved; day-use-fee (500kr) if not staying in a hut. Huts are listed from north to south:

➡ **Hvítárnes**

(N 64°37.007', W 19°45.394'; sites per person 2000kr, dm 6000kr) Has a volunteer warden for most of July and some of August; hut sleeps 30. The kitchen has a gas stove, but no utensils (500kr fee for campers to use it). Beds must be reserved.

➡ **Þverbrekknamúli**

(N 64°43.100', W 19°36.860'; sites per person 2000kr, dm 6000kr) About 4km southeast of the mini ice cap Hrútafell. Sleeps 20; no warden. Beds must be reserved. Generally, not accessible by car.

➡ **Þjófadalir**

(N 64°48.900', W 19°42.510'; sites per person 2000kr, dm 5500kr) Sleeps 11, at the foot of the mountain Rauðkollur, about 12km southwest of Hveravellir. No warden. Beds must be reserved. Not accessible by car.

Getting There & Away

BICYCLE

Of all the interior routes, Kjölur is probably the best for cycling. For a humorous account, read Tim Moore's *Frost on My Moustache*.

Note that the summertime scheduled bus along the Kjölur carries bikes (4000kr) with pre-booking.

BUS

In summer scheduled buses travel along the Kjölur route between Reykjavík and Akureyri (in both directions). You can use it as a day tour, or as a regular bus service. It's also part of Reykjavík Excursions bus passport.

SBA-Norðurleið (www.sba.is) runs Bus 610 Reykjavík–Akureyri, 610a Akureyri–Reykjavík (once daily mid-June to mid-September) SBA's service takes 10½ hours for the complete journey, with half-hour stops at Geysir and Gullfoss. Then it stops at Hvítárnes crossroads and Árbúðir. There's a 15-minute stop at Kerlingarfjöll, and an hour at Hveravellir (time for a dip). The final two stops before Akureyri are Svartá and Varmahlíð. The entire journey costs 17,900kr one way.

Note that the bus may be an appealing option at first; however, we've received comments from readers that while the first hour of outback desolation is riveting, the other nine hours can be bumpy or snooze-inducing if you aren't planning to disembark anywhere along the way.

CAR

The Kjölur route is labelled Rte 35 (not F35), but it is still a mountain road, and while it is technically possible to drive a 2WD along the route, it is absolutely not sanctioned (posted signs are clear on this!). Car-hire companies expressly forbid the use of 2WD rentals on the route and you will be liable for any damage (there are potholes/puddles that could almost swallow a small car, you'll do damage to the car's underside, and your journey will be slow and very bumpy).

Drivers with 4WD vehicles will have no problems on the Kjölur route. If you're in a 2WD and curious for a taste of the highlands, you can drive the first 14km of the route (north of Gullfoss) which are sealed.

Hvítárvatn

The pale-blue lake Hvítárvatn (pronounced *kvi*-towr-vatn), 35km northeast of Gullfoss, is the source of the glacial river Hvítá – a popular destination for Reykjavík-based white-water rafting operators. A glacier tongue of Iceland's second-largest ice cap, Langjökull, calves into the lake and creates icebergs occasionally, adding to the beauty of this spot.

To come by bus, get out at the Hvítárnes crossroads and walk 8km along the 4WD track to the hut.

Kerlingarfjöll

Until the 1850s Icelanders believed that this mountain range (10km off Rte 35 on Rte F347) harboured the worst outlaws. It was thought they lived deep in the heart of the 150-sq-km range in an isolated Shangri-la-type valley. So strong was this belief that it was only in the mid-19th century that anyone ventured into Kerlingarfjöll, and it was only in 1941 that the range was properly explored by Ferðafélag Íslands (Iceland Touring Association).

The colourfully dramatic landscape is broken up into jagged peaks and ridges, the highest of which is Snækollur (1477m), and it's scattered with hot springs. The striated steaming geothermal valley called **Hveradalir** is a highlight.

Access to Kerlingarfjöll is 10km off Rte 35 on Rte F347. The bus stops here.

Note: petrol is not available at Kerlingarfjöll Highland Centre (despite its symbol still appearing on a handful of maps and signs).

Activities

A stunningly colourful but difficult 5km hike ascends from the Kerlingarfjöll Highland Centre to the geothermal area of **Hveradalir**.

KJÖLUR HIKING

Looking for an independent multi-day hike in the area?

Old Kjalvegur route (www.fi.is) An easy and scenic three-day hike (39km) from Hvítárvatn to Hveravellir (or vice versa). The trail follows the original horseback Kjölur route (west of the present road), via the Hvítárnes, Þverbrekknamúli and Þjófadalir mountain huts.

Hringbrautin (www.kerlingarfjoll.is/routes) A challenging three-day circuit (47km) around Kerlingarfjöll, starting and ending at Kerlingarfjöll Highland Centre, with huts at Klakkur and Kisubotnar.

Check on conditions before undertaking it, though – it's usually too muddy to be safe until well into July. Most people opt to drive the 15 minutes to a parking area at Mt Keis, from where Hveradalir is a short, steep walk downhill.

The Highland Centre tour operator, Mountains.is (www.mountains.is) offers tours throughout the area.

Sleeping & Eating

Self-cater (there are cooking facilities at Kerlingarfjöll Highland Centre), or visit the small restaurant here. The breakfast buffet is 2200kr; sandwiches and soups are served during the day; and there are simple, tasty evening options (fish stew, baked salmon, lamb soup).

★**Kerlingarfjöll Highland Centre** GUESTHOUSE €€
(☎summer 664 7878, year-round 664 7000; www.kerlingarfjoll.is; sites per person 2000kr, d with bathroom, incl breakfast 32,850kr; ⊙mid-Jun–mid-Sep; 📶) There is a broad range of hotel, huts and houses at this great, remote centre, with various bathroom configurations and linen options (sleeping-bag accommodation 5900kr to 7900kr). There's also a campsite, guest kitchen with basic utensils, simple restaurant (dinner mains 3100kr to 3800kr) and natural hot-pots. They operate two mountain huts, allowing a three-day loop walk in the area.

Hveravellir

Hveravellir Nature Reserve is a popular geothermal area of fumaroles and hot springs, located about halfway between Gullfoss in the south and the Ring Road in the north. Among its warm pools are the brilliant-blue Bláhver; Öskurhólshver (pronounced *usk*-ur-howls-kver), which emits a constant stream of hissing steam; and a luscious human-made **bathing pool**. Another hot spring, Eyvindurhver, is named after the outlaw Fjalla-Eyvindur. Hveravellir is reputedly one of the many highland hideouts of this renegade.

A service fee (500kr) applies for all day guests using parking, toilets or showers.

Hveravellir HUT €
(☎summer 452 4200, year-round 894 1293; www.hveravellir.is; sites per person 1900kr, dm 7500kr, r incl breakfast 28,500kr; ⊙Jun-Sep, call ahead Oct-May; 📶) The Old Hut sleeps about 30 in dorm beds (linen available for 2000kr) with cooking facilities. The New Hut has private rooms (28,500kr) with shared bathrooms, and no cooking facilities. There's also a campsite, simple cafe and store. Helpful staff assist with information on local hiking trails. They also operate the Áfangi hut, about 38km north, near Blöndulón reservoir.

The small cafe (open 7am to 10pm) offers breakfast (1800kr), and there are soups, sandwiches, cakes, and hot dishes such as fish bake, or chicken and potatoes (mains 2900kr to 3100kr). Offers wi-fi hotspot for a fee.

SPRENGISANDUR ROUTE

To Icelanders, the name Sprengisandur conjures up images of outlaws, ghosts and long sheep drives across the barren wastes. The Sprengisandur route (F26) is the longest north–south trail, and crosses bleak desert moors that can induce a shudder even today in a 4WD.

Sprengisandur offers some wonderful views of Vatnajökull, Tungnafellsjökull and Hofsjökull, as well as Askja and Herðubreið. An older route, now abandoned, lies a few kilometres west of the current one.

The Route

The Sprengisandur route proper begins at Rte 842 near Goðafoss in northwest Iceland. Some 41km later, you'll pass through a metal gate as the road turns into F26. There's a billboard explaining the sights and finer points of the route, and 1km later you'll come upon one of Iceland's most photogenic waterfalls, Aldeyjarfoss (p303). Churning water bursts over the cliff's edge as it splashes through a narrow canyon lined with the signature honeycomb columns of basalt. And just a bit further lies the multiple churning chutes of **Hrafnabjargafoss** (F26), 1km down a signposted turn-off.

After the falls, the Sprengisandur route continues southwest through 240km of inhospitable territory all the way to Þjórsárdalur. There are two other ways to approach Sprengisandur, both of which link up to the main road about halfway through:

Eyjafjörður Approach From the north, the F821 from southern Eyjafjörður (south of Akureyri) connects to the Skagafjörður approach at Laugafell.

Skagafjörður Approach From the northwest, the 81km-long F752 connects southern Skagafjörður (the nearest town is Varmahlíð on the Ring Road) to the Sprengisandur route. The roads join near the lake Fjórðungsvatn (pronounced *fyorth*-ungs-vatn), 20km east of Hofsjökull.

THE BADLANDS

Historically in Iceland, once a person had been convicted of outlawry they were beyond society's protection and aggrieved enemies could kill them at will. Many outlaws (*útilegumenn*), such as the renowned Eiríkur Rauðe (Erik the Red), voluntarily took exile abroad. Others escaped revenge-killing by fleeing into the mountains, valleys and broad expanses of the harsh Icelandic interior, where few dared pursue them.

Undoubtedly, anyone who could live year-round in these bitter, barren deserts must have been extraordinary. Icelandic outlaws were naturally credited with all sorts of fearsome feats, and the general populace came to fear the vast badlands, which they considered to be the haunt of superhuman evil. The *útilegumenn* thereby joined the ranks of giants and trolls, and provided the themes for popular tales such as the fantastic *Grettir's Saga*.

One particular outlaw has become the subject of countless Icelandic folk tales. Fjalla-Eyvindur ('Eyvindur of the Mountains'), a charming but incurable 18th-century kleptomaniac, fled into the highlands with his wife, and continued to make enemies by rustling sheep to stay alive. Throughout the highlands you'll see shelters and hideouts attributed to him and hear tales of his ability to survive in impossible conditions while always staying one jump ahead of his pursuers.

The main route generally opens around the start of July.

Getting There & Away

BUS

In July and August, Reykjavík Excursions (www.re.is/iceland-on-your-own/) operates along the Sprengisandur route (dates determined by road-opening dates).

Reykjavík Excursionsruns Bus 14 Landmannalaugar–Mývatn, 14a Mývatn–Landmannalaugar (one weekly, total journey 10 hours, entire route 16,100kr). Although it's a scheduled bus, it's used as a tour of sorts, with extended pauses at Nýidalur, Aldeyjarfoss and Goðafoss.

These buses along the Sprengisandur carry bikes (4000kr).

CAR

Only true high-suspension (super-Jeep) 4WDs can traverse the Sprengisandur route; large rivers bar the way. Even with a proper 4WD, you will be liable for any damage to a rental vehicle caused by fording rivers, so only do so if you are experienced.

There's no fuel along the route. Goðafoss to Hrauneyjar is 240km, so plan accordingly.

The nearest petrol stations are at Akureyri (from the Eyjafjörður approach); Varmahlíð (from the Skagafjörður approach) or Fosshóll, near Goðafoss (if you're coming from the north along the main route through Bárðardalur). There is petrol at Hrauneyjar if you're driving from the south.

Laugafell

The main site of interest on the Skagafjörður approach is Laugafell, an 879m-high mountain with hot springs bubbling on its northwestern slopes. You can stay nearby at hiker huts, whose best feature is the geothermally heated, natural swimming pool.

Laugafell Hut HUT €

(☎462 2720, Jul & Aug 822 5192; www.ffa.is; N 65°01.630', W 18°19.950'; sites per person 2000kr, dm 7500kr;) Stay near Laugafell at the Ferðafélag Akureyrar hut, with 35 beds, a kitchen and a magnificent, geothermally heated, natural swimming pool. There's a warden on-site in July and August.

Getting There & Away

Laugafell is on both the Skagafjörður approach (93km via Rte 752 and F752) and the Eyjafjörður approach (87km south of Akureyri via Rte 821 and F821) to the Sprengisandur route.

There is no bus service.

A few tour companies out of Akureryi offer 4WD day tours to this area, including the Traveling Viking (p295).

Nýidalur

Nýidalur (also known as Jökuldalur), the range just south of the Tungnafellsjökull ice cap, was discovered by a lost traveller in 1845. With facilities including a campsite and huts, plus appealing hiking trails, it's the most popular rest spot for travellers along the Sprengisandur route. It's about 100km from Hrauneyjar.

You'll need to bring food. The hut has a kitchen (with pots, utensils); note that campers cannot use hut facilities.

There is a **Vatnajökull National Park ranger** (842 4377; www.vjp.is; Jul & Aug) in summer.

Nýidalur Hut HUT €
(Jul & Aug 860 3334; www.fi.is; N 64°44.130', W 18°04.350'; sites per person 2000kr, dm 8500kr) With a campsite, two huts (sleeping up to 79 people) and lots of hiking, Nýidalur makes for a great break in a Sprengisandur journey. The huts have kitchen facilities, showers (500kr) and a summer warden (July and August). Book your bed in advance. Campers cannot use hut facilities.

Getting There & Away

There are two rivers – the one 500m from the hut is usually difficult to cross (even for a 4WD). Ask locally for advice on conditions.

The Sprengisandur buses stop here.

Þórisvatn

Before water was diverted from Kaldakvísl into Þórisvatn (pronounced *thor*-is-vatn) from the Tungnaá hydroelectric scheme in southwest Iceland, it had a surface area of 70 sq km. Now it's one of the country's largest lakes at 85 sq km.

The lake is 11km northeast of the junction between Rte F26 and the Fjallabak route (F208). The closest dining options are found at the Hrauneyjar complex, southwest of the lake.

Veiðivötn

The beautiful area of Veiðivötn (pronounced *veeth*-i-vutn), just northeast of Landmannalaugar (p156), is an entanglement of small desert lakes in a volcanic basin, a continuation of the same fissure that produced Laugahraun in the Fjallabak Nature Reserve. This is a popular place for trout fishing.

The area is about 30km from Hrauneyjar's accommodation, or there are basic huts and camping available in summer (sleeping-bag bed 3500kr, campsite 4000kr), plus fishing licences – see www.veidivotn.is or email ampi@simnet.is. Licences for lakes further south are sold at Landmannahellir.

You will need to be fully self-sufficient. Bring self-catering supplies.

Access to this area is via Rte F228, east of Hrauneyjar.

Hrauneyjar

Somewhat unexpectedly, in the middle of lava and scree fields west of Þórisvatn in the Hrauneyjar region, you'll find a year-round guesthouse and hotel. They lie at the crossroads of the Sprengisandur route (F26) and the F208 to Landmannalaugar, so are handy for highland attractions and have marked walking trails in the area.

There is a **Vatnajökull National Park ranger** (842 4376; www.vjp.is; 9am-5pm mid-Jun–Aug) in summer.

The Hrauneyjar accommodations have high rates, but are in great demand due to their proximity to Landmannalaugar.

There are no cooking facilities at the Highland Center, but they do have two restaurants, and you can buy a few basic supplies, too. Bring most supplies from further afield.

Highland Center Hrauneyjar HOTEL €€€
(487 7782; www.thehighlandcenter.is; Rte 26; d/tr incl breakfast from 24,900/38,800kr, apt 53,500kr;) Hrauneyjar has both a simpler guesthouse building with smaller rooms and sleeping-bag accommodation (13,400kr) and a restaurant (mains 1900kr to 5800kr), as well as a complex with larger, more luxurious rooms; bar and smart gourmet restaurant; hot-pot and sauna about 1.4km away. The latter is only open for groups of eight or more from October to May.

Petrol and diesel are available at Hrauneyjar's Highland Center. There is a sealed road to Hrauneyjar from the west on Rte 32 (it branches off Rte 30 between Selfoss and Flúðir), or you can access it from Rte 26 (off the Ring Road near Hella).

Buses travelling the Sprengisandur route call at Hrauneyjar.

ASKJA ROUTE

The brilliant Askja route (Öskjuleið) runs across the multi-hued highlands to Herðubreið (1682m), the Icelanders' beloved 'Queen of the Mountains', and to the region's most popular marvel, the immense Askja caldera.

The usual access road is Rte F88, which leaves the Ring Road 32km east of Mývatn, but the route slightly east via Rtes F905 and F910 (close to Möðrudalur) has more reliable river crossings.

The Route

Rte F88 leaves the Ring Road at **Hrossaborg**, a 10,000-year-old crater shaped like an amphitheatre, used as a film set for the Tom Cruise sci-fi film *Oblivion* (2013). For much of the way the F88 is a flat journey, following the western bank of the Jökulsá á Fjöllum glacier river, meandering across tephra expanses and winding circuitously through rough, tyre-abusing sections of the 4400-sq-km **Ódáðahraun** (pronounced o-dow-tha-roin; Evil Deeds Lava Field).

Then there are two river crossings, one of which routinely swamps smaller jeeps. Check on conditions before setting out.

After the long journey through hypnotic lava- and flood-washed plains, you reach the lovely verdant oasis of **Herðubreiðarlindir**, at the foot of **Herðubreið**. The route then scoops westwards through ever more remote dunes and lava flows, past the **Drekagil gorge** with its huts and up the hill towards Askja, where you leave your car to walk the remaining 2.5km into the **caldera**.

Note that the approach to Askja via Rtes F905 and F910 (close to Möðrudalur) have more reliable river crossings. Always check before setting out, though.

Activities

For independent hikers, the website of Ferðafélag Akureyrar, the Touring Club of Akureyri (www.ffa.is), outlines details of the **Askja Trail**, known in Icelandic as Öskjuvegurinn. This is the organisation's walking trail with huts across the Ódáðahraun, starting from Herðubreiðarlindir and ending at Svartárkot farm in upper Bárðardalur (pronounced *bowr*-thar-dalur) valley (Rte 843). Hut beds must be booked well in advance with FFA; see the website.

Also see the national-park website (www.vjp.is) for hiking information.

Independent long-distance hikers should inform a park ranger of their plans; leave a travel plan at safetravel.is; and whenever stopping at a hut, write your plan in the guestbook.

For hiker transport in the area, your best best is Mývatn Tours (p368) or Fjalladýrð. They can drop you at a hut and arrange to pick you up a few days later.

Tours

Several operators run super-Jeep tours to Askja, from mid-June (when the route opens) until as late into September/October as weather permits.

From Akureyri it makes for a brutally long day (up to 15 hours); a better base is Reykjahlíð at Mývatn (even then, tour time is around 11 to 12 hours), or better yet Möðrudalur (nine or 10 hours). For a more relaxed pace (and a chance to experience highland evening stillness), consider a two-day tour.

For all tours, you are expected to bring/order a packed lunch and water; some operators stop for a late-afternoon coffee at Möðrudalur en route home; others head further south to the new lava field at Holuhraun. Don't forget your swimsuit and towel, too, should you fancy a chilly dip in Víti crater at Askja.

It's worth noting that with the growth of tourism, many of these companies are offering more highland exploration, including customised multi-day tours, guided hikes, and 4WD treks to lesser-known natural features. There is also a notable growth in winter tours (in huge, weather-defying super-Jeep vehicles or by snowmobile).

See tour company websites for latest prices and offerings, and for advice on what to bring.

★Fjalladýrð JEEP, HIKING

(☎471 1858; www.fjalladyrd.is; Rte 901, Möðrudalur) Based at Möðrudalur farm on Rte 901 these expert, local guides are perfectly placed for Askja tours (36,000kr) via F905 and F910. Tours also visit both Askja and Kverkfjöll (over one/two days 44,000/72,000kr) or hike up Herðubreið (36,000kr). They have excellent accommodation (p313) and eating options (p313) right at the departure point.

Geo Travel JEEP

(☎864 7080; www.geotravel.is) A great small company owned by two local guys. Small-group day tours run from Reykjahlíð and visit Askja and Holuhraun (34,900kr). Also has a two-day tour to Holuhraun, Askja and Kverkfjöll (rates based on passenger numbers).

LUNAR LANDSCAPES

If the infinite grey-sand desert and jagged lava formations of Ódáðahraun appear other-worldly, you'll understand why NASA astronauts of the *Apollo* mission twice visited the area around Askja (more specifically, the area south of the F910 east of Askja and near Drekagil) for astrogeological field trips in the 1960s.

MAJOR HIGHLAND ROUTES

Kjölur route (Rte 35) North–south route across the country. Served by summer buses. All rivers bridged.

Sprengisandur route (Rte F26) North–south route across the country. Served by summer buses.

Askja route (Öskjuleið; Rte F88 or F905/910) Access from Iceland's north to Askja caldera, Herðubreið mountain and the new Holuhraun lava field. Served by numerous tour operators, primarily from Mývatn.

Kverkfjöll route (Rte F905, F910, then F902) Access from Iceland's north or east to Kverkfjöll and its ice caves and glacier Kverkjökull. Served by a few tour operators.

Landmannalaugar and its famous Laugavegurinn Hike, plus Fjallabak Nature Reserve, in the Southwest, and Snæfell, in the East, are also brilliant places to explore.

Wild Boys HIKING
(☎896 4334, 864 7393; www.wildboys.is) This company operates out of Egilsstaðir, so a number of its hiking tours focus on eastern highlands areas like Kverkfjöll and Snaefell. Book multi-day tours, such as three days' hiking around Kverkfjöll (129,900kr), through www.traveleast.is.

Ferðafélag Akureyrar HIKING
(Touring Club of Akureyri; FFA; Map p292; ☎462 2720; www.ffa.is; Strandgata 23, Akureyri) A couple of times a year (in summer), Ferðafélag Akureyrar organises five-day hut-to-hut hiking tours (85,900kr per person) along the Askja Trail. See 'Touring Program' on its website for details; the program is in Icelandic, so look for 'Öskjuvegur' in July and August to see specific dates.

Saga Travel JEEP, BUS
(☎558 8888; www.sagatravel.is) Reliable option departing daily by bus from both Akureyri and Mývatn (from Akureyri/Mývatn 34,900/24,900kr – note that the trip from Akureyri heads off at 6.30am and may be up to 16 hours) and by super-Jeep from Mývatn (34,900kr). Saga also offers longer private multi-day tours.

Jeep Tours JEEP
(☎898 2798; www.jeeptours.is; Egilsstaðir) Jeep Tours runs unique tours out of Egilsstaðir in East Iceland, contrary to the other companies that approach Askja from the north. Day tours to Askja (46,500kr), Kverkfjöll (46,500kr) and the eastern highlands. Tours travel via the (sealed) Rte 910 to Kárahnjúkar dam before tackling lesser-known 4WD tracks.

Fjallasýn JEEP, BUS
(☎464 3941; www.fjallasyn.is) Bus and jeep tours daily to Askja (24,900kr) from Reykjahlíð. Also offers plenty of interior explorations (including a two-day tour to Kverkfjöll upon request) and guided multi-day hiking options. Can depart from the company's base in Húsavík.

North Travel BUS
(☎566 4000; www.northtravel.is) Works with bus company SBA-Norðurleið to run a popular three-day Askja–Kverkfjöll–Vatnajökull tour (including Holuhraun), operating from early July to late August. It departs weekly (Monday) from Akureyri and picks up in Akureyri and Mývatn. Cost is 58,500kr, which includes transport and guide (but not food or accommodation; hut reservations arranged).

Mývatn Tours BUS
(☎464 1920; www.askjatours.is; Mývatn) Tours in a large 4WD bus daily from late June to early September (23,000kr), from Reykjahlíð, plus other packages. This is the best option if you want hikers' transport to the area, and to be picked up another day.

ℹ Information

Askja is part of the vast Vatnajökull National Park, so the park website (www.vjp.is) has excellent information and produces good maps highlighting hiking trails in the area.

There are national park rangers stationed at Drekagil (☎842 4357) in summer, providing information for visitors.

ℹ Getting There & Away

There's no public transport along the Askja route, but there are plentiful tours. Alternatively, hire a large 4WD jeep and prepare for a rocky ride (seek local advice on fording rivers). The route usually opens in mid- to late June.

If you take F88 into Askja, it's a good idea to leave along F910/F905 (with easier rivers) for variety's sake. Other options from Askja include heading east towards Egilsstaðir, or west on the extremely difficult Gæsavatnaleið route (F910 west) to Sprengisandur (ask locally for advice on conditions – it's only for super-Jeeps). To reach Kverkfjöll, head east on F910, then south on F902.

There are no fuel stops anywhere on the route. The nearest ones are at Möðrudalur (90km from Askja) and Mývatn (120km from Askja). Plan accordingly.

Herðubreiðarlindir

The oasis Herðubreiðarlindir, a nature reserve thick with green moss, angelica and the pinky-purple flower of the Arctic river beauty *Epilobium latifolium,* was created by springs flowing from beneath the Ódáðahraun lava. You get a superb close-up view of Herðubreið from here (unless, of course, you're greeted by dense fog and/or a wall of blowing sand).

There's an appealing hut and campground here, and a summertime ranger station. Behind the hut is a Fjalla-Eyvindur 'convict hole'. Outlaw Eyvindur is believed to have occupied it during the winter of 1774–75, when he subsisted on angelica root, raw horsemeat stored on top of the hideout to retain heat inside, and water from the stream running through the hole.

The Þorsteinsskáli hut and camp area are popular, and offer a greener, more welcoming landscape than that encountered at Drekagil.

There is nowhere to buy food. Bring your own self-catering supplies.

Þorsteinsskáli Hut HUT €
(☎ 822 5191; www.ffa.is; N 65°11.544', W 16°13.360'; site/dm per person 2000/7500kr) Verdant Herðubreiðarlindir has an information office staffed by summer wardens, a campsite and the 30-bed Þorsteinsskáli hut, a cosy lodge with showers (500kr) and kitchen. Book your hut beds in advance.

Herðubreiðarlindir is about 60km from Hrossaborg, at the northern point of Rte F88, and another 35km on to Drekagil.

Herðubreið

Icelanders call Herðubreið (pronounced *hair*-the-breth), its most distinctive mountain (1682m), the 'Queen of the Mountains'. Majestic Herðubreið (meaning 'Broad Shoulders') is visible for miles around, and it crops up time and again in the work of local poets and painters, entranced by its beauty.

It's a *móberg* mountain, formed by subglacial volcanic eruptions. In fact, if Vatnajökull was to suddenly be stripped of ice, Grímsvötn and Kverkfjöll would probably emerge looking more or less like Herðubreið.

The hut and camping area for Herðubreið is nearby, at Herðubreiðarlindir.

Drekagil

The name of the gorge Drekagil, 35km southwest of Herðubreið, means 'Dragon Canyon', after the shapes of dragons in the craggy rock formations that tower over it. A hike up the twisting **canyon** (behind the

HIKING HERÐUBREIÐ

If you wish to climb Herðubreið, beware that a topographic sheet won't do you much good here. As serenely beautiful as the queen may be, the hike can be unrelenting, frustrating and dangerous if you're not properly prepared. In the spring, as the weather warms slightly, there are a lot of falling rocks, which alter paths and topography. Clouds often shroud the mountain, which makes it difficult to find your way. A GPS is a must, as is a helmet, plus crampons and an ice axe (and experience in using them).

Herðubreið was once thought to be unclimbable, but it was eventually scaled in 1908. Under optimum conditions you can climb the mountain in summer over one long day. From the Þorsteinsskáli hut, a 12km marked trail runs around Herðubreið to the base at the western slope. From there, a route to the top ascends the western slope. We don't want you to get the wrong idea, however; this climb is demanding, and the threat of snow, rockfall, landslide or bad weather makes it impossible to tackle without the proper mountaineering gear.

Don't go alone, prepare for foul weather, and it is required that you discuss your intentions with the wardens at Herðubreiðarlindir. Consider joining a tour – Fjalladýrð at Möðrudalur can arrange this.

Dreki huts) leads to an impressive waterfall which is only accessible when the canyon's river is low enough to pass.

You can also walk (or drive) 8km up the marked trail to Askja, and there is a marked 20km trail to the Bræðrafell (pronounced *bri*-thra-fetl) hut; consult Dreki rangers first, as the hut is often locked.

The Dreki huts are an ideal base for exploring the area, and day-use of the facilities (bathroom etc) costs 500kr per person.

There is a **ranger station** (☎842 4357; open 8am to 7pm) at Drekagil in the summer.

There is nowhere to buy food. Bring your own self-catering supplies.

Dreki Huts HUT €

(Askja Camp; ☎822 5190; www.ffa.is; N 65°02.503', W 16°35.690'; site/dm per person 2000/8500kr; ⏲mid-/late Jun–early Sep) The Dreki huts, operated by Ferðafélag Akureyrar (Touring Club of Akureyri), sleep a total of 60, and there are showers, a kitchen, a ranger information centre (8am to 7pm) and a warden here. Camping is also permitted, but the wind (bringing dust) and cold may be oppressive for tent campers (consider the lusher site at Herðubreiðarlindir, 35km away).

The Dreki huts and camp area are popular. Book your hut bed in advance.

Getting There & Away

From Drekagil there's an 8km road to reach the Askja car park, and it's then a scenic 2.5km walk across the caldera's lava fields to reach the lake.

At Drekagil the Gæsavatnaleið (pronounced *gi*-sa-vatna-leith) route (F910) turns off the Askja route to cross some intimidating expanses and connect with the Sprengisandur route at Nýidalur, some 125km away. This involves a number of river crossings and is only for large vehicles. Taking the F910 to the east will connect to F902 to Kverkfjöll.

Askja

The utterly remote and inspiring Askja caldera is the main destination for all tours in this northeastern part of the highlands. This immense 50-sq-km caldera shouldn't be missed – as you walk into the multi-coloured snow-rimmed site you'll find it difficult to imagine the sorts of forces that created it.

Your first glimpse of the sapphire-blue lake **Öskjuvatn**, at the heart of the crater, is guaranteed to be a memorable one. The lake stands in contrast to the milky waters inside the small, steep crater known as **Víti**, adjacent to the caldera.

Although a bit on the chilly side (temperatures are currently about 22°C), a dip in Víti's milky blue pool is one of the highlights of an Askja adventure (and is sometimes done sans swimsuit). The route down is slippery and steep, so it may be closed for safety reasons.

Free, ranger-led, one-hour hikes leave from the Askja car park at 1pm daily mid-July to mid-August.

ASKJA HISTORY

The cataclysm that formed the lake in the Askja caldera (and the Víti crater) happened relatively recently (in 1875) when 2 cu km of tephra was ejected from the Askja volcano. The force was so strong that bits of debris actually landed in Continental Europe. Ash from the eruption poisoned large numbers of cattle in northern Iceland, sparking a wave of emigration to America. It's quite daunting to realise that such cataclysmic events could be replayed at any time.

After the initial eruption, a magma chamber collapsed and created a humongous, craterous 11-sq-km hole, 300m below the rim of the original explosion crater. Part of this new depression subsequently filled with water and became the lake Öskjuvatn, the second-deepest in Iceland at 220m.

In the eruption a vent near the northeastern corner of the lake exploded and formed the tephra crater Víti, which contains geothermal water. This is one of two well-known craters called Víti, the other being at Krafla near Mývatn. (FYI: Víti means 'hell' in Icelandic.)

In 1907 German researchers Max Rudloff and Walther von Knebel were rowing on the lake when they completely vanished; their bodies were never found. It was suggested that the lake may have hazardous quirks, possibly odd currents or whirlpools; but a rickety canvas boat and icy water could easily explain their deaths. There's a stone cairn and memorial to the men on the rim of the caldera.

A NEW LAVA FIELD IS BORN

On 16 August 2014, sensors began picking up increased seismic activity in and around Bárðarbunga, one of many volcanoes that lie underneath Vatnajökull ice cap. (This immense volcano system is under the ice cap's northwest area.)

The magma in the Bárðarbunga caldera formed an 'intrusive dike' (tunnel of magma) through the ground under an outlet glacier named Dyngjujökull. On 29 August, the magma surfaced – a fissure eruption, complete with spectacular lava fountains, began in Holuhraun, a 200-year-old lava field about 5km away from the Dyngjujökull glacial edge.

The eruption continued for almost six months and came to be Iceland's largest lava eruption for 230 years. Its stats are impressive: the new basaltic lava field is about 85 sq km in area (considerably larger than the island of Manhattan), is an average of 10m to 14m thick, and weighs about the same as a herd of 600 million elephants. The lava was around 1180°C when it reached the surface. The river system and land around the lava are still undergoing change.

Sleeping & Eating

The closest accommodation is at the Dreki huts and camp area at Drekagil. There is also a hut and camping in the more inviting, fertile area at Herðubreiðarlindir.

There is nowhere to buy food. Bring your own self-catering supplies. You can eat by the Dreki huts, or sit by Öskjuvatn's shores for a picnic on a fine-weather day.

Getting There & Away

From Drekagil there's an 8km road to reach the Askja car park (which has new composting toilets), and it's then a scenic 2.5km walk into and through the caldera (easy to moderate, depending on snow melt and weather conditions) across lava fields to reach Víti and the lake.

Holuhraun

Iceland's huge new lava field dates from 2014–15 (sightseeing flights grant you a sense of its vastness). By road, Holuhraun is accessible from Drekagil; follow the signs to reach a car park and marked trail enabling you to walk on a small section of the lava (it's fragile, and sharp and jagged, so take care). At this access point you can clearly see the difference between the old lava field and the new, and note the interplay of the lava and river.

Park rangers at Drekagil provide information and safety precautions about Holuhraun and offer free one-hour walking tours starting at the car park (once daily, mid-July to mid-August). The area is still volcanically active: stay on the tracks and signed trails at all times.

The closest overnight base is at Dreki huts in Drekagil.

There are no eating options here so bring all supplies.

Getting There & Away

Signs point the way to the Holuhraun car park from Drekagil; head south on the F910 and follow these signs (it's around 24km).

A number of Askja day tours also visit Holuhraun.

KVERKFJÖLL ROUTE

The Kverkfjöll (pronounced *kverk*-fyutl) route creeps across the highlands to the Kverkfjöll area at the northern margins of the Vatnajökull ice cap.

Kverkfjöll is actually a cluster of peaks formed by a large central volcano. It is partially capped by the ice of Kverkjökull (a northern tongue of Vatnajökull). Over time, the name Kverkfjöll has also come to refer to the hot-spring-filled ice caves that often form beneath the eastern margin of the Dyngjujökull ice due to the heavy geothermal activity in this area.

Along the access road F902 (off Rte F910) are several sites of interest, including the twin pyramid-shaped **Upptyppingar hills** near the Jökulsá á Fjöllum bridge, and the **Hvannalindir** oasis, about 20km north of Sigurðarskáli hut (Kverkfjöll's accommodation and information base).

A 2km-return marked hike from behind the hut takes you up **Virkisfell** (1108m) for a spectacular view over Kverkfjöll and the headwaters of the Jökulsá á Fjöllum (pronounced *yuk*-ul-sow ow *fyu*-tloom).

PROPOSED HIGHLANDS NATIONAL PARK

A broad coalition of Icelandic organisations and associations (diverse interest groups including recreational associations, nature conservationists, government agencies and the travel industry) have banded together in the hopes of establishing a national park in the central highlands of Iceland. The goal is to protect the vast wilderness and its unique unspoilt landscapes, plus ensure responsible future management. The area proposed for protection is some 40,000 sq km (including all of the existing Vatnajökull National Park).

As of 2018, the government had formed a committee to work on forming the new park.

The vision of a highlands national park is partially a measure against Iceland's expanding energy and tourism industries. By protecting the area, the coalition hopes to ensure only limited development and construction within the area, and to prevent rivers and geothermal areas from future energy harnessing (which could involve the construction of dams, hydroelectric power stations and high-voltage pylons).

Polls indicate popular support among Icelanders for the creation of such a national park (61% in favour). International backing is also important; and there is a petition seeking support. Read more about the proposal at www.halendid.is.

Kverkfjöll

Besides being the source of the roiling Jökulsá á Fjöllum, central Iceland's greatest river, Kverkfjöll is also one of Iceland's largest geothermal areas.

The lower **Kverkfjöll ice caves** lie 3km from the Sigurðarskáli hut; they're about a 15-minute walk from the 4WD track's end. Here the hot river flows beneath the cold glacier ice, and clouds of steam swirl over the river. It is not possible to enter the caves (they have claimed the life of one person), but depending on the year you can see different openings in the glacier ice.

Ranger-led tours continue up onto the glacier itself. The longer guided tours head over the glacier to the remarkable Hveradalur geothermal area.

Kverkfjöll is part of the vast Vatnajökull National Park; check the park website (www.vjp.is) for information.

There is nowhere to buy food. Bring all your own self-catering supplies.

Sigurðarskáli Hut HUT €
(☎ summer 863 9236, year-round 863 5813; www.ferdaf.is; N 64°44.850', W 16°37.890'; sites/dm per person 2000/8000kr; ⊙ mid-Jun–early Sep) The large Sigurðarskáli hut has comfortable accommodation (sleeps 75) in a new hut, plus a well-maintained campsite. There are cooking facilities, toilets and showers (500kr). Campers pay an additional 800kr if they want access to cabin facilities such as the kitchen.

Tours

Without a robust 4WD vehicle, the only way to visit Kverkfjöll is on a tour. If you do have your own vehicle, you can park and walk up to the viewing area for the mouths of the ice caves (entrance strictly prohibited) – anywhere further is highly ill-advised without a guide.

Some summers, the park rangers stationed at Sigurðarskáli hut offer guided hikes onto the **Kverkjökull outlet glacier** or to the geothermal area at 1700m, known as **Hveradalur** (17,500kr). Email ferdaf@ferdaf.is or call 863 9236 (in summer) to see what tours are being offered.

There are tour packages involving transport and guiding. From the east, Jeep Tours (p368) offers a day trip in a super-Jeep from Egilsstaðir. Wild Boys (p368) has a variety of day and multi-day offerings. Fjalladýrð (p367) has a two-day tour from Möðrudalur. From Mývatn, Geo Travel (p367) has a two-day Askja–Kverkfjöll tour, and there's the popular three-day Askja–Kverkfjöll–Vatnajökull tour run by North Travel (p368), which picks up in Akureyri and Mývatn.

Getting There & Away

The road to Kverkfjöll (F902; in Icelandic known as Kverkfjalaleið) usually opens mid- to late June.

The Kverkfjöll route connects Möðrudalur (70km east of Mývatn, off the Ring Road) with the Sigurðarskáli hut via the F905, F910 and F902. Or, after visiting Askja, follow up with a 70km trip to Kverkfjöll by driving south along the F902.

Drivers note: the petrol stop at Möðrudalur is the last place to fill up.

Understand Iceland

Iceland Today

Iceland's booming tourism (almost 30% growth each year since 2010) has helped the country stabilise its economy following the 2008 banking crash. Tourism has also brought a host of changes, from crowds to more foreign-born workers. Infrastructure and logistical planning rush to keep up. Meanwhile, the populace is pressuring the government to respond to the country's changing situation, protect the environment, and recover from high-profile scandals. All the while being proud of its high-performing football teams.

Best on Film

Heima (2007) Follow band Sigur Rós as they perform throughout Iceland.
Rams (*Hrútar*; 2015) Engrossing tale of two estranged brothers and their sheep.
The Homecoming (*Blóðberg*; 2015) Sly modern comedy-drama where a 'perfect' family's life goes topsy-turvy.
Of Horses and Men (2013) A surreal portrait of the intertwining lives of men and horses.
101 Reykjavík (2000) Dark comedy exploring sex, drugs and the life of a loafer in downtown Reykjavík.
Jar City (2006) Carefully crafted detective thriller based on the novel by Arnaldur Indriðason.

Best in Print

The Draining Lake (Arnaldur Indriðason; 2004) One of many engrossing tales from a master of Nordic Noir.
Independent People (Halldór Laxness; 1934–35) Bleak tragi-comedy from the Nobel Laureate.
The Sagas of Icelanders (Jane Smiley et al; 2005) Excellent, readable translations of Iceland's epic, often brutal, tales.
Devil's Island (Einar Kárason; 1983) American culture clashes with rural tradition in postwar Reykjavík.
The Blue Fox (Sjón; 2003) Poetic 19th-century fantasy-adventure tale.

Tourism Boom

Curious travellers started to arrive en masse following the 2010 Eyjafjallajökull eruption and a smart publicity campaign led by the Iceland tourism board, which helped spread word of Iceland's charms. Tourism saw a 444% increase from 2010 to 2017, with about 2.2 million visitors arriving in 2017, a shocking number when you consider the nation's population is 350,000. Businesses catering to tourists also boomed, and tourism now accounts for 39.2% of Iceland's goods and services (up from 18.8% in 2010) and 8.6% of the GDP, and it employs 14.3% of the country's workforce.

There are some signs of a slowdown, as the strong króna and higher prices have made travel (and life) in Iceland expensive – also potentially shortening visitor stays. Tourism has also hit the regions of the country differently: many tourists stick to the capital area, the Southwest and the Ring Road, so while it's packed there, places like the North, East and Westfjords still remain relatively under-visited.

Tourism Repercussions

The strengthening of the economy as a result of tourism income is indisputable, and many locals appreciate the new services, increase in international profile and wage increases (7.3% from 2017 to 2018) that the industry brings.

But there's a flipside. Short-term apartment rentals in the centre of Reykjavík are pushing locals out of the market. There's also a hotel-building explosion in the capital – by 2020 the number of hotels is due to increase by half – that, too, brings changes.

News reports consistently feature the destruction of the environment (off-road driving, litter, defecation), or rescues of stranded tourists from glaciers, mountainsides and wave-swept beaches by Iceland's search and rescue team (a volunteer- and donation-based operation). In 2016 more than 75% of Icelanders considered the pressure from tourism on the environment to be too high – from whale and puffin consumption to crowds at natural sights.

There is also an impact from the increasing need for foreign labour (who made up about 13% of the workforce in 2018) and the way that changes Icelanders' experience and the use of the Icelandic language (with increased English everywhere).

Responses include limits on short-term apartment rentals, additional cautionary signs and barriers at sights, restrictions on free camping, educational campaigns for tourists and improved methods for learning about safety and logging hikes (www.safetravel.is). Oddly, despite official stances that promote spreading tourism around the country, in 2018 buses were cut back in the North and East.

Protecting Iceland

Important debate is taking place about how Iceland's fragile environment can withstand the pressure it's under. The country's unspoilt natural landscape is both beloved by Icelanders and a major tourist draw. If current growth continues, Iceland could host close to three million visitors in 2020. There's also concern about foreign interests buying vast swaths of land, including important salmon-fishing rivers.

How much tourism can Iceland's waterfalls, trails and lava fields sustain? How can they be adequately protected, for both locals and visitors to enjoy?

Tourism authorities are currently placing huge emphasis on promoting responsible travel and preparing visitors for how to experience and protect the unusual environment. There is also a move to create a Highland National Park (p372), which would protect 40% of the country, and a popular initiative promotes whale watching over eating whale in local restaurants.

Iceland also benefits from its copious sources of renewable energy (primarily geothermal and hydro power). This helps fuel life on the island and also attracts large energy users – (controversial) aluminium smelters (p393) are already in place for cheap power, and lower impact computing 'server farms' are on the rise.

Political Hijinks

One of the world's few nations to prosecute the bankers held responsible for the financial collapse in 2008, Icelanders maintain a sharp watch on their leaders. From the April 2016 Panama Papers scandal that brought down Prime Minister Sigmundur Davíð Gunnlaugsson to the 2017 controversy that brought down the coalition of Prime Minister Bjarni Benediktsson (when his father defended a convicted paedophile), Icelanders hold their leaders to account.

Despite the resulting drama, capital controls (measures limiting the movement of cash and capital in and out of the country) put in place during the recovery after the financial collapse were finally lifted in 2018, and that same year Iceland made grand news when it became the first nation in the world to legislate parity in pay for men and women.

POPULATION: **350,000**

AREA: **103,000 SQ KM**

TOURISTS: **2.2 MILLION (2017)**

SHEEP: **459,000**

ELECTRICITY PRODUCTION FROM RENEWABLES: **100%**

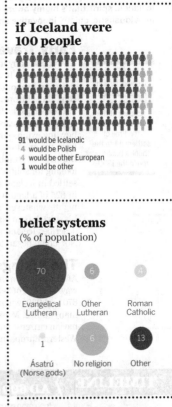

if Iceland were 100 people

91 would be Icelandic
4 would be Polish
4 would be other European
1 would be other

belief systems

(% of population)

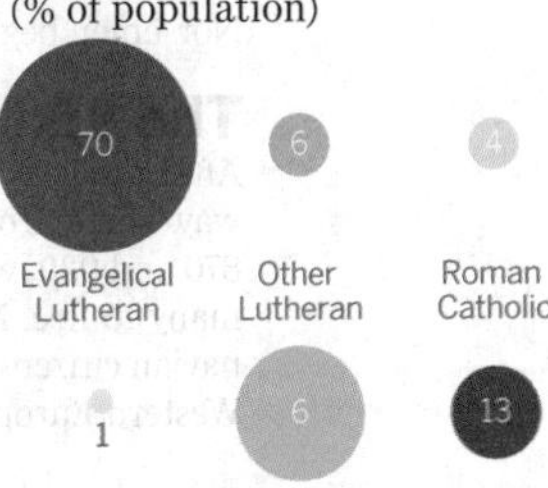

population per sq km

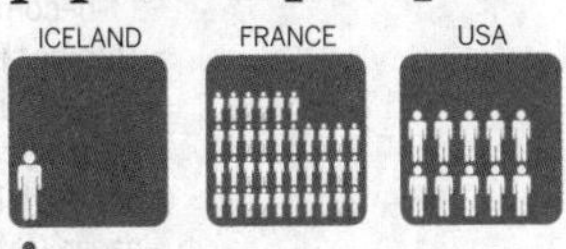

History

Geologically young, staunchly independent and frequently rocked by natural disaster, Iceland has a turbulent and absorbing history of Norse settlement, literary genius, bitter feuding and foreign oppression. Life in this harsh and unforgiving landscape was never going to be easy, but the everyday challenges and hardships have cultivated a modern Icelandic spirit that's highly aware of its stormy past, yet remarkably resilient, fiercely individualistic, quietly innovative and justifiably proud.

Early Travellers & Irish Monks

History of Iceland, by Jon R Hjalmarsson, is an absorbing account of the nation, from the time of settlement to the book's publication in the 1990s.

A veritable baby in geological terms, Iceland was created around 20 million years ago. It was only around 330 BC, when the Greek explorer Pytheas wrote about the island of Ultima Thule, six days north of Britain by ship, that Europeans became aware of a landmass beyond the confines of their maps, lurking in a 'congealed sea'.

For many years rumour, myth and fantastic tales of fierce storms, howling winds and barbaric dog-headed people kept explorers away from the great northern ocean, *oceanus innavigabilis*. Irish monks were the next to stumble upon Iceland: they regularly sailed to the Faroes looking for solitude and seclusion. It's thought that Irish *papar* (fathers) settled in Iceland around the year AD 700. The Irish monk Dicuil wrote in 825 of a land where there was no daylight in winter, but on summer nights 'whatever task a man wishes to perform, even picking lice from his shirt, he can manage as well as in clear daylight'. This almost certainly describes Iceland and its long summer nights. The *papar* fled when the Norsemen began to arrive in the early 9th century.

The Vikings Are Coming!

After the Irish monks, Iceland's first permanent settlers came from Norway. The Age of Settlement is traditionally defined as the period between 870 and 930, when political strife on the Scandinavian mainland caused many to flee. Most North Atlantic Norse settlers were ordinary Scandinavian citizens: farmers, herders and merchants who settled right across Western Europe, marrying Britons, Westmen (Irish) and Scots.

TIMELINE

AD 600–700

Irish monks voyage to uninhabited Iceland, becoming the first (temporary) settlers. There is little archaeological evidence, although the element *'papar'* (fathers) crops up in certain place names.

850–930

Norse settlers from Norway and Sweden arrive, call the island Snæland (Snow Land), then Garðarshólmi (Garðar's Island), and finally Ísland (Iceland). Scattered farmsteads rapidly cover the country.

871

Norwegian Viking Ingólfur Arnarson, credited as the country's first permanent inhabitant, sails to the southwest coast; in time he makes his home in a promising-looking bay that he names Reykjavík.

It's likely that the Norse accidentally discovered Iceland after being blown off course en route to the Faroes. The first arrival, Naddoddr, sailed from Norway and landed on the east coast around 850. He named the place Snæland (Snow Land) before backtracking to his original destination.

Iceland's second visitor, Garðar Svavarsson, circumnavigated the island and then settled in for the winter at Húsavík on the north coast. When he left in the spring some of his crew remained, or were left behind, thus becoming the first Norse to remain.

Around 860 the Norwegian Flóki Vilgerðarson uprooted his farm and family and headed for Snæland. He navigated with ravens, which, after some trial and error, led him to his destination and provided his nickname, Hrafna-Flóki (Raven-Flóki). Hrafna-Flóki sailed to Vatnsfjörður on the west coast but became disenchanted after seeing icebergs floating in the fjord. He renamed the country Ísland (Iceland), and returned to Norway; although he did eventually come back to Iceland, settling in the Skagafjörður district on the north coast.

Credit for the first intentional permanent settlement, according to the 12th-century *Íslendingabók,* goes to Ingólfur Arnarson, who fled Norway with his blood brother Hjörleifur. He landed at Ingólfshöfði (Southeast Iceland) in 871, then continued around the coast and set up house in 874 at a place he called Reykjavík (Smoky Bay), named after the steam from thermal springs there. Hjörleifur settled near the present town of Vík, but was murdered by his slaves shortly after.

As for Ingólfur, he was led to Reykjavík by a fascinating pagan ritual. It was traditional for Viking settlers to toss their high-seat pillars (a symbol of authority and part of a chieftain's paraphernalia) into the sea as they approached land. The settler's new home was established wherever the gods brought the pillars ashore – a practice imitated by waves of settlers who followed from the Norwegian mainland.

Iceland's 1100 Years: The History of a Marginal Society, by Gunnar Karlsson, provides an insightful, contemporary history of Iceland from settlement onwards.

Where to Find Viking Vibes

National Museum (Reykjavík)

Settlement Exhibition (Reykjavík)

Þingvellir National Park (near Selfoss)

Víkingaheimar (Njarðvík)

Eiríksstaðir (reconstruction; Dalir)

Stöng farmstead (Þjórsárdalur)

Settlement Center (Borgarnes)

Njál's Saga sites (Hvolsvöllur)

Assembling the Alþingi

By the time Ingólfur's son Þorsteinn reached adulthood, the whole island was scattered with farms, and people began to feel the need for some sort of government. Iceland's landowners gathered first at regional assemblies to trade and settle disputes, but it became apparent that a national assembly was needed. This was a completely novel idea at the time, but Icelanders reasoned that it must be an improvement on the oppressive system they had experienced under the Nordic monarchy.

In the early 10th century Þorsteinn Ingólfsson held Iceland's first large-scale district assembly near Reykjavík, and in the 920s the self-styled lawyer Úlfljótur was sent to study Norway's law codes and prepare something similar that would be suitable for Iceland.

930

The world's oldest existing parliament, the Alþingi, is founded at Þingvellir. The Icelanders' law code is memorised by an elected law speaker, who helps to settle legal matters at annual parliamentary gatherings.

986

Erik the Red founds the first permanent European colony in Greenland, building the settlements of Eystribyggð and Vestribyggð in the southwest of the country.

999–1000

Iceland officially converts to Christianity under pressure from the Norwegian king, though pagan beliefs and rituals remain. Leif the Lucky lands in Newfoundland, becoming the first European to reach America.

1100–1230

Iceland's literary Golden Age, during which the Old Norse sagas are written. Several are attributed to Snorri Sturluson – historian, poet and the sharpest political operator of the era.

THE VIKINGS

Scandinavia's greatest impact on world history probably occurred during the Viking Age. In the 8th century, an increase in the numbers of restless, landless young men in western Norway coincided with advances in technology, as Nordic shipbuilders developed fast, manoeuvrable boats sturdy enough for ocean crossings.

Norwegian farmers had settled peacefully in Orkney and Shetland as early as the 780s, but the Viking Age officially began in bloodshed in 793, when Norsemen plundered St Cuthbert's monastery on Lindisfarne, an island off Britain's Northumberland coast.

The Vikings took to monasteries with delight, realising that speedy raids could bring handsome rewards. They destroyed Christian communities and slaughtered the monks of Britain and Ireland, who could only wonder what sin they had committed to invite the heathen hordes. However, the Vikings' barbarism was probably no greater than the standard of the day – it was the suddenness and extent of the raids that led to their fearsome reputation.

In the following years Viking raiders returned with great fleets, terrorising, murdering, enslaving and displacing local populations, and capturing whole regions across Britain, Ireland, France and Russia. They travelled to Moorish Spain and the Middle East, attacking Constantinople six times, and even served as mercenaries for the Holy Roman Empire.

Icelandic tradition credits the Norse settlement of Iceland to tyrannical Harald Hårfagre (Harald Fairhair), king of Vestfold in southeastern Norway. Filled with expansionist aspirations, Harald won a significant naval victory at Hafrsfjord (Stavanger) in 890. The deposed chieftains chose to flee rather than surrender, and many wound up in Iceland.

While Viking raids continued in Europe, Eiríkur Rauðe (Erik the Red) headed west with around 500 others to found the first permanent European colony in Greenland in 986. Eiríkur's son, Leif the Lucky, went on to explore the coastline of northeast America in the year 1000, naming the new country Vínland (Wineland). Permanent settlement was thwarted by the *skrælings* (Native Americans), who were anything but welcoming.

Viking raids gradually petered out, and the Viking Age ended with the death of King Harald Harðráði, last of the great Viking kings, who died in battle at Stamford Bridge, England, in 1066.

At the same time Grímur Geitskör was commissioned to find a location for the Alþingi (National Assembly). Bláskógar, near the eastern boundary of Ingólfur's estate, with its beautiful lake and wooded plain, seemed ideal. Along one side of the plain was a long cliff with an elevated base (the Mid-Atlantic Ridge), from where speakers and representatives could preside over people gathered below.

In 930 Bláskógar was renamed Þingvellir (Assembly Plains). Þorsteinn Ingólfsson was given the honorary title *allsherjargoði* (supreme chief-

1104

Hekla's first eruption in human-historical times. The volcano covers Þjórsárdalur valley and its prosperous medieval farms with a thick layer of ash, rock and cinders.

1200

Iceland descends into anarchy during the Sturlung Age. The government dissolves and, in 1281, Iceland is absorbed by Norway.

1241

Seventy armed men arrive at Snorri Sturluson's home in Reykholt, ordered to bring him to Norway to face treason charges. Snorri never leaves – he is stabbed to death in his cellar.

1397

On 17 June the Kalmar Union is signed in Sweden, uniting the countries of Norway, Sweden and Denmark under one king. As part of this treaty, Iceland comes under Danish control.

tain) and Úlfljótur was designated the first *lögsögumaður* (law speaker), who was required to memorise and annually recite the entire law of the land. It was he, along with the 48 *goðar* (chieftains), who held the actual legislative power.

Although squabbles arose over the choice of leaders, and allegiances were continually questioned, the new parliamentary system was a success. At the annual convention of the year 999 or 1000, the assembled crowd was bitterly divided between pagans and Christians, and civil war looked likely. Luckily, Þorgeir, the incumbent law speaker, was a master of tact. The *Íslendingabók* relates that he retired to his booth, refusing to speak to anyone for a day and a night while he pondered the matter. When he emerged, he decreed that Iceland should accept the new religion and convert to Christianity, although pagans (such as himself) were to be allowed to practise their religion in private. This decision gave the formerly divided groups a semblance of national unity, and soon the first bishoprics were set up at Skálholt in the southwest and Hólar in the north.

Over the following years, the two-week national assembly at Þingvellir became the social event of the year. All free men could attend. Single people came looking for partners, marriages were contracted and solemnised, business deals were finalised, duels and executions were held, and the Appeals Court handed down judgements on matters that couldn't be resolved in lower courts.

The word Viking is derived from *vík*, which means bay or cove in Old Norse and probably referred to Viking anchorages during raids.

Anarchy & the Sturlung Age

The late 12th century kicked off the Saga Age, when epic tales of early settlement, family struggles, romance and tragic characters were recorded by historians and writers. Much of our knowledge of this time comes from two weighty tomes, the *Íslendingabók,* a historical narrative from the Settlement Era written by 12th-century scholar Ari Þorgilsson (Ari the Learned), and the detailed *Landnámabók,* a comprehensive account of the settlement.

Despite the advances in such cultural pursuits, Icelandic society was beginning to deteriorate. By the early 13th century the enlightened period of peace that had lasted 200 years was waning. Constant power struggles between rival chieftains led to violent feuds and a flourishing of Viking-like private armies, which raided farms across the country. This dark hour in Iceland's history was known as the Sturlung Age, named for the Sturlungs, the most powerful family clan in Iceland at the time. The tragic events and brutal history of this 40-year era is graphically recounted in the three-volume *Sturlunga Saga.*

The Althing at Thingvellir, by Helmut Lugmayr, explains the role and history of the oldest parliament in the world and includes a section on Þingvellir's unique geology.

1402–04

The Black Death sweeps across Iceland, 50 years after its devastating journey across mainland Europe, and kills around half of the population.

1550

King Christian III's attempts to impose Lutheranism finally succeed after the Catholic bishop Jón Arason is captured in battle and beheaded at Skálholt, along with two of his sons.

1590

Bishop Guðbrandur Þorláksson's lovely – and quite accurate – map of Iceland is published. The sea is sprinkled with whale-like monsters, and it notes that Hekla 'vomits stones with a terrible noise'.

1602

Denmark imposes a trade monopoly, giving Danish and Swedish firms exclusive trading rights in Iceland. This leads to unrestrained profiteering by Danish merchants and Iceland's slow impoverishment.

As Iceland descended into chaos, the Norwegian king Hákon Hákonarson pressured chieftains, priests and the new breed of wealthy aristocrats to accept his authority. The Icelanders, who saw no alternative, dissolved all but a superficial shell of their government and swore their allegiance to the king. An agreement of confederacy was made in 1262. In 1281 a new code of law, the *Jónsbók,* was introduced by the king, and Iceland was absorbed into Norwegian rule.

The Complete Sagas of Icelanders, edited by Viðar Hreinsson, is a must for saga fiends. It's a summary translation of saga tales, featuring all the main yarns, along with a few shorter fantasy tales.

Norway immediately set about appointing Norwegian bishops to Hólar and Skálholt and imposed excessive taxes. Contention flared as former chieftains quibbled over high offices, particularly that of *járl* (earl), an honour that fell to the ruthless Gissur Þorvaldsson, who in 1241 murdered Snorri Sturluson, Iceland's best-known historian and writer.

Meanwhile, the volcano Hekla erupted three times, covering a third of the country in ash; a mini–ice age followed, and severe winters wiped out livestock and crops. The Black Death arrived, killing half the population, and the once indomitable spirit of the people seemed broken.

Enter the Danes

Iceland's fate was now in the hands of the highest Norwegian bidder, who could lease the governorship of the country on a three-year basis. In 1397 the Kalmar Union of Norway, Sweden and Denmark brought Iceland under Danish rule. After disputes between Church and state, the Danish government seized Church property and imposed Lutheranism in the Reformation of 1550. When the stubborn Catholic bishop of Hólar, Jón Arason, resisted and gained a following, he and his two sons were taken to Skálholt and beheaded.

In 1602 the Danish king imposed a crippling trade monopoly whereby Swedish and Danish firms were given exclusive trading rights in Iceland for 12-year periods. This resulted in large-scale extortion, importation of spoilt or inferior goods, and yet more suffering that would last another 250 years. However, one positive eventually emerged from the monopoly. In an attempt to bypass the embargo and boost local industry, powerful town magistrate Skúli Magnússon built weaving, tanning and wool-dyeing factories, which would become the foundations of the modern city of Reykjavík.

Even more Misery

If impoverishment at the hands of Danish overlords was not enough, Barbary pirates got in on the action, raiding the Eastfjords and the Reykjanes Peninsula before descending on Vestmannaeyjar in 1627. The defenceless population attempted to hide in Heimaey's cliffs and caves, but the pirates ransacked the island, killing indiscriminately and loading 242 people onto their ships. The unfortunate Icelanders were taken to Algiers, where most were sold into slavery. Back home, money was

1625–85
Period of the notorious Westfjords witch hunts: 21 Icelanders are executed, beginning with Jón Rögnvaldsson, burned at the stake for 'raising a ghost' and possessing sinister-looking runic writing.

1627
The 'Turkish Abductions' take place: Barbary pirates raid the east of Iceland and the Vestmannaeyjar, taking hundreds of people prisoner and killing anyone who resists them.

1703
Iceland's first census reveals that the country's population is a tiny 50,358; 55% are female. Men – physical labourers – are more affected by malnutrition and famine.

1783–84
The Laki crater row erupts, pouring out poisonous gas clouds that kill 25% of the population and more than 50% of livestock. The haze covers Europe, causing freak weather conditions, flooding and famine.

scrimped and saved for ransom, and eventually 13 of the captives were freed. The most famous was Guðríður Símonardóttir, who returned to Iceland and married Hallgrímur Pétursson, one of Iceland's most famous poets – the three bells in Hallgrímskirkja are named after the couple and their daughter.

During the same period, Europe's witch-hunting craze reached Icelandic shores. Icelandic witches were mostly men – of the 130 cases that appear in the court annals, only 10% involve women. The luckiest defendants were brutally flogged; 21 of the unluckiest were burned at the stake, mostly for supposedly making their neighbours sick or for possessing magical writing or suspicious-looking amulets.

It may have been the Age of Enlightenment in Europe, but it's a wonder any Icelanders survived the 18th century. In this remote outpost in the North Atlantic, the population of 50,000 was holding on for dear life, in the face of a powerful smallpox epidemic, which arrived in 1707 and killed an estimated 18,000 people, and a series of volcanic eruptions: Katla in 1660, 1721 and again in 1755; Hekla in 1693 and 1766; and Öræfajökull in 1727.

Things got worse. In 1783 the Laki crater row erupted, spewing out billions of tonnes of lava and poisonous gas clouds for a full eight months. Fifty farms in the immediate area were wiped out, and the noxious dust and vapours and consequent Haze Famine went on to kill around 9000 Icelanders; first plants died, then livestock, then people. Ash clouds from the eruption affected the whole of Europe, causing freak weather conditions, including acid rain and floods. Authorities in Denmark contemplated relocating the remaining Icelandic population, which by 1801 numbered just 47,000, to Denmark.

Return to Independence

After five centuries of oppressive foreign rule, Icelandic nationalism flourished in the 19th century, conscious of a growing sense of liberalisation across Europe. By 1855 Jón Sigurðsson, an Icelandic scholar, had successfully lobbied for restoration of free trade, and by 1874 Iceland had drafted a constitution and regained control of its domestic affairs.

Iceland's first political parties were formed during this period, and urban development began in this most rural of countries. Still, it wasn't enough to stave off the wave of emigration that had started: between 1870 and 1914, some 16,000 Icelanders left to seek a better life in North America. Reasons for emigrating included lack of opportunity – the growing fishing industry could not employ all the workers who wished to escape the hard labour of rural life and move to the new urban centres – and yet another volcanic eruption, Askja, in 1875, which spewed livestock-poisoning ash.

Iceland Saga, by Magnús Magnússon, offers an entertaining introduction to Icelandic history and literature, and explains numerous saga events and settings. *The Sagas of Icelanders* (Jane Smiley et al; 2001) provides excellent saga translations.

1786

The official founding of Reykjavík (inhabited at the time by fewer than 200 souls). The settlement is granted a trade charter, and merchants are enticed to settle here with tax breaks.

1855–90

Iceland moves towards independence, with the restoration of free trade and a draft constitution. Not everyone sticks around to see it: many Icelanders emigrate to start life afresh in North America.

1917–18

Iceland is struck by the 'Winter of the Great Frosts'. Temperatures plummet to a record low of -38°C (-36.4°F), and icebergs block all ports.

1918

Denmark's grip on Iceland gradually loosens. Following Home Rule in 1904, the Act of Union is signed on 1 December 1918, making Iceland an independent state within the Kingdom of Denmark.

By 1918 Iceland had signed the Act of Union, which effectively released the country from Danish rule, making it an independent state within the Kingdom of Denmark.

Burial Rites, by Hannah Kent, is a novel based on the true story of the last public execution in Iceland. It's set in 1829 and is meticulously researched, evoking the hardships of rural Icelandic life. It's being made into a movie starring Jennifer Lawrence and directed by Luca Guadagnino.

Iceland prospered during WWI as wool, meat and fish exports gained high prices. When WWII loomed, however, Iceland declared neutrality in the hope of maintaining its important trade links with both Britain and Germany.

On 9 April 1940 Denmark was occupied by Germany, prompting the Alþingi to take control of Iceland's foreign affairs once more. A year later, on 17 May 1941, Icelanders requested complete independence. The formal establishment of the Republic of Iceland finally took place at Þingvellir on 17 June 1944 – now celebrated as Independence Day.

WWII & the USA Moves In

As a result of Germany's occupation of Denmark in 1940, Iceland was in charge of its own wartime foreign affairs (and on the path to full independence, to be established before the war's end). Wartime Iceland's complete lack of military force worried the Allied powers and so in May 1940 Britain, most vulnerable to a German-controlled Iceland, sent in forces to occupy the island. Iceland had little choice but to accept the situation, but ultimately the country's economy profited from British construction projects and spending.

When the British troops withdrew in 1941 the government allowed US troops to move in, on the understanding they would move out at the end of the war. Although the US military left in 1946, it retained the right to re-establish a base at Keflavík should war threaten again. Back under their own control, Icelanders were reluctant to submit to any foreign power. When the government was pressured into becoming a founding member of NATO in 1949, riots broke out in Reykjavík. The government agreed to the proposition on the conditions that Iceland would never take part in offensive action and that no foreign military troops would be based in the country during peacetime.

These conditions were soon broken. War with Korea erupted in 1950, and in 1951 at NATO's request the US, jumpy about the Soviet threat, once again took responsibility for the island's defence. US military personnel and technology at the Keflavík base continued to increase over the next four decades, as Iceland served as an important Cold War monitoring station. The controversial US military presence in Iceland only ended in September 2006, when the base at Keflavík finally closed.

1940–41

After the Nazis occupy Denmark, the UK sends British troops to invade and occupy neutral Iceland, concerned Germany might acquire a military presence there. A US base is later established at Keflavík.

1944

A majority of Icelanders vote for independence from Denmark, and the Republic of Iceland is formally established on 17 June. King Christian X telegrams his congratulations.

1966

Icelandic State Television begins its first broadcasts in September.

1974

The Ring Road around the island is completed when the Skeiðarárbrú bridge opens on 14 July. Until now, Höfn has been one of the most isolated towns in Iceland.

Modern Iceland

In the 20th century Iceland transformed itself from one of the poorest countries in Europe to one of the most developed.

Following the Cold War, Iceland went through a period of growth, rebuilding and modernisation. The Ring Road was completed in 1974 – opening up transport links to the remote southeast – and projects such as the Krafla power station in the northeast and the Svartsengi power plant near Reykjavík were developed. A boom in the fishing industry saw Iceland extend its fishing limit in the 1970s to 200 miles (322km). This, however, precipitated the worst of the 'cod wars', as the UK refused to recognise the new zone. During the seven-month conflict, Icelandic ships cut the nets of British trawlers, shots were fired, and ships on both sides were rammed.

The fishing industry has always been vital to Iceland, although it's had its ups and downs – quotas were reduced in the 1990s so stocks could regenerate after overfishing. The industry went into recession, leading to an unemployment rate of 3% and a sharp drop in the króna. The country slowly began a period of economic regeneration as the fishing industry stabilised. Today the industry still provides 33.6% of exports and 12% of GDP, and employs 4% of the workforce. It remains sensitive to declining fish stocks.

In 2003 Iceland resumed whaling as part of a scientific research program, despite a global moratorium on hunts. In 2006 Iceland resumed commercial whaling, in spite of condemnation from around the world. Hunting of minke whales continues, drawing further international rebukes; hunting of endangered fin whales was suspended in 2016 but resumed in 2018.

Wasteland with Words: A Social History of Iceland, by Sigurður Gylfi Magnússon, draws on the detailed diaries and letters of Icelanders in past centuries, with a particular focus on the years from 1850 to 1940.

Financial Crash & Volcanic Eruptions

Iceland's huge dependence on its fishing industry and on imported goods means that the country has always had relatively high prices and a currency prone to fluctuation. Its vulnerability was brought into focus in September 2008, when the global economic crisis hit the country with a sledgehammer blow. Reykjavík was rocked by months of fierce protest, as the then-government's popularity evaporated along with the country's wealth.

Prime Minister Geir Haarde resigned in January 2009. His replacement, Jóhanna Sigurðardóttir, hit international headlines as the world's first openly gay prime minister. Her first major act was to apply for EU membership, with the eventual aim of adopting the euro as the country's new currency, in an effort to stabilise the economy. EU membership was then and continues to be a contentious issue.

Island on Fire, by Alexandra Witze and Jeff Kanipe, examines the 1783 Laki eruptions – the cataclysmic event by which Icelanders measure all other volcanic eruptions.

1975

The third in a series of 'cod wars' takes place between Iceland and the UK. These disputes over fishing rights in the North Atlantic flare up in the 1950s and 1970s, as Iceland expands its territorial waters.

1980

Vigdís Finnbogadóttir becomes president of Iceland, the first woman in the world to become elected head of state.

1986

The beginning of the end of the Cold War? General Secretary Mikhail Gorbachev and President Ronald Reagan agree to meet at a summit in Höfði House, Reykjavík.

2006

The controversial US military base at Keflavík closes down after 45 years in service; the government also approves the resumption of commercial whaling.

ICELAND'S ECONOMIC MELTDOWN

Between 2003 and early 2008, Iceland was full of confidence and riding high. But much of the country's wealth was built over a black hole of debt – its banks' liabilities were more than 10 times the country's annual GDP. The ripples of the worldwide financial crisis became a tidal wave by the time they reached Icelandic shores, washing away the country's entire economy.

By October 2008 the Icelandic stock market had crashed; the króna plummeted, losing almost half its value overnight; all three national banks went into receivership; and the country teetered on the brink of bankruptcy.

Help came for Iceland in November 2008 with a US$2.1 billion International Monetary Fund (IMF) loan and a US$3 billion bailout from Scandinavian neighbours. Nevertheless, spiralling inflation, wage cuts and redundancies meant that Icelanders' incomes fell by a quarter in real terms. Protestors rioted in Reykjavík, furious with a government they felt had betrayed them by not downsizing the bloated banking system.

The crash was a terrible blow to Icelanders – its legacy included high household debt, high inflation, record unemployment (peaking at 9.4% in early 2009) and the need to emigrate for work – some 5000 Icelanders moved to Norway in the four years following the crash.

Incredibly, however, the economic situation has largely been righted. Where other countries in financial straits chose to bail out their financial institutions, the Icelandic government refused to use taxpayers' money to prop up the failing banks. Instead, it made the Icelandic social welfare system its priority, choosing to help those citizens who were worst affected by the crash and let the private banks' creditors take the hit. Iceland's approach won praise from the IMF and from numerous economists.

This unique decision has paid off. While other nations are floundering in the financial mire and dealing with record unemployment rates, Iceland remains on the rise. As of 2018, unemployment continues to be back down to around 2.8% and capital controls (measures limiting the movement of cash and capital in and out of the country) put in place during the recovery are finally lifted.

Iceland again hit global headlines in April 2010, when ash cloud from the eruption under Eyjafjallajökull ice cap shut down European air traffic for six days, causing travel chaos across much of the continent. In comparison, the Grímsvötn volcano, which erupted the following year, was a mere trifle – its ash cloud caused just three days of air-traffic disruption. In 2014, Bárðarbunga's rumblings shone a spotlight onto Iceland's volatility once again, as have Katla's jolts in 2016. In 2018 seismic activity was on the increase in Öræfajökull and continues in Bárðarbunga.

2008

The worldwide financial downturn hits Iceland particularly hard, precipitating the worst national banking crisis ever when all three of the country's major banks collapse.

2009

Iceland formally applies for EU membership – a contentious issue among the population. Formal accession talks begin in 2010, are suspended in 2013, and the application withdrawn by a new government in 2014.

2009

Jóhanna Sigurðardóttir becomes the first female Prime Minister of Iceland and the world's first openly gay head of government of the modern era.

2010

The volcano under Eyjafjallajökull glacier begins erupting in March. In April its 9km-high ash plume brings European flights to a standstill for six days. The eruption is declared over in October.

Tourism Boom & Political Scandals

Events in Iceland have proved there's no such thing as bad publicity. Triggered by the 2010 eruption and the free press it generated for Iceland, plus a concerted Icelandic effort to build airline routes and exposure, tourism has boomed, increasing 440% from 2010 to 2017. The country has become the fastest-growing travel destination in Europe, with all the benefits (economic growth and employment) and headaches (infrastructure issues and environmental impact) that such status entails.

One of the most famous essays on Iceland's financial crash of 2008 is Michael Lewis' 'Wall Street on the Tundra', written for *Vanity Fair* in 2009. Search for it online – it's a cracking read. Follow it with 'Lost', from *The New Yorker* (March 2009).

Icelanders went to the polls in April 2013 with the national economy on the path to recovery, but with the population smarting from the government's tough austerity measures (including higher taxes and spending cuts). The results showed a backlash against the ruling Social Democrats; the centre-right camp (comprising the Progressive Party and the Independence Party) successfully campaigned on promises of debt relief and a cut in taxes, as well as opposition to Iceland's application to join the EU.

The two parties formed a coalition government. In early 2014 the government halted all negotiations with the EU – despite promising a referendum on whether or not to proceed with membership negotiations. Although polls show a majority of Icelanders still oppose joining the EU, making such a move without the promised referendum was deeply unpopular.

In April 2016 the Panama Papers document leak from the law firm Mossack Fonseca revealed financial improprieties implicating three Icelandic ministers, including Prime Minister Sigmundur Davíð Gunnlaugsson. As a result of massive protests, Gunnlaugsson stepped aside as prime minister. Sigurður Ingi Jóhannsson became the acting prime minister, and early elections produced no clear coalition.

In June 2016, on a wave of anti-establishment sentiment, Iceland elected its first new president in 20 years: historian and author Guðni Thorlacius Jóhannesson.

In January 2017, a short-lived coalition formed with only 32 MPs out of 63, headed by the Independence Party and Bjarni Benediktsson, but in September, a scandal surrounding Benediktsson's father's defence of a convicted paedophile brought down that government.

A new government coalition was formed in late 2017, lead by Prime Minister Katrín Jakobsdóttir, the chair of the Left-Green Party, in partnership with the Independence Party and the Progressive Party (Framsóknarflokkurinn), an agrarian-based party.

2013

In parliamentary elections, voters deliver a backlash against the Social Democrats' austerity measures in the wake of the financial crisis. A new coalition of centre-right parties forms government.

2013

The number of international visitors to Iceland numbers 807,000 (up from 320,000 in 2003). A year later, that number hovers around one million, and in 2017 it's 2.2 million.

2014–16

In August 2014, sensors pick up increased seismic activity around Bárðarbunga, a large volcano system under the Vatnajökull ice cap. Eruptions occur through mid-2015. In mid-2016 increased seismic activity is detected at Katla.

2016

As a result of financial improprieties revealed by the Panama Papers document leak from the law firm Mossack Fonseca and the protests that follow, Prime Minister Sigmundur Davíð Gunnlaugsson steps aside.

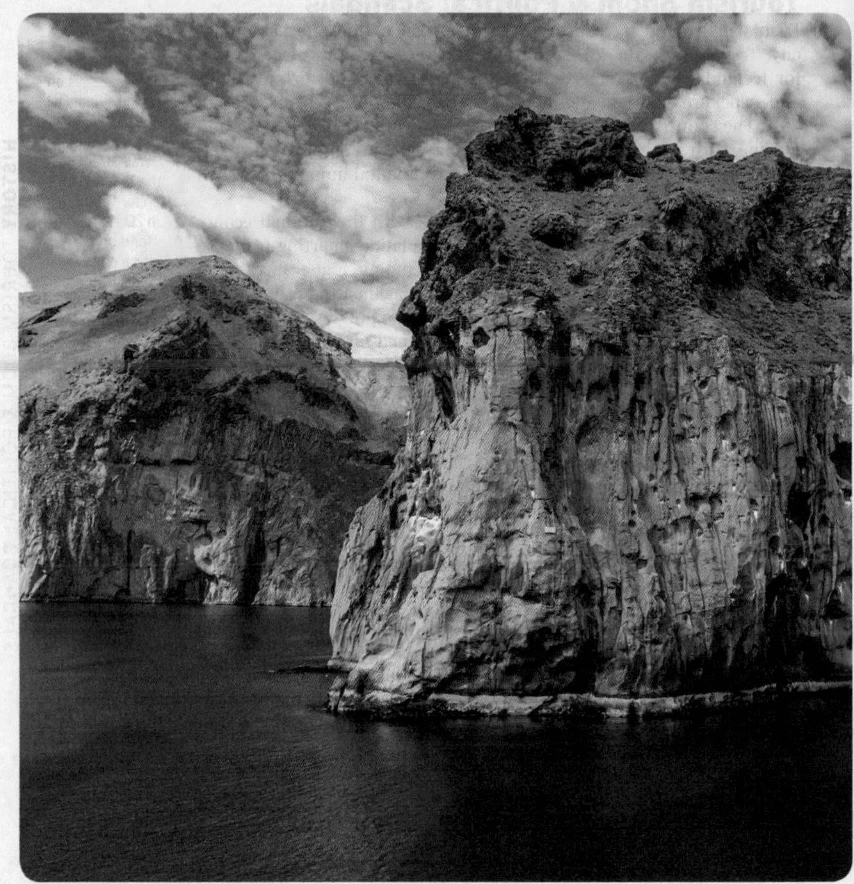

Natural Wonders

It's difficult to remain unmoved by the amazing diversity of the Icelandic landscape. Prepare to explore everything from lunar-like terrain of ornate lava flows and towering volcanoes with misty ice caps to steep-sided glistening fjords, lush emerald-green hills, glacier-carved valleys, bubbling mudpots and vast, desert-like expanses. It is this rich mix of extraordinary scenery and the possibility of experiencing such extremes, so close together, that attracts and then dazzles visitors.

Volatile Iceland

Situated on the Mid-Atlantic Ridge, a massive 18,000km-long rift between two of the Earth's major tectonic plates, Iceland is a shifting, steaming lesson in schoolroom geology. Suddenly you'll be racking your brains to remember long-forgotten homework on how volcanoes work,

Above Heimaey (p171)

what a solfatara is (spoiler: it's a volcanic vent emitting hot gases), and why lava and magma aren't quite the same thing.

Iceland is one of the youngest landmasses on the planet, formed by underwater volcanic eruptions along the joint of the North American and Eurasian plates around 20 million years ago. The Earth's crust in Iceland is only a third of its normal thickness, and magma (molten rock) continues to rise from deep within, forcing the two plates apart. The result is clearly visible at Þingvellir, where the great rift Almannagjá broadens by between 1mm and 18mm per year, and at Námafjall (near Mývatn), where a series of steaming vents mark the ridge.

At 103,000 sq km, Iceland is roughly the size of Portugal, or the US state of Kentucky. Within its borders are some 30 active volcanoes. Its landscape is comprised of 3% lakes, 11% ice caps and glaciers, 23% vegetation, and 63% lava and other raw terrain.

Volcanoes

Thin crust and grating plates are responsible for a host of exciting volcanic situations in Iceland. The country's volcanoes are many and varied – some are active, some extinct, and some are dormant and dreaming, no doubt, of future destruction. Fissure eruptions and their associated craters are probably the most common type of eruption in Iceland. The still-volatile Lakagígar crater row around Laki mountain is the country's most extreme example. It produced the largest lava flow in human history in the 18th century, covering an area of 565 sq km to a depth of 12m.

Several of Iceland's liveliest volcanoes are found beneath glaciers, which makes for dramatic eruptions as molten lava and ice interact. The main 2010 Eyjafjallajökull eruption was of this type: it caused a *jökulhlaup* (flooding caused by volcanic eruption beneath an ice cap) that damaged part of the Ring Road, before throwing up the famous ash plume that grounded Europe's aeroplanes. Iceland's most active volcano, Grímsvötn, which lies beneath the Vatnajökull ice cap, behaved in a similar fashion in 2011.

Iceland not only has subglacial eruptions, but also submarine ones. In 1963 the island of Surtsey exploded from the sea, giving scientists the opportunity to study how smouldering chunks of newly created land are colonised by plants and animals. Surtsey is off-limits to visitors, but you can climb many classical-looking cones such as Hekla, once thought to be the gateway to Hell; Eldfell, which did its best to bury the town of Heimaey in 1974; and Snæfellsjökull on the Snæfellsnes Peninsula.

Recent eruptions in Iceland have tended to be fairly harmless – they're often called 'tourist eruptions' because their fountains of magma, electric storms and dramatic ash clouds make perfect photos but cause relatively little damage. This is partly due to the sparsely populated land, and partly because devastating features such as fast-flowing lava, lahars

GEOLOGICALLY SPEAKING

Everywhere you go in Iceland you'll be bombarded with geological jargon to describe the landscape. These terms will let you one-up geological neophytes.

Basalt The most common type of solidified lava. This hard, dark, dense volcanic rock often solidifies into hexagonal columns.

Igneous A rock formed by solidifying magma or lava.

Moraine A ridge of boulders, clay and sand carried and deposited by a glacier.

Obsidian Black, glassy rock formed by the rapid solidification of lava without crystallisation.

Rhyolite Light-coloured, fine-grained volcanic rock similar to granite in composition.

Scoria Porous volcanic gravel that has cooled rapidly while moving, creating a glassy surface with iron-rich crystals that give it a glittery appearance.

Tephra Solid matter ejected into the air by an erupting volcano.

(mudslides) and pyroclastic surges (like the ones that obliterated Pompeii and Herculaneum) are usually absent in this part of the world.

The main danger lies in the gases that are released: suffocating carbon dioxide, highly acidic sulphur-based gases, and the deadly fluorine that poisoned people and livestock during the Laki eruptions of 1783. The Icelandic Met Office (Veðurstofa Íslands; www.vedur.is) keeps track of eruptions and the earthquakes that tend to precede them, plus the emissions that follow. Its work during 2014–15 Bárðarbunga seismic events and volcanic activity included daily factsheets. As of 2018, the volcanoes to watch are Katla, Hekla and Öræfajökull, all well overdue for eruption.

For background information about the country's diverse geology, check out the revised 2nd edition, 2014 publication of *Iceland – Classic Geology in Europe*, by Þór Þórdarson and Armann Hoskuldsson.

Geysers, Springs & Fumaroles

Iceland's Great Geysir gave its name to the world's spouting hot springs (it comes from the Icelandic for 'to gush'). It was once very active, frequently blowing water to a height of 80m, but earthquakes have altered the pressures inside its plumbing system and today it is far quieter. Its neighbour, Strokkur, now demonstrates the effect admirably, blasting a steaming column into the air every five to 10 minutes.

Geysers are reasonably rare phenomena, with around a thousand existing on Earth. However, in Iceland, water that has percolated down through the rock and been superheated by magma can emerge on the surface in various other exciting ways. Some of it boils into hot springs, pools and rivers – you'll find naturally hot water sources all around Iceland, including the springs at Landmannalaugar, the river at Hveragerði and the warm blue-white pool in the bottom of Víti crater at Askja. Icelanders have long harnessed these soothing gifts of nature, turning them into geothermal swimming pools and spas. The country's smartest spas are Mývatn Nature Baths and the Blue Lagoon, but note that they are not natural hot springs – they are human-made lagoons fed by the water output of the nearby geothermal power plants.

Fumaroles are places where superheated water reaches the surface as steam – the weirdest Icelandic examples are at Hverir, where gases literally scream their way from sulphurous vents in the earth. Lazier, messier bloops and bubblings take place at mudpots, for example, at Seltún (Krýsuvík) on the Reykjanes Peninsula, where heated water mixes with mud and clay. The colourful splatterings around some of the mudpots are caused by various minerals (sulphurous yellow, iron red), and also by the extremophile bacteria and algae that somehow thrive in this boiling-acid environment.

Ice & Snow

Glaciers and ice caps cover around 11% of Iceland; many are remnants of a cool period that began 2500 years ago. Ice caps are formed as snow piles over millennia in an area where it's never warm enough to melt. The weight of the snow causes it to slowly compress into ice, eventually crushing the land beneath the ice cap.

Iceland's largest ice cap, Vatnajökull in the southeast, covers about 8% of the country and is the largest in the world outside the poles. This immense glittering weight of ice may seem immovable, but around its edges, slow-moving rivers of ice – glaciers – flow imperceptibly down the mountainsides. Like rivers, glaciers carry pieces of stony sediment, which they dump in cindery-looking moraines at the foot of the mountain, or on vast gravelly outwash plains such as the Skeiðarársandur in Southeast Iceland. This can occur very quickly if volcanoes under the ice erupt and cause a *jökulhlaup* (flood): the *jökulhlaup* from the 1996 Grímsvötn eruption destroyed Iceland's longest bridge and swept jeep-sized boulders down onto the plain.

Top The iceberg-filled lagoon of Jökulsárlón (p197)
Bottom Hverfjall crater (p307)

Several of Iceland's glaciers have lakes at their tips. Jökulsárlón is a stunning place to admire icebergs that have calved from Breiðamerkurjökull. Luminous-blue pieces tend to indicate a greater age of ice, as centuries of compression squeeze out the air bubbles that give ice its usual silvery-white appearance. Icebergs may also appear blue due to light refraction.

Glaciers have carved out much of the Icelandic landscape since its creation, forming the glacial valleys and fjords that make those picture-postcard photos of today. The ice advances and retreats with the millennia, and also with the seasons, but there are worrying signs that Iceland's major ice caps – Vatnajökull, Mýrdalsjökull in the southwest, and Lang-

WHALING IN ICELAND

In the late 19th century, whale hunting became a lucrative commercial prospect with the arrival of steam-powered ships and explosive harpoons. Norwegian hunters built 13 large-scale whaling stations in Iceland, and hunted until stocks practically disappeared in 1913. Icelanders established their own whaling industry in 1935, until whale numbers again became dangerously low and commercial hunting was banned by the International Whaling Commission (IWC) in 1986. Iceland resumed commercial whaling in 2006, to the consternation of environmentalists worldwide. The question of why Iceland is whaling today is not a simple one to answer.

Iceland's authorities stress that the country's position has always been that whale stocks should be utilised in a sustainable manner like any other living marine resource. Its catch limits for common minke whales and fin whales follow the advice given by the Marine Research Institute of Iceland regarding sustainability – the quota for the 2018 season was for an annual maximum catch of 217 minke whales and 209 fin whales (with an additional 20% – 29 animals – from the previous year's uncaught quota, so a total of 238 fin whales).

Those numbers stir passions, especially given that fin whales are classified as endangered globally on the International Union for Conservation of Nature (IUCN) Red List. In 2016 and 2017 fin whaling was halted due to trade difficulties with Japan (though minke whaling continued), and amid much international outcry fin whaling began again in 2018. Due to the extension of the marine reserve in the eastern part of Faxaflói Bay, near Reykjavík, which is the main place minkes had been caught, minke whaling was halted for the 2018 season after only six animals were killed. A new reserve was also created in North Iceland in Eyjafjörður and Skjálfandi Bay.

Members of Iceland's tourism board are strong objectors to whaling, stating that Iceland's whaling industry will have a detrimental effect on whale watching (although this is disputed by the Ministry of Industries and Innovation). With the boom in tourist numbers, the idea is that a whale is worth more alive (for watching) than dead (for eating). Ironically, estimates are that from 40% to 60% of Icelandic whale-meat consumption is by curious tourists, with only 1% of Icelanders eating whale meat regularly; much is exported to Japan, though demand has declined there, too. In 2012 the International Fund for Animal Welfare (IFAW; www.ifaw.is) and IceWhale (Icelandic Whale Watching Association; www.icewhale.is) launched a high-profile 'Meet Us Don't Eat Us' campaign to encourage visitors to go whale watching rather than whale tasting, and their 2016 petition garnered more than 100,000 signatures. Their website lists whale-friendly restaurants in Iceland.

Icelandic whaling has attracted other international condemnation – in 2014, a formal diplomatic protest (known as a démarche) against whaling was delivered to the Icelandic government from 35 nations, including the US, Australia and members of the EU. And, in 2018, the catching of a rare blue whale/fin whale hybrid received much press coverage, and the company was sued by an environmental group.

A US-based campaign, 'Don't Buy from Icelandic Whalers' (www.dontbuyfromicelandicwhalers.com), encourages the public not to buy fish from suppliers and retailers who source from Icelandic companies linked to whaling. But, for the moment, whaling continues.

jökull and Hofsjökull in the highlands – have been melting at an unprecedented rate since 2000. Glaciologists believe the ice cap Snæfellsjökull in the west (with an average ice thickness of only 30m), as well as some of the outlet glaciers of the larger ice caps, could disappear completely within a few decades. Others have lost their glacier status due to melting, such as West Iceland's Ok (formerly Okjökull) in 2014.

Imported by the Vikings, the purebred Icelandic horse *(Equus scandinavicus)* is a small, tough breed perfectly suited to the country's rough conditions. Icelandic horses have five gaits, including the unusual *tölt* – a running walk so smooth that riders can drink a glass of beer without spilling a drop.

Wildlife

Mammals & Marine Life

Apart from birds, sheep and horses, you'll be lucky to have any casual sightings of animals in Iceland. The only indigenous land mammal is the elusive Arctic fox, best spotted in remote Hornstrandir in the Westfjords – wildlife enthusiasts can apply in advance to monitor these creatures while volunteering at the Arctic Fox Center (www.arcticfoxcenter.com). In East Iceland, herds of reindeer can sometimes be spotted from the road. Reindeer were introduced from Norway in the 18th century and now roam the mountains in the east. Polar bears very occasionally drift across from Greenland on ice floes, but armed farmers make sure they don't last long.

In contrast, Iceland has a rich marine life, particularly whales. On whale-watching tours from Húsavík in North Iceland, you'll have an excellent chance of seeing cetaceans, particularly dolphins, porpoises, minke whales and humpback whales. Sperm, fin, sei, pilot, orca and blue whales also swim in Icelandic waters and have been seen by visitors. Seals can be seen in the Eastfjords, on the Vatnsnes Peninsula in northwest Iceland, in the Mýrar region on the southeast coast (including at Jökulsárlón), in Breiðafjörður in the west, and in the Westfjords.

Birds

Bird life is prolific, at least from May to August. On coastal cliffs and islands around the country you can see a mind-boggling array of seabirds, often in massive colonies. Most impressive for their sheer numbers are gannets, guillemots, gulls, razorbills, kittiwakes, fulmars and puffins. Less numerous birds include wood sandpipers, Arctic terns, skuas, Manx shearwaters, golden plovers, storm petrels and Leach's petrels. In the southern Westfjords you can occasionally spot endangered white-tailed eagles. In addition, there are many species of ducks, ptarmigans, whooping swans, redwings, divers and gyrfalcons, and two species of owls.

Flowers & Fungi

Although Iceland was largely deforested long ago, its vegetation is surprisingly varied – you just need to get close to see it. Most vegetation is low-growing, spreading as much as possible to get a better grip on the easily eroded soil. Wind erosion and damage from off-road drivers are big conservation issues. Even the trees, where there are any, are stunted. As the old joke goes, if you're lost in an Icelandic forest, just stand up.

A Guide to the Flowering Plants and Ferns of Iceland, by Hörður Kristinsson, is the best all-round field guide to Icelandic flowers.

If you're visiting in summer, you'll be treated to incredible displays of wildflowers blooming right across the country. Most of Iceland's 450 flowering plants are introduced species – especially the ubiquitous purple lupin, once an environmental help, now a hindrance. A nationwide poll held in 2004 voted for the mountain avens *(Dryas octopetala)*, known as *holtasóley* (heath buttercup) in Icelandic, as the national flower. Look out for it on gravel stretches and rocky outcrops – its flowers are about 3cm in diameter, each with eight delicate white petals and an exploding yellow-sun centre.

Coastal areas are generally characterised by low grasses, bogs and marshlands, while at higher elevations hard or soft tundra covers the ground.

Another common sight when walking almost anywhere in Iceland is fungi. There are about 2000 types growing here, and you'll see everything from pale white mushrooms to bright orange flat caps as you walk along trails, by roadsides or through fields.

Iceland isn't truly an Arctic country – the mainland falls short of the Arctic Circle by a few kilometres. To cross that boundary, you'll need to travel to the island of Grímsey, Iceland's only real piece of Arctic territory.

In southern and eastern Iceland new lava flows are first colonised by mosses, which create a velvety green cloak across the rough rocks. Older lava flows in the east and those at higher elevations are generally first colonised by lichens. Confusingly, Icelandic moss *(Cetraria islandica)*, the grey-green or pale brown frilly growth that you'll see absolutely everywhere, is actually lichen.

National Parks & Reserves

Iceland has three national parks and more than 100 nature reserves, natural monuments and country parks, with a protected area of 18,806 sq km (about 18% of the entire country). A proposed Highland National Park (www.halendid.is) would protect a vast section of Iceland's interior (40,000 sq km), comprising a full 40% of the country.

Umhverfisstofnun (Environment Agency of Iceland; www.ust.is) is responsible for protecting many of these sites. Its website contains information on its work to promote the protection as well as sustainable use of Iceland's natural resources, including ways travellers can tread lightly. The agency also recruits summer volunteers each year, to work in conservation projects within the parks.

Þingvellir National Park (p119), Iceland's oldest national park, protects a scenic 84-sq-km lake, the geologically significant Almannagjá rift, and is the site of the original Alþingi (National Assembly). The park is a Unesco World Heritage Site.

Snæfellsjökull National Park (p227) in West Iceland was established in June 2001. The park protects the Snæfellsjökull glacier (made famous by author Jules Verne), the surrounding lava fields and coast.

PUFFINS

Cute, clumsy and endearingly comic, the puffin (*Fratercula arctica*, or *lundi* as they're called in Icelandic) is one of Iceland's best-loved birds. Although known for its frantic fluttering and crash landings, the bird is surprisingly graceful underwater and was once thought to be a bird-fish hybrid.

The puffin is a member of the auk family and spends most of its year at sea. For four or five months it comes to land to breed, generally keeping the same mate and burrow (a multiroom apartment!) from year to year.

Until very recently, 60% of the world's puffins bred in Iceland, and you could see them in huge numbers around the island from late May to August. However, over the last decade, the puffin stock has gone into a sudden, sharp decline in the south of Iceland. They still visit the south – Vestmannaeyjar Islands' puffins are the largest puffin colony in the world – but in smaller numbers and with considerably less breeding success. The reason is uncertain, but it's thought that warming ocean temperatures have caused their main food source – sand eels – to decline. It's also possible that hunting and egg collection have had an effect. In 2018, BirdLife International reported that puffins are threatened with extinction globally.

The good news for twitchers is that puffins in the north and west seem less affected (for now). The photogenic birds continue to flitter around the cliffs of Grímsey and Drangey, as well as in Borgarfjörður Eystri, the Westfjords and Snæfellsnes.

Hikers in Skaftafell (p187)

Vatnajökull National Park (p189) is the largest national park in Europe and covers roughly 13% of Iceland. It was founded in 2008 by uniting two previously established national parks: Skaftafell (p187) in Southeast Iceland, and Jökulsárgljúfur (p319) further north. The park protects the entirety of the Vatnajökull ice cap, the mighty Dettifoss waterfall and a great variety of geological anomalies.

Energy Agendas

Iceland's small population, pristine wilderness, lack of heavy industry and high use of geothermal and hydroelectric power (81.2% of their energy use came from renewable sources in 2017) give it an enviable environmental reputation. Its use of geothermal power is one of the most creative in the world, and the country's energy experts are now advising Asian and African industries on possible ways to harness geothermal sources.

However, power supplies provided free by bountiful nature are not just of interest to Icelanders. Foreign industrialists in search of cheap energy also have their eye on the country's glacial rivers and geothermal hot spots. Alcoa, an American aluminium-smelting company, was responsible for one of Iceland's most controversial schemes: the Kárahnjúkar hydroelectric station (p394) in East Iceland, completed in 2009, was the biggest construction project in Iceland's history. It created a network of dams and tunnels, a vast reservoir, a power station and miles of power lines to supply electricity to a fjord-side smelter 80km away in Reyðarfjörður.

Alcoa makes much of its efforts to reduce its carbon footprint including the fact that the aluminium it manufactures in Iceland uses cheap, green energy from renewable sources (this was the whole point of closing two US smelters and setting up here). Environmentalists, however, raised serious objections to the project on a number of grounds, not least

In 2002 scientists discovered the world's second-smallest creature at 0.4 micrometers, *Nanoarchaeum equitans*, living in near-boiling water in a hydrothermal vent off the north coast of Iceland. The name means 'riding the fire sphere'.

that the mega-dam built specifically to power the Alcoa plant has devastated the landscape. Locals though were less vocal – many were grateful for work opportunities coming to the area.

Garden angelica (*Angelica archangelica*) grows wild in many parts of Iceland. It's been valued as a medicinal herb since Viking times, and these days is appearing in more and more recipes. Kaldi beer even has a brew (known as Stinnings Kaldi) with angelica as an ingredient.

The Power of Power

The Kárahnjúkar dam and aluminium smelter are dramatic illustrations of the dilemma Iceland faces.

To ensure economic prosperity, Iceland is seeking to shore up its position as a green-energy superpower. Thanks to its rich geothermal and hydroelectric energy sources, and new wind turbines (read more at www.nea.is), Iceland generates more electricity per capita than any other country in the world – and twice as much as second-placed Norway. Interestingly, Iceland also uses more energy per capita than any other nation. Eighty per cent of Iceland's electricity is sold to a handful of international companies based in Iceland, such as aluminium smelters, but exporting electricity would bring in new revenue.

Iceland and the UK have moved through the initial feasibility studies of exporting clean hydroelectric energy via a 1500km subsea power cable running from Iceland to the UK (read more at www.atlanticsuperconnection.com). Iceland is also continuing to expand its power-intensive industries, including becoming a global data-centre hub, home to servers housing digitised information.

But if such initiatives go ahead, the power must still be harnessed, and power plants and power lines must be built for such a purpose. Where will these be located? What tracts of Iceland's highland wilderness may be threatened by industrial megaprojects? NGO organisation Landvernd (www.landvernd.is), the Icelandic Environment Association, has proposed that the central highlands be protected with the establishment of a national park. Economic profit versus the preservation of nature – it's an age-old battle. Watch this space.

The Impact of Tourism on Nature

More than 2.2 million visitors per year head to Iceland for their dream holiday in a vast natural playground. And guess what? This boom in numbers is threatening the very thing everyone is travelling to see: Iceland's unspoilt nature.

Icelanders are voicing a valid concern that the population of 350,000 and its existing infrastructure is ill-equipped to handle the demands and behaviour of visitors. Media consistently reports instances of tourists disrespecting nature or taking dangerous risks: hiking in poor weather without proper equipment, getting vehicles stuck in rivers, driving cars onto glaciers, falling off cliffs or being swept off beaches. In 2016, 2017 and again in 2018, for example, tourists have been caught hopping across the ice in Jökulsárlón. Footage and social media showing cavalier, risky behaviour like this (see also Justin Bieber rolling in fragile moss in his 2015 'I'll Show You' video) further encourages a disregard for rules, signs and common sense.

The Forlagið (Mál og Menning) series of maps now includes some fun themed ones: *Fuglakort* (Birdwatcher's Map), *Höggunarkort* (Tectonic Map), *Jarðfræðikort* (Geological Map) and *Plöntukort* (Botanical Map). The text is in Icelandic, English and German.

The people on the hook for rescues are the extraordinarily competent and well-respected Icelandic Association for Search and Rescue (ICE-SAR; www.icesar.com). It is an all-volunteer operation funded by donations. A good article on the organisation, 'Life Is Rescues', appeared in *The New Yorker* in November 2015. ICE-SAR puts a huge emphasis on accident prevention and education with its informative website (www.safetravel.is) and '112 Iceland' app that allows travellers to register hikes and trips.

Icelanders have responded by erecting more signs – despite the fact locals tend to abhor them (they mar the landscape); ropes along some walkways – which some visitors continue to flout; and an educational campaign (www.inspiredbyiceland.com/icelandacademy). The govern-

Fimmvörðuháls pass (p153)

ment has also instituted camping rules requiring campervans to spend the night in organised campgrounds rather than on roadsides or in car parks, in part to address the problem of people using the roadside as their toilet. Laws are slightly more relaxed for hikers and cyclists, but they are bound by rules regarding obtaining landowner permission, being an acceptable distance from official campgrounds, ensuring they don't set up more than the allowed number of tents, and ensuring they're not camping on cultivated land.

Ultimately the protection of Iceland's environment will be a joint project between Icelanders and visitors. Icelanders must build on their infrastructure and rules, and foster an attitude of environmental protection, and visitors must heed local advice and respect the country they are visiting.

Dreamland: A Self-Help Manual for a Frightened Nation by Andri Snær Magnason critically examines the government's decisions over Kárahnjúkar dam. The powerful documentary based on the book, *Dreamland* (2009), won critical acclaim.

Proposed Visitor Fees & Caps

A continuously debated proposal involves the introduction of fees to ensure travellers contribute to the protection and maintenance of natural sites, as well as to possibly control visitor numbers to specific sights.

Suggestions include a one-off fee, perhaps an arrival tax payable at the airport, or a nature pass purchased according to the length of your stay. There's also the idea of charging for day-use or parking (already beginning to occur). It doesn't seem like an unreasonable request – especially when one looks at it in the context of Iceland's tiny population, now hosting hordes of trekkers and buses full of holidaymakers all requiring car parks, toilet blocks, picnic tables, litter bins, improved signage, not to mention rangers providing information and safety advice.

There is also occasional talk of lotteries or limits on visitor numbers in certain regions or on certain trails (such as the Laugavegurinn hike), but so far no new policies or legislation have been set down.

Icelandic Culture

Iceland blows away concerns such as isolation, never-ending winter nights and its small population with a glowing passion for all things cultural. The country's unique literary heritage begins with high-action medieval sagas and stretches to today's Nordic Noir bestsellers. Every Icelander seems to play in a band, and the country produces a disproportionate number of world-class musicians. The way of life and grand landscapes inspire visual artists who use film, art and design to capture their unique Icelandic perspectives.

Literature

Bloody, mystical and nuanced, the late 12th- and 13th-century sagas are some of Iceland's greatest cultural achievements. Reverend Hallgrímur Pétursson's 1659 *Passíusálmar* (Passion Hymns) were an Icelandic staple, sung or read at Lent. Nobel Prize–winning author Halldór Laxness put Iceland on the 20th-century literary map. But Icelanders aren't resting on their laurels: today the country produces the most writers and literary translations per capita of any country in the world.

An old Icelandic saying is *Betra er berfættum en bókarlausum að vera* ('It's better to be barefoot than bookless'). Icelanders remain passionate about the written word, so it's fitting that Reykjavík is a Unesco City of Literature, with tours and programs to match.

The Sagas

Iceland's medieval prose sagas are some of the most imaginative and enduring works of early literature – epic, brutal tales that flower repeatedly with wisdom, magic, elegiac poetry and love.

Written down during the 12th to early 14th centuries, these sagas look back on the disputes, families, doomed romances and larger-than-life characters (from warrior and poet to outlaw) who lived during the Settlement Era. Most were written anonymously, though *Egil's Saga* has been attributed to Snorri Sturluson. Some are sources for historical understanding, such as the *Saga of the Greenlanders* and *Saga of Erik the Red,* which describe the travels of Erik and his family, including his son Leif (a settler in North America).

The sagas, written over the long, desperate centuries of Norwegian and Danish subjugation, provided a strong sense of cultural heritage at a time when Icelanders had little else. On winter nights, people would gather for the *kvöldvaka* (evening vigil). While the men twisted horsehair ropes and women spun wool or knitted, a family member would read the sagas and recite *rímur* (verse reworkings of the sagas).

The sagas are very much alive today. Icelanders of all ages can (and do) read them in Old Norse, the language in which they were written 800 years ago. Most people can quote chunks from them, know the farms where the characters lived and died, and flock to cinemas to see the latest film versions of these eternal tales. Check out the Icelandic Saga Database (www.sagadb.org) for more.

Eddic & Skaldic Poetry

The first settlers brought their oral poetic tradition with them from other parts of Scandinavia, and the poems were committed to parchment in the 12th century.

Eddic poems were composed in free, variable meters with a structure very similar to that of early Germanic poetry. Probably the most well known is the gnomic *Hávamál,* which extols the virtues of the common life – its wise proverbs on how to be a good guest are still quoted today.

Skaldic poems were composed by *skalds* (Norwegian court poets) and are mainly praise-poems of Scandinavian kings, with lots of description packed into tightly structured lines. As well as having fiercely rigid alliteration, syllable counts and stresses, Skaldic poetry is made more complex by *kennings,* a kind of compact word-riddle. Blood, for instance, is 'wound dew', while an arm might be described as a 'hawk's perch'.

Iceland publishes the greatest number of books per capita in the world, and the literacy rate is a perfect 100%.

The most renowned *skald* was saga anti-hero Egil Skallagrímsson. In 948, after being captured and sentenced to death, Egil composed the ode *Höfuðlausn* (Head Ransom) for his captor Eirík Blood-Axe. Flattered, the monarch released Egil unharmed.

Modern Literature

Nobel Prize–winner Halldór Laxness is Iceland's modern literary genius. Also well known is the early-20th-century children's writer Reverend Jón Sveinsson (nicknamed Nonni), whose old-fashioned tales of derring-do have a rich Icelandic flavour and were once translated into 40 languages; *At Skipalón* is the only one readily available in English, or you can read his 1894 memoir, *A Journey Across Iceland: The Ministry of Rev. Jon Sveinsson S.J.* Sveinsson's house in Akureyri is now an interesting museum. Two other masters of Icelandic literature are Gunnar Gunnarsson (1889–1975; look for *The Sworn Brothers, a Tale of the Early Days of Iceland,* 2012) and Þórbergur Þórðarson (1888–1974; look for *The Stones Speak,* 2012).

For more contemporary fare, try Einar Kárason's outstanding *Devil's Island,* the first of a trilogy about Reykjavík life in the 1950s; unfortunately, the other two parts haven't yet been translated into English. Hallgrímur Helgason's *101 Reykjavík* is the book on which the cult film was based. It's a dark comedy following the torpid life and fertile imagination of out-of-work Hlynur, who lives in downtown Reykjavík with his mother. Even blacker is *Angels of the Universe,* by Einar Már Gudmundsson, which is about a schizophrenic man's spells in a psychiatric hospital. Svava Jakobsdóttir's *Gunnlöth's Tale* blends contemporary life with Nordic mythology.

TOP ICELANDIC SAGAS

Egil's Saga Revolves around the complex, devious but sensitive Egil Skallagrímsson, and much of it is set near modern-day Borgarnes. A renowned poet or *skald,* triumphant warrior and skilled negotiator, Egil is also the grandson of a werewolf/shapeshifter, and unlike most Saga protagonists, lived to a ripe old age.

Laxdæla Saga A tragic saga set in Northwest Iceland around Breiðafjörður and the Dalir: bitter marriages, thwarted love and murder abound.

Njál's Saga Two of Iceland's greatest heroes, Njál and Gunnar, are drawn into a fatal, 50-year family feud.

Gisli Sursson's Saga The quintessential outlaw story, Gisli's tale involves revenge, fratricide and banishment.

Völsungasaga (Saga of the Völsungs) Parts of this saga may seem familiar – Richard Wagner *(Der Ring des Nibelungen)* and JRR Tolkien *(Lord of the Rings)* both swiped episodes.

Eyrbyggja Saga A minor saga set around the Snæfellsnes Peninsula, worth reading for its offbeat, supernatural tone; definitely the only medieval Icelandic work where ghosts are taken to court over their hauntings.

HALLDÓR LAXNESS

Over his long lifetime, Nobel Prize–winner Halldór Laxness (1902–98) succeeded in reshaping the world of Icelandic literature, and reviving the saga-scale story. Today he is Iceland's most celebrated 20th-century author.

Laxness was born as Halldór Guðjónsson, but he took the name of his family's farm Laxnes (with an extra 's') as his *nom de plume*. Ambitious and inquisitive, Laxness had his first work published at the age of 14, and began his restless wanderings at 17. He wrote his first novel, *Undir Helgahnúk* (Under the Holy Mountain), from a monastery during a period of fervent Catholicism. Laxness then left for Italy, where his disaffection with the Church and increasingly leftist leanings led to the writing of *Vefarinn Mikli frá Kasmír* (The Great Weaver from Kashmir). In the 1930s he moved to America to try his luck in the fledgling Hollywood film industry, before becoming enthralled with communism and travelling widely in the Soviet Bloc. In 1962 the author settled at Laxnes, near Þingvellir, for good; his home is now a museum. It was here that he wrote *Skáldatími* (Poets' Time), a poignant recantation of everything he'd ever written in praise of the Communist Party.

In 1955 Laxness won the Nobel Prize for Literature and became – in true Icelandic style – a hero of the people. His works are masterpieces of irony, and his characters, however misguided, are drawn with sympathy. Unfortunately, only a portion of his 51 novels and countless short stories, articles, plays and poems are currently available in translation, the most famous of which is *Independent People* (1934–35). This bleak tragi-comedy is told in lush, evocative language and deals with the harsh conditions of early-20th-century Icelandic life. It focuses on the bloody-minded farmer Bjartur of Summerhouses and his toiling family, and creates a detailed depiction of traditional farmstead life. Also fascinating is *Iceland's Bell*, a saga-like portrait of extreme poverty and skewed justice, set in an Iceland subjugated by Danish rule. Other translated works are *World Light*, *The Fish Can Sing*, *Paradise Reclaimed*, *The Atom Station* and *Under the Glacier*.

Surfing the Nordic Noir tidal wave is Arnaldur Indriðason, whose Reykjavík-based crime fiction permanently tops the bestseller lists. Many of his novels are available in English, including *Voices*, the award-winning *Silence of the Grave*, *The Draining Lake* and, possibly the best, *Tainted Blood* (also published as *Jar City*, and the inspiration for a film of the same name). Yrsa Sigurðardóttir's thrillers have also been widely translated – her latest are *The Absolution* and *The Hole*. Dip into Ragnar Jónasson's Dark Iceland series with the first, *Snowblind*, set in remote Siglufjörður. Viktor Arnar Ingólfsson's *The Flatey Enigma* has been made into a TV series.

Also look for Guðrún Eva Mínervudóttir's *The Creator*, a dark psychological novel. Former Sugarcube collaborator Sjón's *The Blue Fox* is a fantasy-adventure tale set in the 19th century; or try his most recent: *Moonstone – The Boy Who Never Was*.

Norse Myth

For vibrant retellings of Norse myths try the similarly named:

Norse Mythology by Neil Gaiman

Myths of the Norsemen by Roger Lancelyn Green

Norse Myths by Kevin Crossley-Holland

Music

Pop, Rock & Electronica

Iceland punches above its weight in the pop- and rock-music worlds. Internationally famous Icelandic musicians include (of course) Björk and her former band, the Sugarcubes. From her platinum album *Debut* (1993) to her most recent, *Utopia* (2017), Björk continues to be a force.

Sigur Rós, stars on the international stage, garnered rave reviews with albums such as *Ágætis Byrjun* (1999) and *Takk* (2005). Their most recent, *Route One* (2017), was assembled from music created while they drove the entire Ring Road in midsummer 2016. The band's concert movie *Heima* (2007) is a must-see. Lead singer Jónsi had success with his joyful solo album *Go* (2010).

Reykjavík's cutting-edge Harpa concert hall, with its facade of glimmering hexagons, has four state-of-the art stages and amazing acoustics. It's a great place to catch a show.

Indie-folk Of Monsters and Men stormed the US charts in 2011 with their debut album, *My Head is an Animal.* The track 'Little Talks' from that album reached number one on the Billboard US Alternative Songs chart in 2012. Their latest album, *Beneath the Skin* (2015), debuted at number three on the US Billboard 200.

Ásgeir Trausti, who records simply as Ásgeir, had a breakout hit with *In the Silence* (2014) and sells out concerts internationally. His latest is *Afterglow* (2017).

Reykjavík has a flourishing music scene with a constantly changing line-up of new bands and sounds – see www.icelandmusic.is for an idea of the variety.

Seabear, an indie-folk band, have spawned several top music-makers such as Sin Fang (try *Flowers* from 2013 or *Spaceland* from 2016) and Sóley (*We Sink* from 2012, *Ask the Deep* from 2015 and *Endless Summer* from 2017). Árstíðir record minimalist indie-folk, and had a 2013 YouTube hit when they sang a 13th-century Icelandic hymn a cappella in a train station in Germany. Their album, *Nivalis,* was released in 2018. Kiasmos is a duo mixing moody, minimalist electronica; check out their album also called *Kiasmos* (2014) or the several EPs they've released since.

GusGus, a local pop-electronica act, have 10 studio albums to their credit and opened for Justin Timberlake at his sold-out 2014 concert in Reykjavík. In September 2016, Sturla Atlas, the Icelandic hip hop/R&B phenomenon opened for the other Justin (Bieber); Bieber's video *I'll Show You* was shot in Iceland. Another well-known Icelandic rapper is Gisli Pálmi.

Kaleo, a popular blues-folk-rock band from Mosfellsbær, has hit the international stage with a splash – the song 'No Good' from their 2016 debut studio album *A/B* garnered a Grammy award nomination.

Vestmannaeyjar Islands–born Júníus Meyvant's 2016 debut, *Floating Harmonies,* is a creative blend of beautifully orchestrated folk, funk and soul.

FM Belfast, an electronica band, set up their own recording label to release their first album, *How to Make Friends* (2008); their latest is *Island Broadcast* (2017). Múm makes experimental electronica mixed with traditional instruments (their latest is *Smilewound;* 2013).

Prins Póló, named after a candy bar, records lyric-heavy dance-pop. Also check out Hafdís Huld, whose latest pop album is called *Dare to Dream Small,* and ebullient garage-rockers Benny Crespo's Gang. Just Another Snake Cult heads towards the psychedelic with *Cupid Makes a Fool of Me* (2013). Or check out Singapore Sling for straight-up rock and roll.

The list goes on. And on. Similarly, Reykjavík's live-music venues are ever-changing – the best thing to do is to check the free publication *Reykjavík Grapevine* (www.grapevine.is) or its app (called Appening Today) for current news and listings. Increasingly, live local music can be found all over Iceland. If your trip coincides with one of the country's many music festivals, go! The fabulous Iceland Airwaves (p27) festival (held in Reykjavík in November) showcases Iceland's talent along with international acts, as does Secret Solstice (p25) in June. Þjóðhátíð (p26), aka National Festival, in Vestmannaeyjar, attracts up to 16,000 people for four days of music and debauchery in late July or early August.

Traditional Music

Until rock and roll arrived in the 20th century, Iceland was a land practically devoid of musical instruments. The Vikings brought the *fiðla* and the *langspil* with them from Scandinavia – both a kind of two-stringed box rested on the player's knee and played with a bow. They were never solo instruments but merely served to accompany singers.

Instruments were generally an unheard-of luxury and singing was the sole form of music. The most famous song styles are *rímur* (poetry or stories from the sagas performed in a low, eerie chant; Sigur Rós have dabbled with the form), and *fimmundasöngur* (sung by two people in harmony). Cut off from other influences, the Icelandic singing style barely changed from the 14th century to the 20th century; it also managed to retain harmonies that were banned by the church across the rest of Europe on the basis of being the work of the devil.

Reykjavík Arts Festival (late May/early June) is the perfect chance to see the intersection of Icelandic visual, literary, musical and performing arts.

You'll find choirs around Iceland performing traditional music, and various compilation albums, such as *Inspired by Harpa – The Traditional Songs of Iceland* (2013), give a sampling of Icelandic folk songs or *rímur*.

Cinema & Television

Iceland's film industry is young and strong – regular production started around the early 1980s – and it creates distinctive work. Both short-form and feature-length Icelandic films receive international awards and prestige, and they often feature thought-provoking material and superb cinematography, using Iceland's powerful landscape as a backdrop.

In 1992 the film world first took notice of Iceland when *Children of Nature* was nominated for an Academy Award for Best Foreign Film. In it, an elderly couple forced into a retirement home in Reykjavík make a break for the countryside. The director, Friðrik Þór Friðriksson, is something of a legend in Icelandic cinema circles. *Cold Fever* (1994), *Angels of the Universe* (2000) and *The Sunshine Boy* (2009) are well worth watching, and he also produces many films.

Another film to put Reykjavík on the cinematic map was *101 Reykjavík* (2000), directed by Baltasar Kormákur and based on the novel by Hallgrímur Helgason. This dark comedy explores sex, drugs and the life of a loafer in downtown Reykjavík. Kormákur's *Jar City* (2006) stars the ever-watchable Ingvar E Sigurðsson as Iceland's favourite detective, Inspector Erlendur, from the novels by Arnaldur Indriðason. Kormákur's 2012 film, *The Deep*, based on a true story of a man who saved himself from a shipwreck in the Vestmannaeyjar Islands, was a hit, and in 2013 he launched into Hollywood with *2 Guns*, starring Denzel Washington and Mark Wahlberg. *Everest* (2015) starred Keira Knightley, Robin Wright and Jake Gyllenhaal. Kormákur has established RVK Studios, which also produces the hit TV series *Ófærð* (Trapped; 2015), an excellent, moody crime drama set in Seyðisfjörður in East Iceland (though filmed in Siglufjörður in the north). His latest includes thriller *The Oath* (*Eiðurinn;* 2016) and *Adrift* (2018), starring Shailene Woodley and Sam Claflin.

Director Dagur Kári achieved international success with films including *Nói Albinói* (2003), the story of a restless adolescent in a snowed-in northern fjord town, and the English-language *The Good Heart* (2009). Another RVK Studios production, Kári's *Virgin Mountain* (*Fúsi;* 2015), is a touching portrait of a gentle, isolated man, which played in art houses around the world.

The tiny Museum of Design and Applied Art (www.honnunarsafn.is) in Garðabær, just south of Reykjavík, showcases the local design scene from the early 20th century to today and has a small Kraum design outlet.

Also look out for Hilmar Oddsson's *Cold Light* (*Kaldaljós;* 2004), a slow-moving, poignant film about life in an isolated fjord town, with a stunning performance from the little boy on whom it centres. And, the quirky 2012 documentary *The Final Member* details the bizarre quest for a Homo sapiens penis for the Icelandic Phallological Museum in Reykjavík.

Hafsteinn Gunnar Sigurðsson's first feature film *Either Way* (2011), about two road workers painting stripes on the highway, was remade in the US by David Gordon Green as *Prince Avalanche* (2013). Sigurðsson's *Paris of the North* (2014), a father-son comedy-drama set in remote East Iceland, was a hit at film festivals, and his latest is *Under the Tree* (2017).

READY FOR ITS CLOSE-UP

Iceland has become a Hollywood darling for location shooting. Its immense, alien beauty and the government's 20% production rebate for filmmakers have encouraged Hollywood directors to make movies here. Try to spot the Icelandic scenery in blockbusters such as *Tomb Raider* (2001), *Die Another Day* (2002), *Batman Begins* (2005), *Flags of Our Fathers* (2006), *Stardust* (2007), *Journey to the Centre of the Earth* (2008), *Prometheus* (2012), *Oblivion* (2013), *Thor: The Dark World* (2013), *Star Trek: Into Darkness* (2013), *The Secret Life of Walter Mitty* (2013), *Noah* (2014), *Captain America* (2016), *Justice League* (2017) and the HBO series *Game of Thrones* (locations from Mývatn to Gjáin). Christopher Nolan–hit *Interstellar* (2014) and recent Star Wars instalments *The Force Awakens* (2015) and *Rogue One* (2016) were shot here too. The TV series *Fortitude* is an English production filmed in Reyðarfjörður in East Iceland (though set in Norway). And then there are films such as *Land Ho!* (2014), both set and shot in Iceland.

Film and TV directors aren't the only ones who ditch the CGI and get the real thing in Iceland. Musicians shoot videos here, too, including Icelandic talents Björk, Of Monsters and Men and Sigur Rós. Don't miss Sigur Rós' inspiring concert film *Heima* (2007), starring the Icelandic people and their roaring falls and towering mountains. Bon Iver's 2011 video 'Holocene' is six minutes that the Icelandic Tourist Board should co-opt for its ad campaigns. And Justin Bieber's 2015 'I'll Show You' is an advertisement in what not to do (moss destruction and glacial lagoon bathing).

Some tour companies offer tours tailored to film locations; also check out the app *Iceland Film Locations* (www.filmlocations.is).

Benedikt Erlingsson's 2013 *Of Horses and Men* was an indie sensation for its surreal portrait of the intertwining lives of men and horses, from the horses' perspective. It was nominated as Iceland's entry to the Academy Awards. Erlingsson is also an actor, and had a role in Rúnar Rúnarsson's *Volcano* (*Eldfjall;* 2011), about an ageing couple who evacuate the Vestmannaeyjar islands during the eruption of Eldfjall, and how they reconcile illness with family. *Sparrows (Þrestir)*, Rúnarsson's disturbing portrait of the growing pains of a young man who moves from Reykjavík to a remote town in the Westfjords (much was filmed in Flatey), saw success in 2015.

Rams (*Hrútar;* 2015), directed by Grímur Hákonarson, is an engrossing comedy-drama about two estranged brothers and their sheep. It was a break-out hit internationally, winning the prize Un Certain Regard at Cannes and becoming the Icelandic entry at the 2016 Academy Awards.

Ása Hjörleifsdóttir's *The Swan* (*Svanurinn*; 2018), a story about a young girl sent to live in the northern countryside and what she discovers, premiered at the Toronto Film Festival.

For lighter fare, watch Þórhildur Þorleifsdóttir's *Stella on Holiday* (*Stella í Orlofi*; 1986) full of mistaken-identity hijinks, or *The Homecoming* (*Blóðberg;* 2015), a sly modern comedy-drama where a 'perfect' family's life goes topsy-turvy. Or find 2015's *Albatross,* where city boy Tommi shores up for the summer at the Bolungarvík golf club with a nutty cast of characters.

There are countless other titles that haven't been widely distributed or translated; take a look at www.icelandiccinema.com.

For the latest on Icelandic feature films, documentaries and animation, visit the website www.icelandicfilmcenter.is.

Painting & Sculpture

Many of Iceland's most successful artists have studied abroad before returning home to wrestle with Iceland's enigmatic soul. The result is a European-influenced style, but with Icelandic landscapes and Saga-related scenes as key subjects. Refreshingly, you'll find museums stocked with wonderful works by men and women alike.

Many Icelandic painters and musicians are serious creative artists in multiple disciplines. Some are making a splash overseas, such as Ragnar Kjartansson, who represents a new breed of Icelandic artist: part painter, part actor, director and musician. Reykjavík Art Museum's Hafnarhús and Reykjavík galleries do a great job showcasing such artists.

The first great Icelandic landscape painter was the prolific Ásgrímur Jónsson (1876–1958), who produced a startling number of Impressionistic oils and watercolours depicting Icelandic landscapes and folk tales. You can see his work at the National Gallery in Reykjavík.

One of Ásgrímur's students was Johannes Kjarval (1885–1972), Iceland's most enduringly popular artist, who grew up in the remote East Iceland village of Borgarfjörður Eystri. His first commissioned works were, rather poignantly, drawings of farms for people who were emigrating, but he's most famous for his early charcoal sketches of people from the village and for his surreal landscapes. A whole beautiful building of the Reykjavík Museum of Art (Kjarvalsstaðir) is named for him.

Sculpture is also very well represented in Iceland, with works dotting parks, gardens and galleries across the country. The most famous Icelandic sculptors all have museums dedicated to them in Reykjavík. Notable exponents include Einar Jónsson (1874–1954), whose mystical works dwell on death and resurrection, and Ásmundur Sveinsson (1893–1982), whose wide-ranging, captivating kinetic works celebrate Iceland, its stories and its people. Don't miss Reykjavík Art Museum's Ásmundarsafn, the artist's peaceful former studio that is filled with inspiring sculptures. Sigurjón Ólafsson (1908–92) specialised in busts but also dabbled in abstract forms. Gerður Helgadóttir (1928–75) made beautiful stained glass and sculpture, and has a museum dedicated to her in Kópavogur. You'll also find her work in Reykjavík's Hljómskálagarður Park, along with pieces by Gunnfríður Jónsdóttir (1889–1968), Nína Sæmundson (1892–1962), Þorbjörg Pálsdóttir (1919–2009) and Ólöf Pálsdóttir (1920–).

Iceland's most famous contemporary painter is probably pop-art icon Erró (Guðmundur Guðmundsson, 1932–), who has donated his entire collection to Reykjavík Art Museum's Hafnarhús. Danish-Icelandic artist Olafur Eliasson (1967–) creates powerful installations and also designed the facade of Reykjavík's dazzling concert hall, Harpa. Páll Guðmundsson (1959–) is a working artist in Húsafell who makes evocative sculptures and paintings, and unusual stone and rhubarb *steinharpa* (similar to a xylophone), which he has played with the band Sigur Rós.

Architecture & Design

Iceland's Viking longhouses have succumbed to the ravages of time, but traditional turf-and-wood techniques were used right up until the 19th century. There is a good example at Glaumbær (p277) in North Iceland.

Guðjón Samúelsson (1887–1950), perhaps one of Iceland's most famous 20th-century architects, worked to create a distinctive Icelandic style, and you will find his minimalist buildings all over the country, from Hallgrímskirkja and the nearby swimming pool, Sundhöllin, in Reykjavík, to Þingvallabær (farmhouse at Þingvellir) and Héraðsskólinn, formerly a school in Laugarvatn. *A Guide to Icelandic Architecture* (Association of Icelandic Architects) looks at 250 Icelandic buildings and designs.

Iceland's coterie of unique designers, artists and architects tend to be Reykjavík-based, though that trend is changing with the tourism boom. Many practitioners form collectives and open shops and galleries, which are full of handmade, beautiful works: everything from striking bowls made out of radishes to cool couture. Reykjavík's **Iceland Design Centre** (Hönnunarmiðstöð; ☎771 2200; www.icelanddesign.is; Aðalstræti 2; ⊙10am-6pm Mon-Sat) has loads more information, and its DesignMarch (p24) annual event opens hundreds of exhibitions and workshops to the public.

Icelandic Attitudes

Centuries of isolation and hardship have instilled particular character traits in the small, homogenous Icelandic population. Their connection to their homeland, history and countrypeople is deeply felt, even if the land reciprocates that love with some cruelty (volcanic eruptions and earthquakes, for a start). The nation's 350,000 souls tend to respond to life's challenges with a compelling mix of courage, candour and creativity, edged with a dark, dry humour.

'Þetta reddast' & the National Psyche

Icelanders have a reputation as tough, hardy, elemental types, and rural communities are still deeply involved in the fishing and/or farming industries. Geographically speaking, 'rural' could be said to define most of the country outside the capital region, which is home to only 36% of Iceland's total population.

Naturally enough for people living on a remote island in a harsh environment, Icelanders are self-reliant individualists who don't like being told what to do. But these steadfast exteriors often hide a more dreamy interior world. Iceland has a rich cultural heritage and an incredibly high literacy rate, and its people have a passion for all things artistic. This enthusiasm is true of the whole country, but it's particularly noticeable in downtown Reykjavík, where seemingly everyone plays in a band, dabbles in art or design, makes films or writes poetry or prose – they're positively bursting with creative impulses.

This buoyant, have-a-go attitude was hit hard during the 2008 financial meltdown. Soup kitchens sprang up in the city and thousands of younger people left Iceland to try their luck in Norway. But Icelanders are resilient – within just a few years, emigration rates fell, and confidence started springing up around the country, mushrooming along with new businesses catering to the tourist boom. The country maintains its belief in the old saying *'Þetta reddast'* (roughly translated, 'It will all work out ok'). The phrase is so frequently used it has been described as the country's motto.

Icelanders are happily patriotic. Witness their Euro 2016 football (soccer) victories, with their Viking thunderclap, and the fact that approximately 10% of the country went to France for the tournament. The men's team participated in the World Cup for the first time in 2018, bringing more high spirits. Citizens who achieve international success are quietly feted: celebrities such as musicians Björk and Sigur Rós reflect prestige onto their entire homeland.

Town layouts, the former US military base, and the prevalence of hot dogs and Coca-Cola point to a heavy US influence, but Icelanders consider their relationship with the rest of Scandinavia to be more important. Although they may seem to conform to the cool-and-quiet Nordic stereotype, Icelanders are curious about visitors and eager to know what outsiders think: 'How do you like Iceland?' is invariably an early question. And an incredible transformation takes place on Friday and Saturday nights, when inhibitions fall away and conversations flow as fast as the alcohol.

Iceland is the world's most peaceful country according to the Global Peace Index, which has ranked the country top of the pops every year since 2008. The GPI bases its findings on factors such as levels of violent crime, political instability and the percentage of a country's population in prison.

Iceland has one of the world's highest life expectancies – 80.7 years for men and 83.7 years for women.

Viking sculptures, Saga Museum (p59)

Work Hard, Play Hard

In the last century the Icelandic lifestyle has shifted from isolated family communities living on scattered farms and in coastal villages to a more urban-based society, with the majority of people living in the southwestern corner around Reykjavík. Despite this change, family connections are still very strong. Though young people growing up in rural Iceland are likely to move to Reykjavík to study and work, localised tourism is bringing entrepreneurial and job options to the hinterlands once again.

Icelanders work hard (and long – the retirement age is 67 and soon to be 70), often at a number of jobs, especially in summer's peak when there is money to be made feeding, accommodating, driving and guiding thousands of tourists. The locals have enjoyed a very high standard of living in the late 20th and early 21st centuries – but keeping up with the Jónssons and Jónsdóttirs came at a price. For decades, Icelanders straight out of university borrowed money to buy houses or 4WDs and spent the rest of their days living on credit and paying off loans. Then, in 2008, the financial crash occurred, and huge amounts of debt suddenly had to be paid back. People wondered how Iceland would ever work itself out of its economic black hole. And yet, with characteristic grit, resilience, adaptability and imagination, Icelanders have hauled their country back from economic disaster.

Iceland had just one TV channel until 1988 – and even that went off air on Thursdays so that citizens could do something more productive instead. It's said that most children born before 1988 were conceived on a Thursday...

The Icelandic commitment to hard work is counterbalanced by deep relaxation. The bingeing in Reykjavík on Friday and Saturday nights is an example of R&R gone wild. But, also keep your eye out for the hundreds of summer houses you'll see when you're driving in the country, and the exceptional number of swimming pools, which form the social hub of Icelandic life.

Women in Iceland

In 2017 Iceland held the top spot (for the ninth consecutive year) in the World Economic Forum's Global Gender Gap Index. The index ranked 136 countries on gender equality by measuring the relative gap between women and men across four key areas: health, education, economics and politics. Iceland continues to be the country with the narrowest gender gap in the world – this means Icelandic women have greater access to health and education, and are more politically and economically empowered than women in other countries. In 2018, Iceland became the first country in the world to enact a law requiring that men and women be paid equally for the same job.

The Viking settlement of Iceland clearly demanded toughness of character, and the sagas are full of feisty women (eg Hallgerður Höskuldsdóttir, who declines to save her husband's life due to a slap that he gave her years earlier). For centuries Icelandic women had to take care of farms and families while their male partners headed off to sea.

Though women and men struggled equally through Iceland's long, dark history, modern concepts of gender equality are a pretty recent phenomenon. Women gained full voting rights in 1920, but it wasn't until the 1970s protest movements reached Iceland that attitudes really began to change. Particularly powerful was the 'women's day off' on 24 October 1975: the country ceased to function when 90% of Icelandic women stayed away from work and stay-at-home mums left children with their menfolk for the day.

In 1980 Iceland became the first democracy to elect a female president, the much-loved Vigdís Finnbogadóttir. In 2009 the world's first openly gay prime minister, Jóhanna Sigurðardóttir, came to power. Iceland has among the highest rate of women's participation in the labour market among OECD countries, at 77%.

The social-care system is so good that women have few worries about the financial implications of raising a child alone: maternity-leave provisions are excellent; childcare is affordable; there is no sense that motherhood precludes work or study; and there's no stigma attached to unmarried mothers. The country isn't perfect – sexual harassment and violence are still issues – but Icelandic women are well educated and independent, with the same opportunities as Icelandic men.

Even though Icelanders speak the nearest thing to Viking in existence, Iceland is the least purely Scandinavian of all the Nordic countries. DNA studies have shown that much of Icelanders' genetic make-up is Celtic, suggesting that many Viking settlers had children with their British and Irish slaves.

WHAT'S IN A NAME

Icelanders' names are constructed from a combination of their first name and their father's (or, more rarely, mother's) first name. Girls add the suffix *-dóttir* (daughter) to the patronymic and boys add *-son*. Therefore, Jón, the son of Einar, would be Jón Einarsson. Guðrun, the daughter of Einar, would be Guðrun Einarsdóttir.

Because Icelandic surnames only usually tell people what a person's father is called, Icelanders don't bother with 'Mr Einarsson' or 'Mrs Einarsdóttir'. Instead they use first names, even when addressing strangers. It makes for a wonderfully democratic society when you're expected to address your president or top police commissioner by their first name. And yes, trivia buffs, the telephone directory is alphabetised by first name.

About 10% of Icelanders have family names (most dating back to early Settlement times), but they're rarely used. In an attempt to homogenise the system, government legislation forbids anyone to take on a new family name or adopt the name of their spouse.

There's also an official list of names that Icelanders are permitted to call their children, and any additions to this list have to be approved by the Icelandic Naming Committee. For the 5000 or so children born in Iceland each year, the committee reportedly receives about 100 applications and rejects about half. Among its requirements are that given names 'must be adaptable to the structure of the Icelandic language and spelling conventions', according to the government website portal.

SUPERNATURAL ICELAND: THE HIDDEN PEOPLE

Once you've seen some of the lava fields, eerie natural formations and isolated farms that characterise much of the Icelandic landscape, it will come as no surprise that many Icelanders believe their country is populated by *huldufólk* (hidden people) and ghosts.

In the lava live *jarðvergar* (gnomes), *álfar* (elves), *ljósálfar* (fairies), *dvergar* (dwarves), *ljúflingar* (lovelings), *tívar* (mountain spirits) and *englar* (angels). Stories about them have been handed down through generations, and many modern Icelanders claim to have seen them...or at least to know someone who has.

There are stories about projects going wrong when workers try to build roads through *huldufólk* homes: the weather turns bad; machinery breaks down; labourers fall ill. In mid-2014 Iceland's 'whimsy factor' made international news when a road project to link the Álftanes peninsula to the Reykjavík suburb of Garðabær was halted after campaigners warned it would disturb elf habitat.

As for Icelandic ghosts, they're substantial beings – not the wafting shadows found elsewhere in Europe. Írafell-Móri (*móri* and *skotta* are used for male and female ghosts, respectively) is said to need to eat supper every night, and one of the country's most famous spooks, Sel-Móri, gets seasick when stowing away in a boat. Stranger still, two ghosts haunting the same area often join forces to double their trouble.

Rock stacks and weird lava formations around the country are often said to be trolls, caught out at sunrise and turned to stone. But living trolls are seldom seen today – they're more the stuff of children's stories.

Surveys suggest that more than half of Icelanders believe in, or at least entertain the possibility of, the existence of *huldufólk*. But a word of warning: many Icelanders tire of visitors asking them whether they believe in supernatural beings. Their pride bristles at the 'Those cute Icelanders! They all believe in pixies!' attitude...and even if they don't entirely disbelieve, they're unlikely to admit it to a stranger.

If you want to know more, and ask all the questions you can, join a tour in Hafnarfjörður, 10km south of Reykjavík, or sign up for a course at the Icelandic Elf School (Álfaskólinn; www.elfmuseum.com) in Reykjavík. Yes, there really is such a place, and it runs four-hour introductory classes most Fridays.

Religious Beliefs

Norse

At the time of the Settlement Era, Iceland's religion was Ásatrú, which means 'faith in the Aesir' (the old Norse gods). Óðinn (Odin), Þór (Thor) and Freyr (Frey) were the major trinity worshipped across Scandinavia. Óðinn, their chief, is the god of war and poetry, a brooding and intimidating presence. In Iceland most people were devoted to Þór (Icelandic names such as Þórir, Þórdís and Þóra are still very popular). This burly, red-haired god of the common people controlled thunder, wind, storm and natural disaster, and was a vital deity for farmers and fishers to have on their side. Freyr and his twin sister Freyja (Freya) represent fertility and sexuality. Freyr brought springtime, with its romantic implications, to both the human and the animal world, and was in charge of the perpetuation of all species.

Icelanders peacefully converted to Christianity more than a thousand years ago, but the old gods linger on. The Ásatrú religion re-emerged in the 1970s, almost simultaneously in Iceland, the US and the UK. Whereas membership of other religions in Iceland has remained fairly constant, Ásatrúarfélagið (Ásatrú Association) is growing. It is now Iceland's largest non-Christian religious organisation, with approximately 4126 members in 2018 (an increase of 54% from 2015).

In his book *The Almost Nearly Perfect People* (2014), author Michael Booth seeks to explore 'the truth about the Nordic miracle'. He presents some great stats and entertaining insights on Icelanders, from financial-crash culprits to *huldufólk* (hidden folk) superstitions.

Christianity

Traditionally, the date of the decree that officially converted Iceland to Christianity is given as 1000, but research has determined that it probably occurred in 999. What is known is that the changeover of religions was a political decision. In the Icelandic Alþingi (National Assembly), Christians and pagans had been polarising into two radically opposite factions, threatening to divide the country. Þorgeir, the *lögsögumaður* (law speaker), appealed for moderation on both sides, and eventually it was agreed that Christianity would officially become the new religion, although pagans were still allowed to practise in private.

Today, as in mainland Scandinavia, most Icelanders (around 71%) belong to the Protestant Lutheran Church – but many are nonpractising. Church attendance is very low.

Those interested in exploring their Icelandic heritage should consult the East Iceland Emigration Center (www.hofsos.is), at Hofsós, and the Snorri Program (www.snorri.is).

Icelandic Ancestry & Genetic Research

Biotech research is big in Iceland – thanks, in part, to the 12th-century historian Ari the Learned. Ari's *Landnámabók* and *Íslendingabók* mean that Icelanders can trace their family trees right back to the 9th century.

In 1996, neuroscience expert Dr Kári Stefánsson recognised that this genealogical material could be combined with Iceland's unusually homogenous population to produce something unique – a country-sized genetic laboratory. In 1998 the Icelandic government controversially voted to allow the creation of a single database, by presumed consent, containing all Icelanders' genealogical, genetic and medical records. Even more controversially, the government allowed Kári's biotech startup company deCODE Genetics to create this database, and access it for its biomedical research, using the database to trace inheritable diseases and pinpoint the genes that cause them.

The decision sparked public outrage in Iceland and arguments across the globe about its implications for human rights and medical ethics. Should a government be able to sell off its citizens' medical records? And is it acceptable for a private corporation to use such records for profit?

While the arguments raged (and investors flocked), the company set to work. The database was declared unconstitutional in 2003, deCODE was declared bankrupt in 2010, and sold to US biotech giant Amgen in 2012. By that time, deCODE had built a research database using DNA and clinical data from more than 100,000 volunteers (one-third of the population), and had done work in isolating gene mutations linked to heart attacks, strokes and Alzheimer's disease.

deCODE continues to unravel the mysteries of the human genome and has had 160,000 Icelanders volunteer their data to date. With its completed research, it has also been able to 'impute' the genetic make-up of Icelanders who have not participated at all – leading to ethical questions: should they inform carriers of dangerous gene mutations even if those people have not agreed to participate? In 2018, after much debate, deCODE created a website for informing women who've given samples whether they carry the harmful BRCA2 gene.

The Little Book of the Icelanders, by Alda Sigmundsdóttir, is a wonderful collection of 50 miniature essays on the 'quirks and foibles' of the Icelandic people, written by an insightful Icelander who returned to live in the country after 22 years abroad.

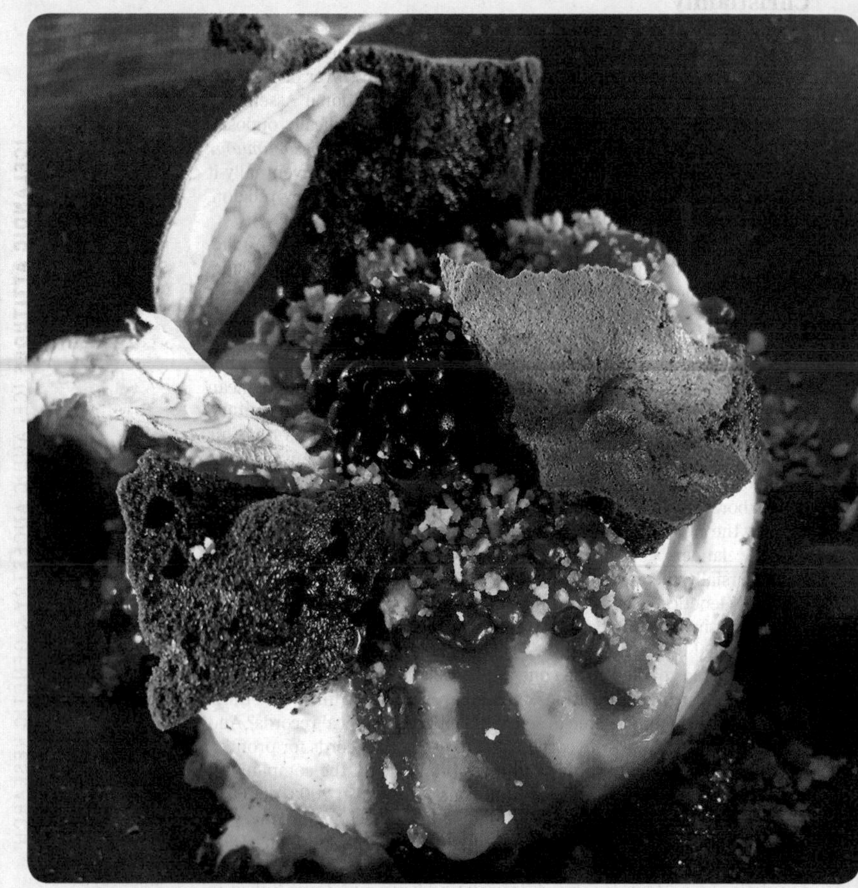

Icelandic Cuisine

If people know anything about Icelandic food, it's usually to do with a plucky population tucking into boundary-pushing dishes such as fermented shark or sheep's head. It's a pity the spotlight doesn't shine as brightly on Iceland's delicious, fresh-from-the-farm ingredients, the seafood bounty hauled from the surrounding icy waters, the innovative dairy products (hello, *skyr!*) or the clever, historic food-preserving techniques that are finding new favour with today's much-feted New Nordic chefs. Reykjavík, especially, has a burgeoning, creative food scene.

Above *Skyr* dessert served at Pakkhús (p205), Höfn

Food Heritage

For much of its history, Iceland was a poverty-stricken hinterland. Sparse soil and cursed weather produced limited crops, and Icelandic farmer-fishers relied heavily on sheep, fish and seabirds to keep them from starving. Every part of every creature was eaten – fresh or dried, salted, smoked, pickled in whey or even buried underground (in the case of shark meat), with preserving techniques honed to ensure food lasted through lean times.

Local food producers and chefs today are rediscovering old recipes and techniques with a renewed sense of pride in the country's culinary heritage, and the results can be quite special. From the capital to select restaurants, sometimes in the most improbably remote locations, you'll find rich, imaginative Icelandic fare. The strong Slow Food Movement prioritises locally grown food over imports, with restaurants proudly flagging up regional treats.

North: The New Nordic Cuisine of Iceland, by chefs Gunnar Karl Gíslason and Jody Eddy, is a beautiful book that profiles traditional Icelandic food producers, many of them suppliers to Gunnar's first-class Dill restaurant.

Staples & Specialities

Fish & Seafood

'Half of our country is the sea', runs an old Icelandic saying. Fish is the mainstay of the Icelandic diet: you'll find it fresh at market stalls and in restaurant kitchens, from where it emerges boiled, pan-fried, baked or grilled.

In the past, Icelanders merely kept the cheeks and tongues of *þorskur* (cod) – something of a delicacy – and exported the rest; but today you'll commonly find cod fillets on the menu, along with *ýsa* (haddock), *bleikja* (Arctic char) and meaty-textured *skötuselur* (monkfish). Other fish include *lúða* (halibut), *steinbítur* (catfish), *sandhverfa* (turbot; non-indigenous), *síld* (herring), *skarkoli* (plaice) and *skata* (skate). During summer you can try *silungur* (freshwater trout) and *villtur lax* (wild salmon). *Eldislax* is farmed salmon; it's available year-round and appears on countless menus in smoked form.

Harðfiskur, a popular snack eaten with butter, is found in supermarkets and at market stalls. To make it, haddock is cleaned and dried in the open air until it has become dehydrated and brittle, then it's torn into strips.

Rækja (shrimp), *hörpudiskur* (scallops) and *kræklingur* (blue mussels) are harvested in Icelandic waters; mussels are at their prime during the very beginning and the end of summer. *Humar* (or *leturhumar*) are a real treat: these are what Icelanders call 'lobster'; the rest of us may know them as langoustine. Höfn, in Southeast Iceland, is particularly well known for *humar* and even has an annual lobster festival.

TASTEBUD TOURING

The incredible local fish and lamb should be high on your hit-list in Iceland. You may be considering the 'novelty value' of sampling the likes of whale, puffin and even *hákarl* (fermented Greenland shark), but please do consider your actions. Try these delicious blasts of local flavour instead.

Skyr Rich and creamy yoghurt-like staple (though actually cheese), sometimes sweetened with sugar and berries. You can consume it in drinks or local desserts, playing a starring role in cheesecake and crème brûlée (or even 'skyramisu') concoctions.

Hangikjöt Literally 'hung meat', usually smoked lamb, served in thin slices (it's traditionally a Christmas dish).

Harðfiskur Brittle pieces of wind-dried haddock ('fish jerky'?), usually eaten with butter.

Pýlsur Icelandic hot dogs, made with a combination of lamb, beef and pork, and topped with raw and deep-fried onion, ketchup, mustard and tangy remoulade (ask for *'eina með öllu'* – one with everything).

Liquorice Salt liquorice and chocolate-covered varieties fill the supermarket sweets aisles.

Rúgbrauð Dark, dense rye bread. Look for *hverabrauð* in Mývatn – it's baked underground using geothermal heat.

A BANQUET OF BODY PARTS

Eyeball a plate of old-fashioned Icelandic food, and chances are it will eyeball you back. In the past nothing was wasted, and some traditional specialities look more like horror-film props than food. You won't be faced with these dishes on many menus, though – they're generally only eaten at *þorramatur* (literally, 'food of *Þorri*') buffets during the Þorrablót midwinter feast (named for the month of *Þorri* in the Old Norse calendar, and corresponding to mid-January to mid-February). Plentiful *brennivín* (caraway-flavoured schnapps) is the expected accompaniment.

Svið Singed sheep's head (complete with eyes) sawn in two, boiled and eaten fresh or pickled.

Sviðasulta (head cheese) Made from bits of *svið* pressed into gelatinous loaves and pickled in whey.

Slátur (the word means 'slaughter') Comes in two forms: *lifrarpylsa* is liver sausage, made from a mishmash of sheep intestines, liver and lard tied up in a sheep's stomach and cooked (kind of like Scottish haggis). *Blóðmör* has added sheep's blood (and equates to blood pudding).

Súrsaðir hrútspungar Rams' testicles pickled in whey and pressed into a cake.

Hákarl Iceland's most famous stomach churner, *hákarl* is Greenland shark, an animal so inedible it has to rot away underground for six months before humans can even digest it. Most foreigners find the stench (a cross between ammonia and week-old roadkill) too much to bear, but it tastes better than it smells... It's the aftertaste that really hurts. A shot of *brennivín* is traditionally administered as an antidote. Note that population numbers of Greenland shark are uncertain.

Meat

Icelandic lamb (promoted here: www.icelandiclamb.is) is hard to beat. During summer, sheep roam free to munch on chemical-free grasses and herbs in the highlands and valleys, before the September *réttir* (sheep roundup), after which they are corralled for the winter. The result of this life of relative luxury is very tender lamb with a slightly gamey flavour. You'll find lamb fillets, pan-fried lamb or smoked lamb on most restaurant menus.

Beef steaks are also excellent but not as widely available, and are consequently more expensive. Horse is still eaten in Iceland, although it's regarded as something of a delicacy; if you see 'foal fillets' on the menu, you're not imagining things.

In East Iceland, wild reindeer roam the highlands, and reindeer steaks are a feature of local menus. Hunting is highly regulated; reindeer season starts in late July and runs well into September.

Birds have always been part of the Icelandic diet. *Lundi* (puffin) used to appear smoked or broiled in liver-like lumps on dinner plates, although it's a rarer sight these days following a worrying crash in puffin numbers. Another seabird is *svartfugl;* it's commonly translated as 'blackbird' on English-language menus, but what you'll actually get is guillemot. High-class restaurants favouring seasonal ingredients may have roasted *heiðagæs* (pink-footed goose) in autumn. Ptarmagin is a Christmas delicacy, though their numbers fluctuate.

Where to Find Fresh...

Langoustines: Höfn

Tomatoes: Flúðir

Reindeer: Egilsstaðir and East Iceland

Hverabrauð ('hot springs bread'): Mývatn

Mussels: Stykkishólmur

Foal: Skagafjörður

Sweets & Desserts

Don't miss *skyr,* a delicious yoghurt-like concoction made from skimmed milk. Despite its rich flavour, it's actually low in fat and high in protein. It's often mixed with sugar, fruit flavours (such as blueberry) and cream to give it an extra-special taste and texture. *Skyr* can be found in any supermarket and as a dessert in restaurants.

Icelandic *pönnukökur* (pancakes) are thin, sweet and cinnamon flavoured. Icelandic *kleinur* (twisted doughnuts) are a chewy treat, along with their offspring *ástarpungar* (love balls), deep-fried, spiced balls of dough. You'll find these desserts in bakeries, along with an amazing array of fantastic pastries and cakes – one of the few sweet legacies of the Danish occupation.

Local dairy farms churn out scrumptious scoops of homemade ice cream, often featured on menus of nearby restaurants.

Sweet, peppery caraway is used to flavour Icelandic cheese, coffee, bread and *brennivín* (schnapps). In late August, after the plant has flowered, some Reykjavikers head to Viðey island to gather caraway seeds.

Drinks

Non-alcoholic

Life without *kaffi* (coffee) is unthinkable. Cafes and petrol stations will usually have an urn of filter coffee by the counter, and some shops offer complimentary cups of it to customers. Snug European-style cafes selling espresso, latte, cappuccino and mocha are ever-more popular, popping up even in the most isolated one-horse hamlets (the coffee isn't always good, though). Tea is available, but ranks as a very poor second choice – the brands sitting on most supermarket shelves make a feeble brew, though that is slowly changing with the increase in tourist demand.

Besides all that coffee, Icelanders drink more Coca-Cola per capita than most other countries. Another very popular soft drink is Egils Appelsín (orange soda) and the home-grown Egils Malt Extrakt, which tastes like sugar-saturated beer.

It isn't a crime to buy bottled water in Iceland, but it should be. Icelandic tap water generally comes from the nearest glacier or spring, and is some of the purest you'll ever drink.

Alcoholic

For some Icelanders, drinking alcohol is not about the taste – getting drunk is the aim of the game. Particularly in Reykjavík, it's the done thing to go out at the weekend and drink till you drop.

You must be at least 20 years old to buy beer, wine or spirits, and alcohol is only available from licensed bars, restaurants and the government-run Vínbúðin liquor stores (www.vinbudin.is). There are roughly 50 shops around the country; most towns have one, and the greater Reykjavík area has about a dozen. In larger places they usually open from 11am to 6pm Monday to Thursday and on Saturdays, and from 11am to 7pm on Fridays (closed Sundays). In small communities, the Vínbúðin store may only open for an hour or two in the late afternoon or evening. Expect queues around 5pm on a Friday. The cheapest bottles of imported wine cost from 1500kr. Beer costs about a third of what you'll pay in a bar.

Chef Anthony Bourdain famously described *hákarl* (fermented Greenland shark) as the worst thing he had ever put in his mouth, and the unusual species lives up to 512 years (the longest-lived vertebrate measured on Earth).

Petrol stations and supermarkets sell the weak and watery 2.2% brew known as pilsner, but most Icelanders would sooner not drink it at all. The main brands of Icelandic beer – Egils, Gull, Thule and Viking – are all fairly standard lager or pils brews; you can also get imported beers. In recent years a slew of good local distilleries and breweries has sprung up all over Iceland, concocting whisky, vodka and dozens of high-calibre

PRICE RANGES

Eating reviews are divided into the following price ranges based on the cost of a main course:

€ Less than 2000kr (€16)

€€ 2000–5000kr (€16–40)

€€€ More than 5000kr (€40)

craft beers – check our cheat sheet (p92) for your next barroom order. Look out, too, for seasonal beers – the ones brewed for the Christmas period are especially popular.

Food lovers may be tempted by food-focused tours such as those out of Akureyri, run by Saga Travel (www.sagatravel.is), or tours around West Iceland, operated by Crisscross (www.crisscross.is).

Reports of astronomical prices for boozing in Iceland arise because a pint of beer in a bar or restaurant costs around 1100kr to 1900kr. In Reykjavík, many venues have early-evening happy hours that cut costs to between 700kr and 900kr per beer. Download the smartphone Reykjavík Appy Hour app to gladden your drinking budget.

The traditional Icelandic alcoholic brew is *brennivín* (literally 'burnt wine'), a potent schnapps made from fermented potatoes and flavoured with caraway seeds. It has the foreboding nickname *svarti dauði* (black death) and it's essential drinking if you're trying any tasty traditional titbits (p410). There are also other local spirits producers, especially of vodka.

Where to Eat & Drink

Restaurants

Iceland's best restaurants are in Reykjavík, but some magnificent finds have also mushroomed up beyond the capital, catering to travellers looking for authentic local flavours. These restaurants are tapping into the network of unsung local producers: barley farmers, mussel harvesters, veggie growers, sheep farmers and fishers. At many places, your meal's food miles will be very low.

Bear in mind that the price difference between an exceptional restaurant and an average one is often small, so it can be well worth going upmarket. Often, though, in rural Iceland you may not have a huge choice – the town's only eating place may be the restaurant in the local hotel, supplemented by the grill bar in the petrol station. And in peak summer, you may struggle to get a table without a reservation, and/or face long waits.

À la carte menus usually offer at least one fish dish, one veggie choice (often pasta) and a handful of meat mains (lamb is the star). Many restaurants also have a menu of cheaper meals such as hamburgers and pizzas. Soup is a mainstay – either as a lunchtime option (perhaps in the form of a soup-and-salad buffet) or as a dinnertime starter. *Fiskisúpa* (fish soup) comes courtesy of various family recipes, while *kjötsúpa* (meat soup) will usually feature veggies and small chunks of lamb.

Peruse *Cool Cuisine: Traditional Icelandic Cuisine* by Nanna Rögnvaldardóttir, *Taste of Iceland* by Úlfar Finnbjörnssonor, or *50 Crazy Things to Taste in Iceland* by Snæfríður Ingadóttir (including great photos by Þorvaldur Örn Kristmundsson) for pictorials and recipes for Iceland's traditional eats.

In Reykjavík, and to a lesser extent Akureyri, there are some ethnic restaurants, including Thai, Japanese, Italian, Mexican, Indian and Chinese. You can also stumble across some welcome surprises – Ethiopian in Flúðir and Moroccan in Siglufjörður.

Opening hours for restaurants are usually 11.30am to 2.30pm and 6pm to 10pm daily. Note that even in summer, restaurants may stop serving meals around 9pm.

Cafes & Pubs

Downtown Reykjavík has a great range of bohemian cafe-bars where you can happily while away the hours sipping coffee, people-watching, scribbling postcards or tinkering on your laptop. Menus range from simple soups and sandwiches to fish dishes and designer burgers. Recent years have seen cafe menus morph into more restaurant-like versions (with an attendant hike in prices). The cafe scene is spreading, too, with cool new spots scattered around the country.

Many of Reykjavík's cafes morph into wild drinking dens in the evenings (mostly on Fridays and Saturdays). DJs suddenly appear, coffee orders turn to beer, and people get progressively louder and less inhibited as the evening goes on, which is usually until sometime between

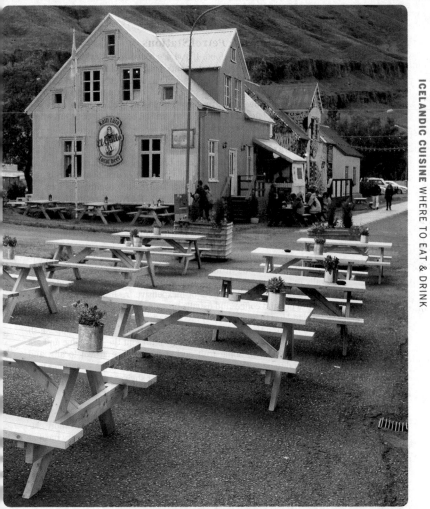

Top Kaffi Lára – El Grilló Bar (p345), Seyðisfjörður

Bottom Icelandic *fiskisúpa* (fish soup) with salmon and prawns

CATCHASNAP/SHUTTERSTOCK ©

4am and 5am. Outside the capital, things are considerably more subdued, although Friday and Saturday nights do see action in Akureyri.

Beer Day (1 March) dates back to the glorious day in 1989 when beer was legalised in Iceland (it was illegal for most of the 20th century). As you'd expect, Reykjavík's clubs and bars get particularly wild.

Hot-Dog Stands & Petrol Stations

Icelanders do enjoy fast food. If you see a queue in Reykjavík, it probably ends at a *pýlsur* (hot dog) stand. Large petrol stations often have good, cheap, well-patronised grills and cafeterias attached. They generally serve sandwiches and fast food from around 11am to 9pm or 10pm. Some also offer hearty set meals at lunchtime, such as meat soup, fish of the day or plates of lamb. Cafeterias at N1 service stations anywhere along the Ring Road are invariably busy.

Supermarkets & Bakeries

Every town and village has at least one small supermarket. The most expensive is 10-11, but it's generally open late hours. Bónus (easily recognised by its yellow-and-pink piggy sign) is the country's budget supermarket chain. Others include Hagkaup, Kjarval, Krónan, Nettó, and Kjörbúðin, formerly known as Samkaup-Strax. Opening times vary greatly; in Reykjavík most are open from 9am to 11pm daily, but outside the capital, hours are almost always shorter. Sunday hours may be limited or nonexistent.

The old-school Icelandic *bakarí* (bakeries) can't be praised enough. Most towns have one (it may be part of a supermarket), which is generally open from 7am or 8am until 4pm on weekdays (sometimes also Saturdays). These sell all sorts of inexpensive fresh bread, buns, cakes, sandwiches and coffee, and usually provide chairs and tables to eat at.

Iceland has to import most of its groceries, so prices are steep – roughly two or three times what you'd pay in North America or Europe. Fish (tinned or smoked) and dairy products represent the best value and are surprisingly cheap. Some fruit and vegetables are grown locally, and these tend to be fresh and tasty, but imported vegetables sometimes look pretty sad by the time they hit supermarket shelves.

Salt Eldhús (www.salteldhus.is) is a small cooking school in Reykjavík that offers hands-on, gourmet cooking classes using local ingredients.

Vegetarians & Vegans

Vegetarians and vegans will have no problem in Reykjavík – there are some excellent meat-free cafe-restaurants in the city, and many more eateries offer vegetarian choices (you'll probably want to eat every meal at Gló). Outside the capital most restaurants have at least one veggie item on the menu – this is routinely cheese-and-tomato pasta or pizza or a salad, though, so you could get bored. Vegans usually have to self-cater, though restaurants are becoming more aware of this food choice.

Survival Guide

Directory A–Z

Accessible Travel

Iceland can be trickier than many places in northern Europe when it comes to access for travellers with disabilities. For details on accessible facilities, contact the information centre for people with disabilities, **Þekkingarmiðstöð Sjálfsbjargar** (Sjálfsbjörg Knowledge Centre; ☎550 0118; www.thekkingarmidstod.is; Hátún 12, Reykjavík). Website God Adgang (www.godadgang.dk), a Danish initiative adopted in Iceland, has instructions for finding Icelandic service providers that have been assessed for the accessibility label.

Particularly good for tailor-made accessible trips around the country are All Iceland Tours (http://alliceland.is) and Iceland Unlimited (www.icelandunlimited.is). Gray Line Iceland (www.grayline.is) and Reykjavík Excursions (www.re.is) run sightseeing and day tours from Reykjavík and will assist travellers with special needs, but they recommend you contact them in advance to discuss your requirements.

Reykjavík's city buses are accessible courtesy of ramps; elsewhere, however, public buses don't have ramps or lifts. Download Lonely Planet's free Accessible Travel guide from http://lptravel.to/AccessibleTravel.

Accommodation

Iceland's accommodation ranges from basic hikers' huts to business-standard hotels, hostels, working farms, guesthouses, apartments, cottages and school-based summer rooms. Luxury and boutique hotels are predominantly found in Reykjavík and tourism hot spots in the southwest, with a select few in regional pockets.

There's been a boom of new hotels and guesthouses, and many existing options have been expanded and upgraded to cater to the rapid increase in visitors. Even still, demand often outstrips sup-

PRACTICALITIES

Discount Cards Students and seniors qualify for discounts on internal flights, some ferry and bus fares, tours and museum entry fees. You'll need to show proof of student status or age.

Laundry Public facilities are tough to find. Campgrounds, hostels and guesthouses may have a washing machine for guest use (for a fee). Business hotels may offer a pricey service. Some rental apartments include a washing machine.

Newspapers & Magazines *Morgunblaðið* (www.mbl.is) has local news in English at www.icelandmonitor.mbl.is/news. *Iceland Review* (www.icelandreview.com) has news and current affairs. *Reykjavík Grapevine* (www.grapevine.is) has excellent tourist-oriented and daily-life articles, plus listings of what's on. Free paper edition of *Grapevine* widely available.

Radio RÚV (Icelandic National Broadcasting Service; www.ruv.is) has three radio stations: Rás 1 (news, weather, cultural programs), Rás 2 (pop music, current affairs) and Rondó (classical music).

Smoking Illegal in enclosed public spaces, including in cafes, bars, clubs, restaurants and on public transport. Most accommodation is nonsmoking.

Weights & Measures The metric system is used.

CAMPING LAWS

New laws regarding camping were introduced in late 2015, primarily to curtail the boom in campervans and caravans pulling over on roadsides or in car parks for the night instead of at organised campgrounds. This habit is offensive to locals, and has resulted in a big increase in people using nature as their bathroom – not cool.

The laws are outlined under the heading 'Where can I camp in Iceland?' on the website of Umhverfisstofnun, the Environment Agency of Iceland (www.ust.is). The bottom line – if you have a camping vehicle of any type (campervan, caravan, tent trailer etc), you must camp in proper, marked campgrounds.

Laws are slightly more relaxed for hikers and cyclists, but there are still rules to follow regarding obtaining landowner permission, being an acceptable distance from official campgrounds, ensuring you don't set up more than the allowed number of tents, and ensuring you're not camping on cultivated land.

ply in popular tourist centres (eg Reykjavík, the south and Mývatn). Summer prices are *high*.

For the cost, accommodation is often of a lower standard than you might expect from a developed European destination, though that is changing in newer hotel construction. In older places, rooms are generally spotless but they are usually small, with thin walls and limited facilities.

- Between June and August travellers should book *all* accommodation in advance (there is no need to prebook campsites). May and September are following this trend. Reykjavík is busy year-round.
- Tourist information centres and the regions' official tourism websites have details of all the accommodation in their town/area.
- The best rate can often be found by contacting the property directly. Some properties don't have their own websites or Facebook page, however,preferring to take bookings via third-party websites like booking.com.
- Prices for summer 2018 are listed in reviews. Expect prices to rise from year to year. Websites list up-to-date prices.
- From September to May, most guesthouses and hotels offer discounts of 10% to 50% on their summer prices.
- Some accommodations close during winter; where this is the case, opening months are given in reviews. Many close over Christmas–New Year, though that is a second high season in Reykjavík, with most hotels open there. If no opening times are given, accommodation is open year-round.
- Some accommodations list prices in euro, to ward against currency fluctuations, but payment is made in Icelandic krónur (kr).
- Guesthouses and farmstays can offer options, eg camping; rooms with/without bathrooms, with made-up beds or sleeping bags; cottages with/without kitchen and/or bathroom. Check websites for full coverage.
- Reviews indicate whether a private bathroom is offered; whether linen is included or if there is a sleeping-bag option; and if breakfast is included in the price.

Camping

Tjaldsvæði (organised campsites) are found in almost every town, at some rural farmhouses and along major hiking trails. The best sites have washing machines, cooking facilities and hot showers, but others just have a cold-water tap and a toilet block. Some are attached to the local *sundlaug* (swimming pool), with shower facilities provided by the pool for a small fee.

Icelandic weather is notoriously fickle, and if you intend to camp it's wise to invest in a good-quality tent. There are a few outfits in Reykjavík that offer rental of camping equipment, and some car-hire companies can also supply you with gear such as tents, sleeping mats and cooking equipment.

With the increase in visitors to Iceland, campgrounds are getting busier, and service blocks typically housing two toilets and one shower are totally insufficient for coping with the demand of dozens of campers. If the wait is long, consider heading to the local swimming pool and pay to use the amenities there.

It is rarely necessary (or possible) to book a camping spot in advance. Many small-town campsites are unstaffed – look for a contact number for the caretaker posted on the service block, or an instruction to head to the tourist information centre or swimming pool to pay; alternatively, a caretaker may visit the campsite in the evening to collect fees.

A few things to keep in mind:

- When camping in parks and reserves the usual rules apply:

SLEEPING PRICE RANGES

The following price categories are based on the high-season price for a double room:

€ less than 15,000kr (€120)

€€ 15,000–30,000kr (€120–240)

€€€ more than 30,000kr (€240)

leave sites as you find them; use biodegradable soaps; and carry out your rubbish.

- Campfires are not allowed, so bring a stove. Butane cartridges and petroleum fuels are available in petrol stations. Blue Campingaz cartridges are not always readily available; the grey Coleman cartridges are more common.
- Camping with a tent or campervan/caravan usually costs 1200kr to 1900kr per person. Electricity is often an additional 800kr. Many campsites charge for showers.
- There's a 'lodging tax' of 333kr per site; some places absorb this cost in the per-person rate, others make you pay it in addition to the per-person rate.
- Consider purchasing the good-value Camping Card (www.campingcard.is), which costs €149 and covers 28 nights of camping at 41 campsites throughout the country for two adults and up to four children from mid-May to mid-September. Note that the card doesn't include the lodging tax, or any charges for electricity or showers. Full details online.
- Most campsites open mid-May to mid-September. Large campsites that also offer huts or cottages may be open year-round. In the off-season ask at tourist offices for info.
- Free accommodation directory *Áning* (available from tourist information centres) lists many of Iceland's campsites, but is not exhaustive.

Emergency Huts

Bright-orange survival huts are situated on high mountain passes and along remote coastlines (and are usually marked on maps of the country). Huts are stocked with emergency rations, fuel and blankets (and a radio to contact help). Note that it is illegal to use the huts in non-emergency situations.

Farmhouse Accommodation

Many rural farmhouses offer campsites, sleeping-bag spaces, made-up guest rooms, and cabins and cottages. Facilities vary: some provide meals or guest kitchen, some have outdoor hot-pots, and many provide horse riding or can organise activities such as fishing. Roadside signs signal which farmhouses provide accommodation and what facilities they offer.

Rates are similar to guesthouses in towns, with sleeping-bag accommodation around 7500kr and made-up beds from 11,000kr to 18,000kr per person. Breakfast is usually included in the made-up room price, while an evening meal (generally served at a set time) costs around 7000kr.

Guesthouses

The Icelandic term *gistiheimilið* (guesthouse) covers a broad range of properties, from family homes renting a few rooms, to self-contained cottages, to custom-built blocks of guest rooms. They vary enormously in character, from stylish options to those with plain or dated decor. A surprisingly high number only have rooms with shared bathroom.

Most are comfortable and cosy, with guest kitchens, TV lounges and buffet-style breakfasts (either included in the price or for around 2200kr extra). If access to a self-catering kitchen is important to you, it pays to ask beforehand to ensure availability. Double rooms in summer cost from 17,000kr to 26,000kr, and self-contained units excluding linen from 19,000kr. Guesthouse rooms with their own bathroom are often similarly priced to hotel rooms.

Hostels

Across the country there are 34 well-maintained hostels administered by Hostelling International Iceland (www.hostel.is). In Reykjavík, Akureyri and a handful of other places, there are also independent backpacker hostels. Bookings are recommended at all of them, especially from June to August. About half the HI hostels open year-round. Check online for opening-date info.

SLEEPING-BAG ACCOMMODATION

Iceland's best-kept secret is the sleeping-bag option offered by hostels and some guesthouses and hotels. For a fraction of the normal cost, you'll get a bed without a duvet; you supply your own sleeping bag. It doesn't mean sleeping in a dorm – generally you book the same private room, just minus linen – BYO towel and pillowcase, too. Prices never include breakfast, but you'll often have the option to buy it. The sleeping-bag option is more prevalent outside peak summer or in more rural places. As a general guide, sleeping-bag accommodation costs about 7500kr per night, per person.

All hostels offer hot showers, cooking facilities and sleeping-bag accommodation, and most offer private rooms (some with private bathroom). Most prices now include linen, but if they don't, the price to hire linen is around 2000kr per person per stay. Breakfast (where available) costs 1700kr to 2300kr.

Join Hostelling International (www.hihostels.com) in your home country to benefit from HI member discounts of 10% per person. Nonmembers pay from about 3800kr to 6500kr for a dorm bed with linen; single rooms start at 7500kr, and double rooms range from 10,000kr to 18,000kr (more for private bathrooms). Children aged four to 12 get a discount of 1500kr.

Hotels

Every major town has at least one business-style hotel, usually featuring comfortable but innocuous rooms with private bathroom, phone, TV and sometimes a minibar and a decent restaurant.

Summer prices for singles/doubles start at around 20,000/28,000kr and usually include a buffet breakfast. Rates for a double room at a nice but non-luxurious hotel in a popular tourist area in peak summer can easily top 34,000kr. Reykjavík high-end hotels and luxury country lodges top 50,000kr. Prices drop substantially outside high season (June to August), and cheaper rates may be found online.

The largest local chains are Icelandair Hotels (www.icelandairhotels.is), Íslandshotel (www.islandshotel.is), which includes the brand Fosshótel, Keahotels (www.keahotels.is) and CenterHotels (www.centerhotels.is). Many international hotel chains are opening in Reykjavík (eg Hilton, Marriott).

BOOK YOUR STAY ONLINE

For more accommodation reviews by Lonely Planet authors, check out http://lonelyplanet.com/hotels/. You'll find independent reviews, as well as recommendations on the best places to stay. Best of all, you can book online.

SUMMER HOTELS

Many boarding schools and colleges become summer hotels offering simple accommodation from early June to late August (some are open longer), and 10 of them are part of a chain called Hótel Edda (www.hoteledda.is), overseen by the Icelandair Hotels chain. Rooms are plain but functional, usually with twin beds, a washbasin and shared bathrooms, although a number of summer hotels have rooms with private bathroom, and a handful offer 'Edda Plus' rooms of a higher standard, with private bathroom, TV and phone. A couple have dormitory sleeping-bag spaces; most have a restaurant. Expect to pay around 4000kr for sleeping-bag accommodation in a dorm (where available); from 21,000/13,500kr for a double room with/without private bathroom; and around 2400kr for breakfast.

Mountain Huts

Private walking clubs and touring organisations maintain *skálar* (mountain huts; singular *skáli*) on many popular hiking tracks. Huts are open to anyone and offer sleeping-bag space in basic dormitories. Some huts also offer cooking facilities, campsites and have a summertime warden.

The huts at Landmannalaugar, Þórsmörk and around Askja are accessible by 4WD; huts in Hornstrandir are accessed by boat; many other mountain huts are on hiking trails and accessible only by foot. GPS coordinates for huts are included in reviews.

The main organisation providing mountain huts is **Ferðafélag Íslands** (Iceland Touring Association; ☎568 2533; www.fi.is; Mörkin 6), which maintains 40 huts around Iceland (some in conjunction with local walking clubs). The best huts have showers (for an additional fee, around 500kr), kitchens, wardens and potable water; simpler huts usually just have bed space, a toilet and a basic cooking area. Beds cost 6000kr to 9000kr for nonmembers. Camping is available at some huts for 2000kr per person.

Other organisations include **Ferðafélag Akureyrar** (Touring Club of Akureyri; ☎462 2720; www.ffa.is; Strandgata 23; ⏰2-5pm Mon-Fri May-Aug, 11am-1pm Mon-Fri Sep-Apr),

ETIQUETTE

Hot-pots & pools Strip and shower thoroughly before entering a hot-pot or pool.

Shoes Remove your shoes when entering someone's home.

Off-roading Don't drive off-road.

Drones Don't use drones in national parks.

Closures Don't ignore signs that advise that roads or sites are closed – this is due to safety.

Climate

Akureyri

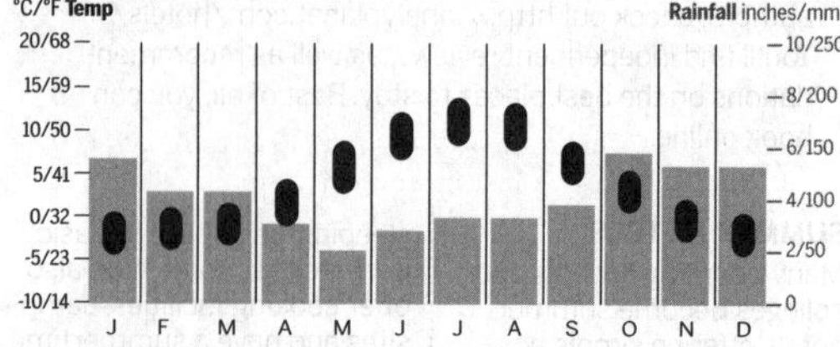

Reykjavík

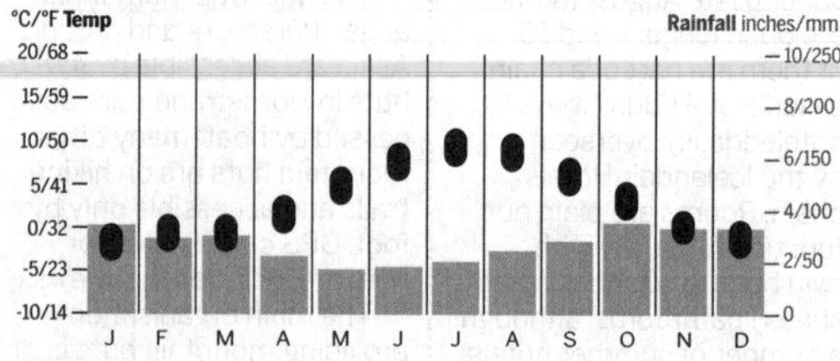

Vík

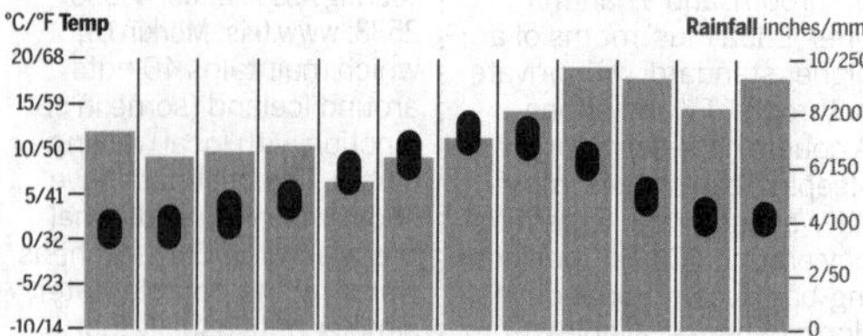

which operates huts in the northeast (including along the Askja Trail), and **Útivist** (☎562 1000; www.utivist.is; Laugavegur 178; ⊙noon-5pm Mon-Fri), which has huts at Básar and Fimmvörðuháls Pass in Þórsmörk.

It's essential to book with the relevant organisation, as places fill up quickly.

Booking Services

Booking.com is widely used across Iceland and is useful for checking all available accommodation in a town/region on a specified date.

Some 170 farm properties are members of Hey Iceland (www.heyiceland.is), formerly called Icelandic Farm Holidays. The company also arranges package self-drive holidays.

Children

Iceland may not be equipped with high-profile attractions for children, but the whole country is an adventure with its wide-open spaces, wildlife and science projects brought to life. It's a fairly easy place to travel with kids, and parents will find it free of most urban dangers, but do keep youngsters away from cliffs and unfenced waterfalls!

Dramatic scenery, an abundance of swimming pools and the friendliness of the locals help keep kids happy, and they will probably love the bird colonies, waterfalls, volcanic areas and glaciers. Or enjoy short hikes, super-Jeep tours, horse riding, whale watching, boat rides and easy glacier walks (for the latter, minimum age is around eight to 10 years).

Reykjavík is the most child-friendly place simply because it has the greatest variety of attractions and facilities. Distances can be long in the rest of the country, so you may want to limit yourselves to one or two regions.

Íslandskort barnanna (Children's Map of Iceland) is aimed at young kids and published by Forlagið (Mál og Menning) with text in Icelandic and English.

Practicalities

- ➡ Admission for kids to museums and swimming pools varies from half-price to free. The age at which children must pay adult fees varies (anywhere from 12 to 18 years).
- ➡ On internal flights and tours with Air Iceland Connect (www.airicelandconnect.is), children aged two to 11 years pay half-fare and infants under two fly free.
- ➡ Most bus and tour companies offer a 50% reduction for children aged four to 11 years; Reykjavík Excursions (www.re.is) tours are free for under 11s, and half-price for those aged 12 to 15.
- ➡ International car-hire companies offer child seats for an extra cost (book in advance).
- ➡ Changeable weather and frequent cold and rain may put you off camping with kids, but children aged two to 12 are usually charged half-price for camping, hostel, farmhouse and other accommodation. Under-twos usually stay for free.
- ➡ Many places offer rooms accommodating families, including hostels, guesthouses and farmstays. Larger hotels often have cots (cribs), but you may not find these elsewhere.
- ➡ Many restaurants in Reykjavík and larger towns offer discounted children's meals, and most have high chairs.

➡ Toilets at museums and other public institutions may have dedicated baby-changing facilities; elsewhere, you'll have to improvise.

➡ Attitudes to breastfeeding in public are generally relaxed.

➡ Formula, nappies (diapers) and other essentials are available everywhere.

Customs Regulations

Iceland has quite strict import restrictions. For a full list of regulations, see www.customs.is.

Alcohol duty-free allowances for travellers over 20 years of age:

➡ 1L spirits and 750mL wine and 3L beer, or

➡ 3L wine and 6L beer, or

➡ 1L spirits and 6L beer, or

➡ 1.5L wine and 12L beer, or

➡ 18L beer

Additionally:

➡ Visitors over 18 years can bring in 200 cigarettes or 250g of other tobacco products.

➡ You can import up to 3kg of food (except raw eggs, some meat and dairy products), provided it's not worth more than 25,000kr. This may help self-caterers to reduce costs.

➡ To prevent contamination, recreational fishing and horse-riding clothes require a veterinarian's certificate stating that they have been disinfected. Otherwise officials will charge you for disinfecting clothing when you arrive. It is prohibited to bring used horse-riding equipment (saddles, bridles etc). See www.mast.is.

➡ Many people bring their cars on the ferry from Europe. Special duty-waiver conditions apply for stays of up to one year.

Electricity

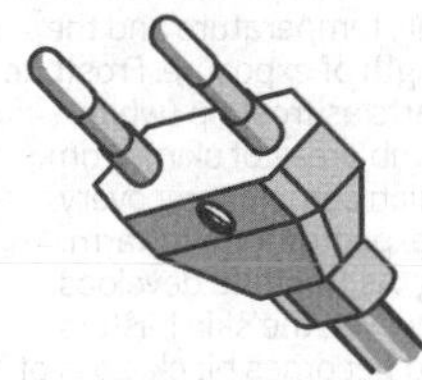

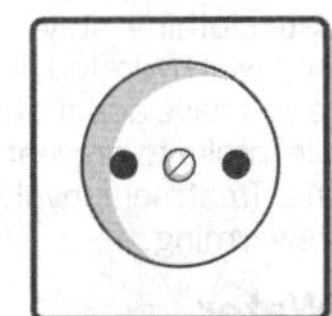

Type C
230V/50Hz

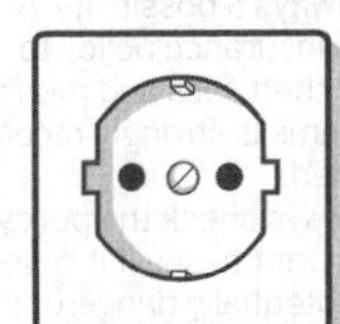

Type F
230V/50Hz

Embassies & Consulates

A handful of countries have formal embassies in Reykjavík. Up-to-date details of embassies and consulates (both Icelandic representation abroad, and embassies in Iceland) can be found on the Icelandic Ministry of Foreign Affairs website (www.mfa.is; click on 'Diplomatic Missions', then 'Foreign Missions').

Health

Travel in Iceland presents very few health problems. Tap water is safe to drink; the level of hygiene is high, and there are no endemic nasties.

Health Insurance

A travel insurance policy that covers medical mishaps is strongly recommended. Always check the policy's small print to see if it covers any potentially dangerous sporting activities you might be considering, such as hiking, diving, horse riding, skiing or snowmobiling.

Vaccinations

There are no required or recommended vaccinations.

Availability & Cost of Health Care

The standard of health care is very high, and English is widely spoken by doctors and medical-clinic staff. Note, however, that there are limited services outside larger urban areas.

For minor ailments, pharmacists can dispense valuable advice and over-the-counter medication; pharmacies can be identified by the sign *apótek*. Pharmacists can also advise as to when more specialised help is required.

Medical care can be obtained by visiting a primary health-care centre, called *heilsugæslustöð*. Find details of centres in greater Reykjavík at www.heilsugaeslan.is; in regional areas, ask at a tourist office or your accommodation for advice on the closest health-care centre.

Citizens of Nordic countries need only present their passport to access health care. Citizens of the European Economic Area (EEA) are covered for emergency medical treatment on presentation of a European Health Insurance Card (EHIC). Apply online for a card via your government health department's website. Holders of an EHIC are charged the same fee as locals.

Citizens from other countries can obtain medical assistance but must pay in full (and later be reimbursed by their insurance provider, if they have one). A standard consultation costs around 10,000kr. Travel insurance is advised. For more detailed information on health care for visitors, see www.sjukra.is/english/tourists.

Hypothermia & Frostbite

The main health risks are caused by exposure to extreme climates; proper preparation will reduce the risks. Even on a warm day in the mountains, the weather can change rapidly – carry waterproof outer gear and warm layers, and inform others of your route.

Acute hypothermia follows a sudden drop of temperature over a short time. Chronic hypothermia is caused by a gradual loss of temperature over hours. Hypothermia starts with shivering, loss of judgment and clumsiness. Unless rewarming occurs, the sufferer deteriorates into apathy, confusion and coma. Prevent further heat loss by seeking shelter; wearing warm, dry clothing; drinking hot, sweet drinks; and sharing body warmth.

Frostbite is caused by freezing and the subsequent damage to bodily extremities. It is dependent on wind chill, temperature and the length of exposure. Frostbite starts as frostnip (white, numb areas of skin), from which complete recovery is expected with rewarming. As frostbite develops, however, the skin blisters and becomes black. Loss of damaged tissue eventually occurs. Your should wear adequate clothing, stay dry, keep well hydrated and ensure you have adequate kilojoule intake to prevent frostbite. Treatment involves rapid rewarming.

Tap Water

Iceland has some of the cleanest water in the world and tap water is completely safe to drink. Locals find it amusing to see travellers buying bottled water when the same quality of water is available from the tap.

Geothermal hot water smells of sulphur, but the cold water doesn't smell.

Insurance

Although Iceland is a very safe place to travel, theft does occasionally happen, and illness and accidents are always a possibility. A travel insurance policy to cover theft, loss and medical problems is strongly recommended.

Always check the policy's small print to see if it covers any potentially dangerous sporting activities you might be considering, such as hiking, diving, horse riding, skiing or snowmobiling.

Worldwide travel insurance is available at www.lonelyplanet.com/travel-insurance. You can buy, extend and claim online anytime – even if you're already on the road.

Internet Access

Wi-fi is common in Iceland.

- Most accommodation and eating venues across the country offer wi-fi, and often buses do, too. Access is usually free for guests/customers. You may need to ask staff for an access code.
- Most of the N1 service stations have free wi-fi.
- The easiest way to get online is to buy an Icelandic SIM card with a data package and pop it in your unlocked smartphone. Other devices can then access the internet via the phone.
- To travel with your own wi-fi hot spot, check out Trawire (http://iceland.trawire.com) for portable 4G modem rental with unlimited usage from US$9 per day (up to 10 laptops or mobile devices can be connected).
- Some car- and campervan-hire companies offer portable modem devices as an optional extra.
- Most Icelandic libraries have computer terminals for public internet access, even in small towns; there's often a small fee.

TAX-FREE SHOPPING

Anyone who has a permanent address outside Iceland can claim a tax refund on purchases when they spend more than 6000kr at a single point of sale. Look for stores with a 'tax-free shopping' sign in the window, and ask for a form at the register.

Before you check in for your departing flight at Keflavík, go to the refund office at Arion Banki (located in the arrival hall opposite the car-rental counter) and present your completed tax-free form, passport, receipts/invoices and purchases. Make sure the goods are unused. Opening hours of the office match flight schedules.

If you're departing Iceland from Reykjavík airport or a harbour, go to the customs office before check-in.

➡ Tourist information centres often have public internet terminals, often free for brief usage.

Legal Matters

Icelandic police are generally low-key and there's very little reason for you to end up in their hands. Worth knowing:

➡ Drink-driving laws are strict. Even two drinks can put you over the legal limit of 0.05% blood-alcohol content; the penalty is loss of your driving licence plus a large fine.

➡ If you are involved in a traffic offence – speeding, driving without due care and attention etc – you may be asked to go to the station to pay the fine immediately.

➡ Drunk and disorderly behaviour may land you in a police cell for a night; you will usually be released the following morning.

➡ Penalties for possession, use or trafficking of illegal drugs are strict (long prison sentences and heavy fines).

LGBT+ Travellers

Icelanders have a very open, accepting attitude towards homosexuality, though the gay scene is quite low-key, even in Reykjavík (p94).

Maps

Online maps are are indeed useful but it's better to obtain paper maps in Iceland, and don't blindly follow GPS mapping instructions (stories abound of online maps sending drivers over mountain passes in winter because it's technically the shortest distance, but definitely not the safest).

Good online maps can be found at ja.is and map.is.

In recent years Iceland has been busy building new roads and tunnels, and sealing gravel stretches. We recommend you purchase a recently updated country map – ensure it shows the rerouted Ring Road (rerouted in East Iceland in late 2017).

Tourist information centres have useful free maps of their town and region. They also stock the free tourist booklet *Around Iceland,* which has information and town plans.

Tourist info centres, petrol stations and bookshops all sell road atlases and maps.

Map publisher Ferðakort (www.mapoficeland.com) sells online and has a dedicated map department at **Iðnú Bookshop** (☎517 7210; www.ferdakort.is; Brautarholt 8; ⌚10am-4pm Mon-Fri) in Reykjavík. Forlagið (Mál og Menning) is another reputable map publisher with a wide range; browse at its **store** (☎580 5000; www.bmm.is; Laugavegur 18; ⌚9am-10pm Mon-Fri, 10am-10pm Sat; Wi-Fi) in the capital or online (www.forlagid.is – click on 'landakort' in the category Bækur & Kort).

Both companies have good touring maps of Iceland (1:500,000 or 1:600,000; approximately 2000kr), useful for general driving. Ferðakort's more in-depth 1:200,000 *Road Atlas* (4000kr) includes details of accommodation, museums and swimming pools.

Both companies also produce plenty of regional maps – Forlagið (Mál og Menning) has a series of eight regional maps *(landshlutakort)* at 1:200,000 (1800kr each). There are also 31 detailed topographic maps at a scale of 1:100,000, covering the entire country – ideal for hikers – plus there are themed maps (eg sagas, geology and birdwatching).

Serious hikers can request maps at local tourist information centres or at national park visitor centres, both of which often stock inexpensive maps detailing regional walks and hikes.

ESSENTIAL: CREDIT CARD PIN

Note: a four-digit PIN is required to make credit- or debit-card purchases, and is essential for operating unstaffed petrol pumps. Ensure you have a PIN-enabled card before you leave home.

Money

ATMs

➡ As long as you're carrying a valid card, you'll need to withdraw only a limited amount of cash from ATMs.

➡ Almost every town in Iceland has a bank with an ATM *(hraðbanki),* where you can withdraw cash using MasterCard, Visa, Maestro or Cirrus cards.

➡ Diners Club and JCB cards connected to the Cirrus network have access to all ATMs.

➡ You'll also find ATMs at larger petrol stations and in shopping centres.

Credit & Debit Cards

➡ Locals use plastic for even small purchases.

➡ Contact your financial institution to make sure that your card is approved for overseas use – you will need a PIN for purchases.

➡ Visa and MasterCard are accepted in most shops, restaurants and hotels. Amex is usually accepted, Diners Club less so.

➡ You can pay for the Flybus from Keflavík International Airport to Reykjavík using plastic – handy if you've just arrived in the country.

➡ If you intend to stay in rural farmhouse accommodation or visit isolated villages, it's a good idea to carry enough cash to tide you over.

TIPS ON SEASONAL OPENINGS

Some regional attractions and tourist-oriented businesses in Iceland are only open for a short summer season, typically from June to August. Reykjavík attractions and businesses generally run year-round. As tourism is growing, businesses are more vague about opening dates; increasingly, they may open sometime in May, or even April, and stay open until the end of September or into October. With the growth of winter tourism, more businesses (especially on the Ring Road) are beginning to open year-round. From September to May some rural museums are happy to open for individuals on request, with a little forewarning – make contact via museum websites or local tourist offices.

Currency

The Icelandic unit of currency is the króna (plural krónur), written as kr or ISK.

➡ Coins come in denominations of 1kr, 5kr, 10kr, 50kr and 100kr.

➡ Notes come in denominations of 500kr, 1000kr, 2000kr, 5000kr and 10,000kr.

➡ Some accommodation providers and tour operators quote their prices in euro to ward against currency fluctuations, but these must be paid in Icelandic currency.

Taxes & Refunds

The standard rate of value-added tax (VAT) in Iceland is 24%. A reduced rate of 11% applies to certain products and services, including books, food and accommodation. VAT is included in quoted prices.

Tipping

➡ As service and VAT taxes are always included in prices, tipping isn't required in Iceland.

➡ Rounding up the bill at restaurants or leaving a small tip for good service is appreciated.

Travellers Cheques

Travellers cheques and banknotes can be exchanged for Icelandic currency at all major banks, but be aware that bank branches are only found in towns of a reasonable size.

Opening Hours

Opening hours vary throughout the year (some places are closed outside the high season). In general hours tend to be longer from June to August, and shorter from September to May. Standard opening hours include the following:

Banks 9am–4pm Monday to Friday

Cafe-bars 10am–1am Sunday to Thursday, 10am to between 3am and 6am Friday and Saturday

Cafes 10am–6pm

Offices 9am–5pm Monday to Friday

Petrol stations 8am–10pm or 11pm (automated pumps open 24 hours)

Post offices 9am–4pm or 4.30pm Monday to Friday (to 6pm in larger towns)

Restaurants 11.30am–2.30pm and 6–9pm or 10pm

Shops 10am–6pm Monday to Friday, 10am–4pm Saturday; some Sunday opening in Reykjavík malls and major shopping strips

Supermarkets 9am–9pm

Vínbúðin (government-run liquor stores) Variable; many outside Reykjavík only open for a couple of hours per day

Post

The Icelandic postal service (www.postur.is) is reliable and efficient, and rates are comparable to those in other Western European countries.

A letter to Europe costs 225kr; to places outside Europe it costs 285kr. A full list of rates, branches and opening hours is available online.

Public Holidays

Icelandic public holidays are usually an excuse for a family gathering or, when they occur on weekends, a reason to head to the countryside and go camping. If you're planning to travel during holiday periods, particularly the Commerce Day long weekend, you should book mountain huts and transport well in advance.

National public holidays in Iceland:

New Year's Day 1 January

Easter March or April; Maundy Thursday and Good Friday to Easter Monday (changes annually)

First Day of Summer First Thursday after 18 April

Labour Day 1 May

Ascension Day May or June (changes annually)

Whit Sunday and Whit Monday May or June (changes annually)

National Day 17 June

Commerce Day First Monday in August

Christmas 24 to 26 December

New Year's Eve 31 December

School Holidays

The main school holiday runs from the first week of June to the third week of August; this is when most of the Edda and summer hotels open.

The winter school holiday is a two-week break over the Christmas period (around 21 December to 3 January). There is also a spring break of about a week, over the Easter period.

Safe Travel

Iceland has a very low crime rate and in general any risks you'll face while travelling here are related to road safety, the unpredictable weather and the unique geological conditions.

- A good place to learn about minimising your risks is Safetravel (www.safetravel.is). The website is an initiative of the Icelandic Association for Search and Rescue (ICE-SAR).
- The website also provides information on ICE-SAR's 112 Iceland app for smartphones (useful in emergencies), and explains procedures for leaving a travel plan with ICE-SAR or a friend/contact.

Road Safety

- Unique hazards (p433) exist for drivers, such as livestock on the roads, single-lane bridges, blind rises and rough gravel roads.
- The numerous F roads (p431) are suitable only for 4WDs, often involve fording rivers, and are often only open for a few months each year, in summer.
- For road conditions, see www.road.is or call 1777.

Weather Conditions

- Never underestimate the weather. Proper clothing and equipment are essential.
- Visitors need to be prepared for inclement conditions year-round. The weather can change without warning.
- Hikers must obtain a reliable forecast before setting off – call 902 0600 for a recorded forecast (press 1 after the introduction) or visit www.vedur.is/english for a forecast in English. Alternatively, download the weather app of the Icelandic Meteorological Office (IMO), called Vedur.
- Emergency huts are provided in places where travellers run the risk of getting caught in severe weather.
- If you're driving in winter, carry food, water and blankets in your car.
- In winter, rental cars are fitted with snow or all-weather tyres.

Geological Risks

- When hiking, river crossings can be dangerous, with glacial run-off transforming trickling streams into raging torrents on warm summer days.
- High winds can create vicious sandstorms in areas where there is loose volcanic sand.
- Hiking paths in coastal areas may only be accessible at low tide; seek local advice and obtain the relevant tide tables.
- In geothermal areas, stick to boardwalks or obviously solid ground. Avoid thin crusts of lighter-coloured soil around steaming fissures and mudpots.
- Be careful of the water in hot springs and mudpots – it often emerges from the ground at 100°C.
- In glacial areas beware of dangerous quicksand at the ends of glaciers, and never venture out onto the ice without crampons and ice axes (even then, watch out for crevasses).
- Snowfields may overlie fissures, sharp lava chunks or slippery slopes of scoria (volcanic slag).
- Always get local advice before hiking around live volcanoes.
- Only attempt isolated hiking and glacier ascents if you know what you're doing. Talk to locals and/or employ a guide.
- It's rare to find warning signs or fences in areas where accidents can occur, such as large waterfalls, glacier fronts, cliff edges, and beaches with large waves and strong currents. Use common sense, and supervise children well.

Telephone

- Public payphones are extremely elusive in Iceland, but you may find them outside larger bus stations and petrol stations. Many accept credit cards as well as coins.
- To make international calls from Iceland, first dial the international access code 00, then the country code, the area or city code, and the telephone number.
- To phone Iceland from abroad, dial your country's international access code, Iceland's country code (354) and then the seven-digit phone number.
- Iceland has no area codes.
- Toll-free numbers begin with 800; mobile (cell) numbers start with 6, 7 or 8.
- The online version of the phone book with good maps is at http://en.ja.is.
- Useful numbers: directory enquiries 118 (local), 1811 (international).

Mobile Phones

Mobile (cell) coverage is widespread. Visitors with GSM phones can make roaming calls; purchase a local SIM card if you're staying a while.

- As of mid-2017, the EU has ended roaming surcharges for people who travel periodically within the EU. Under the 'roam like at home' regulations, residents of the EU and European Economic Area (EEA, which includes Iceland) can use mobile

EMERGENCY NUMBER

For emergency services (police, ambulance, fire, search & rescue) in Iceland, dial ☎112.

devices when travelling in the EU and EEA, paying the same prices as at home.

➡ For non-EU folks, the cheapest and most practical way to make calls at local rates is to purchase an Icelandic SIM card and pop it into your own mobile phone (Tip: bring an old phone from home for that purpose).

➡ Before leaving home, make sure that your phone isn't locked to your home network.

➡ Check your phone will work on Europe's GSM 900/1800 network (US phones work on a different frequency).

➡ Buy prepaid SIM cards at bookstores, grocery stores and petrol stations throughout the country, and also on Icelandair flights. Top-up credit is available from the same outlets.

➡ Iceland telecom Síminn (www.siminn.is/prepaid) provides the greatest network coverage; Vodafone (http://vodafone.is/english/prepaid) isn't far behind. Both have voice-and-data starter packs including local SIM cards; Síminn's costs 2900kr (including either 10GB data, or 5GB and 50 minutes of international talk time). Nova (www.nova.is) is a third player, and is cheap but lacks countrywide coverage.

Phonecards

The smallest denomination phonecard (for use in public telephones – which are very rare) costs 500kr, and can be bought from grocery stores and petrol stations. Low-cost international phonecards are also available in many shops and kiosks.

Time

➡ Iceland's time zone is the same as GMT/UTC (London).

➡ There is no daylight saving time.

➡ From late October to late March, Iceland is on the same time as London, five hours ahead of New York and 11 hours behind Sydney.

➡ In the northern hemisphere summer, Iceland is one hour behind London, four hours ahead of New York and 10 hours behind Sydney.

➡ Iceland uses the 24-hour clock system, and all transport timetables and business hours are posted accordingly.

Toilets

Stories of tourists doing their business in public, in inappropriate places (eg car parks and roadsides), madden the locals. Many Icelanders link this to campers who shun campgrounds, which has led to laws prohibiting such free camping. Reykjavík and larger towns have public restrooms, but natural sights often have too few facilities for the increasing number of visitors. There are also long stretches of road with few facilities. Authorities have built a few new restrooms along the Ring Road (look for blue roadside signs of a black door), but our advice: plan your trip well and be prepared to fork out a small fee (eg 200kr) for the use of some facilities.

Tourist Information

Websites

Official tourism sites for the country:

Visit Iceland (www.visiticeland.com)

Inspired by Iceland (www.inspiredbyiceland.com)

Each region also has its own useful site/s:

Reykjavík (www.visitreykjavik.is)

Southwest Iceland (www.visitreykjanes.is; www.south.is)

West Iceland (www.west.is)

The Westfjords (www.westfjords.is)

North Iceland (www.northiceland.is; www.visitakureyri.is)

East Iceland (www.east.is)

Southeast Iceland (www.south.is; www.visitvatnajokull.is)

Smartphone Apps

Useful and practical smartphone apps include the vital 112 Iceland app for safe travel, Vedur (weather), and apps for bus companies such as **Strætó** (☎540 2700; www.bus.is) and **Reykjavík Excursions** (☎580 5400; www.ioyo.is). Offline maps come in handy.

There are plenty more apps that cover all sorts of interests, from history and language to aurora-spotting, or walking tours of the capital. Reykjavík Grapevine's apps (Appy Hour, Appetite and Appening Today) deserve special mention for getting you to the good stuff in the capital.

Visas

Iceland is one of 26 member countries of the Schengen Convention, under which the EU countries (all but Bulgaria, Croatia, Romania, Cyprus, Ireland and the UK) plus Iceland, Norway, Liechtenstein and Switzerland have abolished checks at common borders.

To work or study in Iceland a permit is usually required – check with an Icelandic embassy or consulate in person or online.

For questions on visa extensions or visas and permits in general, contact the Icelandic Directorate of Immigration, Útlendingastofnun (www.utl.is).

The visa situation for Iceland is as follows:

➡ Citizens of EU and Schengen countries – no visa required for stays of up to 90 days.

➡ Citizens or residents of Australia, Canada, Japan,

New Zealand and the USA – no visa required for tourist visits of up to 90 days.

➡ Note that the total stay within the Schengen area must not exceed 90 days in any 180-day period.

➡ Other countries – check online at www.utl.is.

Volunteering

A volunteering holiday is a worthwhile (and relatively inexpensive) way to get involved with Iceland's people and landscapes.

To prevent any exploitation of volunteers, the union-led website www.volunteering.is outlines the rights of workers.

Iceland Conservation Volunteers (www.ust.is/the-environment-agency-of-iceland/volunteers) Iceland's Environment Agency, known as Umhverfisstofnun (UST), recruits around 150 volunteers each summer for practical conservation projects around the country. Also see Working Abroad (www.workingabroad.com).

SEEDS (www.seeds.is) Iceland-based, organises work camps and volunteering holidays (generally two to three weeks), focusing on the environment, renovation or assistance at events.

Volunteer Abroad (www.volunteerabroad.com) Overview of possible projects in Iceland.

Workaway (www.workaway.info) Promotes exchange between travellers/volunteers and families or organisations looking for help.

Worldwide Friends (www.wf.is) Iceland-based Worldwide Friends runs short-term work camps that supporting the environment and community projects.

WWOOF (www.wwoofindependents.org) World Wide Opportunities On Organic Farms (aka Willing Workers On Organic Farms) has a handful of farm properties in Iceland.

Work

To be hired for in-demand summer seasonal work (eg housekeeping and hospitality in hotels, guesthouses and restaurants) you must be from the EU/EEA. If you're after a professional job, Icelandic language skills may be a prerequisite (exceptions exist in the growing computer programming and gaming industries, and in tourism).

For non-EU/EEA nationals, things aren't so easy – you must have a work permit, which most commonly requires sponsorship from a local company. Full details are outlined on the Directorate of Immigration's site: www.utl.is.

One of the best places to start gathering information and contacts is the website of Vinnumálastofnun, the Icelandic Directorate of Labour (www.vinnumalastofnun.is).

Transport

GETTING THERE & AWAY

Iceland has become far more accessible in recent years, with more flights arriving from more destinations. Ferry transport (from northern Denmark) makes a good alternative for Europeans wishing to take their own car.

Flights, cars and tours can be booked online at lonelyplanet.com/bookings.

Entering the Country

For information see Visas (p18).

Air

Keflavík International Airport (KEF; ☎425 6000; www.kefairport.is; Reykjanesbraut; ⏲24hr) Iceland's main international airport is 48km southwest of Reykjavík.

Reykjavík Domestic Airport (Reykjavíkurflugvöllur; www.isavia.is; Innanlandsflug) Internal flights and those to Greenland and the Faroes use this small airport in central Reykjavík.

A growing number of airlines fly to Iceland (including budget carriers) from destinations in Europe and North America. Some airlines have services only from June to August. Find a list of airlines serving the country at www.visiticeland.com (under Plan Your Trip/Flights).

Air Iceland Connect (☎570 3030; www.airicelandconnect.is; Reykjavík Domestic Airport) The main domestic airline (not to be confused with Icelandair). Also flies to destinations in Greenland and the Faroe Islands.

Eagle Air (☎562 2640; www.eagleair.is; Reykjavík Domestic Airport) Scheduled domestic flights to small airstrips.

Icelandair (www.icelandair.com) The national carrier has an excellent safety record.

WOW Air (www.wowair.com) Icelandic low-cost carrier, serving a growing number of European and North American destinations.

DEPARTURE TAX

There is no departure tax.

Sea

Smyril Line (www.smyrilline.com) operates a pricey but well-patronised weekly car ferry, the *Norröna*, from Hirtshals (Denmark) through Tórshavn (Faroe Islands) to Seyðisfjörður in East Iceland. It operates year-round, although winter passage is weather-dependent – see website for more.

Fares vary greatly, depending on dates of travel, what sort of vehicle (if any) you are travelling with, and cabin selection. Sailing time is around 36 hours from Denmark to the Faroe Islands, and 19 hours from the Faroes to Iceland.

It's possible to make a stopover in the Faroes. Contact Smyril Line or see the website for trip packages.

GETTING AROUND

Air

Iceland has an extensive network of domestic flights, which locals use almost like buses. In winter a flight can be the only way to get between destinations, but weather at this time of year can play havoc with schedules.

Domestic flights depart from the small **Reykjavík Domestic Airport** (Reykjavíkurflugvöllur; www.isavia.is; Innanlandsflug), *not* from the major international airport at Keflavík.

A handful of airstrips offer regular sightseeing flights – eg Mývatn, Skaftafell, and Reykjavík and Akureyri domestic airports – and helicopter sightseeing is increasingly popular.

A list of local airports and useful information about them is found at www.isavia.is.

Air Iceland Connect (☎570 3030; www.airicelandconnect.is; Reykjavík Domestic Airport) Not to be confused with international airline Icelandair. Destinations covered: Reykjavík,

CLIMATE CHANGE & TRAVEL

Every form of transport that relies on carbon-based fuel generates CO_2, the main cause of human-induced climate change. Modern travel is dependent on aeroplanes, which might use less fuel per kilometre per person than most cars but travel much greater distances. The altitude at which aircraft emit gases (including CO_2) and particles also contributes to their climate change impact. Many websites offer 'carbon calculators' that allow people to estimate the carbon emissions generated by their journey and, for those who wish to do so, to offset the impact of the greenhouse gases emitted with contributions to portfolios of climate-friendly initiatives throughout the world. Lonely Planet offsets the carbon footprint of all staff and author travel.

Akureyri, Grímsey, Ísafjörður, Þórshöfn, Vopnafjörður and Egilsstaðir. Offers some fly-in day tours.

Eagle Air (☎562 2640; www.eagleair.is; Reykjavík Domestic Airport) Operates scheduled flights to five small airstrips from Reykjavík: Vestmannaeyjar, Húsavík, Höfn, Bíldudalur and Gjögur. Also runs a number of fly-in day tours.

Bicycle

Cycling is an increasingly popular way to see the country's landscapes, but cyclists should be prepared for harsh conditions.

Gale-force winds, driving rain, sandstorms, sleet and sudden flurries of snow are possible year-round. We recommend keeping your plans relatively flexible so you can wait out bad weather if the need arises.

You'll be forced to ride closely alongside traffic on the Ring Road (there are no hard shoulders to the roads).

The large bus companies carry bikes, so if the weather turns bad or that highlands bike trip isn't working out as planned, consider the bus. Note that space can't be reserved. It's free to take a bike on **Strætó** (☎540 2700; www.bus.is) services; other companies, such as **SBA-Norðurleið** (☎550 0700; www.sba.is) and **Reykjavík Excursions** (☎580 5400; www.ioyo.is), charge 4000kr, and it's advisable to contact them regarding rules and space.

Puncture-repair kits and spares are hard to come by outside Reykjavík; bring your own or stock up in the capital. On the road, it's essential to know how to do your own basic repairs.

If you want to tackle the interior, the Kjölur route has bridges over all major rivers, making it fairly accessible to cyclists. A less-challenging route is the F249 to Þórsmörk. The Westfjords also offers some wonderful, challenging cycling terrain.

Hire

Various places rent out mountain bikes, but in general these are intended for local use only, and often aren't up to long-haul travel.

If you intend to go touring, it's wise to bring your bike from home or purchase one when you arrive; alternatively, Reykjavík Bike Tours (www.icelandbike.com) has touring bikes for rent.

Resources

Cycling Iceland (www.cyclingiceland.is) Online version of the brilliantly detailed *Cycling Iceland* map, published annually.

Icelandic Mountain Bike Club (http://fjallahjolaklubburinn.is) The English-language pages of this website are a goldmine of information.

The Biking Book of Iceland There is a series of cycling books by Ómar Smári Kristinsson, but only one has been translated into English; it covers trails in the Westfjords.

Transporting Bicycles to Iceland

Most airlines will carry your bike in the hold if you pack it correctly in a bike box; contact the airlines for detailed information.

At Keflavík International Airport, a facility (a container 100m east of the Arrivals exit) is available to assemble or disassemble bikes. **Reykjavík City Hostel** (☎553 8110; www.hostel.is; Sundlaugavegur 34; P@; 14) also offers such facilities and will store bike boxes. At Keflavík airport, Bílahótel (www.bilahotel.is) is a garage (in the same building as Geysir Car Rental) that offers luggage storage, including bike boxes. Note: bikes cannot be taken on Strætó bus 55 from Keflavík airport to Reykjavík.

The Smyril Line ferry (www.smyrilline.com) from Denmark transports bikes for €20 each way.

Boat

Several year-round ferries operate in Iceland. Major routes all carry vehicles, but it's worthwhile booking ahead for car passage.

Herjólfur (www.seatours.is) Connecting Landeyjahöfn in South Iceland to Vestmannaeyjar islands.

Sævar (www.hrisey.is) Frequent, easy connections from Árskógssandur in North Iceland, north of Akureyri, to the island of Hrísey.

Baldur (www.seatours.is) Connecting Stykkishólmur in

ESSENTIAL WEB RESOURCES

Five websites every traveller should know about:

Safetravel (www.safetravel.is) Learn about minimising risks while travelling in Iceland.

Icelandic Met Office (www.vedur.is) Never underestimate the weather in Iceland, or its impact on your travels. Get a reliable forecast from this site (or call 902 0600, and press 1 after the introduction). Download its app, too (called Vedur).

Vegagerðin (www.road.is) Iceland's road administration site details road openings and closings around the country. Vital if you plan to explore Iceland's little-visited corners and remote highlands, and for information about winter road access.

Carpooling in Iceland (www.samferda.is) Handy site that helps drivers and passengers link up. Passengers often foot some of the petrol bill. It's a savvy alternative to hitching (for passengers), and a way to help pay for car rental and fuel (for drivers).

Public Transport (www.publictransport.is) An impressive map and searchable database of all public transport services in the country.

West Iceland to Brjánslækur in the Westfjords, via the island of Flatey.

Sæfari (www.saefari.is) Connecting Dalvík in North Iceland to Grímsey island on the Arctic Circle.

From June to August, regular boat services run from Bolungarvík and Ísafjörður to points in Hornstrandir (Westfjords).

Bus

Iceland has a shrinking network of long-distance bus routes, with services provided by a handful of main companies. The free *Public Transport in Iceland* map has an overview of routes; pick it up at tourist offices or view online at www.publictransport.is.

From roughly June to August, regular scheduled buses run to most places on the Ring Road, into the popular hiking areas of the Southwest, and to larger towns in the Westfjords and Eastfjords, and on the Reykjanes and Snæfellsnes Peninsulas. The rest of the year, services range from daily, to a few weekly, to nonexistent.

- At the time of writing, there was no service linking Egilsstaðir in the east with Höfn in the Southeast, making it nearly impossible to complete the Ring Road by bus.
- In summer, 4WD buses run along some F roads (mountain roads), including the highland Kjölur, Sprengisandur and Askja routes (inaccessible to 2WD cars).
- Many bus services can be used as day tours: buses spend a few hours at the final destination before returning to the departure point, and may stop for a half-hour at various tourist destinations en route.
- Many buses are equipped with free wi-fi.
- Bus companies may operate from different terminals or pick-up points. Reykjavík has several bus terminals; in small towns, buses usually stop at the main petrol station or camping ground, but it pays to double-check.
- Many buses have GPS tracking, so you can see when your bus is approaching your stop.

Companies

Main bus companies:

Reykjavík Excursions (☎580 5400; www.ioyo.is) Departs from BSÍ Bus Terminal in Reykjavík.

SBA-Norðurleið (☎550 0700; www.sba.is) Departs from BSÍ Bus Terminal in Reykjavík.

Sterna (☎551 1166; www.icelandbybus.is) Departs from Harpa in Reykjavík; stops at Reykjavík Campsite.

Strætó (☎540 2700; www.bus.is) Main terminal for long-distance buses is at Mjódd.

Trex (☎587 6000; www.trex.is) Hiker transport; has a few departure points in Reykjavík (including the main tourist office and Reykjavík Campsite).

Car & Motorcycle

Driving in Iceland gives you unparalleled freedom to discover the country and, thanks to (relatively) good roads and (relatively) light traffic, it's all fairly straightforward.

- The Ring Road (Rte 1) circles the country and is paved.
- Beyond the Ring Road, fingers of sealed road or gravel stretch out to most communities.
- Driving coastal areas can be spectacularly scenic, and incredibly slow as you weave up and down over mountain passes and in and out of long fjords.
- A 2WD vehicle will get you almost everywhere in summer (note: *not* into the highlands, or on F roads).
- In winter heavy snow can cause many roads to close; mountain roads generally

only open in June and may start closing as early as September. For up-to-date information on road conditions, visit www.road.is.

➡ Don't be pressured into renting a GPS unit – if you purchase a good, up-to-date touring map, and can read it, you should be fine without GPS. If you are planning to take remote trails, a GPS will be worthwhile.

Bring Your Own Vehicle

Car hire in Iceland is expensive, so bringing your own vehicle may not be as crazy as it sounds. The Smyril Line ferry from Denmark is busy in summer bringing vehicles to Iceland from all over Europe (book passage well ahead).

For temporary duty-free importation, drivers must carry the vehicle's registration documents, proof of valid insurance (a 'green card' if your car isn't registered in a Nordic or EU-member country) and a driving licence.

Permission for temporary duty-free importation of a vehicle is granted at the point of arrival for up to 12 months, and is contingent upon agreeing to not lend or sell your vehicle. For more information, contact the Directorate of Customs (www.customs.is).

Winter visitors should have winter tyres fitted (studded tyres are permitted from November to mid-April).

If you're staying for a long period, you might consider shipping your own vehicle via Eimskip (www.eimskip.com) shipping services. Be aware that this is far from cheap, and involves heavy paperwork, but it may be useful for long-stayers who have lots of gear or a well-set-up camper/4WD. Eimskip has five shipping lines in the North Atlantic.

Driving Licences

You can drive in Iceland with a driving licence from the US, Canada, Australia, New Zealand and most European countries. If your licence is not in Roman script, you need an International Driving Permit (normally issued by your home country's automobile association).

Fuel & Spare Parts

➡ Petrol stations are regularly spaced around the country, but in the highlands you should check fuel levels and the distance to the next station before setting off.

➡ At the time of research, unleaded petrol and diesel cost about 220kr (€1.80) per litre.

➡ Some Icelandic roads can be pretty lonely, so carry a jack, a spare tyre and jump leads just in case (check your spare when you pick up your rental car).

➡ In the event of a breakdown or accident, your first port of call should be your car-hire agency.

➡ Although the Icelandic motoring association Félag Íslenskra Bifreiðaeigenda (FÍB; www.fib.is) is only open to locals, if you have breakdown cover with an automobile association affiliated with ARC Europe you may be covered by the FÍB – check with your home association.

➡ FÍB's 24-hour breakdown number is 511 2112. Even if you're not a member, it may be able to provide information and phone numbers for towing and breakdown services.

Car Hire

Travelling by car is the only way to get to some parts of Iceland. Although car-hire rates are very expensive by international standards, they compare favourably to bus or internal air travel, especially if there are a few of you to split the costs. Shop around and book online for the best deals.

F ROADS

We can think of a few choice F words for these bumpy, at times almost-nonexistent tracts of land, but in reality the 'F' stands for fjall (mountain). Do not confuse F roads with gravel stretches of road (regular gravel roads are normally fine for 2WDs, although some of them are bumpy rides for small, low-clearance cars).

➡ F roads are indicated on maps (make sure you use good ones) and road signs with an 'F' preceding the road number (F26, F88 etc).

➡ Opening dates vary with weather conditions, but are generally around mid- to late June.

➡ F roads only support 4WDs. If you travel on F roads in a hired 2WD you'll invalidate your insurance. F roads are unsafe for small cars: do yourself a favour and steer clear, or hire a 4WD (or take a bus or super-Jeep tour).

➡ Before tackling any F road, educate yourself about what lies ahead (eg river crossings) and whether or not the entire route is open. See www.road.is for information.

➡ While some F roads may almost blend into the surrounding nature, driving off marked tracks is strictly prohibited everywhere in Iceland, as it damages fragile ecosystems.

To rent a car you must be 20 years old (23 to 25 years for a 4WD) and hold a valid licence.

The cheapest cars, usually a small hatchback or similar, cost from around 8000kr per day in high season (June to August). Figure on paying around 10,000kr to 12,000kr for the smallest 4WD that offers higher clearance than a regular car but isn't advised for large river crossings, and 15,000kr to 20,000kr for a larger 4WD model.

Rates include unlimited mileage and VAT (a hefty 24%), and usually collision damage waiver (CDW).

Weekly rates offer some discount. From September to May you should be able to find considerably better daily rates and deals.

Check the small print, as additional costs such as extra insurance, airport pick-up charges, and one-way rental fees can add up.

In winter you should opt for a larger, sturdier car for safety reasons, preferably with 4WD (ie absolutely *not* a compact 2WD).

In the height of summer many companies run out of rentals. Book ahead.

Many travel organisations (eg Hostelling International Iceland, Hey Iceland) offer package deals that include car hire.

Most companies are based in the Reykjavík and Keflavík areas, with city and airport offices. Larger companies have extra locations around the country (usually in Akureyri and Egilsstaðir). Ferry passengers arriving via Seyðisfjörður should contact car-hire agencies in nearby Egilsstaðir.

Car-hire companies:

Átak (www.atak.is)

Avis (www.avis.is)

Budget (www.budget.is)

Cars Iceland (www.carsiceland.com)

Cheap Jeep (www.cheapjeep.is)

Europcar (www.europcar.is) The biggest hire company in Iceland.

Geysir (www.geysir.is)

Go Iceland (www.goiceland.com)

Hertz (www.hertz.is)

SADcars (www.sadcars.com)

Saga (www.sagacarrental.is)

CAR SHARING

There are a couple of peer-to-peer car-sharing platforms in Iceland, including Carrenters (www.carrenters.is). There are also locals' cars and campervans occasionally available for rent via airbnb.com.

These platforms offer people the chance to hire privately owned cars from locals. If you take up this option, do your homework and assess the costs and the small print – from our research, some prices were not much different from those of car-hire companies; cars were sometimes quite old; and you don't have the reassurance of a company behind you to help if things go wrong.

Campervan Hire

Combining accommodation and transport costs into campervan rental is a booming option – and has extra appeal in summer, as it allows for some spontaneity (unlike every other form of accommodation, campsites don't need to be prebooked). Travelling by campervan in winter is possible, but we don't recommend it – there are fewer facilities open for campers at this time, and weather conditions may make it unsafe.

Large car-hire companies usually have campervans for rent, but there are also more offbeat choices, offering from backpacker-centric to family-sized, or real 4WD setups for highland exploration. Some companies offer gear rental to help your trip go smoothly (GPS, cooking gear and stove, barbecue, sleeping bags, camping chairs, fishing equipment, portable wi-fi hot spots etc).

There are dozens of companies that can help you get set up. As with rental cars, prices vary depending on size and age of the vehicle, length of rental period, high/low season, added extras etc. Shop around, and read the fine print. Prices for something small and basic can start at around 12,000kr per day.

Camp Easy (www.campeasy.com)

Camper Iceland (www.campericeland.is)

Go Campers (www.gocampers.is)

Happy Campers (www.happycampers.is)

JS Camper Rental (www.jscamper.com) Truck campers on 4WD pick-ups.

Rent Nordic (www.rent.is)

BUYING FUEL

Most smaller petrol stations are unstaffed, and all pumps are automated. There is the (time-consuming) option of going inside a staffed service station to ask staff to switch the pump to manual, enabling you to fill up and pay for your fuel afterwards, but not all places offer such a service.

The first time you fill up, visit a staffed station while it's open, in case you have any problems. Note that you need a PIN for your card to use the automated pumps. If you don't have a PIN, buy prepaid cards from an N1 station that you can then use at the automated pumps.

Motorcycle Hire

Biking Viking (www.rmc.is/en/biking-viking) offers motorcycle rental, tours and service.

Insurance

A vehicle registered in Nordic or EU-member countries is considered to have valid automobile insurance in Iceland. If your vehicle is registered in a non-Nordic or non-EU country, you'll need a 'green card', which proves that you are insured to drive while in Iceland. Green cards are issued by insurance companies in your home country; contact your existing insurer.

When hiring a car, check the small print; most vehicles come with third-party insurance and CDW to cover you for damage to the car. Also check the excess (the initial amount you will be liable to pay in the event of an accident) as this can be surprisingly high.

Hire vehicles are not covered for damage to tyres, headlights and windscreens, or damage caused to the car's underside by driving on dirt roads, through water or in ash- or sandstorms. Many companies will try to sell you additional insurance to cover these possibilities. You need to consider whether this is appropriate for you and your plans, and how prepared you are to cough up in the event of such occurrences (and the cost of the insurance versus factors such as the length of your rental and what regions you plan to visit). There is no way of predicting what climatic conditions you might meet on your trip.

Road Conditions & Hazards

Good main-road surfaces and light traffic (especially outside the capital and Southwest region) make driving in Iceland relatively easy, but there are some specific hazards. Watch the 'Drive Safely on Icelandic Roads' video on www.drive.is for more.

Livestock Sheep graze in the countryside over the summer, and often wander onto roads. Slow down when you see livestock on or near roadsides.

Unsurfaced roads The transition from sealed to gravel roads is marked with the warning sign 'Malbik Endar' – slow right down to avoid skidding when you hit the gravel. Most accidents involving foreign drivers in Iceland are caused by the use of excessive speed on unsurfaced roads. If your car does begin to skid, take your foot off the accelerator and gently turn the car in the direction you want the front wheels to go. Do not brake.

Blind rises In most cases, roads have two lanes with steeply cambered sides and no hard shoulder; be prepared for oncoming traffic in the centre of the road, and slow down and stay to the right when approaching a blind rise, marked as 'Blindhæð' on road signs.

Single-lane bridges Slow down and be prepared to give way when approaching single-lane bridges (marked as 'Einbreið Brú'). Right of way is with the car closest to the bridge.

Sun glare With the sun often sitting low to the horizon, sunglasses are recommended.

Winter conditions In winter make sure your car is fitted with winter tyres, and carry a shovel, blankets, food and water.

Ash- & sandstorms Volcanic ash and severe sandstorms can strip paint off cars; strong winds can even topple your vehicle. At-risk areas are marked with orange warning signs.

F roads Roads (p431) suitable for 4WD vehicles only.

River crossings Few highland roads have bridges over rivers. Fords are marked on maps with a 'V'.

Tunnels There are a number of tunnels in Iceland – a couple are single lane, and a little anxiety-inducing! Before you enter such tunnels, a sign will indicate which direction has right of way. There will be a couple of pull-over bays inside the tunnel (signed 'M'). If the passing bay is on your side in the tunnel, you are obligated to pull in and let oncoming traffic pass you.

Road Rules

- Drive on the right.
- Front and rear seat belts are compulsory.
- Dipped headlights must be on at all times.
- Blood alcohol limit is 0.05%.
- Mobile phone use is prohibited when driving unless you're using a hands-free kit.
- Children under six years must use a car seat.
- Do not drive off-road (ie off marked roads and 4WD trails) – it is an illegal offence and you can be fined.

Speed Limits

- Built-up areas: 50km/h
- Unsealed roads: 80km/h
- Sealed roads: 90km/h

Hitching & Ride-Sharing

Hitching is never entirely safe, and it's not recommended. Travellers who hitch should understand that they are taking a small but potentially serious risk. Nevertheless, we met scores of tourists who were hitching their way around Iceland and most had positive reports. Single female travellers and couples tend to get a lift the quickest.

Patience is a prerequisite of hitching, and logic is important, too – be savvy about where you position yourself. Try standing at junctions, near petrol stations or even by Bónus supermarkets.

When you arrive at your accommodation it can't hurt to let people know where you're aiming for the next day. There may be another traveller going that way who can give you a ride.

Check out Carpooling in Iceland (www.samferda.is) for rides – note there is an

CROSSING RIVERS

While trekking or driving in Iceland's highlands you're likely to face unbridged rivers that must be crossed. There are a few rules to follow.

- Melting snow causes water levels to rise, so the best time to cross is early in the morning before the day warms up, and preferably no sooner than 24 hours after a rainstorm.
- Avoid narrow stretches, which are likely to be deep – the widest ford is likely to be shallowest.
- The swiftest, strongest current is found near the centre of straight stretches and at the outside of bends. Choose a spot with as much slack water as possible.
- Never try to cross just above a waterfall and avoid crossing streams in flood (identifiable by dirty, smooth-running water carrying lots of debris and vegetation).

For Hikers

- A smooth surface suggests that the river is too deep to be crossed on foot. Anything more than thigh-deep isn't crossable without being experienced and having extra equipment.
- Before attempting to cross deep or swift-running streams, be sure that you can jettison your pack midstream if necessary.
- Lone hikers should use a hiking staff to probe the river bottom for the best route and to steady themselves in the current.
- Never try to cross a stream barefoot. Bring wetsuit boots or sandals if you want to keep your hiking boots dry.
- While crossing, face upstream and avoid looking down or you risk getting dizzy and losing balance. Two hikers can steady each other by resting their arms on each other's shoulders.
- If you fall while crossing, don't try to stand up. Remove your pack (but don't let go of it), roll onto your back and point your feet downstream, then try to work your way to a shallow eddy or to the shore.

For Drivers

- If you're not travelling in a convoy, consider waiting for other traffic.
- Watch where and how experienced drivers cross.
- You may need to check the depth and speed of the river by wading into it (using techniques described for hikers, including a hiking staff).
- A good rule of thumb: if you would not want to wade through a river you should not drive through it.
- Work with the water – drive diagonally across in the direction of the current, making sure you're in a low gear. Drive steadily, without stopping or changing gear, just slightly faster than the water is flowing (too slow and you risk getting stuck, or letting water up the exhaust).

expectation that passengers will contribute to fuel costs.

Local Transport

Bus

Reykjavík has an extensive network of local buses connecting all the suburbs, and running to Akranes, Borgarnes, Hveragerði and Selfoss. There are now night services on some routes, running from around 1am to 4.30am on Saturday and Sunday. See www.straeto.is for information on routes, fares and timetables.

Local bus networks operate in Akureyri, Ísafjörður, and the Reykjanesbær and Eastfjords areas.

Taxi

Most taxis in Iceland operate in the Reykjavík area, but many of the larger towns also offer services. Outside of Reykjavík, it's usually wise to prebook.

Taxis are metered and can be pricey. Tipping is not expected.

At the time of research, there were no app-based ride-sharing services (such as Uber and Lyft) in Iceland.

Train

There is no train network in Iceland.

Language

Icelandic belongs to the Germanic language family, which includes German, English, Dutch and all the Scandinavian languages except Finnish. It's related to Old Norse, and retains the letters 'eth' *(ð)* and 'thorn' *(þ)*, which also existed in Old English. Be aware, especially when you're trying to read bus timetables or road signs, that place names can be spelled in several different ways due to Icelandic grammar rules.

Most Icelanders speak English, so you'll have no problems if you don't know any Icelandic. However, any attempts to speak the local language will be much appreciated.

If you read our coloured pronunciation guides as if they were English, you'll be understood. Keep in mind that double consonants are given a long pronunciation. Note also that öy in our pronunciation guides is like the '-er y-' in 'her year' (without the 'r') and that kh is like the 'ch' in the Scottish *loch*. Stress generally falls on the first syllable in a word.

BASICS

Hello.	*Halló.*	*ha*·loh
Good morning.	*Góðan daginn.*	*gohth*-ahn *dai*-in
Goodbye.	*Bless.*	bles
Good evening.	*Gott kvöld.*	khot kverld
Good night.	*Goða nótt.*	*goh*-th-ah noht
Thank you	*Takk./Takk fyrir.*	tak/tak *fi*·rir
Excuse me.	*Afsakið.*	*af*·sa·kidh

WANT MORE?

For in-depth language information and handy phrases, check out Lonely Planet's *Icelandic Phrasebook*. You'll find it at **shop.lonelyplanet.com**, or you can buy Lonely Planet's iPhone phrasebooks at the Apple App Store.

READING ICELANDIC

Letter	Pronunciation
Á á	ow (as in 'how')
Ð ð	dh (as the 'th' in 'that')
É é	ye (as in 'yet')
Í í	ee (as in 'see')
Ó ó	oh (as the 'o' in 'note')
Ú ú	oo (as in 'too')
Ý ý	ee (as in 'see')
Þ þ	th (as in 'think')
Æ æ	ai (as in 'aisle')
Ö ö	eu (as the 'u' in 'nurse')

Sorry.	*Fyrirgefðu.*	*fi*·rir·gev·dhu
Yes.	*Já.*	yow
No.	*Nei.*	nay

How are you?
Hvað segir þú gott? — kvadh *say*·yir thoo got

Fine. And you?
Allt fínt. En þú? — alt feent en thoo

What's your name?
Hvað heitir þú? — kvadh *hay*·tir thoo

My name is ...
Ég heiti ... — yekh *hay*·ti ...

Do you speak English?
Talarðu ensku? — *ta*·lar dhoo *ens*·ku

I don't understand.
Ég skil ekki. — yekh skil e·ki

It will be OK.
Þetta reddast. — *the*-tah *re*-dahst

DIRECTIONS

Where's the (hotel)?
Hvar er (hótelið)? — kvar er (*hoh*·te·lidh)

Can you show me (on the map)?
Geturðu sýnt mér (á kortinu)? — *ge*·tur·dhu seent myer (ow *kor*·ti·nu)

What's your address?
Hvert er heimilisfangið þitt? — kvert er *hay*·mi·lis·fown·gidh thit

EATING & DRINKING

What would you recommend?
Hverju mælir þú með? — *kver*·yu *mai*·lir thoo medh

Do you have vegetarian food?
Eruð þið með grænmetisrétti? — *er*·udh thidh medh *grain*·me·tis·rye·ti

I'll have a ...
Ég ætla að fá ... — yekh *ait*·la adh fow ...

Cheers!
Skál! — skowl

I'd like a/the ..., please.	*Get ég fengið ..., takk.*	get yekh *fen*·gidh ... tak
table for (four)	*borð fyrir (fjóra)*	bordh *fi*·rir (*fyoh*·ra)
bill	*reikninginn*	*rayk*·neen·gin
drink list	*vínseðillinn*	*veen*·se·dhit·lin
menu	*matseðillinn*	*mat*·se·dhit·lin
that dish	*þennan rétt*	*the*·nan ryet
bottle of (beer)	*(bjór)flösku*	(*byohr*)·*fleus*·ku
(cup of) coffee/tea	*kaffi/te (bolla)*	*ka*·fi/te (*bot*·la)
glass of (wine)	*(vín)glas*	(*veen*)·glas
water	*vatn*	vatn
breakfast	*morgunmat*	*mor*·gun·mat
lunch	*hádegismat*	*how*·day·yis·mat
dinner	*kvöldmat*	*kveuld*·mat

EMERGENCIES

Help!	*Hjálp!*	hyowlp
Go away!	*Farðu!*	*far*·dhu
Call ...!	*Hringdu á ...!*	*hring*·du ow ...
a doctor	*lækni*	*laik*·ni
the police	*lögregluna*	*leukh*·rekh·lu·na

I'm lost.
Ég er villtur/villt. (m/f) — yekh er *vil*·tur/vilt

Where are the toilets?
Hvar er snyrtingin? — kvar er *snir*·tin·gin

SIGNS

Inngangur	Entrance
Útgangur	Exit
Opið	Open
Lokað	Closed
Bannað	Prohibited
Snyrting/Salerni	Toilets

NUMBERS

1	*einn*	aydn
2	*tveir*	tvayr
3	*þrír*	threer
4	*fjórir*	*fyoh*·rir
5	*fimm*	fim
6	*sex*	seks
7	*sjö*	syeu
8	*átta*	*ow*·ta
9	*níu*	*nee*·u
10	*tíu*	*tee*·u
20	*tuttugu*	*tu*·tu·khu
30	*þrjátíu*	*throw*·tee·u
40	*fjörutíu*	*fyeur*·tee·u
50	*fimmtíu*	*fim*·tee·u
60	*sextíu*	*seks*·tee·u
70	*sjötíu*	*syeu*·tee·u
80	*áttatíu*	*ow*·ta·tee·u
90	*níutíu*	*nee*·tee·u
100	*hundrað*	*hun*·dradh

SHOPPING & SERVICES

I'm looking for ...
Ég er að leita að ... — yekh er adh *lay*·ta adh ...

How much is it?
Hvað kostar þetta? — kvadh *kos*·tar *the*·ta

That's too expensive.
Þetta er of dýrt. — *the*·ta er of deert

It's faulty.
Það er gallað. — thadh er *gat*·ladh

Where's the ...?	*Hvar er ...?*	kvar er ...
bank	*bankinn*	*bown*·kin
market	*markaðurinn*	*mar*·ka·dhu·rin
post office	*pósthúsið*	*pohst*·hoo·sidh

TRANSPORT

Can we get there by public transport?
Er hægt að taka rútu þangað? — er haikht adh *ta*·ka *roo*·tu *thown*·gadh

Where can I buy a ticket?
Hvar kaupi ég miða? — kvar *keuy*·pi yekh *mi*·dha

Is this the ... to (Akureyri)?	*Er þetta ... til (Akureyrar)?*	er *the*·ta ... til (*a*·ku·ray·rar)
boat	*ferjan*	*fer*·yan
bus	*rútan*	*roo*·tan
plane	*flugvélin*	*flukh*·vye·lin

What time's the ... bus?	*Hvenær fer ... strætisvagninn?*	*kve*·nair fer ... *strai*·tis·vag·nin
first	*fyrsti*	*firs*·ti
last	*síðasti*	see·dhas·ti
One ... ticket (to Reykjavík), please.	*Einn miða ... (til Reykjavíkur), takk.*	aitn *mi*·dha ... (til *rayk*·ya·vee·kur) tak
one-way	*aðra leiðina*	*adh*·ra *lay*·dhi·na
return	*fram og til baka*	fram okh til *ba*·ka

I'd like a taxi ...	*Get ég fengið leigubíl ...*	get yekh *fayn*·gidh *lay*·khu·beel ...
at (9am)	*klukkan (níu fyrir hádegi)*	*klu*·kan (*nee*·u *fi*·rir *how*·de·yi)
tomorrow	*á morgun*	ow *mor*·gun

How much is it to ...?
Hvað kostar til ... ? kvadh *kos*·tar til ...

Please stop here.
Stoppaðu hér, takk. *sto*·pa·dhu hyer tak

Please take me to (this address).
Viltu aka mér til (þessa staðar)? *vil*·tu *a*·ka myer til (*the*·sa *sta*·dhar)

GLOSSARY

See the Icelandic Cuisine chapter (p408) for useful words and phrases dealing with food and dining.

á – river (as in Laxá, or Salmon River)
álfar – elves
austur – east

basalt – hard volcanic rock that often solidifies into hexagonal columns
bíó – cinema
brennivín – local schnapps; often called svartidauði (literally 'black death')
bær – farm/town

caldera – crater created by the collapse of a volcanic cone

dalur – valley

eddas – ancient Norse books
ey – island

fell – see *fjall*
fjall – mountain
fjörður – fjord
foss – waterfall
fumarole – vents in the earth releasing volcanic gas

gata – street
geysir/geyser – spouting hot spring
gistiheimilið – guesthouse
gjá – fissure, rift
goðar – political and religious leaders of certain districts in the times before Christianity (singular *goði*)

hákarl – putrid shark meat
hestur – horse
höfn – harbour
hot-pot – outdoor hot tub or spa pool, found at swimming baths and some accommodation; in Icelandic, hot-pot is *heitur pottur*
hraun – lava field
huldufólk – hidden people
hver – hot spring

ice cap – permanently frozen glacier or mountain top
Íslands – Iceland

jökull – glacier, ice cap

kirkja – church
kort – map

Landnámabók – comprehensive historical text recording the Norse settlement of Iceland
laug – pool; one that is suitable for swimming
lava tube – underground tunnel created by liquid lava flowing under a solid crust
lón – lagoon
lopapeysa/lopapeysur (sg/pl) – Icelandic woollen sweater
lundi – puffin

mudpot – bubbling pool of superheated mud

nes – headland
norður – north

puffling – baby puffin

reykur – smoke, as in Reykjavík (literally 'Smoky Cove')

safn – museum
sagas – Icelandic legends
sandur – sand; can also refer to a glacial sand plain
scoria – glassy volcanic lava
shield volcano – gently sloped volcano built up by fluid lava flows
sími – telephone
skáli – hut (snack bar)
skógur – woods or forest
stræti – street
suður – south
sumar – summer
sundlaug – heated swimming pool

tephra – rock/material blasted out from a volcano
tjörn – pond, lake
torg – town square

vatn – lake, water
vegur – road
vestur – west
vetur – winter
vík – small bay, cove, inlet
vogur – cove, bay

Behind the Scenes

SEND US YOUR FEEDBACK

We love to hear from travellers – your comments keep us on our toes and help make our books better. Our well-travelled team reads every word on what you loved or loathed about this book. Although we cannot reply individually to your submissions, we always guarantee that your feedback goes straight to the appropriate authors, in time for the next edition. Each person who sends us information is thanked in the next edition – the most useful submissions are rewarded with a selection of digital PDF chapters.

Visit **lonelyplanet.com/contact** to submit your updates and suggestions or to ask for help. Our award-winning website also features inspirational travel stories, news and discussions.

Note: We may edit, reproduce and incorporate your comments in Lonely Planet products such as guidebooks, websites and digital products, so let us know if you don't want your comments reproduced or your name acknowledged. For a copy of our privacy policy visit lonelyplanet.com/privacy.

OUR READERS

Many thanks to the travellers who used the last edition and wrote to us with helpful hints, useful advice and interesting anecdotes: Abigail Prince, Adrienne Murray Nielsen, Ben Podborski, Diego Tan, Dolores Schech, Donna Harshman, Erik Verberkt, Gates Dupont, Isabella Pollak, Jared Brooks, Jeroen Castelein, Johan Lupander, Judy Pex, Kathryn Hall, Keith A Liker, Laura Fortey, Nadine Cangi, Peter Kempster, Robin Daus, Sam Rudd-Jones, Sheri St Clair

WRITER THANKS

Alexis Averbuck

Life in Iceland wouldn't be the same without the brilliant support of Carolyn Bain. She shared her friends and her ace tips on this great land with utmost generosity. Folks such as Halldór at Visit North Iceland and Addi, Anton, Stefán, Jóhanna, Finnur, Villi, Elisabet and Odinn and others I met along the way graciously shared their stories and their ideas. Thanks, too, to my own personal peachy King of the Mountains, RVB.

Carolyn Bain

Heartfelt thanks go to Icelandic friends, old and new, for making my relocation to Reykjavík such a rewarding move. As ever, a huge cast of locals, travellers and expats helped make this research project a delight, and I'm grateful to all of them for helping me see more, understand more and enjoy more. Cheers to Clifton Wilkinson for the job, and bouquets to my coauthors for their collaborative spirit, especially to Alexis and Belinda for sparking gin-soaked dreams of future projects.

Jade Bremner

Thanks to Destination Editor Clifton Wilkinson for his superb destination and publishing knowledge. Plus, everyone working behind the scenes on this project – Cheree Broughton, Dianne, Jane, Neill Coen, Evan Godt and Helen Elfer. Last but not least, thanks to my travelling accomplice Harriet Sinclair, who joined me for a few epic days scaling Hekla volcano and walking the legendary Fimmvörðuháls trail.

Belinda Dixon

What an extraordinary opportunity – to drive pitted roads beside vast fjords, soaking in hot-pots along the way. Thanks as big as those mountains go to the whole Lonely Planet team and all who've shared information and inspiration, including Magnus in Djúpavík, Charis in Reykjanes, Kári and Thomas in Ísafjörður and Eyþor in Flateyri. And to the warmest, wisest collaborators a writer could wish for: Alexis Averbuck and Carolyn Bain – raising a *snúður* to you both!

ACKNOWLEDGEMENTS

Climate map data adapted from Peel MC, Finlayson BL & McMahon TA (2007) 'Updated World Map of the Köppen-Geiger Climate Classification', Hydrology and Earth System Sciences, 11, 1633-44.

Cover photograph: Víkurkirkja, Vík, Della Huff/ Alamy ©

THIS BOOK

This 11th edition of Lonely Planet's *Iceland* guidebook was researched and written by Alexis Averbuck, Carolyn Bain, Jade Bremner and Belinda Dixon. The previous two editions were written by Carolyn and Alexis. This guidebook was produced by the following:

Destination Editor Cliff Wilkinson

Senior Product Editor Genna Patterson

Regional Senior Cartographer Valentina Kremenchutskaya

Product Editor Kate Kiely

Book Designer Jessica Rose

Assisting Editors Judith Bamber, Peter Cruttenden, Gabrielle Innes, Kate James, Helen Koehne, Kate Morgan, Charlotte Orr, Susan Paterson, Monique Perrin

Assisting Cartographer James Leversha

Cover Researcher Naomi Parker

Thanks to Sasha Drew, Aomi Ito, Clara Monitto, Martine Power, Kathryn Rowan

Index

ALPHABETICAL ORDER

The Icelandic letters Þ and Ö appear at the end of the alphabet after the letter Z.

Map Pages **000**
Photo Pages **000**

Map Pages **000**
Photo Pages **000**

Map Pages **000**
Photo Pages **000**

Map Pages **000**
Photo Pages **000**